Exam 70-620: *Configuring Windows Vista Client*

Objective	Location in Book
Installing and Upgrading Windows Vista	
Identify hardware requirements.	Chapter 1, Lesson 1
Perform a clean installation.	Chapter 1, Lesson 2
Upgrade to Windows Vista from previous versions of Windows.	Chapter 2, Lesson 1
Upgrade from one edition of Windows Vista to another edition.	Chapter 2, Lesson 2
Troubleshoot Windows Vista installation issues.	Chapter 2, Lesson 3
Install and configure Windows Vista drivers.	Chapter 1, Lesson 3
Configuring and Troubleshooting Post-Installation System Settings	
Troubleshoot post-installation configuration issues.	Chapter 3, Lesson 1
Configure and troubleshoot Windows Aero.	Chapter 3, Lesson 2
Configure and troubleshoot parental controls.	Chapter 4, Lesson 1
Configure Windows Internet Explorer.	Chapter 4, Lesson 2
Configuring Windows Security Features	
Configure and troubleshoot User Account Control.	Chapter 5, Lesson 1
Configure Windows Defender.	Chapter 6, Lesson 1
Configure Dynamic Security for Internet Explorer 7.	Chapter 6, Lesson 2
Configure security settings in Windows Firewall.	Chapter 8, Lesson 1
Configuring Network Connectivity	
Configuring networking by using the Network and Sharing Center.	Chapter 7, Lesson 1
Troubleshoot connectivity issues.	Chapter 7, Lesson 2
Configure Remote Access.	Chapter 8, Lesson 2
Configuring Applications Included with Windows Vista	
Configure and troubleshoot media applications.	Chapter 10, Lesson 1
Configure Windows Mail.	Chapter 9, Lesson 1
Configure Windows Meeting Space.	Chapter 9, Lesson 3
Configure Windows Calendar.	Chapter 9, Lesson 2
Configure Windows Fax and Scan.	Chapter 10, Lesson 2
Configure Windows Sidebar.	Chapter 10, Lesson 3
Maintaining and Optimizing Systems That Run Windows Vista	
Troubleshoot performance issues.	Chapter 11, Lesson 1
Troubleshoot reliability issues by using built-in diagnostic tools.	Chapter 11, Lesson 2
Configure Windows Update.	Chapter 12, Lesson 1
Configure Data Protection.	Chapter 12, Lesson 2
Configuring and Troubleshooting Mobile Computing	
Configure Mobile Display Settings.	Chapter 13, Lesson 1
Configure Mobile Devices.	Chapter 13, Lesson 2
Configure Tablet PC software.	Chapter 14, Lesson 1
Configure Power Options.	Chapter 14, Lesson 2

Exam objectives   The exam objectives listed here are current as of this book's publication date. Exam objectives are subject to change at any time without prior notice and at Microsoft's sole discretion. Please visit the Microsoft Learning Web site for the most current listing of exam objectives: *http://www.microsoft.com/learning/mcp/*.

MCTS Self-Paced Training Kit (Exam 70-620): Configuring Windows Vista™ Client

Ian McLean
Orin Thomas

PUBLISHED BY
Microsoft Press
A Division of Microsoft Corporation
One Microsoft Way
Redmond, Washington 98052-6399

Library of Congress Control Number: 2007924647

Printed and bound in the United States of America.

3 4 5 6 7 8 9   QWT   2 1 0 9 8 7

Distributed in Canada by H.B. Fenn and Company Ltd.

A CIP catalogue record for this book is available from the British Library.

Microsoft Press books are available through booksellers and distributors worldwide. For further information about international editions, contact your local Microsoft Corporation office or contact Microsoft Press International directly at fax (425) 936-7329. Visit our Web site at www.microsoft.com/mspress. Send comments to tkinput@microsoft.com.

Acquisitions Editor: Ken Jones
Developmental Editor: Jenny Moss Benson
Project Editor: Laura Sackerman

Body Part No. X13-68387

If you are just starting out on the certification route and 70-620 is your first Microsoft exam, this book is dedicated to you. You have chosen a career that won't make you rich or leave you lots of spare time, but you'll seldom be bored and you probably won't be unemployed (at least not for long). Good luck.

—Ian and Orin

About the Authors

Ian McLean

Ian McLean, MCSE, MCITP, MCT, has 40 years' experience in industry, commerce, and education. He started his career as an electronics engineer before going into distance learning and then education as a university professor. Currently he runs his own consultancy company. Ian has written 19 books plus many papers and technical articles. He has been working with Microsoft Exchange Server since 1999.

Orin Thomas

Orin Thomas, MCSE, CCNA, CCDA, and Linux+ certified, is an author and systems and database administrator. He is the convener of the Melbourne Infrastructure Administrator's group, the coauthor of several Training Kits for Microsoft Press, and a contributing editor for *Windows IT Pro* magazine.

Contents at a Glance

Table of Contents

What do you think of this book? We want to hear from you!

Microsoft is interested in hearing your feedback so we can continually improve our books and learning resources for you. To participate in a brief online survey, please visit:

www.microsoft.com/learning/booksurvey/

What do you think of this book? We want to hear from you!

Microsoft is interested in hearing your feedback so we can continually improve our books and learning resources for you. To participate in a brief online survey, please visit:

www.microsoft.com/learning/booksurvey/

Introduction

This training kit is designed for information technology (IT) support personnel who support Windows Vista at the Tier 1 or Tier 2 level in a wide range of environments and who plan to take the Microsoft Certified Technology Specialist (MCTS) exam 70-620. We assume that before you begin using this kit you have a solid foundation-level understanding of Microsoft Windows client operating systems and common Internet technologies.

By using this training kit, you will learn how to do the following:

- Install and upgrade Windows Vista
- Configure and troubleshoot post-installation system settings
- Configure Windows Vista security features
- Configure Windows Vista network connectivity
- Configure applications included with Windows Vista
- Maintain and optimize systems that run Windows Vista
- Configure and troubleshoot mobile computers and devices

Hardware Requirements

We recommend that you use an isolated network that is not part of your production network to do the practice exercises in this book. The computer that you use to perform practices requires Internet connectivity. It is possible to perform almost all of the practices in this training kit if you decide to use a virtual machine instead of standard computer hardware. Your computer or computers should meet (at a minimum) the following hardware specification:

- Personal computer with a 1-GHz or faster processor.
- 512 MB of RAM (1.5 GB if you plan to use virtual machine software).
- 40 GB of available hard disk space (80 GB if you plan to use virtual machine software).
- DVD-ROM drive.
- DirectX-capable graphics card with a Windows Display Driver Model (WDDM) driver, Hardware Pixel Shader 2.0 support, and a minimum of 128 MB of graphics memory. Graphics cards with lower specifications might work, but it will not be possible to use Windows Aero.
- Keyboard and Microsoft mouse or compatible pointing device.

- To complete the practice in Lesson 1, "Upgrading and Migrating to Windows Vista," of Chapter 2, you should have access to a Windows XP computer with Service Pack 2 installed. The optional practice involves performing an upgrade of a Windows XP computer, but you should attempt this only under the circumstances outlined in the practice.
- The practices in Chapter 7, "Configuring Network Connectivity," require a wireless router or wireless fidelity interface card.
- The practice in Lesson 3, "Configuring Windows Meeting Space," of Chapter 9 requires a second computer with Windows Vista installed.
- Practices 1 and 2 in Lesson 1, "Configuring and Troubleshooting Media Applications," of Chapter 10 require access to a TV tuner card or universal serial bus (USB) device.
- The practice in Lesson 1, "Troubleshooting Performance Issues," of Chapter 11, requires a USB2 flash memory pen drive that supports ReadyBoost (almost all modern devices do) and a second flash drive that does not support ReadyBoost (less than 256 MB free).
- The practices in Chapter 13, "Configuring Mobile Devices," require Windows Vista running on a mobile PC. You also need a second computer on your network that is acting as a network server (it does not need to be running Windows Vista).
- The practices in Lesson 1, "Configuring TabletPC," of Chapter 14 require access to a Tablet PC that has Windows Home Premium, Business, Enterprise, or Ultimate installed.

Software Requirements

The following software is required to complete the practice exercises:

- Windows Vista Ultimate edition

Using the CD

The companion CD included with this training kit contains the following:

- **Practice tests**   You can reinforce your understanding of how to configure Windows Vista by using electronic practice tests you customize to meet your needs from the pool of Lesson Review questions in this book. Or you can practice for the 70-620 certification exam by using tests created from a pool of 300 realistic exam questions, which give you many practice exams to ensure that you are prepared.
- **An eBook**   An electronic version of this book (eBook) is included for when you do not want to carry the printed book with you. The eBook is in Portable Document Format (PDF), and you can view it by using Adobe Acrobat or Adobe Reader.

How to Install the Practice Tests

To install the practice test software from the companion CD to your hard disk, do the following:

1. Insert the companion CD into your CD drive, and accept the license agreement. A CD menu appears.

NOTE   If the CD menu does not appear

If the CD menu or the license agreement does not appear, AutoRun might be disabled on your computer. Refer to the Readme.txt file on the CD-ROM for alternate installation instructions.

---

2. Click Practice Tests, and follow the instructions on the screen.

How to Use the Practice Tests

To start the practice test software, follow these steps:

1. Click Start/All Programs/Microsoft Press Training Kit Exam Prep. A window appears that shows all the Microsoft Press training kit exam prep suites installed on your computer.
2. Double-click the lesson review or practice test you want to use.

NOTE   Lesson reviews vs. practice tests

Select the (70-620) Configuring Windows Vista Client *lesson review* to use the questions from the "Lesson Review" sections of this book. Select the (70-620) Configuring Windows Vista Client *practice test* to use a pool of 300 questions similar to those that appear on the 70-620 certification exam.

Lesson Review Options

When you start a lesson review, the Custom Mode dialog box appears so that you can configure your test. You can click OK to accept the defaults, or you can customize the number of questions you want, how the practice test software works, which exam objectives you want the questions to relate to, and whether you want your lesson review to be timed. If you are retaking a test, you can select whether you want to see all the questions again or only the questions you missed or did not answer.

After you click OK, your lesson review starts.

- To take the test, answer the questions and use the Next, Previous, and Go To buttons to move from question to question.

- After you answer an individual question, if you want to see which answers are correct—along with an explanation of each correct answer—click Explanation.

- If you prefer to wait until the end of the test to see how you did, answer all the questions and then click Score Test. You will see a summary of the exam objectives you chose and the percentage of questions you got right overall and per objective. You can print a copy of your test, review your answers, or retake the test.

Practice Test Options

When you start a practice test, you choose whether to take the test in Certification Mode, Study Mode, or Custom Mode:

- **Certification Mode**   Closely resembles the experience of taking a certification exam. The test has a set number of questions. It is timed, and you cannot pause and restart the timer.

- **Study Mode**   Creates an untimed test in which you can review the correct answers and the explanations after you answer each question.

- **Custom Mode**   Gives you full control over the test options so that you can customize them as you like.

In all modes the user interface when you are taking the test is basically the same but with different options enabled or disabled depending on the mode. The main options are discussed in the previous section, "Lesson Review Options."

When you review your answer to an individual practice test question, a "References" section is provided that lists where in the training kit you can find the information that relates to that question and provides links to other sources of information. After you click Test Results to score your entire practice test, you can click the Learning Plan tab to see a list of references for every objective.

How to Uninstall the Practice Tests

To uninstall the practice test software for a training kit, use the Add Or Remove Programs option (Windows XP) or the Program And Features option (Windows Vista) in Windows Control Panel.

Microsoft Certified Professional Program

The Microsoft certifications provide the best method to prove your command of current Microsoft products and technologies. The exams and corresponding certifications are developed to validate your mastery of critical competencies as you design and develop, or implement and support, solutions with Microsoft products and technologies. Computer professionals who become Microsoft-certified are recognized as experts and are sought after industry-wide. Certification brings a variety of benefits to the individual and to employers and organizations.

MORE INFO   **All the Microsoft certifications**

For a full list of Microsoft certifications, go to *www.microsoft.com/learning/mcp/default.asp*.

Technical Support

Every effort has been made to ensure the accuracy of this book and the contents of the companion CD. If you have comments, questions, or ideas regarding this book or the companion CD, please send them to Microsoft Press by using either of the following methods:

E-mail: tkinput@microsoft.com

Postal Mail:

Microsoft Press Attn: MCTS Self-Paced Training Kit (Exam 70-620): Configuring Windows Vista Client, *Editor One Microsoft Way Redmond, WA 98052–6399*

For additional support information regarding this book and the CD-ROM (including answers to commonly asked questions about installation and use), visit the Microsoft Press Technical Support website at *www.microsoft.com/learning/support/books/*. To connect directly to the Microsoft Knowledge Base and enter a query, visit *http://support.microsoft.com/search/*. For support information regarding Microsoft software, connect to *http://support.microsoft.com*.

Chapter 1
Installing Windows Vista Client

Exam 70-620, "Configuring Windows Vista Client," is aimed at information technology (IT) professionals who will be installing and supporting the Windows Vista client operating system. The first thing you should recognize is that the installation process is a critical task in a computer's life cycle. How you configure a Windows Vista client computer has significant ramifications for how it is used throughout its lifetime. Today, with more reliable hardware and software, few people will need to have their operating system reinstalled from scratch. It is likely that the configuration decisions you make during the installation of Windows Vista will remain in effect until the computer on which you install it is retired from service.

As an IT pro, you are responsible for making configuration decisions for people who have placed their trust in you. These people might be customers, work colleagues, family members, or friends. These people have given you this responsibility because they lack your expertise and training. They need you to decide whether their current hardware is capable of running Windows Vista. Do you recommend that they upgrade components? Should they purchase a new computer entirely? Will they be best served by dual booting, or should they upgrade from Windows XP to Windows Vista? Which edition of Windows Vista will best suit their needs? What sort of post-installation configuration of device drivers will be necessary? This chapter will help you address all of these questions and will start you on your journey to better understanding the Windows Vista operating system.

Exam objectives in this chapter:
- Identify hardware requirements.
- Perform a clean installation.
- Install and configure Windows Vista drivers.

Lessons in this chapter:

Before You Begin

In this chapter, you will install Windows Vista. You will use this copy of Windows Vista in practice exercises throughout the book. To complete the practices in this and later chapters, you must have a computer capable of running Windows Vista, either directly or within a virtual machine.

Real World

Orin Thomas

I have found virtual machines to be one of the most useful tools in preparing for certification examinations. When I was studying for my Windows NT 4 MCSE, I used a test lab of three spare computers in addition to my normal workstation to practice various configurations. Today, I can achieve all of that using a single computer running Virtual Server 2005 R2. Virtual Server 2005 R2 can be installed on a Windows XP or Windows Server 2003 computer and is freely available from Microsoft's website. After you have installed Virtual Server, you can then create a virtual machine and install an edition of Windows Vista to use with the practices in this book. The main thing to ensure is that your host computer has lots of spare hard disk space and RAM. Adding more RAM and hard disk space is far cheaper than obtaining spare computers! All of my virtual machines are installed on an external universal serial bus (USB) hard disk drive, which is an easy way of expanding your computer's storage capacity. Another benefit of using virtual machines to study with this training kit is the *undo disks* function. If you flub something during a practice, you can reset the virtual machine's state without having to reinstall from scratch. The practice in Lesson 2, "Installing Windows Vista," explaining how to install Windows Vista includes more information about how to configure a virtual machine.

Lesson 1: Identifying Hardware Requirements

The objective of identifying hardware requirements can be boiled down to a single question: "Will this computer run Windows Vista well?" Although it is possible to install Windows Vista on a computer that does not measure up to the *minimum requirements*, the person's experience in using that computer is not going to be as agreeable as it might be. In some situations, hardware that does not meet the minimum requirements will mean that it is simply impossible to install Windows Vista at all. This lesson will help you determine whether a particular hardware configuration is sufficient to run Windows Vista. This lesson will also provide you with an overview of each Windows Vista edition.

After this lesson, you will be able to:
- Determine Windows Vista client hardware requirements.
- Differentiate each edition of Windows Vista based on its feature set.
- Understand the difference between Windows Vista Capable and Windows Vista Premium Ready specifications.
- Run the Upgrade Advisor.

Estimated lesson time: 40 minutes

Assessing Hardware Requirements

At its simplest, assessing hardware requirements means comparing two lists of specifications. The first list of specifications is what you need to run Windows Vista. The second list of specifications shows the current state of the computer on which you want to run Windows Vista. The four primary hardware components that you need to assess in determining whether you can install Windows Vista are:

- Processor
- RAM
- Hard disk drive
- Graphics adapter

Processor

Although there are multiple processor architectures, Windows Vista requires that a processor have a minimum speed of 800 MHz. The recommended processor speed is greater than 1 GHz. Windows Vista will function on both 32-bit and 64-bit architectures. If you want to run Windows Vista on a 64-bit architecture, you should ensure that you obtain the 64-bit edition of Windows Vista rather than the standard 32-bit edition. The 64-bit edition of Windows Vista will provide improved performance on 64-bit hardware over the 32-bit edition.

RAM

Not only do you need enough RAM to run the operating system, but you also need extra RAM to run applications. Most people like to run several applications at once, such as a word processor, e-mail client, web browser, and chat program. When a computer begins running out of available RAM, it begins to use the page file. A page file is a special file, usually hidden, that is used to hold parts of programs and data files that do not fit within the computer's physical memory. Data is moved from the paging file to memory and back again as required. The page file is sometimes called the swap file. The more a computer uses the page file, the slower the computer gets. You can often improve the speed of a computer more by increasing the amount of RAM it has than you can by increasing its processor speed. Windows Vista has a minimum recommended RAM of 512 MB and a recommended RAM of 1 GB.

Hard Disk Drive

Having enough free space on the volume to install the operating system is one thing, but you will need space for an office productivity suite, all that e-mail that arrives, and space to install the latest and greatest games. Although a standard Windows Vista installation will consume approximately 7 GB of hard disk drive space, the recommended minimum is 20 GB hard drive with at least 15 GB of available space, and the recommended amount is 40 GB hard drive with at least 15 GB of available space. If you had only 7 GB of hard disk drive space, you would not be able to install any extra applications!

Graphics Card

Windows Vista has two graphics interfaces: the *basic* interface and the more advanced Windows Aero interface. Windows Aero is more aesthetically pleasing, but Windows Vista is still fully functional if using only the *basic* interface. The minimum requirement to run the *basic* interface is a graphics adapter that is DirectX 9 capable. You can find information on whether a graphics adapter is DirectX 9 capable on the vendor's website or on the product packaging. To run Windows Aero, a graphics adapter needs:

- DirectX 9 capacity
- A WDDM Driver
- Hardware Pixel Shader 2.0
- 32 bits per pixel
- A minimum of 128 MB graphics memory

Comparing Windows Vista Editions

To the uninitiated, one of the most challenging things about Windows Vista is the number of editions it comes in. Each edition, or SKU (Stock Keeping Unit), is aimed at a particular target audience, and each edition has a particular price point. It is likely that in your job as an IT pro, you will have to provide recommendations to friends, family, and customers about which edition of Windows Vista will best suit their needs.

To understand the differences between editions, you should first know the meaning of several terms.

- **Active Directory Domain**   Active Directory directory service domains are rarely used in the home environment but are common in medium and large enterprises. Active Directory domains require a computer running a Windows server operating system.

Exam Tip   Using Windows Vista clients in Active Directory domain environments is covered more fully by the 70-622 and 70-623 exams. Although it is good for you to understand how Active Directory works, you are unlikely to be tested on the technology during the 70-620 exam.

- **Aero**   The new Windows Vista graphical user interface (GUI), which is more efficient and aesthetically pleasing than the Windows XP or Windows 2000 interfaces.
- **Media Center**   Allows a computer to play live and recorded standard and HDTV, movies, music, and pictures all through a single application.
- **Full Hard Drive Encryption**   Enables a hard disk drive to be encrypted on the volume level rather than at the individual file and folder level.
- **Tablet PC capacity**   The ability to run on a Tablet PC and accept pen-based input from the screen.
- **Multiprocessor support**   The ability to use more than one processor.
- **Parental controls**   Allows parents to restrict the websites and games that their children's user accounts can access.

Windows Vista Starter

Windows Vista Starter is the most basic version of Windows Vista. This edition supports only a single 32-bit processor. Starter cannot be used in a domain, cannot run the Aero GUI, does not support Media Center or full hard drive encryption, and cannot be run on a Tablet PC. This edition allows only three applications to run simultaneously and does not support inbound network connections. This edition does not support parental controls. This affordable edition is primarily aimed at computer users in emerging markets.

Windows Vista Home Basic

Windows Vista Home Basic differs from the starter edition in that it comes in both 32-bit and 64-bit editions. Home Basic Edition cannot be used in a domain, cannot run the Aero GUI, does not support Media Center or full hard drive encryption, and cannot be run on a Tablet PC. Home Basic does support parental controls and allows users to have more than three applications open at once.

Windows Vista Home Premium

Like Windows Vista Home Basic, Windows Vista Home Premium cannot be used in a domain. It does, however, support the Aero GUI, it can be run on a Tablet PC, and it supports Media Center functionality. Home Premium supports parental controls and allows users to have more than three applications open at once.

Windows Vista Business

Windows Vista Business supports Aero and Tablet PC functionality. A Windows Vista business PC can also be a member of a domain. Windows Vista Business does not support Media Center and does not support full hard disk drive encryption.

Windows Vista Enterprise

Windows Vista Enterprise supports Aero and Tablet PC functionality. A Windows Vista Enterprise computer can be a member of a domain and can use full hard disk drive encryption. Windows Vista Enterprise does not support Media Center functionality. Windows Vista Enterprise is not available through regular retail channels and is available only to organizations that have their computers covered by Microsoft Software Assurance or a Microsoft Enterprise Agreement.

Windows Vista Ultimate

Windows Vista Ultimate supports all features of Windows Vista Enterprise and Windows Vista Premium. Computers running Windows Vista Ultimate can take full advantage of Media Center functionality and can also be members of an Active Directory domain.

NOTE   **European editions**

European editions also exist of the Home Basic and Business Editions, designated as HOMEBASICN and BUSINESSN on the edition selection screen. These editions lack the other editions' multimedia capabilities in order to comply with EU antitrust restrictions.

32-Bit and 64-Bit Editions

Windows Vista is available in both 32- and 64-bit editions. Although it is possible to run a 32-bit edition of Windows Vista on a computer with a 64-bit processor, it is not possible to run a 64-bit edition of Windows Vista on a computer with a 32-bit processor. The primary advantage of a 64-bit edition of Windows Vista is that it allows a computer to use significantly more RAM than the 32-bit edition. The 64-bit editions of Windows Vista are generally used for specialized computing requirements, such as industrial design or computer generated special effects.

Differentiating Windows Vista Logos

If you have browsed the aisles at your local computer superstore, you will have noticed that many of the computers have a Windows logo attached that designates them as either Windows Vista Capable or Windows Vista Premium Ready. These logos are designed to assure customers that the computer they purchase, even if it has a different operating system installed, is certified as capable of running the Windows Vista operating system. The differences are as follows:

- **Windows Vista Capable** A computer with the Windows Vista Capable PC logo, shown here,

  is certified to meet or exceed the minimum hardware requirements for Windows Vista. A computer with the Windows Vista Capable PC logo might not necessarily be capable of running Windows Aero, but it will still be able to display an interface comparable to that of Windows XP. You generally see this logo on computers that have Windows XP installed.

- **Windows Vista Premium Ready** A computer with the Windows Vista Premium Ready logo, shown here,

  is certified to provide the best Windows Vista experience. The hardware on a computer with this logo exceeds Microsoft's recommended specifications. You generally see this logo on computers that already have Windows Vista installed.

MORE INFO Windows Vista hardware planning

For more information about assessing whether existing computer hardware is capable of running Windows Vista, check out the following website: *http://www.microsoft.com/technet/windowsvista /evaluate/hardware/vistarpc.mspx*

Running Windows Vista Upgrade Advisor

The Windows Vista Upgrade Advisor is a downloadable tool that allows you to determine whether a Windows XP computer is capable of running Windows Vista. The Windows Vista Upgrade Advisor runs only on the 32-bit version of Windows XP and Windows Vista. If the computer that you want to test runs the 64-bit edition of Windows XP, you cannot use the Windows Upgrade Advisor. The Windows Vista Upgrade Advisor will not run on Windows 95, Windows 98, Windows Me, or Windows 2000.

Installing the Windows Vista Upgrade Advisor

Before you install the Windows Vista Upgrade Advisor you need to install Microsoft Core XML Services (MSXML) version 6.0 or later and the .NET Framework version 2 or later. MSXML provides client and server-safe components for Extensible Markup Language (XML) over Hypertext Transfer Protocol (HTTP). The .NET Framework manages the execution of applications written specifically for the framework. Most new Windows Vista applications use it. If you run the installation routine without installing these components, the installation will abort, forwarding you to a page on Microsoft's website that contains the necessary files.

To install the Upgrade Advisor, perform the following steps:

- Download the Windows Vista Upgrade Advisor from the Microsoft website: *http:// www.microsoft.com/windowsvista/getready/upgradeadvisor/default.mspx.*
- Start the installation process by double-clicking the executable file. If you do not have Microsoft Core XML Services 6.0 installed, the installation routine redirects you to a location on Microsoft's website where you can download the installation file. Download the file, and then install it.
- Restart the installation process. If you do not have .NET Framework version 2.0 or higher installed, a dialog box appears. Click Install The .NET Framework. The installation is downloaded from Microsoft's website to the Desktop. Install the .NET Framework by following the prompts. Restart the installation.
- During the installation of the Windows Vista Upgrade Advisor, you are asked to accept a license agreement and to specify an installation folder. You should accept the default values. You should also allow the installation routine to install a Desktop Shortcut.
- When the installation finishes, click Close. You will run the Windows Vista Upgrade Advisor in Practice 2 at the end of this lesson.

> ## Quick Check
> 1. Which operating systems will the Windows Vista Upgrade Advisor run on?
> 2. What is the recommended minimum amount of RAM for Windows Vista?

Quick Check Answers

1. Windows XP 32 bit and Windows Vista 32 bit
2. 512 MB

Running the Upgrade Advisor

The primary purpose of the Upgrade Advisor is to determine whether the current hardware configuration is adequate to run Windows Vista. If your computer is currently unable to run Windows Vista, the Upgrade Advisor informs you, as shown in Figure 1-1. If the current configuration is not adequate, it makes recommendations about what to do to resolve the situation. For example, if your computer has only 256 MB of RAM, the Upgrade Advisor recommends that you upgrade to a minimum of 512 MB of RAM prior to installing Windows Vista.

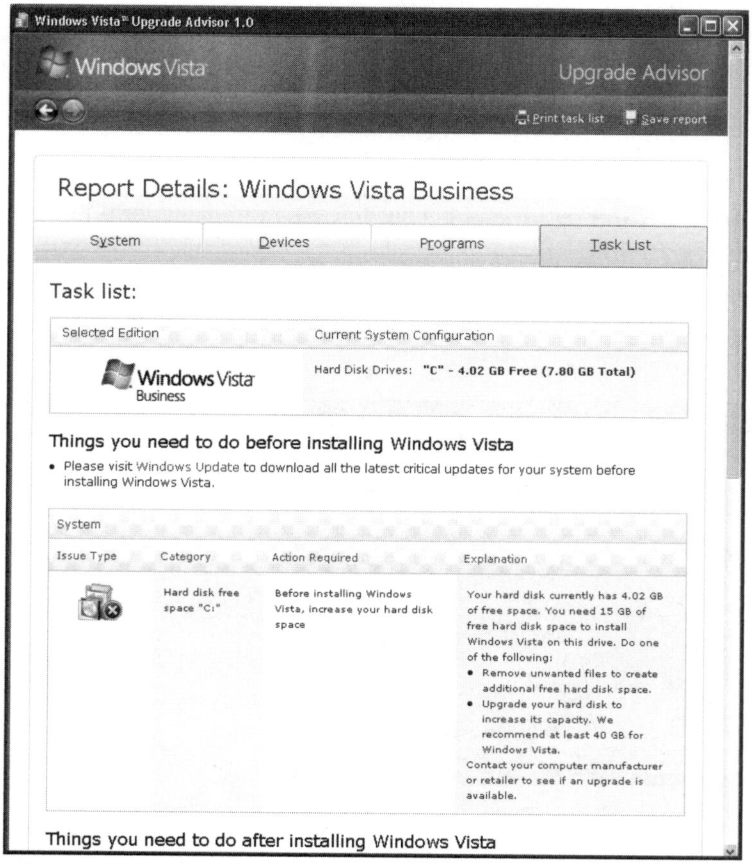

Figure 1-1   Windows Vista Upgrade Advisor report

The Windows Vista Upgrade Advisor also provides a report that explains which edition of Windows will best suit your needs given the configuration of the Windows XP computer on which you ran it. For example, if the Upgrade Advisor detects that a computer is a member of an Active Directory domain, it can discount Home Basic and Home Premium as viable options. Neither edition supports domain membership.

Before you run the Windows Vista Upgrade Advisor you should connect all peripheral devices (such as printers, external hard disk drives, and scanners) to the computer. This allows Upgrade Advisor to take these peripherals into account when making a recommendation.

Practice: Evaluating a Computer Prior to Installing Windows Vista

In these practices, you will evaluate whether or not a computer is capable of running Windows Vista. The first practice is an evaluation of the hardware requirements. The second practice involves running the Upgrade Advisor.

▶ **Practice 1: Evaluate Computer Hardware Prior to Installing Windows Vista**

The Windows Vista Upgrade Advisor is limited in that it can run only on a subset of the operating systems that are actually available. You might be considering, for example, running Windows Vista on a computer that has an operating system such as Linux installed. In this case, you need to make your own evaluation of the computer's hardware capacity.

1. Review the minimum and recommended hardware requirements of Windows Vista.
2. Enter the computer's BIOS. When you power on a computer, it informs you which key to press to enter setup or BIOS.
3. Use BIOS to determine how much RAM is installed on the computer, as shown in Figure 1-2.

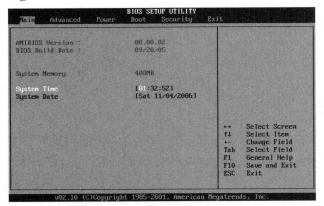

Figure 1-2   Using BIOS to determine the amount of RAM a computer has

4. Use BIOS to determine the size of the hard disk drive installed in the computer.
5. Use BIOS to determine the processor speed of the computer.

6. Log on to the website of the manufacturer of your computer's graphics adapter. Check whether the graphics adapter meets the minimum or exceeds the recommended specifications for Windows Vista.

▶ **Practice 2: Running the Upgrade Advisor**

In this practice, you will run the Upgrade Advisor. To perform this practice, you will need access to a computer that has Windows XP installed. You also need to have downloaded and installed the Windows Vista Upgrade Advisor.

NOTE   Obtaining the Upgrade Advisor

You can download the Windows Vista Upgrade Advisor from the following URL: *http://www.microsoft.com/windowsvista/getready/upgradeadvisor/default.mspx*. The Windows Vista Upgrade Advisor installation routine will assist you in installing any additional components, like the MSXML and .NET Framework that are required to run the application.

---

1. Open the Windows Vista Upgrade Advisor.
2. On the Windows Vista Upgrade Advisor start window, shown in Figure 1-3, click Start Scan.

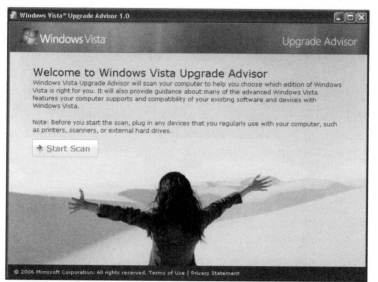

Figure 1-3   Windows Vista Upgrade Advisor start window

3. Depending on the speed of your computer, it might take some time for the scan to complete. During the scan you can click several numbered buttons to learn more about each edition of Windows Vista. When the scan is complete, click the See Details button.
4. The report highlights any problems that the Upgrade Advisor finds and makes a recommendation as to which edition of Windows Vista would best suit the Windows XP

computer based on its current hardware and software configuration. If the Upgrade Advisor reports that the computer is unable to run Windows Vista, you can scroll down and click the See Details button next to the warning sign to determine what course of action you might take to resolve the problem.

Lesson Summary

- Windows Vista's minimum hardware requirements are an 800 MHz or better processor, 512 MB of RAM, 20 GB of hard disk space with at least 15 GB of available space, and support for Super VGA graphics.

- A computer that has the Windows Vista Capable logo meets or surpasses the minimum required hardware configuration to run Windows Vista.

- A computer that has the Windows Vista Premium Ready logo meets or surpasses the recommended hardware configuration of Windows Vista.

- The Windows Vista Upgrade Advisor is a software tool that can run only on 32-bit versions of Windows XP or Windows Vista. It determines whether the current hardware configuration is adequate to run Windows Vista. If the current configuration is not adequate, it makes recommendations about what to do to resolve the situation.

- The Windows Vista Upgrade Advisor also makes a recommendation about which version of Windows Vista would best suit your needs given the configuration of the computer being examined.

Lesson Review

You can use the following questions to test your knowledge of the information in Lesson 1, "Identifying Hardware Requirements." The questions are also available on the companion CD if you prefer to review them in electronic form.

NOTE   Answers

Answers to these questions and explanations of why each answer choice is correct or incorrect are located in the "Answers" section at the end of the book.

---

1. You have several computers that you want to upgrade to Windows Vista Ultimate. Prior to performing the upgrade, you want to run the Windows Vista Upgrade Advisor. Which of the following operating systems can you evaluate using this tool? (Choose all that apply.)

    A. Windows 2000 Professional

    B. Windows XP Professional

    C. Windows Vista Home Basic

    D. Windows Me

2. Which of the following hardware configurations fall below the minimum recommended for Windows Vista?

   A. A computer that has a 10-megabit network interface card

   B. A computer that has a 100-megabit network interface card

   C. A computer that has a 900 MHz Pentium III processor

   D. A computer that has 256 MB of RAM

3. Which of the following processors fall below Windows Vista's minimum recommended requirements? (Choose all that apply.)

   A. 3.0 GHz Pentium IV

   B. 500 MHz Pentium III

   C. 1 GHz Pentium III

   D. 700 MHz Pentium III

Lesson 2: Installing Windows Vista

Although the installation process is straightforward, as an IT pro, you will need to make several important decisions that will influence the configuration of the computer. This includes setting initial disk and volume configuration, security, and network discoverability options. Depending on the hardware configuration of the computer on which you install Windows Vista, performing an installation can take some time. You need to understand the ramifications of each decision. In some cases, if you choose the wrong option, the only remedy will to be to start over from the beginning. In this lesson, you will learn about the Windows Vista installation process, a process that is likely to become very familiar to you over the course of the next few years as an IT pro.

After this lesson, you will be able to:

■ Install Windows Vista Business.

■ Understand how to dual boot Windows Vista with Windows XP.

■ Configure the default operating system in the boot manager.

Estimated lesson time: 75 minutes

Performing the Windows Vista Installation

In this lesson, you will learn the general steps of the Windows Vista installation routine. After you have covered the general steps in the text, the practices at the end of the lesson will walk you through actually how to perform the installation. These practices are important. The practices in all other lessons in this book build on the installation of Windows Vista that you perform at the end of this lesson.

Exam Tip   Prior to taking the exam, you should run through the installation procedure more than once. It will be helpful to be able to differentiate the steps in your mind from those of the Windows XP installation routine. As a rule of thumb, you should have installed Windows Vista at least 10 times prior to taking the 70-620 exam.

The first step in an average Windows Vista clean installation is inserting the installation DVD into the computer's DVD-ROM drive and allowing the computer to boot off the DVD-ROM. Upgrades, covered in detail in Chapter 2, "Windows Vista Upgrades and Migrations," require that you begin the installation from within Windows XP. Some computers will not automatically boot from the DVD-ROM drive. This bypass is often implemented for security reasons because it is possible to boot into an alternate operating system if you can boot from the DVD-ROM drive. To change the computer boot order so that the DVD-ROM drive is checked first, you need to enter the computer's BIOS. From here it is possible to configure the boot order.

MORE INFO Image-based deployment

The 70-620 exam does not cover deploying images of Windows Vista over the network. Enterprise deployment of Windows Vista client is covered by the 70-622 exam. If you are interested in learning more about image-based deployment, consult the following article: *http://www.microsoft.com /technet/windowsvista/deploy/default.mspx*

The first screen in the installation process, shown in Figure 1-4, asks which language you want to install, the time and currency format, and the keyboard layout you want to use. These selections are important because trying to install an operating system in a foreign language is a difficult skill to master! Keyboard layout is also important; even keyboards from other English-speaking countries might superficially seem to use the same layout as a U.S. keyboard, but some of the keys are in different positions. If you are installing Windows Vista for someone who needs access to multiple keyboard layouts, it is possible to add these alternative layouts once Windows Vista is installed. The user can then switch between them as necessary.

Figure 1-4 Select language, time and currency format, and keyboard layout

The next step in the installation process is the Install Windows page. Clicking the Install Now button begins the installation. You also have the option of repairing your computer. The repair process will be covered in detail in Chapter 2, "Windows Vista Upgrades and Migrations," Lesson 3, "Troubleshooting Installations and Upgrades." If you click What To Know Before Installing Windows, you are reminded to:

- Verify that your computer meets the minimum hardware requirements.
- Have your installation media ready. At this point, of course, the media is in the drive!

- Ensure that you have located your 25-character product key.
- Have determined what antivirus software you will install after installation completes. A link to Windows OneCare is provided in the Welcome screen after you complete installation. OneCare is a fully featured subscription-based application available from Microsoft that you can use to protect against viruses and to ensure that your computer has appropriate security settings. You do not have to select OneCare as your antivirus or security solution, and many other vendors have released comparable products.
- Prepare a name for the computer that you will enter during installation. If you are installing in an Active Directory environment, which is not covered on the 70-620 exam, you should also know the name of the domain that you want to join the computer to.
- Ensure that your Internet connection is working.

Clicking Install Now begins the installation process. After a moment, you are asked to enter the 25-character product activation key in the text box shown in Figure 1-5 and to select whether or not you want to automatically activate Windows when the computer connects to the Internet. It is possible to use Windows Vista for 30 days before you need to activate it online or by telephone. Until you are an expert at installing Windows Vista, you should ensure that you are completely happy with the installation and configuration prior to performing activation. That way, if you find something problematic, you will be able to reinstall from scratch without having to worry about a prior activation using your 25-character product key.

If you want to enter the product key later, you receive a dialog box asking if you are sure. After it is installed, Windows Vista reminds you each day until the grace period expires that you need to perform the activation process.

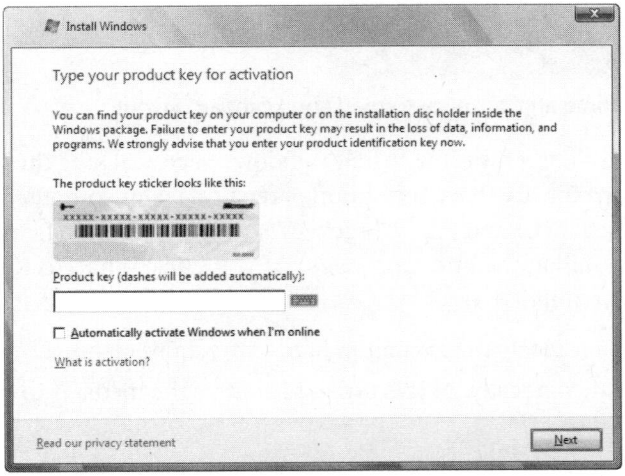

Figure 1-5   Enter the product key

Windows Product Activation

Windows Product Activation (WPA) is the method Microsoft uses to ensure that Windows Vista is installed on only a limited number of computers. You should record each unique key and the computer that it is tied to in a table or in a database in case you misplace the installation media. Several separate identifiers are used in the WPA process:

- **Hardware ID**   An identifier that is generated using information generated from a computer's hardware configuration
- **Product ID**   A 25-character unique key supplied with the installation media
- **Installation ID**   An identifier that Windows Vista creates from the hardware ID and product ID

During the WPA process, the Product ID and Hardware ID are sent to Microsoft. A single Product ID cannot be tied to more than one Hardware ID. If the activation check finds that the Product ID has not been activated and tied to a Hardware ID, both IDs are recorded and the installation is activated. If the activation check finds that the Product ID is tied to a different hardware ID, the activation fails.

MORE INFO   Windows Product Activation

For more information on Windows Product Activation, consult the following website: *http://www.microsoft.com/technet/windowsvista/library/plan/e35edd60-9784-491d-8c51-7affbb42df30.mspx?mfr=true*

Microsoft allows you to reinstall and reactivate Windows Vista on the same computer once. Trying to do so again results in WPA failing, and you need to contact Microsoft support. If you substantially change your hardware configuration, you also need to reactivate Windows Vista. Changing a single component does not force reactivation, but changing multiple components—for example, motherboard, network card, and graphics adapter—forces reactivation. This is to guard against people installing multiple copies of Windows Vista on different computers by swapping hard disk drives around.

NOTE   Wait until your system settles

We have found that until you have installed a new operating system a few times, you are likely to want to reinstall once or twice. With Windows Vista's hardware requirements, you will probably consider upgrading some of your hardware after you have installed to improve your experience. For this reason, we recommend that you do not go through the activation process until you are positive you are happy with your current configuration. That way, if you find you have to revise your hardware configuration, you do not have to worry about activation problems.

Selecting an Edition of Windows Vista

The next stage in the installation process, shown in Figure 1-6, involves selecting the edition of Windows Vista that you will install. The Windows Vista installation media ships with all editions of Windows Vista; however, you can activate only the version of Windows Vista that you have purchased. Each unique 25-character product key is tied to a specific edition of Windows Vista. If you install an edition that does not match your 25-character product key, you will either have to reinstall from scratch after the 30-day activation period has expired or purchase the edition that you have installed. If you purchase a new edition, you will receive a new unique 25-character product key.

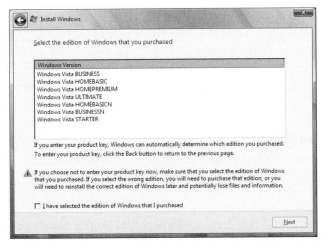

Figure 1-6   Select the edition of Windows Vista that you have purchased

For example, if you install Windows Vista Ultimate but have purchased Windows Vista Business or Home Basic, you will need to reinstall from scratch or purchase a license for Ultimate. There is an exception to this rule. If you purchase Ultimate but accidentally install another edition, you will be able to perform an in-place upgrade to Ultimate. When you are sure, select the I Have Selected The Edition Of Windows That I Purchased check box, and click Next.

Performing a Custom Installation

The option to upgrade is presented only if you run the Windows Vista installation routine from an existing Windows XP or Windows Vista installation, and the computer meets the upgrade requirements. If you have booted off the Windows Vista installation media, only the Custom option is available. Upgrading Windows Vista is covered in Chapter 2, "Windows Vista Upgrades and Migrations," Lesson 1, "Upgrading and Migrating to Windows Vista." This lesson concentrates on the custom install option.

The Where Do You Want To Install Windows page shows a list of all disks and partitions available on the computer. From this page, you can load a driver for a disk drive if one is not already included with Windows. This is often necessary only with special high performance disks or redundant array of independent disks (RAID) arrays. If your hard disk drive is not visible when you reach this part of the installation routine, you need to install the appropriate hard disk driver.

MORE INFO   RAID: redundant array of inexpensive disks

Although Windows Vista supports software RAID, some high performance workstation computers use a hardware RAID array. A hardware RAID array ties multiple identical disks together to increase performance and reliability. In some cases, you might need to load a hardware driver for Windows Vista's installation routine to recognize the RAID array as a valid disk. You can find out more about RAID by referring to the following webpage: *http://www.microsoft.com/technet/technetmag/issues /2005/05/RAID/*

Clicking Drive Options (Advanced) brings up tools, shown in Figure 1-7, that you can use to create a new partition, format, extend a partition across multiple disks, or load a driver. It is not necessary to use the advanced drive options unless you want to create multiple separate partitions. Extending volumes across partitions and disks is beyond the scope of the 70-620 exam. Windows Vista automatically creates and formats a partition if you do not use any of the advanced options.

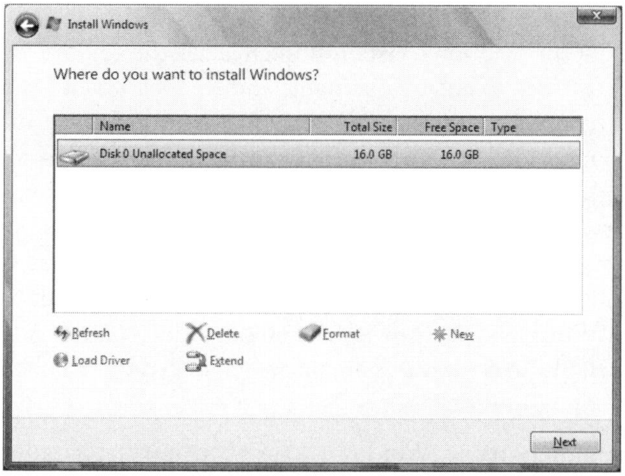

Figure 1-7   Drive options

Generally speaking, you will want to allocate as much space as possible to the partition that will host the Windows Vista volume. By default, all applications are installed onto the volume that hosts Windows Vista. Most people do not delete applications that they have installed unless they have to, which means that over time, the amount of disk space used on the volume that hosts Windows Vista fills. This is especially the case if the person that you are building the computer for likes to play computer games. Modern games take up many gigabytes of disk space. If someone installs a new game each month, that person might use more than 100 GB of storage capacity within a year! If you are ever asked to free up disk space on someone's computer, you should check whether the user has installed any games.

There are also good reasons to partition disks. Windows Vista allows you to create mirrored volumes across separate disks as a way of protecting data. Although you will want to ensure that the volume that hosts Windows Vista has as much space as possible, setting up a separate volume to host data, such as Microsoft Office documents, simplifies setting up redundancy and also greatly simplifies configuring backups.

CAUTION   Disks, partitions, and volumes

These three terms are sometimes used interchangeably in technical documentation. This can be confusing for readers. A disk is the physical hard disk drive. A partition is a logical segmentation of a hard disk drive. A volume is a formatted storage area contained within a partition. If you open Windows Explorer, you are able to view only volumes. The only way that you can view disks and partitions is through the Disk Management tool, which is accessible through the Computer Management console.

After these stages of the process are complete, the installation routine begins copying files from the Windows Vista media to the newly created volume. Features are then installed. After these aspects are completed, the installation reboots.

Your input is not required until the Windows Vista routine reaches the Choose A User Name And Picture page. Here you are asked to enter a username and a password and to select a picture to represent your user account. You will need to enter the password twice and provide a password hint, as shown in Figure 1-8. It is important for you to note that this account automatically becomes a member of the local administrators group. For this reason, you should make the username and password memorable, though be careful to keep them both secured. Whoever has access to this username and password pair has complete control of this computer. For this reason, you should also ensure that the hint you provide is not too obvious. Unlike previous versions of Windows, Windows Vista ships with a built-in Administrator account that is disabled by default. User accounts are discussed in greater detail in Chapter 4, "Configuring and Troubleshooting Internet Access."

The next step is to enter a computer name. Windows Vista offers a name based on the username you entered in the preceding step. You should select a name that is informative rather than wildly imaginative. Good computer names relate to the computer's role. Accounts01 is an excellent name for a Windows Vista computer used in a company's accounting department.

Figure 1-8   Configuring a username and password

NOTE   Label a computer clearly

Although it is not critical in the home, it is easy to lose track of computer names if you work in a large environment. In such an environment, you should label the exterior of a computer with its computer name. That way it is easier to track the computer down when you get a message in the server log that something has gone wrong with a particular client computer.

The next stage of the installation process asks whether you want to install updates. The options are as follows:

- **Use Recommended Settings**   This installs important and recommended updates and helps make Internet browsing safer. It also contacts Microsoft to see if there are solutions to any problems you encounter, such as a missing hardware driver.
- **Install Important Updates Only**   Download and install any important security updates Microsoft has issued since Windows Vista's release.
- **Ask Me Later**   Do nothing at the moment. A warning is provided that the computer might be vulnerable to security threats.

Although it might seem obvious that using the recommended settings is the best solution, there are good reasons why you might select Ask Me Later. If you are installing 100 Windows Vista computers, you will not want each one of them downloading a copy of the same files over your company's Internet connection from the Windows Update servers. Windows Update is a free service through which Microsoft provides patches and updates to your software. It is possible to install Windows Server Update Services (WSUS), an additional component that runs on Windows Server software that allows an organization to have a local Windows Update server. Each of the 100 Windows Vista computers would be able to retrieve all released updates over the company's local area network (LAN) rather than each of them downloading them from the Internet. If your organization is charged for the amount of traffic downloaded over its Internet link, implementing WSUS can bring significant cost benefits. WSUS is not covered on the 70-620 exam but is a technology that you will encounter if you are studying for the Windows Server certification exams.

The installation routine then asks you to review your time and date settings, as shown in Figure 1-9. Be sure to set the correct time zone and date for your computer. If your region shifts to daylight savings during the summer months, ensure that the Automatically Adjust Clock For Daylight Saving Time check box is selected. During installation you do not need to set Windows Vista's time more accurately than the closest minute. When the computer is connected to the Internet, it synchronizes with time servers that keep time using an atomic clock. By default, once a week all Windows Vista computers synchronize with a time server located at *time.windows.com*. Many people use their home computers to tell them the accurate time rather than calling the telephone company's automated service.

Figure 1-9   Setting your computer's time zone

After completing the configuration of the time and date, the installation process presents the Select Your Computer's Current Location dialog box, as shown in Figure 1-10. Setting a computer's location determines how it interacts with the local network. Setting the network to Home configures the network to attempt to discover peer-to-peer network devices. Setting the network to Work configures Windows Vista to attempt to discover domain resources. Configuring the network to Public Location means that the computer will not interrogate other devices on the network. In all cases, the Windows Firewall is active. The settings in this dialog box determine how inquisitive Windows Vista is about other devices on the local network.

Microsoft recommends that if you are unsure of what to choose, you should select Public Location. Making a selection here completes the installation.

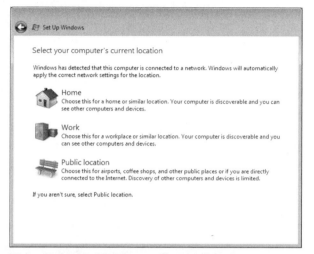

Figure 1-10   Selecting a computer's location

Quick Check

1. How long do you have after installation to activate Windows?
2. You have purchased Windows Vista Ultimate but have accidentally installed Windows Vista Home Premium. What step should you take to remedy the problem?

Quick Check Answers

1. You have 30 days to activate Windows after installing it.
2. Perform an upgrade to Vista Ultimate.

Dual Booting

Dual booting is the process by which you select an operating system to run during boot. When a computer is configured to dual boot, each operating system is installed on a separate volume. Those volumes can be separate partitions on the same hard disk drive or separate partitions on separate hard disk drives. Although virtual machines are making dual booting less popular, there are several reasons to dual boot. These include:

■   Your organization requires you to run either Windows 2000 or Windows XP but has asked you to also test Windows Vista.

■   You are a developer who wants to switch between multiple operating systems, such as Windows Server 2003 and Windows Vista.

■ Your computer does not have enough memory to run different operating systems within virtual machines.

When configuring dual booting, you need to ensure that you install Windows Vista after you install Windows XP. If you have to rebuild a computer that dual boots and you install Windows Vista prior to XP, there might be problems with the way that the boot menu functions.

When you dual boot, you are presented with a text menu asking you which operating system you want to run. To select Windows XP, or any other operating system released prior to Windows Vista, use the arrow keys to select Earlier Version Of Windows, as shown in Figure 1-11. Selecting Earlier Version Of Windows automatically boots Windows XP. If you have multiple earlier operating systems, such as Windows XP and Windows Server 2003, selecting Earlier Version Of Windows brings up the original boot loader. From there you can select between earlier versions of Windows as you would have prior to installing Windows Vista. If you install a version of Windows released after Windows Vista—for example, Windows Longhorn Server—this is listed as an option on the Windows Vista boot menu.

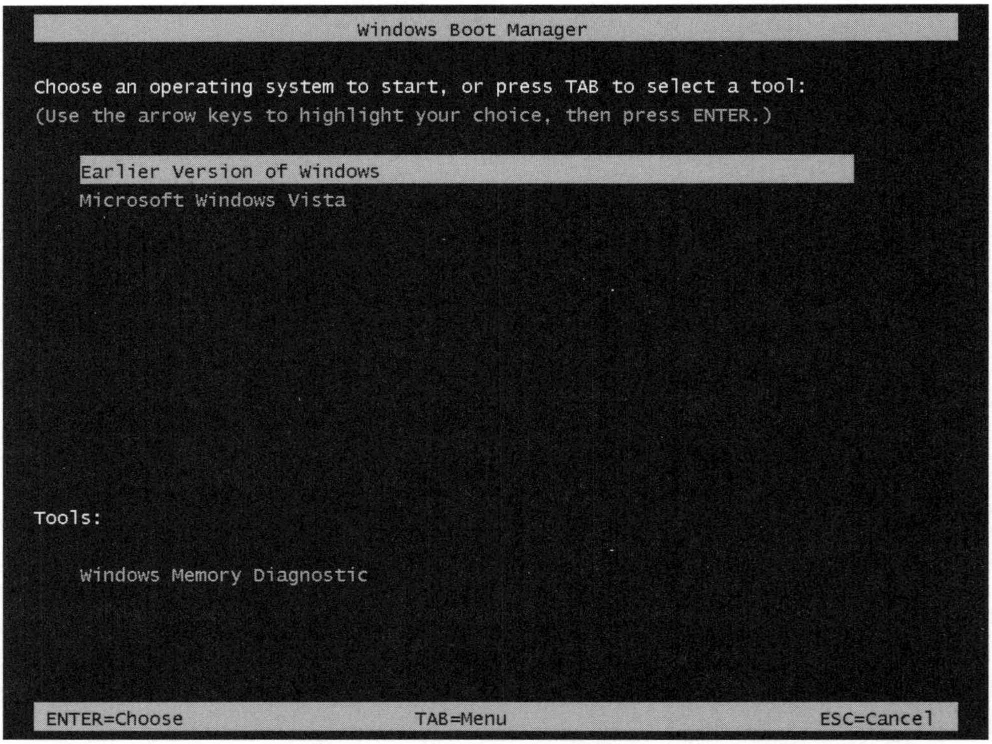

```
                          Windows Boot Manager

  Choose an operating system to start, or press TAB to select a tool:
  (Use the arrow keys to highlight your choice, then press ENTER.)

      Earlier Version of Windows
      Microsoft Windows Vista




















  Tools:

      Windows Memory Diagnostic



  ENTER=Choose                    TAB=Menu                    ESC=Cancel
```

Figure 1-11 Choosing Windows XP by selecting Earlier Version Of Windows in the boot manager

It is possible to change which operating system you want to boot by default in the System Properties dialog box. To configure which operating system to boot by default, perform the following steps.

1. Click Start.
2. Right-click Computer, and then click Properties. This opens the View Basic Information About Your Computer window.

NOTE   Alternative methods

It is also possible to get to this window by opening System in Control Panel. You will find that there are many ways to access important Windows Vista tools. There is no right way to do it; just find what works for you.

---

3. On the Tasks pane, click Advanced System Settings.
4. In the User Account Control dialog box, click Continue.
5. In the Advanced tab of System Properties, click the Settings button in the Startup And Recovery area.
6. Use the Default Operating System drop-down list, shown in Figure 1-12, to select the default operating system for Windows startup.

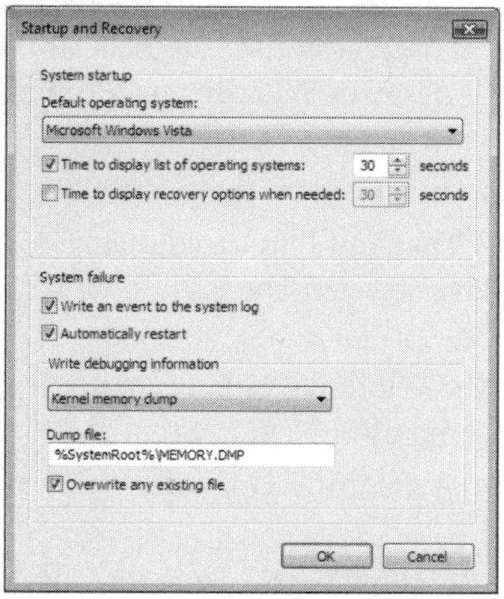

Figure 1-12   Configuring the default startup operating system

Practice: Installing Windows Vista Business

Select Practice 1 or 2, depending on whether you want to install Windows Vista on a computer with or without an existing operating system. If you have a fresh computer or are installing on a virtual machine, you should select Practice 1. If you want to configure Windows Vista in a dual boot configuration with Windows XP, Windows 2000, or Windows Server 2003, do Practice 2. Practice 2 assumes that you have a fresh unpartitioned hard disk drive available.

▶ **Practice 1: Installing Windows Vista Business on a Computer Without an Operating System**

In this practice, you will install Windows Vista Business on a computer that meets the minimum hardware requirements outlined in Lesson 1, "Identifying Hardware Requirements." In Chapter 2, you will upgrade Windows Vista Business to Windows Vista Ultimate edition. If you want to install Windows Vista to dual boot, you should do Practice 2 rather than Practice 1.

NOTE   Windows Vista Virtual Server Settings

If you are using Virtual Server 2005 R2, you should ensure that Virtual Server 2005 R2 is upgraded to SP1. If configuring Windows Vista as a virtual machine, allocate a minimum of 512 MB of RAM to the virtual machine, although 1024 is better. Allocate 25 GB of disk space to the virtual hard disk drive and ensure that Undo Disks are enabled.

---

1. Ensure that the Windows Vista installation DVD is in the DVD-ROM drive and turn on the computer.

2. The Windows Vista installation routine should start automatically, and after several moments you should see the language options screen. Set the options appropriate to your language, currency, and keyboard layout, and click Next.

3. On the Install Windows page, click Install Now. This begins the installation process.

4. The next screen is the WPA page. On this page, clear the Automatically Activate Windows When I'm Online check box. You will perform WPA during a practice in Chapter 3, "Troubleshooting Post-Installation System Settings." Click Next.

5. On the Do You Want To Enter Your Product Key Now page, click No.

6. In the Select The Edition Of Windows That You Purchased dialog box, click Windows Vista Business, and then select the I Have Selected The Edition Of Windows That I Purchased check box.

7. Click Next. On the next page, review the Windows Vista license terms, and then select the I Accept The License Terms check box. Click Next.

8. Because you are installing on a clean system, the Upgrade option is disabled. Click Custom.

9. On the Where Do You Want To Install Windows page, ensure that the disk that you want to install Windows on is selected. Click Drive Options (Advanced).

10. Click New to create a new partition on the allocated space. By default, a new partition is allocated all remaining space on the disk. Click Apply. This creates a new partition.

11. Click Format to create a volume on the newly created partition. A warning, shown in Figure 1-13, informs you that all data stored on the partition will be deleted. Because the partition is newly created, there is no data to lose.

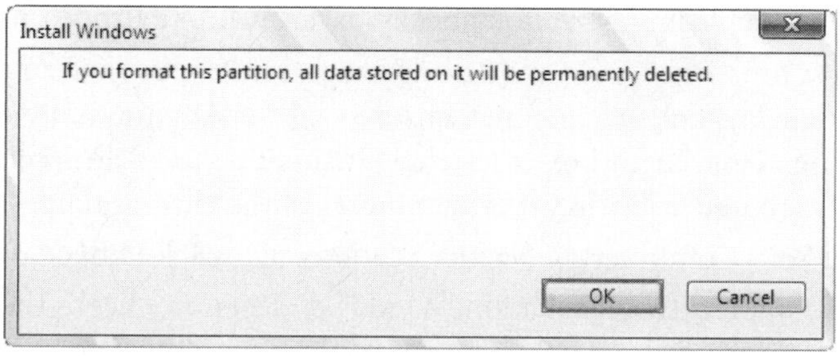

Install Windows

If you format this partition, all data stored on it will be permanently deleted.

OK   Cancel

Figure 1-13   Partition deletion warning

12. Windows automatically formats the partition using the NTFS file system. When the installation routine has finished formatting the partition, click Next.

13. You need to wait for some time while Windows copies files, installs features and updates, and then completes the installation. The installation reboots during this process.

14. In the Choose A User Name And Picture page, assign the username **Kim_Ackers** and the password **P@ssw0rd**. You need to enter the password twice, and you should enter a hint to remind you of what the password is. Click Next.

NOTE   Setting your own username and password

The practice items in this book assume that the initial username set up is **Kim_Ackers** and the assigned password **P@ssw0rd**. If you decide to use a separate username and password pair, substitute it each time you see **Kim_Ackers**.

---

15. In the Type A Computer Name dialog box, shown in Figure 1-14, type **620-Vista**. Select a desktop background, and then click Next.

Figure 1-14   Selecting a computer name and desktop background

16. On the Help Protect Windows Automatically page, click Use Recommended Settings.

17. On the Review Your Time And Date Settings page, select your time zone. If you live in a region that uses daylight savings time, ensure that the Automatically Adjust Clock For Daylight Savings Time check box is selected. Ensure that the date is correct and that the time setting is accurate to within several minutes of the current time. Click Next.

18. On the Select Your Computer's Current Location page, click Public Location.

19. Click Start to complete the installation. Windows Vista now checks the computer's performance and assigns a rating before presenting you with the logon screen.

▶ **Practice 2: Installing Windows Vista Business in a Dual Boot Configuration**

In this practice, you will install Windows Vista on the second hard disk of a computer that already has Windows XP installed. If you have performed the first Windows Vista installation practice, there is no need to perform this practice.

1. Ensure that the Windows Vista installation DVD is in the DVD-ROM drive.

NOTE Preparing for dual boot

This practice is offered for people who do not have enough RAM to run virtual machines or who want to dual boot their current computer with Windows Vista.

There are two basic ways of preparing an existing computer to dual boot. The first is to install a second hard disk drive. The second is to purchase a disk repartitioning tool. Given the licensing fees and the chance of losing data, we recommend that you purchase a second internal hard disk drive.

Several software tools will reliably repartition a disk that currently holds data. The license fee for these tools is around the same cost as a new hard disk drive with several hundred gigabytes of storage.

---

2. Turn on the computer. When you see the prompt:

    Press any key to boot from CD or DVD

    press the spacebar. This starts the Windows Vista installation routine.

3. After several moments, you should see the language options screen. Set the options appropriate to your language, currency, and keyboard layout, and click Next.

4. On the Install Windows page, click Install Now. This begins the installation process.

5. The next screen is the activation page. Clear the Automatically Activate Windows When I'm Online check box. You will perform product activation in Chapter 3, "Troubleshooting Post-Installation System Settings." Click Next.

6. In the Do You Want To Enter Your Product Key Now dialog box, click No.

7. In the Select The Edition Of Windows That You Purchased page, select Windows Vista Business, and then select the I Have Selected The Edition Of Windows That I Purchased check box

8. Click Next, review the Windows Vista license terms, and then select the I Accept The License Terms check box. Click Next.

9. To upgrade to Windows Vista, you need to start the installation process from Windows XP rather than booting off the Windows Vista DVD-ROM. Click Custom.

10. On the Where You Do You Want To Install Windows page, click Drive Options (Advanced).

11. Locate the new drive that you have just installed. In Figure 1-15, you can see that the newly installed drive is Disk 1. The entire drive is unallocated, and it has no partitions. Disk 0, on the other hand, has a single partition of 5.0 GB and a small amount of unallocated space.

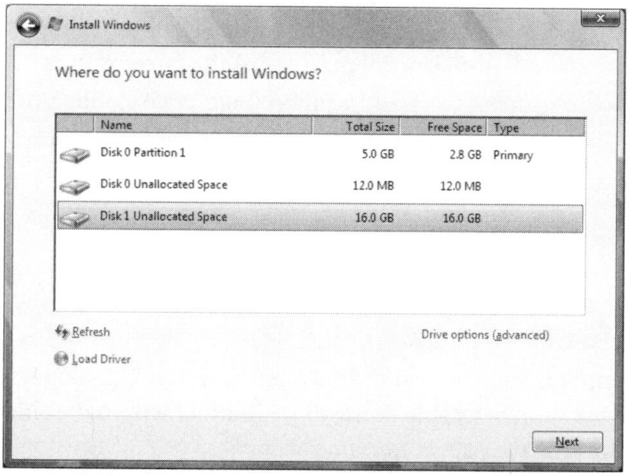

Figure 1-15   Installing Windows Vista on a second disk

12. Ensure that the disk with unallocated space is selected, and click New.

13. By default, all space on the disk is allocated to the new partition on which you install Windows Vista. Click Apply.

14. Click Format to format the newly created partition with the NTFS file system. When the installation routine has finished formatting the partition, click Next.

15. You need to wait for some time while Windows copies files, installs features and updates, and then completes the installation. The installation reboots during this process.

16. At the Choose A User Name And Picture page, assign the username **Kim_Ackers** and the password: **P@ssw0rd**. You need to enter the password twice, and you should enter a hint to remind you of what the password is. Click Next.

NOTE   Setting your own username and password

The practice items in this book assume that the initial username set up is **Kim_Ackers** and the assigned password is **P@ssw0rd**. If you decide to use a separate username and password pair, substitute it each time you see **Kim_Ackers**.

---

17. In the Type A Computer Name dialog box, shown earlier in Figure 1-14, type **620-Vista**. Select a desktop background, and then click Next.

18. On the Help Protect Windows Automatically page, click Use Recommended Settings.

19. On the Review Your Time And Date Settings page, select your time zone. If you live in a region that uses daylight savings time, ensure that the Automatically Adjust Clock For Daylight Savings Time check box is selected. Ensure that the date is correct and that the Time setting is accurate to within several minutes of the current time. Click Next.

20. On the Select Your Computer's Current Location page, click Public Location.

21. Click Start to complete the installation. Windows Vista now checks the computer's performance and assigns a rating before presenting you with the logon screen.

Lesson Summary

- If a computer does not boot directly into the Windows Vista installation routine, you might need to alter the BIOS settings.

- Prior to installation, you should ensure that you have your 25-character product key, have determined what antivirus solution you will implement, have chosen a computer name, and have chosen a user account name and password for the computer.

- Windows Vista allows you a 30-day activation grace period after the completion of the installation process.

- The unique 25-character product key ties you to a specific edition of Windows Vista. If you install an SKU of Windows Vista higher than the one you purchased, you will have to purchase the higher version or reinstall from scratch.

- If the disk that you want to install Windows Vista on is not visible during the installation process, you will have to install the correct driver.

- The user account that you create during the installation process will be the default administrator account for the Windows Vista computer. The default built-in administrator account is disabled in Windows Vista.

- Unless you have a special network configuration, you should use the recommended settings when Windows Vista asks whether you want to download and install updates.

- If you are unsure of which location to specify when the Windows Vista installation routine asks you, select Public Location.

- When a computer is configured to dual boot, each operating system is installed on a separate volume.

Lesson Review

You can use the following questions to test your knowledge of the information in Lesson 2, "Installing Windows Vista." The questions are also available on the companion CD if you prefer to review them in electronic form.

NOTE   Answers

Answers to these questions and explanations of why each answer choice is correct or incorrect are located in the "Answers" section at the end of the book.

---

1. In the next week, you will be responsible for installing Windows Vista Ultimate on 100 computers. Your organization has a Windows Server 2003 computer with WSUS installed. You want each computer to download updates from the WSUS server rather than Microsoft's Windows Update servers on the Internet. Which of the following steps should you take during the installation?

    A. On the Help Protect Windows Automatically page, click Use Recommended Settings.

    B. On the Help Protect Windows Automatically screen, click Ask Me Later.

    C. Configure the computer's current location as Work.

    D. Configure the computer's current location as Public Location.

2. You are performing an installation of Windows Vista Ultimate on a computer that will be used to edit multimedia files for a special effects house. You are using a DVD-ROM as the installation media. The computer is configured with a hardware RAID array. When you reach the portion of the installation routine where you should select a disk on which to install Windows Vista, none is detected. Which step should you take to remedy this?

    A. Configure BIOS to boot off the RAID array.

    B. Configure BIOS to boot off the DVD-ROM drive.

    C. Install the appropriate driver software for the RAID array.

    D. Roll back the driver software for the RAID array.

3. You want to configure a Windows XP Professional computer to dual boot with Windows Vista. Currently the computer has a single disk. The volume that Windows XP is installed on uses all but 3 GB of the disk's total capacity. What step should you take to achieve your goal?

    A. Purchase a second hard disk drive.

    B. Use disk partitioning software to create a new partition.

    C. Upgrade Windows XP to Windows Vista.

    D. Delete the partition containing Windows XP, and install Windows Vista.

Lesson 3: Installing, Updating, and Troubleshooting Windows Vista Device Drivers

Successfully installing Windows Vista does not ensure that all of the hardware devices on the computer will function correctly. Although Windows Vista includes a significant number of hardware drivers, there are likely to be some devices, especially more recent ones, that will require you to manually obtain and install the drivers yourself.

After this lesson, you will be able to:

- Use Device Manager to install drivers.
- Use Device Manager to update drivers.
- Use Device Manager to troubleshoot drivers.
- Use Windows Update to download current drivers.

Estimated lesson time: 75 minutes

Installing Drivers

Device drivers allow the operating system to interact with a specific piece of hardware. Without the device driver, the device often will not work. A scanner without a device driver installed will not scan and a printer without the correct device driver installed will not print.

A good example of how a device driver can make a difference is with graphics adapters. As a part of its hardware configuration, a computer might have a graphics adapter that has more than 256 MB of graphics memory. According to Windows Vista's specifications, that should be more than enough to run Aero. If, however, you are unable to locate a device driver written for Windows Vista for that particular graphics adapter, Windows Vista assigns it a standardized VGA graphics adapter driver. The standard VGA graphics adapter allows you to use Windows Vista but does not allow you to run Aero. Without the correct driver, performance of applications, such as games or Computer Aided Design (CAD) programs, will be poor, and Windows Vista will be able to make only minimal use of the graphics adapter's high performance capability. If you are able to obtain a device driver written for Windows Vista for the graphics adapter, you will experience a massive difference in graphics performance. Aero will run, CAD performance will improve, and your games will display with improved frame rates.

During the setup routine, Windows Vista attempts to locate and install as many hardware device drivers as possible. Most administrators find that most, if not all, of the hardware device drivers their computer requires are already installed the first time they log on. If a particular hardware device driver is not detected and installed automatically, it is possible to use Device Manager to manually install driver software located on CD-ROM or downloaded from the Internet.

Windows Update Driver Settings

When you install a new hardware device, Windows Vista checks its existing set of drivers to see if one is appropriate. By default, Windows Vista also checks with Windows Update in an attempt to locate a newer driver for the device or to see if one has been released if none exists within its existing set. The check with Windows Update behavior is governed by Windows Update Driver Settings, a property dialog box that is accessible through the System Properties. These settings determine how Windows Vista uses Windows Update to locate new drivers when a new device is connected. The three possible Windows Update Driver settings are:

- Check Automatically For Drivers Each Time A Device Is Connected
- Ask The User Whether To Perform The Check When A New Device Is Connected
- Never Check Windows Update For New Drivers

In some cases, you will want to change the default behavior. If you are installing hardware on a series of Windows Vista computers, you already have a copy of the most recent drivers, and your organization's Internet connection is slow, you might want to avoid having each computer contact the Internet when you attach the new hardware. Another reason for disabling the automatic check is that your organization might have a strict testing policy prior to deploying software. Even though Microsoft tests drivers thoroughly prior to uploading them to Windows Update, your organization might use a custom application that Microsoft is unaware of and this application just might conflict with an updated driver. Rather than having new drivers automatically installed, you might allow the installation only of drivers that have been thoroughly tested within your organization's environment.

Manually Installing a Driver

Sometimes no relevant driver is available on the Windows Vista Installation Media or through Windows Update. In this situation, the hardware device is displayed in Device Manager with a yellow warning icon next to it, as shown in Figure 1-16.

In this situation, you might have to install the device driver manually. Almost every hardware device that you purchase comes with a disk or CD-ROM containing device drivers. Alternatively, if you cannot find the disk, you will also usually find the most recent version of the device driver software on the vendor's website. Installing manually involves telling Windows Vista where to look for the drivers and then installing them.

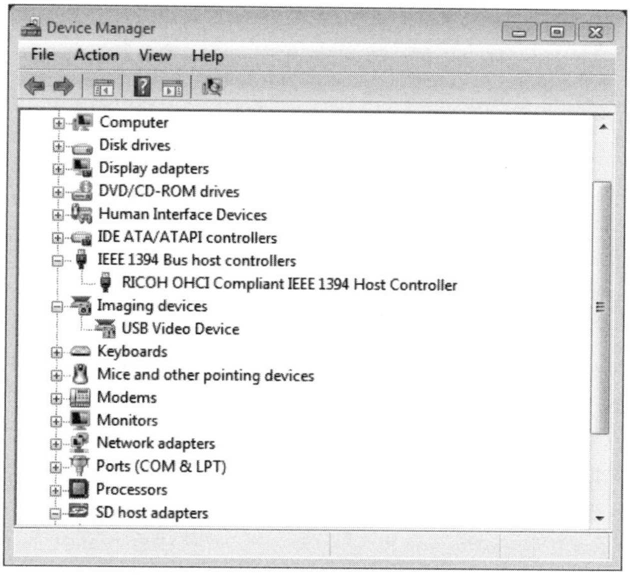

Figure 1-16   Warning icons indicate problems with hardware in Device Manager

To install the driver manually, perform the following steps:

- Make a note of the device driver's location. If you have downloaded the driver off the Internet, it was probably in a compressed format. You need to extract the files from the compressed archive before you can install the device driver.

- In the Start menu, click Control Panel. If the Device Manager icon is not displayed, click Classic View in the left side taskbar. Then, double-click Device Manager. In the User Account Control dialog box, click Continue.

NOTE   User Account Control

You will learn more about the purpose and function of User Account Control in Chapter 5, "User Account Control."

- Locate the device that you want to install the driver for and right-click it. Select Update Driver Software. In this example, the driver for the USB Video Device shown earlier in Figure 1-16 is installed.

- In the Update Driver Software window, click Browse My Computer For Driver Software.

- On the Browse For Driver Software On Your Computer page, shown in Figure 1-17, click Browse, and navigate to the folder containing the driver software. After you have located the folder containing the driver software, click Next.

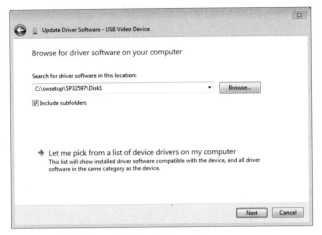

Figure 1-17   Browsing for driver software

The driver software installs, and the computer might request that you reboot.

Driver Signing

Before allowing the installation of a device driver, Windows Vista examines the driver's digital signature. A digital signature is a special block of code used to verify the identity and integrity of a set of files. If a signature is present, Windows Vista validates the integrity of the driver files. Windows Vista then assigns the driver one of the following categories:

- **Signed by Windows Signing Authority**   This driver is either included in Windows Vista or distributed through Windows Update. This driver is signed either by Windows Hardware Quality Lab (WHQL) testing or Windows Sustained Engineering.
- **Signed by trusted publisher**   This driver is signed by a third party (non-Microsoft organization) that the user has explicitly chosen to trust.
- **Signed by untrusted publisher**   This driver is signed by a third party that the user has explicitly chosen not to trust.
- **Signed by publisher of unknown trust**   This driver is signed by a third party that the user has not designated as trusted or untrusted.
- **Altered**   Using the digital signature, Windows Vista has determined that the driver files have been altered since being signed by the publisher.
- **Unsigned**   These drivers do not have a valid digital signature.

If the user attempting to install the driver has no administrative privileges, Windows Vista automatically installs drivers from trusted publishers and silently refuses to install drivers from all other categories. Trusted publishers are designated by a user who has administrator privileges using a special tool called the Certificates console. Using the Certificates console is beyond the scope of the 70-620 exam.

When a user with administrative privileges attempts to install a driver signed by a publisher of unknown trust, Windows Vista prompts the user, asking if he or she wants to install the driver and add the publisher, as shown in Figure 1-18. If a driver lacks a valid signature or has been altered, Windows Vista displays a strong warning against installing the driver, but a user with administrative privileges can still install the software.

Figure 1-18　The warning that Windows Vista displays to a user with administrative privileges who attempts to install a driver from an unknown publisher

Updating Drivers

Updating drivers is the process of replacing older drivers with more recent versions. Windows Vista simplifies the process of updating drivers by making it almost the same process as the one that you use to manually install drivers. Vendors update drivers in an attempt to remove bugs and improve performance. Each hardware device driver has a version number, and Windows Vista examines this version number when it attempts to determine whether a particular driver is an update of another driver. If you download a driver from a vendor's website, it might be more recent than the driver that is available through Windows Update. This might occur because Microsoft puts drivers that appear on Windows Update through a further level of testing after the vendor submits the driver for distribution.

If you have configured the Windows Update Driver Settings to never update drivers, you will have to manually force an update. You will also need to force an update if you have obtained newer drivers for a device if those drivers are not yet hosted on the Windows Update site. The process of updating to drivers that you have downloaded from the Internet or which are stored on CD-ROM is the same as the process for installing drivers by specifying the location of the folder that holds them. This process was covered earlier in this chapter, in the section on installing drivers.

To manually update drivers from the Internet, perform the following steps:

- In the Start menu, click Control Panel. If the Device Manager icon is not displayed, click Classic View in the left side taskbar.
- In Control Panel, double-click Device Manager. Click Continue to close the User Account Control dialog box.

- Locate the device for which you want to update the driver.
- Right-click the device, and select Update Driver Software.
- Click Search Automatically For Updated Driver Software. This makes Windows search your computer, including the CD or DVD-ROM drive and the Windows Update website, for updated drivers. If Windows locates an updated driver, it automatically installs it, as shown in Figure 1-19.

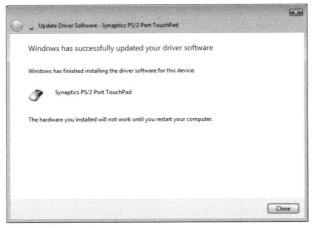

Figure 1-19   Downloading and installing an updated driver from the Internet

New drivers appear as optional updates in Windows Update. You can initiate Windows Update by opening the Start menu, clicking All Programs, and then clicking Windows Update. After Windows Update has opened, click Check For Updates.

To determine which drivers are available, click View Available Updates. This opens the View Available Updates window shown in Figure 1-20. Select the check box next to the update you want to install, and then click Install.

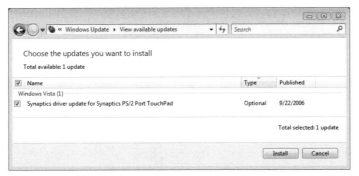

Figure 1-20   Viewing driver updates as optional updates in Windows Update

---

Quick Check

1. Which categories of drivers does Windows Vista allow users without administrator privileges to install?
2. What are the three Windows Update Driver Settings?

Quick Check Answers

1. Drivers signed by the Windows Signing Authority and drivers signed from sources on the trusted publishers list
2. Check Automatically For Drivers Each Time A Device Is Connected, Ask The User Whether To Perform The Check When A New Device Is Connected, and Never Check Windows Update For New Drivers

---

Troubleshooting Drivers

Troubleshooting drivers is the art of determining which hardware device driver is causing a system stability problem. Often, it is quite easy to figure this out. If the hardware works on a computer with a different operating system but not on Windows Vista, you can conclude that the hardware is not broken. If the hardware does not work on any operating system, you would suspect that the hardware was causing the problem.

Hardware device driver problems manifest in several ways:

- **The device the driver manages does not work**   This diagnosis is relatively simple to make. For example, when connected to a Windows XP Professional computer, documents sent to a color laser printer print successfully. When the same printer is connected to a Windows Vista computer, documents sent to the color laser printer do not print. In this situation, you would suspect the driver.

- **The device the driver manages works erratically**   This is more difficult to diagnose because it might not happen every time. Over time, however, you would notice that the computer would sometimes crash when you tried to do the same thing. If the computer crashed once every five times you tried to print a document, you would eventually figure out that there was something wrong with the printer driver.

- **Windows Vista encounters a STOP error when the device is being used**   STOP errors manifest themselves as a blue screen with white text. Often, the text provides a hint as to what has caused the STOP error. By default, Windows Vista dumps kernel memory to %SYSTEMROOT%\MEMORY.DMP and then reboots. One way of ensuring that you get the details of a STOP error down is to prevent Windows Vista from automatically rebooting. This procedure is discussed in this lesson's practice session.

- **Error or warning dialog boxes appear on the screen when the device is in use**   The error message might relate to something else, or a program might crash when you attempt something involving the device. For example, if an application crashes every time you try to use one scanner but works fine when you use another, you would suspect that the driver for the first scanner might be faulty.

■ **After a long period of stability, the installation of a new driver causes the computer to become unstable** If a computer has been stable for a long time prior to the installation of a new driver and errors and crashes start to occur, it is likely that the new driver is causing the problem.

When you have determined that a hardware device driver is causing the problem, you have three options. The first is to update to a newer version of the same driver. Updating drivers was covered earlier in this lesson. The second option is to roll back the driver to a previous version, one that you know works and does not cause errors. The third option is to completely uninstall the hardware device driver. The second and third options are discussed in the remainder of this lesson.

Rolling Back Drivers

Driver rollback allows you to return to using a previous version of a hardware driver, should you find that the drivers you have installed are either not working or are causing errors or system instability. Driver rollback was a feature introduced with Windows XP. Prior to Windows XP, returning a computer to an earlier version of a driver was a nightmare. Often, it was simpler to reinstall the entire operating system from scratch! You can roll back a driver by editing a device's properties in Device Manager. It is possible to use driver rollback only if a previous version of the driver had been installed on the computer. If no previous version exists, the Roll Back Driver button in the Driver tab of the device's Properties dialog box is dimmed.

To roll back a device driver, perform the following steps:

1. In the Start menu, click Control Panel. If the Device Manager icon is not displayed, click Classic View in the left side taskbar.

2. In Control Panel, double-click Device Manager. Click Continue to close the User Account Control dialog box.

3. Locate the device for which you will roll back the driver.

4. Right-click the device, and select Properties.

5. In the device's Properties dialog box, shown in Figure 1-21, on the Driver tab, click Roll Back Driver.

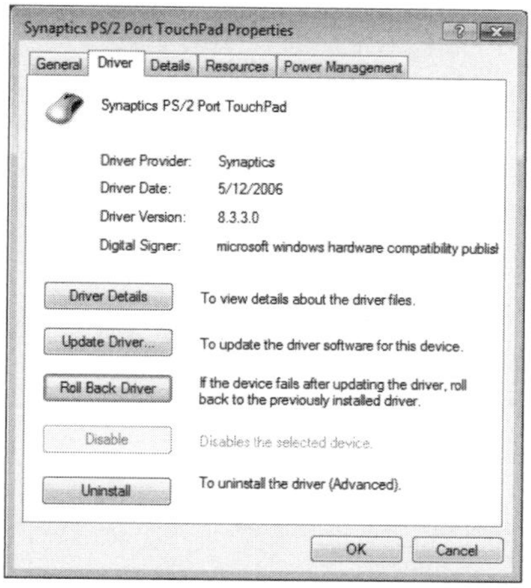

Figure 1-21   The device's Properties dialog box

6.   Click Yes to the Warning. The driver is now rolled back.

7.   Click Close to close the device properties. In some cases, you will need to reboot the computer for the change to take effect.

If a recently installed driver is stopping Windows Vista from finishing the boot process and you are therefore unable to roll the driver back, you can use the Last Known Good Configuration boot option. The Last Known Good Configuration option is present as a boot option in the event that Windows Vista was unable to complete the startup process the last time that process was attempted. The Last Known Good Configuration is written after the logon process is completed. If the computer allows you to log on, the previous Last Known Good Configuration is overwritten to include the problematic driver software.

Real World

Orin Thomas

Being a regular gamer, I frequently check the website of the manufacturer of my gaming computer's graphics card to see if an updated device driver has been released. When an updated driver is released, I immediately download and install it, hoping to squeeze a few more frames per second out of my favorite graphically intensive games. Sometimes an updated driver means that I can turn on a few more details in the game's 3D engine, making my experience just a little more immersive. In general, my impatience has been rewarded. Once or twice, the manufacturer has not ironed out all the bugs in the driver, and I have to use the driver rollback feature to return to the previous version until the issue is resolved.

Removing a Driver

In some situations, it is impossible to roll back a driver. This often happens when you have installed a vendor's driver manually for a device because Windows Vista and Windows Update have failed to locate one. If this manually installed driver is causing system instability and you cannot roll it back, you need to uninstall it. You should remove a driver only when you are unable to roll the driver back.

1. In the Start menu, click Control Panel. If the Device Manager icon is not displayed, click Classic View in the left side taskbar.
2. In Control Panel, double-click Device Manager. Click Continue to close the User Account Control dialog box.
3. Locate the device for which you will roll back the driver.
4. Right-click the device, and select Properties.
5. In the device's Properties dialog box, click the Driver tab.
6. Click Uninstall. A warning, like the one in Figure 1-22, is shown. Click OK.

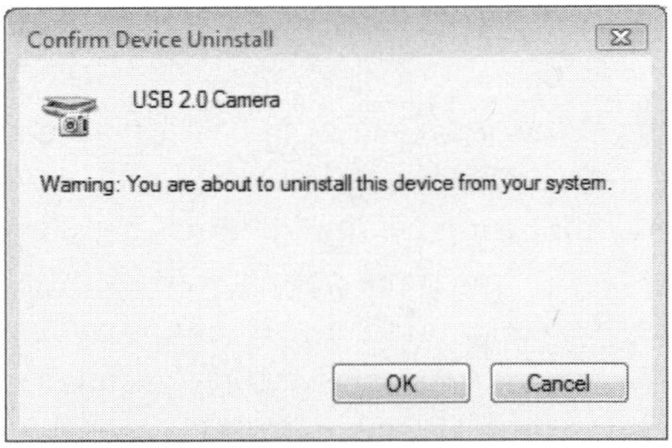

Figure 1-22   Warning presented when uninstalling a driver

7. The device driver is removed from the system. If you refresh Device Manager, you will see the yellow warning icon next to the device you removed the driver from. Windows attempts to reinstall the driver when it detects the device, but because the driver has been uninstalled, it will be unable to do so.

Practice: Managing Windows Vista Device Drivers

In these two practices, you will perform two tasks that are integral to managing and trouble-shooting Windows Vista device drivers. The first practice task involves configuring Windows Update Driver Settings. These settings control Windows Vista's behavior in looking for new drivers when a new hardware device is detected. The second practice involves configuring Windows Vista's system failure settings.

▶ **Practice 1: Configuring Windows Update Driver Settings**

In this practice, you will configure the Windows Update Driver Settings. These settings determine how Windows Vista will use Windows Update to locate new drivers when a new device is connected. The possible settings are to check automatically for drivers each time a device is connected, to ask whether the check should be performed when a new device is connected, or to never perform the check. To configure the Windows Update Driver settings, perform the following steps:

1. In the Start menu, click Control Panel. If the Device Manager icon is not displayed, click Classic View in the left pane.
2. Double-click System.
3. Under Tasks, click Advanced System Settings. Click Continue to close the User Account Control dialog box.
4. Click the Hardware tab.
5. Click the Windows Update Driver Settings button.
6. In the Windows Update Driver Settings dialog box, select the Ask Me Each Time I Connect A New Device Before Checking For Drivers option, as shown in Figure 1-23.

Figure 1-23   The Windows Update Driver Settings dialog box

7. Click OK to close the dialog box.
8. Click OK again to close the System Properties dialog box.

▶ **Practice 2: Configuring System Failure Options**

The Windows Vista system failure setting determines the amount of debugging information that Windows Vista provides if a STOP error occurs. By default, Windows Vista performs a kernel memory dump and then automatically reboots. If you are trying to determine which driver is causing the STOP error to occur, you will want the STOP error screen to remain displayed until you have had time to jot down as much information about the error as possible.

For this to happen, you need to stop Windows Vista from automatically rebooting. Dumping all memory also allows you to more thoroughly debug what is going on, although examining Windows memory dump files is beyond the scope of the 70-620 exam. To configure the Windows Vista system failure settings, perform the following steps:

1. In the Start menu, click Control Panel. If the Device Manager icon is not displayed, click Classic View in the left side taskbar.

2. Double-click System.

3. Under Tasks, click Advanced System Settings. Click Continue to close the User Account Control dialog box.

4. Click the Advanced tab, and then click the Settings button in the Startup And Recovery section.

5. Clear the Automatically Restart check box.

6. From the Write Debugging Information drop-down list, select Complete Memory Dump.

7. Click OK twice to close the Startup And Recovery dialog box and the System Properties dialog box.

Lesson Summary

- The majority of hardware device driver software is installed automatically during the installation process.

- Windows Update Driver Settings determine whether Windows Vista will contact the Windows Update website to locate drivers when new hardware is detected.

- The primary tool used to install, configure, and manage device drivers is the Device Manager console.

- To install driver software obtained from the hardware vendor, right-click in Device Manager, and select update software. From there, specify the location of the driver files.

- If a driver causes system instability, edit the driver properties in Device Manager, and roll the driver back to a previous version.

- If a driver cannot be rolled back to a previous version but is still causing system instability, it is possible to uninstall the driver completely by editing the device properties in Device Manager.

Lesson Review

You can use the following questions to test your knowledge of the information in Lesson 3, "Installing, Updating, and Troubleshooting Windows Vista Device Drivers." The questions are also available on the companion CD if you prefer to review them in electronic form.

NOTE **Answers**

Answers to these questions and explanations of why each answer choice is correct or incorrect are located in the "Answers" section at the end of the book.

1. Which of the following items in the Control Panel can you use to determine whether or not updated device drivers are available for the hardware on your Windows Vista computer? (Choose all that apply.)

    A. Windows Update

    B. Device Manager

    C. Network and Sharing Center

    D. Add Hardware

2. Last week you updated your graphics adapter manually after downloading new device driver software from the vendor's website. This is the third time you have done this since you purchased your Windows Vista computer. Until now, you have never experienced any system instability. Since the installation of the latest version of the driver, the computer appears to crash randomly. You suspect the new driver. What should you do?

    A. Uninstall the driver.

    B. Run Windows Update to obtain a new driver.

    C. Roll back the device driver.

    D. Roll back using System Restore.

3. You are working on installing a new hardware device on 1000 Windows Vista computers. Because you have a copy of the latest signed device drivers for this hardware on a USB thumb drive, you do not want Windows Vista automatically querying Windows Update looking for new drivers. You want to configure Windows Vista to ask you whether it should check Windows Update for new drivers when you attach a new hardware device. Which of the following steps should you take to ensure that this happens?

    A. Configure Windows Update Driver Settings.

    B. Configure User Account Control.

    C. Configure Device Manager.

    D. Configure Startup and Recovery.

Chapter Review

To further practice and reinforce the skills you learned in this chapter, you can perform the following tasks:

- Review the chapter summary.
- Review the list of key terms introduced in this chapter.
- Complete the case scenarios. These scenarios set up real-world situations involving the topics of this chapter and ask you to create a solution.
- Complete the suggested practices.
- Take a practice test.

Chapter Summary

- Performing a hardware evaluation involves comparing Windows Vista's minimum and recommended specifications against the hardware configuration of the computer on which you intend to install Windows Vista.
- The Windows Vista Upgrade Advisor is a software tool that you can use to help determine a computer's capacity to run Windows Vista.
- The user account created during the installation process has local administrator privileges.
- Dual booting allows a user to run Windows Vista while retaining the ability to run another operating system.
- Unlike previous versions of Windows, Windows Vista uses the Windows Updates process to stay current with the latest drivers.
- Drivers that cause problems with system stability can be rolled back to previous versions or uninstalled completely.

Key Terms

Do you know what these key terms mean? You can check your answers by looking up the terms in the glossary at the end of the book.

- Aero
- BIOS
- DirectX
- driver rollback
- driver signing
- dual booting
- Hardware Pixel Shader

- Media Center
- multiprocessor support
- Stock Keeping Unit (SKU)
- Tablet PC
- Windows Product Activation (WPA)
- Windows Vista Display Driver Model (WDDM)

Case Scenarios

In the following case scenarios, you will apply what you have learned about different editions of Windows Vista and how to troubleshoot problems with hardware device drivers. You can find answers to these questions in the "Answers" section at the end of this book.

Case Scenario 1: Recommending Windows Vista Editions

You work as a senior technician at the local computer superstore. The sales department has asked you to help them with a Windows Vista promotion where they can match customer needs with specific editions of the Windows Vista client operating system.

1. Which edition of Windows Vista should be recommended to users in a home environment who do not have a high performance graphics card, do not require multimedia functionality, and only want to run multiple Office 2007 applications while surfing the Internet?
2. Which edition of Windows Vista should be included on Tablet PC computers aimed at home users who do not need to connect their computers to an Active Directory domain?
3. Which edition of Windows Vista should be included on mobile computers that will be used by executives who want to connect to both their home and business networks while retaining Media Center functionality?

Case Scenario 2: Diagnosing and Troubleshooting Device Driver Problems

You work as a senior technician for a large computer superstore. You have three computers that you suspect are having problems with hardware device drivers. The problems are as follows:

1. The owner of computer one purchased a printer a year ago, prior to upgrading to Windows Vista. Since upgrading to Windows Vista six months ago, the user has been unable to print. What step should you first try to resolve this problem?
2. The owner of computer two has installed the latest version of a vendor's graphics adapter driver. Since performing this installation, the computer has begun to freeze

every time the owner's mother attempts to print from Microsoft Word. Which course of action should you pursue?

3. Computer three has what appears to be random STOP errors. Unfortunately, the computer restarts before you have time to read any of the information displayed in the STOP error message. What steps could you take to ensure that you can see the text of the STOP error message?

Suggested Practices

To help you successfully master the exam objectives presented in this chapter, complete the following tasks.

Identify Hardware Requirements

■ **Practice 1: Evaluate existing hardware**   Evaluate five separate Windows XP computers owned by you, your organization, or your friends to determine whether they would qualify for the Windows Vista Premium Ready certification as outlined in Lesson 1, "Identifying Hardware Requirements."

■ **Practice 2: Using the Windows Vista Upgrade Advisor**   Install and run the Windows Vista Upgrade Advisor on three separate Windows XP computers owned by you, the organization you work for, or your friends. Use the advisor to determine which edition of Windows Vista would best suit each computer based on its current usage profile.

Perform a Clean Installation

Because the practice in this section will take a significant amount of time, only one is listed.

■ **Practice: Wipe and Redo**   Perform a second installation of Windows Vista Business. Do this by deleting and then re-creating the partition and volume you created when installing Windows Vista Business in Lesson 2, "Installing Windows Vista."

Install and Configure Windows Vista Drivers

■ **Practice 1: Updating drivers using the Internet**   Run Windows Update, and use the optional updates to install any updated drivers.

■ **Practice 2: Driver rollback**   Use the driver rollback feature to roll back any driver that you updated in Practice 1 to its initial state. After you have rebooted, reinstall the driver by right-clicking it in Device Manager and selecting Update.

Take a Practice Test

The practice tests on this book's companion CD offer many options. For example, you can test yourself on just one exam objective, or you can test yourself on all the 70-620 certification exam content. You can set up the test so that it closely simulates the experience of taking a certification exam, or you can set it up in study mode so that you can look at the correct answers and explanations after you answer each question.

MORE INFO **Practice tests**

For details about all the practice test options available, see the "How to Use the Practice Tests" section in this book's Introduction.

Chapter 2

Windows Vista Upgrades and Migrations

Although consumers start buying and using a new operating system from the day it appears, most large organizations take their time moving to the new technology. A consumer who upgrades a PC to Windows Vista is already enthusiastic about learning the new ways to do old things and exploring the limits of the new features. Organizations move slower than consumers, and many will not get around to adopting Windows Vista until it has been available for several years. When large organizations move to a new operating system, they rarely replace their existing hardware. This means that information technology (IT) pros who support desktop operating systems need to be conversant with moving people from Microsoft Windows XP to Windows Vista. The first lesson in this chapter explores the two processes by which this is achieved: migration and upgrade.

Unlike several years ago, when a computer had to be upgraded or replaced every few years to remain capable of running the latest productivity software, today's computers are powerful enough that they are likely to be capable of running the latest productivity software well into the next decade. With this in mind, it is likely that the needs that lead a person to choose a specific edition of Windows Vista at the beginning of their computer's life cycle might have expanded as that person becomes more familiar with the operating system's capabilities. The second lesson in this chapter explores the process of moving from one edition of Windows Vista to another.

Unfortunately, not all installations and upgrades will complete successfully. Sometimes this is because the person performing the upgrade forgets an important fact; sometimes it is due to an event beyond your control, such as a power failure during the installation. The chapter's final lesson examines methods that can be used to troubleshoot the Windows Vista upgrade and installation process.

Exam objectives in this chapter:
- Upgrade to Windows Vista from previous versions of Windows.
- Upgrade from one edition of Windows Vista to another edition.
- Troubleshoot Windows Vista installation issues.

Lessons in this chapter:

Before You Begin

To complete the lessons in this chapter, you must have done the following:

- Completed the installation practices in Chapter 1, "Installing Windows Vista Client," Lesson 2, "Installing Windows Vista." The result of this practice is that you have installed Windows Vista Business on a personal computer or in a virtual machine.
- To complete the practice in Lesson 1, you should have access to a Windows XP computer with Service Pack 2 installed. The optional practice involves performing an upgrade of a Windows XP computer, but you should attempt this only under the circumstances outlined in the practice.

No additional configuration is required for this chapter.

Real World

Orin Thomas

Recently, I was asked by friends and family who have computers that are a couple of years old but still meet the recommended requirements for Windows Vista and who want to get Vista, whether they should upgrade their current operating system to Vista or buy a new PC and migrate their data. To answer this question, I take a three-year view. I ask myself, "How will they be using their computer in three years time?" My brother-in-law, who loves to play computer games as much as I do, would be better off getting a new computer that runs Vista and migrating his data. If he upgraded his current computer to Vista, given the type of games he likes to play, he'd probably need a new one within 18 months anyway. If I recommended that he upgrade his current computer, he would end up buying Vista twice and still have to perform the migration of data to his new computer! My neighbors, on the other hand, do not do anything other than a bit of e-mail and word processing. If they wanted Vista, perhaps because they want to use Media Center or really like Aero, I'd recommend that they upgrade. It is highly likely that they will still be happy with the performance of their current hardware in several years time—something I am sure would not apply to my brother-in-law!

Lesson 1: Upgrading and Migrating to Windows Vista

Whether you upgrade or migrate to Windows Vista depends on the hardware and software configuration of the computer you're going to work with. In Chapter 1, "Installing Windows Vista Client," we discussed dual booting, which is when a computer is configured to run both Windows Vista and another operating system. Upgrading and migrating differ from dual booting because both involve having the user's data, such as Microsoft Internet Explorer bookmarks and desktop settings, included in the new Windows Vista installation. When upgrading or migrating to Windows Vista, the user forgoes using the existing operating system.

After this lesson, you will be able to:
- Determine valid upgrade paths.
- Explain the difference between an upgrade and a migration to Windows Vista.
- Understand the functionality of the Windows Easy Transfer tool.
- Use the Windows Easy Transfer tool to migrate data to Windows Vista.
- Identify application compatibility requirements.

Estimated lesson time: 30 minutes

NOTE   The lesson time will be longer if you perform the optional upgrade from Windows XP to Windows Vista.

Upgrade and Migration Concepts

Some of the questions in the 70-620 exam involve your understanding the difference between an upgrade and a migration. When explaining upgrades and migrations, it is important to be precise with definitions. This first section clarifies some concepts that will be useful throughout the rest of the chapter. These terms build on each other and are defined as follows:

- **Original operating system**   This is the operating system that users have been using and which hosts their data until they upgrade or migrate. In the 70-620 exam, the original operating system can be Windows 2000, Windows XP, and Windows Vista.
- **Destination operating system**   The operating system that the user will be using when the upgrade or migration process is completed. For the purposes of the 70-620 exam, the destination operating system will always be Windows Vista.
- **Upgrading**   Upgrading is the process by which the original operating system is directly converted to Windows Vista. All data and user settings are retained, although it is possible that application compatibility problems might arise. Application compatibility problems are covered in more detail later in this lesson.

- **Migrating**   Migrating is the process by which the user's settings and data are moved to a new Windows Vista installation. There are two types of migration: side-by-side and wipe-and-load. A side-by-side migration is one in which you migrate files from one computer to a separate computer. A wipe-and-load migration is one in which you migrate data off a computer, perform a clean installation of a new operating system on that computer, and then migrate the data back.

Here are some examples that might help you understand the differences between an upgrade and a migration:

- If you purchased a second computer that had Windows Vista pre-installed and you moved all of your data from your original computer, regardless of what operating system is on the original computer, you are performing a migration. This type of migration is a side-by-side migration.

- If you add a new hard disk drive to your existing computer, install Windows Vista in a dual boot configuration, and move your settings and data across to Windows Vista, you are also performing a migration. This type of migration is a side-by-side migration.

- If you back up your data to a DVD-ROM, format your hard disk drive, and then perform a clean install of Windows Vista, you are performing a migration. This is a wipe-and-load migration.

- If you back up your data to a DVD-ROM and then upgrade the original operating system, you are performing an upgrade.

- If you use the Custom Install option to install Windows Vista on top of the partition that currently hosts Windows XP, you are performing a migration. In this scenario, your original Windows folder will be renamed Windows.old. Although your applications will still be located in the Program Files folder, they need to be reinstalled to be recognized by the new installation of Windows Vista.

CAUTION   Perform a full backup!

Prior to migrating or upgrading, you should take a full backup of the original operating system, including all user data. You should get into the habit of backing up important user data regularly. Although using one of the migration tools is likely to be all that you need, you should take a full backup prior to performing a migration or upgrade. Having a full backup gives you a fallback position if something goes catastrophically wrong.

Identifying Valid Upgrade Paths

Direct upgrades to Windows Vista from previous versions of Windows are the exception rather than the rule. In general, unless you are running Windows XP, it will be necessary to perform a migration rather than an upgrade. It is also important to consider that it is not possible to upgrade from a 32-bit operating system to a 64-bit or from a 64-bit operating system to a 32-bit. Moving between operating system architectures requires a clean install on a new volume. Following is a list of previous versions of Windows and the Windows Vista migration and upgrade options that are available for them.

- **Windows 95 / 98 / Me**   It is not possible to directly upgrade to any edition of Windows Vista from Windows 95, 98, or Me. It is possible to use earlier versions of the User State Migration Tool to migrate data from these operating systems to any edition of Windows Vista, but Microsoft does not support such a migration. It is not possible to use Windows Easy Transfer to migrate data from these operating systems.

- **Windows NT 4 Workstation**   It is not possible to upgrade directly from Windows NT® 4 Workstation to any edition of Windows Vista. It is possible to use the User State Migration Tool to migrate data from Windows NT 4 to any edition of Windows Vista, but Microsoft does not support such a migration.

NOTE   Unsupported migrations

Version 2.x of the User State Migration Tool works perfectly well with Windows 95 / 98 / Me and NT 4 and was used to migrate data from these operating systems to Windows XP when it was released. Version 3.x of the tool is unsupported on these earlier operation systems. It is important to note that the most recent versions of the User State Migration Tool are able to import files generated by the version 2.x tool.

- **Windows 2000 Professional**   It is impossible to directly upgrade to Windows Vista from Windows 2000 Professional. If Service Pack 4 is installed, it is possible to use Windows Easy Transfer to migrate data and user settings from Windows 2000 Professional to any edition of Windows Vista. It is also possible to use the User State Migration Tool to migrate data and user settings from Windows 2000 Professional to any edition of Windows Vista.

NOTE   Bridgehead migrations

Although it requires a significant amount of effort, if you have the required software, it is of course possible to upgrade Windows 98, Me, NT 4.0, and 2000 to Windows XP and then to upgrade Windows XP to Windows Vista. Because this type of technique is not in any way supported by Microsoft, it will not be on the 70-620 exam.

- **Windows XP Home**   It is possible to directly upgrade to all 32-bit editions of Windows Vista from Windows XP Home. It is possible to use both the User State Migration Tool and Windows Easy Transfer to migrate data from Windows XP Home to any edition of Windows Vista.

- **Windows XP Professional**   Unlike Windows XP Home, it is possible to upgrade Windows XP Professional only to the 32-bit Business, Enterprise, and Ultimate editions of Windows Vista. It is possible to use the User State Migration Tool or Windows Easy Transfer to migrate data from Windows XP Professional to any edition of Windows Vista.

■ **Windows XP Professional 64-bit edition**   It is only possible to upgrade to the 64-bit Business, Enterprise, and Ultimate editions of Windows Vista from Windows XP Professional 64-bit. It is not possible to upgrade from Windows XP Professional 64-bit to a 32-bit edition of Windows Vista. It is possible to use the User State Migration Tool or Windows Easy Transfer to migrate data from Windows XP 64-bit edition to any edition of Windows Vista.

■ **Windows XP Media Center**   It is possible to upgrade Windows XP Media Center only to the 32-bit Home Premium and Ultimate editions of Windows Vista. This is because these editions are the only ones that have Media Center functionality. It is possible to use the User State Migration Tool or Windows Easy Transfer to migrate data from Windows XP Media Center to any edition of Windows Vista.

■ **Windows XP Tablet PC**   It is possible to upgrade Windows XP Tablet PC only to the 32-bit Business, Enterprise, and Ultimate editions of Windows Vista. Only these editions of Windows Vista have Tablet PC functionality. It is possible to use the User State Migration Tool or Windows Easy Transfer to migrate data from Windows XP Tablet PC to any edition of Windows Vista.

Upgrading from Server Operating Systems

Sometimes, especially in environments where the person who is responsible for IT support does not have a background in IT, you will encounter a situation where someone is using a server operating system on a workstation. It is not unheard of to encounter a receptionist using a computer running Small Business Server 2003 with Microsoft Office installed. You will not encounter such a scenario on the 70-620 exam, but you will be surprised what you will encounter working on as an IT pro in the real world. You can use the User State Migration Tool to remedy this situation. Although such a scenario is unlikely to occur on the exam, in the real world, knowing how to migrate data off a server configured as a workstation will be a valuable, if only occasionally used, skill.

Migrating to Windows Vista

Both the User State Migration Tool and Windows Easy Transfer can use three methods of transferring data from the original operating system to the new Windows Vista installation. The tool that you select depends heavily on the situation. For most scenarios covered by the 70-620 exam, the Windows Easy Transfer tool is appropriate. For the sake of completeness, the following section also covers the more advanced User State Migration Tool.

Windows Easy Transfer

Windows Easy Transfer is the tool that you should use when you have only a few users to migrate from the original operating system to the destination operating system. Windows Easy Transfer is very similar to the Windows XP File Settings And Transfer Wizard. Windows Easy Transfer has the following properties:

- Windows Easy Transfer writes data only to computers running Windows Vista.

- You can use Windows Easy Transfer only to transfer files from a computer running Windows 2000 SP4. You cannot use it to transfer other settings.

- Windows Easy Transfer can transfer user accounts, files, and settings from computers running Windows XP SP2 and Windows Vista. When you use it to transfer data from Windows XP SP2 or Windows Vista, Windows Easy Transfer can migrate Internet Explorer bookmarks, music files, pictures, documents, desktop settings, application settings, mail account settings, and mail.

- Windows Easy Transfer does not migrate password settings to the new computer.

- It is possible using Windows Easy Transfer to create a CD-ROM on a computer with a CD-ROM writer that you can use to install Windows Easy Transfer on a computer running Windows 2000 SP4 or Windows XP SP2.

- During the Windows Easy Transfer process, no files or settings will be deleted from the computer running the original operating system.

Windows Easy Transfer allows you to move data between computers using four methods:

- **Windows Easy Transfer Cable**   Available from hardware vendors, this special cable, illustrated in Figure 2-1, plugs into the source and destination computer's universal serial bus (USB) ports. If both computers have USB 2 ports, it is possible to transfer up to a gigabyte of data between them every minute. Unless you are performing this function regularly, you might not want to purchase the cable. If you are performing transfers regularly, using a cable is simpler than performing network configuration or organizing removable media.

Figure 2-1   Windows Easy Transfer Cable

- **Local area network**   It is possible to transfer data over a local area network using the Windows Easy Transfer tool.
- **Optical media**   If the computer with the original operating system has a CD or DVD-ROM recorder, it is possible to burn transferred data to this media and then import it on the computer with the destination operating system. The downside with this method is that optical media can hold only a limited amount of data.
- **Removable storage**   USB devices or removable hard disk drives can also be used to migrate data using the Windows Easy Transfer Tool.

When running the Windows Easy Transfer tool, you usually start by running the application on the destination operating system and selecting a transfer medium, as shown in Figure 2-2. You also need to generate a Windows Easy Transfer Key on the destination computer. This key is used to protect files and settings using encryption when they are transferred across the network. That way, if the files and settings are intercepted, the person who intercepted them would not be able to access them. It is necessary to generate a key prior to starting Windows Easy Transfer on the original computer.

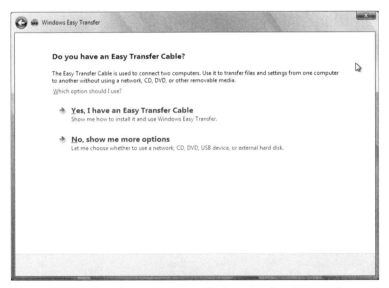

Figure 2-2   Performing an easy transfer by selecting the transfer method on the destination computer first

If an upgrade is impossible, it's also possible to use Windows Easy Transfer when moving a computer from Windows XP to Windows Vista. In this case, you do not start Windows Easy Transfer on the destination operating system because it does not exist until you finalize the installation of Windows Vista. For example, a computer running Windows XP has two hard disk drives. A disk drive is partitioned in such a way that, because of disk space limitations on the volume hosting Windows XP, it is impossible to perform an upgrade to Windows Vista. If you repartitioned the disk hosting the volume with Windows XP, meaning that the volume hosting Windows XP would be lost, it would be possible to install Windows Vista on the newly repartitioned volume. In this case, you first use Windows Easy Transfer to write the migration data to a removable storage device, repartition the computer's disk, perform a clean install of Windows Vista, and then run Windows Easy Transfer to import the migration data from the removable storage device you saved it to.

NOTE Repartitioning

Repartitioning is the process by which you reconfigure how a physical disk drive is mapped out with logical volumes. Unless you use special tools, all data on a volume that is repartitioned will be lost.

You have two options when migrating account data to the new computer using Windows Easy Transfer:

- Migrate a user account on the original computer to a newly created user account on the destination computer.
- Migrate a user account on the original computer to an existing local account on the destination computer, as shown in Figure 2-3.

If you choose the second option, all of the original computer user account files and settings will be added to the account files and settings of the specified user on the destination computer. For example, Ian has a user account on a Windows XP computer that contains important documents and Internet Explorer bookmarks. Ian also has a user account on a new computer running Windows Vista that has existing bookmarks and other important documents. Using Windows Easy Transfer, Ian can add all of the documents, bookmarks, and settings from his account on the Windows XP computer to the new computer running Windows Vista.

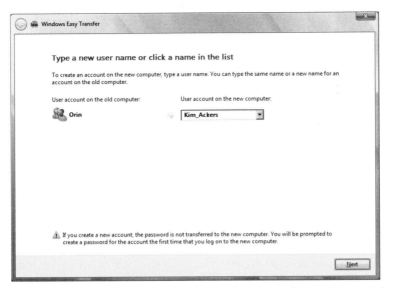

Figure 2-3   In this transfer, all the files and settings of user account Orin on the Windows XP computer are migrated to the Kim_Ackers account on the Windows Vista computer

If you create a new account on the destination computer, you should be aware that no password will be transferred. When the user tries to log on using the new account on the destination computer, the user is prompted to create a new password.

MORE INFO   **Windows Easy Transfer tool**

For more information on the Windows Easy Transfer utility, visit the following webpage on the Microsoft website: *http://www.microsoft.com/windowsvista/community/ready_winvista.mspx*.

User State Migration Tool

You can use Version 3 of the User State Migration Tool to automate the migration of large numbers of user accounts on Windows XP and Windows Vista operating systems. In general, the tools can migrate the same type of information from a computer running Windows XP to a computer running Windows Vista. Some differences between the tools include the following:

■ The User State Migration Tool can be completely automated by creating a migration rule. Windows Easy Transfer requires a significant amount of user interaction. This means that the User State Migration Tool can be used to automate large deployments.

NOTE   **Migration rule**

A migration rule is an Extensible Markup Language (XML) file that specifies precisely which user accounts, settings, and files are migrated and how this migration is to occur.

- The User State Migration Tool can migrate user data from a computer running Windows Vista to a computer running Windows XP.

- The User State Migration Tool can migrate digital certificates between computers if the target computer is Windows Vista. Windows Easy Transfer cannot migrate digital certificates.

- The User State Migration Tool can migrate encrypted files and folders between computers. Windows Easy Transfer cannot migrate encrypted files.

- The User State Migration Tool does not work with a Windows Easy Transfer Cable.

- The User State Migration Tool cannot automatically detect its partner computer over the network like Windows Easy Transfer can.

Unlike Windows Easy Transfer, the User State Migration Tool requires that you be familiar with the command line. There are two primary components:

- **Scanstate.exe**   Scanstate.eXE is used to capture migration data on the original computer.

- **Loadstate.exe**   Loadstate.eXE is used to import migration data onto the new computer.

Migration data can be saved to a network location, removable storage media, or the local hard disk using the Scanstate.eXE tool. When the migration is complete, you use the Loadstate.eXE tool to load the migrated data onto the destination computer.

MORE INFO   User State Migration Tool

For more information on version 3.0 of the User State Migration Tool, access the following page on Microsoft's website: *http://www.microsoft.com/technet/WindowsVista/library/usmt/91f62fc4-621f-4537-b311-1307df010561.mspx?mfr=true.*

Quick Check

1. In which situations would you consider using the User State Migration Tool instead of Windows Easy Transfer?
2. To which versions of Windows Vista can you upgrade Windows XP Media Center edition?

Quick Check Answers

1. The User State Migration Tool is suitable when you have many computers and users to migrate from Windows 2000 or XP to Windows Vista. The Windows Easy Transfer tool is best used when a small number of users and computers need to be migrated to Windows Vista.
2. You can upgrade Windows XP Media Center to either Windows Vista Home Premium or Windows Vista Ultimate.

Upgrading to Windows Vista

The practice at the end of this lesson provides detail on the exact procedure you use to upgrade from Windows XP to Windows Vista. The software for an upgrade edition of Windows Vista is approximately two-thirds of the cost of the full edition, although this might vary depending on your location. The upgrade editions require that you have Windows XP; you cannot perform a clean installation without the presence of Windows XP.

If the hard disk drive holding your upgraded copy of Windows Vista fails completely, you do not need to reinstall Windows XP and then install Windows Vista. You will be able to perform a clean installation using the Windows Vista upgrade edition. However, you will be asked to provide your original Windows XP product key as well as your Windows Vista product key during the installation.

Upgrade Considerations

You should keep the following points in mind prior to and during the upgrade from Windows XP to Windows Vista.

- Perform a full backup of your computer before beginning the upgrade.
- If you are in a domain environment, note the name of the computer that you are going to upgrade.
- Ensure you have the product key available prior to installing Windows Vista.
- Run the Windows Vista Upgrade Advisor to determine if any program or device driver problems that might occur will arise if you perform the upgrade. If there are, check the vendor's website for an update or a workaround.
- Ensure that there are at least 11 GB of free space on the volume that hosts the Windows XP installation. Although the Upgrade Advisor recommends that you have around 40 GB of space, it is possible to upgrade from Windows XP to Windows Vista if more than 11 GB are free. If you start the upgrade process and do not have at least 11 GB free, the option to perform an upgrade will be unavailable, and you will be able to perform only a custom installation. If you select a custom installation, none of your programs or user data will be present when the installation completes.
- Any FAT32 volumes on your Windows XP computer will be automatically converted to NTFS during the upgrade to Windows Vista.

NOTE   FAT32 and NTFS

FAT32 is an older file system that has been in use since Windows 95. NTFS has many benefits over FAT32 and allows user and group level security, encryption, and file-level compression.

■ If a Windows XP computer has a partitioned hard disk, it might be possible to repartition the hard disk and extend the volume hosting Windows XP so that you can upgrade the computer to Windows Vista. For example, say that a computer running Windows XP has a hard disk drive with a capacity of 40 GB. This hard disk drive is partitioned into two volumes of 20 GB each. The volume hosting Windows XP has only 5 free gigabytes of space. The second partition hosts a small amount of unimportant data. If you backed up this data, you could then use the Disk Management tool to delete the second partition and then to extend the first one so that the volume hosting Windows XP had 25 free gigabytes of space.

Real World

Orin Thomas

I've been keeping an eye on the Windows Vista newsgroups and forums for a while. During the beta and release candidate period, it was possible to download an evaluation copy of Windows Vista from Microsoft's website. What some people did not realize was that they also had to apply to Microsoft to get a product key so that they could use this evaluation software. Because they had not read the documentation as carefully as they should have, they were flummoxed that the Windows Vista upgrade routine would not accept their product key. Where were they getting the product keys if they had not applied for them from Microsoft? From the Windows XP product key sticker that was attached to their computer! Needless to say, you cannot use a Windows XP product key as a substitute for a Windows Vista one!

Rolling Back a Failed Upgrade

Windows Vista is designed to automatically roll back to Windows XP if there is a failure during the installation process. It is possible to roll back to Windows XP up until the point where a successful logon occurs. After a successful logon occurs, it is impossible to return to Windows XP without performing a clean installation of that operating system.

For example, when upgrading a computer from Windows XP to Windows Vista, you ignore warnings in the compatibility report about your graphics adapter driver. When Windows Vista tries to boot for the first time, all you are able to view is a blank screen. When you reboot, a text-based menu gives you the option of rolling back to Windows XP. This option is provided until you successfully log on to a normal session of Windows Vista. Unlike with the upgrade from Windows 2000 Professional to Windows XP, if you decide after a few days of using Windows Vista that you really do not like it, you're stuck. After you have successfully logged on to an upgraded Windows Vista installation, there is no going back to Windows XP!

MORE INFO   Zero Touch Installation

Although not covered by the 70-620 exam, Zero Touch Installation is a toolset that you can use to automate the process of upgrading many computers from Windows XP to Windows Vista. If you are in a situation where you need to perform a significant number of migrations in which the hardware and software configurations of the original computers are similar, you should investigate Zero Touch Installation. For more information, consult the following TechNet article: *http://www.microsoft.com/technet/technetmag/issues/2006/09/ZeroTouch/*.

Identifying Application Compatibility Requirements

A nightmare scenario for anyone who has upgraded to Windows Vista is to find that a mission-critical application no longer functions. In your role as a Windows IT professional, you will be required to advise people who are considering upgrading to Windows Vista about the degree to which their current set of applications will function under the new operating system. Although it might seem that most applications will function without a problem under Windows Vista, if they run under Windows XP or other previous versions of Windows, this will not always be the case.

To get a good idea of whether existing Windows XP applications are compatible with Windows Vista, you should run the Windows Vista Upgrade Advisor. When you run the advisor, it downloads the latest information about application compatibility from Microsoft's website. The Windows Vista Upgrade Advisor makes recommendations about which programs might have compatibility problems when run on Windows Vista.

When an application crashes on Windows Vista, a user has the option to send a report on the crash to Microsoft. From this collected data, Microsoft is able to get a picture of which applications encounter problems when executed on Windows Vista. Although the Windows Vista Upgrade Advisor will not identify every application that might encounter problems running on Windows Vista, it will identify the vast majority.

NOTE   Test it yourself

The only way to be absolutely certain that an application runs on Windows Vista is to test it on Windows Vista yourself. If you are unable to perform testing yourself, you can check with the vendor who supplied the application to see if there are any known problems.

NOTE   Use a search engine

Typing in the application name and Vista as terms into a search engine is a quick way of determining whether a particular application functions on Windows Vista. It is very likely that someone before you has attempted to run on Windows Vista the application that you are interested in. It is also likely that if they have encountered problems with that application, they have made a comment about it on a forum or a blog somewhere on the World Wide Web.

Even if you do not run the Windows Vista Upgrade Advisor, a compatibility report is generated during the upgrade process, as shown in Figure 2-4. This compatibility report will be saved to the desktop of the account that you used to perform the upgrade on after the upgrade is completed. The compatibility report displayed during installation might differ from the compatibility report generated by the Windows Vista Upgrade Advisor depending on whether you're using updated installation files. This is not a problem with the Windows Vista Upgrade Advisor because this application downloads the most up-to-date information possible from Microsoft's website prior to generating its compatibility report.

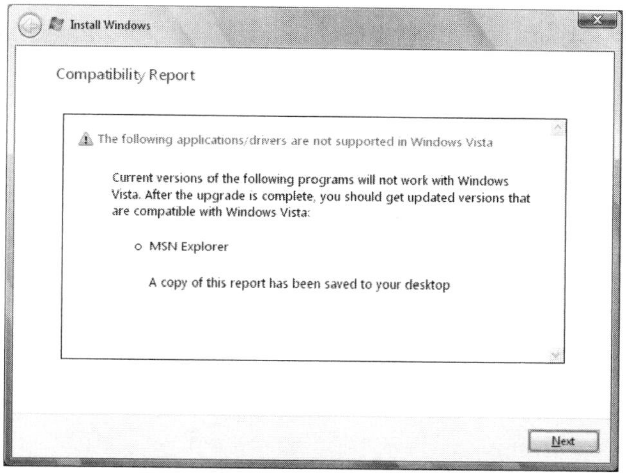

Figure 2-4   A compatibility report generated during an upgrade from Windows XP to Windows Vista

Practice: Migrating and Upgrading

In this set of practices, you will be performing both a migration and an upgrade. You will perform the migration using the Windows Easy Transfer utility. Both practices require a computer running Windows XP SP2. In the second, optional practice, you will actually be upgrading a computer running Windows XP.

▶ **Practice 1: Using Windows Easy Transfer to Move Files Between Computers**

This first practice allows you to transfer files from a Windows XP computer that is connected by a network to the Windows Vista Business computer that you created during the practices in Chapter 1, "Installing Windows Vista Client." This practice assumes that networking is configured on both the original and destination computers. If you are unsure about the configuration of networking, you might want to review Chapter 7, "Configuring Network Connectivity."

1. Log on to the computer running Windows Vista Business using the **Kim_Ackers** account. The password for this account is **P@ssw0rd**.

2. Click the Start menu, All Programs, Accessories, System Tools, and then click Windows Easy Transfer.

3. Click the Continue button in the User Account Control dialog box. The first page of the Windows Easy Transfer wizard, shown in Figure 2-5, is displayed.

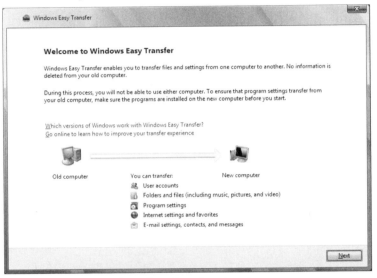

Figure 2-5   The Windows Easy Transfer wizard

4. Click Next.

5. On the Do You Want To Start A New Transfer Or Continue One In Progress page, click Start A New Transfer.

6. On the Which Computer Are You Using Now page, click My New Computer.

7. On the Do You Have An Easy Transfer Cable page, click No, Show Me More Options.

8. In the Is Windows Easy Transfer Installed On Your Old Computer page, click No, I Need To Install It Now.

9. On the Choose How To Install Windows Easy Transfer On Your Old Computer page, click Windows Installation Disc or Windows Easy Transfer CD.

10. On the Are Your Computers Connected To A Network page, click Yes, I'll Transfer Files And Settings Over The Network.

11. In the dialog box asking you to unblock Windows Easy Transfer from the firewall, shown in Figure 2-6, click Yes.

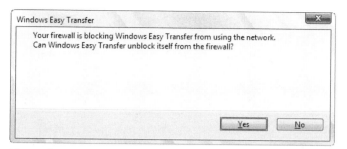

Figure 2-6   For easy transfer to work over the network, the settings on the firewall must be modified

12. On the Do You Have A Windows Easy Transfer Key page, click No, I Need A Key.

13. Make a note of the key, and then move to the computer from which you will be migrating data. In this case, it is the Windows XP computer.

14. Insert the Windows Vista installation media into the optical drive of a computer running Windows XP.

15. When the Windows Vista window appears, click Transfer File And Settings From Another Computer.

16. On the Welcome To Windows Easy Transfer page on the computer running Windows XP, click Next.

17. On the Choose How To Transfer Files And Settings To Your New Computer page on the computer running Windows XP, click Transfer Directly, Using A Network Connection.

18. On the Choose How To Transfer Files And Settings Over A Network page, click Use A Network Connection.

19. Click Yes at the Firewall prompt.

20. On the Do You Have A Windows Easy Transfer Key page, click Yes, I Have A Key.

21. On the Type Your Windows Easy Transfer Key page, enter the Windows Easy Transfer key that you wrote down in step 13 of this practice. Click Next.

22. The computer running Windows XP now connects to the network and attempts to locate the computer running Windows Vista.

23. When the computers connect to each other, you see the What Do You Want To Transfer To Your New Computer page. Click Advanced Options.

24. This brings up the Select User Accounts, Files, And Settings To Transfer page, as shown in Figure 2-7. Select all user accounts, program settings, and data that you want to transfer, and click Next.

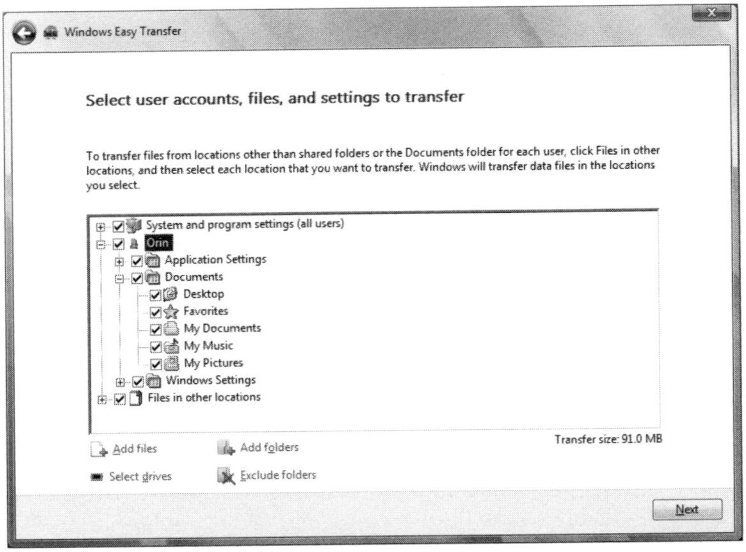

Figure 2-7   Windows Easy Transfer options

25. On the account mappings page, create a new account for each user that you are going to migrate to Windows Vista. Click Next.

26. The transfer between the computers now finishes. You should not use either computer until the entire process is finished. If a transfer fails, you will need to start it over.

27. When you see the message on the original computer that you're ready to transfer files and settings to your new computer, move to the destination computer.

28. You might have to wait at the new computer until the transfer is complete. When the transfer is complete, a summary will be displayed on the destination computer. Click Close.

29. You will be asked to log off or restart for the changes to take effect. Click Yes.

30. On the Windows XP computer, click Close.

▶ **Practice 2: Upgrading from Windows XP Professional to Windows Vista Ultimate**

This practice is provided for readers who want to take the next step in their exam preparation and actually perform an upgrade of Windows XP to Windows Vista. To complete the practice, perform the following steps:

1. Start Windows XP Professional. Insert the Windows Vista installation media. Open My Computer. Double-click the DVD-ROM drive hosting the Windows Vista installation media. This opens the Windows Vista window. (If the Windows Vista window does not automatically appear, double-click on Setup.exe to start the installation.)

2. Click Install Now.

3. On the Get Important Updates For Installation page, shown in Figure 2-8, click Do Not Get The Latest Updates For Installation.

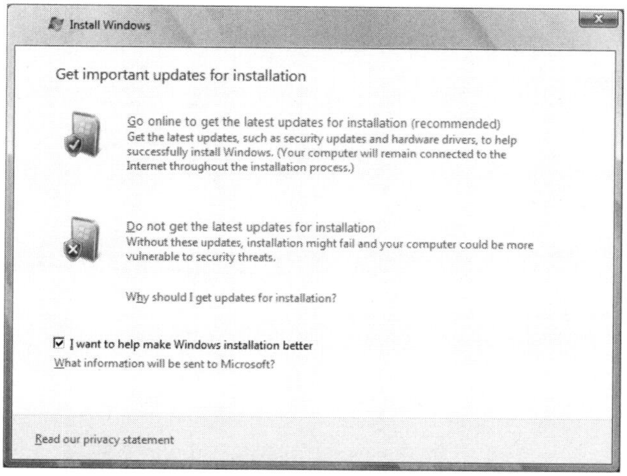

Figure 2-8 Configuring whether the upgrade process should get the latest updates

---

NOTE   Updates and the installation process

Although the safest way to upgrade is to install any newly released updates as soon as possible, there are reasons why you might avoid this path. If you have a slow connection to the Internet or you work in an organization that has a Windows Server Update Services (WSUS) server, it might make sense to obtain these updates later.

---

4. On the Type Your Product Key For Activation page, clear the Automatically Activate Windows When I'm Online check box. Click Next.

CAUTION   Using the grace period

Until you become experienced in performing upgrades of Windows XP to Windows Vista, use the 30-day activation to ensure that the upgrade functions properly. You do not want to be in the position of performing product activation just to figure out that you need to restart the upgrade or install process again from scratch.

---

5. In the Do You Want To Enter Your Product Key Now dialog box, click No.
6. On the Select The Edition Of Windows That You Purchased page, select Windows Vista ULTIMATE. Select the I Have Selected The Edition Of Windows That I Purchased check box, and click Next.
7. On the Please Read The License Terms page, review the license, and select the I Accept The License Terms check box. Click Next.

8. On the Which Type Of Installation Do You Want page, shown in Figure 2-9, click Upgrade.

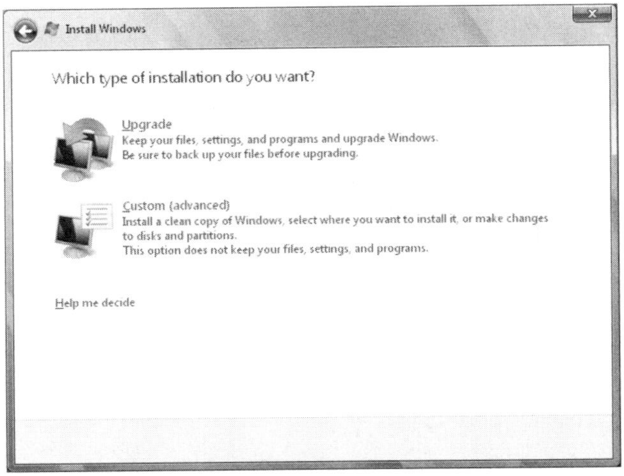

Figure 2-9 Selecting an upgrade or a custom installation

9. Review the Compatibility Report, and click Next.

NOTE   Different information

If the information presented in this compatibility report is different from the information in the Windows Upgrade Advisor, it is because the Upgrade Advisor downloads the most recent information from Microsoft.

---

10. The upgrade process starts. Depending on the speed of the computer that you are performing the upgrade on, this can take some time. During the upgrade, the computer will reboot several times.

11. On the Help Protect Windows Automatically page, click Ask Me Later.

12. On the Review Your Time And Date Settings page, verify that the settings are correct. These settings should be correct because they will have been taken from Windows XP's settings prior to the upgrade.

13. On the Select Your Computer's Current Location page, click Public Location.

14. The upgrade will inherit the previous computer name and local user account settings from Windows XP.

15. On the Thank You page, click Start. This will conclude the installation. Before allowing a logon using an existing Windows XP account, Windows Vista benchmarks the upgraded system to generate a performance rating. This performance number is available through the Performance Information item in the classic view of the control panel.

Lesson Summary

- It is possible to perform a direct upgrade to Windows Vista only from Windows XP. You can upgrade Windows XP Tablet PC only to the Business, Enterprise, or Ultimate editions of Windows Vista. You can upgrade Windows XP Media Center only to the Home Premium or Ultimate editions of Windows Vista.

- Prior to performing an upgrade, ensure that at least 11 GB of free space is available on the volume that hosts Windows XP. Also, use the Windows Vista Upgrade Advisor to confirm that your computer is capable of running Windows Vista and that you will not encounter critical hardware or software incompatibilities.

- You can migrate Windows 2000 Professional SP4 user files and accounts to Windows Vista using Windows Easy Transfer. You can migrate Windows XP user files, settings, and accounts to Windows Vista using Windows Easy Transfer. A Windows Easy Transfer Cable connects to each computer's USB ports. It is also possible to migrate data over the network and write it to removable media.

- The User State Migration Tool is recommended for migrations of multiple computers. The tool consists of two command-line utilities, scanstate.exe and loadstate.exe, and is able to migrate encrypted files and digital certificates. It is possible to use this tool to migrate user data and settings from Windows 2000 SP4 computers.

- Prior to upgrading, run the Windows Vista Upgrade Advisor to check for application compatibility issues.

Lesson Review

You can use the following questions to test your knowledge of the information in Lesson 1, "Upgrading and Migrating to Windows Vista." The questions are also available on the companion CD if you prefer to review them in electronic form.

NOTE Answers

Answers to these questions and explanations of why each answer choice is correct or incorrect are located in the "Answers" section at the end of the book.

---

1. Your organization has just purchased 50 new computers that run Windows Vista Business. Employees are currently using computers running Windows 2000 Professional. These computers are incapable of running Windows Vista and will have their hard disk drives formatted and then donated to a local charity. It is necessary to move all of the user's local user account data to the new Windows Vista computers before this happens. Local user data includes mail settings, mail, Internet Explorer settings, and desktop settings. Which of the following tools should you use to perform this migration?

    A. Windows Easy Transfer

    B. File Settings and Transfer Wizard

    C. Windows Anytime Upgrade

    D. User State Migration Tool

2. An executive at your company has a Tablet PC computer running Windows Vista Ultimate. A problem with the computer's fingerprint reader means that it needs to be sent back to the manufacturer for repair. This repair will take three weeks. In the meantime the executive will be given a replacement Tablet PC running Windows XP Tablet PC. Which of the following tools could you use to transfer the executive's data?

    A. User State Migration Tool

    B. Windows Easy Transfer

    C. Windows Anytime Upgrade

    D. File Settings and Transfer Wizard

3. You have been asked to find out whether it is possible to upgrade several computers used by workers in a small business from Windows XP to Windows Vista. All the workers use several off-the-shelf applications as a part of their job tasks. Which methods can you use to determine if these applications will work with Windows Vista? (Choose all that apply.)

    A. Check with the vendors.

    B. Run the User State Migration Tool.

    C. Run the Windows Vista Upgrade Advisor.

    D. Run Windows Anytime Upgrade.

4. A customer recently purchased a laptop that has Windows XP installed as its operating system. The laptop is marked with the Windows Vista Capable logo. The customer works as a wedding videographer and uses the laptop to edit and create DVDs for his clients. He recently purchased an upgrade version of Windows Vista Ultimate from your store. He attempted to upgrade the laptop to Windows Vista but could not do it. Which of the following should you check in an attempt to resolve this problem?

    A. Verify that the laptop has enough RAM to run Windows Vista.

    B. Verify that there is enough free hard disk space to upgrade to Windows Vista.

    C. Verify that a Windows Display Driver Model (WDDM) driver exists for the laptop's graphics adapter.

    D. Verify that the customer has activated his copy of Windows XP.

Lesson 2: Upgrading Between Windows Vista Editions

In the course of studying for the 70-620 exam, you have come to understand the benefits and limitations of each edition of Windows Vista. Unfortunately, not everyone who selects an edition of Windows Vista will do so with full knowledge of the feature limitations it might have. After using Windows Vista for some time, users might find that the edition of Windows Vista that best meets their needs is not the edition of Windows Vista that is installed on their computers. These users might want to use features such as Media Center or BitLocker drive encryption. Because their computers are already capable of running Windows Vista, there is no need to perform a migration; these users can gain access to the enhanced feature set by upgrading to another edition. In this lesson, we look at the processes by which you can upgrade one edition of Windows Vista to another.

After this lesson, you will be able to:

- Understand which upgrade options are available for any given edition of Windows Vista.
- Understand how to use Windows Anytime Upgrade to upgrade to a different edition of Windows Vista.
- Understand the hardware requirements of performing an in-place upgrade between Windows Vista editions.
- Troubleshoot upgrades between Windows Vista editions.

Estimated lesson time: 70 minutes

Upgrading Windows Vista Editions

Unlike previous versions of Windows, Windows Vista is modular. That means that each edition shares a common base and the difference between the editions is the modular components that are added to that common base. Therefore, unlike when you perform an upgrade between Windows XP and Windows Vista, replacing almost all files in the original installation, you can view a Windows Vista upgrade as essentially adding extra components to the existing installation. The process is in some ways similar to turning on a feature using Programs And Features in the Control Panel.

There are limitations to upgrades. It is not possible to pick and choose which components are added. Each edition comprises a specific set of components. It is impossible to mix and match, and the edition that is currently installed determines the edition to which you can upgrade Windows Vista. Prior to performing an upgrade, be sure to take a full backup and to manually create a restore point as described in Chapter 1, "Installing Windows Vista Client," Lesson 3, "Installing, Updating, and Troubleshooting Windows Vista Device Drivers."

Supported Upgrade Paths

As mentioned, it is not possible to upgrade any edition of Windows Vista to any other edition. The options for upgrading are limited by the edition that is currently installed on your computer. The rules about upgrading between editions are as follows:

- It is possible only to upgrade from a 32-bit edition to another 32-bit edition and from a 64-bit edition to another 64-bit edition. It is not possible to upgrade a 32-bit edition to a 64-bit edition, nor is it possible to upgrade a 64-bit edition to a 32-bit edition.

- You can upgrade from Windows Vista Home Basic to Windows Vista Home Premium or Windows Vista Ultimate.

- You can upgrade from Windows Vista Home Premium to Windows Vista Ultimate.

- You can upgrade from Windows Vista Business to Windows Vista Enterprise or Windows Vista Ultimate.

- You can upgrade from Windows Vista Enterprise to Windows Vista Ultimate.

NOTE Downgrading

It is not possible to perform a downgrade from one edition of Windows Vista to another. The only way to go from a more fully featured version of Windows Vista to a less fully featured version of Windows Vista is to migrate data and perform a clean install.

One way of remembering legitimate upgrade paths is to think of Windows Vista as coming with two tracks, a home track and a business track, with the Ultimate edition being where the tracks meet. An upgrade must stay on its own track and cannot cross onto the opposing track. Finally, keep in mind that the 32-bit and 64-bit editions are incompatible when it comes to upgrades.

Upgrade Methods

For the purposes of the 70-620 exam, there are two primary methods of upgrading from one edition of Windows Vista to another. If you were to take the 70-622 exam, you would also need to be aware of how to perform edition upgrades using network based deployment. The two upgrade methods are:

- **Windows Anytime Upgrade** Windows Anytime Upgrade is a feature available in all editions of Windows Vista except Ultimate. Anytime Upgrade can work in two ways. Users can purchase a Windows Anytime Upgrade disc at a retail store or run Windows Anytime Upgrade and purchase the edition to which they want to upgrade online. After the license has been obtained, they can perform the upgrade using the original Windows Vista media or the Windows Anytime Upgrade disc. Windows Anytime Upgrade is cheaper than an in-place upgrade because the price of an upgrade is cheaper than the full price of the corresponding edition.

■ **In-place Upgrade**   An in-place upgrade requires a full version of the edition that the user wants to upgrade to. In-place upgrades take significantly longer to perform than Windows Anytime Upgrades and are more expensive because they require purchasing a full version of the edition to be upgraded to. In-place upgrades are likely to be used by organizations that have a software license agreement with Microsoft but have obtained a fleet of computers with an original equipment manufacturer (OEM) version of Windows Vista that does not meet their needs. Unlike Windows Anytime Upgrade, it is not necessary to activate Windows prior to performing an in-place upgrade.

Windows Anytime Upgrade

Windows Anytime Upgrade is the simplest way for average users to upgrade from one edition of Windows Vista to another. Users with more than 20 computers with a similar configuration to upgrade at once should consider using a network-based upgrade solution. Windows Anytime Upgrade is located in the All Programs area of the Start Menu under Extras and Upgrades.

When you run Windows Anytime Upgrade, you are presented with a window, shown in Figure 2-10, that informs you of your upgrade options. For example, when you run Windows Anytime Upgrade on a computer running Home Basic, it tells you that you can upgrade to Home Premium or Ultimate. You can review the differences between the current edition that you are running and the one to which you are considering upgrading. When you are sure about your selection, you can begin the upgrade process.

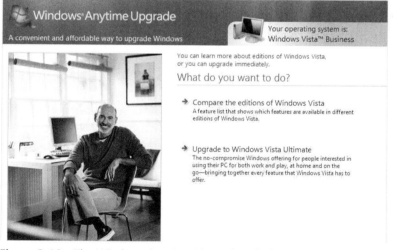

Figure 2-10   The Windows Anytime Upgrade splash screen

To complete the Windows Anytime Upgrade process, complete the following steps:

1. Ensure that your copy of Windows Vista is activated. It is impossible to use Windows Anytime Upgrade on a computer that has not gone through the Windows Product Activation process.

2. Purchase the Windows Vista Upgrade online. After the purchase is complete, you can download software containing the new license key. This software begins the upgrade process.

3. You need to ensure that the Windows Vista installation media is in the DVD-ROM drive. The upgrade process uses this media to install the additional features.

If you are uncomfortable or unable to perform an online transaction, you can purchase an appropriate edition of the Windows Anytime Upgrade CD-ROM. Inserting the Anytime Upgrade CD-ROM starts the upgrade process. If you have an Anytime Upgrade CD-ROM it is not necessary to insert the original Windows Vista installation media because all of the optional components are included on the Anytime Upgrade media.

Quick Check

1. What is the pre-condition on using Windows Anytime Upgrade?
2. You have the 64-bit edition of Windows Vista Home Basic. You want to upgrade. Which editions of Windows Vista can you upgrade to?

Quick Check Answers

1. The computer that you want to upgrade must have completed Windows Product Activation.
2. You can upgrade to the 64-bit edition of Windows Vista Home Premium or Windows Vista Ultimate.

In-Place Upgrade

An in-place upgrade does not simply add the new edition's components to the existing edition; it replaces all of the original installation's files while retaining its settings and data. For this reason, an in-place upgrade takes significantly longer than a Windows Anytime Upgrade, which simply adds the new edition's components to the existing installation.

An in-place upgrade requires at least 11 GB of free space. This space is used to expand files and migrate current applications and settings to the new edition of Windows Vista. Although this is an upgrade in the sense that it is not necessary to separately migrate user data, when you perform this operation a parallel version of the new edition of Windows Vista is installed that replaces the existing edition. During the upgrade, these 11 GB of free space are used to store temporary files and data.

Practice: Upgrading Windows Vista Business to Windows Vista Ultimate

In the real world, when dealing with only a small number of computers, you would choose to use the Windows Anytime Upgrade option to upgrade from Business to Ultimate. However, to fully use that option requires you to purchase the upgrade license online or to possess a copy of the Windows Anytime Upgrade disc. Because we don't expect you to purchase a second Windows Vista license to complete the practices in this book, we will perform an in-place upgrade. In-place upgrades with a single license can be performed under very specific conditions.

IMPORTANT   This practice is required

Because you have so far installed only Windows Vista Business and many of the practice exercises in later chapters require that you have access to Windows Vista Ultimate, you are required to complete this practice. Only if you have ignored the practices in Chapter 1, "Installing Windows Vista Client," and installed Ultimate without installing Business can you skip this practice exercise.

▶ **Practice 1: Performing an In-Place Upgrade of Windows Vista Business to Windows Vista Ultimate**

In this practice, you will upgrade Windows Vista Business, which was installed in Chapter 1, "Installing Windows Vista Client," Lesson 2, "Installing Windows Vista," to Windows Vista Ultimate. To perform the practice, complete the following steps:

1. Boot into Windows Vista, and log on using the Kim Ackers account.

2. Insert the Windows Vista installation media.

3. The AutoPlay dialog box appears. Click Run Setup.exe, and continue on to step 4. If the AutoPlay dialog box does not appear, from the Start menu, open the Computer item, and double-click the Windows Vista installation media. In the User Account Control dialog box, click Allow.

4. The Windows Vista window appears. Click Install Now.

5. On the Get Important Updates For Installation page, click Do Not Get The Latest Updates For Installation.

NOTE   Installing updates

This is done in the interest of making this practice as quick as possible. In real-world situations, you might want to install updates at this stage.

---

6. On the Type Your Product Key For Activation page, clear the Automatically Activate Windows When I'm Online check box. Click Next.

7. In the Do You Want To Enter Your Product Key Now dialog box, click No.

8. On the Select The Edition Of Windows That You Purchased page, click Ultimate, and then select the I Have Selected The Edition Of Windows That I Purchased check box. Click Next.

9. On the Please Read The License Terms page, review the license, and then select the I Accept The License Terms check box. Click Next.

10. On the Which Type Of Installation Do You Want page, click Upgrade, as shown in Figure 2-11. When you click Upgrade, the process starts. This process might take some time.

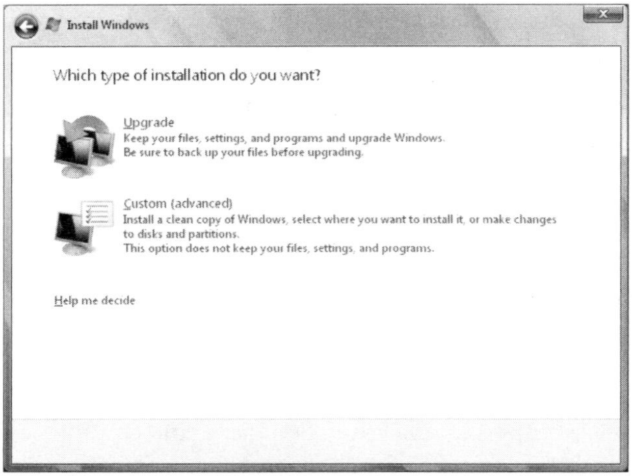

Figure 2-11   Selecting Upgrade and beginning the process

11. Eventually you are presented with the Help Protect Windows Automatically screen. Click Use Recommended Settings.

12. Review the time and date settings to ensure that they are correct, and then click Next.

13. Click Start. Windows Vista rebenchmarks the computer to generate the performance index number.

14. Log onto Windows Vista using the username **Kim_Ackers** and the password **P@ssw0rd**.

15. When you log on with this account, the Welcome Center opens. You can verify in the Welcome Center that Windows Vista Ultimate is installed, as shown in Figure 2-12.

Figure 2-12   The Windows Vista Welcome Center

Lesson Summary

- It is not possible to upgrade from a 32-bit edition of Windows Vista to a 64-bit edition of Windows Vista; nor is it possible to upgrade from a 64-bit edition of Windows Vista to a 32-bit edition of Windows Vista.

- Home Basic can be upgraded only to the Home Premium and Ultimate editions. Home Premium can be upgraded only to Ultimate. Business can be upgraded only to Enterprise and Ultimate. Enterprise can be upgraded only to Ultimate.

- Windows Anytime Upgrade allows you to upgrade only after you have activated your current Windows Vista installation.

- There are two methods of performing Windows Anytime Upgrade. The first is to purchase a Windows Anytime Upgrade CD-ROM from a computer retailer and use it to perform the upgrade. The second method is to use the Windows Anytime Upgrade application to purchase and download the license to the upgraded edition of Windows Vista over the Internet and use the Windows Vista installation media to perform the upgrade.

- Prior to performing an upgrade, you should perform a full backup.

- Performing an in-place upgrade requires at least 11 GB of free disk space.

- If you upgrade a Windows XP computer that has volumes formatted with the FAT32 filesystem to Windows Vista, the volumes will automatically be converted to NTFS.

Lesson Review

You can use the following questions to test your knowledge of the information in Lesson 2, "Upgrading Between Windows Vista Editions." The questions are also available on the companion CD if you prefer to review them in electronic form.

NOTE Answers

Answers to these questions and explanations of why each answer choice is correct or incorrect are located in the "Answers" section at the end of the book.

---

1. A customer of yours has a computer with Windows Vista Home Basic installed. He has installed several important applications that have complex activation and licensing requirements. Because of these requirements, he needs to perform an upgrade rather than a migration. Which of the following editions of Windows Vista is it possible to upgrade his computer to? (Choose all that apply.)

    A. Home Premium

    B. Business

    C. Enterprise

    D. Ultimate

2. Which if the following must you do prior to using Windows Anytime Upgrade?

    A. Purchase a new copy of the edition of Windows Vista that you want to upgrade to.

    B. Activate your current edition of Windows Vista.

    C. Run the Windows Vista Upgrade Advisor.

    D. Install MSXML 6.0 and .NET Framework 2 or higher.

3. An executive at your company has asked that you install Media Center on his Windows Vista Business Tablet PC computer. Which of the following strategies could you use to achieve this?

    A. Upgrade the computer to Windows Vista Home Premium.

    B. Upgrade the computer to Windows Vista Ultimate.

    C. Upgrade the computer to Windows Vista Enterprise.

    D. Upgrade the computer to Windows Vista Home Basic.

Lesson 3: Troubleshooting Installations and Upgrades

After you have logged on successfully to a computer that you have upgraded to Windows Vista, the only way back to Windows XP is to format the hard disk drive and to reinstall from scratch. If you have a significant number of applications installed and you find that some of the most critical ones do not work, you might begin to regret starting the upgrade process in the first place. In this lesson, we examine several techniques that you can employ to get recalcitrant applications working with Windows Vista. We also examine the techniques that you can employ to recover Windows Vista when something goes horribly awry.

After this lesson, you will be able to:
- Resolve application compatibility problems.
- Troubleshoot Windows Vista installations.
- Troubleshoot Windows Vista upgrades.
- Select an appropriate System Recovery Tool option.
- Create and use system restore points.

Estimated lesson time: 30 minutes

Resolving Application Compatibility Problems

Applications that were written for previous versions of Windows will not always work with Windows Vista. The primary reason for this is that Windows Vista is a significantly more secure operating system than previous versions of Windows. Programming techniques that worked in prior versions of Windows no longer work because the methods that the application used to interact with the operating system were similar to methods used by viruses and worms to infect the operating system.

Application compatibility problems generally come in two varieties:

- The application expects to run in an environment like that of an earlier version of Windows.
- There are problems with User Account Control.

When Windows Vista notes that there is a problem running an older program, it invokes the Program Compatibility Assistant. This automatic function attempts to resolve conflicts with User Account Control or run the program in a mode that simulates an earlier version of Windows. Sometimes the assistant does not get it right, and you have to manually alter settings to get the program to run yourself.

Configuring Application Compatibility Mode

Compatibility mode allows an application installed on a computer running Windows Vista to run in an environment that emulates a previous version of Windows. Windows Vista's compatibility modes can emulate the following environments:

- Windows 95
- Windows 98 / Windows Me
- Windows NT 4.0 (Service Pack 5)
- Windows 2000
- Windows XP (Service Pack 2)
- Windows Server 2003 (Service Pack 1)

It is possible to configure compatibility only for programs that are not a part of Windows Vista. For example, you can configure compatibility options for a program that you download and install from the Internet, but it is not possible to configure compatibility options for Internet Explorer or Windows Mail.

Other program compatibility features involve fixing how Windows Vista displays the application. If the program appears to function but there are errors in the way it displays, the problem might be resolved by altering the display settings. The alterations that can be made are:

- Force the application to run in 256 color mode.
- Force the application to run in 640 x 480 resolution.
- Disable Windows Vista visual themes for the application. This is useful if the buttons or title bar do not display correctly.
- Disable Desktop Composition and Disable Display Scaling On High DPI Settings.

It is also possible to have the program run as though it was executed by an administrator. Older versions of Windows, specifically Windows 95, 98, and Me, gave all users administrative privileges. Although you will be prompted by the User Account Control dialog box, the application will fail to run because of the way Windows Vista security works. Selecting the Run This Program As An Administrator check box means that you still need to be an administrator to run the program but that some of the UAC security is bypassed in order to get the application to function.

MORE INFO   Applications that need administrator privileges

To find out more about getting applications that require administrator privileges to run without compromising security, consult the following article: *http://www.microsoft.com/technet/windowsvista /library/00d04415-2b2f-422c-b70e-b18ff918c281.mspx.*

To configure the compatibility for a program, perform the following steps.

1. On the Start menu, right-click the program for which you want to want to configure compatibility options.
2. Click Properties. This will open the Properties dialog box.
3. Click the Compatibility tab.
4. Select the Run This Program In Compatibility Mode For check box, and use the drop-down list to select a previous version of Windows, as shown in Figure 2-13. Click OK to save the settings.

Instead of editing the program properties manually, it is also possible to run the Program Compatibility Wizard. You can start the Program Compatibility Wizard from Windows Help by entering the terms "Program Compatibility Wizard." A link will be provided to run the wizard. The wizard asks you the location of the program, the operating system that it was designed for, and any of the other display settings mentioned earlier. The Program Compatibility Wizard does not add anything new; it just provides a simpler way of configuring compatibility.

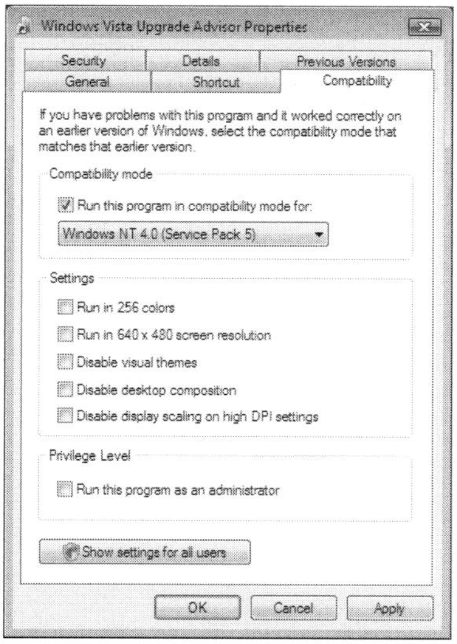

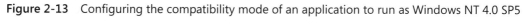

Figure 2-13   Configuring the compatibility mode of an application to run as Windows NT 4.0 SP5

Troubleshooting Windows Vista Installation and Upgrades

Sometimes installations or upgrades fail. The following list is a set of observations on what is most likely to cause an installation or upgrade of Windows Vista to fail and what you can do about it.

■ The most likely thing that will cause an installation or upgrade to Windows Vista to fail is a lack of hard disk drive space. Prior to performing either an upgrade or a clean install, ensure that there is enough space on the volume on which you are going to install Windows Vista.

■ Ensure that you disable all antivirus and anti-spyware software prior to performing an upgrade.

■ If you cannot boot off the Windows Vista installation media when attempting to perform a new installation, check the computer's BIOS configuration. You need to configure the BIOS to allow you to boot off the optical media drive prior to booting off the hard disk drive. If BIOS appears to be configured correctly, as shown in Figure 2-14, physically check that all cables and connectors to the optical media drive are securely connected.

```
                       BIOS SETUP UTILITY
                      Boot

                                                   Specifies the boot
  1st Boot Device          [CDROM]                 sequence from the
  2nd Boot Device          [Floppy Drive]          available devices.
  3rd Boot Device          [Hard Drive]
  4th Boot Device          [PXE UNDI(Bus0 Slot]



                                                   ↔     Select Screen
                                                   ↑↓    Select Item
                                                   +-    Change Option
                                                   F1    General Help
                                                   F10   Save and Exit
                                                   ESC   Exit

         v02.10 (C)Copyright 1985-2001, American Megatrends, Inc.
```

Figure 2-14   Ensuring that the optical media drive is configured to boot before the hard disk drive

■ If, when performing an installation or an upgrade, the volume that you want to install does not appear in the Where Do You Want To Install Windows dialog box, you will need to load a hardware device driver so Windows Vista can recognize the hard disk. Alternatively, shut down the computer and check that the hard disk that hosts the destination volume has all cables firmly connected.

■ Be sure to run the Windows Vista Upgrade Advisor against your computer prior to performing the installation and check the compatibility report. It is possible that Windows Vista drivers do not exist for a critical piece of hardware. Until these drivers are available, your computer might not function. Alternatively, if the computer is used for a particular purpose, such as interfacing with special equipment, the computer might function fine, but with no drivers the equipment will not. From the perspective of those who need the equipment, this would be a failed upgrade.

■ It is impossible to perform an in-place upgrade unless there are at least 11 GB of free space on the volume containing the original installation of Windows Vista. If you have fewer than 11 GB free, you will need to use Windows Anytime Upgrade.

■ If the Windows Vista installation media is damaged and you cannot perform an installation, you will need to contact the vendor you purchased it from for a replacement.

- If the Windows Vista installation media has become damaged and you want to upgrade from one version of Windows Vista to another, it is still possible to use the Windows Anytime Upgrade media to perform an upgrade.

- If you do not have access to the Internet, it is possible to upgrade to another edition of Windows Vista only if you perform an in-place upgrade or if you have the Windows Anytime Upgrade media.

- You can only perform an upgrade from within Windows. You will not have the option of upgrading if you boot off the installation media.

- If you are configuring a computer to dual boot with Windows XP, ensure that you install Windows Vista after you install Windows XP. If you reinstall Windows XP after you have installed Windows Vista, it will cause problems with the boot menu. You can resolve this problem by running Startup Repair off the installation media. It is also possible to resolve this problem using the bcdedit.exe application, although this involves complex operations from the command line.

Real World

Orin Thomas

In some cases, a failed upgrade is in the eye of the beholder. While writing this book, I purchased a Tablet PC so that I could test out some of the technologies I write about in Chapter 13, "Configuring Mobile Devices." The Tablet PC came with a pre-installed copy of Windows XP Tablet PC. In Windows XP the tablet worked great. Flipping the screen around resulted in an automatic change from portrait to landscape mode, and the tablet was able to seamlessly connect to the local 802.11g wireless local area network (WLAN). When I upgraded to Windows Vista Ultimate, I learned that the software that told Windows to shift from portrait to landscape and allowed the WLAN to be started did not work with Vista. I could change the screen manually by going through the Control Panel, but I'd have to wait until drivers were released before the WLAN was fixed. I can live with that because I am aware that a problem with being an early adopter of technology is that not everything will work from the beginning. However, if I had been upgrading the Tablet PC for someone else, say a company executive or someone from a sales department, that person would probably have considered the upgrade a failure. The success of an upgrade depends on whether a user is happy with the result. Someone who is used to Tablet PC functionality is not going to be too excited when told that it will not behave like a tablet until the vendor gets around to releasing some updated drivers at some undefined point in the future.

> ### Quick Check
>
> 1. You have a computer that is already running Windows Vista Business and you want to perform an in-place upgrade to Windows Vista Ultimate. What is the only hardware component that can prevent this upgrade from succeeding?
> 2. At what point during an upgrade of Windows XP to Windows Vista does it become impossible to roll back the installation to Windows XP?
>
> ### Quick Check Answers
>
> 1. If the computer already runs Windows Vista, the only thing that would stop an in-place upgrade from succeeding would be a lack of hard disk space.
> 2. It is impossible to roll back to Windows XP if you have upgraded to Windows Vista after a successful logon to Windows Vista has occurred.

Configuring System Recovery Options

The Windows Vista installation media includes five tools you can use to repair a computer if something goes wrong that you cannot fix from a normal Windows session or by booting into safe mode or the Last Known Good Configuration.

NOTE   **Safe mode and Last Known Good Configuration**

Safe mode and Last Known Good Configuration are startup options presented at boot time when Windows Vista fails to start properly. Safe mode allows Windows to boot with a minimal set of drivers. Safe mode and Last Known Good Configuration were discussed in Chapter 1, "Installing Windows Vista Client," Lesson 3, "Installing, Updating, and Troubleshooting Windows Vista Device Drivers."

You almost always access System Recovery Options by booting off the Windows Vista installation media. Sometimes vendors install the System Recovery tools on a separate partition, but performing such an operation is beyond the scope of the 70-620 exam. Rather than selecting Install Vista after the language selection dialog box, you click Repair Your Computer, and then select the installation of Windows Vista you want to repair. If the computer you are attempting to repair requires specialized drivers to access the hard disk drive, it is possible to load the device driver software during this step. After you have selected the installation that you will repair, you are presented with the menu shown in Figure 2-15. Each of the tools in the System Recovery Options menu is covered in the following paragraphs.

Figure 2-15   System Recovery tools

Startup Repair

You can use Startup Repair to fix most startup problems and you should consider it a first port of call if you encounter a Windows Vista computer that fails to boot properly. The Startup Repair process is able to restore missing system files or repair basic disk errors that stop Windows Vista from booting properly. The Startup Repair process is automatic and requires no user intervention once it has been initiated. Startup Repair cannot be used to fix hardware failures and is unlikely to be helpful if the Windows Vista computer is infected with a virus or a worm.

System Restore

System Restore is a process you can use to return a computer's system files to an earlier point in time. For example, you create a restore point prior to installing a program that installs newer versions of Windows Vista system files. If those new system files cause problems, System Restore allows you to roll back to the original version of the system files as they existed just before you installed the program. System restore points are automatically captured prior to the installation of drivers or applications. This is a significant advantage because people generally think of making a restore point only after something has gone catastrophically wrong. It is possible to perform a system restore from the System Recovery Tools or from within Windows Vista using the System Restore Utility.

Windows Complete PC Restore

In earlier versions of Windows a tool called Automated System Recovery allowed you to completely rebuild your Windows installation provided you had a full backup, some special disks, and the Windows Vista installation media. Windows Complete PC Restore is similar. As long as you have taken a complete backup of your computer and stored it somewhere safe, it is possible to completely restore the computer using the Windows Vista Installation Media and this backup set. It is important to note that the size of a complete backup is equivalent to the size of the operating system, all applications, and their data. Such a backup is likely to be written to an external hard disk drive rather than to optical media or a USB flash drive. Windows Backup is covered in more detail in Chapter 12, "Configuring Updates and Protecting Data."

Windows Memory Diagnostic Tool

Errors with a computer's physical memory can be very difficult to diagnose. A computer that has RAM problems can work perfectly for weeks and then randomly freeze three times in half an hour. Crashes are usually easier to diagnose because they occur when the same set of actions are replicated. As mentioned in Chapter 1, "Installing Windows Vista Client," prior to upgrading to the WDDM graphics adapter, my laptop computer would always crash if I tried to play video files. Crashes caused by RAM hardware errors are so frustrating because they seem to occur randomly. You might be playing a video when the first crash occurs, browsing a website when the second crash occurs, and playing solitaire when the third crash occurs. When you encounter a computer that appears to crash almost at random, run the Windows Memory Diagnostic Tool, shown in Figure 2-16. This tool is specifically designed to detect errors on physical memory. After you activate it, the computer will reboot and perform a series of memory tests. Depending on the amount of RAM and the speed of the processor, this check can take some time.

If the Windows Memory Diagnostic Tool detects an error, your only recourse is to replace the RAM. Hardware errors in RAM chips cannot be repaired. If you have multiple RAM chips in your computer, it is likely that only one of them has the error. For this reason, once you have determined by running the diagnostic utility that there is a problem with the RAM, you should carefully remove the chips and check them one at a time to determine which of them is faulty. By checking only one stick of RAM at a time, you can determine if all the RAM has errors or if the error is confined to a single chip. When replacing the RAM, you need to ensure that the replacement RAM has identical characteristics, such as RAM frequency. If the replacement RAM does not have identical characteristics, it could cause more problems.

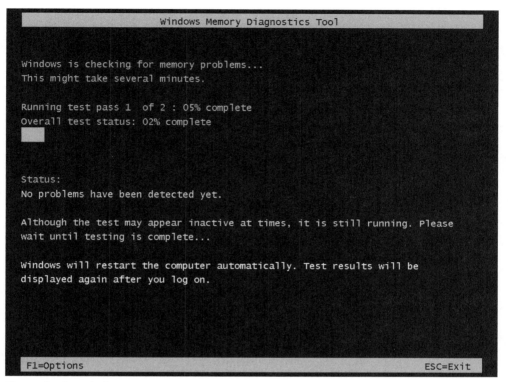

Figure 2-16 Windows Memory Diagnostic Tool

Command Prompt

Although Startup Repair does an excellent job of replacing missing system files, it will occasionally be unable to detect a corrupt system file. In this case, you can manually replace files by using the System Recovery command prompt tool. After you enter the command prompt, it is possible to copy files directly from the Windows Vista installation media to the volume that hosts the Windows installation.

Practice: Creating and Reverting to a System Restore Point

In this practice, you will explore the functionality of System Restore. System Restore allows you to take a snapshot of a computer at a particular point in time. If the system becomes unstable, it is possible to return to this snapshot, undoing all changes to system files that have been made since the snapshot was taken.

▶ **Practice 1: Creating a System Restore Point**

In this practice, you will manually create a system restore point. After you create the restore point, you will add some Windows Vista components. This practice sets up Practice 2, which will restore Windows Vista to the configuration at the system restore point.

1. Log on to Windows Vista Ultimate using the Kim_Ackers account and the password P@ssw0rd.

2. Click Start, All Programs, Accessories, System Tools, and then System Restore.

3. In the User Account Control dialog box, click Continue.

4. On the Restore System Files And Settings page, click Open System Protection.

5. This will open the System Protection tab of the System Properties dialog box, shown in Figure 2-17.

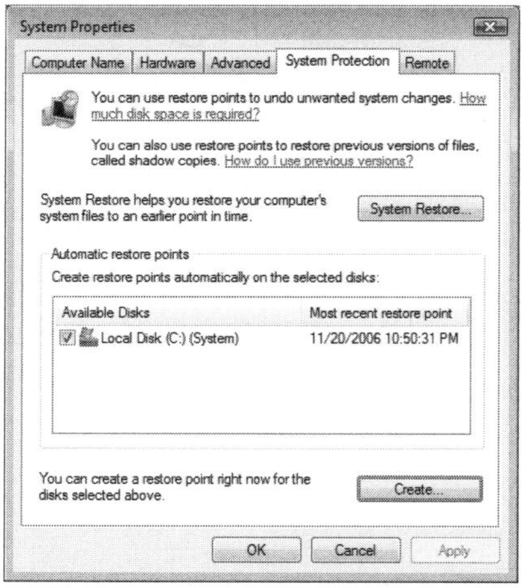

Figure 2-17 Creating restore points by using the System Protection tab of the System Properties dialog box

6. Select the check box next to Local Disk (C:) (System). If Windows Vista is installed on another volume, ensure that the volume marked with (System) is selected.

7. Click Create to create the system restore point.

8. In the Create A Restore Point dialog box, shown in Figure 2-18, enter the description Chapter 2 Lesson 2 Restore Point, and click Create. Windows Vista now creates a restore point.

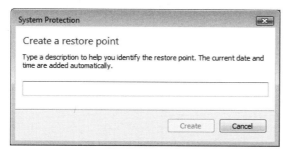

Figure 2-18 To create a restore point, enter a description

9. Click OK to close the dialog box informing you that the restore point was created successfully.

10. Click OK to close the System Properties dialog box.

11. Close the System Restore wizard.

12. Open the Control Panel. If the Control Panel does not display the Classic View, click Classic View.

13. Double-click Programs And Features.

14. Click Turn Windows Features On Or Off.

15. Click Continue in the User Account Control dialog box.

16. Select the Telnet Server and TFTP Client check boxes. Click OK.

17. Windows Vista installs these features.

18. After the features are installed, close the Programs And Features dialog box.

▶ **Practice 2: Reverting to a System Restore Point**

In this practice, you will use the restore point created in Practice 1 to restore the components that you installed after you created the restore point. Although it is possible to perform a system restore from within Windows Vista itself by opening the System Restore item, this practice will simulate a Windows Vista problem that prevents the computer from booting up fully. In this case, it is possible to perform a system restore from the Windows Vista installation media.

1. Insert the Windows Vista installation media into the DVD-ROM drive.

2. Restart the computer. At the Press Any Key To Boot From CD Or DVD prompt, press the spacebar. This will boot the Windows Vista installation media.

3. On the Windows Vista Language Preferences page, click Next.

4. On the Install Windows page, click Repair Your Computer.

5. On the System Recovery Options page, shown in Figure 2-19, ensure that the Windows Vista installation is selected, and click Next.

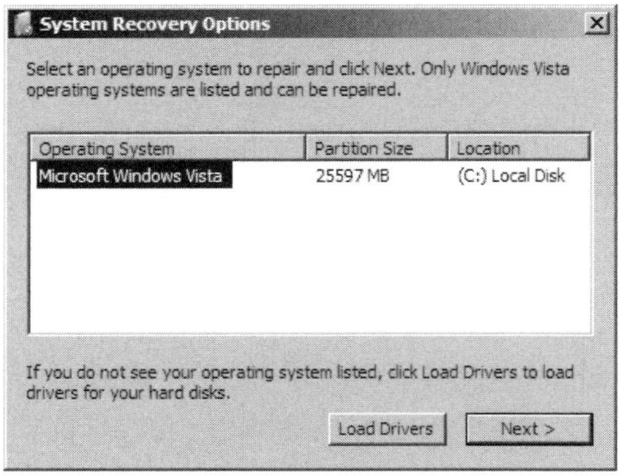

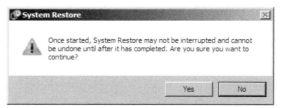

Figure 2-19   Selecting the installation of Windows Vista that you want to repair using System Recovery Options

6. In the System Recovery Options dialog box, click System Restore.

7. In the Restore System Files And Settings dialog box, click Next.

8. On the list of restore points, select Manual: Chapter 2 Lesson 2 Restore Point. Click Next. When the new components were added to Windows, a new restore point was created. Do not select this new restore point, but select the one that you manually created.

9. On the Confirm Disks To Restore page, click Next.

10. Click Finish. Click Yes in the warning dialog box displayed in Figure 2-20.

Figure 2-20   System Restore warning dialog box

11. The system restore process will take some time to complete. When the restore is completed, you are informed that your documents have not been affected. Click Restart to restart the computer.

12. When the computer has booted, log on as Kim_Ackers. When you log on, you are presented with a System Restore dialog box informing you that System Restore completed successfully. Click Close.

13. Open the Programs And Features item in Control Panel.

14. Click Turn Windows Features On Or Off.
15. Click Continue to close the User Account Control dialog box.
16. Verify that the Telnet Server and TFTP Client components that were enabled in Practice 1 are no longer active on the computer.
17. Click OK to close the Windows Features dialog box.

Lesson Summary

- If an application has problems running on Windows Vista, you might resolve the problem by using compatibility mode. Windows Vista can run programs in the following compatibility modes: Windows 95, Windows 98/Me, Windows NT 4.0 Service Pack 5, Windows 2000, Windows XP (Service Pack 2), and Windows Server 2003 (Service Pack 1).

- System Recovery Options can be accessed by booting off the Windows Vista Installation Media.

- The Startup Repair system recovery option is used to automatically fix problems that prevent Windows Vista from starting.

- The System Restore system recovery option is used to roll back Windows Vista to an earlier state.

- The Windows Complete PC Restore system recovery option is used to restore the entire operating system and application from a backup.

- The Windows Memory Diagnostic Tool system recovery option is used to check RAM for errors.

- The Command Prompt system recovery option can be used to open a command prompt from where it is possible to copy files from the Windows Vista media to the volumes on the computer.

Lesson Review

You can use the following questions to test your knowledge of the information in Lesson 3, "Troubleshooting Installations and Upgrades." The questions are also available on the companion CD if you prefer to review them in electronic form.

NOTE Answers

Answers to these questions and explanations of why each answer choice is correct or incorrect are located in the "Answers" section at the end of the book.

1. Your Windows Vista computer has been hit by a virus. The damage is localized to a particular application that you installed a week ago. You want to return the computer to the state it was in prior to the installation of the application. Which of the following techniques could you employ?

   A. Boot off the installation media, and perform a system restore.

   B. Boot off the installation media, and perform a startup repair.

   C. Boot off the installation media, and run the command prompt.

   D. Boot off the installation media, and run Windows Complete PC Restore.

2. A customer has brought in a laptop computer that has problems. The computer appears to power on successfully and passes the POST test, but it is unable to start loading Windows Vista. Which of the following System Recovery Options should you try first in an attempt to resolve this issue?

   A. Startup Repair

   B. System Restore

   C. Windows Complete PC Restore

   D. Windows Memory Diagnostic Tool

3. A user complains that an application that worked perfectly well on her old Windows 98 computer does not work at all on her new Windows Vista computer. The user has local administrator rights on her computer. Even though she is prompted by the User Account Control dialog box, she is unable to install the application in question. Which modifications might you make to get the application to install?

   A. Configure the application to run under Windows 98 / Me compatibility mode.

   B. Configure the application to run in 256 colors.

   C. Configure the application to run in 640 x 480 resolution.

   D. Configure the application to run this program as an administrator.

Chapter Review

To further practice and reinforce the skills you learned in this chapter, you can perform the following tasks:

- Review the chapter summary.
- Review the list of key terms introduced in this chapter.
- Complete the case scenarios. These scenarios set up real-world situations involving the topics of this chapter and ask you to create a solution.
- Complete the suggested practices.
- Take a practice test.

Chapter Summary

- It is possible to upgrade Windows XP only to Windows Vista. You should carefully check the features of the version of Windows XP that you are going to upgrade because this will determine which edition of Windows Vista should be installed.
- Windows Easy Transfer can be run from the Windows Vista installation media on Windows XP and Windows 2000 SP4 computers. The application is used to migrate files (Windows 2000), settings, and application data (Windows XP). When you're using Windows Easy Transfer, the target computer must be running an edition of Windows Vista.
- The Windows Vista Upgrade Advisor can be used to determine if an existing application running on Windows XP is incompatible with Windows Vista.
- There are two methods for performing an upgrade from one edition of Windows Vista to another. Using Windows Anytime Upgrade requires that you either purchase a license from a retailer over the Internet or purchase a Windows Anytime Upgrade disk from a traditional retail outlet. An in-place upgrade is similar to an upgrade from Windows XP to Windows Vista and needs at least 11 GB of free space.
- If an application will not run, it is possible to run it in a compatibility mode that emulates a previous version of Windows.
- Booting off the Windows Vista installation media and selecting Repair This Computer allows you to access the System Recovery tools. You can use these recovery tools to repair startup problems, return to a prior restore point, perform a full system recovery, and test the computer's physical memory.

Key Terms

Do you know what these key terms mean? You can check your answers by looking up the terms in the glossary at the end of the book.

- compatibility mode
- destination operating system
- migration
- original operating system
- rollback
- side-by-side
- System Restore
- upgrade
- User State Migration Tool
- Windows Anytime Upgrade
- Windows Easy Transfer
- wipe-and-load

Case Scenarios

In the following case scenarios, you will apply what you have learned about upgrading to Windows Vista, migrating to Windows Vista, and troubleshooting installations and upgrades. You can find answers to these questions in the "Answers" section at the end of this book.

Case Scenario 1: Upgrading and Migrating

You work for the local electronics superstore. Your manager has received many inquiries from customers about having Windows Vista installed on their existing computers. All their computers run Windows XP. In each of the three following cases, assess whether you should perform an upgrade or a migration and which edition of Windows Vista you would recommend the customer move to.

- Pentium IV 3.0 GHz CPU, 2 GB RAM, 256 MB PCIe graphics card with Hardware Pixel Shader 2.0 and DirectX 9 support, 200 GB HDD with 70 GB free. Operating System: Windows 2000 Professional. Primary use: games. Secondary use: DVD playback.
- 2 GHz Core 2 CPU, 1 GB RAM. Windows XP Tablet PC. 128-MB graphics chipset with WDDM support. Used to connect to Small Business Server 2003 domain through a virtual private network (VPN).

- Laptop computer with 1.5 GHz Core Duo CPU, 512 MB RAM. 64-MB graphics chipset. No WDDM support. Owned by a couple who have purchased a new scanner that comes only with Windows Vista drivers. They are unable to use the scanner with Windows XP. They have an OEM version of Microsoft Encarta® installed on their computer that they like to use, but the CD-ROM they used to install it has become misplaced. They also want to use Windows Mail to send messages to their children and grandchildren.

Case Scenario 2: Troubleshooting

Several Windows Vista computers are experiencing unexplained failures. Examine the symptoms listed below, and select the appropriate system recovery option.

- Computer freezes at random times after bootup. The only way to restore functionality is to reboot the computer.
- Computer gets halfway through the bootup process and then crashes.
- Several important files have become corrupted and cannot be repaired using Startup Repair.

Suggested Practices

To help you successfully master the exam objectives presented in this chapter, complete the following tasks.

Upgrade to Windows Vista from Previous Versions of Windows

- **Practice 1: Windows Easy Transfer**   Create three separate local user accounts on a computer running a previous version of Windows. Create some unique temporary documents and Internet Explorer bookmarks for each of these accounts. Use the Windows Easy Transfer tool to migrate these accounts to the Windows Vista Ultimate computer that you are using for the practices in this training kit.
- **Practice 2: User State Migration**   Create three new separate local user accounts, different from the ones you created in Practice 1, on a computer running a previous version of Windows. Create some unique temporary documents and Internet Explorer bookmarks for each of these accounts. Use the User State Migration Tool to migrate these accounts to the Windows Vista Ultimate computer that you are using for the practices in this training kit. Compare this tool to the Windows Easy Transfer tool in terms of ease of use and overall functionality.

Upgrade from One Edition of Windows Vista to Another Edition

- **Practice 1: Upgrade Windows Vista Home Basic to Windows Vista Home Premium**   Create a new Windows Vista Home Basic virtual machine using Windows Vista installation software purchased from a retail location. Perform an in-place upgrade to update this virtual machine to Windows Vista Home Premium.
- **Practice 2: Upgrade Windows Vista Home Premium to Windows Vista Ultimate**   Perform an in-place upgrade on the Windows Vista Home Premium virtual machine that you created in Practice 1. Upgrade the operating system to Windows Vista Ultimate.

Troubleshoot Installation Problems

- **Practice 1: Compatibility Mode**   Download and install an application from the Internet, and configure it to run in a compatibility mode that emulates Windows NT 4.0.
- **Practice 2: System Recovery**   Boot off the Windows Vista installation media, and run the memory checking utility to verify that the RAM on your computer has no errors.

Take a Practice Test

The practice tests on this book's companion CD offer many options. For example, you can test yourself on just one exam objective, or you can test yourself on all the 70-620 certification exam content. You can set up the test so that it closely simulates the experience of taking a certification exam, or you can set it up in study mode so that you can look at the correct answers and explanations after you answer each question.

MORE INFO   Practice tests

For details about all the practice test options available, see the "How to Use the Practice Tests" section in this book's Introduction.

Chapter 3
Troubleshooting Post-Installation System Settings

Although you can usually resolve all problems with a computer during or just after performing an installation, some problems become apparent only after you have used the new operating system for a few days. The same applies to purchasing a car. A problem that you might not notice when you drive around the block with the salesperson might become obvious after you have driven the car for a week. Post-installation troubleshooting is about finding the initial quirks that you missed and personalizing the computer so that it best meets your needs. Primarily, this is going to be ensuring that all hardware that is installed on the computer is actually working and that the computer's display settings suit the person using the computer rather than the person who set up the computer. In this chapter, we also examine Microsoft Windows Aero. Aero makes Windows Vista look significantly different from earlier versions of Windows. If you are working in a job trying to sell new computers to customers, you can underline the difference between the new and the old by demonstrating some of Windows Aero's functionality. Finally, this chapter looks at the Windows Product Activation and Windows Genuine Advantage processes.

Exam objectives in this chapter:
- Troubleshoot post-installation configuration issues.
- Configure and troubleshoot Windows Aero.

Lessons in this chapter:

Before You Begin

To complete the lesson in this chapter, you must have done the following:

- Completed the installation and upgrading practices in Chapter 1, "Installing Windows Vista Client," and Chapter 2, "Windows Vista Upgrades and Migrations." As a result, you will have installed Windows Vista Ultimate edition on a personal computer or on a virtual machine. This computer should also have a working connection to the Internet.

No additional configuration is required for this chapter.

Real World

Orin Thomas

As a part of my preparation for writing Chapter 14 of this book, "Working with Tablet PC," I purchased a new Tablet PC. Although I was able to install Windows Vista to dual boot with the existing Windows XP Tablet PC edition without any problem, upon logging on for the first time, I noticed that several hardware devices did not work. Tablet PCs automatically change the display from portrait to landscape mode when you convert the screen from laptop to tablet mode. This worked fine on Windows XP but would not work with Windows Vista Ultimate. A hardware button that allowed me to configure this change manually also did not function. Because it was tedious to manually switch between the two modes, to solve this problem, I used Windows Vista's voice recognition functionality to configure a set of vocal shortcuts that allowed me to switch the screen from portrait to landscape mode without having to mess about with the pen input device. Sometimes successful post-installation troubleshooting amounts to finding another way to make something work until a better solution becomes available.

Lesson 1: Troubleshooting Post-Installation Configuration Issues

Post-installation troubleshooting involves ensuring that all devices and applications installed on the Windows Vista computer are working properly. Often, you can ascertain this only by using the computer for some time after the initial installation. Only if you have used the computer for some time can you be sure that a particular hardware device is unreliable or that a particular application seems to be in the habit of failing. Post-installation troubleshooting also involves tailoring the computer to best suit your needs. This often means adjusting the screen resolution, color settings, desktop background, and refresh rate to something you feel comfortable with, just as you'd adjust all the settings—like mirrors, seat, and steering wheel—in your car to ensure that you are not uncomfortable when driving.

After this lesson, you will be able to:

- Resolve device configuration issues.
- Resolve display settings issues.
- Resolve visual appearance issues.

Estimated lesson time: 40 minutes

Device Manager Troubleshooting

Although Windows Vista makes it very simple to connect and use a hardware device, a lot of complex behind-the-scenes activities occur when you perform such a connection. The device and Windows Vista must negotiate which hardware resources the device will use to communicate with the computer. In the past it was necessary for the person installing the hardware device to manually configure its settings by configuring hardware jumpers. Today, hardware device resource allocation is accomplished through software. Windows Vista's Device Manager is the primary tool used to perform this management and configuration. Device Manager is also the tool that you will most likely use to resolve device configuration issues.

Opening Device Manager

Although Device Manager has its own separate console, it is also visible as a node of the Computer Management Console. To open Device Manager, use one of the following methods:

Method One: Using the Control Panel

1. Click Start, and then click Control Panel.
2. Ensure that the Control Panel is configured to use Classic View.
3. Double-click the Device Manager icon.
4. Click Continue to close User Account Control.

Method Two: Using the Computer Management Console

1. Click Start, and right-click the Computer item.
2. Click Manage. This opens the Computer Management Console.
3. In the left pane, click the Device Manager node.

The advantage of viewing Device Manager alongside other items in the Computer Management Console is that you have quick access to items such as the Event Viewer, Services and Applications, and Reliability and Performance.

Device Manager Basics

Device Manager allows you to manage the hardware and software resources used by drivers. Device Manager is helpful in performing post-installation troubleshooting tasks by indicating which hardware devices have issues that require addressing. For example, Figure 3-1 shows Windows Vista's Device Manager. From examining the exhibit, you can see that there is a problem with the Multimedia Audio Controller. Device Manager highlights this problem by the placement of the warning icon, a black exclamation mark on a yellow background.

Figure 3-1   Device Manager showing a problem with a device

Device Manager reports problems with a device by displaying a warning icon next to it. You can find out more about that problem by right-clicking the device and viewing the device's properties. To continue from the earlier example, as you can see in Figure 3-2, the Device Status box in the General tab of the device's Properties dialog box indicates that the drivers for this particular device are not installed.

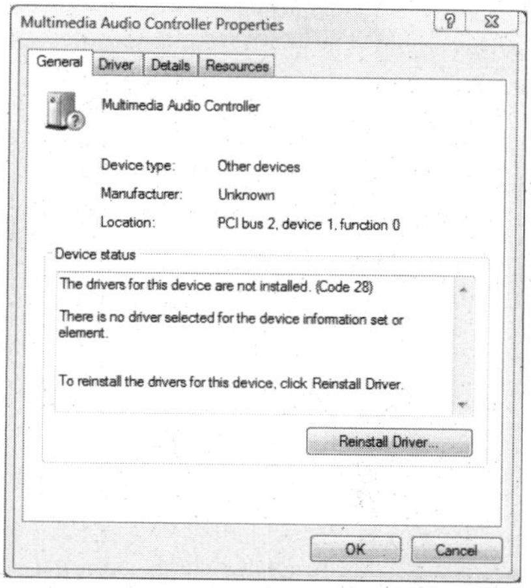

Figure 3-2 Using the General tab of a device's Properties dialog box to get information on device problems

It is important to note that only users with elevated privileges are able to uninstall devices or modify device driver or hardware properties. To find out more about rights and permissions in Windows Vista, see Chapter 5, "User Account Control." Standard users are able to view the Device Manager. You should remember this because it means that you can query anyone about what they see in the Device Manager if they are asking you for technical support over a help desk telephone line. In the next section, we look at the other tabs of the Device Manager and how they can aid in post-installation troubleshooting of devices.

Understanding Device Properties

The tabs that are available in the Properties dialog box when you edit a device's properties depend on the device and the driver that is installed. Although these tabs can vary from device to device, the four most common tabs are:

- **General** This tab provides basic information about the device. If the device has a problem, this tab provides some details on the problem and also provides an error code that you can use to troubleshoot the problem by searching on Microsoft's website.
- **Driver** This tab was covered in Chapter 1, "Installing Windows Vista Client," Lesson 3, "Installing, Updating, and Troubleshooting Windows Vista Device Drivers." It allows you to view details about the driver, update the driver, roll back the driver, disable the device, or uninstall the driver.
- **Details** The Details tab provides information on device properties. Use the drop-down list, as shown in Figure 3-3, to view extremely detailed information on the device.

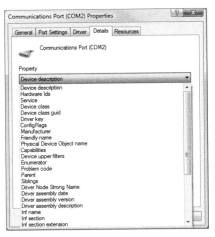

Figure 3-3   Using the Details tab to view detailed properties of a device through a drop-down list

■ **Resources**   Resources are parts of the computer's hardware that the device interacts with. The resources used are heavily dependent on the device. A COM port requires access to a specific input/output (I/O) range and an interrupt request (IRQ); a graphics adapter requires access to these things and to specific memory ranges. On some devices it is possible for you to manually set the hardware resources a device uses by clearing the Use Automatic Settings check box, as shown in Figure 3-4. From this point, it is possible either to set a basic configuration using the drop-down list or to manually enter settings for the device. Although Windows Vista will do its best to manage how devices interact with the computer, post-installation troubleshooting might involve changing the resource settings manually to resolve conflicts. Not all devices allow manual resource configuration.

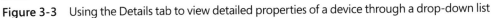

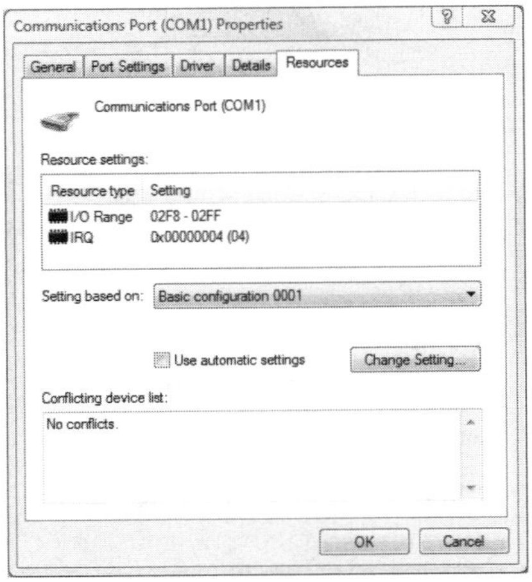

Figure 3-4   Clearing Automatic Settings to manually configure the hardware resources a device uses

As mentioned earlier, some devices have extra tabs that are not mentioned above. For example, some devices also have a Power Management tab, shown in Figure 3-5, that you can use to configure whether Windows Vista can turn off a device to save power. You might examine this setting if a user reports that a device seems to fail after a certain amount of time. It might simply be that the device is configured to turn itself off after a particular period has elapsed in an effort to reduce power consumption.

Figure 3-5 Configuring a device to turn off to save power when not in use

Understanding Hardware Resources

The settings of up to three types of resources are reported on the Resources tab of a device's properties. Not all devices that connect to a Windows Vista computer use all three types of resources. These resources are:

- **I/O range** Input/output range. The range of addresses through which data is exchanged between the device and the computer.
- **IRQ** Interrupt request. The standard x86 architecture has 16 IRQs (0 to 15). A hardware device uses an IRQ to notify the CPU that it requires attention. The Advanced Programmable Interrupt Controller (APIC) architecture manages IRQ settings on modern computers, even allowing devices to share the same IRQ in some instances.
- **Memory range** A specific area of the computer's memory allocated for the device to use.

In general, it is not necessary for you to configure resources manually on a Windows Vista computer after you install the operating system. This is because almost all hardware devices designed for computers that run Windows Vista are plug and play compatible. When you connect a plug and play device to the computer, Windows automatically detects and identifies the device and then searches the set of existing drivers that come with the operating system for a match. If no driver is found among the existing set, Windows Vista extends that search to Windows Update. After Windows Vista locates and installs the driver, the computer allocates hardware resources. If Windows Vista is unable to locate a driver, the device is marked with a warning icon and is not allocated resources.

Although almost all hardware devices that people use with Windows Vista will be plug and play compliant, it is possible that unusual hardware—for example, custom-designed scientific equipment—might still require you to adjust hardware settings through the device's Properties dialog box in Device Manager. Sometimes Windows Vista simply does not detect non-plug and play hardware. In order to install a non-plug and play device that is not detected automatically on a computer running Windows Vista, you must manually get Windows to search for the new hardware. To do this, open Device Manager, right-click the computer name at the very top of the device tree, and then click Add Legacy Hardware. This starts the Add Hardware Wizard. A practice that involves manually adding a legacy hardware device to Windows Vista is at the end of this lesson.

Exam Tip   In the old Windows NT 4.0 certification exams, some questions had answers that suggested manually changing jumper settings on hardware to reconfigure which resources it used. In this Windows Vista exam, all hardware configuration settings are managed through Windows. You do not have to worry about questions that suggest removing hardware from the computer and configuring settings manually.

Disabling a Device

Sometimes the stability of a Windows Vista installation is undermined by a particular hardware device that you cannot remove from the computer. For example, a network adapter integrated into the motherboard causes the computer to encounter STOP errors. To resolve such an issue, you might disable the device using Device Manager. To disable a device, right-click it in Device Manager, and then click Disable. When you disable a device, Device Manager places a down arrow icon next to the device, as shown in Figure 3-6, to indicate its disabled status. This differentiates it from a device that was disabled in another manner, such as through a computer's basic input/output system (BIOS). A device that was disabled using the computer's BIOS will not appear in Device Manager.

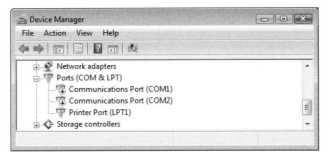

Figure 3-6   The down arrow icon, which indicates that a device has been disabled using Device Manager

NOTE   Mystery items: the question mark icon

The question mark icon appears next to a device when Windows Vista cannot identify what the device is. Using the Update Driver Software option on such devices is rarely helpful because without knowing what the device is, Windows Vista cannot ask for a driver for it from the Windows Update servers. In doing your own troubleshooting, you will have to figure out which devices are installed on the computer that do not appear within Device Manager and are not functioning. You will then need to download the device drivers for this item from the manufacturer's website. If you cannot figure out what the device is that is generating the question mark icon, be sure to download and install the Windows Vista drivers for your motherboard from the appropriate manufacturer's website. We have found through experience that unusual and unidentifiable devices always turn out to be some extra device that you do not really need that is soldered on to the motherboard.

Using the Reliability Monitor in Post-Installation Troubleshooting

The Reliability Monitor is an excellent tool for diagnosing the worst problem a technician faces, the intermittent failure. Although a hardware device or an application will usually fail immediately after you have installed Windows Vista, sometimes the fault might be more intermittent. Intermittent failures are the worst problem for a technician because when you examine the computer yourself, everything seems to be working fine. You can use the Reliability Monitor, shown in Figure 3-7, to get an overview of failures over a configurable period of time.

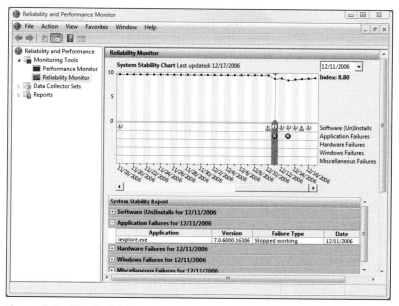

Figure 3-7   The Reliability Monitor

The Reliability Monitor can be very helpful for IT professionals who have to maintain computers that are in an environment that is unmanaged, such as computers that are used in the home or in a small business environment without an Active Directory directory service domain. In enterprise environments, system administrators are generally able to control what software, features, and hardware are installed on computers in the environment. The 70-620 exam deals with Windows Vista computers in less structured environments, such as the home and small businesses. In these environments, the person who uses the computer usually has administrator privileges on that computer and is responsible for installing all applications and hardware. This can make troubleshooting more difficult than it is in an enterprise environment because in the enterprise environment, you have a level of control over what people can and cannot install. In an unmanaged environment, you cannot entirely be sure of what has happened to the computer that has caused the problem that you have been asked to fix because with full administrator rights, the user could have done anything!

The Reliability Monitor reports on the following:

- **Software installation and removal** An information event or warning sign indicates when software has been installed or removed. This is not limited to the installation or removal of applications but also applies to installing, updating, rolling back, or removing device drivers.
- **Application failures** When applications such as Internet Explorer crash or freeze, a red X icon is shown in the Application Failures row.
- **Hardware failures** Records when a hardware device has failed or become unavailable. Very useful for troubleshooting hardware problems.
- **Windows failures** Records events such as boot failures or operating system crashes, including STOP errors.
- **Miscellaneous failures** Records when a failure occurs that does not fit into the category of application, hardware, or Windows failure. This includes events such as the computer being disruptively shut down during a power outage.

If you have installed Windows Vista for someone and that person returns a few days later complaining of crashes or hardware problems, you can quickly verify these claims by examining the log in Reliability Monitor. Reliability Monitor also provides the system stability graph. You can use this graph to visually determine when system stability started to deteriorate. You then match this up with events that occurred around the same time. To view the Reliability Monitor, perform the following steps:

1. Click Start, and then click Control Panel.
2. Ensure that the Control Panel is switched to Classic View.

3. Double-click Administrative Tools, and then double-click Reliability And Performance.

4. Under the Monitoring Tools node, click Reliability Monitor.

Configuring the settings of the Reliability Monitor and how it works is covered in more detail in Chapter 11, "Maintaining and Optimizing Windows Vista."

Problem Reports and Solutions

When an application crashes or something else goes wrong, Windows Vista is able to send a report on the problem to Microsoft. It is possible to tease out the detail of these problems using the Reliability Monitor, but Problem Reports And Solutions provides a convenient summary, shown in Figure 3-8, of all current and past issues that have occurred with Windows Vista, also detailing how the problems were resolved. An example of a resolution might be that a device driver for a hardware component that did not exist when Windows Vista was installed became available through Windows Update at a later time. Windows resolved the problem by automatically installing the updated driver on the computer, which made the hardware device functional.

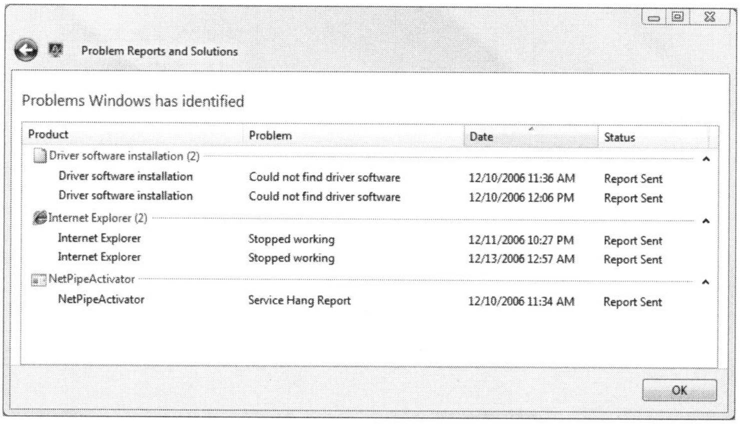

Figure 3-8 A list of problems that have occurred on a Windows Vista computer

To view Problem Reports and Solutions, perform the following steps:

1. Click Start, and then click All Programs.

2. Click Maintenance, and then click Problem Reports And Solutions.

3. Click View Problem History. This presents a list of all problem reports that have been sent or not sent to Microsoft.

The Problem Reports And Solutions feature of Windows Vista is covered in more depth in Chapter 11, "Maintaining and Optimizing Windows Vista."

Quick Check

1. What technology is used to automatically allocate hardware resources to devices to ensure that no conflicts occur?
2. What does a yellow warning sign icon next to a device in Device Manager indicate?

Quick Check Answers

1. Plug and play
2. That the device has a problem. You can determine the nature of this problem by examining the error information in the device's properties.

Display Settings

Even with the same monitors, a display configuration that works well for a 19-year-old college student is not going to work well for a 79-year-old great-grandmother. The student might be completely happy with a resolution of 1600 by 1200 pixels on a standard 19-inch CRT monitor because the student is young and has good vision. The great-grandmother might prefer the significantly lower resolution of 800 by 600 pixels when using the same equipment because her vision is not so great, and to use the computer, she needs things displayed in a larger way. Part of the post-installation troubleshooting process is configuring Windows Vista in such a way that it best meets the needs of the person who will be using the computer. Because the primary sense most people use to receive information from a computer is eyesight, the importance of configuring Windows Vista's display settings cannot be understated.

The first thing to note is that it is reasonably hard to configure display settings in such a way as to render Windows Vista unusable. Whenever you change screen resolution, the number of colors, or the monitor refresh rate and click Apply or OK, Windows switches to the new setting and then displays a prompt asking you to confirm this, as shown in Figure 3-9.

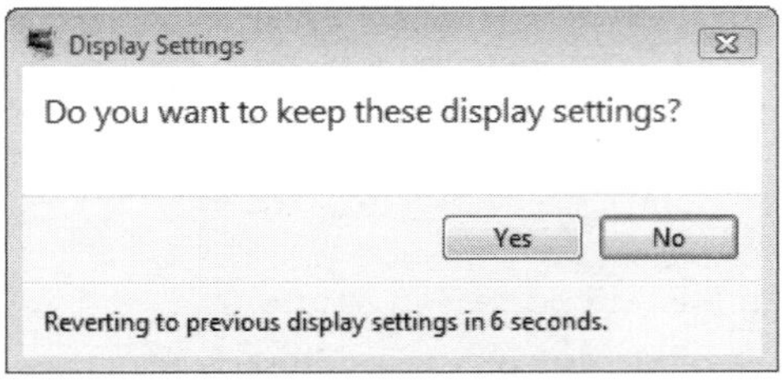

Figure 3-9   Windows Vista reverts to the original display settings in 15 seconds unless you confirm the change

The reason for this is fairly straightforward. In earlier versions of Windows (with the exception of Windows 2000/XP/2003), this prompt did not exist. It was possible to configure the resolution of Windows to a setting that the monitor did not support. You changed the setting, clicked OK, and then suddenly, you could not see anything. You had to then reset the computer and boot into safe mode to fix the problem. Once the new change has been made, Windows now displays a prompt for 15 seconds asking you to confirm your decision. If you do not click Yes, which is difficult if you cannot see the dialog box, Windows Vista reverts to your original settings after the 15-second countdown has concluded. The dialog box is configured with the focus on the No button, saving you from accidentally confirming an incompatible resolution should you accidentally press the Enter key during the 15-second grace period.

Resolution

Monitor resolution is always measured by two numbers of pixels. The first number describes the number of pixels displayed horizontally. The second number describes the number of pixels displayed vertically. Hence, a monitor configured with a resolution of 1600 x 1200 has a display that is 1600 pixels wide and 1200 pixels tall. In total, a monitor configured with a resolution of 1600 x 1200 displays 1,920,000 pixels!

NOTE   **What is a pixel?**

Pixel is short for picture (pix) element. Each image on a monitor is made up of thousands (sometimes millions) of elements. These individual elements are known as pixels. The width and height of a pixel is dependent on the size of the display device and the set resolution. Hence, the size of a pixel on a 19-inch monitor set to a resolution of 1024 x 768 is larger than that of a pixel on the same monitor set to a resolution of 1600 x 1200.

Microsoft recommends the resolutions based on monitor size, as shown in Table 3-1.

Table 3-1   Recommended Resolutions Based on Monitor Size

Monitor Size (Diagonal)	Recommended Resolution
15-inch monitor	1024 x 768 pixels
17-inch to 19-inch monitor	1280 x 1024 pixels
20-inch and larger monitor	1600 x 1200 pixels

Although these are recommended settings, cathode ray tube (CRT) monitors always support resolutions lower than the recommended one. Most monitors also support resolutions that are higher than these recommended figures. In terms of post-configuration troubleshooting, you need to set a resolution that suits the person using the computer. You also have to be sure that the monitor the person is using supports the resolution that you are going to set. When people buy new computers, they do not always purchase new monitors. This can mean that someone running the latest and greatest computer hardware is connecting it to a 21-inch monitor that the user might have purchased in the late 1990s. This monitor might work perfectly fine but might not support the highest resolutions that the graphics adapter can output. The reason that someone can use only a 21-inch monitor at a resolution of 1024 x 768 might be that the monitor is 15 years old. If a person in this situation wants to use the computer with a higher display resolution, that person needs to purchase a new monitor. Users without administrator privileges are able to change monitor resolution settings. Unlike other settings available through the Personalization item in Control Panel, resolution, number of colors displayed, and monitor refresh rates apply to all users of the computer. That means that if you and your great-grandmother share a single Windows Vista computer, you will have to come to a compromise on what monitor settings suit you both because otherwise you will have to keep adjusting them each time one of you logs in after the other.

Quick Check

- A friend of yours has just purchased a new computer but has not purchased a monitor. This computer has a very powerful graphics card that your friend will use in her job designing webpage animation. She has a large monitor she purchased some years ago that she wants to continue using with the newly purchased computer. Although the display settings show a maximum resolution of 2048 x 1536, whenever she attempts to set the resolution above 1600 x 1200, the screen goes blank. Why might this happen?

Quick Check Answer

- The monitor might simply not support resolutions beyond a certain level. Although a monitor might be very large, it might not support high resolutions and refresh rates.

Liquid crystal display (LCD) monitors are different from standard CRT monitors in that they have a native resolution that is dependent on their size and the way that they are manufactured. For example, a 22-inch (measured diagonally) monitor from one manufacturer might have a different native resolution than a 22-inch monitor from another. Knowing the native resolution is important. If the LCD monitor is not configured to use native resolution, the display can appear to be blurry or blocky. You can determine the native resolution of an LCD monitor by consulting the documentation that it shipped with or by checking the manufacturer's website.

Real World

Orin Thomas

As mentioned earlier, LCD monitors look best if run in their native resolution. I have a widescreen LCD monitor attached to one of my computers. Its native resolution is 1680 x 1050. This computer is configured to boot between Windows XP, Windows Server 2003, and Windows Vista Ultimate. In Windows XP and Windows Server 2003 I can configure the display settings so that the monitor can run in its native resolution. Even though the Windows Vista display adapter driver and monitor drivers have been installed, I cannot configure the display adapter to run in native resolution. After searching the web, I found that the problem is with my display adapter drivers. Other people had encountered the same problem. In testing, they had found that by using a graphics adapter with an alternative chipset, they were able to get the monitor working in its native resolution using Windows Vista. For me, it is a matter of waiting until the vendor of the particular graphics adapter I use gets around to updating its Windows Vista drivers. Interestingly enough, the appropriate drivers became available the day I submitted the first draft of this chapter.

Colors

When Windows Vista runs normally, it displays either 16-bit or 32-bit color. Sixteen-bit color means that the monitor displays 65,536 colors, and 32-bit color means that the monitor displays 16,777,216 colors. Almost all modern monitors display 32-bit color, and generally speaking it is better to have your monitor configured to display as many colors as possible. There are some situations in which you might have to switch from 32-bit color to 16-bit color. For example, your monitor might fail, and you cannot afford a new one for a couple of weeks. As an alternative, you have a 10-year-old monitor in the garage that you hook up to your Windows Vista computer. The monitor cannot display very high resolutions and can display only a diminished number of colors, but this will be an acceptable solution until you can acquire a replacement monitor.

MORE INFO Legacy applications

Some applications fail when attempting to display more than 256 colors. To deal with these situations, you should configure the application's compatibility settings to run the application only in 256-color mode. Application compatibility settings were covered in more detail in Chapter 2, "Windows Vista Upgrades and Migrations."

Multiple Monitor Settings

To increase their productivity, people are increasingly connecting more than one monitor to their computers. Many desktop graphics adapters ship with the ability to output two separate signals to monitor devices. Almost all laptop and Tablet PC computers also have the ability to support an ancillary display. For laptop and Tablet PCs, this is generally used to connect directly to a projector device. As far as Windows Vista is concerned, an attached projector is treated as just another display.

MORE INFO   Network projectors

Connecting laptop and Tablet PCs to network projectors, which do not connect to graphic adapter display outputs, is covered in more detail in Chapter 13, "Configuring Mobile Devices."

Although Windows Vista supports as many monitors as you can fit graphics adapters onto your motherboard, this support requires each graphics adapter to use the same chipset and the same Windows Display Driver Model (WDDM) driver. Thus it is possible to have an Accelerated Graphics Port (AGP) graphics adapter with two outputs and two further adapters, each with two outputs, in Peripheral Component Interconnect (PCI) slots to run a total of six monitors if, and only if, all three graphics adapters use the same WDDM driver. If your computer has two x16 PCIe slots and your graphics adapters use separate chipsets, Windows Vista will disable one of the graphics adapters even if the same hardware configuration allowed you to use multiple monitors in Windows XP. There are some things you cannot do in Windows Vista that you could do in Windows XP. Occasionally these items turn up in certification exams. The error message displayed when two disparate graphics chipsets are used is shown in Figure 3-10.

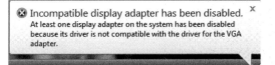

Figure 3-10   An additional graphics adapter disabled by Windows Vista because it requires an alternate graphics adapter

---

NOTE   No mix and match

In general, this means that you can run adapters with nVidia chipsets together or adapters with ATI chipsets together, but you cannot mix and match the two. Although you can mix within the same family, mixing graphics adapters that were released several years apart, even if they have the same chipset, is likely to cause a problem because different WDDM drivers will be used. Because most graphics adapters have multiple outputs, it will only be in a situation where someone needs more than three or more monitors running off the same computer that you will have to be careful. For more information, consult the following URL: *http://www.microsoft.com/whdc /device/display/multimonVista.mspx*.

When you connect multiple monitors to a computer, the Display Settings dialog box changes, as shown in Figure 3-11.

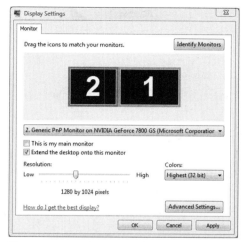

Figure 3-11   The Display Settings dialog box when two monitors are connected to Windows Vista

The new items in the display settings dialog box, compared to a single display dialog box, are as follows:

- **Identify Monitors button**   This button is used to help you determine which physical monitor corresponds to which numbered monitor in the dialog box.
- **This Is My Main Monitor check box**   Selecting this check box means that this monitor will be used as the primary multimedia display device.
- **Extend The Desktop Onto This Monitor check box**   Selecting this check box allows you to make an extended desktop. This means that you can seamlessly drag a window from one screen to another. When the item that you are moving passes the center edge on one display, it begins to be drawn on the other display. This allows you to easily move items between each display as needed.

After you have connected multiple monitors to the computer running Windows Vista, you need to determine which monitor in the Display Settings Properties represents which physical monitor sitting in front of you. Windows makes a guess, but depending on which way your cables are configured, that guess might not reflect reality. It can be disconcerting to drag a window to the right edge of the right monitor only to have it appear on the left edge of the left monitor. If this happens, it is because the computer believes these two monitors are in different positions.

NOTE   **Windows Vista default behavior**

Although Windows Vista does not allow wraparound movement of windows, some applications do. For example, you can keep dragging a window from left to right indefinitely. As you reach the right edge of the right monitor, the window wraps around to the left edge of the left monitor. You can then keep dragging it right, where it passes from the left monitor to the right monitor and so on, ad infinitum, ad absurdum.

To determine which monitor is actually in front of you and to rectify the situation if it is not correct, perform the following steps:

1. Right-click the desktop, and then click Personalize.
2. Click Display Settings.
3. Click Identify Monitors. A large number appears on each monitor. If it represents the current placement of your monitors, the configuration is correct.
4. If the number order on the screen does not represent the placement of your monitors, drag the items representing the monitors into the order that represents the actual monitor placement..

Advanced Settings

The Advanced Settings option allows all users of a Windows Vista computer to modify color management and the monitor's refresh rate and view information about the graphics adapter connected to their computer. As with Personalization settings, almost all items in the Advanced Settings dialog box can be configured by a user with a standard set of permissions. Any item that requires administrative privileges displays the User Account Control shield icon. User Account Control and the shield icon are discussed in greater detail in Chapter 5, "User Account Control." Each of these options is covered in more detail in the following section.

Adapter Properties   The Adapter tab, shown in Figure 3-12, allows you to see information about the graphics adapter installed on the computer. This can be helpful if you are unsure of what adapter is installed or if you want to verify that the adapter included in the computer that you are about to buy is the one that was actually advertised as being included. Clicking the List All Modes button displays all output resolutions and monitor frequencies that the adapter supports.

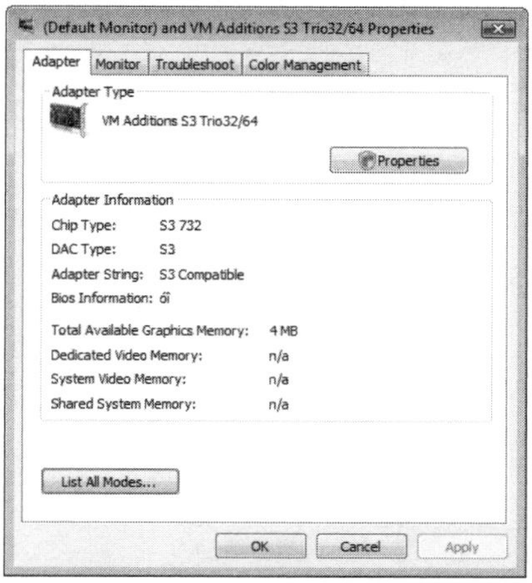

Figure 3-12   Graphics adapter properties

Color Management   The purpose of color management is to ensure that colors look the same across all devices used with the Windows Vista computer. For example, a printer produces a different set of colors than a monitor does. A scanner uses a different set of colors than a printer does. Windows Vista's color management maintains the color relationships between devices so that the image you see on the screen matches the output that you get from the printer as closely as possible. Because most printers are unable to display as many colors as a monitor, configuring this setting can reduce the number of colors a monitor displays. This setting is really used only by people who professionally work with images and print and is likely to be irrelevant to most people who use Windows Vista.

Monitor   You set the refresh rate used by a monitor in the Monitor tab of an adapter's advanced properties, as shown in Figure 3-13. The set refresh rate determines how quickly the monitor updates the image on the screen. The appropriate refresh rate for a person depends on that person's vision. The higher the set refresh rate, the smaller the amount of screen flicker. Some people do not perceive any flicker on a CRT monitor at 60 Hz; other people perceive flicker on the same monitor at 90 Hz. Some people get headaches if they perceive the flicker, and others do not.

Figure 3-13   Configuring the screen refresh rate

In many cases, the higher that you set the refresh rate on a CRT monitor, the lower the maximum resolution that is available. A 19-inch monitor might be able to support only a resolution of 1600 x 1200 at an 85 Hz refresh rate but supports a high resolution like 2048 x 1536 at a lower refresh rate of 60 Hz. When performing a post-installation tuning for someone, find that person's preferred graphical resolution and then set the refresh rate as high as possible. LCD monitors use a different technology than CRT monitors. This means that they very rarely have refresh rates that you can change from the factory setting. Because of the way that LCD monitors are updated, they do not flicker in the same way that CRT monitors do and are less likely to cause headaches.

Troubleshooting   Clicking the Change Settings button in the Troubleshoot tab of the graphics adapter properties requires that the user have administrative permissions. Assuming that the user does have these permissions, clicking this item presents the Display Adapter Troubleshooter, shown in Figure 3-14. The only modification that you can make to troubleshoot your display adapter is to adjust your hardware acceleration settings. By default, the hardware acceleration settings are set to full acceleration. Only if the picture on the display is encountering problems, such as moving a window and having its afterimage drag across the screen leaving a trail, would you reduce the hardware acceleration. It might be that by accelerating the hardware, the graphics adapter is overheating or malfunctioning, causing images to not be drawn correctly on the screen. Reducing the graphics adapter's hardware acceleration might solve the problem.

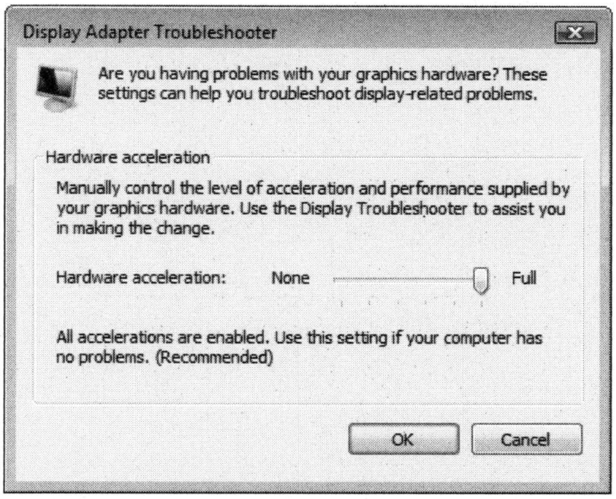

Figure 3-14 Disable hardware acceleration if images are not being drawn correctly on the screen

Visual Appearance Settings

Although it might seem odd, you will find that many users of Windows Vista will put as much stock in how their computer looks as they do in how quickly it functions. In the following sections we discuss several methods that you can use to individualize an installation of Windows Vista. Users can configure all these settings with a standard set of permissions. It is also important to note that unlike monitor resolution and refresh rates, these personalization settings apply only to a single user's profile. This means that if one person sets a particular desktop background and color scheme, it applies only to that person's profile. Other users who log on to the same computer will have their own desktop background, screen saver, and color settings.

Window Color and Appearance

Window Color And Appearance, shown in Figure 3-15, allows you to change the color settings of the default Windows Vista theme. It is also possible to modify the transparency settings, making it easier, or harder, to see through each window's title bar. Accessed through the Personalization dialog box, you can configure one of 12 default colors or build your own color using the color mixer.

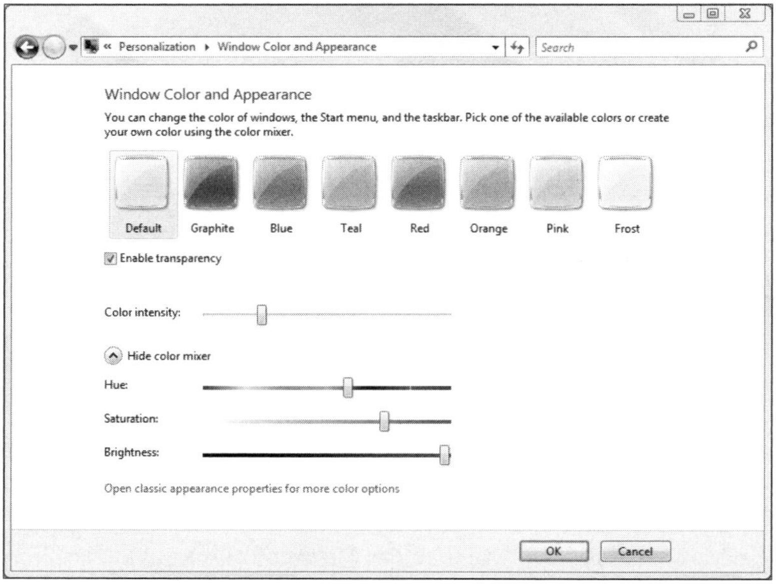

Figure 3-15   Configuring Windows Color And Appearance to find a color that suits your own sense of style

If your computer is not running the Aero interface, clicking Window Color And Appearance takes you to the appearance settings screen that was in Windows XP and Windows Server 2003. You can alter color schemes in the same manner that worked with these older operating systems. Practice 3, at the end of this lesson, further explores the options for modifying Windows Vista's color and appearance.

Desktop Background

Windows Vista allows you to set your desktop background using almost all popular image formats. You can either select a background from a large number of built-in wallpaper images or select your own picture by clicking Browse and navigating to a folder containing your own set of pictures. It is also possible to right-click on an image you have located on the Internet and to set it as a desktop background. In general, you should download an image and set it as a background rather than setting it as a background using Internet Explorer. If you use Internet Explorer and you set a new desktop background, only to change your mind later, you will have to remember where on the Internet you found your previous image. If you save the image file to your hard disk drive, you can simply reload it.

Screen Saver

Although today's modern displays have hardware that protects them from the problem of image burn-in, many users still like having a screen saver become active after their computer has been idle for some time. Burn-in occurred on older monitors, where a static image that did not change would become "burned in" to the monitor's display. Windows Vista comes with several default screen savers. It is also possible to download screen savers from the Internet, although you should caution users about doing that because nefarious third parties often use free screen saver software on the Internet as a way of installing Trojan applications on a computer.

Screen savers have a security benefit in a corporate environment. You can configure a screen saver so that the computer becomes locked when the computer has been idle. For example, say that someone employed in an organization that uses an open plan environment is working on sensitive payroll information using a Windows Vista computer. This person gets called away from the computer and forgets to lock the screen. Without a screen saver, a curious coworker might wander by and be able to view the sensitive information. However, if the screen saver is configured correctly, the computer automatically locks itself. This minimizes the chance that someone unauthorized will gain access to the computer.

Screen saver configuration is available through the Personalization item in the Control Panel. As with the configuration of desktop background and other Windows Vista personalization tasks, a user with standard privileges can perform this task. Practice 4, at the end of this lesson, walks through the screen saver configuration process.

NOTE 3D screen savers

Many of the default screen savers that ship with Windows Vista require a card capable of displaying 3D effects. This is unlikely to be a problem unless you are running Windows Vista in a virtual machine environment.

Practice: Post-Installation Troubleshooting

In these practices, you will perform several exercises that will familiarize you with tools that are useful in performing post-installation troubleshooting. These include the installation of legacy hardware, examining system stability, and configuring personalized settings.

▶ **Practice 1: Add Legacy Hardware**

In this practice, you will use the Add Hardware Wizard to search for legacy hardware. A legacy device is one that will work with Windows Vista but that is not automatically detected and installed by the operating system. Legacy devices are not plug and play compatible. In this practice, you will install a legacy loopback adapter. Although they are virtual devices, you can use loopback adapters to perform network diagnostics. Performing this exercise will give you an understanding of the manual installation process. To complete this practice, perform the following steps:

1. Click Start, and then click Control Panel.
2. Ensure that Control Panel is set to Classic View.
3. Open Device Manager.
4. Right-click the Computer Name at the top of the device tree, and then click Add Legacy Hardware.
5. In the Welcome To The Add Hardware Wizard page, shown in Figure 3-16, click Next.

Figure 3-16   Adding legacy hardware using the Add Hardware Wizard

6. Select Install The Hardware That I Manually Select From A List (Advanced), and then click Next.
7. Scroll down through the Common Hardware Types list, and then select Network Adapters. Click Next.
8. In the Select Network Adapter dialog box, select Microsoft in the Manufacturer List, and then select Microsoft Loopback Adapter, as shown in Figure 3-17. Click Next.

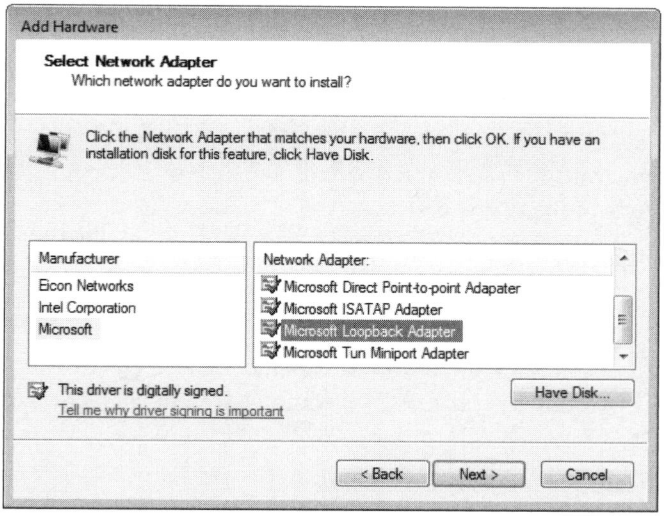

Figure 3-17   Adding the Microsoft Loopback Adapter

9. Click Next again to install the hardware.

10. Click Finish to exit the wizard.

11. In Device Manager, verify that the Microsoft Loopback Adapter is installed under the Network Adapters node.

▶ **Practice 2: Examine the System Stability Chart**

The System Stability Chart, a component of the Reliability Monitor, gives you a graphical representation of a Windows Vista computer's stability. It gives technicians visual cues on what might be causing post-installation problems. For example, has the computer been unstable since Windows Vista was installed, or has something else, perhaps the installation of an application or device driver software, caused instability to occur? To access the System Stability Chart, perform the following steps:

1. Click Start, and then click Control Panel.

2. Ensure that the Control Panel is set to Classic View.

3. Double-click Administrative Tools, and then double-click Reliability And Performance. Click Continue.

4. Click Reliability Monitor, and then view the System Stability chart.

5. Note where the graph representing system stability drops. Check what software was installed at this point; it is likely to be causing the problem you are troubleshooting.

▶ **Practice 3: Changing Windows Vista Color and Appearance**

Windows Vista allows users to personalize their copy of Windows Vista by selecting a set of colors that they find appealing. In this practice, you will change the color and appearance of Aero from its default settings. To complete this practice, perform the following steps:

1. Right-click the desktop, and then click Personalize.
2. Click the Windows Color And Appearance item.
3. Click the downward pointing arrow next to Show Color Mixer.
4. Move the Hue, Saturation, and Brightness sliders until you find a color that you like.
5. Select and then clear the Enable Transparency check box. Note the changes this makes in the appearance of the dialog box.

▶ **Practice 4: Changing Screen Saver Settings**

In this practice, you will change the screen saver from the default to the 3D Text screen saver, which you will configure to display the time. You will configure the screen saver to activate if the computer has not been used for 15 minutes. Finally, you also ensure that the logon screen is displayed after the computer is resumed. To complete the practice, perform the following steps:

1. Right-click the desktop, and then click Personalize.
2. Click the Screen Saver item.
3. In the Screen Saver drop-down list, select 3D Text.
4. Click Settings.
5. In the 3D Text Settings dialog box, select Time, and then click OK.
6. In the Wait box, change the setting to 15 Minutes.
7. Select the On Resume, Display Logon Screen check box. When complete, the dialog box should look like Figure 3-18. Click OK to accept the new settings.

Figure 3-18   Increasing security by configuring the screen saver to require the user to log back on

Lesson Summary

- A warning icon in Device Manager indicates that a hardware device is experiencing a problem. This problem could be related to a software driver or to a conflict with the hardware configuration.
- The General tab of a device's properties in Device Manager provides information on a problem.
- The Resources tab of a device's properties in Device Manager can be used to configure automatic or manual device resource allocation.
- You must run the Add Hardware Wizard to manually add any legacy hardware that Windows Vista has not automatically detected.
- If you cannot remove a problematic device from a computer, it is possible to manually disable it using Device Manager. Device Manager assigns disabled devices down arrow icons.
- The Reliability Monitor records significant events, such as software installation and crashes, as well as hardware installation and failures. The system stability index provides a graphical representation of system stability that you can use to pinpoint when stability started to degrade.
- Problem Reports And Solutions can provide a summary of problems and resolutions that have occurred since installation.
- It is possible to personalize Windows Vista to a user's taste by configuring an appropriate color scheme and desktop background. These settings are specific to each user's accounts.
- It is possible to customize monitor resolution and flicker rate to suit a person's needs. Resolution and refresh rate apply to all users of the system.

Lesson Review

You can use the following questions to test your knowledge of the information in Lesson 1, "Troubleshooting Post-Installation Configuration Issues." The questions are also available on the companion CD if you prefer to review them in electronic form.

NOTE Answers

Answers to these questions and explanations of why each answer choice is correct or incorrect are located in the "Answers" section at the end of the book.

1. A customer has come into the computer superstore in which you work seeking technical assistance. The customer purchased a laptop computer with a widescreen monitor. The laptop came with Windows XP installed but also came with a voucher allowing the customer to upgrade to Windows Vista. The customer has since purchased Windows Vista and installed it but complains that the screen looks blurry and blocky compared with the way it looked when running Windows XP. Which of the following is likely to be the cause of the customer's problems? (Choose all that apply.)

    A. The refresh rate is set incorrectly.

    B. The number of colors is set incorrectly.

    C. The monitor is not configured to use its native resolution.

    D. The monitor is incompatible with Windows Vista.

2. You work as a technician at the local computer superstore. Two weeks ago, you installed Windows Vista Ultimate edition for a customer on her computer. Since then, she has gradually been installing hardware and applications on her computer. She has asked for your help because in the last few days, applications have begun to freeze and Windows Vista has crashed twice. You suspect the addition of a new application or hardware device is at the root of the problem. Which of the following tools could you use to determine which device has caused the instability? (Choose all that apply.)

    A. Device Manager

    B. Add New Hardware Wizard

    C. Problem Reports And Solutions

    D. Reliability Monitor

3. You work on the technical support desk at the local computer superstore. A customer has called complaining that he is getting a headache from the flickering of his monitor. What advice should you give him?

    A. Adjust the number of colors displayed.

    B. Adjust the monitor's resolution.

    C. Adjust the refresh rate.

    D. Adjust the color management settings.

4. A graphic designer is having trouble with her Windows Vista laptop. She is trying to design a logo with a specific set of colors. When she prints out her work, the colors do not match the design on the screen. Which of the following adjustments can you make to Windows Vista to ensure that the colors on the screen match the colors output to the printer?

   A. Change the number of colors displayed from 32-bit to 16-bit.

   B. Use the Color Management utility.

   C. Change the refresh rate of the monitor.

   D. Change the screen resolution.

5. A customer has come to you for help with a device that he purchased from the Tailspin Toys website. The device is a non-plug and play PCI card that interfaces with a remote-controlled helicopter. The device comes with drivers that are designed to work with Windows Vista, but although the customer has installed the device, he was never prompted to install the drivers. You check Device Manager for the device and see that it is not there. Which of the following courses of action should you pursue?

   A. Install the drivers manually.

   B. In Device Manager, manually configure the resources the device uses.

   C. In Device Manager, execute Scan For Hardware Changes.

   D. In Device Manager, execute Add Legacy Hardware.

6. Due to a programming error, a device driver for a particular critical device on a customer's Windows Vista computer defaults to using a specific I/O range. Unfortunately, another critical hardware device already uses that I/O range. It will be several weeks until the driver can be updated. In the meantime, which strategy should you pursue first?

   A. Using Device Manager, disable the problematic device.

   B. Using Device Manager, uninstall the driver.

   C. Using Device Manager, uninstall the device.

   D. Using Device Manager, alter the device's resource settings.

Lesson 2: Configuring and Troubleshooting Windows Aero

Aero is the most noticeable visual difference between Windows Vista and earlier releases of Windows. Many people, when they log on to Windows Vista for the first time, are going to be looking for Aero. They will have seen demonstrations of the operating systems, either from a salesperson or on TV, and they will want to try the Flip 3D feature for themselves. If Aero is not working and they cannot flip their Windows in 3D, these people are going to want to know why. In this lesson, we discuss the hardware and software requirements for running Aero and techniques that you can use to get Aero running if a computer meets these requirements but does not display Aero. This lesson also discusses the Windows Product Activation (WPA) process and the Windows Genuine Advantage (WGA) process. Finally, we examine how you can run the System Performance Rating tool and how you can use the figures it generates to determine whether your computer is capable of running specific software.

After this lesson, you will be able to:

- Identify hardware requirements for Windows Aero.
- Troubleshoot graphics card issues.
- Identify WDDM drivers.
- Configure Windows Genuine Advantage.
- Run the System Performance Rating tool.
- Change the desktop theme to Windows Aero.

Estimated lesson time: 40 minutes

Troubleshooting Windows Aero

As you learned in the previous lesson, ordinary users are able to modify their display preferences. Some modifications will automatically force the computer to stop using Aero and shift to the Vista Basic desktop theme. If the user who made the changes did not keep track of what he or she was doing, it is possible that the user will not be able to get the computer back to running Aero. In this section, we look at how you can troubleshoot Windows Aero. We cover how you can be sure that Aero will actually work on your computer and explain the steps that you can take to get Aero back if you have configured Windows Vista not to use it.

Identifying Aero Hardware Requirements

Before wondering whether a computer has the hardware capacity to run Aero, you need to ensure that the edition of Windows Vista that is installed on the computer is actually able to run Aero. If a computer has the Starter or Home Basic editions of Windows Vista installed, it will not matter how awesome its graphics adapter is. These editions of Windows Vista do not support Aero.

When you are sure that the edition of Windows Vista you are working with does support Aero, you need to ensure that the graphics adapter hardware also supports Aero. To run Aero, the graphics adapter on the Windows Vista computer must meet the following criteria:

- **DirectX 9 capable**   Unless a graphics adapter is very old indeed, it is likely to be DirectX 9 capable. Any new graphics adapter will be DirectX 9 capable, and the only users who will have to worry about this condition are the ones using a previous version of Windows, such as Windows 2000 or Windows XP. If you have a computer that has either of these operating systems installed and you want to determine whether your graphics adapter is DirectX 9 capable, you can download DirectX 9 from Microsoft's website. DirectX 9 is also distributed with most games. You can check whether a Windows XP computer is already running DirectX 9 by using the Dxdiag.exe utility.

- **A WDDM driver**   WDDM stands for Windows Display Driver Model. A WDDM driver is one that has been specifically written for Windows Vista. Although it might be possible to get Windows Vista to work using a display driver written for Windows XP, it will not be possible to use the Aero interface with this XP driver. A WDDM driver for the graphics adapter must exist if the adapter is going to be used to run Aero.

- **Hardware Pixel Shader 2.0**   Hardware Pixel Shader is a set of mathematical routines incorporated into a graphics adapter's programming that is used to generate visual effects on a per-pixel basis. Version 2.0 allows a greater set of visual effects than version 1.0. Almost all graphics adapters released after 2006 include Hardware Pixel Shader 2.0 support. If you are unsure, check the graphics adapter's technical specifications. These either come with the adapter itself or can be found on the vendor's website.

- **32 bits per pixel**   The graphics adapter must support 32-bit color. A graphics adapter or monitor that supports only 16-bit color is incapable of displaying the Aero interface. If you switch the graphics adapter from 32-bit to 16-bit color in the Display Settings dialog box on a computer running Aero, Windows Vista automatically shifts down to the Vista Basic interface.

- **Minimum of 64 MB graphics memory**   Although Aero displays on a computer with 64 MB of graphics memory, it can display only low resolutions. The graphics memory does not need to be dedicated memory. Many graphics adapters, primarily those on notebook computers, use shared system memory (RAM) to supplement the dedicated video memory, as shown in Figure 3-19.

Figure 3-19   A graphics adapter with 32 MB of dedicated video memory and 271 MB of shared system memory (a total of 303 MB of graphics memory), which is more than enough to run Aero in high resolutions

---

Exam Tip   If you are given the specifications of a graphics adapter in the exam, look for any obvious violations of the above list. Exam questions tend to have answers that are obvious if you know the theory behind them. You will not get a question about a graphics adapter with 63 MB of total memory. If a figure indicating that the answer is wrong is given, it will be 16 or 32 MB, which is clearly less than what is required for Aero.

Quick Check

1. Which editions of Windows Vista are unable to run Aero under any circumstances?
2. What happens if you are running Aero and you change the graphics adapter settings from 32-bit to 16-bit?

Quick Check Answers

1. The Starter and Home Basic editions are unable to run Windows Vista with Aero, no matter how capable their graphics adapter is.
2. Aero stops running and the computer begins to use the Windows Vista Basic interface.

Checking Whether Aero Is Running

After you have determined that the graphics adapter meets the necessary specifications to run Aero and you have installed Windows Vista, you will need to actually check that Aero is running. At a superficial level, Windows looks the same when it is using either Aero or the Vista Basic theme. When you are more familiar with Aero, you will more easily notice what separates Aero from other options. The easiest way to determine whether Aero is working on a computer is to use the Flip 3D function. Flip 3D, shown in Figure 3-20, is a feature that allows a user to switch between applications. Each application is cascaded in three dimensions and keeps running even when displayed in this three-dimensional cascade.

Figure 3-20 Browsing open windows three-dimensionally in Flip 3D

To use Flip 3D, hold down the Windows key, and then press the tab key. If Windows Aero is working, you will see the 3D window cascade. If Aero is not working, nothing will happen. Another quick way to tell if Aero is running is to look at the title bar. An Aero title bar is usually transparent, but when the Vista Basic theme is running, the title bar is opaque. Title bar transparency is not always an accurate method of determining whether Aero is running because it is possible to disable transparency and still run Aero.

NOTE   Not always Aero

Sometimes, when a particular type of application is running, Windows Vista shifts to the Vista Basic interface. This generally happens when the application that is running is graphically intense. When the application finishes executing, Aero is automatically restored.

Setting Aero as the Desktop Theme

Earlier we mentioned that it was possible to disable Aero on a computer that was capable of running it by switching from 32-bit to 16-bit color mode. It is also possible to disable Aero by switching to an alternate theme, such as Windows Vista Basic, Windows Standard, or Windows Classic. If a computer is capable of displaying Aero but is not doing so, you can switch to Aero by performing the following steps:

1. Right-click the desktop, and select Personalize.
2. In the Personalization dialog box, click Window Color And Appearance.
3. Click Open Classic Appearance Properties For More Color Options.
4. In the Appearance Settings dialog box, shown in Figure 3-21, select Windows Aero in the Color Scheme box, and click Apply.

Figure 3-21   Using the Appearance Settings dialog box to set the color scheme to Windows Aero

If the computer is incapable of running Aero because the color settings are configured to use 16-bit or for some other reason, the Windows Aero color scheme will not be available in this dialog box.

> **Real World**
>
> *Orin Thomas*
>
> I had Windows Vista installed on several computers when the operating system was in the beta and release candidate stages. During these stages the graphics adapter on one of my laptop computers went from not having an available WDDM driver to having one. When a driver finally became available through Windows Update and I installed it, I noticed some unusual behavior with my computer. When I created a new account and logged on with it, I would be presented with the Aero interface. When I logged on using the accounts that existed prior to the installation of the WDDM driver, I was presented with the Basic interface. Despite trying everything mentioned in this chapter, there was no option to change the interface to Aero. Eventually, I migrated all my existing settings using the Easy Transfer Wizard to a USB device, removed the existing logon profile, and logged on with the existing account. When I did this, I found that the computer had defaulted to the Aero interface. I was able to import my data and begin using Aero on that computer. Although this technique is unlikely to turn up on the exam and might have itself been unique to the beta and release candidate process, I included it here so that you can employ it as a strategy should you ever encounter Windows Vista behaving in a similar manner.

Windows Genuine Advantage

Windows Genuine Advantage (WGA) is one method Microsoft uses to try to ensure that only legitimate users of the Windows operating system gain access to several services, such as Windows Update, and downloads, such as the latest version of Internet Explorer, Windows Media Player, Windows Defender, and Windows OneCare Live.

To pass a WGA requires that the computer has passed through the WPA process. Although the details of WPA were covered in Chapter 1, "Installing Windows Vista Client," here is a summary of the main points:

- As a part of the activation process, a unique hardware ID is generated based on a computer's hardware configuration. Although two computers might have exactly the same parts, these parts have different identification information, such as serial numbers, that ensure that each hardware ID is unique.

- During the WPA process, the product ID that comes with the Windows Vista installation media and the unique hardware ID are sent to Microsoft.

- A check is performed on the Microsoft servers to determine whether the product ID has been used before.
- If it turns out that the product ID has been used before and is paired in the activation database with a different hardware ID, the WPA process fails.
- If it turns out that the product ID has never been used before, the product ID and hardware ID are recorded together in Microsoft's activation database and the WPA process succeeds.
- If it turns out that the product ID has been used before, but the hardware ID matches the hardware ID that is paired with the product ID in the activation database, the WPA process succeeds. This is to allow you to reinstall Windows on the same hardware once. If you need to perform reinstallation more than once, you will need to call the WPA hotline.
- You can change computer components once without forcing reactivation. If you change multiple components at the same time, you will need to reactivate Windows.

In Chapter 1, we suggested that you do not activate your copy of Windows immediately. This allowed you to upgrade from the Business to the Ultimate edition of Windows Vista in Chapter 2, "Windows Vista Upgrades and Migrations." The 30-day WPA grace period also allows your system configuration to settle prior to performing activation. For example, if you find that your computer requires more memory, a faster processor, or a better graphics card after you install Windows Vista, you should install these components prior to performing the WPA process.

If you are performing technical support for someone and want to know whether they have activated their copy of Windows, you should perform the following steps:

1. Click the Start menu, and then click Control Panel.
2. Double-click System.
3. A screen that looks similar to the one in Figure 3-22 appears. If you look toward the bottom of the screen, you see a section entitled Windows Activation. The information in this section tells you whether or not this copy of Windows Vista has successfully completed WPA.

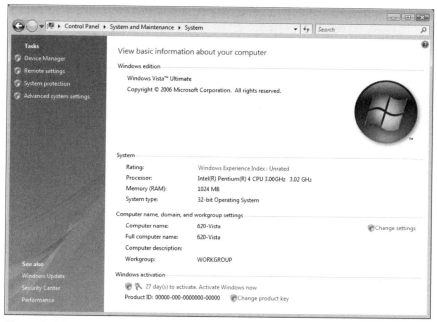

Figure 3-22   A computer that has yet to complete the WPA process

If you have already entered your product key, you can choose to activate at any time in the 30 days after the installation was completed. If you did not enter your product key, entering it by selecting the Change License Key option forces the activation process to occur immediately. If you do not enter the product key during setup, enter it only when you are ready to perform the WPA process.

The WGA process is initiated when you visit Microsoft's website and attempt to download an application or feature for Windows Vista that requires a WGA check. During the WGA process, a special add-on component for Internet Explorer is installed. Your permission will be sought to install this add-on and your permission will again be sought to go through the WGA process. The WGA process involves the add-on component collecting information from your computer and then sending that information to Microsoft. During the WGA process, the add-on will collect the following information:

- Your computer's make and model
- Operating system version and any existing WGA software
- Region and language settings
- A unique WGA identifier created by the add-on component
- An encrypted version of your product key and product ID

- BIOS information such as name, revision number, and revision date
- Encrypted primary hard disk drive volume serial number

It is important to note that the WGA process does not collect your name, address, e-mail address, or any other information that Microsoft could use to identify you.

If someone bypasses the WPA process using some form of circumvention technology and is running an unlicensed version of Windows Vista, the WGA process will not be able to verify that person. In addition to receiving regular notifications that the installation of Windows is not genuine, he or she will be able to download only certain updates from the Windows Update servers. All updates released by Microsoft fit into one of the three following categories:

- **Critical**   These updates should be installed immediately because an attacker could exploit the vulnerabilities that they remedy.
- **Important**   These updates should be installed as soon as possible. They differ from updates in the Critical category because exploits that take advantage of these vulnerabilities have yet to appear.
- **Moderate**   These updates generally fix usability problems rather than possible security exploits.

The Automatic Updates function on a computer that has not completed the WGA process limits downloads to critical updates only.

NOTE   Manual installation only

Users who have not completed the WGA process are able to manually install important and moderate updates, hotfixes, and patches after downloading the required files from Microsoft's website.

WGA validation is an ongoing process. A validation is performed each time you use Microsoft's website to obtain software that requires validation. During this process, your current configuration is assessed against the past data collected during WGA validation. Microsoft occasionally updates the add-on control, which requires you to install the new version. Other than this occasional instance, the WGA process is designed to be as unobtrusive as possible. A demonstration of the WGA process is provided in Practice 3 at the end of this lesson.

NOTE   Ongoing validation process

The reason that the validation process is ongoing is that it would be significantly easier to circumvent if it were a one-off process. Microsoft becomes aware of newly pirated product keys on an ongoing basis. These product keys are systematically excluded in the WGA process.

The System Performance Rating Tool

The System Performance Rating tool is used to generate the Windows Experience Index number. The Windows Experience Index number can be used to determine whether a computer running Windows Vista has enough capacity to run a particular application. The idea is simple. An application has a recommended Windows Experience Index rating. If your computer meets that figure, the application should perform adequately. If your computer has a Windows Experience Index number below that rating, the application might still run, but it is unlikely to do so in acceptably.

The components that are tested as a part of generating the Windows Experience Index number are shown in Table 3-2.

Table 3-2 Components Used to Determine System Performance

Component	Measurement
Processor	Calculations per second
Physical memory (RAM)	Memory operations per second
Graphics	Windows Aero desktop performance
Gaming graphics	3D graphics performance
Primary hard disk	Disk data transfer rate

The Windows Experience Index score is determined by the score of the lowest-rated component. A computer that is rated between 1 or 2 can perform basic tasks adequately but should not be used for games or multimedia. A computer rated at 3 can run Aero and play DVDs well but might have problems displaying HDTV. A computer rated above 4 runs software and multimedia applications well. At Windows Vista's release, the only way to achieve an index score of 5 was to be running a state-of-the-art high-performance workstation.

The Windows Experience Index score is generated automatically as the installation of Windows Vista finalizes. You can have your computer reevaluated at any time. You should do this if you add a newer graphics adapter, processor, motherboard, RAM, or hard disk drive. To generate a new Windows Experience Index score, perform the following steps:

1. Click Start, and then click Control Panel.
2. Ensure that the Control Panel is set to use Classic View.
3. Open the System item.
4. Click Windows Experience Index.
5. In the Rate And Improve Your Computer's Performance dialog box, shown in Figure 3-23, click Update My Score.

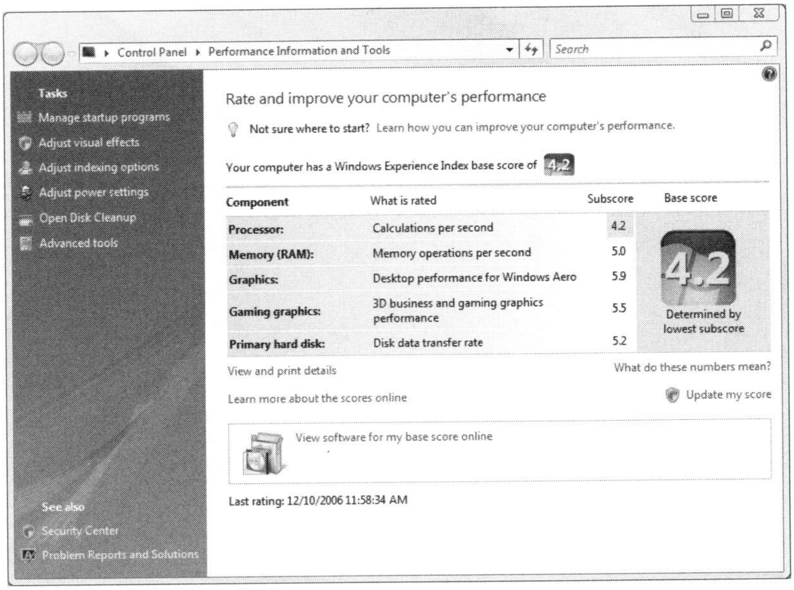

Figure 3-23   The Rate And Improve Your Computer's Performance dialog box, which shows how each specific component rates

6. The assessment takes place. It takes a few minutes to complete. If there has been an improvement in the hardware that has the lowest score, the Windows Experience Index number increases.

Practice: Product Activation and Windows Genuine Advantage

In these practices, you will perform WPA, either over the Internet or by using the telephone. Once you have completed activation, you will pass through the WGA process.

▶ **Practice 1: Performing Windows Product Activation over the Internet**

To perform this practice, your Windows Vista computer must have an active Internet connection. Verify that the connection is working by navigating to *http://www.microsoft.com* using Internet Explorer. If your Windows Vista computer does not have a connection to the Internet, you must perform Practice 2 instead of Practice 1. To perform Practice 1, follow these steps:

1. Click the Start menu, and then click Control Panel.
2. Double-click System.
3. In the Windows Activation section, click Change Product Key.
4. Click Continue in the User Account Control dialog box.
5. In the Change Your Product Key For Activation dialog box, shown in Figure 3-24, enter your Windows Vista product key, and click Next.

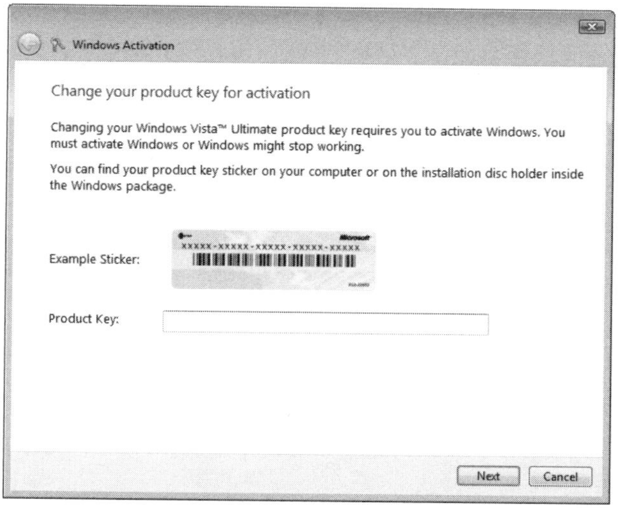

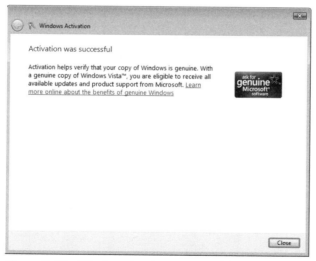

Figure 3-24 Enter your product key in the Change Your Product Key For Activation dialog box

6. If you are connected to the Internet, the Activating Windows dialog box is displayed for a few minutes. During this time, Windows Vista goes through the entire WPA process.

7. After the WPA process completes, a message is displayed telling you that activation was successful. The Genuine Microsoft Software logo is displayed, as shown in Figure 3-25. If activation is not successful, you might have to phone Microsoft support to resolve the situation.

Figure 3-25 Windows has been successfully activated

▶ **Practice 2: Performing Windows Product Activation over the Telephone**

Perform this practice instead of Practice 1 only if your Windows Vista computer does not have a connection to the Internet.

1. Click the Start menu, and then click Control Panel.
2. Click System And Maintenance.
3. Click the text that says See The Name Of This Computer.
4. On the View Basic Information About Your Computer screen, click Activate Windows Now.
5. Click Continue in the User Account Control dialog box.
6. In the Windows Activation dialog box, shown in Figure 3-26, click Show Me Other Ways To Activate.

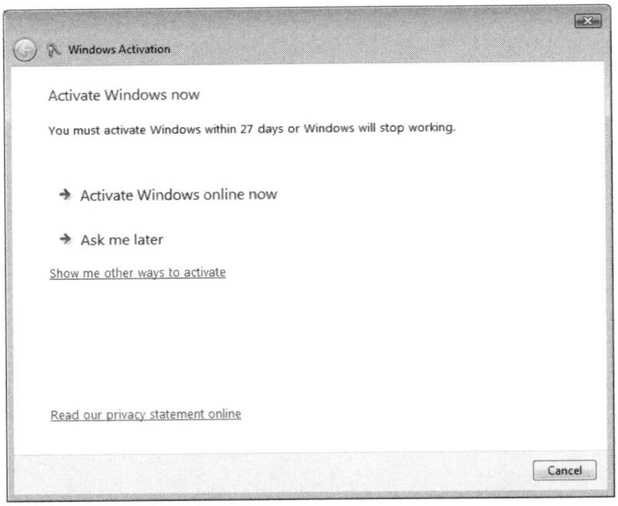

Figure 3-26   Selecting an alternative activation method

7. On the How Do You Want To Activate Windows screen, click Use The Automated Phone System.
8. On the Find Available Phone Numbers For Activation screen, click the drop-down menu to select your country, and then click Next.
9. Call the displayed phone number, as shown in Figure 3-27. Follow the instructions on the phone, and then enter the confirmation ID that the automated phone system gives you. After you have entered all numbers, click Next to activate.

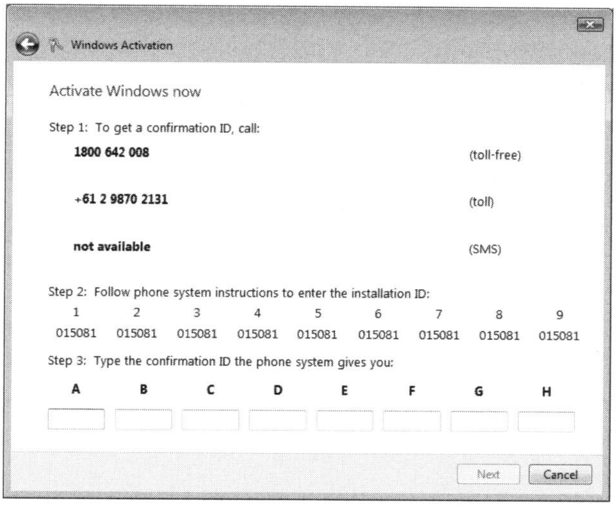

Figure 3-27   Follow the automated telephone instructions to receive the confirmation ID

▶ **Practice 3: Windows Defender and Windows Genuine Advantage**

This practice consists of a series of steps that will demonstrate a typical WGA check. In this practice, you begin the process of obtaining Windows Defender, a freely available Microsoft product that is used to protect against spyware. To get to the point of actually downloading Windows Defender, your computer must pass a WGA check. With Windows Vista, you would not actually do this because Windows Defender is already included. This practice demonstrates the WGA check and is not about Windows Defender. This practice requires that your computer be connected to the Internet. To complete this practice, perform the following steps:

1. Open Internet Explorer, and navigate to the following URL: *http://www.microsoft.com /athome/security/spyware/software/default.mspx*

2. Click Download It Here.

3. In the area of the webpage that has a Continue button next to Validation Required, as shown in Figure 3-28, click Continue.

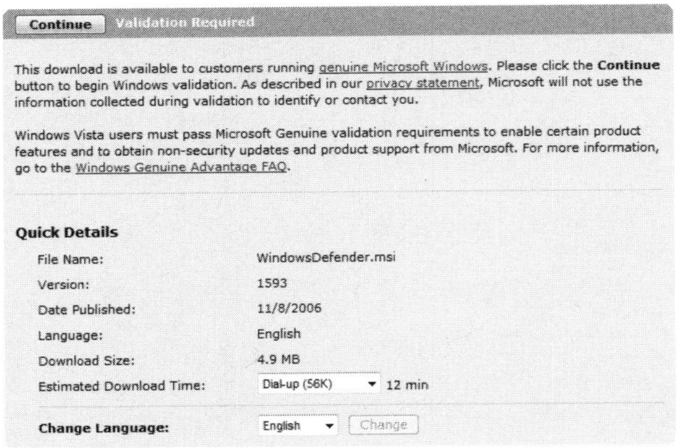

Figure 3-28   Validation Required message

4. This takes you to the Install The Genuine Windows Validation Component page. You will most likely need to close an information bar dialog box by clicking the Close button.

5. Click the message at the top of the page that says "This website wants to install the following add-on: 'Windows Genuine Advantage' from 'Microsoft Corporation'. If you trust the website and the add-on and want to install it, click here ...". Select the Install ActiveX Control option.

6. Click Continue in the User Account Control dialog box.

7. In the Internet Explorer Add-On Installer – Security Warning dialog box, shown in Figure 3-29, click Install. This installs the Genuine Windows Validation Component Internet Explorer add-on.

Figure 3-29   You are asked whether you want to install the software

8. The component is installed. After it has been installed, the WGA check is performed. When this check succeeds, you are taken to a page on Microsoft's website that allows you to download Windows Defender.

Lesson Summary

- Before you try to troubleshoot Aero, make sure that the edition of Windows Vista that you are using supports it.
- To support Aero, a graphics adapter must be DirectX 9 capable, have a WDDM driver, have Hardware Pixel Shader 2.0 support, support 32-bit color, and have at least 128 MB of graphics memory.
- You can check whether Aero is running by pressing both the Windows and the Tab key at the same time.
- Setting Windows to use 16-bit color disables Aero.
- Windows Genuine Advantage checks allow you to download extra applications and operating system components if you have a genuine copy of Windows.
- The WGA check does not send your personal information to Microsoft.
- If your computer fails a WGA check, you will be able to download from Windows Update only updates that are rated as critical by Microsoft. Updates that are rated as important or moderate will not be available through Windows Update.
- The System Performance Rating tool generates the Windows Experience Index number by evaluating a computer's processor, RAM, graphics adapter, and hard disk drive performance. The Index rating is the lowest number of all of these components.

Lesson Review

You can use the following questions to test your knowledge of the information in Lesson 2, "Configuring and Troubleshooting Windows Aero." The questions are also available on the companion CD if you prefer to review them in electronic form.

NOTE   Answers

Answers to these questions and explanations of why each answer choice is correct or incorrect are located in the "Answers" section at the end of the book.

1. You share a Windows Vista computer with several other postgraduate students at the local university. You logged on to the computer this morning and found that the Aero interface is no longer functioning. Which of the following will restore Aero with a minimum of effort?

    A. Update to a WDDM graphics adapter driver.

    B. Change the theme to Windows Aero.

    C. Change the monitor refresh rate.

    D. Change the number of displayed colors.

2. Your computer has the Windows Experience Index score shown in Figure 3-30.

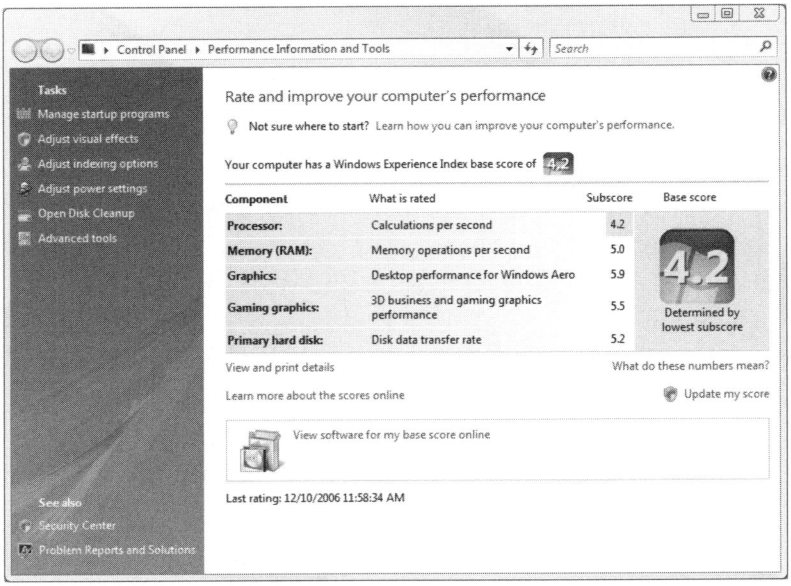

Figure 3-30   Example of a Windows Experience Index score

Which component would you upgrade to improve the score?

- **A.** Processor
- **B.** RAM
- **C.** Graphics adapter
- **D.** Hard disk drive

3. Which of the following information is not collected when your computer passes through a WGA check? (Choose all that apply.)

- **A.** The computer name
- **B.** Your name
- **C.** BIOS revision date
- **D.** Your computer's Internet Protocol (IP) address

4. Which of the following graphics adapters is capable of running Windows Aero? (Choose all that apply.)

- **A.** Dedicated video memory 32 MB. Shared system memory 0 MB. System video memory 0 MB.
- **B.** Dedicated video memory 128 MB. Shared system memory 0 MB. System video memory 0 MB.

     C. Dedicated video memory 128 MB. Shared system memory 128 MB. System video memory 0 MB.

     D. Dedicated video memory 32 MB. Shared system memory 0 MB. System video memory 16 MB.

5. After you install Windows Vista, how long is the grace period before you must activate the product?

     A. 10 days

     B. 15 days

     C. 30 days

     D. 180 days

Chapter Review

To further practice and reinforce the skills you learned in this chapter, you can perform the following tasks:

- Review the chapter summary.
- Review the list of key terms introduced in this chapter.
- Complete the case scenarios. These scenarios set up real-world situations involving the topics of this chapter and ask you to create a solution.
- Complete the suggested practices.
- Take a practice test.

Chapter Summary

- If screen artifacts are being displayed, reduce or disable hardware acceleration in the graphics adapter's advanced properties.
- Increasing the refresh rate can reduce the amount of visible flicker on CRT monitors.
- To modify Windows Vista's background and desktop settings, right-click the desktop, and then select Personalize.
- By editing a hardware device's properties in Device Manager, it is possible to resolve resource conflicts.
- You can determine that Aero is running by attempting to perform a 3D flip.
- It is possible to change the theme to Aero only if the computer meets the necessary requirements, and 32-bit color is being used.
- The Windows Experience Index is the lowest value generated when the System Performance Rating tool is run.

Key Terms

Do you know what these key terms mean? You can check your answers by looking up the terms in the glossary at the end of the book.

- flicker
- legacy hardware device
- plug and play
- Power Management
- refresh rate
- resolution
- resources

Case Scenarios

In the following case scenarios, you will apply what you have learned about troubleshooting post-installation configuration issues and troubleshooting Windows Aero. You can find answers to these questions in the "Answers" section at the end of this book.

Case Scenario 1: Post-Installation Troubleshooting

You are preparing 10 Windows Vista computers that will be used as workstations in an Antarctic research outpost. You need to ensure that all hardware and software works correctly before shipping the computers to the South Pole. When configuring the computers, you have come up against the following problems:

1. One type of legacy device, installed in five of the Windows Vista computers, does not appear in the Device Manager. What steps should you take to install it?

2. On three of the computers there is a conflict between two scientific devices. What method could you take to resolve this conflict?

3. One special device conflicts with COM1. You are unable to modify the resources used by either the device or the COM port. What course of action could you take to ensure that the device works?

Case Scenario 2: Troubleshooting Aero and Display Settings

You are developing guidelines for a group of postgraduates who share several Windows Vista computers in a lab. You want to give them information so that they know the effect that making changes to display settings and themes has on other users. As a part of this process, you need to answer the following questions:

1. Under what conditions could a user with standard privileges accidentally disable Aero for all the others?

2. One student gets headaches because she perceives the monitor to be flickering. What is a possible drawback to increasing the refresh rate?

3. One student has visual difficulties and needs the monitor set to a low resolution. Will this affect the other students?

Suggested Practices

To help you successfully master the exam objectives presented in this chapter, complete the following tasks.

Troubleshoot Post-Installation Configuration Issues

■ **Practice 1: Maximum Refresh Rates for Each Resolution**   If you have a CRT monitor, make a table for the maximum possible refresh rate for each resolution that your graphics adapter and monitor is capable of displaying.

Alter the refresh rate of your CRT monitor at your preferred resolution. See if you can notice the difference. You might have to manually adjust your monitor's horizontal and vertical settings.

■ **Practice 2: Alter Hardware Settings Using Device Manager**   Use hardware manager to alter the settings of LPT1. Disable the device, and then view the icon that appears next to the device.

Change the resource settings of a device from manual to automatic. Attempt to change the resources to different settings. Note what happens when you attempt to make this change.

■ **Practice 3: Change Visual Settings in Windows Vista**   Download an image from the Internet, and set it as your desktop background using the Desktop Background item in the Personalization item in Control Panel. Do not right-click an image in Internet Explorer, and use the Set As Background option!

Configure Windows Vista to use the Frost color and appearance.

Configure Windows Vista to use the Classic Windows 2000 Theme.

Configure and Troubleshoot Windows Aero

■ **Practice 1: Perform a 3D Flip**   Perform a 3D flip to verify that Aero is functioning.

■ **Practice 2: Aero and 16-bit Color**   After verifying that Aero is functioning, set the graphics adapter to use 16-bit rather than 32-bit color. Note the effect of this action on Aero.

Take a Practice Test

The practice tests on this book's companion CD offer many options. For example, you can test yourself on just one exam objective, or you can test yourself on all the 70-620 certification exam content. You can set up the test so that it closely simulates the experience of taking a certification exam, or you can set it up in study mode so that you can look at the correct answers and explanations after you answer each question.

MORE INFO   Practice tests

For details about all the practice test options available, see the "How to Use the Practice Tests" section in this book's Introduction.

Chapter 4
Configuring and Troubleshooting Internet Access

When you install Windows Vista (as described in Chapter 1, "Installing Windows Vista Client"), the installation program asks you whether your computer is in a home, business, or public environment. If you choose a business or a public environment and setup detects an Active Directory directory service domain, your computer joins that domain and accesses the Internet through the business local area network (LAN).

Exam Tip   The 70-620 examination objectives do not specify Windows Vista as an Active Directory client operating system. Examination 70-622 tests this configuration.

In the home environment, or if your computer is part of a small business network that uses a workgroup rather than a domain, the computer is configured to access the Internet either through a direct connection to your Internetservice provider (ISP) or through another computer that provides Internet Connection Sharing (ICS). Your computer also might share its direct Internet connection with other clients in its workgroup. The Network And Sharing Center, accessible from Control Panel, together with software provided by your ISP, helps you configure Internet access. Internet Gateway Device Discovery And Control (IGDDC) is used when you enable ICS on your computer and turn on network sharing in the Network And Sharing Center.

MORE INFO   IGDDC

For more information on IGDDC, search for "Using Internet Gateway Device Discovery and Control" in Windows Help and Support or access *http://207.46.197.98/Windows/en-US/Help/670718ec-7d51-49ed-87f1-b8a98ced11a41033.mspx*.

When access to the Internet is configured, your interface to the World Wide Web (WWW) is the Internet Explorer 7+ (IE7+) web browser. This chapter discusses how you configure IE7+ to provide access to appropriate web content by using Parental Controls and Content Advisor, how you subscribe to news feeds to obtain the latest information from websites that provide that service, and how you configure print and viewing controls.

Exam objectives in this chapter:
- Configure and troubleshoot parental controls.
- Configure Windows Internet Explorer.

NOTE Internet Explorer 7+

This chapter discusses Internet Explorer 7+, as specified in the 70-620 examination objectives. If you want to download and use another browser, you are, of course, perfectly at liberty to do so.

Lessons in this chapter:

Before You Begin

To complete the lesson in this chapter, you must have done the following:

- Completed the installation and upgrading practices in Chapter 1, "Installing Windows Vista Client," and Chapter 2, "Windows Vista Upgrades and Migrations." As a result, you will have installed Windows Vista ultimate edition on a personal computer. You should also have a working connection to the Internet because this is required for Windows Vista installation.

No additional configuration is required for this chapter.

Real World

Ian McLean

I take the view that the Internet, and in particular the World Wide Web, is one of the best educational tools ever created. From the comfort and safety of their own homes and schools, children have access to more information than they could find in even the largest library—and kids who would never consider going into some dusty old library *want* to access the web.

Of course the Internet is a dangerous place—just as the world is. Responsible parents and teachers ensure that the children in their charge do not access sites that contain content that they consider inappropriate, and carefully monitor the use of chat and bulletin board sites.

Lesson 1: Configuring and Troubleshooting Parental Controls and Content Advisor

Parental Controls lets parents decide how their children use the computer. As an IT professional you might be asked to advise parents on how to configure Parental Controls or to configure the facility for less computer-aware parents. You might need to answer more general questions related to Internet safety and safety strategies. This is one of the most significant areas of concern that purchasers of home computers have and they often need a lot of information and reassurance. You might also need to configure restrictions for your own children.

MORE INFO   Internet safety

For more information on Internet safety, you should seriously consider purchasing the book "Look Both Ways: Help Protect Your Family on the Internet" by Linda Criddle and Nancy Muir (Microsoft Press, 2006) and reading it carefully. This inexpensive paperback gives you a lot of information that will help you in your chosen career. It might also help you protect your own children.

Schools can also use Parental Controls to limit the web content, games, and programs that pupils can access on a per-child basis, although they are more likely to ask you to limit access to certain types of web content on a per-machine basis, in which case you would configure Content Advisor.

You can configure Parental Controls to set limits on children's access to the web, the hours that they can log on to the computer, and which games they can play and programs they can run. When Parental Controls blocks access to a webpage or game, the computer displays a notification. The child can click a link in the notification to request permission for access to that webpage or program. A responsible adult who has an account with administrator credentials can then allow access by entering a password. Thus a parent can control what his or her children can access.

Content Advisor, a separate feature from Parental Controls in Windows Vista, works with websites that supply content ratings for potentially unacceptable content. When a user attempts to access such content or to access a site that has no ratings configured, IE7+ might block access depending on the Content Advisor settings. In this case a responsible person can allow access by supplying a supervisor password. You can also configure Content Advisor to permit access to sites that have no content ratings configured. Unlike Parental Controls, Content Advisor addresses only browsing the Internet and does not address broader parental concerns, such as time logged on, access to certain applications, and so on. It also works on a per-machine basis, not a per-user basis.

NOTE   **Supervisor passwords and administrator credentials**

You define a supervisor password when you (or a parent or teacher you are assisting) activate and configure Content Advisor. Supplying the supervisor password enables a user to view web content that Content Advisor blocks. An administrator password, on the other hand, enables you to log on by using an administrator account, or (by default) to perform administrator tasks when logged on as a standard user. Administrator credentials (that is, a password) can also be supplied to allow a child to access web content, games, or programs that Parental Controls would otherwise block.

After this lesson, you will be able to:
- Create an administrative account for a parent and standard user accounts for both a parent and his or her children.
- Limit the hours during which a particular child can use a computer.
- Limit and control the websites that the child can access.
- Limit and control the programs that the child can run.
- Limit and control the games that the child can play.
- Generate activity reports for specified users.
- Use Content Advisor to control the sites that any user on a computer can access.

Estimated lesson time: 60 minutes

Setting Up Users and Configuring System Access

Before you configure Parental Controls you need to make sure that each child has a standard user account because you can apply Parental Controls only to standard user accounts. To set up Parental Controls you need an administrator user account. You cannot apply Parental Controls to an administrator user account.

A user account is a collection of information that tells Microsoft Windows which user rights and access permissions you have on the computer. The user account records your user name, password, and a unique number that identifies your account. You use your user account when you enter your user name and password to log on to the computer.

There are three kinds of accounts:

- Standard
- Administrator
- Guest

Each account type has different rights and restrictions. The standard account is the account to use for everyday computing. The administrator account provides more control over the computer and should be used only when necessary. The guest account is used primarily for people who need temporary use of the computer.

Administrator Accounts

An administrator account is a user account that lets you make changes that affect other users. Administrators can change security settings, install software and hardware, and access all files on the computer. Administrators can also make changes to other user accounts.

When you install Windows Vista, you specify an administrator account. A built-in administrator account also exists but is disabled by default. You can create additional administrator accounts on the computer, but they are not the same as the built-in administrator account. The built-in administrator account might not be protected by User Account Control (UAC), and you should enable and use it only when it is absolutely necessary. Chapter 5, "User Account Control," discusses UAC in detail. Unlike previous versions of Windows, the administrator account that you specify during Windows Vista installation is an ordinary administrator account and not the built-in account that has special privileges.

The Principle of Least Privilege

When you install Windows Vista, you create an administrator account for your own use or for the use of the person for whom you are setting up the computer. The nominated administrator should use the administrator account (or account credentials) when performing tasks such as changing system time, installing software, or creating standard accounts.

However, one of these standard accounts should be for the nominated administrator. The Principle of Least Privilege states that a user should never have more privileges than are needed to carry out a task. A user should not be logged on as an administrator if the user is, for example, creating or editing a document in Microsoft Word. A person with an administrator account might sometimes find it convenient to log on with these credentials if he or she is carrying out a lot of administrative tasks, but that person should otherwise use a standard account. If the user needs to perform an administrative task, UAC (by default) prompts for administrator account credentials and the user does not need to log out from his or her standard account.

The Principle of Least Privilege is important for two reasons. First, if a user leaves a machine unattended while logged on as an administrator, an unauthorized person could access the machine before it times out and could make changes. Second, if a user accidentally launches a destructive virus (or other malware) while logged on as an administrator, the effects are usually much worse than if that user were logged on as a standard user because the virus can run with elevated privileges.

Standard Accounts

A standard account lets you use most of the capabilities of the computer, but you cannot make changes that might affect other users or the security of the computer unless you provide administrator account credentials (the password that corresponds to an administrator account name). When you use a standard account, you can use most of the software that is installed on the computer but you cannot install or uninstall software and hardware, delete files that are required for the computer to work, or change settings on the computer that affect other users.

Standard accounts help protect your computer by preventing users from making changes that affect everyone who uses the computer. Microsoft recommends creating a standard account for each user, including the nominated administrator.

Guest Account

The guest account is an account for users who do not have a permanent account on a computer. It allows people to use the computer without having access to regular users' personal files. People using the guest account cannot install software or hardware, change settings, or create a password. Typically, the guest account is used on a kiosk computer or in a school, college, or other institution that runs night school courses. A kiosk computer is a computer that is in a public place and is accessed by the general public. Kiosk computers are used for limited purposes, such as browsing the web and checking webmail.

CAUTION   **Do not enable the guest account**

The guest account should be disabled. For security reasons, you should not enable this account unless you have specific reasons for doing so.

Addressing Web Browsing Issues

The Internet is a valuable resource for children, offering a wealth of information and experience. However, it can also expose vulnerable youngsters to information that might not be appropriate for them.

The Parental Controls feature enables you to determine how children use a computer. You can use Parental Controls to set limits on the hours that children can access the computer, the types of games that they can play, the websites they can visit, and the programs they can run.

Time Limits

You can control when children can use a computer by specifying time limits that prevent them from logging on during specified hours. You can set different logon hours for every day of the week, and you can block all the rest. If a child is logged on when his or her allotted time ends,

Windows Vista automatically logs that child off. You can change the settings if a user needs more (or less) time. Activity reports show you how long each child spends logged on to the computer.

Activity Reports

Activity reports enable you to view children's online activities. To activate activity reports, you open Parental Controls from the Control Panel and then click the account of the user for whom you want to turn on activity reporting. You activate Parental Controls (if necessary) and, under Activity Reporting, select On, Collect Information About Computer Usage.

To view activity reports, you open Parental Controls, click the account for which you want to view activity reports, and then click View Activity Reports, as shown in Figure 4-1.

Figure 4-1   The View Activity Reports control

Website Access

You can set limits on how children access the web. You can restrict the websites that they visit, make sure they visit only age-appropriate websites by selecting an age rating, indicate whether you want to allow file downloads, and set up which content you want the content filters to block and allow. You can also block or allow specific websites.

Content Advisor allows you to control the types of Internet content that users can view on a computer. Depending on how you configure it, Content Advisor blocks or allows certain content by using ratings that websites voluntarily provide. Because not all websites are rated, Content Advisor automatically blocks unrated websites (unless you configure Content Advisor to allow them). When you configure the settings and turn Content Advisor on, it checks websites as users visit them.

You can use either Parental Controls or Content Advisor to limit web access. Parental Controls limits access on a per-user basis and you can set different levels of restriction for different users. Content Advisor implements the same level of restriction for all users of a specific computer, including administrators.

MORE INFO   Content Advisor

For more information about Content Advisor, search for "Internet Explorer Content Advisor: frequently asked questions" in Windows Help and Support.

Controlling Program Access

Parental Controls enables you to specify the programs a child can use. You can permit (select) all programs and then block (clear) any that you do not want a child to run, or you can block (clear) all programs and specify (select) those that a child is permitted to run.

NOTE   Use Parental Controls with care

Sometimes Parental Controls does not provide the best method of preventing children from accessing prohibited information. Suppose, for example, a parent uses a Microsoft Office Excel spreadsheet to keep track of his or her finances and wants to prevent children from viewing this financial information. Parental Controls can block Excel, but this would be a great pity because it is a program that children should learn to use. The parent can permit the use of blocked programs by supplying administrator credentials, but this is not always convenient.

In this case the best solution is probably to allow children to run Excel but to advise the parent to protect sensitive and confidential Excel spreadsheets by using the password facility that Excel provides.

To control which programs children can run, you open Parental Controls under User Accounts And Family Safety in Control Panel. You then click a child's user account and ensure that On, Enforce Current Settings is selected. This setting enables Parental Controls for that child. You can then configure web restrictions, time limits, games ratings, and program limits for that child. If you click Allow And Block Specific Programs and select *Person's Name* Can Only Use The Programs I Allow, you can then click Check All to permit all programs and then clear the check boxes for those you want to block; or you can click Uncheck All to block all programs and then select the check boxes for those you want to permit.

If a program that you want to block or allow does not appear in the list, you can click Browse to locate the program. Typically, you would use the Browse facility if you have recently added a new application to the computer. Whether programs installed after the initial configuration are automatically blacklisted (prohibited) or whitelisted (allowed) is determined by a number of factors—for example, how you implement the software installation. You should use Browse to add all such programs to the list presented by the Parental Controls list. Then you can specify whether they are blocked or not.

NOTE Ensure that you select all the programs you want children to run

If you choose the *Person's Name* Can Only Use The Programs I Allow In This List option, you need to select all of the programs that you want a child to be able to run. Parental Controls will block any program you do not include in the list. Suppose, for example, a parent forgets to specify Word and a child has a homework assignment to complete. If you are the person who set up Parental Controls, or helped the parent to do so, the blame will be shifted to you. If you are that parent, you have only yourself to blame.

Addressing Gaming Issues

You can use Parental Controls to prevent children from playing games that their parents do not want them to play. You can control access to games, choose an age rating level, choose the types of content you want to block, and specify whether you want to allow or block specific games. To do this you double-click Parental Controls in Control Panel, click the account of the child for whom you want to set up Parental Controls, and then click Games Control. You configure Games Control and other Parental Controls settings in the practice session later in this lesson.

You can block:

- All games
- Specific games that you choose
- Specific games based on age ratings
- Specific games based on content ratings

You can use these four methods in combination. You can, for example, block games based on both content and age ratings.

Quick Check
- What four factors can you configure by using Parental Controls that control how a child uses a computer?

Quick Check Answer
- Logon hours
- Access to web content
- Access to games
- Access to executable programs

Troubleshooting Parental Controls and Content Advisor

If you, or more probably, users you are advising, have problems with Parental Controls or Content Advisor, the probable cause is that the configuration is incorrect. A user might not understand, for example, that blocking all programs except those specified means just that (except Internet Explorer cannot be blocked because it is considered to be an integral part of the operating system [OS]). A user might choose an age rating for games that is inappropriate for his or her children.

This is an area where there is scope for subjective judgment. What one person considers obscene, another might consider harmless or "good fun." You need to tactfully find out exactly what a parent or teacher who comes to you for advice actually wants. It is also an area where there is a lot of scope for human error. A parent might find it inconvenient to enter credentials every time a child needs to run a program—so she adds the child's account to the local Administrators group. Later, she calls for help because the child is no longer banned from playing unsuitable games.

Problems with Content Advisor often stem from a misunderstanding of what this tool can or cannot do. Site ratings are voluntary. Some sites are not rated—often perfectly reputable bulletin board or information sites. If you, or a user you are advising, decide to allow access to sites with no rating for that reason, it is possible that Content Advisor might also allow access to an adult site that has omitted to set a content rating. No system is infallible.

When troubleshooting, you need to check settings, check membership of the local Administrators group, and try to get the user you are advising to tell you calmly and unemotionally exactly under what circumstances a child accessed unsuitable material or was unable to access a good educational site. In this area, possibly as much as or more than any other, the PLBSM principle applies—the problem lies between seat and mouse.

Practice: Configuring Parental Controls and Content Advisor

In this practice session you create an administrator account for the nominated administrator (the parent) to use, log on by using that account, and create four standard accounts. One of the standard accounts is for the parent's use, and the other three are for his or her (notional) children. You then set up Parental Controls on one of the child accounts. Finally, you use Content Advisor to control the types of Internet content that can be viewed on the computer.

NOTE Control Panel view

All practices in this chapter assume that Control Panel opens with the default (category) view. If Control Panel is showing the Classic view, click Control Panel Home in the left pane.

You can extend the practice by setting up different levels of control for each of the three accounts—supposing, for example, that you are configuring Parental Controls for three children aged 7, 12, and 15 years. You can then test the settings by logging on with each child account.

NOTE   You can choose more sensible account names

For legal reasons this book uses generic account names—for example, parent_standard. If you prefer, you can use real names and specify passwords that are different from those in the practice session. However, if you do so you need to ensure that you use your chosen account names and passwords in every practice session that specifies account logons. These accounts are used in several chapters of this book.

▶ **Practice 1: Creating an Administrator Account**

In this practice you create an administrator account for the nominated administrator. You will use this account in this and subsequent chapters. You could use the account that you created when you installed Windows Vista, but in the practices you are simulating setting up the computer for a parent and creating an administrator account for the parent's use.

1. Log on by using the account that you created when you installed Windows Vista.
2. From Settings on the Start menu, click Control Panel.
3. Under User Accounts And Family Safety, click Add Or Remove User Accounts.
4. Click Continue in the User Account Control dialog box.
5. Click Create A New Account, as shown in Figure 4-2.

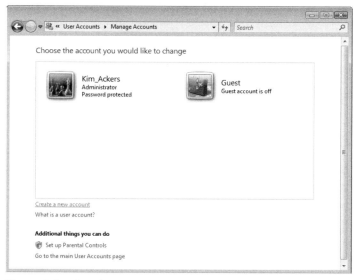

Figure 4-2   Creating a new account

6. In the New Account Name text box, type **parent_admin**.

7. Select Administrator as the account type, as shown in Figure 4-3.

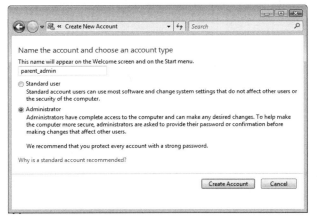

Figure 4-3   Specifying the account name and type

8. Click Create Account.

9. The dialog box previously shown in Figure 4-2 appears, with the parent_admin account added. Click the parent_admin account.

10. Click Create A Password.

11. In the Create A Password dialog box, click How To Create A Strong Password. Read the information in the Help window carefully. Close the Help window.

12. In the Create A Password dialog box, specify and confirm **P@ssw0rd** as the password for the parent_admin account.

Real World

Ian McLean

Any security text that you read will tell you that you should always protect an administrative account with a strong password. The supervisor password you specify for Content Advisor should also adhere to the strong password rules. I have always found this a very difficult idea to sell to parents (and even more so to teachers). They are reluctant to memorize "this rubbish" and even more reluctant to type it in every time they need to supply administrator credentials. Advise them that they should change the password every three months or so and watch your popularity plummet.

In cultures where the partaking of moderate quantities of alcoholic beverages on social occasions is permissible (we call this "a small refreshment" in Scotland), I have found the phrase, "look after your passwords like you look after the key to your liquor cabinet," particularly effective in getting this message across. When they grasp this concept, adults are much less likely to set weak passwords or to write their strong passwords on sticky notes and stick them on to their monitors.

This worked beautifully until I came across a teacher who was a dedicated and vociferous teetotaler. Oh well, you can't win them all!

13. Click Create Password. Close the Change An Account dialog box.
14. Press Ctrl+Alt+Del, and click Switch User.
15. Check that you can log on using the parent_admin account.

▶ **Practice 2: Adding the Run Command to the Start Menu**

By default, the Run command is not directly available from the Start menu. You can access this command by clicking Accessories on the Start menu and then clicking Run. However, this is inconvenient if you use the command frequently. In this practice you add the Run command to the Start menu, which you need for other practices.

1. If necessary, log on by using the parent_admin account.
2. Right-click the Start button, and select Properties.
3. Click Customize.
4. In the list of Start menu options, select the Run Command check box.
5. Click OK.
6. Click OK to close the Taskbar And Start Menu Properties dialog box.

NOTE Customizing the Start menu

Customizing the taskbar and Start menu is done on a per-user basis. If you want to access the Run command directly from the Start menu while logged on with another user account, you need to add it to the Start menu for that account.

▶ **Practice 3: Creating Standard Accounts**

In this practice you create standard accounts for one parent and three children. The practice demonstrates an alternative method of creating user accounts by using the Microsoft Management Console (MMC). You should not attempt this practice until you have successfully completed Practices 1 and 2.

1. If necessary, log on by using the parent_admin account.
2. From the Start menu, select Run. In the Run box, type **mmc**.

3. Click Continue in the User Account Control dialog box.
4. Under the File menu, select Add/Remove Snap-in.
5. In the Available Snap-ins pane, select Local Users And Groups, as shown in Figure 4-4.

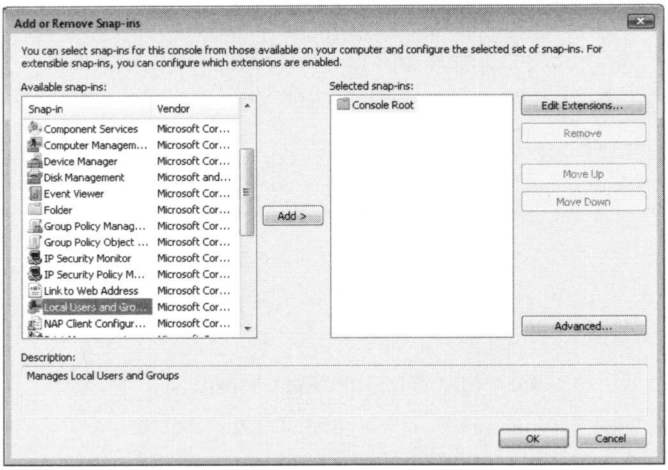

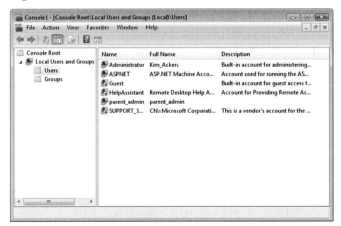

Figure 4-4   Selecting the Local Users And Groups snap-in

6. Click Add. In the Choose Target Machine dialog box, make sure that Local Computer (The Computer On Which This Console Is Running) is selected, and click Finish.
7. Click OK to close the Add Or Remove Snap-Ins dialog box.
8. Under Console Root, expand Local Users And Groups and click Users, as shown in Figure 4-5.

Figure 4-5   The Users container

9. Right-click Users, and select New User.

10. Create an account with the account name parent_standard and the password parentpass. Set the account so that the password does not expire and the user cannot change the password (you first need to clear the User Must Change Password At Next Logon check box). Figure 4-6 shows these settings.

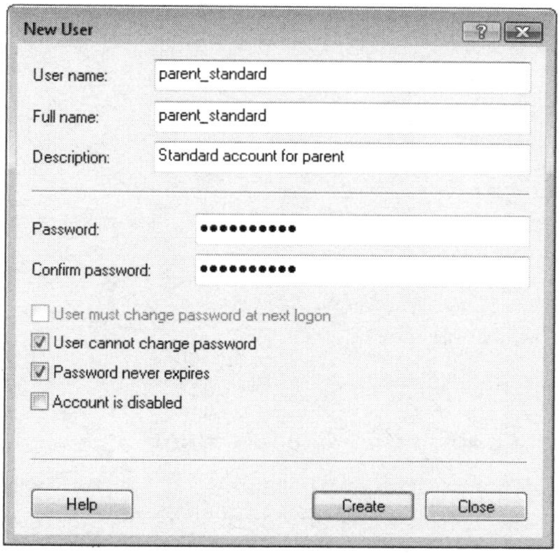

Figure 4-6   Creating the parent_standard account

11. Click Create.

12. Use the New User dialog box to create accounts for the following. In all cases, the user should not be able to change the password and the password should not expire.

   ❏ Account name: child1; Password child1pass

   ❏ Account name: child2; Password child2pass

   ❏ Account name: child3; Password child3pass

NOTE   These are not typical settings

Typically, a user is required to change his or her password at first logon and passwords expire after (for example) 180 days. Parents might, however, choose to create passwords for their children and not permit the children to change them. The Password Does Not Expire setting is used here for convenience while you are studying this book. In the real world it is highly advisable to set a password expiry period.

---

13. Close the New User dialog box. Figure 4-7 shows the accounts you have created in this practice session.

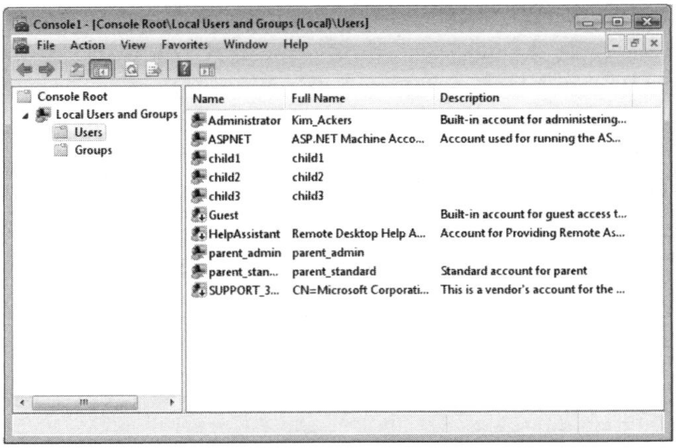

Figure 4-7   User accounts created

14. Test these accounts by logging on with them.

▶ **Practice 4: Configuring Parental Controls on a Child Account**

In this practice you configure Parental Controls on the child1 account. The practice asks you to log on by using the administrator account (parent_admin) that you created in Practice 1. Alternatively, you can log on by using the parent_standard account that you created in Practice 3 and supply the password for the parent_admin account whenever you are prompted to do so. Using the parent_standard account complies with the Principle of Least Privilege but adds steps to the procedure. You need to complete Practices 1, 2, and 3 before attempting this practice.

1. If necessary, log on by using the parent_admin account.
2. From Settings on the Start menu, select Control Panel.
3. Under User Accounts And Family Safety, click Set Up Parental Controls For Any User.
4. Click Continue in the User Account Control dialog box.
5. In the Choose A User And Set Up Parental Controls dialog box, click the child1 account.
6. In the User Controls dialog box shown in Figure 4-8, select On, Enforce Current Settings. Under Activity Reporting, select On, Collect Information About Computer Usage.

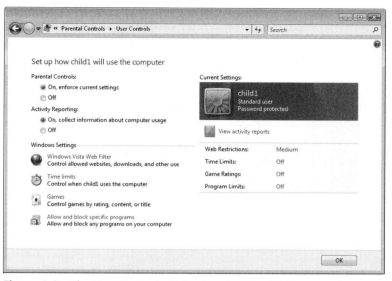

Figure 4-8   The User Controls dialog box for the child1 account

7. Click Windows Vista Web Filter.

8. In the Web Restrictions dialog box, ensure that Block Some Websites Or Content is selected. Choose a web restriction level of High and block file downloads. Figure 4-9 shows these settings.

Figure 4-9   Setting web restrictions for the child1 account

CAUTION   The web filter does not offer absolute protection

Turning on the web filter significantly reduces the number of websites children might view that contain content you have decided is objectionable. However, the filter does not offer absolute protection. Because new pages are published continuously and objectionable content is subjective, the filter might not block all of the content that you want it to block.

---

9. The settings shown block all websites except those specifically approved for use by children. However, you do not want child1 to be able to access the website www.contoso.com, even though this website is approved. (You might prefer to substitute a website of your own choosing for www.contoso.com.) Click Edit The Allow And Block List.

10. In the Website Address text box, specify www.contoso.com and click Block. Figure 4-10 shows this website added to the block list. Click OK.

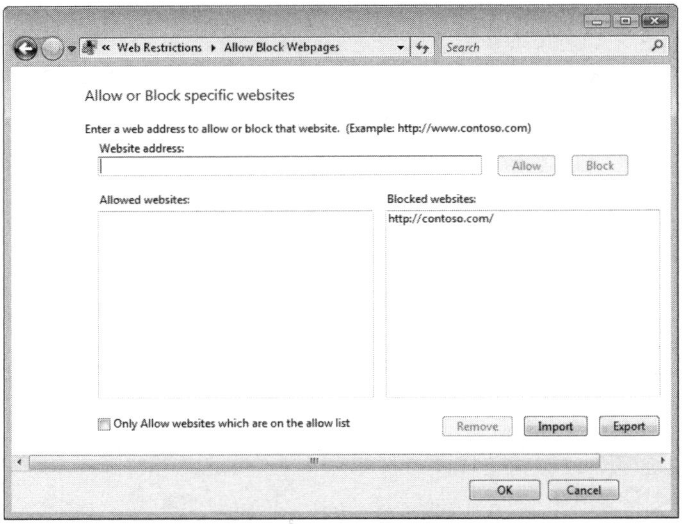

Figure 4-10   Adding a website to the block list

11. Click OK to close the Web Restrictions dialog box.

12. In the User Controls dialog box, click Time Limits.

13. By default, all hours are allowed. Click and drag to specify the hours you want to block, as shown in Figure 4-11.

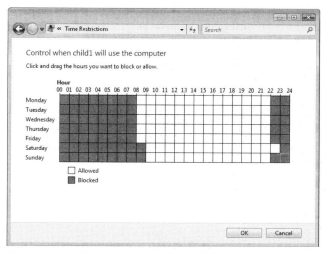

Figure 4-11   Time restrictions for child1

14.   Click OK to close the Time Restrictions dialog box.

15.   In the User Controls dialog box, click Games.

16.   In the Game Controls dialog box, ensure that child1 is permitted to play games. Click Set Game Ratings.

17.   In the Game Restrictions dialog box, select Block Games With No Rating and the EVERYONE classification, as shown in Figure 4-12.

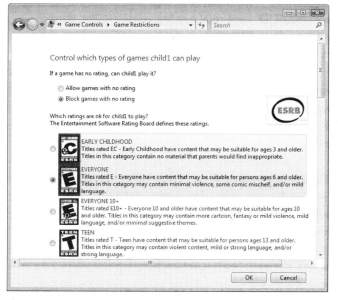

Figure 4-12   Specifying a games rating

NOTE   Classifications vary with geographic area

You might see a different set of rating classifications depending on your geographical area. For example, in the United Kingdom and most of Europe the equivalent to the EVERYONE classification is Universal (BBFC).

NOTE   Games ratings

The default games rating system for U.S. users is Entertainment Software Rating Board (ESRB). If you want to, however, you can change the rating system you use. To do this, open Control Panel and click Set Up Parental Controls For Any User. In the list of Tasks on the left side of the panel, click Select A Games Rating System.

---

18.   Scroll down the Game Restrictions dialog box until you see the Block These Types Of Content list. Block all types of unacceptable content, with the exception of Some Adult Assistance May Be Needed, as shown in Figure 4-13. This might be unnecessary with an EVERYONE classification, but it gives additional protection. If you do not live in North America, the list you see might be different from that shown in Figure 4-13.

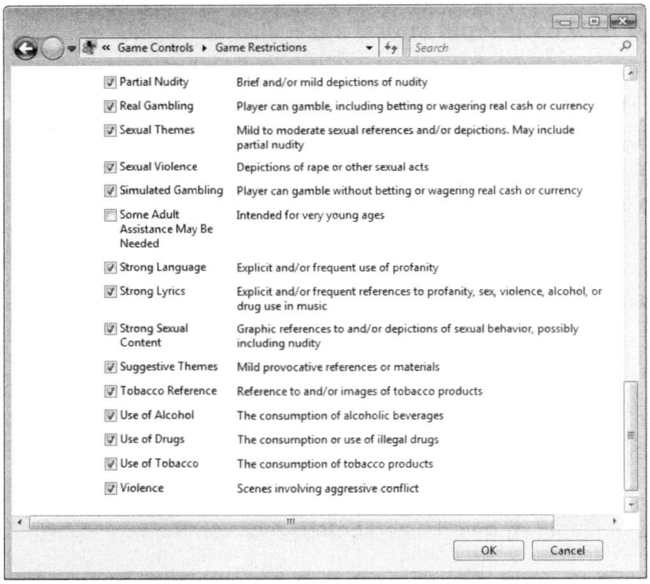

Figure 4-13   Blocking unacceptable games content

19. Click OK to close the Game Restrictions dialog box. In the Game Controls dialog box, click Block Or Allow Specific Games.

20. In the Game Overrides dialog box, block FreeCell, Hearts, Solitaire, and Spider Solitaire, as shown in Figure 4-14.

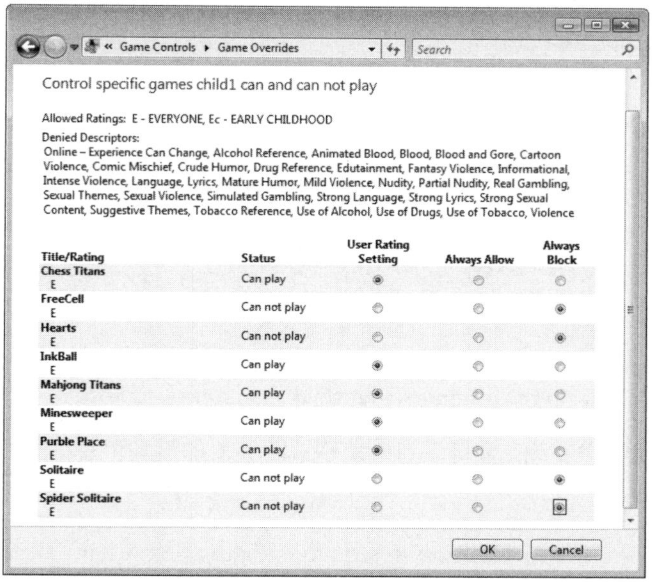

Figure 4-14   Blocking specific games

21. Click OK to close the Game Overrides dialog box. Click OK to close the Game Controls dialog box.

22. In the User Controls dialog box, click Allow And Block Specific Programs.

23. In the Application Restrictions dialog box, shown in Figure 4-15, select Child1 Can Only Use The Programs I Allow, and then select the programs you want to allow. The list of programs on your computer is probably different from that shown in Figure 4-15. Optionally, experiment with the use of the Browse control.

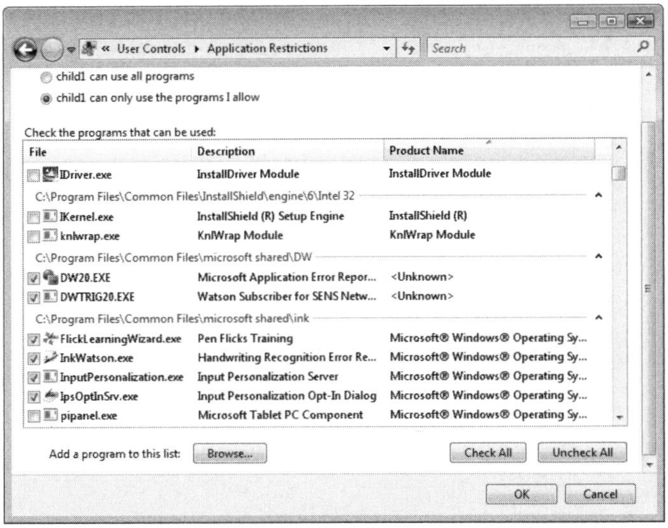

Figure 4-15   Specifying the programs that child1 can run

24. Without careful research into what programs child1 requires, it is unwise to block programs. When you believe you are familiar with this dialog box, select Child1 Can Use All Programs.

25. Click OK to close the Application Restrictions dialog box. Click OK to close the User Controls dialog box. Close the Parental Controls dialog box.

26. Test your settings by switching the user to child1 and attempting to access various websites and play games.

27. Switch to the parent_admin account and view the activity report for child1.

MORE INFO   Activity reports

For more information about viewing activity reports, search for "Set up Parental Controls activity reports" in Windows Help and Support and expand "To view activity reports."

---

28. If you need more practice, set up Parental Controls for child2 and child3.

▶ **Practice 5: Configuring Content Advisor**

In addition to (or possibly instead of) setting web filters for specific users on a computer, you can specify Content Advisor settings that apply to all users. If you want to view a website that Content Advisor blocks, or if you want to allow another user to do so, you can supply a supervisor password. In this practice you enable Content Advisor, specify a supervisor password, and configure the filters for the various types of content that you can block or allow. Setting a supervisor password also allows you to prevent other administrators from changing settings in Content Advisor.

Before you attempt this practice you should have successfully completed Practices 1 and 2. If you do not want to complete these practices, you can still carry out Practice 5 by using the administrator account you created when you installed Windows Vista.

1. If necessary, log on by using the parent_admin account.
2. Open Internet Explorer.
3. Click the Tools button, and then click Internet Options, as shown in Figure 4-16.

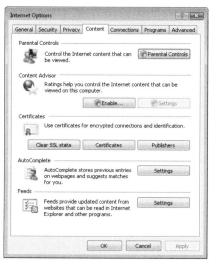

Figure 4-16 Accessing Internet Options

4. In the Internet Options dialog box, click the Content tab.
5. Under Content Advisor, click Enable. Figure 4-17 shows the Content Advisor Enable control.

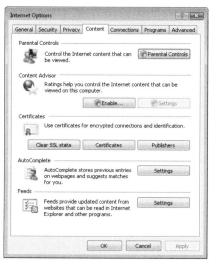

Figure 4-17 The Content Advisor Enable control

6. Click Continue in the User Account Control dialog box.

7. In the Content Advisor dialog box, click the General tab. Ensure that the Supervisor Can Type A Password To Allow Users To View Restricted Content check box is selected.

8. Click Create Password.

9. In the Create Supervisor Password dialog box, type a password, confirm the password, and type a password hint. The supervisor password should not be the same as the password with which you protected the parent_admin account. When you have set your supervisor password for Content Advisor, either memorize it or store it securely. You will need it if you want to disable or change settings in Content Advisor in the future. Click OK.

10. Click OK to close the Content Advisor message box.

11. Click Apply.

12. In the Content Advisor dialog box, click the Ratings tab. When you enable Content Advisor, it is configured by default with the settings least likely to offend. In addition to blocking objectionable content, it also blocks any unrated content.

13. Select a category in the Select A Category To View The Ratings Level list, as shown in Figure 4-18, and then move the slider to adjust the level. You can specify None, Limited, or Unrestricted.

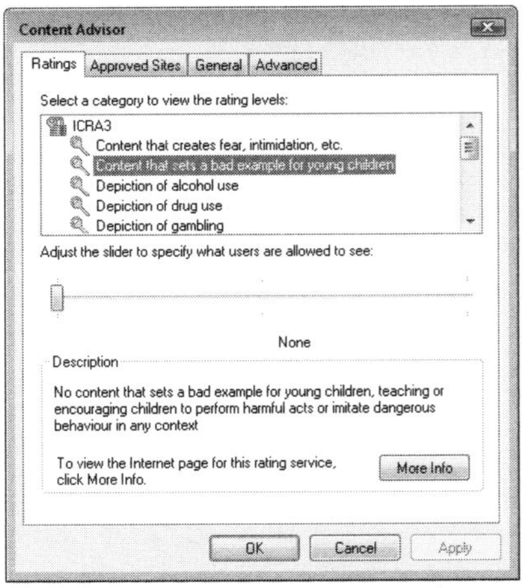

Figure 4-18   Selecting a category

14. Specify the level of restriction you require for each category. When you have set a level for a category, click Apply.

15. Optionally, you can click the General tab and allow users to view sites that have no rating. The creators of commercial sites typically set ratings, but often creators of personal websites, blogs, and bulletin boards do not configure any ratings. You can also click the Approved Sites tab and specify sites that you always want users to be able to access and

sites that you never want users to be able to access. Approved Sites settings override any ratings that the sites might have.

16. When you have finished configuring Content Advisor, click OK. This closes the Content Advisor dialog box and saves your settings. Read the text in the Content Advisor message box and then click OK.

17. Click OK to close the Internet Options dialog box. Close and reopen your browser. Attempt to browse to a site that contains potentially offensive content. You need to supply the supervisor password before you can do so.

IMPORTANT   Now disable Content Advisor

For convenience, while you are studying this book and carrying out practices, you should now access the Content tab in the Internet Options dialog box and disable Content Advisor.

Lesson Summary

- You can create standard and administrator accounts.
- You should always disable the guest account and the built-in administrator account unless specifically required.
- You can perform most administrative functions when logged on with a standard account if you supply the account name and password of an administrator account.
- You can configure Parental Controls to limit the hours during which a user can be logged on to the computer, what websites a user can access, what games a user can play, and what programs a user can run. Parental Controls is configured on a per-user basis.
- You can view activity reports for users for whom you have configured Parental Controls.
- You can enable and configure Content Advisor to control the website content that all users of your computer can access.

Lesson Review

You can use the following questions to test your knowledge of the information in Lesson 1, "Configuring and Troubleshooting Parental Controls and Content Advisor." The questions are also available on the companion CD if you prefer to review them in electronic form.

NOTE   Answers

Answers to these questions and explanations of why each answer choice is correct or incorrect are located in the "Answers" section at the end of the book.

---

1. You are creating a standard user account by using the Local Users And Groups MMC snap-in. In the New User dialog box, shown in Figure 4-19, you want to specify that the user cannot change the password and the password never expires, but these check boxes are inactive. What should you do in order to create the account with the required specifications?

Figure 4-19   Creating an account for Mark Hanson

    A. Enable and switch to the built-in administrator account.

    B. You cannot use this method to create a standard account. Use the Add Or Remove User Accounts control that you access through the Control Panel.

    C. Clear the User Must Change Password At Next Logon check box.

    D. Change the user name to Mark_Hanson.

2. You have set Content Advisor so that IE7+ can access websites with medium ratings for potentially offensive content. You discover that you need to supply a supervisor password to access a bulletin board website that you know contains no offensive content. You access a considerable number of bulletin board and technical information websites in the course of your job. How can you solve this problem with the least amount of administrative effort?

    A. Add the bulletin board site to the list of approved websites in Content Advisor.

    B. Switch to the administrator account that you created when you installed Windows Vista before attempting to access bulletin board websites.

    C. Change the rating for user-generated content to High.

    D. Configure Content Advisor to allow access to sites that have no rating.

3. You have configured Parental Controls to block games with no rating and specified the EVERYONE classification for the account used by a seven-year-old child. However, the child's parents disapprove of card games in general and want to ensure that their child cannot play them. You do not want to block all games. How do you prevent the child from accessing card games?

    A. In the Game Overrides dialog box, block specified card games such as FreeCell, Hearts, Solitaire, and Spider Solitaire.

    B. In the Game Restrictions dialog box, block specified card games such as FreeCell, Hearts, Solitaire, and Spider Solitaire.

    C. In the Game Overrides dialog box specify EVERYONE 10+.

    D. In the Game Restrictions dialog box specify EVERYONE 10+.

4. You want to prevent a child from running three specific programs by using Parental Controls. You enable Parental Controls and navigate to the Application Restrictions dialog box and specify that the child can use only the programs you allow. How do you specify the programs that you want to block by using the least administrative effort?

    A. Select the check boxes beside the programs you want to block.

    B. Click Select All. Clear the programs you want to block.

    C. Click Uncheck All. Individually select the check boxes beside all the programs you want to allow.

    D. Click Browse and browse to the three programs you want to block. Right-click each of the executable files and select Block.

5. You want to configure Parental Controls on an existing user account. Which of the following methods can you use to access the User Controls dialog box? (Choose all that apply.)

    A. In Control Panel, click Set Up Parental Controls For Any User. When the User Account Control dialog box appears, click Continue or supply administrator credentials. Click the user account.

    B. In Control Panel, click Set Up Parental Controls For Any User. When prompted, type in the supervisor password and click OK. Click the user account.

    C. Open an MMC. When the User Account Control dialog box appears, click Continue or supply administrator credentials. Add the Local Users And Groups snap-in. Click Finish. Click OK. Expand Local Users And Groups. Click Users. Right-click the user account and select Parental Controls.

    D. In Control Panel, click Classic View. Double-click Administrative Tools. Double-click Computer Management. When the User Account Control dialog box appears, click Continue or supply administrator credentials. Expand Local Users And Groups. Click Users. Right-click the user account and select Parental Controls.

    E. In Control Panel, click Add Or Remove User Accounts. When the User Account Control dialog box appears, click Continue or supply administrator credentials. Click Set Up Parental Controls. When the User Account Control dialog box appears, click Continue or supply administrator credentials. Click the user account.

6. You are using Parental Controls to configure web restrictions for a six-year-old child. You want to block all web content except websites approved for children. What web restriction level should you choose?

    A. Custom

    B. None

    C. Medium

    D. High

Lesson 2: Configuring Internet Explorer 7+

News feeds—also known as really simple syndication (RSS) feeds—contain frequently updated content published by a website. Typically, you can find them on news websites and blogs (online diaries), but webmasters also use them to distribute other types of digital content—for example, pictures, audio files, or video clips.

NOTE   Alternative names

News feeds are sometimes called Extensible Markup Language (XML) feeds, syndicated content, or web feeds.

You can configure IE7+ to poll websites that provide news feeds to which you have subscribed. As an information technology (IT) professional, you need to access technical news feeds—for example, those provided by professional magazines or by Microsoft MSN. You also need to be able to advise any users you support (possibly a work colleague or a customer covered by an extended warranty agreement) how they can set up news feeds.

NOTE   RSS web feed formats

RSS is a family of web feed formats. The acronym RSS can refer to the following standards: really simple syndication (RSS 2.0); rich site summary (RSS 0.91, RSS 1.0); and resource description framework (RDF) site summary (RSS 0.9 and 1.0).

IE7+ also providesenhanced Print Preview controls that enable you to print webpages to your specifications and a Search facility that allows you to select the search provider of your choice and add other search providers as necessary. As with news feeds, you need to use these facilities on your own computer and to advise customers and colleagues on how to configure them. This lesson describes how you subscribe to and access news feeds, how you configure webpage printing, and how you specify search providers. You need an Internet connection to complete the practices in this lesson.

After this lesson, you will be able to:

- Subscribe to a news feed.
- Access a news feed to which you have subscribed.
- Refresh a news feed (if necessary).
- Configure the Print Preview feature in IE7+.
- Specify headers and footers for webpage printouts.
- Configure the search bar and search providers.

Estimated lesson time: 75 minutes

Configuring News Feeds (RSS Feeds)

IE7+ can discover and display news feeds as you visit websites. When you subscribe to feeds, IE7+ automatically checks for and downloads updates that you can view later. The browser looks for news feeds on every webpage you visit. When it finds available feeds, the Feeds button on the Internet Explorer toolbar changes from gray to orange and the browser generates a sound (if audio is enabled).

When you click the Feeds button you see a list of available feeds. If more than one feed is available, you can select the feed you want to view. If only one feed is available, your browser goes directly to the page for that feed. You then see a list of items (topics and articles) that you can read, and you can subscribe to the feed.

Managing Subscriptions

When you subscribe to a feed, IE7+ adds it to the common feed list. Updated information from the feed is automatically downloaded to your computer and you can view this information in IE7+. When you access the list of items in a feed, you can subscribe by clicking the Subscribe To This Feed link. You then provide a name for the feed and select a folder to contain the information. Finally, you click Subscribe. Subscriptions to a feed are usually free.

A news feed typically contains the same content that is displayed on a webpage, but the format is often different. When you subscribe to a feed, IE7+ automatically checks the website and downloads new content so you can see what is new since you last visited the feed. You can view your subscribed feeds on the Feeds tab in the Internet Explorer Favorites Center by clicking the Favorites Center (star-shaped) button and then clicking Feeds.

MORE INFO   RSS feeds

For more information about RSS feeds, search for "Using feeds (RSS)" in Windows Help and Support.

Configuring Feed Updates

In the early days of news feeds a subscriber was notified if a feed was updated, usually through e-mail or Internet messaging (IM). The subscriber would then go online to refresh the news feed. He or she had the option of reading the updated news feed online or offline.

This so-called "pull" system can be clumsy and inconvenient, and it led to the development of *aggregators*. An aggregator or news aggregator (sometimes called a feed reader) is client software that uses a web feed to poll news feed sites and retrieve syndicated web content. Aggregators work in the background, invisible to the user, while that user is online. As a result, the user can read up-to-date information supplied by a news feed without needing to go online specifically to refresh the feed. In effect, this is a "push" system that enables subscribed news feeds to send updated information to the user without the need for that user to refresh the news feed.

NOTE Search aggregator

A search aggregator works in the same way as a news aggregator but provides a customized set of search results.

Aggregators minimize the time and effort that you spend regularly checking websites for updates and create a unique information space or "personal newspaper." When you subscribe to a feed, an aggregator checks for new content at regular intervals and downloads any updates. The aggregator function also permits a user to easily unsubscribe from a feed.

Modern web browsers, and in particular IE7+, incorporate built-in aggregator functions. When you access a subscribed news feed from IE7+, you have the option of refreshing it (assuming you are online) but typically you do not need to. By moving your mouse cursor over the feed icon, you can find out when the feed was last refreshed and whether any new items were added. IE7+ displays all your subscribed feeds as a convenient folder structure, effectively implementing the personal newspaper function.

NOTE Other built-in aggregators

Aggregator features are also built into portal sites such as My Yahoo! and Google, e-mail programs such as Mozilla Thunderbird, Apple's iTunes (a podcast aggregator), and other applications. Devices such as mobile phones or TiVo video recorders (which already aggregate television programs) can incorporate XML aggregators.

Clouds

Some news aggregators can register to Clouds. Clouds is a web service, introduced in 2000, that notifies the aggregator of updates to a feed and eliminates the need for periodic polling. In theory, this approach should provide a more efficient use of bandwidth. In practice, the overhead associated with registration can mean no net bandwidth saving. Clouds also introduces issues of scalability and a single point of failure. You need to be aware that this service exists, but IE7+ does not implement it.

MORE INFO Aggregators and the RSS 2.0 specification

For more information about aggregators, access *http://en.wikipedia.org/wiki/News_aggregator*. For more information about the RSS 2.0 specification, access *http://www.rssboard.org/rss-specification*.

Configuring Print and Viewing Controls

Typically, printing webpages is a frustrating activity. Unlike Word document files and Portable Document Format (PDF) files, webpages do not fit into convenient letter-sized (or A4-sized) chunks. Often when you print a webpage that looks OK on your screen, you find that it does not quite fit inside your print margins and you lose a few characters at the end of each line. Without the controls that programs such as Word provide, page breaks can also occur in inconvenient places.

IE7+ addresses these issues with an enhanced set of Print Preview functions. These functions provide almost the same control over webpage printing that you previously had over printing document pages. You can also control how you view a webpage in Print Preview without affecting how the webpage prints out.

Using Print Preview

When you print a webpage, IE7+ automatically scales it to fit within the margins of your paper. IE7+ also reduces the size of a page slightly if a single line of text (an orphan) would otherwise print at the foot of a page. You can use Print Preview to see how a printed webpage looks and to adjust page orientation, scaling, and margins.

When you browse to the webpage you want to print, you can click the arrow to the right of the Print button and then click Print Preview. You can also select Page Setup from this list, or you can access the Page Setup dialog box from Print Preview.

The Print Preview controls enable you to do the following:

- Print the page vertically (portrait orientation).
- Print the page horizontally (landscape orientation).
- Change paper size, orientation, or margins, and specify headers or footers.
- Turn specified headers or footers on or off.
- Stretch or shrink the page size to fill the printed page. (This feature replaces the zoom feature that previous versions of Internet Explorer provided.)
- Adjust margins by dragging horizontal or vertical markers to change where the page will print.
- Print the webpage using the current settings.

If the webpage uses multiple frames, you can apply these settings to the webpage as it is laid out on the screen or only on selected frames. This powerful feature allows you to print some frames with portrait orientation and some with landscape orientation.

Print Preview also lets you change how a webpage is displayed on the screen. The following controls affect how things look only in the Print Preview window—they do not affect the printed copy.

- View Full Width
- View Full Page
- Show Multiple Pages
- Specify The Page To Display
- Display The First Page
- Display The Previous Page
- Display The Next Page
- Display The Last Page

Specifying Headers and Footers

The Page Setup dialog box enables you to specify the contents of headers and footers by using a combination of words and symbols. Table 4-1 lists the (case sensitive) variables that you use to print the date or time, page numbers, Window titles, or page addresses on headers or footers on your printed pages. For example, if you wanted to print the page number and the total number of pages on the footer of a document, you would specify Page &p of &P.

Table 4-1   Header and Footer Variables

To Print This:	Type This:
Window title	&w
Page address (URL)	&u
Date in short format	&d
Date in long format	&D
Time	&t
Time in 24-hour format	&T
Current page number	&p
Total number of pages	&P
Right-aligned text	&b <text to right align>
Centered text	&b <text to center> &b
A single ampersand (&)	&&

Exam Tip   Examination questions that test your knowledge of variables such as those listed in Table 4-1 are easy to write and have been popular with examiners in previous examinations.

You can specify the long and short formats of the date and the format for the time (not the 24-hour format) by accessing Regional And Language Options from Control Panel. Typically, when you browse to a webpage you find that it already specifies its headers and footers. The

Page Setup dialog box lets you change this specification if you like. Print Preview lets you control whether or not the specified header and footer is printed.

Quick Check

■ What can you specify when you access the Page Setup dialog box from the Print Preview tool in IE7+?

Quick Check Answer

■ The widths of the left, right, top, and bottom margins

■ The contents of the header and footer

■ Orientation (landscape or portrait)

■ Page size

■ Paper source

Troubleshooting Print Preview Issues

Before Microsoft introduced the Print Preview browser feature, printing webpages was difficult and frequently resulted in calls to the help desk. You will still get enquiries. Some webpages are exceptionally dynamic and are designed to be viewed, not printed. Nevertheless, the Print Preview feature should result in a much higher success rate, with far fewer webpages printed with characters missing at the margins.

Troubleshooting problems generally occur when users change the defaults. If a user chooses to alter the Stretch Or Shrink The Page Size To Fill The Printed Page default, some of the pages might not fit. Users might not realize that dragging the margins to new positions or altering page orientation affects every page and not just the page they are looking at. Most websites provide reasonable defaults for headers and footers, but users can change these. The variables used to specify headers and footers are not as complex as they first appear. Nevertheless, users will get them wrong. You need to be familiar with these variables so that you can advise users about the correct formula, possibly by e-mail or telephone. Users have also been known to disable headers and footers and then change the format and call the help desk when the headers and footers do not print.

As with all troubleshooting issues, one of your primary tasks is to educate your users.

Configuring the IE7+ Search Bar and Adding Search Providers

By default, the IE7+ Search bar (or toolbar instant search box) uses the Microsoft Live Search. You can switch to Google search engine, carry out a local search on the webpage, change the default provider, or add new search providers—for example AOL Search, Ask Jeeves, and Yahoo Search.

You type a keyword or phrase into the Search bar and then press Enter, or you can press Alt+Enter to display the search results in a new tab. Pressing Ctrl+E takes you to the Search bar without using the mouse.

NOTE   You can also use the Address bar

If you prefer, you can use the IE7+ Address bar instead of the Search bar. Type **Find**, **Go**, or **?** followed by a keyword, website name, or phrase, and then press ENTER. If you want the search results to display in a new tab, press Alt+Enter after typing the phrase.

Search Providers

If you do not find what you're looking for with a particular search provider, you can search using a different one. The IE7+ Search bar lets you add search providers and switch between them to improve your search results. If you want to become familiar with different search providers, you should install new search providers and experiment with changing the search provider that IE7+ uses by default. Some websites offer their own special searches for activities such as hobbies, shopping, fashion, and so on. When you locate search providers on websites that you visit, you can add these to your list of search providers.

When you browse to a webpage that offers a search provider and you want this search provider to be available in IE7+ all the time and not just for the current browsing session, you can type TEST into the search box on that webpage and copy the resulting Uniform Resource Locator (URL). You can then click the arrow to the right of your Search bar, select Find More Providers, and add the search provider to your list by pasting the URL into the Create Your Own section on the Add Search Providers To Internet Explorer 7 webpage, supplying a name for the search provider, and then clicking Install.

MORE INFO   Tips for searching the Internet

For more information about how to make your Internet searches more efficient, search for "Tips for searching the Internet" in Windows Help and Support.

Practice: Configuring News Feeds, Webpage Printing, and the IE7+ Search Bar

In this practice session you subscribe to a news feed and access the information that the feed provides. You also configure the Print Preview settings for a webpage and add search providers to the Search bar. You do not need administrator privileges to do either of these tasks, and the practice session uses the parent_standard account that you created in the previous lesson. If you want to, you can use any account configured on your computer. If, however, you use a child account for which you configured Parental Controls, you might not be able to access some websites.

If you choose to use the parent_standard account, you need to have successfully completed Practices 1, 2, and 3 of Lesson 1.

▶ **Practice 1: Subscribing to a News Feed**

In this practice you subscribe to a news feed.

1. If necessary, log on by using the parent_standard account.

2. Browse to a website that provides one or more news feeds, for example *http://channel9.msdn.com/*.

NOTE   Internet addresses can change

Internet addresses (URLs) are notoriously transient and no guarantee can be given that *http://channel9.msdn.com/* will still be there by the time you read this book. However, it is a Microsoft-owned site and probably more stable than most. If the URL does not work, almost all online magazine sites provide news feeds.

---

3. Click the Feeds button, as shown in Figure 4-20. If the site provides more than one feed, these are listed. In this case click a topic that interests you.

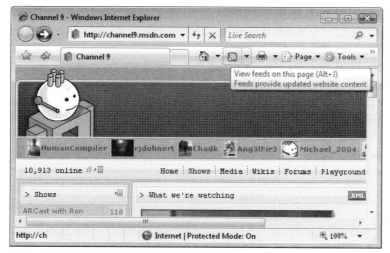

Figure 4-20   The Feeds button

4. Click Subscribe To This Feed, as shown in Figure 4-21.

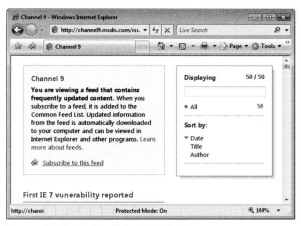

Figure 4-21   Subscribing to a feed

5. From the Create In drop-down list, select Microsoft Feeds, as shown in Figure 4-22. Click New Folder and type a folder name—for example, Channel 9 Feeds. Click Create.

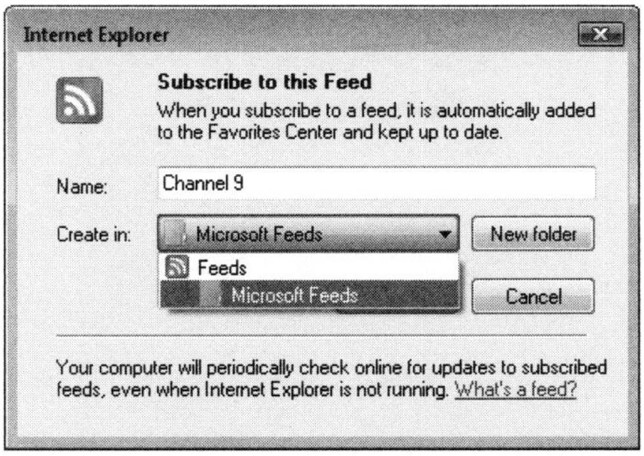

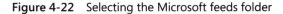

Figure 4-22   Selecting the Microsoft feeds folder

6. Click Subscribe.

The website informs you that your subscription is successful.

▶ **Practice 2: Accessing a News Feed**

In this practice you access a news feed. IE7+ will poll any subscribed news feeds and update the information automatically. You can then read this information even if you are offline.

1. If necessary, log on by using the parent_standard account.
2. Open IE7+.

3. Click the Favorites button.

4. Click Feeds. If necessary, expand Microsoft Feeds and then Channel 9 Feeds (or whatever you named your folder).

5. Move your mouse cursor over the news feed that you subscribed to—for example, Channel 9. As shown in Figure 4-23, a pop-up message box tells you whether there have been any new items and when the feed was last updated. The refresh symbol to the right of the feed name allows you to refresh the feed if you are working online.

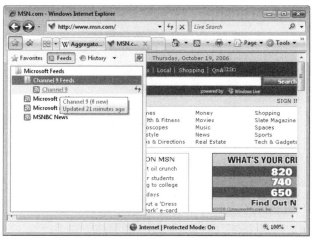

Figure 4-23   Information about the feed

6. Click the news feed. This lets you read the latest information whether you are online or not.

▶ **Practice 3: Printing a Webpage**

In this practice you access a webpage and configure Print Preview so that you can print it to your specification.

1. If necessary, log on by using the parent_standard account.

2. Open IE7+ and browse to a website of your choice—for example, *http://www.msnbc.msn.com*.

3. Click the down arrow to the right of the printer symbol and select Print Preview. The Print Preview dialog box opens, as shown in Figure 4-24.

Figure 4-24   The Print Preview dialog box

4. Click the Landscape button and select a multiple page view. All the pages are now landscape, as shown in Figure 4-25.

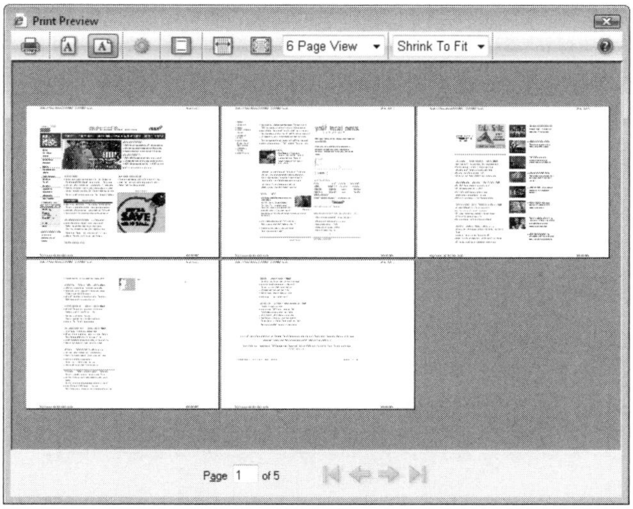

Figure 4-25   Multiple page view

5. Click the Portrait button and select a single page view. Use the controls at the foot of the dialog box to go through the pages.

6. Drag the margin controls to adjust the top, bottom, right, and left margins, as shown in Figure 4-26. Either use a multiple page view or select each page in turn to ensure that all pages have the new margin settings. Restore the margins to (approximately) where they were before.

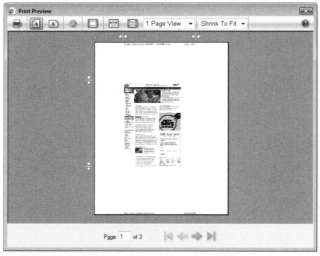

Figure 4-26 Adjusting margins

7. Select single page view (if necessary). Click the View Full Width button. Click the Turn Headers And Footers On Or Off button. Verify that headers and footers no longer appear, as shown in Figure 4-27.

Figure 4-27 Turning off headers and footers

8. Turn headers and footers back on. Experiment with the settings in the Shrink To Fit box. Restore the Shrink To Fit setting.

9. Click the Page Setup button. As shown in Figure 4-28, the Page Setup dialog box lets you select landscape and portrait orientation, specify page size (for example letter or A4), and specify paper source. It also provides a nongraphical (and more accurate) method of specifying margin settings. Finally, it allows you to specify the header and footer formats.

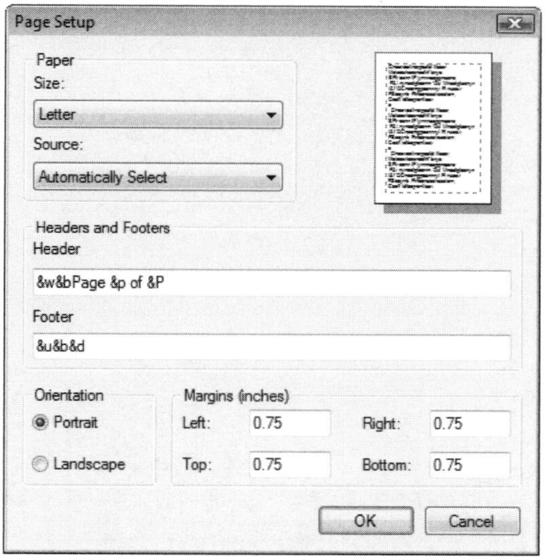

Figure 4-28   The Page Setup dialog box

10. Experiment with the header and footer specification by using the variables listed in Table 4-1. In the dialog box shown previously in Figure 4-28, for example, a footer specification of &u&b&d&b would center-justify rather than left-justify the date at the bottom of the page.

11. When you are happy with your Print Preview settings, print the webpage.

▶ **Practice 4: Adding Search Providers to the Search Bar**

In addition to searching Windows Help And Support for a word or phrase that you type into the Search bar (or toolbar search box), Windows Vista can use a search provider (for example, Google or Live Search) to find the information online. In this practice, you add search providers to your Search bar.

1. If necessary, log on by using the parent_standard account.

2. Open IE7+.

3. Click the arrow to the right of the Search bar, and select Find More Providers.

4. A webpage appears, as shown in Figure 4-29. Click the search provider that you want to add.

Figure 4-29   Selecting a search provider that you want to add

5. The Add Search Provider dialog box opens, as shown in Figure 4-30. If you want to use the provider that you have specified by default, select the Make This My Default Search Provider check box.

Figure 4-30   The Add Search Provider dialog box

6. Click Add Provider.

7. Use the same procedure for each provider that you want to add.

Lesson Summary

- When you browse to a webpage that provides news feeds, you can subscribe to one or more of these feeds.
- You can access subscribed feeds through the Favorites Center in IE7+.
- IE7+ updates the information from subscribed feeds in the background whenever you are logged on.
- You can read the information provided by subscribed news feeds whether you are logged on or logged off.
- The Print Preview and Page Setup controls enable you to configure how a webpage appears when you print it out.
- You can enter variables in the Page Setup dialog box that control the content and format of the page headers and footers.
- You can add other search providers to the IE7+ Search bar.

Lesson Review

You can use the following questions to test your knowledge of the information in Lesson 2, "Configuring Internet Explorer 7+ ." The questions are also available on the companion CD if you prefer to review them in electronic form.

NOTE Answers

Answers to these questions and explanations of why each answer choice is correct or incorrect are located in the "Answers" section at the end of the book.

---

1. You have subscribed to a news feed. You want the information provided by the news feed to be refreshed automatically in the background whenever you are offline. You should not have to navigate to the news feed site in order to refresh the feed information. You want to be able to read the news feed contents whether you are connected to the Internet or not. What is the easiest way of meeting these requirements?

    A. Download and install a third-party news aggregator.

    B. You do not need to take any action. IE7+ does all this automatically.

    C. Download and install a third-party search aggregator.

    D. Register your IE7+ browser with Clouds.

2. You want to change the margin settings before you print a webpage. You want the left and right margins to be 0.25 inches smaller and the top and bottom margins to be 0.2 inches larger. How can you do this?

   A. In Print Preview click the View Full Width button. Drag the margins to the new positions.

   B. In Print Preview click the View Full Page button. Type new values for the margin sizes in the margin boxes.

   C. In Print Preview click the Page Setup button. Type new values for the margin sizes in the margin boxes.

   D. In Print Preview click each margin symbol in turn and drag them to their new positions.

3. You want a webpage to print with a footer that contains the word "Page" followed by a space, the page number, a space, the word "of," a space, and then the total number of pages—for example, "Page 6 of 10." You want this to be center-justified. What do you type into the footer specification box?

   A. &bPage &p of &P&b

   B. &bPage &p of &P

   C. &bPage &P of &p&b

   D. &bPage &P of &p

4. In IE7+ you browse to a webpage that has its own search provider. You type **TEST** into the webpage search box and copy the URL that results from the search. How do you then add the provider to your search providers list?

   A. Click the arrow to the right of your Search bar. Select Change Search Defaults. Paste the URL into the Search Providers list.

   B. Click Tools and expand Internet Options. Select the General tab and select Change Search Defaults.

   C. Click the arrow to the right of your Search bar and select Find More Providers. On the Add Search Providers webpage scroll to the foot of the page and click Add To Favorites. Paste the URL in the box provided.

   D. Click the arrow to the right of your Search bar and select Find More Providers. On the Add Search Providers to Internet Explorer 7 webpage, in the Create Your Own dialog box, paste the copied URL into the box provided, type a name for the search provider, and then click Install.

Chapter Review

To further practice and reinforce the skills you learned in this chapter, you can perform the following tasks:

- Review the chapter summary.
- Review the list of key terms introduced in this chapter.
- Complete the case scenarios. These scenarios set up real-world situations involving the topics of this chapter and ask you to create a solution.
- Complete the suggested practices.
- Take a practice test.

Chapter Summary

- You can configure Parental Controls for a standard account but not for an administrator account. You can limit logon hours and control access to websites, games, and executable programs on a per-user basis. You can also generate and view activity reports. You can use Content Advisor to control website access for all users.
- IE7+ allows you to contribute to news feeds and provides aggregator functions that update news feeds automatically and let you read them offline.
- You can use the Print Preview and Page Setup controls to configure how a webpage appears when you print it out and to configure the webpage headers and footers.
- You can enter variables in the Page Setup dialog box that control the content and format of the page headers and footers.
- You can configure the IE7+ Search Bar by adding search providers and specifying defaults.

Key Terms

Do you know what these key terms mean? You can check your answers by looking up the terms in the glossary at the end of the book.

- age rating
- aggregator
- Content Advisor
- content rating
- Internet connection sharing (ICS)
- Internet device discovery and control (IGDDC)
- Parental Controls

- RSS feed (news feed)
- search provider

Case Scenarios

In the following case scenarios, you will apply what you have learned about configuring and troubleshooting Parental Controls and configuring IE7+. You can find answers to these questions in the "Answers" section at the end of this book.

Case Scenario 1: Advising Users on How to Configure Parental Controls

You provide technical support to the help desk at Northwind Traders, a retail company that sells computers and computer equipment at retail outlets throughout the United States. The company has recently started selling computers with Windows Vista operating systems, and customers are asking for help in configuring Parental Controls. Answer the following questions:

1. A customer has three children aged 6, 11, and 15. He does not want to prevent them from playing games, but neither does he want them exposed to games that are unsuitable for their age groups. He is a pacifist and does not want any of his children to play violent games (although mild cartoon violence is acceptable). The customer's computer is configured to use the ESRB games ratings. How should he set up Parental Controls?

2. A user has configured the Medium web restriction level for her 12-year-old son. She is concerned to discover that he has accessed an educational bulletin board site where various scientific theories are discussed, including Darwin's theory of evolution. This conflicts with her religious beliefs. She concedes that the site is carefully monitored and contains no offensive language or overt sexual content. She has added the site to the block list she has created for her son but wants to ensure that, as far as is possible, he cannot access sites of a similar nature. What do you advise?

3. A customer has set up Parental Controls for his son and has blocked his son's access to all programs except those that he specifies. He has enabled his son to access a number of educational programs that are installed on his computer. However, his son can no longer open Word to edit his homework assignments. What do you advise?

Case Scenario 2: Printing Webpages

You provide technical assistance to your work colleagues at Trey Research through an internal help desk. Trey Research employees frequently print out complex webpages generated by other research and academic organizations. They find it easier to read paper copy than a computer screen, especially when traveling. Sometimes the webpage printouts are unsatisfactory and colleagues ask for your assistance. Answer the following questions:

1. A colleague accesses a webpage that uses a number of frames. She finds the frame layout difficult to read and wants a printout that shows all frames individually, one after the other. How can she do this?

2. A co-worker has been experimenting with the Change Print Size control to try to improve the look of his printout. He has decided that none of the print sizes settings is satisfactory, and he therefore selects 100%. He finds that he is losing characters at the edge of the printed page and that the orphan control no longer works. What should he do?

3. A research team member does not like the positions of the page breaks on a webpage printout. She has used the Shrink To Fit print size setting, but this is not entirely satisfactory. What do you advise?

4. Your boss wants to change the header of a webpage so that the title is right-justified and the page number and total number of pages (for example Page 1 of 10) are left-justified. What should he type in the Page Setup header box?

Suggested Practices

To help you successfully master the exam objectives presented in this chapter, complete the following tasks.

Configure and Troubleshoot Parental Controls

- **Practice 1: Configure Web Access for Children of Various Ages**   Experiment with the Parental Control web access settings, assuming that you are setting them up for children aged 5, 7, 11, and 15. If necessary, create more standard accounts to do this. In addition to configuring Parental Controls, enable and configure Content Advisor. Experiment until you feel confident about how the two controls interact.

- **Practice 2: Configure Game Controls for Children of Various Ages**   Experiment with the Parental Control game controls settings, assuming that you are allowing access to games for the same child accounts for which you configured web access in Practice 1. Specify games rating systems other than ESRB.

- **Practice 3: Configure Application Restrictions**   Configure application restrictions on one or more child accounts. Experiment with the use of the Browse facility.

Configure Internet Explorer 7+

- **Practice 1: Subscribe to News Feeds**   Use the search facility to find websites that provide news feeds and subscribe to the feeds of your choice. Access a news feed while you are online and refresh it. Access a news feed while you are offline and read it.

- **Practice 2: Configure Print Preview for a Webpage**   Find a webpage that provides a lot of information in a complex frame structure. Experiment with making the orientation of some frames portrait and others landscape. Use the Page Setup dialog box to reconfigure the headers and footers.
- **Practice 3: Add Search Providers**   Add search providers listed in the Add Search Providers To Internet Explorer 7 webpage to your search providers list. Access websites that implement search providers and add these to your search providers list.

Take a Practice Test

The practice tests on this book's companion CD offer many options. For example, you can test yourself on just one exam objective, or you can test yourself on all the 70-620 certification exam content. You can set up the test so that it closely simulates the experience of taking a certification exam, or you can set it up in study mode so that you can look at the correct answers and explanations after you answer each question.

MORE INFO   **Practice tests**

For details about all the practice test options available, see the "How to Use the Practice Tests" section in this book's Introduction.

Chapter 5
User Account Control

User Account Control (UAC) segregates Windows tasks into two groups: those that standard users can accomplish and those that only administrators can accomplish. In addition, UAC causes administrator accounts to run as standard accounts most of the time.

When an administrator-level task is initiated, a user receives a prompt so that he or she can temporarily elevate his or her privileges in order to complete that single task. If the user is logged on with an administrator account, the user grants permission to continue with the task. If, on the other hand, the user is logged on with a standard account, the user needs to provide administrator credentials (by selecting an administrator account and entering a password) in order to continue.

This default user experience is called Admin Approval mode. In this mode, applications require specific permission to run as an administrator application—an application that requires a full administrator access token (or elevated access token) and has the same access privileges as an administrator.

NOTE Administrator accounts

In this context, administrator accounts are accounts that are added to the local Administrators group. UAC does not operate on the built-in Administrator account because Admin Approval mode does not apply to this account by default.

A user who is logged with administrative credentials but is performing a user-level task does so in the context of a standard user. In this case, if the user initiates an administrator-level task, the system (by default) asks for permission to continue but does not ask for additional credentials. UAC also warns both standard and administrator users if they attempt to execute an application that has not been digitally signed.

Exam objectives in this chapter:
- Configure and troubleshoot User Account Control.

Lessons in this chapter:

Before You Begin

To complete the lesson in this chapter, you must have done the following:

■ Installed Windows Vista Ultimate edition on a personal computer, as described in Chapter 1, "Installing Windows Vista Client" and Chapter 2, "Windows Vista Upgrades and Migrations."

■ Created an administrator account and standard accounts and enabled the Run command on the Start menu, as described in Practices 1, 2, and 3 of Chapter 4, "Configuring and Troubleshooting Internet Access," Lesson 1, "Configuring and Troubleshooting Parental Controls and Content Advisor."

No additional configuration is required for this chapter.

Real World

Ian McLean

A tendency exists, even among experienced administrators, to look at the addition of yet more security features in a new operating system (OS) and shudder. However, sometimes a feature comes along that provides immediate and obvious benefits and is well worth the effort of coming to grips with. Previous Windows client OSs made it easy for users to configure accounts with administrative privileges. As a result, many Windows applications assume that the user is a local administrator. However, when ordinary users typically have administrator access, every application and service that runs on the system—including worms, Trojan horses, and other forms of malware—also does so with complete administrator privileges.

Earlier OSs—for example, Windows XP—offered the runas feature. This was designed to escalate user privileges and enable software to run when the logged-on account did not have a high privilege level, but it was a plaster to cover a gaping wound. It was awkward, and many applications simply could not use it. On several occasions I have been asked to survey the wreck of a network and noted that all users had administrative privileges. "They need to," I am assured, "because we have to run ...."

Windows Vista confronts this problem head on. Its architecture incorporates a number of technologies that Microsoft has designed specifically to lock down the system but still provide compatibility features that help applications written for previous operating systems continue to load and run as they always did. The key technology in this group is UAC. The security benefits of UAC far outweigh whatever annoyances its dialog boxes might cause, and I recommend it.

NOTE   Designed for Windows logo

Any application that carries the "Designed for Windows 2000 / XP / Vista" logo will run without requiring that the user is a local administrator.

Lesson 1: Configuring and Troubleshooting User Account Control

This lesson discusses how UAC works; what types of tasks require elevated privileges; the differences between standard accounts, administrator accounts, and the built-in Administrator account; how you elevate user privileges; how you configure UAC by using local security policies; and how you disable Secure Desktop. It also looks at problems related to UAC and how you would troubleshoot such problems.

After this lesson, you will be able to:
- Explain how UAC enhances security while maintaining backward compatibility.
- Distinguish between standard accounts, administrator accounts, and the built-in Administrator account.
- Elevate user privileges for a standard user.
- Configure UAC by using local security policies.
- Disable UAC.
- Disable Secure Desktop.
- Use the Program Compatibility Wizard to enable legacy programs to run in Windows Vista.

Estimated lesson time: 85 minutes

How User Account Control Works

UAC is invisible to both standard users and administrators while they are performing nonadministrative tasks—for example, creating and editing Microsoft Word documents, changing power management settings, or adding a printer. Suppose, however, that you log on with a standard user account and attempt to perform an administrative-level task—for example, installing an application or changing the system date or time. As shown in Figure 5-1, Microsoft automatically applies a Windows shield icon to user interface (UI) elements that require account escalation.

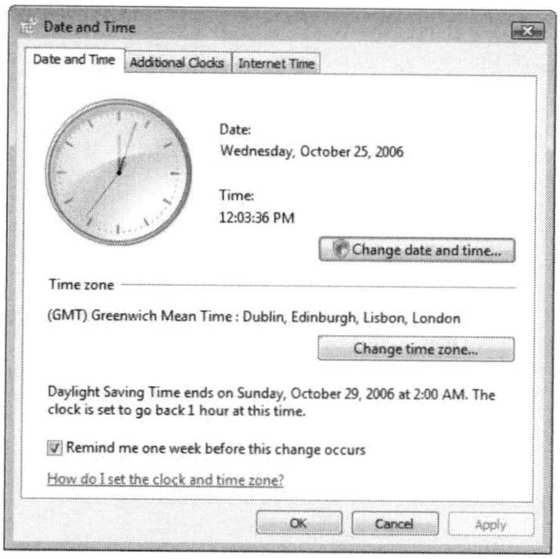

Figure 5-1   Windows Shield icon

When you click this icon, a dialog box opens. It requires you to select an administrator account and to enter the corresponding password—or insert a smart card and enter a personal identity number (PIN)—in order to complete the selected task. Figure 5-2 shows this dialog box.

Figure 5-2   Prompt for an administrator password

If, on the other hand, you logged on as an administrator, clicking the shield icon results (by default) in the dialog box shown in Figure 5-3. You are not required to reenter your credentials but instead to click Continue.

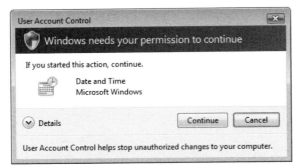

Figure 5-3 Giving Windows permission to continue

NOTE Increasing UAC security

You can increase security by configuring Windows Vista to always prompt for administrative credentials, even when the logged-on user has administrator privileges. You do this in the practice session in this chapter.

If an administrator attempts to execute an application that has not been digitally signed or validated, the UAC dialog box shown in Figure 5-4 appears. If a standard user attempts to access the same program, the dialog box requires the user to select an administrator account and supply a password.

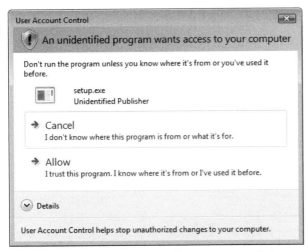

Figure 5-4 Giving an unsigned program permission to continue

If, on the other hand, the program is digitally signed, the UAC dialog box shown in Figure 5-5 appears (by default) for administrator accounts. Users logged on with standard accounts are required to select an administrator account and enter a password.

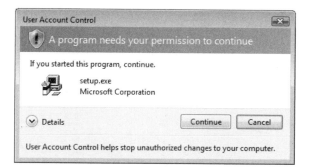

Figure 5-5   Giving a signed program permission to continue

> ## Digital Signatures
>
> For an executable program (for example, an application, driver, or macro) to be trusted, it is not sufficient for it to have a digital certificate issued by any source. The publisher needs to be trusted. Trusted publishers are held in a trusted publishers list on your computer. This list can include reputable software suppliers such as Microsoft Corporation and trusted external certificate providers such as Thawte or VeriSign.
>
> Even when executable code is digitally signed, it might not be validated because the signature is not from a trusted source. If you receive a warning to this effect, you have the option of running the program or canceling the operation. If you trust the software provider, you can add this provider to the trusted publishers list by selecting the Always Trust Applications From This Source check box.

MORE INFO   **Digital signatures**

For more information about digital signatures, access *http://windowshelp.microsoft.com/Windows /en-US/Help/077238d3-2e78-4655-872c-6d59462840111033.mspx.*

When any of the UAC dialog boxes appears, Windows Vista takes a screenshot of your desktop and switches into Secure Desktop (which is also used by Windows Vista's welcome/logon window). You cannot perform any other operations on your computer until you have dealt with the dialog box. Microsoft implements UAC in this way because the corporation's security researchers recognized that it might be possible to spoof UAC if it appeared on screen as a normal Windows dialog box. Also, if a user has a lot of windows open simultaneously, a UAC consent dialog box in a standard window could get buried under other windows, and the user might not realize that authorization is required.

NOTE UAC increases parental control

UAC makes it possible for parents to configure standard user accounts for their children. When, for example, a child wants to install an application, a parent can first review the application and then provide credentials for the installation only when he or she is sure that it is safe.

Backward Compatibility

Most programs written for earlier OSs—for example, Windows XP—also work in Windows Vista, but some older programs might run poorly or not run at all. If an older program does not run correctly, you can start the Program Compatibility Wizard, shown in Figure 5-6. Program compatibility is a Windows mode that lets you run programs written for earlier versions of Windows. Chapter 2, "Upgrading Windows Vista," introduced the Program Compatibility Wizard, and you use this wizard in the practice session later in this chapter.

Figure 5-6 The Program Compatibility Wizard

NOTE The Program Compatibility Wizard vs. the Program Compatibility Assistant

The Program Compatibility Assistant is a feature of Windows that runs automatically if it detects a compatibility problem when you run a legacy program. The Program Compatibility Wizard is a tool you can run manually on a program if you notice compatibility issues. If the Program Compatibility Assistant does not fix the program automatically without user intervention, you should run the Program Compatibility Wizard.

CAUTION   Program Compatibility Wizard limitations

Do not use the Program Compatibility Wizard if you are attempting to run antivirus programs, backup programs, disk utilities, or other system programs. This might cause data loss or create a security risk.

MORE INFO   Updating drivers

Some compatibility problems might be caused by drivers. If an older driver is causing problems, you need to update it manually. For more information, search Windows Help And Support for "Update drivers: recommended links."

Unlike previous Microsoft client OSs—for example, Windows XP—which typically grant applications complete control over the system and permit them to read and write information anywhere in both the registry and the file system, Windows Vista locks down the registry and file system. To ensure backward compatibility, UAC provides registry and file system virtualization services that silently redirect read and write operations from protected portions of the registry and file system to unprotected locations in the user's profile. These locations are hidden and the whole process is automatic and invisible to the user.

Running User Accounts as Standard Users

UAC increases Windows Vista security by causing administrator accounts to run as standard users, elevating account privileges only when required and prompting the user before doing so. Conversely, standard users can perform most (but not all) administrator tasks by providing administrator account credentials. For example, a standard user can supply administrator credentials and then change system time, but you need to be logged on as an administrator to configure local security policy.

In previous client OSs that do not have UAC (or in Windows Vista with UAC disabled), an administrator is automatically granted full access to all system resources. Most users do not require such a high level of access to the computer, and even users who do sometimes need to perform administrator functions typically spend most of their time on nonadministrator tasks.

Without UAC, a user who is logged on as an administrator can install software, often without receiving a prompt or warning, and as a result can unintentionally or intentionally install a malicious program that might compromise the computer and affect all users.

In Windows Vista Admin Approval mode, the access control model has changed to help mitigate this problem. In this mode, both administrator and standard user accounts run by default as standard users. If a user needs to perform an administrator function, he or she needs to elevate his or her privileges. If the user is an administrator, the UAC dialog box asks the user to click Continue when trying to start an administrator application before the application can use the user's full administrator access token. The user has the option of clicking Cancel if he or she has doubts about performing the operation. If the user is not an administrator, the user must provide administrator credentials to run the program.

Because Admin Approval mode requires an administrator to approve application installations, unauthorized applications cannot be installed automatically or without the explicit consent of an administrator. Administrators always receive a warning and need to take affirmative action before any software can be installed.

Elevating User Privileges

UAC, by default, gives a user the option of elevating his or her privileges in order to perform an administrator task. A standard user needs to supply the password of an administrator account. An administrator needs only to give the program permission to continue. When the task is complete, the user account reverts to running as a standard account.

As Figure 5-7 shows, four types of user accounts exist: the built-in Administrator account, administrator accounts, standard accounts, and the built-in Guest account.

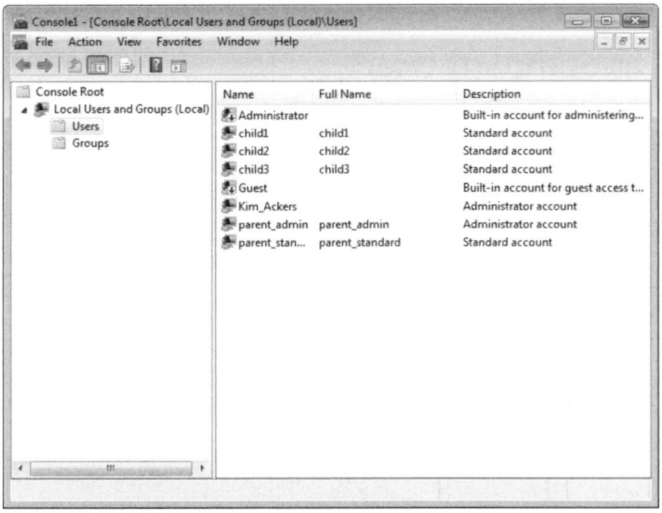

Figure 5-7   Types of user accounts

The built-in Guest account is a member of the Guests group. Windows Vista disables this account by default. Even when it is enabled, users logged on with the Guest account cannot perform administrator tasks. Chapter 4, "Configuring and Troubleshooting Internet Access," discussed the Guest account. This account allows users who do not have a permanent account to use the computer without having access to regular users' personal files. For example, you might enable and use the Guest account for students' use in a school or college that runs night school courses.

Administrator accounts are members of the Administrators and Users groups, as shown in Figure 5-8. They run as standard users except when performing administrator tasks, when they run as administrators with elevated privileges.

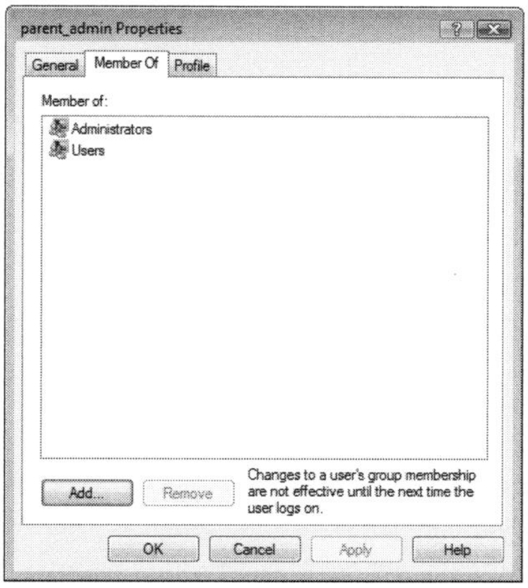

Figure 5-8   Administrator account group membership

Standard accounts are members of the Users groups, as shown in Figure 5-9. They run as standard users. If a user logged on with a standard account wants to perform an administrator task, he or she selects an administrator account and types in the password. The task runs under the elevated privileges of the administrator account.

Figure 5-9   Standard account group membership

As Figure 5-10 demonstrates, the built-in Administrator account is a member of only the Administrators group. By default, this account does not run as a standard user account and always has elevated privileges. UAC does not, by default, protect this account. You should not enable or use the built-in Administrator account unless you have good reasons for doing so.

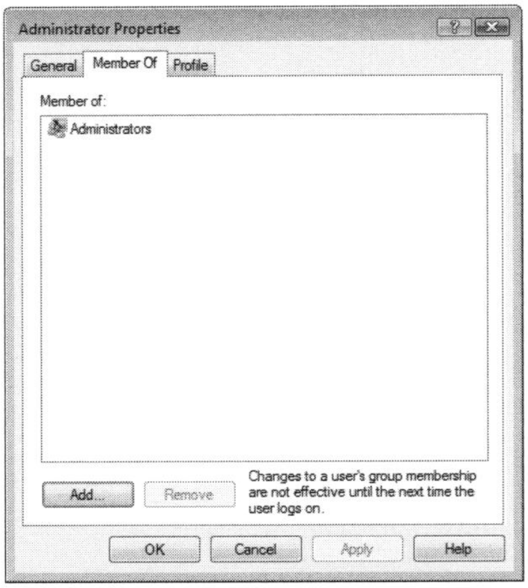

Figure 5-10   Built-in Administrator account group membership

IMPORTANT   **Rename and protect the built-in Administrator account**

Even if you never intend to enable the built-in Administrator account, you should rename it and give it a complex password. An account called Administrator, with no password and permanently elevated privileges, is a dangerous entity. It requires only one check box selection to enable it.

Using Local Security Policies to Configure User Account Control

If your Windows Vista PC is operating in stand-alone mode or as part of a workgroup (that is, it is not a member of an Active Directory directory service domain), you can configure UAC by using the Local Security Policy console, shown in Figure 5-11. You access this console in the practice session later in this chapter, but if you want to take a look at it now, open the Run box, type **Gpedit.msc**, click Continue to close the UAC dialog box, expand Computer Configuration, expand Windows Settings, expand Security Settings, expand Local Policies, and click Security Options.

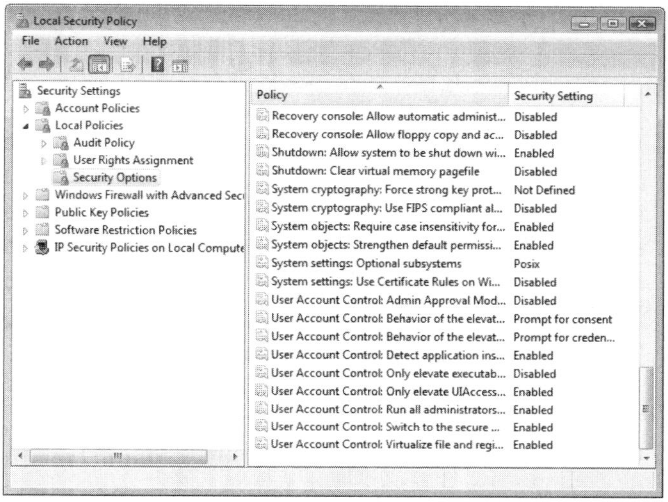

Figure 5-11   Local Security Policy in the Group Policy Object Editor console

The following UAC settings are listed under Local Policies, Security Options:

- User Account Control: Admin Approval mode for the Built-in Administrator Account
- User Account Control: Behavior of the elevation prompt for administrators in Admin Approval mode
- User Account Control: Behavior of the elevation prompt for standard users
- User Account Control: Detect application installations and prompt for elevation
- User Account Control: Only elevate executables that are signed and validated
- User Account Control: Only elevate UIAccess applications that are installed in secure locations
- User Account Control: Run all administrators in Admin Approval mode
- User Account Control: Control Switch to the Secure Desktop when prompting for elevation
- User Account Control: Virtualize file and registry write failures to per-user locations

Admin Approval Mode for the Built-in Administrator Account

This setting determines whether the UAC Admin Approval mode is applied to the built-in Administrator account. The default setting is Disabled. By default, the built-in Administrator account lets a user log on in Windows XP compatible mode and run all applications by default with permanently elevated privileges.

If the setting is Enabled, the built-in Administrator account lets the user log on in Admin Approval mode. In this mode, any operation that requires elevation of privilege prompts for consent, and the user can click Continue or Cancel.

Behavior of the Elevation Prompt for Administrators in Admin Approval Mode

This setting determines the user experience of administrators when performing an operation that requires elevated privileges. The default setting is Prompt For Consent. The following options are available:

- **Prompt For Consent**   An operation that requires elevation of privilege prompts the user to click either Continue or Cancel. If the administrator selects Continue, the operation continues with elevated privileges.
- **Prompt For Credentials**   An operation that requires elevation of privilege prompts the administrator to enter a password. If the user enters valid credentials, the operation will continue with elevated privileges.
- **Elevate Without Prompting**   The administrator can perform an operation that requires elevation without consent or credentials (XP-compatible mode). This setting gives an administrator the same user experience that the built-in Administrator account offers by default. The user could accidentally install malware without receiving a prompt or warning. For this reason, you should not select this option unless you have a good reason for doing so.

Behavior of the Elevation Prompt for Standard Users

This setting determines the user experience of standard users when performing an operation that requires elevated privileges. The default setting in Windows Vista Ultimate is Prompt For Credentials. The following options are available:

- **Prompt For Credentials**   An operation that requires elevation of privilege prompts the user to select an administrator account and enter a password. If the user specifies valid credentials, the operation will continue with elevated privileges.
- **Automatically Deny Elevation Requests**   This option results in a standard user receiving an access denied error message when he or she tries to perform an operation that requires elevation of privilege. This setting is typically used in the enterprise environment where the clients are in an Active Directory domain, and users do not perform administrator tasks.

Quick Check

- You want to ensure that standard users cannot perform tasks that require elevated privileges and are not prompted for administrator credentials when they attempt to carry out such tasks. What UAC setting should you configure?

Quick Check Answer

- Set User Access Control: Behavior Of The Elevation Prompt For Standard Users to Automatically Deny Elevation Requests.

Detect Application Installations and Prompt for Elevation

This setting determines whether signed and unsigned application installs trigger a UAC elevation dialog box. The setting affects the entire system, and the default on a Windows Vista Ultimate client running in a workgroup is Enabled. The following options are available:

- **Enabled**   UAC detects application installation packages that require an elevation of privilege to install and triggers the relevant elevation prompt. The prompt depends upon whether the user has logged on by using a standard or an administrator account and whether the application is signed.
- **Disabled**   Typically, a domain administrator would disable this setting in an enterprise environment with standard user desktops that leverage delegated installation technologies such as Group Policy Software Install (GPSI) or Systems Management Server (SMS). In this case, installer detection is unnecessary.

MORE INFO   GPSI and SMS

You can obtain more information about GPSI by accessing *http://support.microsoft.com/default.aspx /kb/816102* and about SMS by accessing *http://www.microsoft.com/smserver/default.mspx*. However, these technologies are unlikely to be featured in the 70-620 examination.

Only Elevate Executables That Are Signed and Validated

This setting determines whether UAC enforces public key infrastructure (PKI) signature checks on any interactive application that requests elevation of privilege. If such checking is enforced, only signed application installs can trigger a UAC elevation dialog box and receive permission to continue. The default setting for a PC running Windows Vista Ultimate in a workgroup is Disabled. The following options are available:

- **Disabled**   UAC does not enforce PKI certificate chain validation before an executable can run. A user with elevated privileges can run unsigned executable files on the computer.

- **Enabled**   PKI certificate chain validation is required before an executable can run. This setting is appropriate in the enterprise environment where a domain administrator publishes PKI certificates in a local computer's trusted publisher store to permit executables to run.

MORE INFO   Public key infrastructure

You can obtain more information about public key infrastructure and application signing by accessing *http://www.microsoft.com/windowsserver2003/technologies/pki/default.mspx*. However, the 70-620 examination is unlikely to test PKI in any depth.

Only Elevate UIAccess Applications That Are Installed in Secure Locations

This setting enforces the requirement that applications that request execution with a user interface access (UIAccess) integrity level must reside in a secure location on the file system. Secure locations are limited to the following directories:

- *xxx*\Program Files\, including subdirectories
- *xxx*\Windows\system32\r-
- *xxx*\Program Files (x86)\, including subdirectories for 64-bit versions of Windows

The default setting is Enabled. The following options are available:

- **Enabled**   An application can launch with UIAccess integrity only if it resides in a secure location in the file system.
- **Disabled**   An application can launch with UIAccess integrity even if it does not reside in a secure location in the file system.

NOTE   PKI signature checks on UIAccess applications

Windows Vista enforces a PKI signature check on any interactive application that requests execution with UIAccess integrity level, regardless of the state of this security setting.

NOTE   User Interface Automation and the UIAccess attribute

You can obtain more information about UI Automation and the UIAccess attribute by accessing *http://windowssdk.msdn.microsoft.com/en-gb/library/ms742884.aspx*. However, the 70-620 examination is unlikely to test this topic in depth.

Run All Administrators in Admin Approval Mode

This setting determines the behavior of all UAC policies for the entire system. It specifies whether all administrator accounts run in Admin Approval mode, which generates UAC consent dialog boxes for administrator tasks. The default setting is Enabled.

Admin Approval mode and all other UAC policies are dependent on this setting being enabled. Disabling the setting effectively switches UAC off. If you do so, the Security Center will notify you that the overall security of the OS has been reduced. Changing this setting requires a system reboot.

Quick Check

- You do not want a standard user to be able to perform any administrator-level tasks, even by providing administrator credentials. What two UAC settings prevent this?

Quick Check Answer

- User Access Control: Run All Administrators In Admin Approval Mode set to Disabled. This disables UAC.
- User Access Control: Behavior Of The Elevation Prompt For Standard Users set to Automatically Deny Elevation Requests. This setting results in a standard user receiving an access denied error message when he or she tries to perform an operation that requires elevation of privilege.

Control Switch to the Secure Desktop When Prompting for Elevation

This setting determines whether the Secure Desktop environment appears whenever a UAC prompt is initiated by the system and whether the elevation request will prompt on the interactive user's desktop or the Secure Desktop. The default setting is Enabled.

The reasons for using Secure Desktop were discussed earlier in this chapter. If you disable this setting, your computer could fall victim to external attacks that spoof a UAC dialog box.

Real World

Ian McLean

When the beta version of a new OS is released, one of my responsibilities is to write a report on the new features for distribution to colleagues. Typically, such reports are required within days, or even hours, of my getting my hands on the software.

Naturally, I need screenshots. So I log on, attempt to perform an administrator task, and happily press the Print Screen button to capture the resulting UAC dialog box. Of course, this does not work. Secure Desktop blocks all applications from running—including the Print Screen function.

> Screen cameras are time-consuming and awkward to set up, and I never seem to get good results. Photography is not one of my skills. However, I persevere and eventually get some rather poor-quality screenshots.
>
> Then, I look at the UAC configuration options, and almost the first thing I spot is the User Account Control: Switch To The Secure Desktop When Prompting For Elevation policy. Oops!
>
> The moral of the story: no matter how short time might be, always find out what a new feature can do *before* you start to use it.

Virtualize File and Registry Write Failures to Per-User Locations

This setting determines whether UAC virtualizes the registry and file system for legacy applications that attempt to read or write from private parts of the system. The default setting is Enabled, which redirects legacy application writes to both the registry and file system to locations in the user's profile. This feature permits a user to run legacy applications that historically ran in the context of the administrator account and wrote run-time application data back to either %ProgramFiles%, %Windir%, %Windir%\system32, or HKLM\Software\.

Virtualization facilitates the running of pre-Windows Vista applications that would otherwise fail. An administrator running only Windows Vista-compliant applications might choose to disable this feature (although this is not recommended). If the feature is disabled, applications that write data to protected locations will fail, as they did in previous versions of Windows.

NOTE **Do not disable the Virtualize File And Registry Write Failures To Per-User Locations policy**

For compatibility reasons, Microsoft recommends that you do not disable this policy.

Quick Check

- You have moved an application that opens a user interface from C:\Program Files\MyApp to D:\MyStuff\MyApp and created a shortcut on your desktop to the application. You find that the application no longer runs. What UAC setting could be causing this?

Quick Check Answer
- The User Access Control: Only Elevate UIAccess Applications That Are Installed In Secure Locations policy is Enabled by default. This prevents applications that access user interfaces from running unless they are installed in secure locations (such as a subdirectory of All Programs). Although you could change this UAC setting, it is probably a bad idea to do so because this would affect the security of all such applications. Restoring the application to its original location is likely to be a better solution.

Exam Tip   UAC is an exceptionally important new feature of Windows Vista. The 70-620 examination is likely to test UAC and, in particular, UAC policy settings extensively. Make sure that you are thoroughly familiar with these settings.

Troubleshooting UAC and Program Compatibility

Sometimes the user experience in Windows Vista is not what you expect it to be. Users are prompted for credentials when they believe they should not be or not prompted for credentials when they should be. Programs do not run and software cannot be installed. Programs that should not be permitted to run do so.

NOTE   Check for negatives

Users will tell you quickly enough if they do not have the privileges that they think they should or if they cannot install or run software that they believe they should be able to. They are less likely to tell you that they have more privileges than they expect, are not prompted for credentials, and can install and run software when they expect this to be prohibited.

As an IT professional, you should periodically check that users cannot do more than you expect them to. If you have blocked unsigned programs, for example, you should check that such programs cannot run. Users report faults that do not enable them to do what they expect. You need to determine whether they can do more than you expect.

Check Group Membership

In the domain environment group, membership tends to be strictly controlled by the domain administrators. In a workgroup environment, a (regrettable) tendency still exists to grant a user administrator rights on his or her workstation. If you are called on to work on a home network under a service agreement, at least one member of the household will be an administrator.

In such a situation, check the membership of the localAdministrators group. A parent might have placed a child's account in this group because he or she could not be around to supply an administrator password. The child could then have reconfigured some computer settings. If a user is not being prompted to click Continue when starting administrator tasks, has the built-in Administrator account been enabled?

Check Software Status

If a user attempts to install software by using an unsigned setup program, the user experience is different from what it would be if the program were signed. If the setting User Account Control: Only Elevate Executables That Are Signed And Validated is Enabled, unsigned installation software will not run. However, the process of validating software and obtaining a digital signature is a lengthy one, and even the most reputable software suppliers sometimes release unsigned programs. If software behaves as if it is unsigned, then it is likely that it actually is unsigned. If it is from a reputable and trusted source, it is unlikely to harm your computer.

By default, UAC specifies that UIAccess applications can run with elevated privileges only if they are installed in secure locations. This prohibition applies whether the application is digitally signed or not. By default, these applications are installed in secure locations, but sometimes they are moved or copied. If such an application is giving problems, check its location.

Windows Vista runs most legacy software that was designed for use on earlier OSs. Some third-party applications designed for use with Windows 95 (or earlier) attempt to access the hard disk directly. Such programs do not run, nor should they. Third-party disk manager and virus-checking software might have compatibility problems. You should not attempt to run such programs. Windows Vista offers virtualization of secure locations and the Program Compatibility Wizard. If neither of these facilities permits a legacy program to run, it probably is just as well.

Check the UAC Settings

If UAC is not operating as expected, check the UAC settings. The default settings typically work well, and it is probably a good idea to restore the defaults, after first noting any changes that have been made. If you consider it wise, you can then try changing settings one at a time to what they were when you started the investigation. You can then locate the setting that caused the reported problem.

Also, remember that you must configure UAC in a workgroup on a per-computer basis. If a user is accustomed to using one workstation and decides to use another, the user experience might be different. A reported fault might not be a fault at all, but merely somebody else's settings.

Sometimes a local administrator might not understand the effects of UAC settings. Such a user might, for example, disable the Virtualize File And Registry Write Failures To Per-User Locations setting because "I didn't understand what it did, so it seemed like a good idea to disable it." The user then reports that important legacy software no longer runs. A user might disable Run All Administrators In Admin Approval Mode, believing this setting applies only to administrators, and then report that standard users can no longer run programs by supplying administrator credentials.

Restoring UAC defaults gives you a sensible starting point. You can then take it from there.

Practice: Configuring UAC and Testing Your Settings

In this practice session, you configure UAC settings and test them while logged on as a standard user, an administrator, and the built-in Administrator. The practice session uses the user accounts you created in Chapter 4, "Configuring and Troubleshooting Internet Access." To perform the practices as written, you need to have successfully completed Practices 1, 2, and 3 of Chapter 4, "Configuring and Troubleshooting Internet Access," Lesson 1, "Configuring and Troubleshooting Parental Controls and Content Advisor."

At a minimum you need to have created one standard user account. If you want to, you can use the administrator account that you created when you installed Windows Vista.

▶ **Practice 1: Adding Administrative Tools to All Programs on the Start Menu**

In Chapter 4, "Configuring and Troubleshooting Internet Access," you added the Run command to the Start menu and accessed tools such as Local Users And Groups by opening the Microsoft Management Console (MMC) from the Run box and installing the required snap-in. Adding Administrative Tools to All Programs on the Start menu provides a more convenient method of accessing these tools.

1. Log on by using the parent_admin account that you created in Chapter 4, "Configuring and Troubleshooting Internet Access." (This user's password is P@ssw0rd.)
2. Right-click the Start button, and select Properties.
3. On the Start Menu tab, click Customize.
4. Scroll down to System Administrative Tools, and select Display On The All Programs Menu, as shown in Figure 5-12.

Figure 5-12　Displaying Administrative Tools on All Programs

5. Click OK.

6. Click OK to close the Taskbar And Start Menu properties dialog box.

▶ **Practice 2: Enabling the Built-In Administrator Account**

For testing purposes only, this practice enables the built-in Administrator account. First, however, you rename the account and assign a complex password. This account should always be password-protected and should *not* be called Administrator.

1. If necessary, log on by using the parent_admin account.

2. On the Start, All Programs menu, click Administrative Tools, and select Computer Management.

3. Click Continue in the UAC dialog box.

4. Expand Local Users And Groups, and click Users.

5. In the details pane, right-click the Administrator account and select Rename, as shown in Figure 5-13.

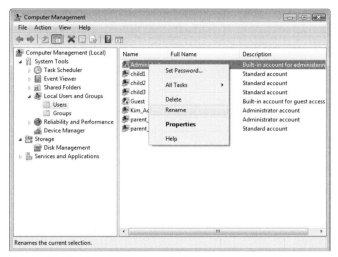

Figure 5-13   Renaming the Administrator account

6. Rename the Administrator account Don_Hall.

7. Right-click Don_Hall, and select Set Password.

8. Read the message in the Warning box, and then click Proceed.

IMPORTANT   Changing a user's password

If you, as an administrator, change a user's password, that user will no longer be able to read his or her files if these files have been encrypted by using the Microsoft encrypting file system (EFS). If, on the other hand, a user changes his or her own password, specifying the previous password to do so, EFS encrypted files remain accessible and readable. In the first instance, the files will need to be decrypted by a decryption agent and, if required, encrypted with the user's new encryption key. Hopefully, this should motivate users not to forget their passwords. Refer to *http://technet2.microsoft.com/WindowsServer/en/library /b505401c-5ec8-4f0f-b82b-ea24b28bfbad1033.mspx?mfr=true* for more details.

---

9. Specify and confirm a complex password—for example, P@ssAdm1n.

10. Click OK, and then click OK to close the message stating that the password has been set.

11. Right-click Don_Hall, and select Properties.

12. In the General tab, clear the Account Is Disabled check box, and then click OK.

13. Switch user to Don_Hall.

14. Perform an administrator task—for example, changing system time. A UAC dialog box does not appear, and you do not need to give permission to continue.

15. Run an application file—for example, the Setup.exe file on almost any Microsoft software installation CD-ROM. The UAC dialog box does not appear.

16. Switch user to parent_admin.

▶ **Practice 3: Configuring UAC Settings**

In this practice, you configure UAC settings and test them by logging on as a standard user, as an administrator, and as the built-in Administrator. The practice does not reconfigure every setting but selects a subset as examples. You can expand the practice by experimenting with the settings it does not reconfigure.

Do not attempt this practice until you have successfully completed Practices 1 and 2.

1. If necessary, log on by using the parent_admin account.

2. On the Start, All Programs menu, click Administrative Tools, and select Local Security Policy. If you have not added Administrative Tools to the All Programs menu, you can open this tool by typing **Secpol.msc** in the Run box and then clicking OK.

3. Click Continue in the UAC dialog box.

4. Expand Local Policies, and select Security Options.

5. Scroll down to the end of the list of policies.

6. Double-click User Account Control: Admin Approval Mode For The Built-In Administrator Account.

7. On the Local Security Setting tab, select Enabled, as shown in Figure 5-14, and then click OK.

Figure 5-14   Enabling Admin Approval mode for the built-in Administrator account

8. Switch user to Don_Hall. Attempt to change system time and to run an application file. UAC now prompts you to Continue or Cancel.

9. Switch user to parent_admin.

10. Restore the User Account Control: Admin Approval Mode For The Built-In Administrator Account to its default setting (Disabled).

11. In the Local Security Policy console, double-click User Account Control: Behavior Of The Elevation Prompt For Administrators In Admin Approval Mode.

12. From the drop-down list, select Elevate Without Prompting, as shown in Figure 5-15. Click OK.

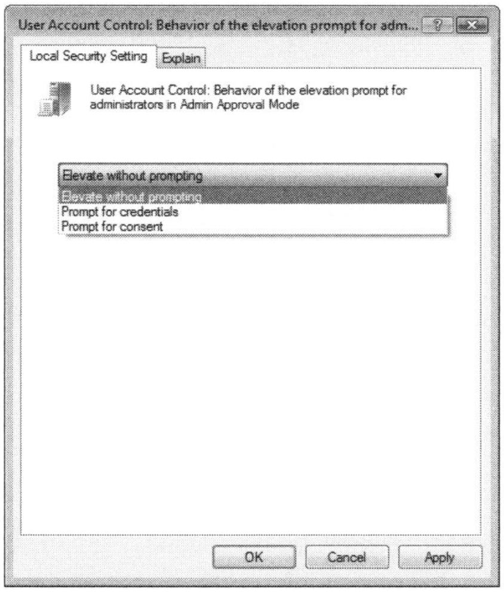

Figure 5-15 Specifying that an administrator account runs with elevated privileges without a prompt

13. Attempt to run an application file. You are now able to do this without receiving a UAC prompt and clicking Continue. The parent_admin account is automatically granted elevated credentials without a UAC warning.

14. Switch user to a standard user—for example, parent_standard.

15. Attempt to run an application file. In this instance there is no change to the user experience. A standard user needs to specify an administrator account and supply the password for that account.

16. Switch user to parent_admin.

17. In the Local Security Policy tool, double-click User Account Control: Behavior Of The Elevation Prompt For Administrators In Admin Approval Mode.

18. From the drop-down list, select Prompt For Credentials, as shown in Figure 5-16. Click OK.

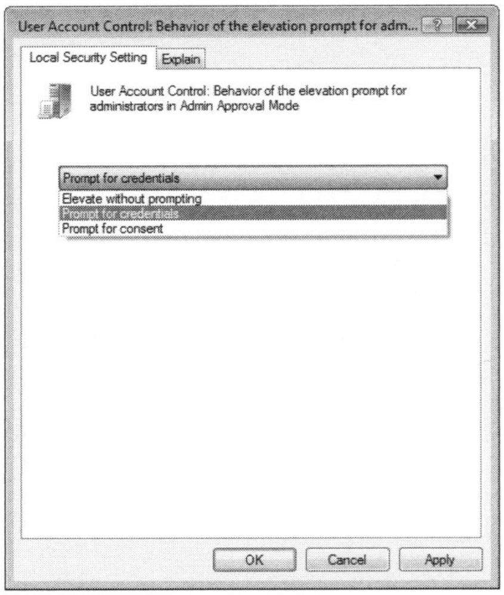

Figure 5-16 Specifying that an administrator needs to supply credentials

19. Attempt to run an application. You now need to supply an administrator password in order to continue. The same user experience occurs if you perform an administrative task such as changing system time. This setting does not affect the user experience of a standard user.

20. In the Local Security Policy console, double-click User Account Control: Behavior Of The Elevation Prompt For Administrators In Admin Approval Mode.

21. From the drop-down list, select Prompt For Consent (the default setting). Click OK.

22. In the Local Security Policy console, double-click User Account Control: Behavior Of The Elevation Prompt For Standard Users.

23. From the drop-down list, select Automatically Deny Elevation Requests, as shown in Figure 5-17. Click OK.

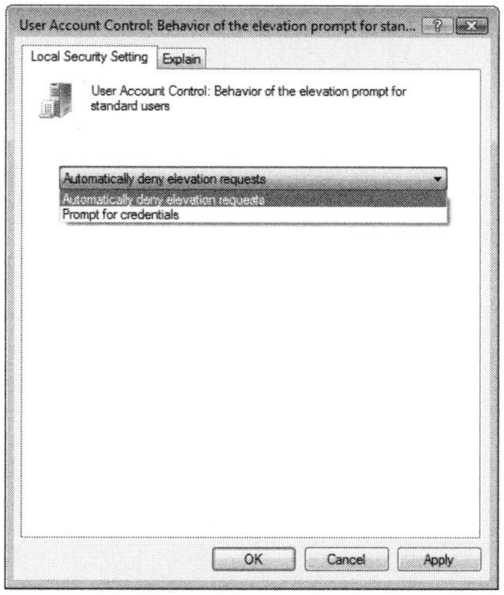

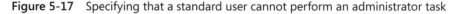

Figure 5-17   Specifying that a standard user cannot perform an administrator task

24. Switch user to parent_standard, and attempt to change the system time. You can no longer specify administrator credentials to elevate your privileges.

NOTE   Denying elevation requests

Although at first sight it seems that automatically denying elevation requests increases system security because standard users cannot perform administrator tasks, this setting also prevents an administrator from logging on with a standard account and temporarily elevating his or her privileges as required. It results in administrators always using administrator accounts. UAC mitigates this situation by ensuring that the administrator account runs most of the time with standard account privileges, but automatically denying elevation requests is not generally considered to be good security practice.

25. Switch user to parent_admin.

26. In the Local Security Policy console, double-click User Account Control: Behavior Of The Elevation Prompt For Standard Users.

27. From the drop-down list, select Prompt For Credentials. Click OK.

28. Use the procedures described in this practice to configure and test other UAC settings.

29. Disable the built-in Administrator account (Don_Hall). If you are not sure how to do this, see Practice 2.

▶ **Practice 4: Disabling Secure Desktop**

In this practice, you configure UAC settings to disable Secure Desktop. This lets you perform other tasks (for example, screen captures) while a UAC dialog box is open.

Do not attempt this practice until you have successfully completed Practices 1 and 2.

1. If necessary, log on by using the parent_admin account.
2. On the Start, All Programs menu, click Administrative Tools, and select Local Security Policy.
3. Click Continue in the UAC dialog box.
4. Expand Local Policies, and select Security Options.
5. Scroll down to the end of the list of policies. Double-click User Account Control: Switch To The Secure Desktop When Prompting For Elevation.
6. On the Local Security Setting tab, select Disabled, as shown in Figure 5-18. Click OK.

Figure 5-18   Disabling Secure Desktop

7. Perform an administrator task, such as changing system time, or run an application. The desktop is no longer dimmed, and you can perform other tasks when the UAC dialog box is on the screen.
8. Restore the setting to its default.

▶ **Practice 5: Disabling UAC**

In this practice you disable UAC. As a result, user accounts run in legacy Windows XP mode. You then reenable UAC. Do not attempt this practice until you have successfully completed Practices 1 and 2.

1. If necessary, log on by using the parent_admin account.
2. On the Start, All Programs menu, click Administrative Tools, and select Local Security Policy.
3. Click Continue in the UAC dialog box.
4. Expand Local Policies, and select Security Options.
5. Scroll down to the end of the list of policies. Double-click Run All Administrators In Admin Approval Mode.
6. On the Local Security Setting tab, select Disabled, as shown in Figure 5-19. Click OK.

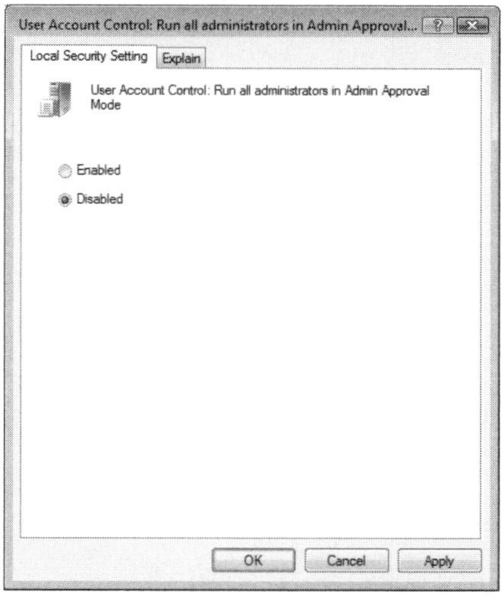

Figure 5-19   Disabling UAC

7. Access the Windows Security Center by clicking Security in the Control Panel. As shown in Figure 5-20, Windows Vista warns you that User Account Control is turned off.

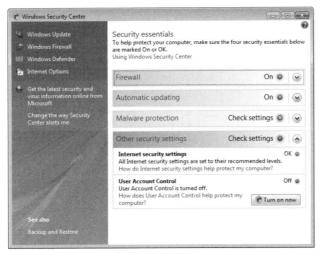

Figure 5-20 Disabling UAC compromises system security

8. Close all windows and reboot the computer.

9. Log on by using the parent_admin account.

10. Perform an administrator task, such as changing system time, or run an application. The parent_admin account is now running continuously with elevated privileges, and you no longer need to give permission to continue.

11. Switch user to parent_standard.

12. Attempt to perform an administrator task, such as changing system time, or run an application. As Figure 5-21 demonstrates, a user logged on with a standard account cannot perform administrator tasks and is not prompted for administrator credentials.

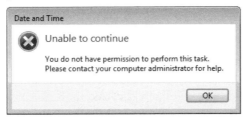

Figure 5-21 A standard user can no longer supply administrator credentials

13. Switch user to parent_admin.
14. Restore the Run All Administrators In Admin Approval mode setting to Enabled.
15. Restore to their defaults any other UAC settings that you have changed.
16. Close all windows and reboot the computer.

Optional Practice: Configuring Legacy Software to Run In Windows Vista

In this practice session, you use the Windows Vista Program Compatibility Wizard to configure legacy software so that it runs in Windows Vista. You should carry out this practice only if you have legacy software—typically, a third-party program—that you want to run in Windows Vista. If you have no such requirement, you do not need to perform the practice. If in the future you need to run such software or if a user you are supporting has this requirement, then you can do the practice.

▶ **Practice 1: Running the Program Compatibility Wizard**

In this practice you use the Program Compatibility Wizard. The practice also demonstrates that you can often run a utility from the same Windows Vista Help and Support screen that you use to obtain information about it.

1. If necessary, log on using the parent_admin account.
2. Locate the software that you want to run. Typically, this will be on an installation CD-ROM or possibly in the Windows.old subdirectory. The software must not be an anti-virus program, a disk utility, or any other system program.
3. In Windows Vista Help And Support, search for "Compatibility Wizard."
4. Click the Start The Program Compatibility Wizard link.
5. Click the Click To Open The Program Compatibility Wizard link.
6. The Welcome page appears. Click Next.
7. Select an option from the page shown in Figure 5-22. The option you select depends on the location of your legacy software. If in doubt, select I Want To Locate The Program Manually, click Next, and then click Browse.

Figure 5-22   Selecting a program location

8. Select the legacy program you want to run, as shown in Figure 5-23. Your legacy program will almost certainly be different from the one shown in the figure. Click Next.

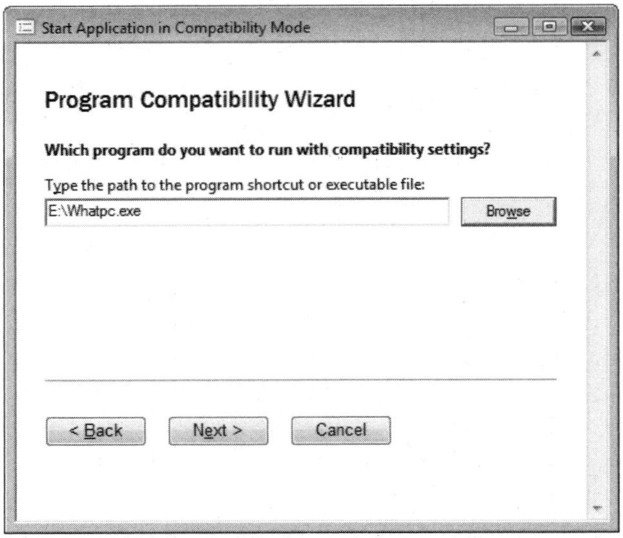

Figure 5-23   Selecting a program

9. Select the OS that is recommended for the program or that previously successfully supported the program. Click Next.

10. Specify display settings, as shown in Figure 5-24. Click Next.

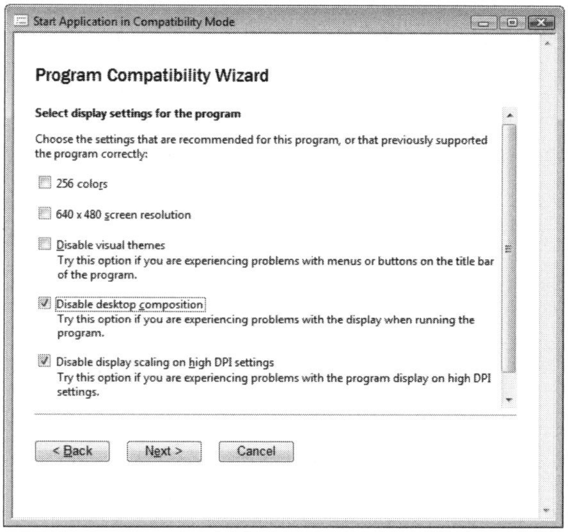

Figure 5-24   Specifying display settings for legacy software

11. Many legacy programs (unfortunately) can run only in the context of an administrator account. If this is the case with your legacy program, select the Run This Program As An Administrator check box. Click Next.

12. If you are happy with your settings, click Next.

13. In the UAC dialog box, click Allow.

14. If you have configured the settings correctly, the legacy program should run. If it is an installation program, you can install the software.

15. You are prompted to inform Windows Vista whether the compatibility settings you configured were satisfactory, as shown in Figure 5-25. If so, select Yes, Set This Program To Always Use These Compatibility Settings. Click Next.

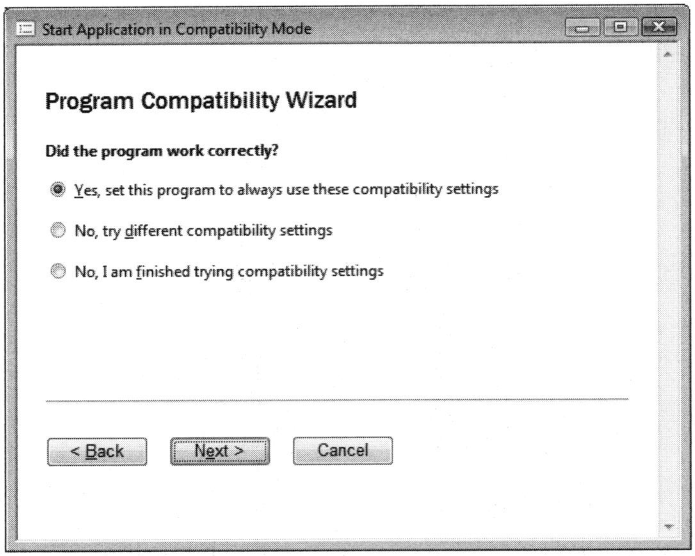

Figure 5-25 Setting the legacy program to use the specified settings

16. If you want to, send information about your program compatibility settings to Microsoft. Select either Yes or No, and then click Next.

17. Click Finish to close the wizard.

Lesson Summary

- You can use the Program Compatibility Wizard to run legacy programs in Windows Vista. Where such programs write to protected areas, Windows Vista sets up directories in the user profile to clone the protected areas.

- By default, UAC ensures that an administrator account runs without elevated privileges except when such privileges are required to perform an administrator task. The user grants permission for this to happen.

- A standard user is, by default, prompted to supply administrator credentials if he or she attempts to perform an administrator task.

- The built-in Administrator account is disabled by default. When enabled, it does not, by default, use UAC and always runs with elevated privileges.

- You can configure UAC settings to change the user experience of administrators, standard users, and the built-in Administrator.

- You can configure UAC settings to change how Windows Vista handles unsigned application files and UIAccess applications.

- You can disable Secure Desktop. You can also disable UAC entirely, but this is not recommended.

Lesson Review

You can use the following questions to test your knowledge of the information in Lesson 1, "Configuring and Troubleshooting User Account Control." The questions are also available on the companion CD if you prefer to review them in electronic form.

NOTE   Answers

Answers to these questions and explanations of why each answer choice is correct or incorrect are located in the "Answers" section at the end of the book.

---

1. Ian McLean is writing Chapter 5 of a book about Windows Vista. He wants to generate a figure that shows a UAC dialog box. He has not changed any UAC settings. He logs on with the administrator account he created when he installed Windows Vista and attempts to change the system time. When the UAC dialog box appears, he presses Print Screen, and then clicks Cancel to close the box. He opens Microsoft Paint and selects the Edit menu, but Paste is not available. What has he done wrong?

    A. He should not have clicked Cancel on the UAC dialog box.

    B. He should have disabled Secure Desktop.

    C. He should have logged on as a standard user. UAC does not apply to administrators.

    D. He should have logged on with another administrator account. UAC does not apply to the administrator account that he created when he installed Windows Vista.

2. What setting disables UAC?

    A. User Account Control: Run All Administrators In Admin Approval Mode is Disabled

    B. User Account Control: Run All Administrators In Admin Approval Mode is Enabled

    C. User Account Control: Behavior Of The Elevation Prompt For Administrators In Admin Approval Mode is set to Elevate without prompting

    D. User Account Control: Behavior Of The Elevation Prompt For Administrators In Admin Approval Mode is set to Prompt For Credentials

3. You want to ensure that legacy applications that attempt to write to protected parts of the registry or file system cannot run in Windows Vista. What UAC setting do you configure?

    A. User Account Control: Only Elevate Executables That Are Signed And Validated is Enabled

    B. User Account Control: Only Elevate Executables That Are Signed And Validated is Disabled

    C. User Account Control: Virtualize File And Registry Write Failures To Per-User Locations is Enabled

    D. User Account Control: Virtualize File And Registry Write Failures To Per-User Locations is Disabled

4. You want to configure UAC settings. You open Local Security Policy from the Administrative Tools menu and expand Security Settings. How do you access the UAC settings?

    A. Expand Local Policies, and select Security Options.

    B. Expand Local Policies, and select Audit Policy.

    C. Expand Local Policies, and select User Rights Assignment.

    D. Select Software Restriction Policies.

5. You have installed Windows Vista Ultimate on a computer that is part of a workgroup. Which of the following UAC settings are enabled by default? (Choose all that apply.)

    A. User Account Control: Admin Approval Mode For The Built-In Administrator Account

    B. User Account Control: Virtualize File And Registry Write Failures To Per-User Locations

    C. User Account Control: Only Elevate Executables That Are Signed And Validated

    D. User Account Control: Only Elevate UIAccess Applications That Are Installed In Secure Locations

    E. User Account Control: Run All Administrators In Admin Approval Mode

    F. User Account Control: Switch To The Secure Desktop When Prompting For Elevation

6. You are having difficulty running a legacy Windows 95 program in Windows Vista. You discover that the program will run only in the context of an administrator account. How do you run this program?

    A. You cannot run legacy programs that run only in the context of an administrator account.

    B. You need to enable the User Account Control: Virtualize File And Registry Write Failures To Per-User Locations setting.

    C. You need to run the Program Compatibility Wizard and select the Run This Program As An Administrator check box.

    D. You need to enable the User Account Control: Only Elevate Executables That Are Signed And Validated setting.

Chapter Review

To further practice and reinforce the skills you learned in this chapter, you can perform the following tasks:

- Review the chapter summary.
- Review the list of key terms introduced in this chapter.
- Complete the case scenarios. These scenarios set up real-world situations involving the topics of this chapter and ask you to create a solution.
- Complete the suggested practices.
- Take a practice test.

Chapter Summary

- UAC ensures that user accounts runs without elevated privileges unless the task the user wants to carry out requires such privileges. By default, administrators grant permission for this to happen while standard users need to supply the credentials of an administrator account. UAC does not apply to the built-in Administrator account by default.
- Windows Vista permits legacy software that attempts to write to protected areas by virtualizing these areas in the user's profile. You can use the Program Compatibility Wizard to run legacy programs that have compatibility issues.
- UAC settings determine how Windows Vista handles unsigned application files and UIAccess applications and whether Secure Desktop is enabled when a UAC dialog box is generated.

Key Terms

Do you know what these key terms mean? You can check your answers by looking up the terms in the glossary at the end of the book.

- access token
- account escalation
- Admin Approval mode
- administrator application
- context
- credentials
- digitally signed
- legacy programs
- local Administrators group

- privileges
- Secure Desktop
- User Account Control (UAC)

Case Scenarios

In the following case scenarios, you will apply what you have learned about configuring and troubleshooting UAC and running legacy applications. You can find answers to these questions in the "Answers" section at the end of this book.

Case Scenario 1: Giving Advice On User Account Control

You are an IT professional for a company that provides equipment for home and small business users. Your company's customer installations typically consist of between four and eight workstations configured as a workgroup. Your company has recently been supplying workstations that run Windows Vista, and you have been asked to give advice about UAC. Answer the following questions:

1. Don Hall, the Chief Executive of Margie's Travel, is not convinced about UAC. He wants to know why he, as an administrator, needs to click Continue every time he wants to perform an administrator-level task. What do you tell him?

2. Don is unconvinced. As an administrator he wants to be able to perform all tasks without prompting. What setting can he change to accomplish this with the least impact on network security?

3. Don does not want any users logged on with standard accounts to be able to change configurations that affect any other user. As an IT professional, part of whose job specification is to advise on security, what do you tell him? If he insists on reconfiguring UAC, how best can he achieve his objectives with the least impact on network security?

4. Don wants to make the minimum number of changes to UAC configuration while assuring that he, as an administrator, is not prompted to give permission while performing administrative tasks while standard users are prohibited from initiating such tasks. How can Don reconfigure UAC to meet this goal, and what warning would you give?

Case Scenario 2: Running Legacy Programs

As an IT professional providing customer support, you need to advise customers about running legacy programs. Answer the following questions:

1. Kim Ackers wants to prohibit any legacy program that attempts to write to protected registry locations from running. What UAC setting should she configure?

2. Don Hall cannot run a legacy program because it needs to run with a full administrator access token. How can he run the program?

3. You have a legacy virus protection program that you want to run in Windows Vista. You have read that the Windows Vista Program Compatibility Wizard can help configure legacy software so it can run. Should you use this wizard in this instance? If not, why not?

Suggested Practices

To help you successfully master the exam objectives presented in this chapter, complete the following tasks.

Configure and Troubleshoot User Account Control

■ **Practice: Investigate Additional UAC Settings**   The first practice session in this chapter asks you to reconfigure the UAC settings most commonly changed and investigate the results. Reconfigure the settings not specified in the practices and investigate the results.

Configure Legacy Programs to Run in Windows Vista

■ **Practice: Locate and Configure Legacy Programs**   Locate some legacy programs. If you or some friends and colleagues have old software installation CD-ROMs for Windows 95, Windows 98, or Windows ME, you can use setup programs on those disks. Configure the software so it runs in Windows Vista.

Take a Practice Test

The practice tests on this book's companion CD offer many options. For example, you can test yourself on just one exam objective, or you can test yourself on all the 70-620 certification exam content. You can set up the test so that it closely simulates the experience of taking a certification exam, or you can set it up in study mode so that you can look at the correct answers and explanations after you answer each question.

MORE INFO   Practice tests

For details about all the practice test options available, see the "How to Use the Practice Tests" section in this book's Introduction.

Chapter 6
Configuring Internet Explorer Security

Any computer that accesses the Internet comes under attack when a user browses webpages. Spyware can be covertly installed on your computer, often when you download and install other programs, such as music or video file sharing programs. It can generate annoying advertisements (this type of spyware is sometimes called adware), collect personal information, or change the configuration of your computer, generally without your consent.

Eliminating all spyware is exceptionally difficult. However, Microsoft Windows Defender, which ships with Windows Vista, can scan for, identify, and eliminate most spyware. In this chapter, you learn how to configure Windows Defender, update your spyware definitions, and manage applications by using the Software Explorer feature.

Spyware is only one of the several ways that your computer can be attacked while browsing the Internet. Internet Explorer 7+ (IE7+) offers a number of features that dynamically protect you from unwanted Internet content and other attacks. You can invoke protected mode, block pop-up windows, configure security zones and privacy settings, manage add-ons, and configure the phishing filter service. Phishing is a type of scam that attempts to lure Internet users into disclosing personal information, such as their social security numbers, bank account details, or credit card numbers.

Exam objectives in this chapter:
- Configure Windows Defender.
- Configure Dynamic Security for Internet Explorer 7.

Lessons in this chapter:

Before You Begin

To complete the lessons in this chapter, you must have done the following:

- Installed Windows Vista Ultimate on a personal computer, as described in Chapter 1, "Installing Windows Vista Client," and Chapter 2, "Windows Vista Upgrades and Migrations."

- Created an administrator account and standard accounts and enabled the Run command on the Start menu, as described in Practices 1, 2, and 3 of Chapter 4, "Configuring and Troubleshooting Internet Access," Lesson 1, "Configuring and Troubleshooting Parental Controls and Content Advisor."

No additional configuration is required for this chapter.

Real World

Ian McLean

Not all software that generates advertisements or tracks your online activities is necessarily unauthorized. For example, you might sign up for a free music service and consent to receive targeted advertisements as part of your agreement. Removing the software that generates the advertising would breach your agreement and result in your no longer being able to download music files. Always read download agreements carefully and be wary of anything that is offered "for free."

Lesson 1: Configuring Windows Defender

Windows Defender helps protect your computer against pop-ups, slow performance, and security threats caused by spyware and other unwanted software. It features real-time protection and a monitoring system that recommends actions against spyware when it is detected. It also minimizes interruptions and helps you stay productive.

As an information technology (IT) professional, you should run antispyware software such as Windows Defender regularly. You would find it extremely embarrassing and unprofessional if your own machine became seriously infected. However, your first duty is to protect your colleagues by ensuring that Windows Defender is correctly configured on their machines. You might also provide help desk support to customers, possibly as part of a warranty agreement, and advise them on how best to protect their systems.

Spyware and other potentially unwanted software can attempt to install itself any time you connect to the Internet. It can also infect your computer when you install some programs using a CD-ROM, DVD-ROM, or other removable media. Unwanted or malicious software (malware) can also run at unexpected times, not only when it is installed.

This lesson explores Windows Defender features—for example, real-time protection, IE7+ integration, and Software Explorer. It describes how you configure custom scans, update your spyware definitions, and address definition update issues. It looks at the facilities that Windows Defender provides for managing applications.

> **After this lesson, you will be able to:**
> - Configure Windows Defender real-time protection.
> - Configure and run a custom scan.
> - Schedule a scan and specify actions to be taken based on the alert level of potential threats.
> - Schedule spyware definition updates.
> - Troubleshoot definition update issues and spyware removal.
> - Use Software Explorer to manage applications.
>
> **Estimated lesson time: 50 minutes**

Real-Time Protection

Windows Defender provides real-time protection whether or not you have opened the Windows Defender program from the All Programs menu and whether or not you are logged on. Windows Defender real-time protection alerts you when spyware or potentially unwanted software attempts to install or run on your computer. It also alerts you when programs attempt to change important Windows settings. Not all programs are necessarily malicious, and real-time protection provides a number of alert levels, as listed in Table 6-1.

Table 6-1   Windows Defender Real-Time Protection Alert Levels

Alert Level	What Has Been Detected	What You Need To Do
Severe	Widespread or exceptionally malicious programs—for example, viruses, Trojan horses, or worms—that affect your privacy and the security of your computer and could damage your computer.	Remove this software immediately.
High	Programs that potentially collect personal information and affect your privacy or damage your computer—for example, by changing settings without your knowledge or consent.	Remove this software immediately.
Medium	Programs that potentially affect your privacy or make changes to your computer that could affect your computing experience—for example, by collecting personal information or by changing settings.	Review the alert details to see why the software was detected. If you do not like the way that the software operates or if you do not recognize and trust the publisher, consider blocking or removing the software.
Low	Software that might collect information about you or your computer or change how your computer works but is operating in agreement with licensing terms displayed when you installed the software.	This software is typically benign when it runs on your computer, unless it was installed without your knowledge. If you are unsure whether to allow it, review the alert details or check to see if you recognize and trust the publisher of the software.
Not yet classified	Programs that are typically benign unless they are installed on your computer without your knowledge.	If you recognize and trust the software, allow it to run. If you do not recognize the software or the publisher, review the alert details to decide what action to take. If you are a SpyNet community member, check the community ratings to see if other users trust the software.

Depending on the alert level, you can choose one of the following actions:

- **Ignore**   Allows the software to be installed or run on your computer. If the software is still running during the next scan or if the software tries to change security-related settings on your computer, Windows Defender will alert you about this software again.
- **Quarantine**   Moves the software to another location on your computer and then prevents the software from running until you choose to restore it to its original location or remove it.
- **Remove**   Permanently deletes the software.
- **Always Allow**   Adds the software to the Windows Defender allowed list and allows it to run on your computer. Windows Defender no longer alerts you to risks that this software might pose. You should add software to the allowed list only if you trust both the software and the software publisher.

Windows Defender real-time protection also alerts you if software attempts to change important Windows settings. In this case, the software is already running on your computer and you can choose one of the following actions:

- **Permit**   Allows the software to change security-related settings on your computer.
- **Deny**   Prevents the software from changing security-related settings on your computer.

Quick Check

- You receive a Windows Defender real-time protection alert that warns you that a potentially malicious program is attempting to run on your computer. You can choose one of several options. What choices do you have?

Quick Check Answer

- Ignore
- Quarantine
- Remove
- Always Allow

You can configure real-time protection by clicking Tools in Windows Defender, clicking Options, and scrolling to the Real-Time Protection Options settings, as shown in Figure 6-1.

Figure 6-1   Real-Time Protection Options dialog box

In the dialog box shown in Figure 6-1, you can choose the software and settings that you want Windows Defender real-time protection to monitor. However, Microsoft recommends that you use all of the real-time protection options, called agents. For this reason, the practice session later in this lesson does not ask you to reconfigure real-time options. Table 6-2 lists these agents and states the purpose of each.

Table 6-2   Windows Defender Real-Time Protection Agents

Real-Time Protection Agent	Purpose
Auto Start	Monitors programs that are allowed to automatically run when you start your computer. Spyware and other malware are often configured to run automatically when Windows starts, enabling them to run without your knowledge and collect information. Programs configured in this way can also make your computer start or run slowly.
System Configuration (Settings)	Monitors security-related settings in Windows. Spyware and other malware can change hardware and software security settings and then collect information that can be used to further undermine security.
Internet Explorer Add-ons	Monitors programs that automatically run when you start IE7+. Spyware and other malware can masquerade as web browser add-ons and run without your knowledge.

Table 6-2   Windows Defender Real-Time Protection Agents

Real-Time Protection Agent	Purpose
Internet Explorer Configurations (Settings)	Monitors browser security settings, which are your first line of defense against Internet attacks. Spyware and other malware can try to change these settings without your knowledge.
Internet Explorer Downloads	Monitors files and programs that are designed to work with IE7+, such as ActiveX controls and software installation programs. The browser itself can download, install, or run these files. Spyware and other malware can be included with these files and installed without your knowledge.
Services and Drivers	Monitors services and drivers. Because services and drivers perform essential computer functions, they have access to important routines in the operating system (OS). Spyware and other malware can use services and drivers to gain access to your computer or to run undetected on your computer as if they are normal OS components.
Application Execution	Monitors when programs start and any operations they perform while running. Spyware and other malware can use vulnerabilities in programs that you have installed to run without your knowledge. Windows Defender real-time protection monitors your programs and alerts you if it detects suspicious activity.
Application Registration	Monitors tools and files in the OS. Programs that purport to be part of the OS can run at any time, not just when you start Windows or another program. Spyware and other malware can register programs to start without notice and run, for example, at a scheduled time each day without your knowledge.
Windows Add-ons	Monitors Windows add-on programs (also known as software utilities). Add-ons are designed to enhance your computing experience in areas such as security, browsing, productivity, and multimedia. However, add-ons can also install programs that collect information about you or your online activities and expose sensitive personal information—often to advertisers.

MORE INFO   Windows Defender real-time protection

For more information, search Windows Help and Support for "Understanding Windows Defender real-time protection."

The SpyNet Community

The online Microsoft SpyNet community helps you see how other people respond to software that has not yet been classified for risks. If you can determine whether other community members allow or block software, this can help you choose whether to allow it on your computer. If you participate in the community, your choices are in turn added to the community ratings to help other people choose what to do.

Spyware is continually being developed, and SpyNet ratings help Microsoft determine which software to investigate. For example, if members of the community identify suspicious software that has not yet been classified, Microsoft will analyze the software, determine if it is spyware, and, if needed, update the Windows Defender definitions. Up-to-date definitions help Windows Defender detect the latest spyware threats and prevent spyware from infecting your computer. Even if software is not spyware, Windows Defender alerts you if it detects that software is operating in a way that might be malicious or unwanted.

If you join SpyNet, Windows Defender automatically sends information to Microsoft about spyware, potentially unwanted software, and software that has not yet been analyzed for risks. The actions that are applied to the software are also reported to Microsoft.

To join the Microsoft SpyNet community, you open Windows Defender from the Start, All Programs menu, click Tools, and then click Microsoft SpyNet. On the resulting window, shown in Figure 6-2, you can select your level of participation or decide that you do not want to participate. By default, you are registered with a basic membership. If you want to change this, select one of the other options and click Save. You need to supply administrator credentials or, if you are an administrator, click Continue in the User Access Control (UAC) dialog box.

Figure 6-2   Selecting the level of SpyNet participation

If Windows Defender subsequently detects software on your computer that has not yet been classified for risks, you might be asked to send a sample of the software to Microsoft SpyNet for analysis. In this case, Windows Defender displays a list of files that can help analysts determine if the software is malicious. You can choose to send some or all of the files in the list.

If you suspect that a file or program on your computer might be spyware, you can send it to Microsoft by following the online instructions at *http://www.microsoft.com/athome /security/spyware/software/support/reportspyware.mspx.*

If Windows Defender alerts you about software that you do not believe to be malicious or unwanted, you can report this to Microsoft by completing the False Positive report form at *http://www.microsoft.com/athome/security/spyware/software/isv/fpform.aspx.*

Internet Explorer Integration

Windows Defender integrates with IE7+ to enable files to be scanned when they are downloaded. This helps ensure that a user does not accidentally download malicious software. Windows Defender can block suspicious downloaded files when you attempt to execute them. If, for example, you manually choose to install an IE7+ add-on or other type of Web download and Windows Defender has marked the file as suspicious, it blocks that installation.

The Windows Defender service runs constantly in the background regardless of which type of user account you are using or whether you have opened the application from the All Programs menu. It also works when no one is logged on. Windows Defender attempts to work mainly in the background like any other integrated IE7+ component, requiring as little user intervention and generating as few pop-ups as possible. The developers have made a genuine attempt to make the application less annoying than the spyware it blocks.

Windows Defender also integrates tightly with Microsoft's PC health subscription service, Windows Live OneCare, and with the SpyNet community. The SpyNet community was described earlier in this chapter.

Windows Live OneCare

Windows Live OneCare is a subscription service, so you need to pay for it. It integrates tightly with Windows Defender and extends the protection that Windows Defender provides. Windows Live OneCare helps protect your computer and provides automated optimization features that should keep your PC running at its optimum speed. It also regularly backs up files and settings to CD-ROM, DVD-ROM, or external hard disk.

The service provides virus and spyware scanners and a managed, two-way firewall. These features help protect your computer from viruses, worms, Trojan horses, hackers, and other threats. It runs continuously in the background, but you can scan individual files and folders for viruses on demand. You can also scan attachments you receive through Windows Live Messenger or MSN Messenger.

Windows Live OneCare regularly defragments your computer's hard disk and removes any unnecessary files. It helps ensure that important security updates from Microsoft are installed efficiently and on time.

Finally, the service provides an online help service available 24 hours a day, 7 days a week.

> **CAUTION   Online help services can sometimes fail**
>
> A 24-hours-a-day, 7-days-a-week online help service implies that no service downtime is scheduled. However, an online service can sometimes fail for reasons that are outside the service provider's control. Do not, therefore, assume the service will always be available when you need it. If the service is down, wait for a while, and then try again.

Many of the services that Windows Live OneCare provides (backup, updates, virus scanning, spyware detection, and so on) are already available for free, but you need to configure and maintain them. It is unarguably convenient to have everything in the one package, but whether you choose to pay the subscription is up to you (or your employer). You can obtain more information about Windows Live OneCare at *http://www.windowsonecare.com/*.

NOTE   Further IE7+ integration

In Windows Defender Beta 1, users were able to use software explorers to browse downloaded ActiveX controls and track eraser activities (which erase all tracking of a user's Internet activity). The reason that Microsoft gives for removing the ActiveX and tracks eraser functionality is that this functionality is now found in IE7+. This is a further example of the tight integration between Windows Defender and IE7+.

Configuring Custom Scans

You can use Windows Defender to scan for spyware and other potentially unwanted software that might be installed on your computer, to schedule regular scans, and to automatically remove any malicious software that is detected during a scan.

You can choose to scan only specified locations on your computer. This is known as a custom scan. However, if a custom scan detects potentially unwanted or malicious software, Windows Defender then automatically runs a quick scan so it can remove the detected items from other areas of your computer if required.

You can configure a custom scan by opening Windows Defender, clicking the arrow next to the Scan button, and then clicking Custom Scan. You can then select Scan Selected Drives And Folders and click Select. The resulting dialog box is shown in Figure 6-3.

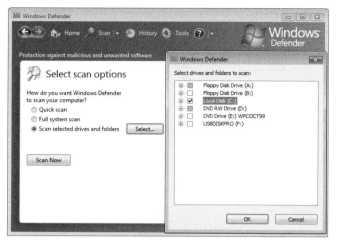

Figure 6-3   Configuring a custom scan

You can then select the drives and folders that you want to scan, click OK, and then click Scan Now. You configure a custom scan in the practice session later in this chapter.

Choosing Advanced Scanning Options

When you configure Windows Defender to scan your computer, you can select advanced options. You access these options by clicking Tools in Windows Defender, clicking Options, and scrolling to Advanced Options, as shown in Figure 6-4.

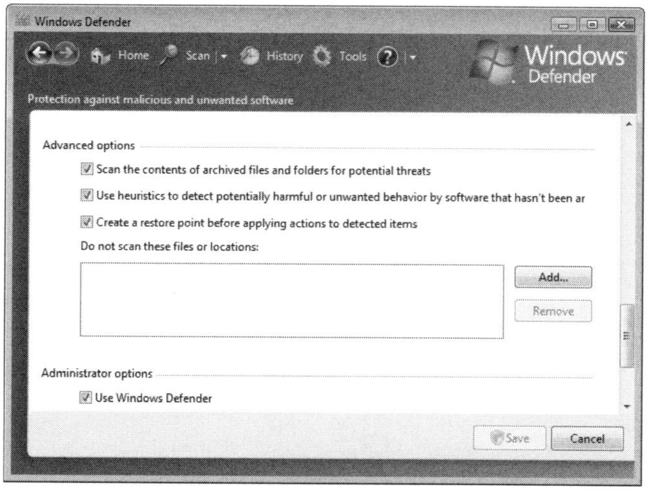

Figure 6-4   Specifying advanced scanning options

The following advanced options are available:

- **Scan The Contents Of Archived Files And Folders For Potential Threats** Scanning these locations might increase the time required to complete a scan, but spyware and other potentially unwanted software can install itself in these locations.

- **Use Heuristics To Detect Potentially Harmful Or Unwanted Behavior By Software That Has Not Been Analyzed For Risks** Windows Defender uses definition files to identify known threats, but it can use heuristics to detect and alert you about potentially harmful or unwanted software that is not yet listed in a definition file.

- **Create A Restore Point Before Applying Actions To Detected Items** Because you can set Windows Defender to automatically remove detected items, this option is provided to enable you to restore system settings if you want to use software that you did not intend to remove.

- **Do Not Scan These Files Or Locations** Use this option to specify any files and folders that you do not want Windows Defender to scan.

NOTE Heuristics

Heuristics is the application of experience-derived knowledge to a problem. Heuristics software looks for known sources, commonly used text phrases, and transmission or content patterns that experience has shown to be associated with potentially harmful or unwanted software. In simple terms, heuristics is what a program uses to obtain the best possible answer when it does not have enough information to guarantee a correct one.

Configuring Administrator Options

The Administrator Options section is located below the Advanced Scanning Options in the Windows Defender Options dialog box. If you select the Use Windows Defender check box, all users are alerted (if Windows Defender is on) when spyware or other potentially harmful software attempts to install or run on the computer. Windows Defender checks for new definitions, scans the computer regularly, and automatically removes harmful software. However, if only this option is selected, elevated privileges are required to configure Windows Defender and determine when scans occur.

If, in addition, you select the Allow Everyone To Use Windows Defender check box, this allows all users, including standard users, to scan the computer, configure how Windows Defender deals with potentially harmful software, and review all Windows Defender activities.

Scheduling Windows Defender Scans

You cannot schedule custom scans, but you can schedule either quick scans or full system scans. Microsoft recommends that you schedule a daily quick scan. This checks the areas of your computer that spyware and other potentially unwanted software is most likely to infect. If you want Windows Defender to check all files and programs on your computer, you can instead run or schedule a full scan.

Based upon the alert level, you can choose to automatically remove spyware and other potentially unwanted software if it is detected during a scan, to ignore items, or to perform a default action that Windows Defender determines based on the definition of the software it detects. Figure 6-5 shows the relevant dialog box, which you access by clicking Tools on the Windows Defender menu and then clicking Options. You perform this configuration in the practice session later in this chapter.

Figure 6-5   Scheduling scans and specifying actions depending upon the alert level

NOTE   Severe alert items

You cannot select a default action for software items with a severe alert rating because Windows Defender automatically removes such an item or alerts you to remove it. If software has not yet been classified for potential risks to your privacy or your computer, you need to review information about the software and then choose an action.

Working with Windows Defender Definitions

Definitions are files that identify and describe potential software threats. Windows Defender uses definitions to determine if software that it detects is spyware or other potentially unwanted software and then to alert you to potential risks. To help keep your definitions up-to-date, Windows Defender works with Windows Update to automatically install new definitions as they are released. You can also configure Windows Defender to check online for updated definitions before scanning.

Controlling Definition Downloads

When you use Windows Defender, you need to keep definitions up-to-date. Because spyware is continually being developed, Windows Defender relies on up-to-date definitions to determine if software that is trying to install, run, or change settings on your computer is potentially unwanted or malicious. Windows Defender works with your Windows Update settings to automatically install the latest definitions.

You can set Windows Vista to automatically install important and recommended updates or to install important updates only. Important updates can offer significant benefits, such as improved security and reliability. Recommended updates can address noncritical problems and help enhance your users' computing experience.

If you do not want Windows Vista to install updates automatically, you can instead configure a notification that warns you when your computer requires updates, so you can download and install them yourself. Alternatively, you can set Windows Vista to automatically download updates and then notify you so you can install them yourself.

To do this, you open Windows Update from the All Programs menu and click Change Settings. You can then select the automatic updating option that you want in the dialog box shown in Figure 6-6. These options apply to all Windows updates, not only to spyware definitions. To get important and recommended updates for your computer, select the Include Recommended Updates When Downloading, Installing, Or Notifying Me About Updates check box under Recommended Updates.

You can also automatically check for new spyware definitions before carrying out scheduled scans. To do this, you open Windows Defender, click Tools, and then click Options. You can then scroll to Automatic Scanning, ensure that the Automatically Scan My Computer (Recommended) check box is selected, and select the Check For Updated Definitions Before Scanning check box. This check box was shown in Figure 6-5. You then click Save and either supply administrator credentials or give permission to continue as prompted.

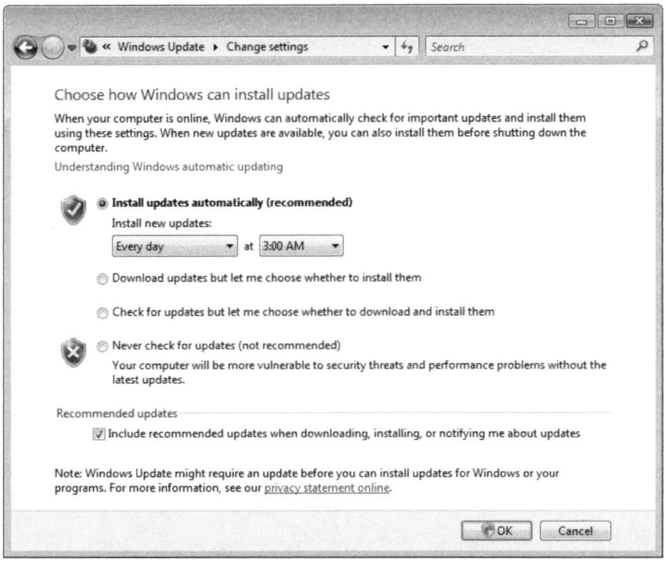

Figure 6-6   Selecting an update option

Troubleshooting Definition Update Issues

Issues related to definition updates typically occur if the updates are incorrectly configured and either are not downloaded at all or are downloaded but not installed. Issues can also arise if a user has mis-scheduled either Software Update or scheduled Windows Defender scan times. If the user has scheduled both update and scan times at 3:00 P.M. instead of 3:00 A.M., for example, the user could notice performance degradation in the middle of the afternoon. This becomes particularly inconvenient if a downloaded software update requires a reboot on installation, although this happens far less often with Windows Vista than with previous OSs. Conversely, problems can occur if a user schedules software updates and scans that require definition updates for a time when the computer is offline.

If a colleague or a customer reports update problems, or if a computer is found to be badly infected with spyware, your first task should be to check the Windows Defender and Software Update configurations to ensure that definitions are being downloaded and installed. In order to scan a computer for the latest threats, you might need to check for and download updated and new definitions manually. To do this, you open Windows Defender, click the arrow to the right of the Help button, and then click Check For Updates. As prompted, you need either to provide administrator credentials or click Continue. Windows Defender checks the definitions on the computer against an online database and notifies you if an update is required. You can then manually update the definitions.

NOTE   Optional updates

Optional updates are not downloaded or installed automatically. If you want to install optional updates, you need to do this manually.

Real World

Ian McLean

If a user you support does not want to update his or her software or spyware definitions automatically, possibly because that user connects to the Internet only intermittently through a dial-up connection, you should recommend frequent update checks (at least once per week). This can be a difficult situation, particularly if the user does not have administrator privileges and you need to supply administrator credentials every time an update is needed. When you are dealing with inexperienced or unsophisticated users, this is much less a technical problem than a people problem.

Such users are often nervous about "things" happening on their computer while they are asleep. They are typically unsure about allowing their workstations to be updated automatically when they are not using them. They are particularly worried if, when they start working with their computer in the morning, they are told it requires a reboot (although this happens less often with Windows Vista than with other OSs). If they have left work unsaved on the computer overnight, this can compound the problem.

As a support technician and an administrator, you need people skills as well as technical skills. You need to convince users that they should let operations such as updates happen automatically and tactfully warn them of the consequences of a malware infection on their computer. Automatic updates at nonpeak times make life easier for the users you support—and for you.

As far as persuading your users to back up their work regularly and especially before they leave their machines last thing in the afternoon or evening is concerned—any administrator will tell you that's the hardest job of all!

You can quickly obtain information about whether Windows Defender is protecting a computer, whether automatic updating is configured, and other security information by clicking Security in Control Panel and opening the Windows Security Center, as shown in Figure 6-7. The Windows Security Center provides links that let you configure Windows Defender, Windows Firewall, Windows Update, and Internet settings as well as links to the Windows Help and Support files that describe these settings.

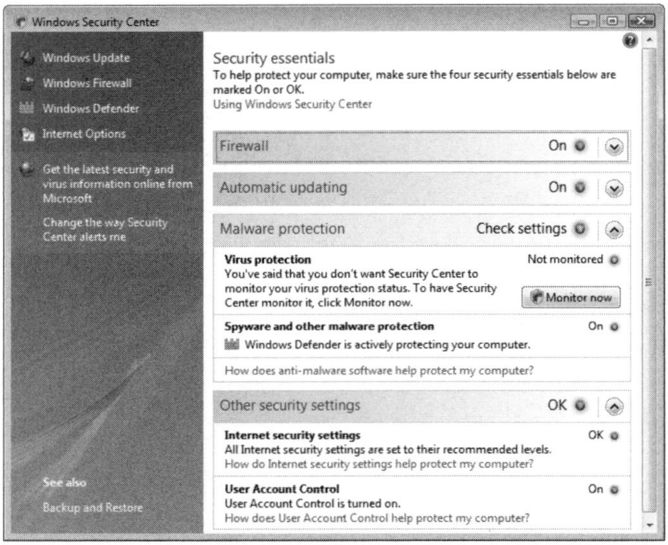

Figure 6-7   The Windows Security Center

You can obtain information about Windows Defender activities by opening Windows Defender and clicking History. The Windows Defender History window is shown in Figure 6-8. From this window, you can obtain information about when Windows Defender scanned a computer, what items were allowed, and what items were quarantined. Optionally, you can clear the history records.

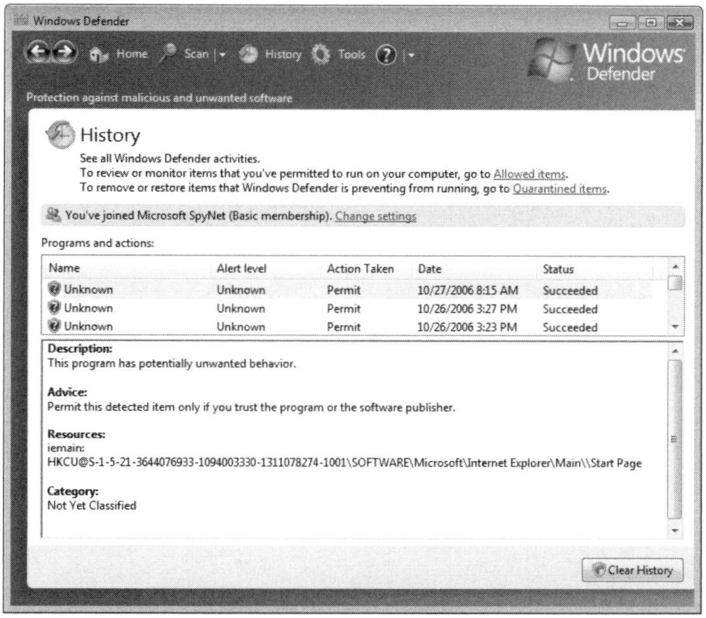

Figure 6-8 Windows Defender History

Troubleshooting Spyware Removal

Spyware can sometimes infect areas of your computer (for example, the boot sector or system files) that are difficult to clean without causing further problems. If Windows Defender informs you that it cannot remove spyware automatically and you cannot remove it manually by following any directions that Windows Defender might provide, you can click Uninstall A Program In Control Panel and remove any programs that you do not believe should be on your computer.

You should use this method very carefully. Control Panel lists many programs, most of which are not spyware, and some spyware programs use special installation methods to avoid showing up in the list. If the spyware program offers an uninstall option, you should remove it with this method. Take care to remove only those programs you can positively identify as spyware. Do not remove programs that you might want to keep, even if you use them infrequently. If you are not sure what a program does or why it is on your system, try typing its filename into a search engine.

MORE INFO   Uninstalling programs

For more information about uninstalling programs, search for "Uninstall or change a program" in Windows Help and Support.

Some spyware can hide so well that it cannot be removed, either through Windows Defender or by uninstalling programs. If you still see evidence of spyware after trying these methods, you can try rolling back to a restore point. If this does not work, you might need to reinstall your OS.

Rolling back to a restore point might remove malware, but it will also undo any changes you made and delete any software you installed since you created the restore point. Reinstalling Windows Vista removes spyware but also deletes your files and programs. In either case, make sure that you back up your documents and files and that you have access to the installation discs you will need to reinstall your programs.

Evidence of Spyware

Windows Defender and other antispyware programs can detect most spyware and remove most of what it detects. However, even if Windows Defender tells you your system is clean, spyware could still be lurking somewhere. You might have some form of spyware on your computer if you notice any of the following:

- You see new toolbars, links, or favorites that you did not add to your web browser.
- Your home page, mouse pointer, or search program changes unexpectedly.
- You type the address for a website but are taken to a different website without notice.
- You see pop-up advertisements, even when you are not accessing the Internet.
- Your computer suddenly starts running slower than usual.

If you see any or all of these symptoms and Windows Defender does not detect spyware, ensure that your spyware definitions are up-to-date and run a full system scan. If the spyware cannot be removed, you might need to delete it manually (if you can find it) or, as a last resort, reinstall the OS.

Managing Applications by Using Software Explorer

You can use Software Explorer—or, to be accurate, a series of software explorers—in Windows Defender to view detailed information about software that is currently running on your computer and to distinguish between legitimate applications and executable code that can affect your privacy or your computer's security. You can discover, for example, which programs run automatically when you start Windows, and you can obtain information about how these programs interact with Windows programs and services.

You access Software Explorer by opening Windows Defender, clicking Tools, and then clicking Software Explorer. If you are logged on with a standard user account, you can use Software Explorer to view and manage the programs that you use. If you want to view and manage programs and other software for all users on the computer, you can click Show For All Users. In this case, you are, by default, prompted to select an administrator account and supply a password. If you are logged on as an administrator, you need to give Software Explorer permission to run with elevated privileges by clicking Continue. The resulting dialog box is shown in Figure 6-9.

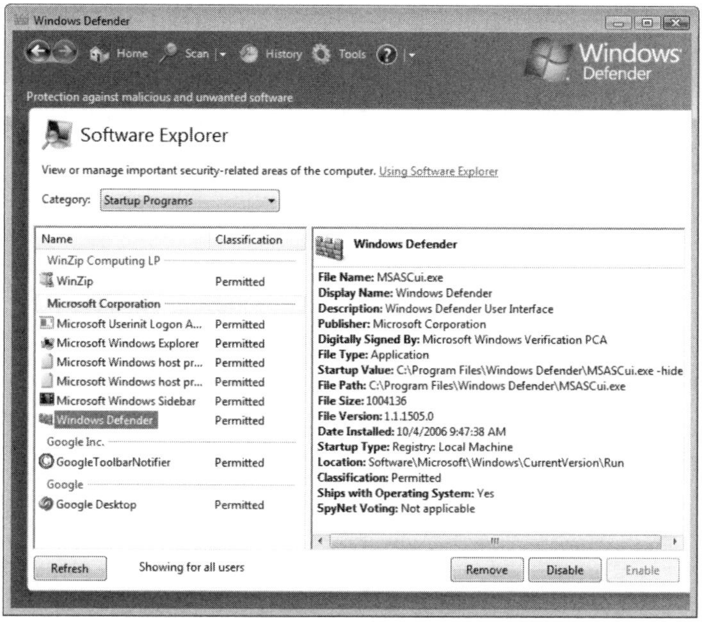

Figure 6-9 Software Explorer

NOTE   Show For All Users

The Show For All Users button will not appear if you have only one user account enabled on your Windows Vista PC. If you do not see this button, create additional accounts as described in Chapter 4 and log on at least once with one of these accounts.

If you are an administrator, the ability to manage programs for all other users of a computer is an important feature. Software Explorer is a component of Windows Defender, and its main purpose is to detect spyware and other malware that, for example, runs automatically when you start Windows. However, it is convenient, particularly in a computer that has multiple users, to be able to view all the software on a computer and obtain information about each application.

Exam Tip   The Show For All Users feature in Software Explorer might not appear—for example, it can be disabled in the enterprise environment. However, the 70-620 exam tests your knowledge of Windows Vista Ultimate in a small office/home office (SOHO) or stand-alone environment, and you need to know that this feature exists and that it requires elevated privileges.

Software Explorer helps you monitor the following items, which you can select from the Category drop-down list in the Software Explorer dialog box:

- **Startup Programs**   Programs that run automatically with or without the user's knowledge when Windows starts.
- **Currently Running Programs**   Programs that are currently running on the screen or in the background.
- **Network Connected Programs**   Programs or processes that can connect to the Internet or to a home or office network.
- **Windows Sockets (Winsock) Service Providers**   Programs that perform low-level networking and communication services for Windows and programs that run on Windows. These programs often have access to important areas of the OS.

For each type of item (which, in effect, has its own software explorer), every element is rated as "Permitted," "Not yet classified" or "Potentially Unwanted." The first and last categories carry a link that lets you learn more about the particular item. The second category invites you to submit the program to SpyNet for further analysis.

Displaying Software Explorer Details

Software Explorer displays basic information about programs—for example, the program name, publisher, and version. Depending on the type of software you choose in the category list, you might also see the information listed in Table 6-3.

Table 6-3   Information Returned by Software Explorer

Title	Description
Auto Start	Indicates whether the program is registered to start automatically when Windows starts.
Startup Type	The location where the program is registered to start automatically when Windows starts–for example, in the registry or the All Users Startup folder.
Ships With Operating System	Indicates if the program was installed as part of Windows–for example, Windows Defender ships with Windows Vista.
Classification	Indicates whether the program has been analyzed for risks to your privacy and the security of the computer.
Digitally Signed By	Indicates if the software has been signed and, if so, the publisher that signed it. If the publisher is not on the trusted publishers list and is not a source you trust, you need to obtain more details (for example, from SpyNet) before deciding whether you trust the software.

Quick Check

A Windows Defender scan has located an unclassified program that you do not recognize. You decide to quarantine the program, but first you want to know more about it.

1. How do you find out whether it is configured to run automatically when Windows starts?
2. If the program is configured to run automatically when Windows starts, how do you discover the location in which the program is registered to start automatically?
3. How do you find out if the program is digitally signed and who signed it?
4. How do you find out whether the program is spyware?

Quick Check Answers

1. Locate the program in the Currently Running Programs category in Software Explorer, and check the Auto Start information.
2. Locate the program in the Startup Programs category in Software Explorer, and check the Startup Type information.
3. Locate the program in Software Explorer (any category), and check the Digitally Signed By information.
4. Submit the program to SpyNet for assessment.

MORE INFO   **The Windows Malicious Software Removal Tool**

In addition to Windows Defender, Microsoft provides the Malicious Software Removal Tool (MSRT) for free, and the latest version of this tool is downloaded as part of Microsoft Update. For more information about the MSRT, access *http://www.microsoft.com/downloads/details.aspx?FamilyId =47DDCFA9-645D-4495-9EDA-92CDE33E99A9&displaylang=en*.

Practice: Configuring Windows Defender Scans

In this practice session, you configure and carry out a Windows Defender custom scan. You also configure a full system scan to occur at 1:00 A.M. every day and specify the action that you want Windows Defender to take for each alert level. These practices ask you to log on by using a standard account—for example, the parent_standard account that you created in Chapter 4, "Configuring and Troubleshooting Internet Access." If you prefer, you can use the administrator account (Kim_Ackers) that you created when you installed Windows Vista. If you use an administrator account, the UAC dialog box prompts you to click Continue, and you do not need to provide administrator credentials.

▶ **Practice 1: Configuring a Custom Scan**

In this practice, you configure a custom scan and then scan the computer.

1. If necessary, log on by using the parent_standard account.
2. On the Start, All Programs menu, select Windows Defender.
3. Click the arrow to the right of Scan, and select Custom Scan. In the dialog box shown in Figure 6-10, ensure that Scan Selected Drives And Folders is selected.

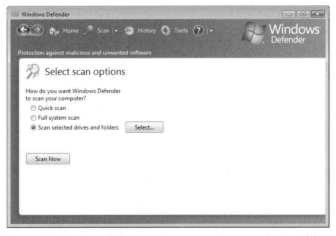

Figure 6-10   Specifying a custom scan to scan selected drives and folders

4. Click Select. You can select the drive or drives you want to scan, as shown in Figure 6-11. Removable media drives, such as CD-ROM and DVD-ROM drives, are active only if media are inserted. For this practice, select the Local Disk (C:) check box.

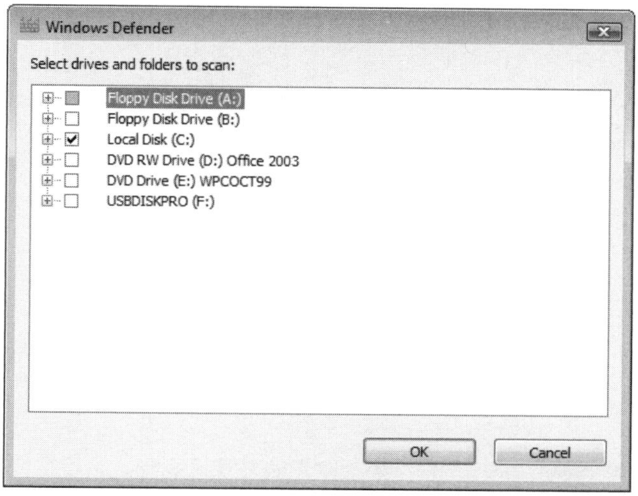

Figure 6-11 Specifying a drive

5. If you do not want to scan all folders on a drive, you can expand the drive and select the check boxes for the folders you want to scan, as shown in Figure 6-12. In this practice, you will scan all of drive C.

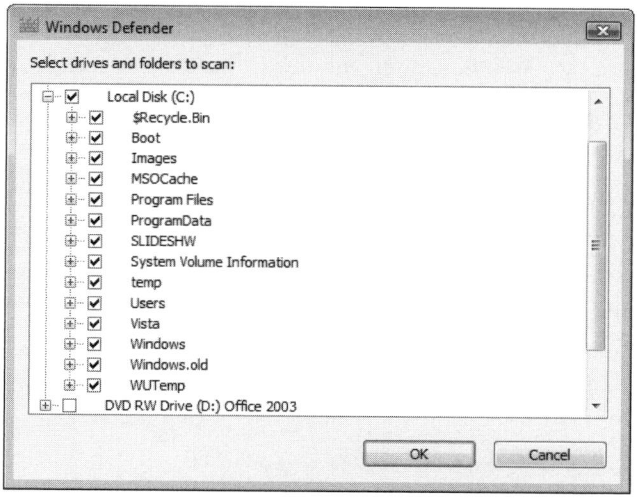

Figure 6-12 Specifying folders

6.   Click OK. In the Select Scan Options dialog box, click Scan Now.

7.   Windows Defender scans the selected drive. This can take some time. Figure 6-13 shows that no spyware was detected in the scanned computer. You might obtain different results. If Windows Defender detects suspect files, follow the prompts.

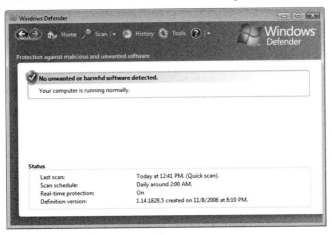

Figure 6-13   The scan completes

▶ Practice 2: Scheduling a Full System Scan and Specifying Actions

In this practice, you schedule a full system scan and specify the action that Windows Defender should take if it finds any suspect executable files, based on the alert level. You do not need to complete Practice 1 before you attempt this practice.

1.   If necessary, log on by using the parent_standard account and open Windows Defender.

2.   Click Tools, and then click Options.

3.   In the Automatic Scanning section select Daily, 1:00AM, and Full System Scan.

4.   Ensure that the Check For Updated Definitions Before Scanning check box is selected.

5.   Ensure that the Apply Default Actions To Items Detected During A Scan check box is selected.

6.   In the Default Actions section, select Remove for High Alert Items, as shown in Figure 6-14.

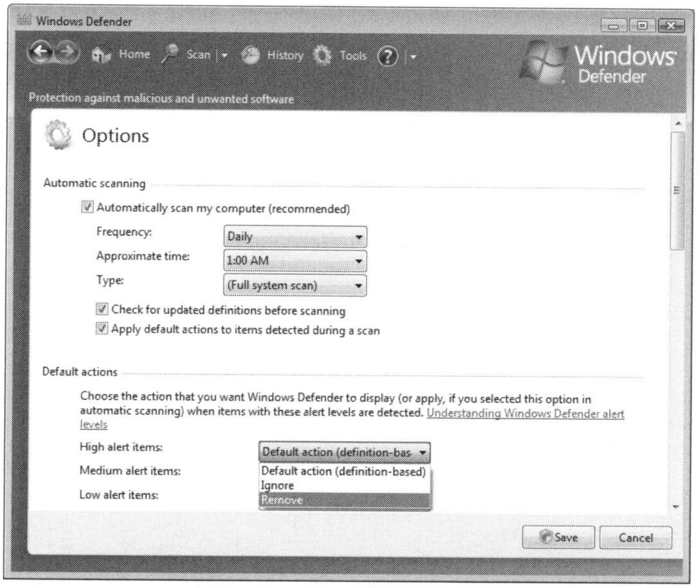

Figure 6-14   Specifying the default action for high alert items

7. In Default Actions, select Ignore for Low Alert Items. Leave the Medium Alert Items setting at Default Action (Definition-Based). The dialog box should look similar to Figure 6-15.

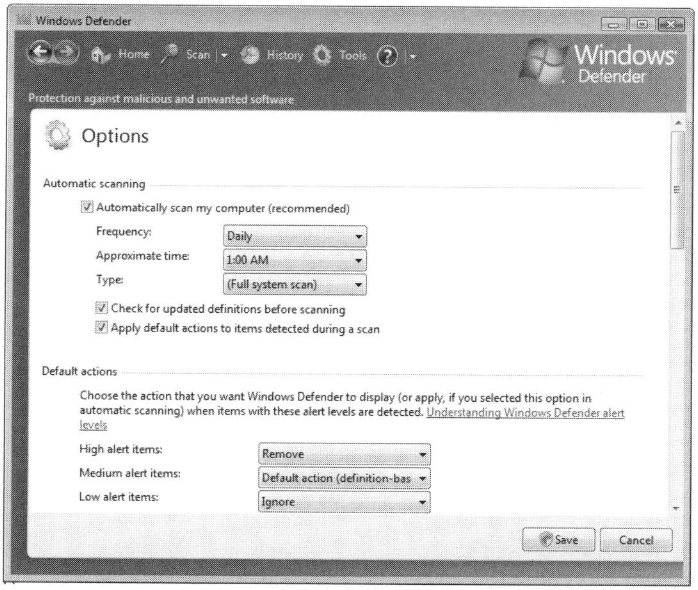

Figure 6-15   Scheduled scan specification

8. Click Save. When prompted, select an administrator account in the UAC dialog box and enter the account password. If you logged on by using an administrator account, you need to click Continue at this point.

Lesson Summary

■ Windows Defender provides real-time protection against spyware and other malware whether or not the program has been opened and whether or not any user is logged on to the computer.

■ Windows Defender uses spyware definitions and heuristic algorithms to identify malware and potential malware. New Windows Defender definitions can be downloaded through Windows Update or Microsoft Update. You can configure Windows Defender to download new definitions before starting a scan.

■ You can use a custom scan to scan your computer immediately, and you can also configure Windows Defender to scan at regular intervals, typically every 24 hours.

■ You can configure Windows Defender to ignore, quarantine, or remove suspected software, depending upon the alert level that the software generates. By default, Windows Defender decides the action to take depending on the type of threat and the alert level.

■ You can use Software Explorer to view and manage the programs that you use. If your computer has multiple users, you can use Software Explorer to view and manage all programs installed on the computer.

■ Microsoft provides the online SpyNet community to help you see how other people respond to software that has not yet been classified for risks. You can submit unclassified programs to SpyNet, and Microsoft will analyze them for risks.

Lesson Review

You can use the following questions to test your knowledge of the information in Lesson 1, "Configuring Windows Defender." The questions are also available on the companion CD if you prefer to review them in electronic form.

NOTE Answers

Answers to these questions and explanations of why each answer choice is correct or incorrect are located in the "Answers" section at the end of the book.

1. You want Windows Defender real-time protection to notify you about software that has not yet been classified for risks. How do you configure this setting?

   A. No such setting exists. Windows Defender always notifies you about software that has not yet been classified for risks.

   B. Open Windows Defender, click Tools, and then click Options. Under Real-Time Protection Options, select the Choose If Windows Defender Should Notify You About Software That Has Not Been Classified For Risks check box.

   C. Open Windows Defender, and click the arrow beside Scan. Select Custom Scan. In the Scan Options dialog box, select the Scan For Software That Has Not Been Classified For Risks check box.

   D. Open Windows Defender, click Tools, and then click Software Explorer. In all four categories, list the programs that are not yet classified.

2. Which of the following can you select in the Categories box in Software Explorer? (Choose all that apply.)

   A. Startup Programs

   B. Currently Running Programs

   C. Auto Start Programs

   D. Network-Connected Programs

   E. Programs that ship with the operating system

   F. Windows Sockets (Winsock) Service Providers

3. You are scheduling a quick scan in Windows Defender and specifying actions depending upon the alert level of any suspect items that the scan discovers. For which of the following alert levels are you unable to specify an action?

   A. Severe alert items

   B. High alert items

   C. Medium alert items

   D. Low alert items

4. You have configured Windows Defender to remove any items with a severe or high alert level. You are, however, concerned that an item might be removed that you want to keep. What advanced option should you set so you can restore any items that should not have been deleted?

   A. Scan The Contents Of Archived Files And Folders For Potential Threats

   B. Use Heuristics To Detect Potentially Harmful Or Unwanted Behavior By Software That Has Not Been Analyzed For Risks

   C. Create A Restore Point Before Applying Actions To Detected Items

   D. Do Not Scan These Files Or Locations

Lesson 2: Configuring Dynamic Security for Internet Explorer 7+

Browser security has become increasingly important in recent years as the frequency and severity of Internet attacks has increased. You need to protect your own computer and, as an IT professional, you need to advise colleagues how to best configure their security settings. If you give assistance through a help desk or as part of an extended warranty agreement, many of the questions you are asked and concerns that you need to allay will be about browser security. IE7+, which ships with Windows Vista, offers the following security features to help protect security and privacy when a user browses the web:

- **Protected mode**   Provides protection from websites that try to save files or install programs on a computer
- **Phishing filter**   Provides protection from online phishing attacks, fraud, and spoofed websites
- **Pop-up blocker**   Blocks most pop-up windows
- **Security zones**   Let you define security restrictions for specific websites and for unspecified websites encountered while browsing the Internet
- **Privacy settings**   Let you define what information your computer sends to websites—for example, by controlling the use of cookies
- **Manage add-ons**   Lets you disable or allow web browser add-ons and delete unwanted ActiveX controls

In this lesson, you learn how to configure IE7+ security features and to address issues related to browser security.

After this lesson, you will be able to:

- Enable and disable protected mode and resolve any issues users might have with this feature.
- Configure the phishing filter and report suspected phishing websites.
- Configure the pop-up blocker so users see the minimum number of pop-ups.
- Configure security zones so security settings are automatically applied to websites.
- Configure privacy settings—for example, by controlling the use of cookies.
- Manage add-ons—for example, ActiveX controls.

Estimated lesson time: 60 minutes

Resolving Protected Mode Issues

IE7+ protected mode makes it more difficult for malware to be installed on a computer. If any malicious programs are installed, protected mode makes it more difficult for them to significantly damage a user's files or OS. The Windows Help and Protected mode allows a user to install wanted software when logged on as a standard user by supplying administrator credentials. This allows a user to browse the Internet normally and install the desired software without putting the computer at risk by logging on with an administrator account.

UAC ensures that an administrator account runs as a standard account except when enhanced privileges are required. The difference is that if a user supplies administrator credentials or gives a task permission to run with elevated privileges, these elevated privileges apply until the task completes. Protected mode, on the other hand, prompts the user every time a program running in the browser needs to write to any area other than the Temporary Internet Files folder. In this way, any rogue add-ons or other malware that attempt a covert installation through IE7+ are blocked before they are installed, so Windows Defender does not need to detect or remove them. Protected mode recognizes that packages installed from the Internet pose more risk to the OS and user files than do packages installed from CD-ROM or administrator tasks, like changing system time.

NOTE   IE7 vs. IE7+

Internet Explorer 7 (IE7) is available for earlier OSs—for example, Microsoft Windows XP. However, the browser ships with Windows Vista. IE7, running on Windows Vista, becomes IE7+. The difference is that IE7+ supports protected mode and IE7 does not. This situation is currently under review and could have changed by the time you read this book.

Protected mode is enabled by default for Internet, local intranet, and restricted sites, but not for trusted sites. The Internet Protected Mode: On icon appears on your browser status bar (the bottom-right of your browser window), and you can double-click this icon if you want to change this setting. You can also access the control for enabling or disabling protected mode by clicking Tools on your browser, clicking Internet Options, and selecting the Security tab, as shown in Figure 6-16.

Figure 6-16   The Enable Protected Mode check box

In addition to warning users when webpages try to install software, as shown in Figure 6-17, and giving users the option of always trusting software from a particular source, IE7+ warns when webpages try to run software programs outside the browser and outside protected mode because such programs might have access to user files or to the OS. If a user trusts a program, the user can choose to allow any website to use the program to open web content. You need to warn users to consider carefully before deciding to always trust software from a particular source or allowing any website to use a particular program to open web content.

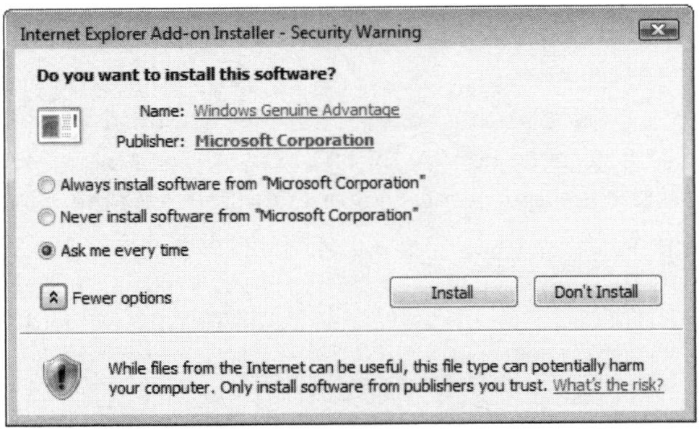

Figure 6-17   Warning that a webpage is trying to install software

Protected mode and UAC enable accounts to run as standard user accounts, and users cannot install programs without supplying administrator credentials or, at worst, giving permission to continue. This protects the computer from software installing itself silently without a user's knowledge or permission. However, if malware bypasses this protection, it could attack user files.

For example, a program could hijack a browser and "sniff" the user's keystrokes in order to steal or delete personal data or encrypt data for ransom. With protected mode, an exploited browser is only able to exploit that current browser session and sniff key strokes entered into the browser. It cannot sniff keystrokes outside the browser and use this information to damage system files or user data.

It would, of course, be preferable if such malware were kept out altogether, and Windows Vista offers several layers of protection. However, no system is completely secure. Browser session key logging is the unfortunate result of such a program sneaking through the defenses, but protected mode prevents system level infection, system level key logging, and compromised user data. Also, a browser that gets infected in protected mode is not persistently infected, and restarting the browser flushes the infection. The main advantage of protected mode is that it prevents privilege escalation (a process hijacking the elevated privileges associated with a user or system account) through IE7+.

Protected mode should not raise a large number of issues with your users. The protected mode symbol is not particularly intrusive in normal operation. Issues can arise if a user with administrator privileges (for example, on a home network) disables protected mode because the user does not understand what it does. As with any security feature, issues can also arise if a user expects perfect security. There is no such thing as perfect security.

Configuring the Phishing Filter

Phishing is a type of scam that attempts to lure you into disclosing personal information, such as your social security number, bank account details, or credit card number. In a typical phishing attack, an e-mail appears to come from your bank telling you to change your online banking password. You click on the site and it looks the same as your bank website but is in fact a phishing site designed to steal your confidential details. Microsoft is committed to helping to protect Internet users worldwide from becoming victims of phishing scams through consumer education, industry collaboration, legislation, enforcement, and technology innovation. In particular, IE7+ provides a phishing filter that helps determine whether a website is a legitimate site or a phishing site. Microsoft and MSN also provide simulated phishing and suspected phishing websites to let you test your settings.

IMPORTANT   Pronunciation

Phishing is pronounced "fishing." If you are supporting a telephone help desk service, do *not* mispronounce this word.

The IE7+ phishing filter blocks websites and cautions users about both reported and suspected phishing websites. The filter uses a combination of dynamic reputation services and heuristics. It provides Internet service providers (ISPs) and web service providers with a mechanism to clarify whether a site is a phishing site or not, and it gives legitimate website providers the opportunity to correct any incorrect identification of site content. Microsoft recognizes that legitimate web service providers whose sites mistakenly fall under suspicion are as much victims of phishing as users who suffer identity theft.

Real World

Ian Mclean

Identity theft is not new, although Internet browsing and e-mail communication make it a more widespread problem than it used to be. Long before personal computers became common, scam artists (or con artists as they were called in those days) pretending to be bank employees or other trustworthy persons would telephone unsuspecting consumers and convince some of them to divulge private information. However, online personal computing has expanded the problem. Media outlets report that phishing-related scams have resulted in more than $2 billion in fraudulent bank and financial charges to date.

As an IT professional, you need to warn colleagues and customers of the dangers of identity fraud and explain how they can filter out the worst examples. However, some people just cannot be helped. In a survey, one newspaper put reporters on the street who pretended to be carrying out a survey and asked people at random to complete a survey form that asked them for their credit and debit card personal identity numbers (PINs). A worrying percentage happily gave this information. The incentive for completing the survey was a bar of chocolate.

I've spent years trying to persuade computer users that if some stranger on the Internet asks for their bank account details, it is not so they can put money in. I confess I've sometimes been tempted to buy three small cups and a ball and change my line of business.

The phishing filter is enabled by default. This setting is on the Advanced tab of the Internet Options dialog box, which you can access by selecting Phishing Filter on the IE7+ Tools menu and clicking Phishing Filter Settings. This dialog box is shown in Figure 6-18.

If the filter is disabled or if automatic website checking is turned off, you enable both of these features by selecting Turn On Automatic Website Checking and clicking OK. You then see the information box shown in Figure 6-19. You can also enable the phishing filter by selecting Phishing Filter on the IE7+ Tools menu, clicking Turn On Automatic Website Checking, and then selecting Turn On Automatic Phishing Filter (Recommended).

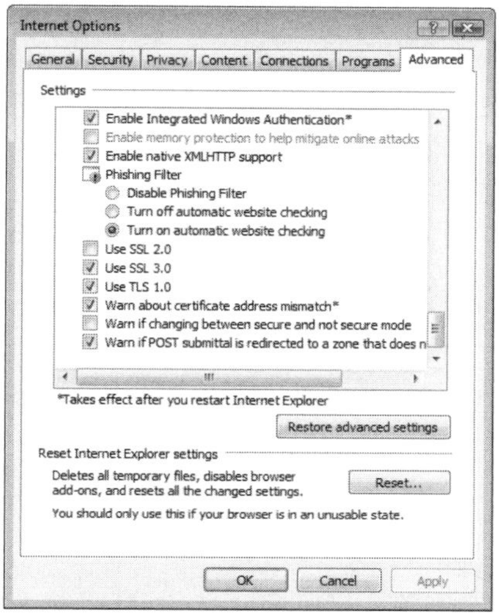

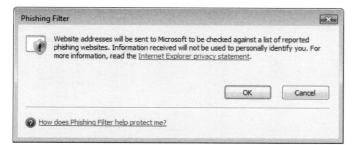

Figure 6-18 Phishing filter controls

When the phishing filter is enabled, Microsoft checks any Uniform Resource Locator (URL) that you access against a list of reported phishing websites and tells you if the website is on the list. The phishing filter also uses heuristics to determine whether the website might be suspect, even though it is not on any list. You investigate the effect of the other phishing filter controls in the practice session later in this lesson.

Figure 6-19 Phishing filter information message

The phishing filter is integrated into IE7+ but stays in the background until a user visits a suspect website. If the user has enabled automatic web checking, IE7+ issues either a red or a yellow warning.

If the website has been confirmed as a reported phishing site (based on an online list of sites that are updated several times every hour), the red warning shown in Figure 6-20 appears. This warning page offers users the option to close the webpage immediately or continue at their own risk to the site.

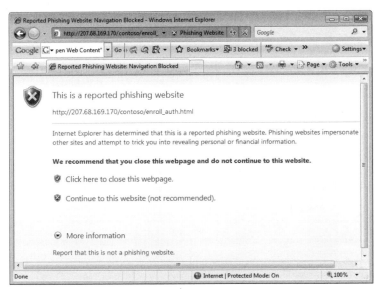

Figure 6-20 The red warning

If, on the other hand, the phishing filter detects a website that contains characteristics similar to a phishing site and the user has enabled automatic web checking, IE7+ displays a yellow warning, shown in Figure 6-21. This does not block access to the site but instead recommends that users avoid entering any personal information on the site, especially bank account or social security details.

Figure 6-21 The yellow warning

NOTE **MSN search toolbar phishing filter**

You need to be aware that the MSN search toolbar can also provide phishing filter functionality through the downloadable Microsoft Phishing Filter Add-in for MSN. However, if you are using IE7+ (or IE7) with the browser phishing filter enabled, the MSN add-in is probably unnecessary.

In order to protect legitimate websites, Microsoft provides access to a web form that web providers can complete if their nonphishing website comes under suspicion. The web form, shown in Figure 6-22, is accessible from both the red and yellow warning dialog boxes.

Figure 6-22   Reporting an incorrectly classified website

MORE INFO   Online resources

Microsoft offers a number of online resources to help educate consumers about online safety issues such as phishing. For more information, access *http://www.microsoft.com/athome/security /email/phishing.mspx*.

Using the Pop-Up Blocker

A pop-up is a web browser window that appears on top of the website a user is currently viewing. Usually, advertisers create pop-up windows. IE7+ pop-up blocker lets you block most pop-ups on your own computer, and you will probably be asked to advise other users how they should configure pop-up blocking. Users can choose the level of blocking they prefer, either blocking all pop-up windows or allowing pop-ups they want to see. When the IE7+ pop-up blocker is enabled (the default), a user can still see a pop-up by clicking the IE7+ Information bar. Pop-unders are a variant of pop-ups that appear on the screen under the current webpage and can be seen only when you close or minimize the webpage. If a user browses several sites, it is difficult to determine which site generated the pop-under. The pop-up blocker blocks both pop-ups and pop-unders.

CAUTION **Not all pop-ups are bad**

You might need to enable pop-ups on certain sites in order for the sites to work properly. For example, if users get their e-mail through Outlook Web Access (OWA) while out of the office, they need to allow pop-ups on the OWA site in order to reply to messages. This is a common cause of help desk calls.

You can configure pop-up blocker by clicking Tools in IE7+, selecting Pop-Up Blocker, and clicking Pop-Up Blocker Settings. The Pop-Up Blocker Settings dialog box is shown in Figure 6-23.

Figure 6-23 Pop-Up Blocker Settings dialog box

From this dialog box, you can disable pop-up blocker or enable it if it has been disabled. If the blocker is enabled, you can add websites whose pop-ups you want to allow. You can use the * wildcard when doing this—for example, *.woodgrovebank.com allows pop-ups from all sites with URLs that end in woodgrovebank.com. This setting would typically be used by Woodgrove Bank employees who want to access their work e-mail through OWA.

You can also set the level of pop-up blocking. The following options are available:

- High: Block All Pop-ups (Ctrl+Alt to override)
- Medium: Block Most Automatic Pop-ups
- Low: Allow Pop-ups From Secure Sites

The default setting is Medium.

Exam Tip   It is a good idea to know what the default settings are for features such as Windows Defender, protected mode, the phishing filter, and the pop-up blocker. Traditionally, some examination questions are based on what happens by default and whether settings need to be changed. You can get this information from books such as this one, but you should also get as much hands-on practice with Windows Vista as you can. Experienced users develop a "feel" for the default behavior of a system.

A user can see blocked pop-ups by clicking the browser Information bar or by pressing Ctrl+Alt when accessing a website. If the pop-up blocking level is set to High, you need to use the latter method. By default, pop-ups display in separate windows. If you (or users you are supporting) prefer to have pop-ups display in tabs, you can configure this by opening Internet Options from the IE7+ Tools menu, selecting the General tab, clicking Settings in the Tabs section, and selecting Always Open Pop-Ups In A New Tab.

Users might have issues if pop-ups that they expect do not appear, for example, in OWA. They might also have issues if pop-ups do appear when they do not expect them. The default pop-up blocker settings do not block all pop-ups. Adware or other spyware can sometimes bypass the blocker and open pop-up windows. In this instance, you need to remove the offending software. Refer to Lesson 1 of this chapter, "Configuring Windows Defender."

In addition, some windows with active content are not blocked, and IE7+ does not block pop-ups from websites that are in the Local Intranet or Trusted Sites security zones. If you want to block the pop-ups from these websites, you need to remove the websites from these zones. Security zones are discussed later in this lesson.

If the user still complains about seeing block-ups, you can block all pop-ups (except possibly those generated by malware) by setting the filter level to High: Block All Pop-Ups. You need to explain to the user that the functionality of some sites might diminish if this setting is selected.

> ## Quick Check
> 1. What security settings are available on the pop-up blocker and which setting is the default?
> 2. How can you view the pop-ups that a website provides?
>
> ### Quick Check Answers
> 1. High, Medium, and Low. The default is Medium.
> 2. You can press Ctrl+Alt when you access the site. You can also click the Information bar. If the security setting is High, you need to use Ctrl+Alt.

Utilizing Security Zones

You can use a security zone to configure security settings for a number of websites, or all web-sites not included in other zones, in a single operation. IE7+ assigns all websites to one of four security zones:

- Internet
- Local Intranet
- Trusted Sites
- Restricted Sites

The zone to which a website is assigned specifies the security settings that IE uses for that site. You can choose websites to assign to the Local Intranet, Trusted Sites, or Restricted Sites zones. All other websites are assigned to the Internet zone. For example, if you have a list of websites that you visit and you completely trust those sites, add those sites to the Trusted Sites zone, or, if you are really confident about your judgment, to the Trusted Sites zones for the users you support.

You can add a website to a security zone or configure the security settings by accessing Inter-net Options and selecting the Security tab. Figure 6-16 showed the Internet security zone. The Sites button on this zone is disabled because you cannot add sites to the Internet zone. This zone contains all sites except those you have added to one of the other three zones. Figure 6-24 shows the Trusted Sites zone.

Figure 6-24   The Trusted Sites zone

You can add a site to the Trusted Sites zone or to the Restricted Sites zone by browsing to that site, opening Internet Options in your browser, selecting the Security tab, and clicking the selected zone. The URL of the website then appears in the Add This Website To The Zone box, and you can click Add. Alternatively, if you already know the URL of a site you want to add, you can type it in the Add This Website To The Zone box and again click Add.

A further restriction exists when adding sites to the Trusted Sites zone, however. By default, you can add only secure sites (sites with URLs beginning with https:) to this zone. If you wanted to add the site specified in Figure 6-25 to the Trusted Sites zone, you would first need to clear the Require Server Verification (Https:) For All Sites In This Zone check box.

Figure 6-25   Adding a site to a zone

Typically, a site on an intranet can be identified by its URL. The Local Intranet zone therefore offers automatic detection of intranet sites, as shown in Figure 6-26. If you prefer to specify sites manually, as you can for the Trusted Sites and Restricted Sites zones, you can click the Advanced button.

Figure 6-26   Automatic detection of Local Intranet zone sites

The following five levels of predefined security settings exist for security zones:

- High
- Medium-high
- Medium
- Medium-low
- Low

By default, the High security level applies to the Restricted Sites zone, the Medium-high to the Internet zone, the Medium to the Trusted Sites zone, and the Medium-low to the Local Intranet zone. You can change the setting for a zone by dragging the slider control. You can restore all zones to their default security levels by clicking Reset All Zones To Default Level. You can also view the security settings specified for a predefined security level or define a custom setting by selecting a zone and clicking Custom Level. Figure 6-27 shows the resulting dialog box. If you change the settings, the Reset button enables you to reset your changes if necessary. You need to restart your browser before any changes made to security zone settings or security levels apply.

Figure 6-27   The Security Settings dialog box for the Trusted Sites zone

A lot of security settings exist, and it is possible that users might select an inappropriate security level for a zone or add sites to the Trusted Sites zone list that should not be trusted. The defaults are sensible, and you can usually resolve most of the issues that users might have by restoring these defaults.

Security zone settings apply on a per-user basis, so if several users access the same computer, IE7+ could have different security settings for each user. More responsible and experienced users could be given, or more likely give themselves, less restrictive settings. In some ways, this is similar to parental controls, discussed in Chapter 4, "Configuring and Troubleshooting

Internet Access." However, the two features are not directly related. You cannot use security zones to determine what games a user plays, and a user who is blocked from downloading a program from the Internet through security zone settings cannot specify administrator credentials to enable the download.

Configuring Privacy Settings

IE7+ provides a number of features that can help protect your users' privacy when they are online. Privacy settings let you specify how a computer handles cookies. Privacy alerts warn users when they try to access a website that does not meet privacy settings criteria. Users can also view a website's privacy statement.

You can configure privacy settings by accessing Internet Options from the IE7+ Tools menu and selecting the Privacy tab, as shown in Figure 6-28.

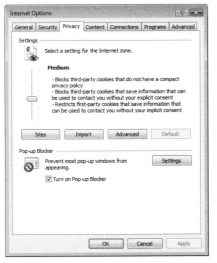

Figure 6-28   The Privacy tab

Cookies

Cookies are small files that some websites put on a computer to store user information. Cookies can make browsing more convenient by letting users return to websites without needing to log on again or by remembering preferences. Most cookies are harmless and useful. Sometimes, however, advertisers create cookies that track a user's browsing and shopping habits without the user's knowledge or permission. IE7+ privacy settings define how cookies are handled on a per-user basis.

> The following types of cookies exist:
>
> ■ Temporary or session cookies are removed from a user's computer when the browser closes. Websites use them to store temporary information, such as items in your shopping cart.
>
> ■ Persistent or saved cookies remain on a computer after the browser closes. Websites use them to store information, such as the user's sign-in name and password, so users do not need to sign in each time they go to a particular site. Persistent cookies can remain on a computer for a significant length of time.
>
> ■ First-party cookies come from the website that a user is viewing and can be either persistent or temporary. Websites might use these cookies to store information that they reuse the next time the user goes to that site.
>
> ■ Third-party cookies come from other websites' advertisements (such as pop-up or banner ads) that are on the website that the user is currently viewing. Websites might use these cookies to track a user's browsing pattern for marketing purposes.

You can define how IE7+ handles cookies by configuring privacy settings for the Internet security zone. Six settings are available:

■ Block All Cookies
■ High
■ Medium High
■ Medium
■ Low
■ Accept All Cookies

The default setting is Medium. You can view the details of each setting by moving the slider control. If you want to change the setting, drag the slider to the setting you require and click Apply.

You can also block or allow cookies for specific websites by clicking the Sites button, typing the appropriate URL, and clicking either Block or Allow. If you want to disable automatic cookie handling and specify how your browser handles cookies, you can click Advanced and select the Override Automatic Cookie Handling check box in the Advanced Privacy Settings dialog box shown in Figure 6-29. If you do this, the Default button in the Internet Options Security tab becomes active, enabling you to restore the default settings. The Privacy tab also provides an alternative method of accessing the pop-up blocker settings discussed earlier in this lesson.

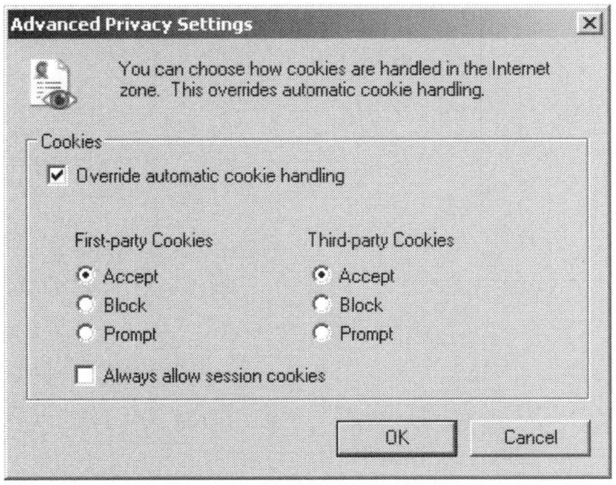

Figure 6-29   The Advanced Privacy Settings dialog box

MORE INFO   Custom Privacy Preferences files

The Import button lets you import Internet Explorer Privacy Preferences files to configure custom privacy settings. These files are written in Extensible Markup Language (XML). The structure and use of Custom Privacy Preferences files is beyond the scope of this book and the 70-620 examination. However, if you want more (highly technical) information, access *http://msdn.microsoft.com/library /default.asp?url=/workshop/security/privacy/reference/privacy_ref_entry.asp.*

Privacy Policies

Websites that collect personal information typically publish privacy policies that describe how the site uses this information. You should advise users to read the privacy statement carefully before entering any personal information into an unfamiliar website. Users need to look for conditions, such as allowing the website to share information with others or the requirement that they should accept unsolicited e-mail messages or advertising. Privacy policies are usually found in the website's Help section. If you want to read the privacy policies of one of the world's best known online sales sites, access *http://pages.ebay.com/help/policies/privacy-policy .html* and *http://pages.ebay.com/securitycenter/privacy_central.html.*

You can also access the privacy policy for a specific webpage by clicking Page in IE7+ and selecting Web Page Privacy Policy. This opens the Privacy Report dialog box, which gives you a list of the items that the site you have accessed owns. You can then select a webpage item and click Summary. Typically, however, a website's Help page gives you more information than the IE7+ privacy report feature. Clicking the Settings button in the Privacy Report dialog box lets you view the privacy settings on your computer.

You need to advise users that even though a website has a privacy statement, this does not mean that the web service provider will not misuse information. Users should not give personal information to a website they do not trust.

MORE INFO   Trusting a website

For more information, look up "When to trust a website" in Windows Help and Support.

Secure Websites

Secure websites provide an encrypted connection between IE7+ and the site. Encrypted connections make it difficult for a hacker to intercept a user's personal or financial information. This encryption is provided by a security certificate, which is an electronic document that identifies the website. Although encryption can help protect user information as it travels over the Internet, it does not guarantee that the website is reputable or that the website owners protect confidential information when they receive it.

When you access a secure website, IE7+ displays a lock in the Security Status bar at the top of the browser window. Clicking the lock lets the user view a security report that displays the identity information for the website, as shown in Figure 6-30.

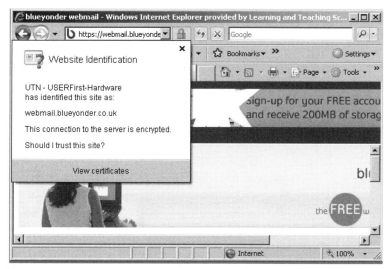

Figure 6-30   Identity information for a secure website

MORE INFO   Privacy and online safety

The Microsoft Security at Home website provides tools, tips, and links to help home users access the Internet more safely. Much of the information on this site is also applicable to small business users. You can access this site at *http://www.microsoft.com/athome/security/default.mspx*.

Managing Add-Ons

Add-ons—for example, ActiveX controls, browser extensions, browser helper objects, or tool-bars—can improve user experience on a website by providing multimedia or interactive content. However, some add-ons can cause a computer to stop responding or to display undesirable content, such as pop-up advertisements.

ActiveX Controls

ActiveX is a set of technologies that Microsoft developed in order to share information among different applications. ActiveX controls use these technologies and can be automatically downloaded and executed by a web browser, such as IE7+. Programmers develop ActiveX controls in a variety of languages, including C, C++, Visual Basic, and Java.

ActiveX controls have full access to the Windows OS. With this power comes a certain risk that the control might damage a user's software or data. To lessen this risk, Microsoft developed a registration system so that browsers can identify and authenticate an ActiveX control before downloading it.

If you, or users whom you support, encounter problems that you think might be related to an add-on, you can use the Manage Add-Ons dialog box to disable that add-on. If you do not know which add-on is causing problems, you can disable them one at a time. You can also enable add-ons one at a time, delete ActiveX controls if required, and download any new add-ons that are available. To access the Manage Add-Ons dialog box, shown in Figure 6-31, you select Tools in IE7+ and then click Manage Add-Ons.

In the Show drop-down list, you can choose to view add-ons that have been used by Internet Explorer. This displays all add-ons installed on the computer. You can also view add-ons currently loaded in Internet Explorer. This displays only those add-ons that are needed for the current webpage or a recently viewed webpage. You can view add-ons that run without requiring permission. This displays add-ons that were preapproved by Microsoft, your computer manufacturer or a service provider, and have typically been checked and digitally signed. Finally, you can view downloaded ActiveX controls.

You can disable any add-on, but you can delete only user-installed ActiveX controls in the Manage Add-Ons dialog box. If you want to remove an add-on, as opposed to merely disabling it, you need to use the Add Or Remove Programs tool in Control Panel.

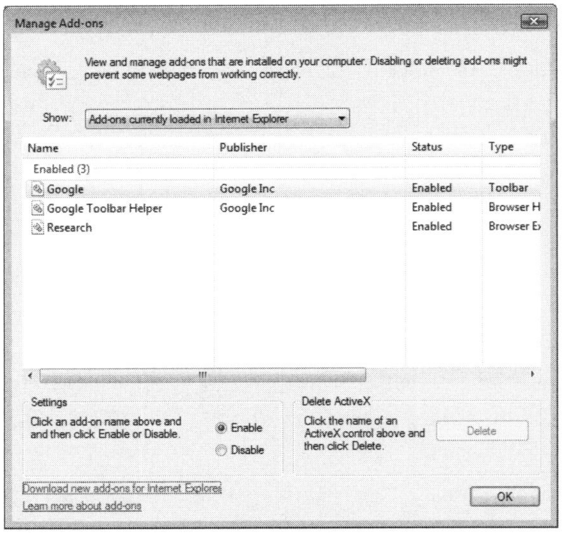

Figure 6-31 Identity information for a secure website

NOTE Temporarily disabling all add-ons

If you think a problem might be caused by an add-on, but you do not know which one, you can temporarily disable all add-ons by selecting Accessories from All Programs on the Start menu, clicking System Tools, and then selecting Internet Explorer (No Add-ons).

Some add-ons are digitally signed. This means that there is a specially encoded tag in the file that identifies the publisher. If an add-on is not digitally signed, (Not Verified) is displayed in the Publisher column, as shown in Figure 6-32. This does not necessarily mean that there is anything wrong with the add-on.

Web browser add-ons can add useful features—for example, extra toolbars, animated mouse pointers, and pop-up ad blockers. A user can download add-ons from the Internet but usually needs to provide administrator credentials in order to install them. Problems can arise when an add-on is installed without the user's knowledge. This can happen if the add-on is part of another program that the user gave permission to install. Some add-ons ship with Windows Vista and install at the same time as the OS.

Typically, add-ons seldom cause problems, but sometimes an add-on can force IE7+ to shut down unexpectedly. This can happen if the add-on was created for an earlier version of Internet Explorer or has a programming error. If an add-on causes problems, you can disable it and, if prompted, report the problem to Microsoft. These reports are anonymous and are used to improve Microsoft's products and to encourage other companies to update and improve theirs.

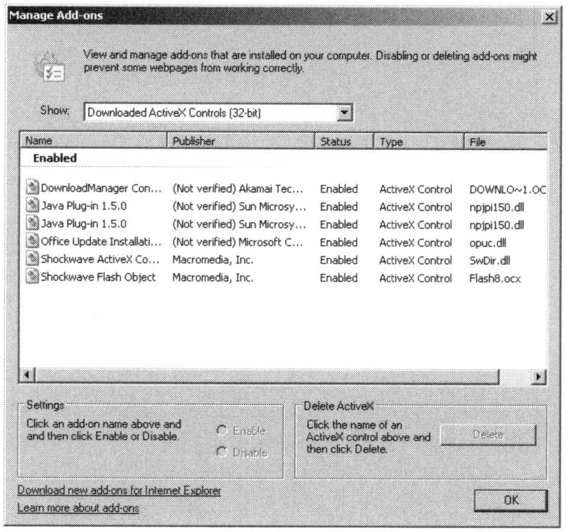

Figure 6-32   Add-ons that are not verified

Practice: Configuring and Testing the Phishing Filter

In this practice session, you configure the phishing filter and test the result of your configuration. The practice asks you to log on by using a standard account—for example, the parent_standard account that you created in Chapter 4, "Configuring and Troubleshooting Internet Access." If you prefer, you can use the administrator account (Kim_Ackers) that you created when you installed Windows Vista. No administrator permissions are needed to carry out the practice.

▶ **Practice: Testing the Effect of Phishing Filter Settings**

In this practice, you test the effect of the three possible settings for the phishing filter by accessing the phishing and suspicious sites that Microsoft and MSN provide for this purpose.

1. If necessary, log on by using the parent-standard account.
2. Open IE7+.
3. From the Tools menu, click Phishing Filter, and then select Phishing Filter Settings.
4. In the Internet Options dialog box, scroll down to Phishing Filter.
5. Ensure that Turn On Automatic Website Checking is selected, and then click OK.
6. If a Phishing Filter information box appears, click OK to close it.
7. In the Address bar, type **http://207.68.169.170/contoso/enroll_auth.html**, and then press Enter. (This is a phishing site that MSN maintains for test purposes.)
8. The red warning appears. This window was shown in Figure 6-20.
9. Click the Security Report control (labeled Phishing Website) to the right of the Address bar. The message shown in Figure 6-33 appears.

Figure 6-33   Security report

10. In the Address bar, type **http://207.68.169.170/woodgrovebank/index.html.html**, and then press Enter. (This is a suspected phishing site that Microsoft maintains for test purposes. Note that .html appears twice at the end of the URL.)

11. The yellow warning appears. This was shown in Figure 6-21. The Address bar background turns yellow.

12. Close the warning report window.

13. From the Tools menu, click Phishing Filter, and then select Phishing Filter Settings.

14. In the Internet Options dialog box, scroll down to Phishing Filter.

15. Select Turn Off Automatic Website Checking, and then click OK.

16. In the Address bar, type **http://207.68.169.170/contoso/enroll_auth.html**, and then press Enter. Note that a Click This Icon To Check Whether This Is A Reported Phishing Website icon appears, as shown in Figure 6-34.

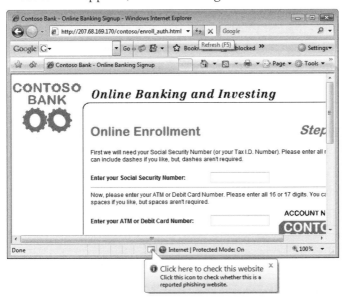

Figure 6-34   The Click This Icon To Check Whether This Is A Reported Phishing Website icon

17. Click the icon, and select Check This Website. Read the information in the Phishing Filter information box, and then click OK to close the box. The red warning now appears telling you that this is a phishing site.

18. In the Address bar, type **http://207.68.169.170/woodgrovebank/index.html.html**, and then press Enter.

19. Click the icon at the foot of the webpage to check whether this is a reported phishing site, and select Check This Website.

20. Read the information in the Phishing Filter information box, shown in Figure 6-35, and then click OK to close the box.

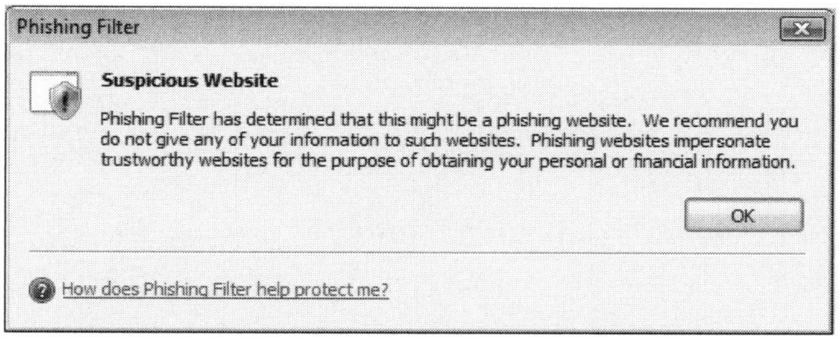

Figure 6-35   Suspicious website warning information

21. From the Tools menu, click Phishing Filter, and then select Phishing Filter Settings.

22. In the Internet Options dialog box, scroll down to Phishing Filter.

23. Select Disable Phishing Filter, and then click OK.

24. Access the *http://207.68.169.170/contoso/enroll_auth.html* site and the *http://207.68 .169.170/woodgrovebank/index.html.html* site in turn. You now receive no indication that either site is a phishing site.

25. Restore the phishing filter setting to the default value (Turn On Automatic Website Checking).

Lesson Summary

- IE7+ protected mode provides protection from websites that try to save files or install programs on a computer. If such a program succeeds in installing itself, protected mode ensures that it can operate only inside the browser and cannot damage user files or the OS. Protected mode is enabled by default for the Restricted Sites, Internet, and Local Intranet security zones.

- The IE7+ phishing filter provides protection from online phishing attacks, fraud, and spoofed websites. By default, the filter provides a red warning when it detects a known phishing site and blocks access to that site. If the site is a suspected phishing site, a yellow warning appears. You can configure the filter not to scan websites but instead to generate an icon that you can access to learn a site's phishing status. You can also disable the filter and scan websites on a site-by-site basis.

■ The IE7+ pop-up blocker blocks most pop-up windows by default. You can configure the level of pop-up blocking and specify websites from which you accept pop-ups.

■ You can specify the security level that is applied to a site by placing it in the IE7+ Restricted Sites, Trusted Sites, and Local Intranet security zones. Any site not in one of these zones is in the Internet zone. You can accept the default security level for each of these zones, specify another security level for a zone, or configure individual security settings within a security level.

■ IE7+ privacy settings let you define what information your computer sends to websites—by controlling the use of cookies, for example. You can specify one of six privacy settings for the Internet security zone and allow or block cookies from specified websites. You can also disable automatic cookie handling and specify how you want IE7+ to handle cookies.

■ The IE7+ add-on manager lets you disable or allow individual web browser add-ons. You can allow or disable add-ons that have been used by IE7+, add-ons currently loaded in IE7+, and add-ons that run without requiring permission. You can allow, disable, or delete downloaded ActiveX controls.

Lesson Review

You can use the following questions to test your knowledge of the information in Lesson 2, "Configuring Dynamic Security for Internet Explorer 7+." The questions are also available on the companion CD if you prefer to review them in electronic form.

NOTE Answers

Answers to these questions and explanations of why each answer choice is correct or incorrect are located in the "Answers" section at the end of the book.

---

1. You are configuring protected mode for IE7+ security zones. For which security zone is protected mode *not* enabled by default?

    A. Internet

    B. Local Intranet

    C. Trusted Sites

    D. Restricted Sites

2. You receive a help desk call from a user who has set her pop-up blocker filter level to High. She wants to view the pop-ups on a particular site. She does not want to view pop-ups from other sites. She does not always want to automatically view pop-ups from the site she specifies but just to view them when she needs to. What do you advise?

    A. Access the site, and then click the Information bar.

    B. Press Ctrl+Alt when accessing the site.

    C. Add the site to the Allowed Sites list.

    D. Set the filter level to Medium.

3. Which phishing filter setting does not block access to an identified phishing site with a red warning but instead generates an icon at the foot of the browser window to warn the user about the site's phishing status?

    A. Turn Off Automatic Website Checking

    B. Turn On Automatic Website Checking

    C. Disable Phishing Filter

    D. Check This Website

4. A user you support has identified a website that he says gives him useful information. However, you have doubts about some of the utilities and ActiveX controls that the site offers. You do not think it is a good idea for the user to be able to download anything, either accidentally or on purpose, from that site. What do you advise the user to do?

    A. Add the site to the Internet security zone.

    B. Set the security level of the Internet security zone to High.

    C. Add the site to the Trusted Sites zone.

    D. Add the site to the Restricted Sites zone.

Chapter Review

To further practice and reinforce the skills you learned in this chapter, you can perform the following tasks:

- Review the chapter summary.
- Review the list of key terms introduced in this chapter.
- Complete the case scenarios. These scenarios set up real-world situations involving the topics of this chapter and ask you to create a solution.
- Complete the suggested practices.
- Take a practice test.

Chapter Summary

- Windows Defender ships with Windows Vista and is tightly integrated with IE7+ to provide real-time protection against spyware and other malicious software.
- Windows Defender definitions need to be regularly updated. You can configure this to happen automatically. You can configure regular Windows Defender scans and specify how the software handles programs it detects depending on their alert levels. You can obtain further information about unspecified programs through Microsoft SpyNet.
- IE7+ provides a number of configurable security utilities. Protected mode provides protection from websites that try to upload malicious software and limits the damage that such software can do. The phishing filter provides protection from online phishing attacks. The pop-up blocker blocks most pop-up windows by default.
- You can specify the security level that is applied to a site by placing it in the appropriate IE7+ security zone. By default, websites are in the Internet zone unless you place them in one of the other zones. IE7+ privacy settings define what information your computer sends to websites. The IE7+ for add-on manager lets you disable or allow individual web browser add-ons and allow, disable, or delete ActiveX controls.

Key Terms

Do you know what these key terms mean? You can check your answers by looking up the terms in the glossary at the end of the book.

- ActiveX
- add-on
- heuristics
- malware
- phishing

- pop-ups
- security zone
- spyware

Case Scenarios

In the following case scenarios, you will apply what you have learned about configuring Internet Explorer security. You can find answers to these questions in the "Answers" section at the end of this book.

Case Scenario 1: Giving Advice on a Windows Defender Setting

You are an IT professional providing frontline support for Margie's Travel, a small business that does not have an Active Directory directory service domain but instead uses workstations configured in a workgroup. The company has recently upgraded the OS on all its computers to Windows Vista. Company employees are becoming familiar with Windows Defender, and you are supporting them. Answer the following questions:

1. A colleague has been using Windows Defender and reports that an application that he uses regularly has been deleted. He has used default settings, except he has specified that items with a high alert level should be removed. He has forgotten where he got the useful application. What do you tell him?

2. A colleague is configuring a nightly Windows Defender scan. She is unsure about specifying the default action to detect high alert items and wants to make sure they cannot harm her system. At the same time, she does not want to remove them completely in case Windows Defender deletes items in error. What do you advise?

3. A colleague runs a Windows Defender scan. The scan identifies an application that is not classified. The user is not sure whether to delete the item or not. What do you advise?

Case Scenario 2: Advising Customers About IE7+ Security Settings

You are an IT professional working for a computer systems retailer. You provide telephone help desk support to home and small business users as part of an extended warranty contract. Your employer has recently started selling computers that have Windows Vista installed, and customers sometimes require assistance with their security settings. Answer the following questions:

1. A customer has received an e-mail telling him his bank account might have been hacked by international terrorists. The e-mail gives him a URL to access in order to confirm his account details. When he clicks on the link, he sees a window with a red shield that allows him to continue to the website but says that this is not recommended. He is very

worried about his account but is also concerned that the message does not recommend that he accesses the website. What do you tell him?

2. A Windows Defender scan runs on a customer's computer every night. It has identified a number of suspicious downloads. The customer tells you she has been experimenting with the custom settings on her security zones. What do you advise?

3. A customer accesses her work e-mail at home by using OWA. She is having problems replying to e-mails. When she clicks Reply, the reply window does not appear. What do you advise?

4. A customer has been investigating add-on manager settings and finds a list of add-ons that run without requiring permission. He is concerned about this. What do you tell him?

Suggested Practices

To help you successfully master the exam objectives presented in this chapter, complete the following tasks.

Learn More About Windows Defender Settings

- **Practice 1: Investigate Windows Defender Options**   Open Windows Defender, click Tools, and select Options. Investigate all the settings in the Options dialog box. Click the Understanding Windows Defender Alert Levels link and read the information in the Windows Help and Support file.

- **Practice 2: Access the Windows Defender Website**   Open Windows Defender, click Tools, and select the link to the Windows Defender website. Investigate this site. Repeat this practice regularly because this site is frequently updated.

Experiment with Dynamic Security Settings for IE 7+

- **Practice 1: Investigate the Advanced Settings**   In IE7+ click Tools, click Internet Options, and select the Advanced tab. You saw this tab when you configured the phishing filter earlier in this chapter. Investigate and experiment with the other settings. If you do not know what a setting does, look it up in Windows Help and Support. If you change any settings, click Restore Advanced Settings when you are finished.

- **Practice 2: Investigate the Detailed Security Settings for Security Zones**   In IE7+ click Tools, click Internet Options, and select the Security tab. Click each zone in turn and click Custom Level to view the individual settings. In particular, note which zones enable the user to download files and ActiveX controls (signed and unsigned). If you decide to experiment with the settings, remember to click Set All Zones To Default Level and then for each zone click Details and click Reset. Finally, restart your browser when you are finished.

Take a Practice Test

The practice tests on this book's companion CD offer many options. For example, you can test yourself on just one exam objective, or you can test yourself on all the 70-620 certification exam content. You can set up the test so that it closely simulates the experience of taking a certification exam, or you can set it up in study mode so that you can look at the correct answers and explanations after you answer each question.

MORE INFO   Practice tests

For details about all the practice test options available, see the "How to Use the Practice Tests" section in this book's Introduction.

Chapter 7
Configuring Network Connectivity

As an information technology (IT) professional providing frontline desktop support and help desk advice, you will mostly be involved with applications, application settings, security settings, upgrades, backups, and users who have forgotten their passwords. However, you might have to set up a workgroup that uses Internet Connection Sharing (ICS) or configure wireless connectivity. You will become involved with networking if a client computer loses connectivity or if your small office/home office (SOHO) network loses its connection to the Internet. This chapter discusses how you configure networking in the SOHO environment and how you troubleshoot connectivity issues.

Exam objectives in this chapter:
■ Configuring networking by using the Network And Sharing Center.
■ Troubleshooting connectivity issues.

Lessons in this chapter:

Before You Begin

To complete the lesson in this chapter, you must have done the following:

■ Installed Windows Vista Ultimate on a personal computer, as described in Chapter 1, "Installing Windows Vista Client," and Chapter 2, "Windows Vista Upgrades and Migrations."

■ Created an administrator account and standard accounts and enabled the Run command on the Start menu, as described in Practices 1, 2, and 3 of Chapter 4, "Configuring and Troubleshooting Internet Access," Lesson 1, "Configuring and Troubleshooting Parental Controls and Content Advisor."

■ Installed a wireless router—sometimes called a wireless access point (WAP)—on your network by following manufacturer's instructions. Alternatively, if you have a computer running Windows Vista that has a wireless fidelity (Wi-Fi) interface card installed, you can use this to implement wireless connectivity. The wizard that you use to configure a Wi-Fi–enabled computer is described in Lesson 1, "Using the Network And Sharing Center to Configure Networking." Whatever method you use, you need wireless connectivity to complete the practices in this chapter.

- The practice session in Lesson 1 asks you to connect to your network a wireless-ready computer with Windows Vista Ultimate installed. If the computer you intend to use for this purpose is not wireless-ready, you will need to install a wireless card, a wireless local area network (LAN) adapter (for a laptop), or a universal serial bus (USB) wireless adapter.

- You can carry out the practice with a single computer that you connect to your network first with a wired connection and then wirelessly. However, you will find the practice session more satisfactory if you have two computers, both running Windows Vista Ultimate, one of which you connect to your network through a wired connection and the other that you can connect wirelessly.

Real World

Ian McLean

I have been teaching networking for some considerable time, and I make knowledge of the binary and hexadecimal numbering systems a prerequisite of my courses. Nevertheless, I've grown used to the glazed look in some candidates' eyes when I start talking about subnet masks or subnetting. I then ask these candidates to stay late and endeavor to explain why 255 (decimal) equals 11111111 (binary) equals FF (hexadecimal).

Sometimes I encounter resistance. People see numbers theory as impractical, confusing, or useless. It is none of these things. If you want to make progress as a network engineer, you need to be as comfortable using the binary numbering system as you are using the decimal. Network design using supernetting and subnetting looks like a black art to the uninitiated. It seems complex and difficult, and if you can master it you deserve promotion and more pay. Actually, if you know binary it is quite easy.

Many online resources exist to help you learn binary and hexadecimal—for example, *http://www.learntosubnet.com, http://technet2.microsoft.com/WindowsServer/f/?en/library /50173c0e-d7ff-4788-a9a7-363de8d72f0c1033.mspx* and *http://www.math.grin.edu/~rebelsky /Courses/152/97F/Readings/student-binary.html.* I do not intend duplicating this information here.

However, I would urge you to learn binary and hexadecimal if you have not already done so. Remember that there are 10 types of people in the world—those who understand binary and those who do not.

Lesson 1: Using the Network And Sharing Center to Configure Networking

As you progress in your chosen career, you will need to know a lot more about networking. You will need to know how to create a subnet, how to divide a subnet into smaller subnets (subnetting), and how to combine several subnets to make a larger one (supernetting). You will become familiar with the components of a network—for example, client PCs, servers, switches, routers, firewalls, and so on. You will learn about protocols—in particular, those that make up the Transmission Control Protocol/Internet Protocol (TCP/IP) protocol stack.

A sound knowledge of networking and TCP/IP is essential to your career progress. These topics are unlikely to be tested in depth in the 70-620 examination, and only an introduction is included in this chapter. To deal with TCP/IP thoroughly would need a book as long as this one. (I know. I wrote that book.)

This chapter starts with an introduction to TCP/IP, in particular IP addresses, subnet masks, and default gateways. It continues with the practical aspects of configuring and managing a network.

After this lesson, you will be able to:
- Explain the functions of an IP address, a subnet mask, and a default gateway, and interpret the dotted decimal format.
- Connect workstations to a wired network and set up ICS on that network.
- Add a device to a wireless network.
- Manage connections for both wired and wireless networks.
- Manage preferred wireless networks.
- Share resources so that other users can access them and their owner can access them from other computers on the network.

Estimated lesson time: 70 minutes

Introduction to Networking and TCP/IP

The list of protocols in this section is not exclusive. The TCP/IP protocol stack is extensive and contains a large number of protocols and subprotocols that have no place in a brief introduction. Internet Protocol (IP) is the protocol that you need to be familiar with when you are setting up a network, and this section discusses it first. It then summarizes the protocols and services that combine with IP to ensure that information passes accurately and efficiently across a network and between networks.

Internet Protocol

IP controls packet sorting and delivery. Each incoming or outgoing packet, or IP datagram, includes the source IP address of the sender and the destination IP address of the recipient. IP is responsible for routing. If information is being passed to another device within a subnet, the datagram is sent to the appropriate internal IP address. If the datagram is sent to a destination that is not on the local subnet (for example, when you are accessing the Internet), IP examines the destination address, compares it to a route table, and decides what action to take. Windows Vista supports both Internet Protocol version 4 (IPv4) and Internet Protocol version 6 (IPv6). IPv6 is configured automatically, and you are unlikely ever to need to carry out a manual IPv6 configuration. This lesson therefore concentrates on IPv4.

Exam Tip   The 70-620 examination is unlikely to test IPv6 configuration. However, you do need to know that IPv6 exists and how to check whether it is enabled because the protocol is used to implement features in Windows Vista—for example, Windows Meeting Space.

You can view the IP configuration on a computer by opening the Command Prompt window. You can access it either by selecting Accessories and then Command Prompt on the All Programs menu, or by entering **cmd** in the Run box.

If you are examining command outputs from the Command Prompt window, it is useful to redirect them to a text file. You would not do this if you were using the Command Prompt window to enter configurations, but it is useful for studying the detailed information that some commands return. We shall try it initially with a fairly small output file, but it is particularly useful for commands that return a lot of information (for example, ipconfig /all or ipconfig /?).

The ipconfig command displays a computer's IP settings. To capture the output of the ipconfig command in a text file, follow these steps:

1. Open the Command Prompt window.
2. Type **ipconfig > ipconfig.txt**, as shown in Figure 7-1.

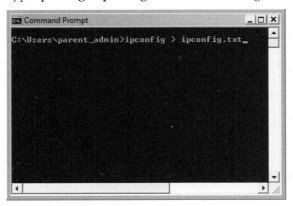

Figure 7-1   Output redirected to a text file

Use Microsoft Notepad to open the ipconfig.txt file, which you will find on the directory from which you ran the command. (In the example shown, this is C:\Users\parent_admin.) The information in the file depends on the interfaces that are configured on the computer, but you should obtain an output similar to Figure 7-2.

```
ipconfig - Notepad

File  Edit  Format  View  Help

windows IP Configuration

Ethernet adapter Local Area Connection:

    Connection-specific DNS Suffix  . : tailspintoys.com
    Link-local IPv6 Address . . . . . : fe80::dcfa:ae07:5484:a86b
    IPv4 Address. . . . . . . . . . . : 10.16.10.143
    Subnet Mask . . . . . . . . . . . : 255.255.255.0
    Default Gateway . . . . . . . . . : 10.16.10.1
```

Figure 7-2   Ipconfig command output

Let's leave the connection-specific Domain Name System (DNS) suffix and the link-local IPv6 address until later. The IPv4 address identifies the computer and the subnet that the computer is on. An IP address must be unique within a network. Here it is unique within a private network (the number 10 at the start of the address tells us that). If the IP address is a public address on the Internet, it needs to be unique throughout the Internet. We look at public and private addresses later in this chapter.

There is nothing magical about the IPv4 address. It is simply a number in a very large range of numbers. It is expressed in a format called dotted decimal notation because that gives us a convenient way of working with it. An IP address is a number defined by 32 binary digits (bits), where each bit is a one or a zero. Consider the binary number:

00001010 00010000 00001010 10001111

The spaces are meaningless. They make the number easier to read.

The decimal value of this number is 168,823,439. In hexadecimal it is 0A100A8F. Neither of these ways of expressing the number is memorable or convenient.

Binary digits, however, are generally divided into groups of eight, called octets (an electronics engineer would call them bytes). So let's group this number into four octets and put a dot between each, because dots are easier to see than spaces.

00001010.00010000.00001010.10001111

Convert the binary number in each octet to a decimal and you get:

10.16.10.143

Exam Tip   Microsoft examinations that require number conversion typically give you access to an on-screen scientific calculator. This is very similar to the calculator you can access from the Windows Vista Accessories menu. If you're not familiar with scientific calculators, practice with this one—for example, enable binary (Bin) and type 11111111. Enable decimal (Dec) and then hexadecimal (Hex), and ensure that you get 255 and FF, respectively.

Binary, decimal, hexadecimal, and dotted decimal are all ways of expressing a number. The number uniquely identifies the computer (or other network component) within a network and the specifically identifiable network (or subnet) that it is on.

A network is divided into one or more subnets. Small networks—for example, SOHO networks—might consist of only a single subnet. Subnets are connected by a router (for example, a WAP, a Microsoft server configured as a router, or a hardware device such as a Cisco or 3Com router). Each subnet has its own subnet address within the network and its own gateway or router connection. In large networks some subnets can connect to more than one router, but this configuration is outside the scope of the 70-620 examination. Figure 7-3 shows two subnets connected through a router. You can also regard the connection through a modem to an Internet service provider (ISP) as a subnet, and this subnet, in turn, connects to the Internet through a router at the ISP.

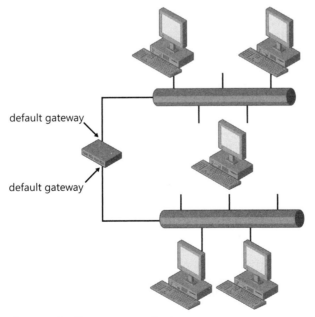

Figure 7-3   Two connected subnets

So what identifies the computer and what identifies the subnet? To discover this we need to look at the next value, the subnet mask.

Subnet masks are most peculiar numbers. They represent binary numbers that consist of all ones followed by all zeros. For example:

255.255.255.0 is the binary number 11111111 11111111 11111111 00000000.

The actual value of this number is irrelevant. What matters is the number of ones and zeros. A one says that the corresponding bit in the IPv4 address is a network address bit. A zero says that the corresponding bit in the IPv4 address is a computer or host address bit.

In the example given, the last eight bits of the subnet mask are all zero. So, the host address is the final octet of the subnet address, or 143. The network address of the subnet is 10.16.10.0. Because hosts are defined by a single octet in this example, the 10.16.10.0 subnet contains 254 host addresses. The first IPv4 address in the subnet is 10.16.10.1. The last is 10.16.10.254. The number 10.16.10.0 identifies the subnet and is called the subnet address. The number 10.16.10.255 is called the broadcast address and is used when a datagram needs to be sent to every host on a subnet.

Subnetting and Supernetting

You can split a subnet into smaller subnets by adding ones to the end of the ones in the subnet mask. If you have two (or more) suitable contiguous subnets, you can merge them into a single subnet by changing one or more ones at the end of the ones in the subnet masks to zeros. These techniques are known as subnetting and supernetting, respectively.

If an organization has a significant number of computers on its network (say more than 100—this number varies depending on the type, volume, and pattern of traffic on the network) or if it has several geographic locations, the organization will probably create several subnets. If a subnet contains too many computers and other devices, it tends to slow down because there is a greater chance of two computers trying to put data onto the network simultaneously and causing a collision. Dividing a network into several subnets reduces the likelihood of such collisions.

At the router that connects to the Internet, however, the organization will use supernetting to combine (or summarize) the subnets so that they can be defined with a single network address that will be translated to a public address on the Internet. Public addresses and address translation are discussed later in this lesson.

Supernetting, subnetting, and the related classless interdomain routing (CIDR) and variable length subnet mask (VLSM) technologies are unlikely to be tested in the 70-620 examination. Nevertheless, if you want to find out more (and I recommend that you do), access *http://www.howtosubnet.com* and *http://support.microsoft.com/kb/164015*.

NOTE   CIDR notation

Because the subnet mask 255.255.255.0 consists of 24 ones followed by 8 zeros, you can also write it as /24. A subnet with a network address 192.168.0.0 and a subnet mask 255.255.255.0 (for example) is then designated 192.168.0.0/24. This is sometimes called CIDR notation. A subnet mask with 25 ones followed by 7 zeros is a /25 subnet mask. In dotted decimal this would be 255.255.255.128.

The final value, shown in Figure 7-2, is the default gateway. This is the IP address of the router connection on the same subnet as the IP address of the host computer. If an IP datagram does not have a destination address in its own subnet, it is routed through other subnets until it finds the destination it is looking for. If you browse to a website, for example, you need to send data to the web server for that site, which has an IP address somewhere on the Internet.

Put simply, some datagrams need to get out of your subnet and go to another network (for example, the Internet). Your computer sends these datagrams to a routing device. This can be a hardware router (for example, a Cisco or 3Com router), a server that is configured as a router, or the computer or wireless router through which the other computers in a SOHO access the Internet—for example, through ICS. The default gateway is the address within the subnet of the routing device (which will have at least one more IP address on another subnet). It is where outgoing datagrams leave the subnet. It is also where incoming datagrams from other networks enter the subnet.

Quick Check

1. What is the binary number 00001010 11110000 10101010 01000000 in dotted decimal notation?
2. Are the IPv4 addresses 192.168.1.200 and 192.168.1.24 on the same subnet? Both have a subnet mask of 255.255.255.0.

Quick check answers:

1. 10.240.170.64.
2. The subnet mask specifies that the final octet holds the host address. Therefore, the first three octets hold the subnet's network address. In both cases this is 192.168.1.0, so the computers are on the same subnet.

Internet Control Message Protocol

Internet Control Message Protocol (ICMP) provides maintenance and routing facilities for IP. ICMP messages that are encapsulated within IP datagrams and can be routed throughout a network. The protocol builds and maintains route tables, performs router discovery, adjusts flow control to prevent link or router saturation, and provides diagnostic tools, such as ping and tracert. Arguably the best known application of ICMP is the ping command, which checks network connectivity. For example, in the configuration shown previously in Figure 7-2, you could check that your computer can connect to the default gateway by pinging the IP address 10.16.10.1, as shown in Figure 7-4. The tracert command (pronounced traceroute) checks connectivity to a device on a distant network and returns details of any intermediate networks (hops).

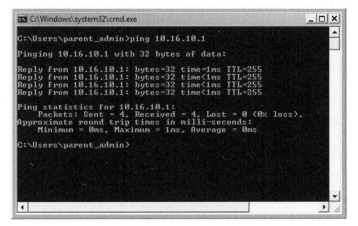

Figure 7-4   The ping command

NOTE **Ping and firewalls**

Sometimes firewalls are configured to block ICMP. If you want to test connectivity by using ping, you might need to allow ICMP in one or more firewalls or turn the firewalls off. Chapter 8, "Configuring Firewall and Remote Access," discusses firewall configuration. By default, Windows Firewall on Windows Vista computers permits ICMP traffic.

Internet Group Management Protocol

Internet Group Management Protocol (IGMP) provides support for IP multicasting, which is the transmission of an IP datagram to a host group—that is, a number of hosts identified by a single multicast IP destination address. For example, an Active Directory directory service domain controller uses multicasting to replicate Active Directory information to other domain controllers.

Address Resolution Protocol

Address Resolution Protocol (ARP) resolves IP addresses to media access control (MAC) addresses used by network hardware devices, such as network interface cards (NICs). A MAC address identifies a device within its own physical network by using a six-byte (48 bit) number programmed into the device's read-only memory (ROM). MAC addresses are typically displayed in hexadecimal notation (for example, 00-CF-62-E5-82-3B). The MAC address of the computer's NIC is listed as the physical address in the listing returned by the **ipconfig /all** command.

IPv6

IPv6 was originally developed because the IPv4 address space was running short of addresses. An IPv6 section of the Internet (the 6bone) exists. IPv6 can generate IPv4 compatible addresses that ensure that IPv4 datagrams can be directed through an IPv6 network. Eventually, IPv6 will be the IP protocol of choice (some argue that it is already), but IPv4 is unlikely to disappear for some time.

Where IPv4 uses 32-bit addresses, IPv6 uses 128 bits, giving an almost incomprehensible number of possible addresses. You write IPv6 addresses in hexadecimal rather than dotted decimal notation. IPv6 uses multicast Neighbor Solicitation messages rather than ARP broadcasts, and IGMP is replaced with multicast listener discovery (MLD) messages.

MORE INFO   IPv6

For more information about IPv6, look up "IPv6: Frequently Asked Questions" in Microsoft Windows Help and Support. For more detailed information, access *http://technet2.microsoft.com /WindowsServer/en/library/cba5a7ac-742a-49a6-8212-3844c768a0f81033.mspx?mfr=true.*

Transmission Control Protocol

Transmission Control Protocol (TCP) provides a reliable, connection-based service to applications. It is used for logon, file and print sharing, and other common functions. It can be used only for one-to-one communications where the start and endpoints are defined and the transmission route is established by a handshake protocol.

User Datagram Protocol

User Datagram Protocol (UDP) provides a connectionless, unreliable transport service and is generally used for one-to-many communications that use broadcast or multicast IP datagrams. Because delivery of UDP datagrams is not guaranteed, applications that use UDP must supply their own reliability mechanisms. UDP can be used for browsing, e-mail, and video streaming.

Network Services

TCP/IP provides a large number of services, the more significant of which are described briefly in this overview. TCP/IP services include the following:

- **Dynamic Host Configuration Protocol (DHCP)** Automatically assigns IP addresses to DHCP-enabled hosts. It assigns IP addresses from one or more scopes and handles IP address leasing and renewal. Exclusion ranges can be defined for non DHCP-enabled hosts, and static assignments can be made to specific MAC addresses. DHCP can also specify the IP address of the default gateway(s) and DNS server(s).

- **Domain Name Service** Resolves both local host names and fully qualified domain names (FQDNs)—for example, www.contoso.com—to IP addresses (and vice versa). A local DNS server can perform this function on its own subnet. For example, if you enter **ping Glasgow** in the Command Prompt window, DNS resolves the computer name Glasgow to its IP address. DNS also works over the Internet to resolve the FQDNs of remote websites to their IP addresses. DNS provides a connection-specific DNS suffix (refer to Figure 7-2) for e-mail addresses. If you had an e-mail server (for example, a Microsoft Exchange server) on your network, the connection-specific DNS suffix would be the section of the e-mail address after the @ symbol (for example, don.hall@tailspintoys.com). The Dynamic Domain Name Service (DDNS) uses the concept of a dynamic database and enables dynamic updates.

- **Automatic Private IP Addressing (APIPA)** Configures an internal private network when DHCP is not provided. If you have a network with no connection to any other network and you want the computers on that network to see one another, you can connect them by using an Ethernet hub and allow them to configure themselves without requiring DHCP services. APIPA configures a computer's IP settings with an IP address in the range 169.254.0.1 through 169.254.255.254 and a subnet mask of 255.255.0.0. APIPA does not configure a default gateway because an APIPA-configured network does not send IP datagrams to, or receive them from, any other networks.

- **Windows Internet Name Service (WINS)** Resolves network basic input/output system (NetBIOS) names to IP addresses. It provides a dynamic database, in which each client registers its NetBIOS name and IP address on power-up or if either is changed. NetBIOS name resolution was widely used in Microsoft Windows NT and earlier versions of Windows.

MORE INFO NetBIOS

For more information about NetBIOS, access *http://technet2.microsoft.com/WindowsServer /f/?en/library/4fbaebbb-6334-4b26-8118-cb36a261978a1033.mspx.*

- **Network Address Translation (NAT)** Allows many devices on a private network to gain access to the Internet through one public IP address. NAT translates between private IP addresses used internally in a local network and public addresses used on the Internet. When you send a request to the Internet—for example, by typing a URL into a browser— the information that the request returns (the webpage) needs to find its way back to your computer, which has an internal IP address on your LAN. Typically, your ISP allocates only one public IP address that all the computers on your LAN share when accessing the Internet. NAT deals with this situation and ensures that IP datagrams from the Internet reach the correct LAN destinations.

NOTE Network Address Translation

For more information about NAT, access *http://technet2.microsoft.com/WindowsServer /en/library/bd8a2548-25a8-4a4c-ad5c-c2719add9fd21033.mspx?mfr=true.*

Public and Private IPv4 Addresses

Every device on the Internet has its own unique public IPv4 address that is shared with no other device (a LAN also has at least one IPv4 address that is unique on the Internet). For example, if you type a URL such as http://www.adatum.com into your web browser, the FQDN www.adatum.com identifies a web server that has a public IPv4 address—for example, 207.46.197.32.

Any organization that has an Internet presence is allocated one or more public IP addresses that that organization and only that organization can use. The Internet Assigned Numbers Authority (IANA) issues and controls public IPv4 addresses through various agencies—for example, the United Kingdom Education and Research Network (UKERNA). In the case of a SOHO network, the ISP will allocate one public IPv4 address from a range that IANA or one of its agencies has allocated to the ISP.

Most organizations do not have enough public IP addresses to allocate one to every device on their networks. Also, issuing public IPv4 addresses to computers in an organization's network has security implications. Instead, organizations use private IPv4 addresses for their internal networks and use NAT to translate these addresses to a public address or addresses for Internet access.

Private IP addresses should never be used on the Internet, and typically a router on the Internet ignores private IP addresses. An organization can use whatever private IPv4 address range it chooses without requiring permission from IANA. Because private IPv4 addresses are internal to an organization, many organizations can use the same range of IPv4 addresses without causing IP conflicts. Most computers on internal networks do not need a unique public address but instead share a single public address that identifies their LAN and that NAT translates to their private addresses. Only devices on a LAN that have an Internet presence—for example, web servers, e-mail servers, and DNS servers—require a unique public address mapped through NAT to their internal private address.

IANA has reserved the following three blocks of IPv4 address space for private networks:

- 10.0.0.0/8 (10.0.0.1 through 10.255.255.254)
- 172.16.0.0/12 (172.16.0.1 through 172.31.255.254)
- 192.168.0.0/16 (192.168.0.1 through 192.168.255.255)

In addition, the APIPA range 169.254.0.0/16 (169.254.0.1 through 169.254.255.254) is also considered private because these addresses should never appear on the Internet. However, you should use this range only for automatic IPv4 address allocation through APIPA in an isolated subnet. You should not use this range in private networks that configure their devices though DHCP or manual (static) configuration and use NAT to implement Internet access.

Most organizations use only a small subsection of the private address space. For example, the 10.0.0.0/8 network contains more than 16 million host addresses, and very few organizations need that many. A commercial company with two private subnets might, for example, use 10.0.10.0/24 (10.0.10.1 through 10.0.10.254) and 10.0.20.0/24 (10.0.20.1 through 10.0.20.254) for these subnets. ICS uses the 192.168.0.0/24 address range (192.168.0.1 through 192.168.0.254), and most WAPs also use this range of addresses.

MORE INFO   Private networks—the definitive document

The accurate definition of a private network is a network that uses Request for Comments (RFC) 1918 IP address space. As you progress in your career as a network engineer, you will refer more and more frequently to RFCs like RFC 1918. To view this RFC, access *http://tools.ietf.org/html/rfc1918*.

Connecting to a Network

If you are setting up a wired SOHO network from scratch, you will likely start with a single computer connected to your cable or dial-up modem, which in turn provides a connection to the Internet. Typically, most networks are connected to the Internet, either directly or through other networks. If your network is completely isolated, with no connections to either the Internet or other LANs, then it is usually sufficient to let it configure itself through APIPA.

More commonly, you are adding a computer to an existing network (for example, a SOHO network). In this case a DHCP service probably already exists on the network. When you connect to the Internet, your ISP automatically configures your modem connection. If you set up Internet Connection Sharing (ICS), the computer on your network that directly accesses your modem automatically configures all the other computers on its LAN.

MORE INFO   Internet Connection Sharing

For more information about ICS and an excellent illustrative diagram, search for "Using ICS (Internet Connection Sharing)" in Windows Help and Support.

Typically, the computers on a SOHO are set to receive their IP configurations automatically. In an isolated network that does not use APIPA you might need to configure each computer manually, but that's unusual. By default, when you install Windows Vista it configures your network adapter (or adapters) to get IP configurations automatically.

You can check this by opening the Network And Sharing Center. You do this by opening Control Panel, clicking Network And Internet, and then clicking Network And Sharing Center. In the Network And Sharing Center, click View Status beside the Local Area Connection that connects to your SOHO network and click Properties in the Local Area Connection Status dialog box. (You can also click Manage Network Connections in the Network And Sharing Center, right-click the relevant Local Area Connection, and click Properties). You need to supply administrator credentials or click Continue in the UAC dialog box. After you have done so, the Local Area Connection Properties dialog box appears, as shown in Figure 7-5.

Figure 7-5   Local Area Connection Properties dialog box

In this dialog box you can select Internet Protocol Version 4 (TCP/IPv4) and click Properties. Unless you have chosen manual configuration by selecting the Use The Following IP Address option, you should see that IPv4 is set up for automatic configuration, as shown in Figure 7-6. If you click the Alternate Configuration tab, you will see that APIPA is used by default if DHCP information is not available.

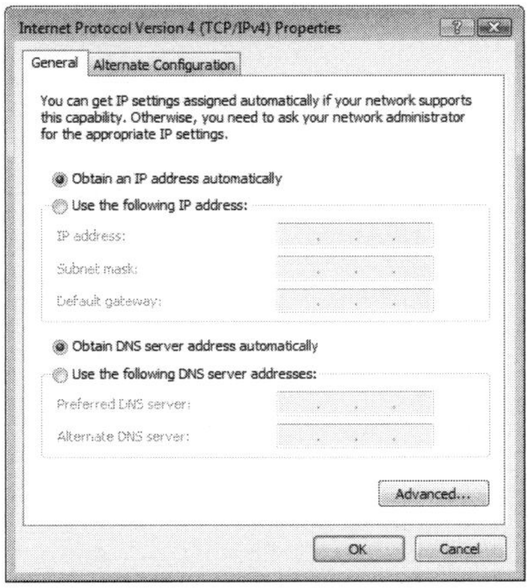

Figure 7-6   Automatic IPv4 configuration

You can do the same for Internet Protocol Version 6 (TCP/IPv6). This will almost certainly be set up for automatic configuration. It is most unlikely that you will need to configure IPv6 manually or that IPv6 configuration will feature in the 70-620 examination.

In a wireless SOHO you typically connect your wireless router—sometimes known as a wireless access point (WAP)—to your cable or dial-up modem. The other devices on your network—for example, computers or printers—then connect to the WAP. In this case the computers on the network all connect to the Internet through the WAP. You can use a third-party WAP or configure a Wi-Fi–enabled Windows Vista computer to implement wireless access. A third-party WAP is configured by default to provide TCP/IP configuration; a Wi-Fi–enabled Windows Vista computer is configured to provide TCP/IP configuration through ICS. If you are setting up from scratch, you are using a third-party WAP, and your ISP does not provide a modem, you can purchase a combined modem and WAP.

You can also implement a hybrid network. In this case, the WAP is typically connected to the modem as before and computers in fixed locations are connected using wired connections to Ethernet ports on the WAP. Most third-party WAPs have several Ethernet ports in addition to the wide area network (WAN) port that connects to the modem. You can wire the fixed computers directly to the WAP or you can connect them by using a switch (or a hub) and connect the switch to the WAP.

Wireless-enabled devices connect directly to the WAP, and both wired and wireless devices are on the same network and obtain their IP configuration from the WAP, which provides DHCP and internal DNS services (in the case where a Wi-Fi–enabled computer provides wireless access, DHCP and DNS services are provided through ICS). The WAP forwards any datagrams that need to go to the Internet (for example, browser requests) through the modem to your ISP, which provides external DNS resolution. Typically, you configure a third-party WAP by accessing a webpage interface and a Wi-Fi adapter card through a dialog box. Refer to the manufacturer's documentation for details.

MORE INFO Internal vs. external resolution

If you need to resolve a computer name on your internal network to an IP address (for example, if you entered **ping Glasgow** in the Command Prompt window), then the DNS service on your WAP or ICS computer provides the IPv4 address that corresponds to the computer name. If, on the other hand, you needed to resolve an FQDN on the Internet (if you entered **http://www.contoso.com** in your browser, for example), then that FQDN is resolved over the Internet. FQDNs are resolved over the Internet using a DNS server hierarchy and an iterative process.

Although it is unlikely that the 70-620 examination will test your knowledge of iterative DNS queries, you will need to know how DNS works over the Internet if you intend to develop your career as a network engineer. For more information, access *http://technet2.microsoft.com/WindowsServer /en/library/0bcd97e6-b75d-48ce-83ca-bf470573ebdc1033.mspx?mfr=true.*

Traditionally, an ICS computer provided DNS, DHCP, and Internet connectivity for a wired SOHO network and a third-party WAP performed the same function for a wireless network. However, many modern computers (both desktop and laptop) include a built-in Wi-Fi adapter card, which means that the computer itself can act as a WAP. Windows Vista provides a wizard that lets you easily configure wireless access for such a computer. The same wizard lets you save wireless settings on a USB flash drive to enable you to join other wireless-enabled computers to your network. If you use this facility, the computer that you configure to provide wireless access is also configured for ICS, so it provides DHCP and DNS services on the SOHO network. Figure 7-7 shows the SOHO network configurations described in this lesson.

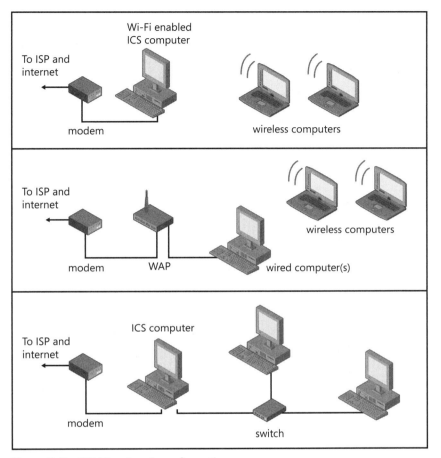

Figure 7-7   SOHO network configurations

Exam Tip   The 70-620 examination is likely to test the configuration in which a computer running Windows Vista is configured to provide both wireless access and DHCP and DNS services.

Setting Up a Network Connection

The first computer you install on a wired SOHO network will likely be connected to a modem through a USB or Ethernet connection. It will also have an Ethernet connection to enable computers and other devices to connect to it through a hub. Your ISP will give you instructions about how to establish an Internet connection and will provide a username and password.

To connect to the Internet, you access the Network And Sharing Center from Control Panel, click Set Up A Connection Or Network, select Connect To The Internet, and click Next. You then select the method you are using to connect—for example, Broadband Point-To-Point Protocol Over Ethernet (PPPoE)—and enter the name and password that your ISP provided, as shown in Figure 7-8. If you choose to allow other people to use the connection, a UAC dialog box appears. When you click Connect, the wizard configures your Internet connection.

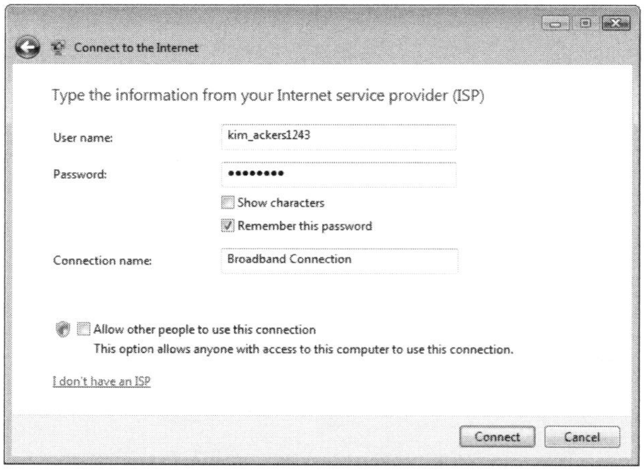

Figure 7-8   Providing information from your ISP

You can specify a name for your network by opening the Network And Sharing Center and clicking Customize. You then select Public or Private (Private for a SOHO) and type a network name—for example, tailspintoys.com. On the next wizard page you click Close to confirm your settings. The Network And Sharing Center now displays your network connected to the Internet, as shown in Figure 7-9. You can get details about the Sharing And Discovery settings and change a setting if you need to by clicking the arrow beside each setting.

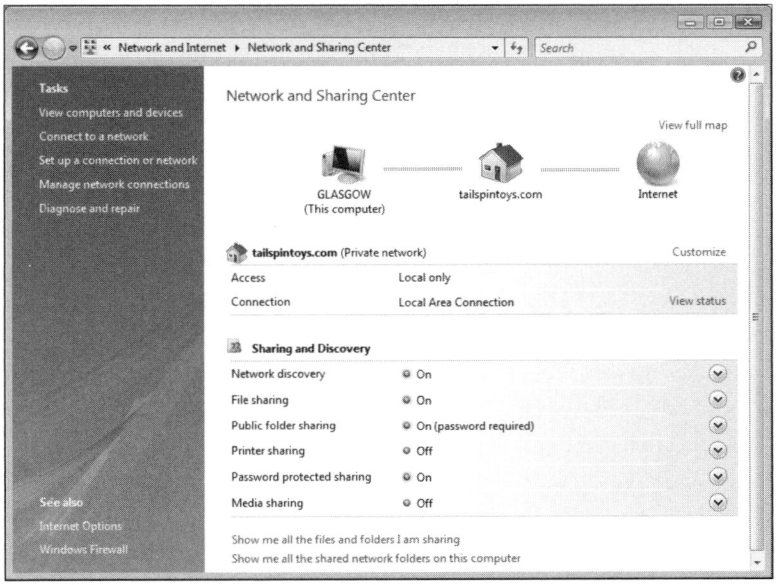

Figure 7-9   The Network And Sharing Center

Typically, other computers on a wired SOHO will connect to the Internet through the first computer that you configure on the network. To enable this to happen, you need to configure ICS on that computer. You also enable ICS in the configuration where a computer with a Wi-Fi adapter is providing both ICS and wireless connectivity. To enable ICS, follow these steps:

1. Open the Network And Sharing Center and click Manage Network Connections.
2. Right-click the connection you want to share and click Properties.
3. As prompted, either provide administrator credentials or click Continue in the UAC dialog box.
4. Click the Sharing tab, and then select the Allow Other Network Users To Connect Through This Computer's Internet Connection check box.

NOTE   **The Sharing tab**

The Sharing tab is not available if you have only one network connection. You cannot configure ICS unless you have both a connection to the Internet and a connection to other computers on your network.

---

5. If you want to, you can also select the Allow Other Network Users To Control Or Disable The Shared Internet Connection check box. This is sometimes known as making the connection universal, and it is necessary if you want to determine whether someone else has been making changes to network connection settings.

6. Optionally, you can allow other network users to use services running on your network by clicking Settings and selecting the services you want to allow.

When you enable ICS, your LAN connection is configured with a new static IP address (192.168.0.1) and other settings—for example, subnet mask, default gateway, and DNS server address. The static address (192.168.0.1) is used as the default gateway for the subnet—default gateway addresses need to be static. If you connect other computers to your network before you enable ICS, you might need to change their TCP/IP settings, typically by rebooting. As a general rule it is preferable to add other computers to your network after you have configured ICS.

To add a computer to a wired network you need only connect it to the network and turn it on. Provided the computer is set to receive its configuration automatically and the computer's name is not the same as that of another computer already on the network, the computer will join the network and receive its configuration through ICS. If you have changed the default workgroup name (WORKGROUP) on your network, you also need to change this setting on any computer you add.

Adding a computer through a wired connection to a hybrid network is the same as adding it to a fully wired network. You simply plug it in and turn it on. By default it should be configured to obtain its IP settings automatically. In this case, however, it obtains them from the WAP (either a third-party WAP or a Wi-Fi–enabled computer configured to provide wireless access and ICS).

MORE INFO **Setting up a virtual private network (VPN) connection**

If your business network supports a VPN connection, you might want to connect to the business network from home by using the VPN connection. You also need to be able to advise users you support on how to do this. For more information, search for "Set up a connection to your work-place by using VPN" in Windows Help and Support.

Exam Tip The 70-620 examination probably will not ask you how to set up a VPN server. It could, however, test your knowledge of how to connect through a VPN connection.

Adding a Wireless Device to a Network

If you have a wireless network, you can run the Set Up A Wireless Router Or Access Point Wizard on one computer that is already on your network and save network settings to a USB flash drive. This is the same wizard that you would use to configure a computer with a Wi-Fi adapter to provide wireless access for a network. The steps you follow are almost identical except that in one case you are configuring settings to create a file on a USB drive that enables other computers to connect to a configured wireless network. In the other case you are configuring the actual wireless settings.

You can add a wireless-enabled computer to your network by plugging the USB flash drive into that computer and clicking Wireless Network Setup Wizard in the AutoPlay dialog box. You save wireless settings to a USB drive and add a wireless-enabled computer to your network in the practice session later in this lesson. If you are setting up a WAP on a computer with a Wi-Fi interface that is running Windows Vista, you follow much the same procedure except you do not specify saving the settings to a USB flash drive. (You also need to configure ICS on that computer.) However, you can save settings to a flash drive if your Windows Vista computer is Wi-Fi enabled and provides wireless access itself or if it is not Wi-Fi enabled but is connected to a third-party WAP. Saving settings to a USB flash drive is therefore the more universal procedure, which is why it has been chosen for the practice session.

Alternatively, you can manually add a wireless computer running Windows Vista to your network by clicking Connect To on the Start menu, choosing the wireless network from the list that appears, and then clicking Connect. You then type the network security key or passphrase (if prompted) and click OK.

NOTE   Network security key

By default, a WAP is set to permit open access by any wireless-enabled computer within its range. You can set up your WAP to require a security key and ensure that any user who wants to add a computer to the network needs to provide a passphrase. Refer to the manufacturer's instructions for details. For more information about wireless network security, search for "Set up security for your wireless network" in Windows Help and Support.

Quick Check

■ You are adding a new computer to a wired network that connects to the Internet through a cable modem attached to one of your computers by a USB cable. The new computer is configured to obtain its IP configuration automatically. When you turn the new computer on, it is configured with an IP address, a subnet mask, and IP addresses for its default gateway and DNS server. Where does it get this information?

Quick Check Answer

■ From the computer attached to the modem, which is configured to run ICS

To add a wireless device other than a computer to a network, you need to follow the manufacturer's instructions that came with the device. You might be able to add the device using a USB flash drive. If the device is a printer, you might need to enable printer sharing so that other computers on the network can use it. If you want to add a Bluetooth enabled device to your network, you need a Bluetooth network adapter.

MORE INFO   **Bluetooth**

For more information about Bluetooth, search for "Bluetooth" in Windows Help and Support.

Wireless Networks

In a wireless network the computers are connected by radio signals instead of wires or cables. Advantages of wireless networks include mobility and easy physical installation (you do not need to run cables under the floor). Disadvantages include a slower connection (typically) than a wired network and interference from other wireless devices, such as cordless phones.

Currently three types of wireless network technologies are in common use:

- **802.11b**   Up to 11 megabits per second (Mbps); good signal range; low cost. This technology allows fewer simultaneous users than the other two options and uses the 2.4 gigahertz (GHz) frequency. This frequency is prone to interference from microwave ovens, cordless phones, and other appliances.
- **802.11a**   Up to 54 Mbps; more simultaneous users than 802.11b but a smaller signal range; expensive. This option provides a fast transmission speed and uses the 5 GHz frequency, which limits interference from other devices. However, its signal is more easily obstructed by walls and other obstacles and it is not compatible with 802.11b network adapters, routers, and access points.
- **802.11g**   Up to 54 Mbps (under optimal conditions); more simultaneous users than 802.11b; very good signal range; not easily obstructed. This option is compatible with 802.11b network adapters, routers, and access points, but it uses the 2.4 GHz frequency and has the same interference problems as 802.11b. It is also more expensive than 802.11b.

802.11b is adequate for most home and many small office applications. If, however, your network carries a high volume of streaming media (video or music) traffic or if interference is a major problem, you might consider 802.11a. If you already have 802.11b devices on your network but require high-speed transmission between specified network points, you might consider 802.11g. Most modern WAPs on sale from computer equipment retailers are now 802.11g.

If you have more than one wireless network adapter in your computer or if your adapter uses more than one standard, you can specify which adapter or standard to use for each network connection.

NOTE   802.11n

The 802.11n standard is still in draft format and cannot currently be described as being "in common use." However, a number of vendors are manufacturing equipment using the current draft 802.11n standard. Most 802.11n devices are compatible with 802.11b and 802.11g.

Exam Tip   Several 802.11 standards exist in addition to 802.11a, 802.11b, and 802.11c. However, the standards described in this lesson are those in common use. If you see any other standard (for example, 802.11d) given as a possible answer in the examination, that answer is almost certainly wrong. Whether this statement should include 802.11n is debatable because it is possible to buy an adapter that conforms to the draft 802.11n standard.

Managing Network Connections

You can view a list of all the connection interfaces (wired and wireless) on a computer by opening the Network And Sharing Center and clicking Manage Network Connections. This opens the Network Connections folder that stores all the connections that enable your computer to connect to the Internet, a network, or another computer. When you install a network adapter in your computer, Windows creates a connection for it in the Network Connections folder. A local area connection is created for an Ethernet network adapter (or any other hard-wired network adapter), and a wireless network connection is created for a wireless network adapter.

You can right-click any network connection and select Status. If you click Details in the Local Area Connection Status dialog box, you access the Network Connection Details dialog box, shown in Figure 7-10.

The information in the Network Connection Details dialog box for any connection on your computer will almost certainly differ from that shown in Figure 7-10, but it is instructive to look at the information in that figure. In this case, the workstation is on a small business network that connects to another (probably larger) network that provides DNS, WINS, and DHCP services. It is likely that workstations on the small business network access other networks, including the Internet, through the second network. The computer is on the 10.16.10.0 subnet, with an IP address of 10.16.10.143. This subnet accesses other subnets, in particular the 10.16.10.30 subnet, through a gateway with an IP address of 10.16.10.1. The 10.16.30.0 subnet contains a server with the IP address 10.16.30.10 that provides DHCP, DNS, and WINS services. (The router is configured to pass DHCP broadcasts between the networks.) A server with the IP address 10.16.30.11 also provides WINS and DNS services. Figure 7-11 shows this network structure. This type of setup is common in a business or educational environment, but you are unlikely to come across it on a home network.

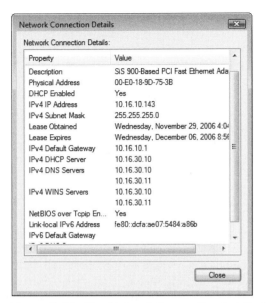

Figure 7-10 The Network Connection Details dialog box

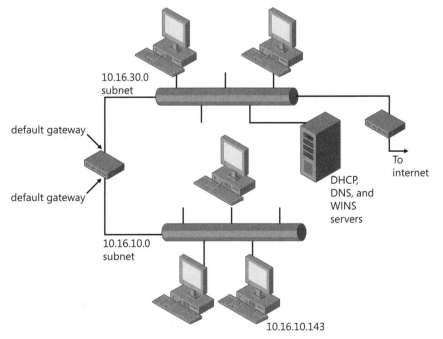

Figure 7-11 Typical network structure in a business or educational environment

On a wired home network with ICS enabled, a workstation typically has an address on the 192.168.0.0 network with its default gateway 192.168.0.1. A WAP is typically not configured with the 192.168.0.1 address but might instead have, for example, the IP address 192.168.123.254. This is then the default gateway for the computers and other devices on the network. Whatever the settings on your network are, you should take a note of them when everything is working correctly. This information is invaluable if something goes wrong.

Figure 7-10 also shows that NetBIOS over TCP/IP is enabled. Some services and applications use NetBIOS names rather than DNS hostnames, and enabling this setting allows these applications to work. The Physical Address value in Figure 7-10 is the MAC address of the NIC.

Exam Tip   The 70-620 examination is most unlikely to contain questions related to NetBIOS over TCP/IP or MAC addresses. This book defines them but does not discuss them in depth.

Clicking Close in the Network Connection Details information box returns you to the Local Area Connection Status dialog box. Clicking Properties and supplying administrator credentials or clicking Continue in the UAC dialog box accesses the Local Area Connections Properties dialog box. From this dialog box you can enable or disable the items shown or install more items (client services, server services, or protocols) by clicking Install.

Typically, the Local Area Connection Status dialog box (for both wired and wireless connections) might contain the following items:

- **Client For Microsoft Networks**   Enables the computer to access resources on a Microsoft network.
- **Quality Of Service (QoS) Packet Scheduler**   Provides traffic control. This can be significant if you have high-bandwidth traffic, such as video streaming, on your network.
- **File And Printer Sharing for Microsoft Networks**   Enables other computers to access resources on your computer in a Microsoft network (and other networks).
- **Internet Protocol Version 6 (TCP/IPv6)**   IPv6 configuration.
- **Internet Protocol Version 4 (TCP/IPv4)**   IPv4 configuration.
- **Link-Layer Topology Discovery Mapper Input/Output (I/O) Driver**   Discovers and locates other computers, devices, and network infrastructure components on the network and determines network bandwidth.
- **Link-Layer Topology Discovery Mapper Responder**   Allows the computer to be discovered and located on the network.

If an item is configurable, selecting the item activates the Properties button, and you can click this to configure the item's properties. You can also configure the adapter itself (for example, update the driver) by clicking Configure in the Local Area Connections Properties dialog box.

Take a note of the items that have been installed and enabled on your computer while it is working correctly. It is probable that all the other computers on a network you are administering have similar settings (apart from their IP addresses). It is a good idea to check this, possibly by using Remote Desktop. You might not change these settings very often, but if something goes wrong you can find out what the original settings were.

Quick Check

■ From which dialog box can you add a new protocol, server service, or client service?

Quick Check Answer

■ The Local Area Connections Properties dialog box

You can also right-click a connection in the Network Connections dialog box and select Diagnose. Lesson 2 of this chapter, "Using the Network And Sharing Center to Configure Networking," discusses troubleshooting connections.

If you have more than one network connection, you can create a network bridge by selecting two or more connections (click each connection in turn while holding down the Ctrl key), right-clicking, and selecting Bridge Connections. This task requires elevated privileges and you need to provide credentials or click Continue in the UAC dialog box as prompted.

A network bridge is software or hardware that connects two or more networks so that they can communicate. If you are managing a SOHO network that has different types of networks (for example, wired and wireless), you would typically use a bridge when you want to exchange information or share files among all of the computers on those networks. If you use the network bridge software built into Windows, you do not need to buy additional hardware.

Managing Preferred Wireless Networks

If you have a wireless-enabled mobile computer—for example, a laptop—you can take it to various locations and connect to whatever wireless networks are available at any location. You can see the available networks by opening the Network And Sharing Center, clicking Connect To A Network, and selecting Wireless in the Show list to view a list of the currently available wireless networks. You can then select a network and click Connect.

If you do not see the network that you want to connect to, you can click Set Up A Connection Or Network in the Network And Sharing Center. You can select from a list of available options (for example, Connect To The Internet) and manually search for and connect to a network. You can also create a new network connection.

Some networks require a network security key or passphrase. To connect to a secure network that you do not administer, you need to ask the network administrator or the service provider for the key or passphrase.

CAUTION   Choose a security-enabled wireless network

When you are connecting to a wireless network that is not your own, you should always choose a security-enabled wireless network if it is available. If you connect to a network that is not secure, someone with the right tools can see everything that you do, including the websites you visit, the documents you work on, and the user names and passwords that you use.

If you have previously connected to various wireless networks, the list of these networks is known as your preferred list. The wireless networks on your preferred list are your preferred wireless networks. You can click Manage Wireless Networks in the Control Panel and view saved wireless networks. You can change the order in which your computer attempts to connect to preferred networks by dragging the networks up or down in the list. You can also change preferences for the network by right-clicking the network and selecting Properties.

NOTE   Manage wireless networks

This icon appears in Control Panel only if your computer is wireless-enabled.

Exam Tip   If you are asked how to set up an automatic connection to a specific wireless network in the 70-620 examination, one of the steps you need to take is to drag the network to the top of the list of saved wireless networks.

Preventing Your Computer from Switching Between Wireless Access Points

When you, or users you support, move around with a mobile wireless-enabled computer, the computer will switch from one wireless network to another in order to stay connected. This is normal behavior. However, problems can occur when the same location is within range of several wireless networks and a computer tries to switch between these access points even though the user has not changed location. This can cause temporary interruptions to the user's connection, or the computer might lose the connection entirely.

With 802.11b or 802.11g (or 802.11n) routers and access points, the maximum range is up to 150 feet (46 meters) indoors and 300 feet (92 meters) outdoors. With 802.11a routers and access points, the maximum range is 50 feet (15 meters) indoors and 100 feet (30 meters) outdoors. These ranges are in optimal conditions with no interference. If a wireless-enabled computer is, for example, on a desktop that is 50 feet away from one WAP and 70 feet away from another, problems can occur. You can ask the user to move (usually impractical) or turn off automatic switching in one or both of the network profiles. Lesson 2 of this chapter, "Using the Network And Sharing Center to Configure Networking," discusses wireless network troubleshooting.

Networks with the Same Service Set Identifier (SSID)

The SSID is the identity of your wireless network. If a network on your list of preferred wireless networks has the same SSID as another network that is in range of your computer, Windows might try to switch between the two WAPs because it considers them to be the same network. Typically, the default SSID of a WAP is Default. If several people set up wireless networks—for example, in an apartment block or in a building that contains several small business offices—and none of them change the default, problems can occur. In this case, the solution is to give each WAP a unique SSID. Check the manufacturer's documentation that came with a device for instructions about how to change the SSID.

Real World

Ian McLean

I have a friend who used to work in the customer support section of a computer equipment retailer. Some time ago, when wireless home networks were comparatively rare, he received three calls on the same day from customers reporting problems with delays and loss of connectivity in their wireless networks. In one case the network had been working perfectly for just over a week before the problems occurred. In the other two cases the networks had been newly installed.

My friend took the precaution of checking the addresses of the customers. They all lived in the same apartment block. Apparently one of them had set up a wireless network and had been so impressed with it that he had invited his immediate neighbors in to have a look at it. They too had been impressed and had purchased exactly the same equipment—with exactly the same defaults.

Hardware and Interference Problems

Problems can also occur if the wireless adapter in a computer, or the WAP to which it connects, is not working properly. Lesson 2 of this chapter, "Using the Network And Sharing Center to Configure Networking," addresses this situation. Even if the hardware is functioning properly, interference from other devices can cause problems.

802.11b and 802.11g use the 2.4 GHz frequency. Microwave ovens and cordless phones also use this frequency. 802.11a uses the 5 GHz frequency. Some cordless phones also use this frequency. If these devices cause interference between a computer and the network it is connected to, the computer might try to switch to another nearby network. It is impractical to ask your friends not to phone or your neighbors not to use their microwave while you are browsing the Internet. The solution here is to change the WAP settings to use a different wireless channel or to configure the channel to be selected automatically if it is set to a fixed channel number. In the United States and Canada you can use channels 1, 6, and 11. Check the manufacturer's information that came with your WAP (or Wi-Fi adapter) for instructions about how to set the wireless signal channel.

Sharing Files and Folders

Users you support typically want to share files and folders so that their colleagues can view and, if appropriate, amend their files or, more commonly, so that they can work with their own files while using another computer on the network. Sharing files and folders on a network from any folder on a computer requires elevated privileges, so unless your users are local administrators on their own computers, you will be involved. At the very least you will need to supply administrator credentials, but typically you will also set up permissions that determine whether other users with accounts on the same computer and other users on the network are permitted to view, or to view and alter, shared files.

With your assistance, your users can share files and folders from any folder on their computers. They can also share files by placing them in the Public folder. Either method allows them to share files or folders with other users logged on to the same computer or with other users on the network. Users do not need to supply administrator credentials to place files in the Public folder, but elevated privileges are required to specify whether these files can be opened (or opened and amended) by users logged on to other computers on the network.

Configuring File and Folder Sharing

Typically, unless every computer in the workgroup has its own local printer, you will also need to share printers so that all users on your local network can print their documents. Network discovery needs to be enabled so that a user can view and access other computers, devices, and shares on the network. If enabled, password-protected sharing permits only users who have an account on the computer and can therefore supply credentials to access shared resources. Typically, in a workgroup users have accounts on several computers. A user can log on at one workstation and access his or her shared files on another workstation by supplying credentials for his or her account on the second computer. If you want to grant access to users logged on to another workstation who do not have accounts on the computer that stores the files, you can turn password-protected sharing off. Media sharing allows you to share music, picture, and video files across a network.

You can enable or disable Network Discovery, File Sharing, Public Folder Sharing, Printer Sharing, Password Protected Sharing, and Media Sharing in the Network And Sharing Center by clicking the arrow next to the feature you want to configure (see Figure 7-9). You can configure Public Folder Sharing so anyone logged on to any computer on the network can open, change, or create files, or you can specify that only read access is permitted. Even when Public Folder Sharing is disabled, users logged on to the computer locally can access files in the

Public folder. Configuration is an administrator function, and you need to either provide credentials or click Continue as prompted in the UAC dialog box.

Quick Check

- You want all users on a network configured as a workgroup to have access to shared resources on a workstation, whether they have accounts on the workstation or not. Currently, the default settings are configured in the Network And Sharing Center. How do you enable the specified access?

Quick Check Answer

- Disable Password Protected Sharing.

You might also need to configure Windows Firewall to allow users logged on to other computers on a network to access files. To do this, you open Control Panel and, under Security, click Allow A Program Through Windows Firewall. If prompted, you need to either provide administrator credentials or click Continue in the UAC dialog box. In the Program Or Port list, select the File And Printer Sharing check box and then click OK.

Configuring Sharing Permissions

Users can share files by copying or moving them into the Public folder. To access this folder and its subfolders, such as Public Documents, the user opens Windows Explorer, selects Documents, and then selects Public in the navigation pane. The sharing permissions on files shared by using this method are determined by the Public Folder Sharing and Password Protected Sharing settings in the Network And Sharing Center. Users typically use this method if they want to share only a few files or if they do not want other users to access folders like My Documents.

Users who choose to share files from any folder on the computer typically log on to different computers on a network and want to access their working files from any of these computers. They usually want the shares created for their own use, although they might make selected files and folders available for their colleagues to read or to read and amend. This sharing method is useful when other users are permitted access to only some of the shared files and different users or groups are granted different levels of access (assuming Password Protected Sharing is enabled). As an administrator, you typically assist users to configure this type of sharing and set up the sharing permissions depending upon user requirements.

The owner of a file or folder has, by default, full permissions on the share and is granted the Owner role. Any group or user that is added can be granted the Reader, Contributor, or Co-Owner role on a shared folder. Readers can read files in the folder, Contributors can amend the files, and Co-Owners can also change the sharing permissions (by providing administrator credentials or clicking Permission if prompted). File roles are Reader and Co-Owner. Typically, folder sharing is more common than individual file sharing and only files in folders such as My Documents can be shared. File sharing can be used when you share a folder but want to set different permissions on a file in that folder.

Other Methods of Sharing Files

In addition to creating shares and copying files to their Public folder structure, copying files to removable media, or e-mailing them to each other, users can share information by using the following methods:

- **Ad hoc networks** When users need to share files between two computers that are not currently on the same network but are physically close to each other—30 feet (9 meters) apart or closer—they can use a computer-to-computer network, also known as an ad hoc network. An ad hoc network is a temporary wireless connection between computers (and other devices) and can be used, for example, to share documents during a meeting.

MORE INFO Ad hoc networks

For more information, search for "Set up a computer-to-computer (ad hoc) network" in Windows Help and Support.

- **Windows Meeting Space** Allows users to set up a session where they can share documents, programs, or their desktops with other session participants. Windows Meeting Space automatically sets up an ad hoc network and requires wireless connections.

MORE INFO Windows Meeting Space

For more information, search for "Windows Meeting Space: frequently asked questions" in Windows Help and Support and refer to Lesson 2, "Configuring Windows Contacts and Windows Calendar," of Chapter 9, "Configuring Communications Applications."

- **Windows-compatible file-sharing programs** Third-party software designed to share files. Search for "file-sharing programs" on the Internet or access *http://www.internet-guide.co.uk/file-sharing.html*.
- **Websites** Many websites are devoted to sharing photos and other types of files. Care is required when using this method because sometimes there is very little control over what other contributors post on such websites.
- **Instant messaging** Most instant messaging programs (for example, Windows Live Messenger) allow users to share files while chatting online.

Practice: Joining Devices to a Wireless Network

In this practice session you save wireless network settings to a USB flash drive and use these settings to join a wireless-enabled computer to the network.

▶ **Practice 1: Saving Wireless Network Settings to a USB Flash Drive**

In this practice you generate settings that enable you to connect wireless-enabled devices—for example, computers and printers with wireless cards installed—to your wireless network. You can use the same technique to configure your wireless router if wireless routing is implemented by a Windows Vista computer with a Wi-Fi adapter. When you install them on a network, you configure third-party wireless routers by following the manufacturer's instructions. This practice assumes you have configured a wireless router and have a computer running Windows Vista connected to your network. As stated in the "Before You Begin" section at the beginning of this chapter, you can carry out the practice by first connecting your wireless-enabled computer to the network with a hard-wired connection and then disconnecting it and connecting it wirelessly. However, it is a lot easier if you use two computers, the first connected with a wired connection and the second you intend to connect wirelessly.

1. If necessary, log on by using an administrator account. You can use the parent_admin account that you created in Chapter 4 or the Kim_Ackers account that you created when you installed Windows Vista.

2. Open the Control Panel and click Network And Internet.

3. Click Network And Sharing Center. Under Tasks, select Set Up A Connection Or Network.

4. In the Set Up A Connection Or Network Wizard, shown in Figure 7-12, select Set Up A Wireless Router Or Access Point. Click Next.

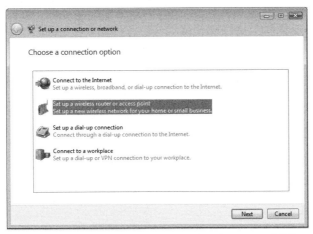

Figure 7-12   The Set Up A Connection Or Network Wizard

5. The Set Up A Wireless Router Or Access Point Wizard opens, as shown in Figure 7-13. Click Next.

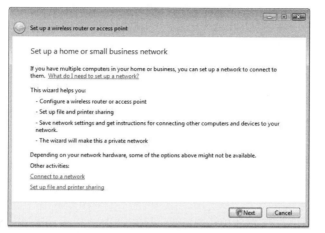

Figure 7-13   The Set Up A Wireless Router Or Access Point Wizard

6. If a UAC dialog box appears, click Continue.

7. The wizard searches for a wireless access device by running the Detecting Network Hardware And Settings utility, as shown in Figure 7-14.

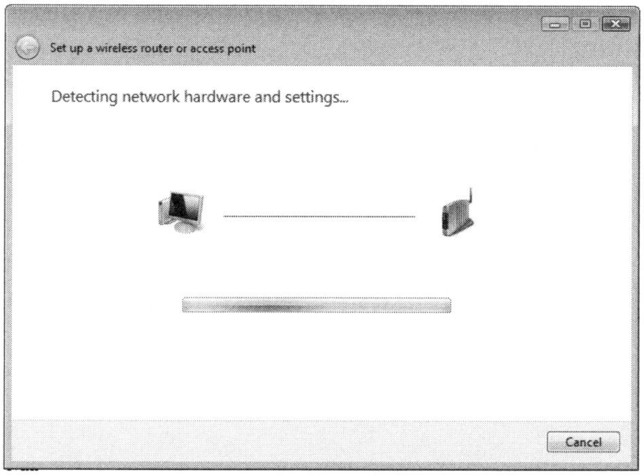

Figure 7-14   Searching for a wireless access device

8. If the wizard asks you if you want to turn on network discovery for all private networks, as shown in Figure 7-15, click No, Make The Network I Am Connected To A Private Network.

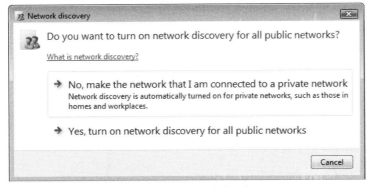

Figure 7-15   The Network Discovery dialog box

9. Click Create Wireless Network Settings And Save To USB Flash Drive.

10. The wizard asks for a name for your wireless network, as shown in Figure 7-16. This network name can contain only letters, numbers, and underscores. Specify a name and click Next. The name you specify becomes the wireless network's SSID.

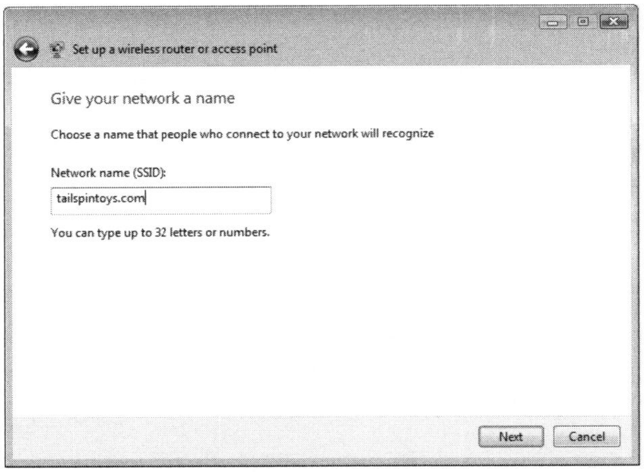

Figure 7-16   Specifying a network name

11. The wizard suggests a passphrase, as shown in Figure 7-17. You can accept this passphrase, ask the wizard to generate another one by clicking Create A Different Passphrase For Me, or type in your own passphrase. Either amend the passphrase or accept the one the wizard provides, and then click Next.

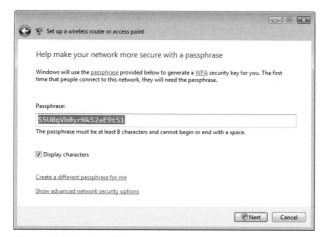

Figure 7-17 Specifying a passphrase

12. If prompted, click Continue in the UAC dialog box. The next wizard page, shown in Figure 7-18, lets you specify file and printer sharing settings. Typically, you would use the custom settings on your computer (the default). Click Next.

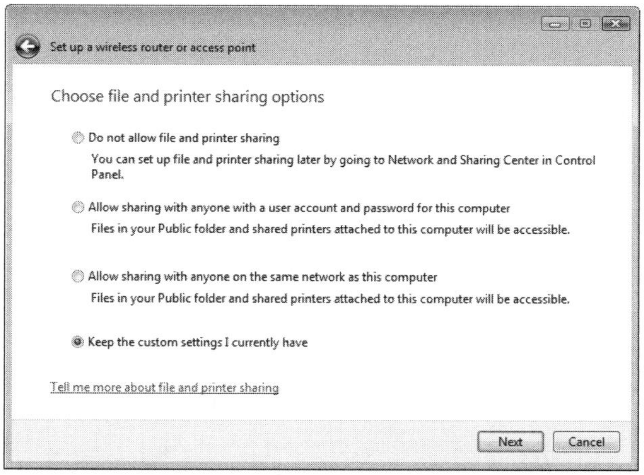

Figure 7-18 Specifying file and printer sharing sessions

13. When prompted, plug the USB device into your computer (if necessary) and specify the drive location.

14. The wizard gives you instructions on how to add a device or computer, as shown in Figure 7-19. Click the link to obtain more detailed instructions.

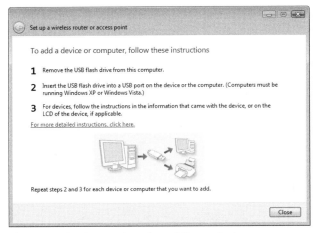

Figure 7-19   Instructions for adding a device

15. Read the Wordpad document, shown in Figure 7-20. Close the document. Click Close to close the wizard.

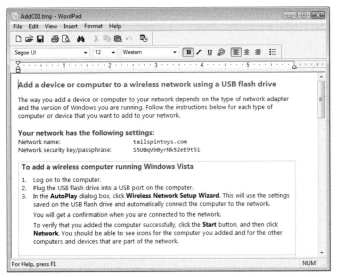

Figure 7-20   More detailed setup instructions

▶ **Practice 2: Adding a Computer to a Wireless Network**

In this practice you use the settings you have configured on your USB drive to add a wireless-enabled computer to your wireless network. It is recommended that you use a second computer running Windows Vista that is already wireless-enabled. The practice asks you to log on with a standard account. You can use an administrator account if you want to, but you do not need to be an administrator to add a computer to a wireless network.

1. If necessary, log on by using a standard account—for example, the parent_standard account that you created in Chapter 4, "Configuring and Troubleshooting Internet Access."

2. Plug in the USB flash drive. In the Autoplay dialog box, shown in Figure 7-21, click Wireless Network Setup Wizard.

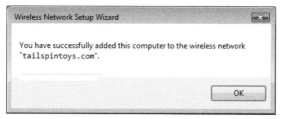

Figure 7-21   The Autoplay dialog box

3. When prompted, click Yes to join your computer to the specified wireless network.

4. The information box, shown in Figure 7-22, appears when your computer has successfully joined the network. Click OK.

Figure 7-22   Your computer is added to the network

Lesson Summary

- IP is responsible for ensuring that a datagram sent across a network reaches its destination. TCP and UDP are transport protocols. ICMP implements TCP/IP messaging and is used by the ping command. DHCP automatically configures computers on a network with their TCP/IP settings. DNS resolves a hostname or FQDN to an IP address. ARP resolves an IP address to a MAC address.

- An IP address identifies a computer (or other network device) on a subnet. A subnet mask defines the range of IP addresses on a subnet.

- A wired SOHO that contains more than one computer typically implements TCP/IP configuration through ICS. Computers and other devices on a wireless or hybrid SOHO obtain their configurations from the WAP. If wireless access is implemented by using a Wi-Fi-enabled Windows Vista computer, this computer should also be configured to provide ICS.

- You use the Network And Sharing Center to view computers and devices on a network, connect to a network, set up a connection or network, and manage network connections.

- You also use the Network And Sharing Center to enable or disable network discovery and configure file, folder, printer, and media sharing.

- A standard user can share files on a network by copying them into his or her public folder hierarchy. Sharing any file or folder on a computer requires administrator privileges, as does configuring share permissions.

Lesson Review

You can use the following questions to test your knowledge of the information in Lesson 1, "Using the Network And Sharing Center to Configure Networking." The questions are also available on the companion CD if you prefer to review them in electronic form.

NOTE   Answers

Answers to these questions and explanations of why each answer choice is correct or incorrect are located in the "Answers" section at the end of the book.

---

1. Which command-line command displays the IP configuration of a computer's interfaces?
   A. ping
   B. tracert
   C. ipconfig
   D. cmd

2. Which of the following methods can you use to display the properties of a LAN connection? (Choose all that apply.)
   A. In the Network And Sharing Center, click Internet Options. In the Connections tab of the Internet Properties dialog box, click LAN Settings.
   B. In the Network And Sharing Center, click View Status beside the connection. In the Local Area Connection Status dialog box, click Properties.
   C. In the Network And Sharing Center, click Manage Network Connections. In the Network Connections dialog box, right-click the connection and select Properties.
   D. In the Network And Sharing Center, click Manage Network Connections. In the Network Connections dialog box, right-click the connection and select Status. In the Local Area Connection Status dialog box, click Properties.

3. Which of the following wireless LAN hardware standards can achieve bandwidths of up to 54 Mbps? (Choose all that apply.)

   A. 802.11a

   B. 802.11b

   C. 802.11d

   D. 802.11g

4. Which of the following wireless LAN hardware standards is the least prone to being affected by interference from domestic devices?

   A. 802.11a

   B. 802.11b

   C. 802.11d

   D. 802.11g

5. A user who does not have administrator privileges wants to be able to share files on her computer by using a simple copy and paste operation without requiring administrator intervention. She wants to be able to access and edit her files from other computers in the workgroup on which she has accounts. She wants access to her shared files to be restricted to users who have accounts on the computer on which she shares them. How do you configure sharing on this user's computer?

   A. Enable File Sharing; disable Public Folder Sharing; enable Password Protected Sharing; enable Network Discovery

   B. Enable File Sharing; enable Public Folder Sharing; disable Password Protected Sharing; enable Network Discovery

   C. Disable File Sharing; enable Public Folder Sharing; enable Password Protected Sharing; disable Network Discovery

   D. Disable File Sharing; enable Public Folder Sharing; enable Password Protected Sharing; enable Network Discovery

Lesson 2: Troubleshooting Connectivity Issues

As an IT professional, one of the most common problems you will encounter is computers not being able to connect to one another, to other internal networks within your organization, or to the Internet. In this lesson you look at general troubleshooting tools that help you debug both wired and wireless network connectivity, issues specific to wireless connections, and the Diagnose Internet Connection tool that Windows Vista provides. The lesson also discusses Windows Firewall settings and public and private networks.

After this lesson, you will be able to:
- Perform basic network infrastructure troubleshooting.
- Use command-line tools to troubleshoot IP configuration and connectivity.
- Troubleshoot problems specific to wireless networks.
- Use the Diagnose Internet Connection tool to troubleshoot connectivity issues.
- Configure network settings in Windows Firewall.
- Distinguish between public and private network profiles.

Estimated lesson time: 60 minutes

Real World

Ian McLean

This lesson is about troubleshooting network connectivity and the tools available to you for this task. However, before you start to troubleshoot any sort of problem, you need to find out exactly what it is. Always try to take a commonsense approach and remember that the least reliable part of any system is located between the mouse and the seat. You should ask a number of questions:

- Did it ever work?
- What is still working?
- What has stopped working?
- How are the things that work related to the things that do not work?
- What's it doing now that it did not do before?
- What's it not doing now that it did do before?
- What was changed just before the problem occurred?

- Does the problem occur only on one computer or is it common to all users and all computers?

  Then, ask yourself two questions:

- Have I solved this problem before and documented the solution?
- Has someone else solved the problem and documented it in TechNet?

This leads to the other important thing you need to do, and I cannot emphasize this enough: *document the problem and the solution*. A job is not complete unless it is documented. It is not easy for the harassed IT professional to find the time to do the documentation. Find the time. It pays handsomely in the long run.

Basic Troubleshooting

Connection problems can have many possible causes. In wired networks a cable could be faulty or might not be connecting properly to its socket. Interfaces that should get their IP configurations dynamically (automatically) could be set with a static (manual) configuration. Where two or more interfaces form a network bridge, one or more interfaces could have been removed from the bridge. ICS might be set up incorrectly or not set up at all. A third-party WAP could have been added to a wired network so that wireless computers can connect, but the computer previously configured to provide ICS might not be reconfigured to obtain its configuration from the WAP. A WAP, NIC, or modem could be faulty. Your ISP could be suffering an outage. Newly installed software might have changed your connection properties. The list is practically endless.

First principles always apply. Start with the network and ensure that no cables have been pulled out or are half-way out and causing unreliable connections. Make sure all the appropriate light-emitting diodes (LEDs) on the modem, WAP, and network interfaces are lit when they should be lit and flickering when they should be flickering. If a device shows no sign of life, check that its power supply is connected to the mains and to the device. Check out any illuminated red LEDs. A red light does not always indicate a fault, but red frequently signifies danger.

If all the lights on your cable modem are on except the online light, your modem could be on standby or your ISP might be suffering an outage. Many modems have a button that switches from standby to online mode. If pressing this button does not solve the problem, phone your ISP's helpline before you waste time checking out your equipment.

If you are using a dial-up modem, try unplugging it from the phone socket and plugging in an ordinary phone instead. If you get a dial tone, your telephone connection is okay.

You can sometimes solve modem problems by turning off any computer directly connected to the modem and then turning off the modem itself. Wait a few minutes, turn the modem back on, and then restart the computer. If other computers on a wired or hybrid network obtain their configuration through ICS from the computer attached to the modem, reboot these computers when the ICS computer is back online.

If you are having problems with wireless connections, try switching the WAP off—or powering down if wireless connectivity is implemented by a Wi-Fi–enabled Windows Vista computer. You should then power down any computers that connect to the WAP through Ethernet cables and possibly your wireless computers as well. Wait a few minutes, switch the WAP back on, and reboot the computers. If you suspect the modem, switch off the modem, the WAP, and all network computers and then turn them on again in that order. Check the WAP settings.

MORE INFO   Basic fault finding

For more information and hints on diagnosing problems caused by a malfunctioning cable modem, dial-up modem, WAP, or network cable or by an ISP outage, search for "Troubleshoot network and Internet connection problems" in Windows Help and Support.

Checking Computer-to-Computer Connectivity

Before you start to use the tools Windows Vista provides to check computer-to-computer connectivity, first make sure the computer you are trying to connect to is switched on. In a wired network, make sure it is plugged into the network. If you are using ICS, make sure the ICS computer is switched on and running, otherwise none of the other computers will connect to the Internet. If the computers on your network get their TCP/IP connections from a third-party WAP, make sure the WAP is switched on and connected to the modem. For a computer running Windows Vista to connect to other computers on a LAN, Network Discovery needs to be enabled on both the source and destination computers. Network Discover is enabled by default, but if you are having problems accessing other computers, check this setting in the Network And Sharing Center.

You can see other computers on a network only if at least one folder on each computer is shared. You might be able to ping the computer by IP address and by name (see later in this lesson) but you will not see the computer in the Network dialog box unless it is sharing resources on the network.

NOTE   Viewing the Full Network Map

You can view all the computers and other network-enabled devices on your subnet or SOHO by clicking Network in the Start menu. If a computer on your network does not display, its network discovery setting might be set to Off. To change the network discovery setting on another computer, log on to the computer, open the Network And Sharing Center, expand Network Discovery, click Turn On Network Discovery, and then click Apply.

Troubleshooting Device Drivers

If a network connection is suffering intermittent problems, it is sometimes sufficient to disable and then enable the connection in the Network Connections dialog box. However, if this does not help, the device driver might be corrupt or out of date. If you have configured the computers on your network to use Microsoft Update, the drivers should be updated as required. Nevertheless, you might sometimes find it necessary to locate and reinstall the latest driver.

To do this, right-click Computer on the Start menu, and select Properties. Click Device Manager and enter administrator credentials or click Continue to close the UAC dialog box. In Device Manager expand Network Adapters, right-click the relevant adapter, and click Properties. In the General tab of the Network Adapter Properties dialog box you should get an indication of whether the device is working properly. In the Driver tab, shown in Figure 7-23, you can click Update Driver and then click Search Automatically For Updated Driver Software.

Figure 7-23   Network Adapter Properties dialog box, Driver tab

If Windows Vista finds a more up-to-date driver, it installs it; otherwise it tells you that you have the most up-to-date driver. If, in the latter case, you still want to reinstall the driver, you can access the Driver tab of the Network Adapter Properties dialog box and click Uninstall. When you have uninstalled the driver, you can click Update Driver in the same tab to locate, download, and install the latest driver.

MORE INFO   **Troubleshooting device drivers**

For more information on troubleshooting device drivers, refer to Lesson 3, "Installing, Updating, and Troubleshooting Windows Vista Device Drivers," of Chapter 1, "Installing Windows Vista Client" and Lesson 1, "Troubleshooting Post-Installation Configuration Issues," of Chapter 3, "Troubleshooting Post-Installation System Settings."

CAUTION   Deleting network adapter device driver software

The Uninstall function gives you the option of deleting the network adapter device driver software from the computer. You might want to do this if you suspect this software is corrupt. However, be aware that if you delete the driver software for an interface, you will no longer be able to connect to your network or to the Internet through that interface to download a new interface driver. You need either to use a second interface (if the computer has one) or install the driver from removable media.

Sometimes problems can occur with a wired connection because by default the computer can turn the connection off to save power. If you want to change this behavior, access the Network Adapter Properties dialog box, select the Power Management tab, clear the Allow The Computer To Turn Off This Device To Save Power check box, and then click OK.

Troubleshooting IP Configuration

Command-line tools for troubleshooting IP configuration have been around for some time and are well-known. The ping tool was mentioned in Lesson 1, "Using the Network And Sharing Center to Configure Networking." It is traditionally one of the most commonly used tools for testing connectivity, although more firewalls block ICMP than used to be the case so perhaps the use of the tool is no longer universal. However, even if you cannot get past a firewall on your organization's network, ping is still useful.

You can check that TCP/IP is working on a computer by entering **ping 127.0.0.1**. The IPv4 address 127.0.0.1 is called the loopback address and always identifies the device from which the ping command is issued.

You can then ping the IPv4 address of the computer. You can find out what this is either by using the ipconfig command or by accessing the Network Connection Details dialog box (see Figures 7-2 and 7-10). For the configuration shown in these figures, this command is **ping 10.16.10.143**. If your computer has more than one interface combined in a network bridge, you can ping the IPv4 address of the network bridge. When you have established that you can ping your computer using an IPv4 address, you can test that DNS is working internally on your network by pinging your computer name—for example, **ping Glasgow**.

You can also use the ipconfig command for troubleshooting. The command **ipconfig /all** gives you the same information that you obtained from the Network Connection Details dialog box in Figure 7-10, but for all interfaces. Figure 7-24 shows the output from an ipconfig /all command redirected for clarity into a text file. The computer whose configuration is shown here is a different computer with a different configuration from the one whose connection details were shown in Figure 7-10. It is a wireless-enabled laptop used on a home network. It obtains its configuration through DHCP from a third-party WAP with an IPv4 address 192.168.123.254, which is the subnet's gateway to the modem and the Internet. The WAP also provides internal DNS services. However, the resolution of FQDNs such as www.contoso.com is provided by the ISP's DNS server with the public IPv4 address 62.31.64.39.

```
all - Notepad
File  Edit  Format  View  Help

Windows IP Configuration

    Host Name . . . . . . . . . . . . : Melbourne
    Primary Dns Suffix  . . . . . . . :
    Node Type . . . . . . . . . . . . : Hybrid
    IP Routing Enabled. . . . . . . . : No
    WINS Proxy Enabled. . . . . . . . : No

Wireless LAN adapter Wireless Network Connection:

    Connection-specific DNS Suffix  . :
    Description . . . . . . . . . . . : Cisco Systems 350 Series PCMCIA Wireless
    Physical Address. . . . . . . . . : 00-11-21-A1-A4-1D
    DHCP Enabled. . . . . . . . . . . : Yes
    Autoconfiguration Enabled . . . . : Yes
    Link-local IPv6 Address . . . . . : fe80::e98d:979d:a523:2b12%10(Preferred)
    IPv4 Address. . . . . . . . . . . : 192.168.123.111(Preferred)
    Subnet Mask . . . . . . . . . . . : 255.255.255.0
    Lease Obtained. . . . . . . . . . : Tuesday, December 12, 2006 9:24:54 PM
    Lease Expires . . . . . . . . . . : Tuesday, January 23, 2007 1:24:53 PM
    Default Gateway . . . . . . . . . : 192.168.123.254
    DHCP Server . . . . . . . . . . . : 192.168.123.254
    DHCPv6 IAID . . . . . . . . . . . : 167776545
    DNS Servers . . . . . . . . . . . : 62.31.64.39
                                        192.168.123.254
    NetBIOS over Tcpip. . . . . . . . : Enabled

Ethernet adapter Local Area Connection:

    Media State . . . . . . . . . . . : Media disconnected
```

Figure 7-24   Ipconfig /all output for a wireless-enabled laptop on a home network

When you are debugging connection problems by using the ipconfig /all command, look out for an address in the APIPA range 169.254.0.1 through 169.254.255.254. Windows Vista assigns an APIPA address if your computer has not received a configuration through DHCP, either from the computer running ICS on a wired network, the WAP on a wireless or hybrid network, or the ISP (in the case when the network consists of a single home computer connected directly through a modem). Unless your network is completely isolated and never accesses any other network, including the Internet, an APIPA address indicates a connection error.

You should also look out for the IPv4 address 192.168.0.1. If you are using ipconfig on a computer that is providing ICS for a wired network, this is what the computer's IPv4 address should be. If, on the other hand, you are adding a workstation to a wired or wireless network that obtains its configuration from a WAP and you find the workstation has this IP address, you likely need to change its IPv4 properties so that it obtains its configuration dynamically. The computer was previously used to provide ICS for a network and has been statically configured with the 192.168.0.1 IP address. This sometimes happens when you install a third-party WAP on an existing wired network to create a hybrid network—the other wired computers and the wireless mobile computers all get their configurations from the WAP, but you forget to reconfigure the computer that previously provided ICS.

Real World

Ian McLean

I recently came across the problem of a statically configured computer in my own home network, although the situation was a bit different. The computer that was connected directly to the Internet and providing ICS was experiencing memory problems. I had a newer and more powerful computer that I wanted to use for this purpose anyway so I replaced the old computer. I then bought some RAM, installed it on the old computer, and decided I might as well plug it into a spare port and use it as an ordinary workstation.

Did I remember to reconfigure the interface so the computer obtained its TCP/IP settings dynamically? Well, put it this way—it wasn't just the computer that had memory problems.

If you can successfully ping your computer by name and IPv4 address and are happy with the results obtained by ipconfig, you can then try pinging other workstations on your network by IPv4 address and computer name. Finally, you should check that you can ping your default gateway from all the computers in your network. You can then test connectivity to your ISP by pinging the ISP's DNS server.

NOTE   Ipconfig and connectivity

In general, if ipconfig /all identifies a default gateway and an internal and external DNS server, the computer is likely to be able to connect to them. However, IP configuration is refreshed periodically and it is possible that connectivity has been lost after the last refresh. It is worthwhile pinging the default gateway and DNS servers to check this out.

If you cannot ping a computer on your network to test connectivity, make sure your internal fire-walls are not blocking ICMP. (On a computer running Windows Vista, Windows Firewall permits ICMP by default.) If the problem still exists with the firewalls reconfigured or disabled (please remember to enable them afterward), check the physical network connections again (you should have done this first) and use ipconfig on the computer you cannot reach to check its IP settings.

Quick Check

- You have purchased a second-hand computer and are connecting it to a hybrid network that obtains its configuration from DHCP provided by a third-party WAP. The computer is not wireless-enabled, so you plug it into an Ethernet hub and switch it on. It cannot access the Internet. You enter ipconfig from the Command Prompt console and discover that the computer has an IP address of 10.1.10.231. You know the WAP is working properly and the Ethernet connection is okay. What should you check next?

> **Quick Check Answer**
> - Check that the computer is set to receive its TCP/IP configuration dynamically. It has not been reconfigured by DHCP on the WAP and its previous owner has probably configured it statically with the 10.1.10.231 address. You need to reconfigure the computer to receive its TCP/IP settings dynamically.

If you want to reconfigure IP settings on a workstation on your network, you can reboot it. If this is not convenient, the commands **ipconfig /release** and **ipconfig /renew** release the old configuration and obtain a new one. (In theory, **ipconfig /renew** should be sufficient, but I always use both commands.) Sometimes when you renew a computer's configuration, it does not immediately register its new settings in DNS and you cannot ping it by computer name. In this case, **ipconfig /registerdns** forces registration.

NOTE   Opening the administrator Command Prompt Console

The **ipconfig /registerdns** and **ipconfig /flushdns** commands require that you run the Command Prompt Console as an administrator. To do this, select Accessories from the All Programs menu, right-click Command Prompt, and click Run As Administrator. As with all administrator level prompts, the UAC dialog box will, by default, prompt you to provide administrator credentials or click Continue.

If you try to ping a computer by name or access a website from a workstation and DNS cannot resolve the computer name or URL, then information that resolution has failed is stored (cached) in the workstation. If you try to do the same thing again, the workstation will not attempt to obtain name resolution but will instead use the cached information and again fail the request. This is known as negative caching. However, name resolution might have failed because of a temporary glitch in the internal or external DNS service. Even though DNS is now working, the computer name or FQDN will not be resolved to an IPv4 address because of the cached information. The problem will disappear in 30 minutes or so because the workstation's DNS resolver cache is regularly cleared. However, if you do not want to wait this long, you can solve the problem immediately by using the **ipconfig /flushdns** command to flush the DNS cache.

NOTE   The /allcompartments switch

If you use the /allcompartments switch after the ipconfig command, you can apply the command to all network adapter compartments—that is, universally across all interfaces. For example, **ipconfig /allcompartments /all** or **ipconfig /allcompartments /renew**.

If you want to trace the route of an IP datagram through an internetwork (a series of networks or hops), you can use the tracert command to list the path the datagram took and the delays encountered at each hop. To generate the tracert output, shown in Figure 7-25, the command

tracert 62.31.64.39 was issued from the wireless laptop whose configuration was shown in Figure 7-24. The tracert output was redirected into a text file for two reasons. First, it is easier to read. Second, I am not permitted for legal reasons to use the actual names of my ISP or telecommunications company (telco). Therefore, I have changed these in the text file to the fictitious names contoso and adatum respectively in order to protect the innocent (me).

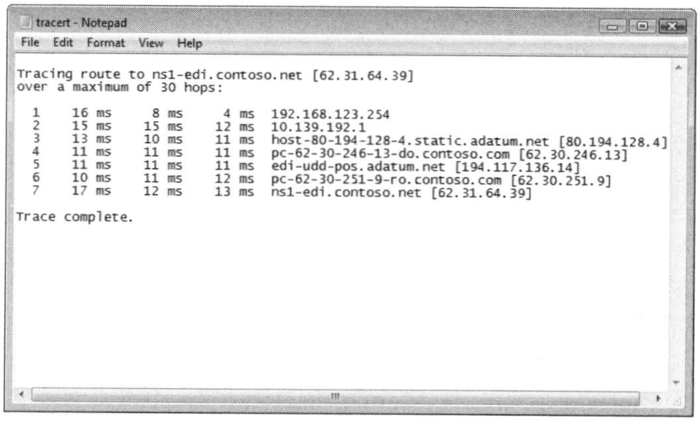

Figure 7-25   Tracert output

NOTE   Pathping

The pathping command traces a route in much the same way as the tracert command but gives more detailed statistics about each hop. Try this command for yourself—for example, **pathping www.contoso.com**.

Troubleshooting Wireless Network Settings

In general, wireless adapters have the same type of IPv4 configurations as Ethernet adapters and you can check connectivity by using the same command-line tools. However, certain problems are peculiar to wired connections. We discussed these briefly in Lesson 1, "Using the Network And Sharing Center to Configure Networking."

Problems can occur when a wireless-enabled laptop is within range of more than one preferred network. This can happen in business premises that are too large to be covered by the one network. When you move from one part of the building to another, you can switch to a second network and retain Internet connectivity. However, the networks typically overlap, and employees can experience connectivity problems if they use their laptops in an overlap area.

To prevent this from happening you can disable automatic switching in one or both of the network profiles. You do this by selecting Manage Wireless Networks in the Network And Sharing Center, right-clicking the network whose profile you want to alter, and selecting Properties. You carry out this procedure in the practice session later in this chapter.

CAUTION   Disabling automatic switching is not always a good idea

You can disable automatic switching between preferred networks to solve the problems that occur when a user is working in an overlap area. However, be very cautious about doing this as a matter of course. A doctor working in a hospital will not want to manually connect to another WAP point when she moves from one ward to another. A teacher will not want to change his settings when moving between classes. Always ensure that your users understand the disadvantages of this "fix."

To reduce interference from devices such as mobile phones and microwave ovens, you can change the channel that your WAP uses. Some channels are less interference-prone than others. If wireless access is provided by a computer with a Wi-Fi interface, you can access the dialog box for that interface. To configure a third-party WAP, follow the manufacturer's instructions. You can configure most third-party WAPs through a web interface from any computer on the network. If, for example, a WAP has an IPv4 address of 192.168.123.154, then entering **http://192.168.123.254** should access configuration controls similar to those shown in Figure 7-26.

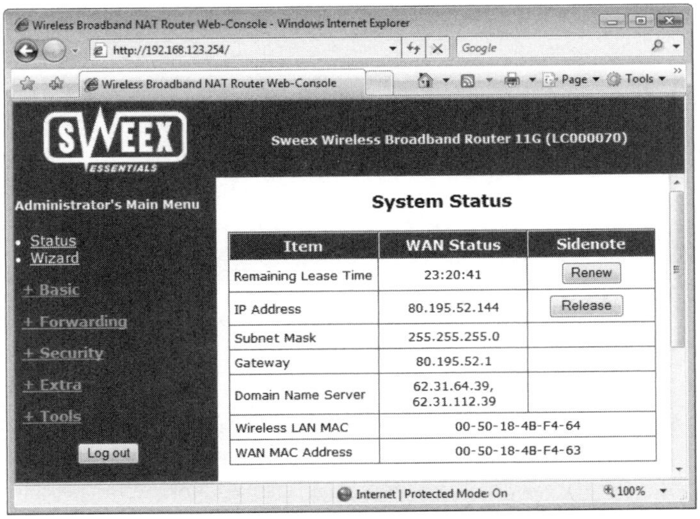

Figure 7-26   A typical third-party WAP configuration interface

A number of factors determine which channel gives you the least interference—for example, your location and the type of devices that are causing interference. You need to experiment with channel settings until you find the best one.

Figure 7-27 shows the basic setup page for a third-party WAP with default settings. When you install a WAP, you should change the SSID and configure security settings.

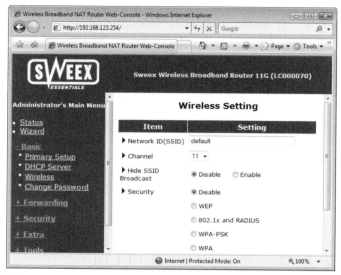

Figure 7-27   SSID, network, and encryption settings on a typical third-party WAP

Changing the SSID prevents problems arising because your network is near others that are configured with the default SSID. If you do not secure your wireless network, a thief no longer needs to break into your home. He or she can sit in an automobile outside your front gate, turn on a wireless-enabled laptop, steal your passwords, and empty your bank account. If you are configuring a wireless network for your company and do not secure it, your company could be out of business and you could be out of a job.

Configuring Wireless Network Security

Many wireles connection problems are related to security. The precise steps involved in setting up security depend on the type of WAP (third-party WAP device or Wi-Fi–enabled Windows Vista computer) you have installed on your network. This section discusses the settings available in most WAPs and ways in which you can increase wireless network security. You can take the following steps to increase security in your own or your employer's wireless network:

- **Change the default SSID**   As previously discussed in this lesson, you should do this anyway so that nearby networks with default settings do not interfere with your wireless network. Changing an SSID improves network security because hackers who see a network with a default SSID deduce that it is a poorly configured network and are more likely to attack it.

- **Turn on Wi-Fi Protected Access (WPA) or Wired Equivalent Privacy (WEP) encryption**   All wireless equipment supports some form of encryption that scrambles messages sent over wireless networks so they cannot be easily read if they are intercepted. You should choose the strongest form of encryption that works with your wireless network. However, all wireless devices on your LAN must share the identical encryption settings. Therefore, you need to find the most secure setting that you can configure on both your WAP and your wireless adapters.

- **Change default administrator passwords**   The webpage interface that allows you to configure a third-party WAP usually presents you with a logon dialog box that requires at least a password (typically admin) and sometimes a user name. The default settings are well known to hackers. Change them.

- **Enable MAC address filtering**   This is regarded as a fairly complex configuration because MAC addresses—48-bit hexadecimal numbers—look daunting. Many administrators believe they need to go round all their network devices, enter the **ipconfig /all** command, write down the MAC addresses, and then type this information into the WAP configuration website interface. In fact, this time-consuming operation is not necessary. ARP resolves IP addresses to MAC addresses and caches the results. So, all you need to do is sit at a single station on your network, ping all the network devices (by name if you prefer; DNS resolves names into IP addresses), and then capture the contents of the ARP cache into a text file from which you can copy them and paste them into the WAP interface. You do this in a practice later in this lesson. (Sometimes knowing about protocols and what they do can be very useful.) Unless you have the requirement that other laptops should be able to use a wireless network (in a hotel, for example) you should configure MAC filtering to help secure your network.

- **Disable SSID broadcast**   A WAP typically broadcasts its SSID at regular intervals. This feature is designed for businesses and mobile hotspots where wireless clients might come and go. In a home network and many small office networks, this feature is unnecessary and increases the likelihood that a hacker will try to log on.

- **Do not auto-connect to open wireless networks**   Connecting to an unsecured wireless network exposes a computer to security risks. Some network adapters have a setting that prohibits this. This is a setting specific to the adapter, not to Windows Vista, although Windows Live One-Care, if installed, increases browser and firewall security if a computer connects to an unsecured network.

- **Enable firewalls**   Ensure that Windows Firewall is enabled on wireless computers. If the WAP has an inbuilt firewall or is implemented on a Windows Vista computer protected by Windows Firewall, also check that this firewall is enabled.

- **Position the WAP centrally**   Wireless signals normally reach to the exterior of a home or office, but you should minimize the outdoor leakage as much as possible. Position the WAP near the center of the building. Do not put it on your front windowsill.

- **Turn off the network during extended periods of nonuse**   It is often impractical to turn a WAP off frequently, but consider doing so during extended periods offline (for example, during holiday closures).

- **Consider assigning static IP addresses to wireless devices**   DHCP makes setup easy and comparatively error-free. However, network attackers can obtain valid IP addresses from a network's DHCP pool. Most WAPs let you disable DHCP. If you have configured a Windows Vista computer to provide wireless access, you can disable ICS on that computer. You can then assign private static IP addresses (possibly in the 10.0.0.0 network) to all your network devices. This increases security, but static setup is inconvenient and error-prone. You should consider this option only in networks where security is a highly critical consideration or in networks where your WAP appears to have problems configuring (for example) external DNS settings through DHCP.

Connecting to a Network that Does Not Broadcast its SSID

Some wireless networks do not advertise their SSIDs for security reasons. However, if you know the network details, you can connect to it. To do this, open Network And Sharing Center and click Set Up A Connection Or Network. Select Manually Connect To A Wireless Network and click Next. Type the network's name and select the security type. The encryption type is typically entered automatically. You type the security key or passphrase and decide whether to connect to the network automatically. If the network is secure, this is the default. For unsecured networks the default is not to connect automatically. When you have completed all the fields, click Next. Your computer detects and (if specified) connects to the network.

Using the Diagnose Internet Connection Tool to Troubleshoot Connectivity Issues

There has never been a substitute for good basic faultfinding. However, after you have gone through the basic checks Window Vista provides automated assistance with the Windows Network Diagnostics tool, sometimes known as the Diagnose Internet Connection tool.

You can access the automated Network Diagnostics tool if you fail to connect to a website on the Internet. The webpage that appears in your browser gives you a direct link to the tool when you click Diagnose Connection Problems, as shown in Figure 7-28.

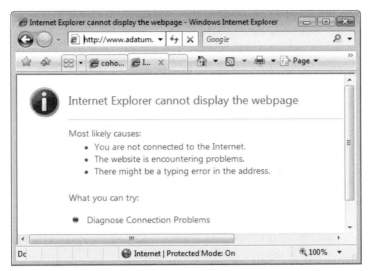

Figure 7-28   The Diagnose Connection Problems link

Network Diagnostics returns a message that might help you diagnose the problem, as shown in Figure 7-29.

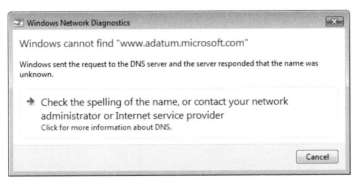

Figure 7-29   Diagnosing a failure to locate a website

You can diagnose connection problems by running the Network Diagnostic tool from the Network And Sharing Center by clicking Diagnose And Repair. You can also run the Network Diagnostics tool against a specific interface or interface bridge by clicking Manage Network Connections in the Network And Sharing Center, right-clicking the relevant connection, and selecting Diagnose. If you are prompted for administrator credentials or confirmation, close the UAC dialog box by providing credentials or by clicking Continue. Figure 7-30 shows the result of a network diagnostic run against a wireless interface.

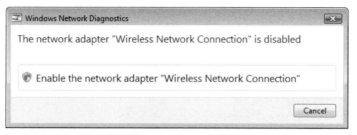

Figure 7-30   Diagnosing a disabled wireless connection

Configuring Network Settings in Windows Firewall

Chapter 8, "Configuring Firewall and Remote Access Settings," discusses firewalls and firewall configuration in detail. This chapter therefore provides only a brief introduction and discusses firewall settings only in so far as they affect network connectivity and your ability to test and troubleshoot this connectivity.

Microsoft Windows Firewall is enabled by default in Windows Vista. It blocks all incoming traffic other than traffic that meets the criteria defined in the exceptions. You can configure an exception by allowing a program to send information back and forth through the firewall—sometimes called unblocking. You can also allow a program through the firewall by opening one or more ports.

Enabling, disabling, and configuring Windows Firewall are administrator-level functions, so you will be involved in any firewall changes if you support a business network. In the home environment at least one account with administrator privileges typically exists, so your involvement will probably be to give advice through help desk calls. The defaults are sensible, and often you will be able to solve home users' problems by telling them how to restore these defaults.

The default firewall settings depend on the network location you defined when you installed Windows Vista. The firewall is on for all network locations (home or work, public place, or domain) but with separate profiles for each location. It is on for all network connections and blocks inbound connections that do not match an exception.

The function of the firewall in its default configuration is to prevent hackers or malware (such as worms) from gaining access to a computer. You can also configure the firewall to prevent a hacker or careless user from sending malware from his or her computer to your subnet and to other networks, including the Internet. In some network attacks—for example, distributed denial of service (DDoS)—an attacker takes control of unprotected computers (zombies) and uses them to attack a network. Configuring inbound and outbound firewall rules provides additional protection against such attacks. You can, for example, configure Windows Firewall to allow or block incoming or outgoing packets (or both incoming and outgoing) that use a particular TCP or UDP port number.

Unlike more advanced firewalls, such as the one implemented by Microsoft Internet and Security Acceleration (ISA) Server, Windows Firewall cannot examine the contents of e-mail messages, so you need virus-scanning software to detect and delete suspicious attachments and to disinfect a computer if a virus gets through the defenses. You also need to remind any users you support not to open attachments unless they fully trust the e-mail's source—and keep reminding them.

No firewall can guarantee to stop all malware, and you need to configure Windows Defender (or third-party software) to provide continuous protection and perform regular scans and definition updates. You also need to ensure that phishing filters are in place and content filtering is configured appropriately on any network you support. On networks accessed by children you need to advise parents or teachers about how to set up parental controls or possibly configure the controls for them. You should never fall into the trap of thinking that because the firewall is on everything, it is perfectly safe—nor should you let your users believe this.

Configuring Exceptions

You can configure exceptions by clicking Allow A Program Through Windows Firewall in the Control Panel and clearing the UAC dialog box in the normal way. Figure 7-31 shows the Exceptions tab of the Windows Firewall Settings dialog box.

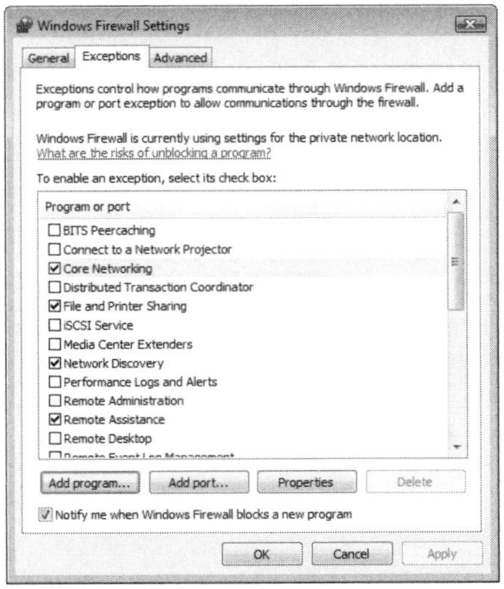

Figure 7-31   The Windows Firewall Settings Exceptions tab

You can select any of the exceptions on the list (whether enabled or not) and click Properties to obtain details about the exception. If you click Add Program, you can use the Add A Program dialog box to add to the exceptions list. If the program you want to add is not on the list of programs, you can browse for it.

Clicking Add Port allows you to add a port to the exceptions list. If you enable a port, traffic associated with that port is allowed through the firewall. Ports are associated with protocols, so if, for example, you added TCP (and possibly UDP) ports 20 and 21 to the exceptions, you would enable File Transfer Protocol (FTP) traffic to pass through the firewall.

Exam Tip   The 70-620 examination does not require a detailed knowledge of protocols and ports. Nevertheless, if you are interested in what ports are used by a particular protocol, access *http://www.iana.org/assignments/port-numbers*.

In both the Add A Program and Add A Port dialog boxes you can click Change Scope. This lets you define the range of computers to which the exception applies. You can specify only computers on the local subnet, any computer, or a list of computers identified by IPv4 address or IPv4 address and subnet mask. You can also specify computers by IPv6 address.

Finally, if you access the Advanced tab you can click the Restore Defaults button. This is a valuable feature when you are assisting users who have messed up their firewall settings.

Examining Advanced Security Settings

You can obtain more information about configured exceptions and perform advanced security configuration by accessing the Windows Firewall with Advanced Security Microsoft Management Console (MMC). This tool enables you to set up and view detailed inbound and outbound rules. You can open the tool from Administrative Tools. If you have not added Administrative Tools to your All Programs menu, you can access the menu by clicking System And Maintenance in Control Panel. You close the UAC dialog box in the normal way and the console appears. Selecting Inbound Rules results in the window as shown in Figure 7-32.

Advanced firewall configuration is beyond the scope of this chapter. However, Figure 7-32 shows that File And Printer Sharing (Echo Request - ICMPv4-In) is enabled. Double-clicking this item accesses the dialog box shown in Figure 7-33. You can experiment by accessing all the tabs in this dialog box, but the important setting as far as troubleshooting connections is concerned is that enabling file and printer sharing enables ICMPv4 echo requests, so we can use the ping, tracert, and pathping tools.

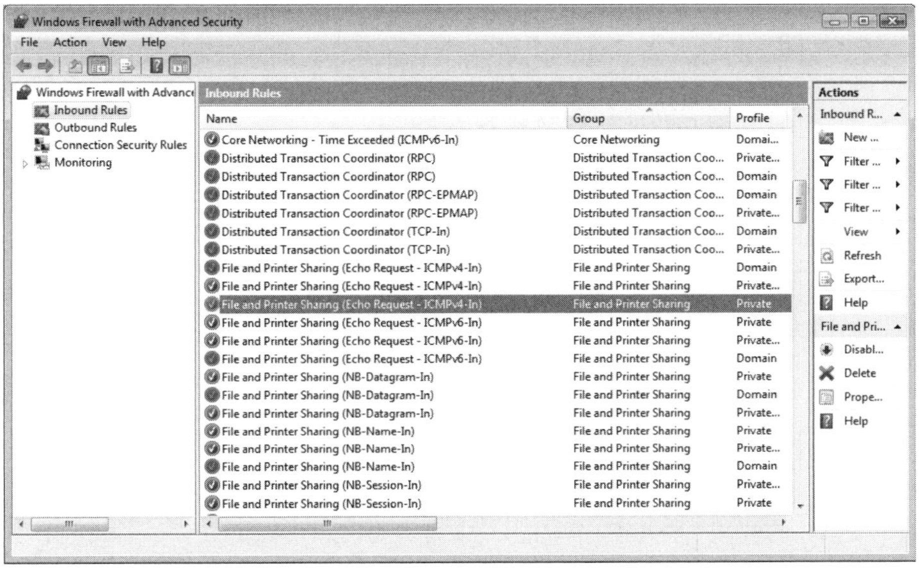

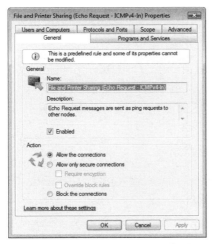

Figure 7-32   Inbound firewall rules

Figure 7-33   File and Printer Sharing (Echo Request - ICMPv4-In) Properties

MORE INFO   **Advanced firewall configuration**

For more information, access *http://go.microsoft.com/fwlink/?LinkId=64343* and *http://go.microsoft.com/fwlink/?LinkId=64382*.

> ## Quick Check
> - How do you restore the default firewall settings?
>
> ## Quick Check Answer
> - From Control Panel click Allow A Program Through Windows Firewall. This opens the Windows Firewall Settings dialog box. In the Advanced tab click Restore Defaults.

Applying Public and Private Firewall Settings

You can configure different groups of firewall settings (profiles) depending on the location that you choose for your network. You can specify this when installing Windows Vista and change your network location by clicking Customize in the Network And Sharing Center.

MORE INFO   Network location

For more information, search for "Choosing a network location" in Windows Help and Support.

You can configure different rules and settings for the Domain, Public, and Private firewall profiles. Domain profiles are outside the scope of this book and the 70-620 examination. We shall therefore consider Private and Public profiles.

Private profile settings apply when a computer is connected to a private network behind a private gateway or router. Public profile settings apply when a computer is connected directly to a network in a public location. The Public profile is active when there is at least one public network or unidentified connection.

If, for example, you access the Advanced tab of the dialog box shown in Figure 7-31, you will see that this exception applies only to Private network locations. Figure 7-34 illustrates this. You can specify that the rule applies to the Public (and Domain) profiles and further refine it by specifying the types of interface to which it applies—by default LAN, Remote Access, and Wireless.

You can create a profile for each network category, with each profile containing different firewall policies. For example, Windows Firewall can automatically allow incoming traffic for a specific logging tool when the computer is on private networks but block similar traffic when the computer is connected to public networks. This provides flexibility on your internal network without sacrificing security for mobile users. A public network profile typically has strict firewall policies to protect against unauthorized access. A private network profile typically has less restrictive firewall policies to allow (for example) file and print sharing and peer-to-peer discovery. Only one profile is applied at any one time.

By default, all incoming traffic is blocked except for core networking traffic. On the Private profile, network discovery and remote assistance traffic is allowed. You need to create specific rules if you want to allow other authorized traffic to pass through the firewall into the computer. The default settings allow all outgoing traffic. If you want to control outgoing traffic through the firewall, you need to specifically block programs or types of traffic.

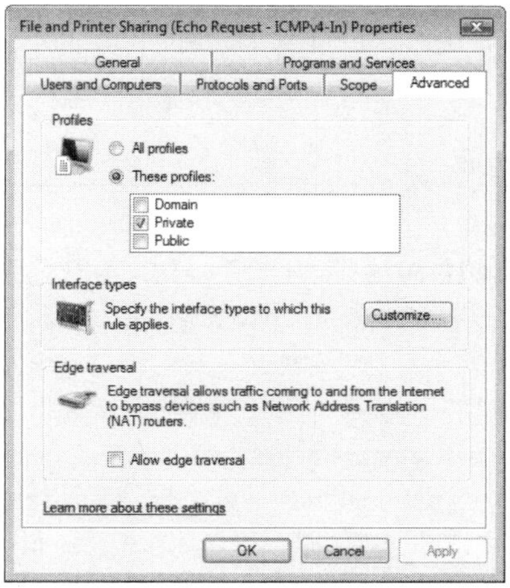

Figure 7-34   File and Printer Sharing (Echo Request - ICMPv4-In) Advanced Properties

To view the controls for configuring profiles, open the Windows Firewall with Advanced Security MMC and click Windows Firewall Properties in the Overview pane. This opens the Windows Firewall With Advanced Security On Local Computer dialog box, shown in Figure 7-35. This dialog box has a tab for each of the three available profiles (Domain, Private, and Public) and a tab for Internet Protocol Security (IPSec) settings. You will look at the settings in detail in Chapter 8, "Configuring Firewall and Remote Access Settings."

Figure 7-35   Windows Firewall With Advanced Security On Local Computer dialog box

Practice: Configuring MAC Security on a WAP and Disabling Automatic Switching

In this practice session you configure your WAP so that only computers with specified MAC addresses can access your wireless network. You also disable automatic switching on a wireless computer so that it does not attempt to switch between two preferred networks that are within range.

▶ **Practice 1: Configuring MAC Security on a WAP**

In this practice you capture the IPv4 addresses and MAC addresses of the wireless computers on your network in a text file and paste this information into the configuration webpage for a third-party WAP. If you have implemented wireless access by using a Wi-Fi–compatible Windows Vista computer, you need to paste the same information into the relevant tab of your Wi-Fi configuration dialog box.

Configuring MAC Security helps ensure that unauthorized users cannot connect their computers to your wireless network. You can complete this practice logged on as a standard user, provided you know the logon credentials for the WAP interface. However, this is a task that typically an administrator would perform, and the practice asks you to log on by using an administrator account.

1. If necessary, log on by using an administrator account—for example, the Kim_Ackers account that you created when you installed Windows Vista or the parent_admin account that you created in Chapter 4, "Configuring and Troubleshooting Internet Access."

2. Open the Command Prompt Console either from Accessories on the All Programs menu or by entering **cmd** in the Run box.

3. Enter **arp -a**. This should show two static entries. The entry with 224 in the first IPv4 octet is the multicast address. The second static entry with 255 in the final IPv4 octet is the broadcast address. You can ignore both entries for the purposes of this exercise. You probably have an entry for the WAP itself, which you can also ignore.

4. Ping your local computer by hostname—for example, **ping Melbourne**.

5. Ping all the other wireless-enabled computers on your network by hostname.

6. If you have any other wireless devices on your network—for example, a wireless-enabled network printer—ping these devices also.

7. Enter **arp –a > arp.txt**.

8. Use Notepad to open the arp.txt file. Depending on the account you logged on with, this should be in C:\Users\Kim_Ackers or C:\Users\parent_admin. The text file should be similar to that shown in Figure 7-36.

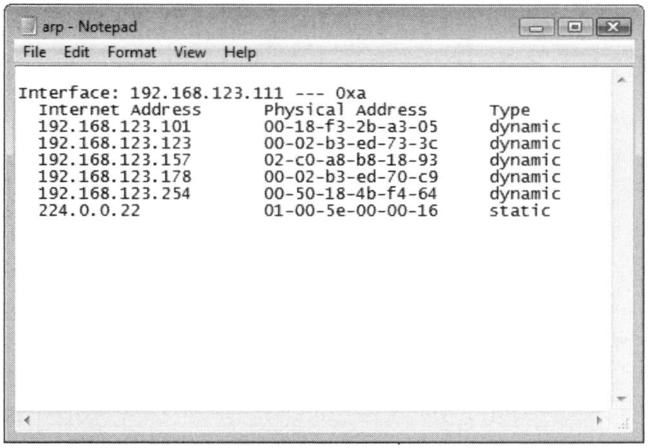

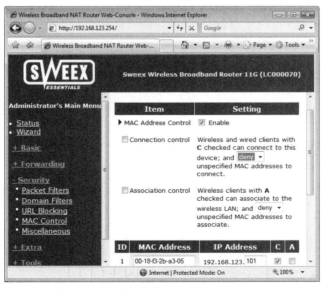

Figure 7-36 Arp –a output in a text file

9. Open your browser and enter the URL for your WAP web interface—for example, **http://192.168.123.254**. Alternatively, open the dialog box for the Wi-Fi adapter card if it is installed on your computer.

10. Access the MAC Address Control page (or tab) and enable MAC Address Control. This should look similar (but probably not identical) to Figure 7-37.

Figure 7-37 MAC Address Control page on a typical third-party router

11. Copy the details for the MAC addresses of the computers and other devices from the text file and paste them into the MAC Address Control page. If required, type in the IPv4 addresses. You likely need to type in only the final octet.

12. Complete the configuration on the web interface or dialog box. Typically, you do this by means of a configuration wizard.

13. Test the configurations by ensuring that all the computers you have specified can still access the network. If you have access to another wireless-enabled computer whose details you did not enter in the MAC Address Control page, check that this computer cannot access your network.

▶ **Practice 2: Disabling Automatic Switching**

In this practice you disable automatic switching on a wireless-enabled computer. The practice asks you to log on by using a standard account—for example, the parent_standard account that you created in Chapter 4, "Configuring and Troubleshooting Internet Access." If you prefer, you can use the administrator account (Kim_Ackers) that you created when you installed Windows Vista. However, no administrator permissions are needed to carry out the practice.

1. If necessary, log on by using a standard account—for example, the parent_standard account that you created in Chapter 4.

2. Open the Network And Sharing Center and click Manage Wireless Networks.

3. Right-click the preferred network to which you want to remain connected even when there is another preferred network within range. Select Properties.

4. In the Wireless Network Properties dialog box on the Connection tab, shown in Figure 7-38, clear the Connect To A More Preferred Network If Available check box.

Figure 7-38   The Wireless Network Properties dialog box

5. Click OK.

Lesson Summary

- The ipconfig command displays a computer's TCP/IP settings, and you can use it to detect incorrect configuration. The ping command tests connectivity. The tracert and pathping commands trace the path of an IP datagram through an internetwork.

- You can access the Windows Network Diagnostics tool from the Network And Sharing Center to troubleshoot a faulty network connection. If you fail to connect to a website, you can access the same tool by clicking Diagnose Connection Problems.

- Problems with wireless connectivity can occur if a computer is within range of two preferred networks or two networks that have the same SSID. Interference from domestic devices can also cause problems.

- Using an unsecured wireless network can create significant security risks. If you configure a wireless network, always ensure that it is secure.

- Windows Firewall blocks all incoming traffic except that which meets exception rules. You can configure rules by allowing specified programs through the firewall. You can also allow all traffic that uses specified ports through the firewall. Optionally, you can configure the firewall to control outgoing traffic.

- You can configure different firewall settings (profiles) depending on whether the computer is in a public or private location. Public profiles are typically more restrictive than Private profiles.

Lesson Review

You can use the following questions to test your knowledge of the information in Lesson 2, "Troubleshooting Connectivity Issues." The questions are also available on the companion CD if you prefer to review them in electronic form.

NOTE Answers

Answers to these questions and explanations of why each answer choice is correct or incorrect are located in the "Answers" section at the end of the book.

1. You open the browser on a computer on your wired SOHO and attempt to access a website. You receive a message that Internet Explorer cannot display the webpage. You remember that the computer that provides ICS on your network is switched off. You restart this computer and again try to access the webpage at the computer from which you tried to access it before. You are sure the URL is correct. You can access other websites from this computer. What can you do to get to the website? (Choose all that apply.)

   A. Reboot your modem.

   B. Reboot the computer.

   C. Access the website from another computer on your network.

   D. Open the Command Prompt console from the Run box and enter **ipconfig /flushdns**. Refresh the browser.

   E. Open the Command Prompt console by right-clicking the item in the Accessories menu and selecting Run As Administrator. Enter **ipconfig /flushdns**. Refresh the browser.

   F. Wait for a while and try again.

2. One of the users you support uses a wireless laptop in the office and also takes it with her on business trips. She reports that when she uses the laptop in the lounge area of a hotel in which she frequently stays she experiences delays and connection problems. She has no problems when using the laptop in her hotel room or when she returns to the office. What should you do to help solve the problem?

   A. Change the SSID of your office network.

   B. Advise the user to change the order in which her laptop attempts to access preferred networks.

   C. Disable network switching on one or both of the preferred networks that the user connects to in order to access the Internet from her hotel.

   D. Update the device driver for the user's wireless LAN adapter.

3. You want to ensure that only certain designated wireless laptops can connect to your network. What do you need to enable?

   A. MAC address control

   B. IPv4 address control

   C. WEP

   D. WPA

4. You are having problems with a connection and want to run the Network Diagnostics tool. How can you access this tool? (Choose all that apply.)

   A. On the Accessories menu, select System Tools.

   B. On the Administrative Tools menu, select Task Scheduler. Schedule the Network Diagnostic tool to start immediately.

   C. In the Network And Sharing Center click Diagnose And Repair.

   D. Access the Local Area Connections Properties dialog box and click Configure. In the General tab, click Repair.

   E. On the message returned by the browser when it cannot access a webpage, click Diagnose Connection Problems.

   F. Open the Network Connections dialog box by selecting Manage Network Connections on the Network And Sharing Center. Right-click a connection and click Diagnose.

5. Which of the following locations are available when you configure profiles in Windows Firewall? (Choose all that apply.)

   A. Public

   B. Wireless

   C. Domain

   D. External

   E. Private

Chapter Review

To further practice and reinforce the skills you learned in this chapter, you can perform the following tasks:

- Review the chapter summary.
- Review the list of key terms introduced in this chapter.
- Complete the case scenarios. These scenarios set up real-world situations involving the topics of this chapter and ask you to create a solution.
- Complete the suggested practices.
- Take a practice test.

Chapter Summary

- The protocols and services in the TCP/IP protocol stack control device configuration, package routing, and package transmission through an internetwork.
- You use the Network And Sharing Center to configure networks and network connections, connect to networks, configure sharing and network discovery, and access Network Diagnostics.
- You can use command-line tools such as ping, pathping, tracert, and ipconfig to diagnose connectivity problems in both wired and wireless networks. Wireless networks can experience problems due to network switching or interference. Unsecured wireless networks can pose security risks.
- By default, Windows Firewall controls incoming traffic and allows only traffic that meets exception rules. You can enable exceptions, create exception rules, control outgoing traffic, and configure Private and Public profiles.

Key Terms

Do you know what these key terms mean? You can check your answers by looking up the terms in the glossary at the end of the book.

- binary digit (bit)
- default gateway
- Internet Protocol (IP) address
- Internet Protocol (IP) datagram
- octet
- preferred wireless network
- private network

- protocol
- protocol stack
- public address
- subnet
- subnet mask
- wireless fidelity (Wi-Fi)
- wireless router

Case Scenarios

In the following case scenarios, you will apply what you have learned about configuring and troubleshooting network connectivity. You can find answers to these questions in the "Answers" section at the end of this book.

Case Scenario 1: Advising Customers About Network Configuration

You are an IT professional working for Northwind Traders. Your company supplies computer systems on a contract basis. You provide telephone help desk support to small business users as part of an extended warranty contract. Typically, your customers configure their networks as workgroups rather than as Active Directory domains. Most of the systems your company provides run Windows Vista Business or Ultimate. Answer the following questions:

1. A customer runs a very small business from his home. Until recently he used a single computer connected directly to his cable modem to access the Internet. His business has expanded and now he uses three computers. He has connected them with an Ethernet hub and now connects to his modem through a USB cable. He reports that the computer connected to the modem can access the Internet but the others cannot. What do you advise?

2. A customer has set up a wireless network in her office. She is pleased with the ease with which she set up her third-party WAP by clicking a single button in the web interface. However, she reports that workers in the office next door to her can access and use her network. What do you advise?

3. A business customer with four employees wants to access information on his own workstation from other workstations on his office. He has administrator and standard accounts on all the workstations on his network. He uses file and folder sharing because he does not want to copy or move a large amount of information into his public folder structure. He wants his deputy to be able to access the information but not to change it. What do you advise?

Case Scenario 2: Troubleshooting a Network

You are an IT professional providing frontline support for Trey Research, a small research organization that has recently upgraded the operating system (OS) on all its computers to Windows Vista. Trey Research does not have an Active Directory domain but instead uses workstations configured in a workgroup. Some of the company computers are desktops and are wired to the hybrid office network. However, some employees frequently travel to the premises of Trey Research's clients and use wireless laptops both while on business and in the office. One of your tasks is to troubleshoot network connectivity problems.

1. The wireless adapter on a colleague's laptop failed while he was away from the office and he replaced it. He could connect to the wireless network at the client's premises but is unable to connect to the Trey Research network. What is likely to be the problem and how do you solve it?

2. You have set up Trey Research's wireless network securely. However, your boss is concerned that wireless networks at client premises might not be so secure. She wants firewall settings on laptop computers to allow only the minimum level of exceptions when the laptops are used on client premises. At the same time, she does not want you to reconfigure firewalls every time an employee visits a client and again when that employee returns to the office. What do you tell her?

3. An employee's desktop computer cannot connect to the Internet or to other computers on the internal network. You inspect the computer's configuration and find it has an IPv4 address 169.254.16.221 with a subnet mask 255.255.0.0. None of the other desktop or laptop computers in the office are experiencing problems. What is likely to be wrong with the computer?

Suggested Practices

To help you successfully master the exam objectives presented in this chapter, complete the following tasks.

Learn More About Network Configuration

- **Practice 1: Investigate Network Addressing**   Access one of the many websites on the Internet that discuss binary numbers, network addresses, and subnet masks. Make sure you are comfortable with these concepts.

- **Practice 2: Use the Network And Sharing Center**   You can do a lot with this versatile and powerful Windows Vista tool. Investigate all its functions thoroughly and become familiar with its screens, wizards, and dialog boxes. Investigate the Sharing and Discovery settings and make sure you are comfortable with the functions of each setting.

- **Practice 3: Investigate the WAP Web Interface or Wi-Fi Dialog Box**   Although you might not use every function that a third-party WAP configuration web interface or a Wi-Fi adapter dialog box provides, make sure you know what wireless access settings are available. Become familiar with the configuration pages (or tabs) on your interface and with the manufacturer's documentation.

- **Practice 4: Set Up an Ad Hoc Network**   Refer to Windows Help and Support and set up an ad hoc network between two wireless-enabled computers. Share files between the computers.

Become Familiar with Troubleshooting and Firewall Configuration

- **Practice 1: Use the Command-Line Debugging Tools**   Become familiar with all the switches available with ping, tracert, arp, ipconfig, and pathping. Use the command-line help (for example, **ping /?**).

- **Practice 2: Find Faults by Using Windows Network Diagnostics**   Generate some faults on your interfaces (for example, by unplugging Ethernet cables and misconfiguring adapters). Use the Network Diagnostic tool to find these faults.

- **Practice 3: Investigate the Windows Firewall with Advanced Security Tool**   Become familiar with this powerful and complex tool, which this chapter introduced only briefly. This practice should set you up nicely to tackle the next chapter, "Configuring Firewall and Remote Access Settings."

Take a Practice Test

The practice tests on this book's companion CD offer many options. For example, you can test yourself on just one exam objective, or you can test yourself on all the 70-620 certification exam content. You can set up the test so that it closely simulates the experience of taking a certification exam, or you can set it up in study mode so that you can look at the correct answers and explanations after you answer each question.

MORE INFO   Practice tests

For details about all the practice test options available, see the "How to Use the Practice Tests" section in this book's Introduction.

Chapter 8

Configuring Firewall and Remote Support Settings

Microsoft Windows Firewall is an integral part of protecting your computer from people of nefarious intent. From the moment your computer connects to a public network, automated scanners probe its network interfaces looking for weaknesses to exploit. Protection is increasingly important with the proliferation of publicly accessible Wi-Fi networks. You do not know who in your local coffee shop is running packet sniffing equipment, attempting to compromise other users' computers. The firewall in Windows Vista rises to this challenge. The firewall includes the ability to filter incoming and outgoing traffic as well as to use more complex rules than earlier versions. This greatly enhances the protection of users and their computers and provides a more secure working environment.

Remote Assistance and Remote Desktop are two technologies that appear superficially similar but are used for quite different purposes. Remote Assistance is used by people who need help from someone who cannot come and provide it in person. Remote Assistance allows two people to view the same desktop, which is not only useful in troubleshooting scenarios but is also useful if a user needs to be taught something quickly that would not otherwise warrant an on-site visit. Remote Desktop, on the other hand, can be used by only one person at a time. It allows a user to connect remotely to, and take over a session on, a computer or to connect to a computer to which no one has logged on and start a new session.

Exam objectives in this chapter:

- Configure security settings in Windows Firewall.
- Configure Remote Access.

Lessons in this chapter:

Before You Begin

To complete the lessons in this chapter, you must have done the following:

- Completed the installation and upgrading Practices in Chapter 1, "Installing Windows Vista Client," and Chapter 2, "Windows Vista Upgrades and Migrations." As a result, you will have installed Windows Vista Ultimate on a personal computer or within a virtual machine. This computer should also have a working connection to the Internet.

No additional configuration is required for this chapter.

Real World

Orin Thomas

When I first started providing professional technical support, as opposed to amateur support, which was paid for with cups of coffee and the occasional chocolate cookie, there was no such thing as being able to remotely view someone's desktop. Rather than being able to see it on our own screen, we had to imagine what the person on the other end of the telephone was actually seeing. This was made even more exciting by the fact that the people we were supporting were using multiple versions of Windows (Windows 3.11, Windows NT 3.5, Windows NT 4, and Windows 95) and multiple versions of the Macintosh operating system. It was necessary to have memorized all possible menu and interface configurations. In those days, most people were not as computer literate as they are today, so they'd describe dialog boxes as "thingies" and "doodads." This meant that over the telephone you could solve basic problems such as printing issues, but providing more complex support usually necessitated an on-site visit. As I was working at a university at the time, this could mean a walk to another office in the same building but usually meant a half-hour walk across campus to help someone with a solution that was almost impossible to describe over the telephone. Remote Assistance changed support dramatically. It was possible to see the user's desktop as the user did, and, in some cases, it was possible to directly interact with it. Remote Desktop also allows help desk staff to provide a small amount of training, helping users learn program features that would otherwise necessitate a separate on-site visit.

Lesson 1: Configuring Security Settings in Windows Firewall

Modern computers are increasingly required to interact with networks, be those the protected networks of the workplace or home or the less safe network of the Internet. Unfortunately, not everyone connected to networks has your best interest at heart. If you have ever monitored a firewall connected to the Internet, you will have noticed that scans and probes wash up against it like waves on a beach. A lot of people out there would love to take control of your computer, and they constantly run scans against known Internet service provider (ISP) address ranges looking for new computers to take over. The firewall that ships with Windows Vista is designed to keep your computer secure in the anarchic maelstrom that is the public Internet. It will not protect you if you open an e-mail containing a virus, but it will act as a wall, stopping those on the outside from getting in.

After this lesson, you will be able to:
- Configure Security Settings in Windows Firewall.
- Configure firewall rules.
- Configure firewall exceptions.

Estimated lesson time: 40 minutes

Firewall Basics

A firewall restricts network traffic on the basis of a set of configurable rules. The Windows Firewall is present by default on all of a computer's network interfaces. Firewalls work in the following way: when traffic reaches the interface, the firewall analyzes it, either dropping the traffic or allowing it past on the basis of the configured rules. Windows Vista uses two firewalls that work in concert, the Windows Firewall and Windows Firewall with Advanced Security. The primary difference between them is the complexity of the rules that they use in determining whether to let network traffic cross the interface that they protect.

What makes the Windows Vista Firewall different from the one that was included with Windows XP is that it functions in a bidirectional manner. The Windows XP firewall worked only on network traffic coming toward the computer from the network. If you think of a firewall as a gate on a road, the Windows XP firewall would allow in only traffic that met a set of rules, but it would let all traffic out without any checks.

The Windows Vista Firewall applies rules to traffic in both directions. Unless there is a rule that grants an exemption, any traffic that Windows Vista transmits to the network will be dropped by the firewall, just as incoming traffic will be dropped if no rule exists to allow it to pass. When thinking about active firewalls, always remember that unless a rule exists to allow a particular form of traffic, the firewall drops the traffic. You must explicitly allow traffic to pass across a firewall rather than specifically denying traffic. Occasionally there is a need to use deny rules, and this will be described later in this lesson.

Another important feature of the Windows Vista Firewall is full stealth. Stealth is a feature that stops an external *host* from performing what is called an OS fingerprint. OS fingerprinting is the process through which an external host is able to determine a computer's operating system (OS) by sending special traffic to its external network interface. OS fingerprinting is one of the first steps in preparing an attack. After an attacker knows the operating system that a host is using, the attacker can attempt exploits that are known to be effective against that operating system. The stealth feature of Windows Vista means that any external attacker is unsure which operating system or firewall is in use. The stealth feature of Windows Vista cannot be disabled.

Boot time filtering is another new feature of the Windows Vista Firewall. In previous versions of Windows the computer was open to network traffic from the moment it booted up. Firewall software, either built into Windows or from a third-party vendor, would only become operational once the operating system had finished the startup process. This left a window of opportunity between the network interface becoming operational during the startup process and the firewall becoming active. Clever attackers were able to exploit this window and compromise the security of computers. With boot time filtering, there is no such window of opportunity; the computer's network interfaces are protected from the instant that they become active.

To understand the operation of the Windows Vista Firewall, you need to be familiar with some core networking concepts. If you have a lot of experience with networks, you might want to skip ahead to the next section. These concepts are:

- **Protocol**   In terms of Windows Firewall there are only two protocols, Transmission Control Protocol (TCP) or User Datagram Protocol (UDP). TCP is more reliable and is used for the majority of Internet traffic. UDP is used for broadcast and multicast data, as well as for the sort of traffic associated with online games.
- **Port**   A port is an important number that is located in the header of a TCP or UDP datagram. Ports are used to map network traffic to particular services or programs running on a computer. For example, port 80 is reserved for World Wide Web traffic and port 25 for the transmission of e-mail across the Internet.
- **IPSec (Internet Protocol Security)**   A method of securing Internet traffic using encryption and digital signing. If an IPSec datagram is captured, its contents cannot be read. IPSec also provides sender verification, which allows the receiver to be certain of the datagram's origin.
- **Network address**   Each computer on a network has a network address. Firewalls sometime treat traffic differently based on the network address the traffic originates from.
- **Inbound traffic**   Inbound traffic is network data that comes from an external computer and is addressed to your Windows Vista computer.

- **Outbound traffic**   Outbound traffic is network data that your Windows Vista computer sends to other computers on local or remote networks through a network interface.
- **Network interface**   This can be a local area network (LAN) connection, a wireless connection, a modem connection, a virtual private network (VPN) connection, or a FireWire connection.

Profiles and Network Location Awareness

Network Location Awareness (NLA) is a process in which Windows Vista assigns a network profile depending on the current network environment. There are three possible profiles called Public, Private, and Domain. Profiles become active according to the following rules:

- **Private profile**   The Private profile becomes active when the network types of all active network connections are categorized as Private by NLA. Active network connections include LAN, Wireless, VPN, Modem, and FireWire. The key is active. If a network interface is in the disconnected state, such as when you are not connected to a wireless LAN or are not using your modem, it does not count toward the profile designation. When a computer connects to a new network, Windows Vista queries the user, asking whether the network is Public, Home, or Work. If the user designates the network as Home or Work, it will be categorized by Windows Vista as Private. It is important to note that if a network is incorrectly designated, this will influence the function of NLA.
- **Public profile**   Windows Vista activates the Public profile in any situations where the Private or Domain profiles do not apply. If one network interface out of five on a Windows Vista computer is designated Public when the others are designated Private, the Public profile will apply. By default, when the Public profile is in force, the firewall rules are the most restrictive.
- **Domain profile**   The Domain profile is active when the Windows Vista computer has authenticated with a domain controller on all active network interfaces. Because the 70-620 exam does not deal with Windows Vista in domain environments, you should be aware of this profile but not be too concerned about its details.

Windows Firewall

By default, Windows Firewall protects all modem, cabled network, wireless, and FireWire connections to a computer. Unlike Windows XP, where firewall settings were configured by editing the properties of an interface, you configure Windows Vista's basic firewall centrally using a Control Panel item. When viewing the status of Windows Firewall or editing the firewall configuration, it is possible to view the settings only for the current network profile, whether Public, Private, or Domain.

Checking and Modifying the State of Windows Firewall

You can enable or disable Windows Firewall either completely or on a per-connection basis. To view the status of Windows Firewall, open the Control Panel in Classic View and then double-click the Windows Firewall item. The details pane, shown in Figure 8-1, shows whether or not Windows Firewall's current configuration includes the current network location.

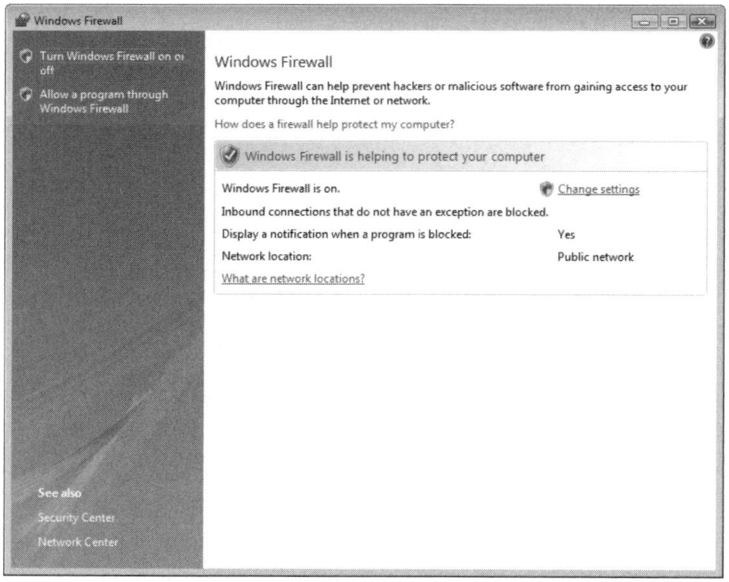

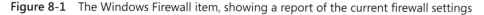

Figure 8-1 The Windows Firewall item, showing a report of the current firewall settings

Modifying the properties of Windows Firewall requires a user account with the ability to elevate privileges. You can enable or disable the firewall from the Windows Firewall Settings dialog box, as shown in Figure 8-2. From the Windows Firewall item in Control Panel, you can access this dialog box by clicking Turn Windows Firewall On Or Off or Change Settings.

Selecting the Block All Incoming Connections check box in the General tab of the Windows Firewall Settings dialog box blocks any exceptions that you might have configured for incoming traffic. This includes blocking connections from Remote Assistance and Remote Desktop that might have previously been configured. Selecting the Block All Incoming Connections check box is most appropriate when you use the computer in an unsecured area, such as a laptop computer in a café with free wireless access. You will remember from earlier chapters that when you connect to a new network Windows Vista asks you whether it is public, home, or work. The designation that you apply directly influences which Windows Firewall profile is active. If you choose the wrong designation, the computer that you are using in a public place might not be as well protected as you want it to be.

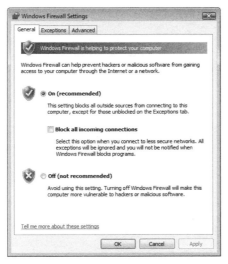

Figure 8-2   The Windows Firewall Settings dialog box

Selecting the Off option completely disables Windows Firewall. The most likely reason why you might want to disable Windows Firewall is if you want to install a third-party software firewall on your Windows Vista computer and you want to allow this firewall, rather than the one that ships with Windows Vista, to manage your computer's network security. It is important to note that you should not disable Windows Firewall just because you have another firewall between your computer and the network, such as a small office/home office (SOHO) router or Network Address Translation (NAT) device. It is perfectly normal to have firewalls active even when your computer is on a protected network. It might be that another computer on your protected network is infected by a worm. Dropping your firewall could lead to your computer becoming infected, even though the protected network is theoretically safe. Using a firewall is not always a sign of paranoia. On the network, anyone could be out to get you!

To apply Windows Firewall to certain connections only, you should click the Advanced tab, as shown in Figure 8-3. You can remove or apply the firewall to each configured network connection on your computer by selecting or clearing the check box next to its name. From this tab, it is also possible to restore Windows Firewall to its default settings. You should click this button if you are concerned that specific exceptions have made the computer insecure. The problem with doing this is that you will need to re-create all necessary exceptions as the need for them arises.

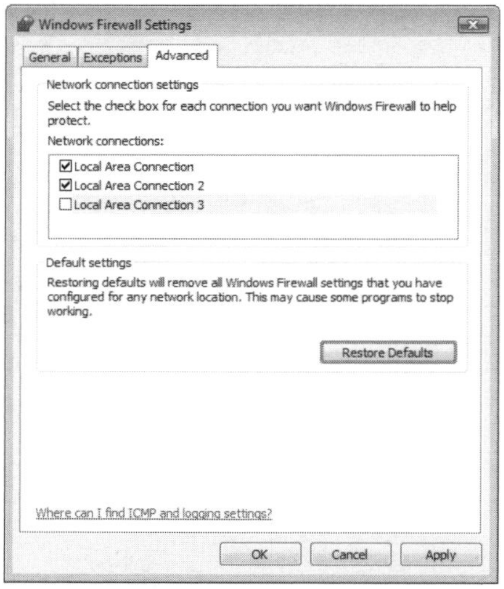

Figure 8-3   Applying Windows Firewall to specific network connections

Configuring Exceptions

Exceptions are used to allow incoming network connections for specific programs or services running on the Windows Vista computer. The Exceptions tab, shown in Figure 8-4, allows users who can elevate privileges to manually add exceptions to the default block rule. You can configure these exceptions on the basis of a particular program or a particular TCP or UDP port. If the Notify Me When Windows Firewall Blocks A New Program check box is cleared, Windows Firewall silently blocks the traffic. Notifications are enabled by default.

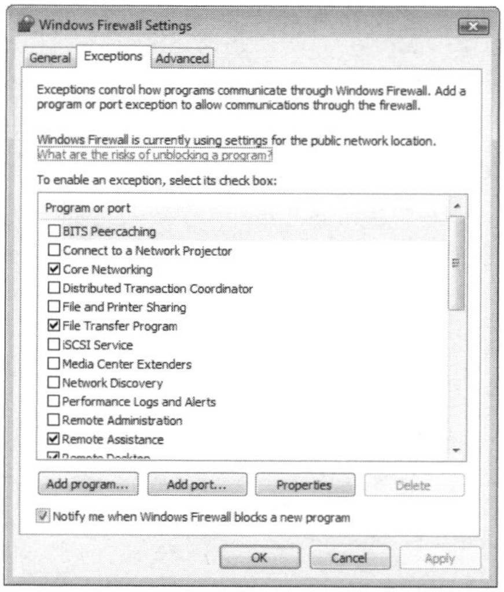

Figure 8-4   Configure exceptions by either selecting a preconfigured program or manually adding a port and protocol

Most programs you use already have a preconfigured exception in the list. Clicking Properties on any existing exception tells you more about that exception—for example, the location of the program or the port type and number. To add a new program and configure the scope of its rule, perform the following steps:

1. In the Exceptions tab of the Windows Firewall Settings dialog box, click Add Program.

2. If the program is in the list, select it. Otherwise, click Browse, and locate the program.

3. Click Change Scope to bring up the Change Scope dialog box shown in Figure 8-5.

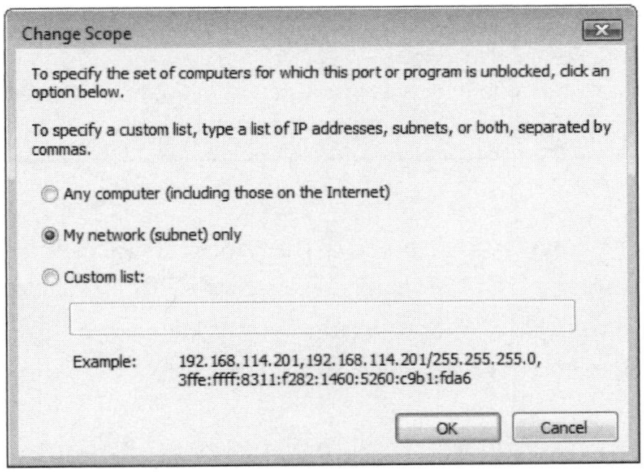

Figure 8-5   The Change Scope dialog box

4. In the Change Scope dialog box, select the set of computers that this exception applies to. This can be all computers, computers on the same subnet, or a subnet defined by entering either an IPv4 address, an IPv6 address, or networks defined by addresses and subnet masks. Click OK to close the Change Scope dialog box. Click OK again to close the Add A Program dialog box.

As shown in Figure 8-6, adding a new port is very similar to adding a new program. It is necessary to specify a name, which should represent the service or protocol that you are opening the port for. You also need to specify the port number and whether it uses the TCP or UDP transport protocol. The Change Scope button allows you to specify the remote computers that the rule applies to based on their Internet address in the same way that it does for program exceptions.

It is important to remember that it is possible to view and edit the Windows Firewall settings only for the current profile. Any configuration settings you make to the firewall when the network location is a public network will not be present when the network location changes to a private network.

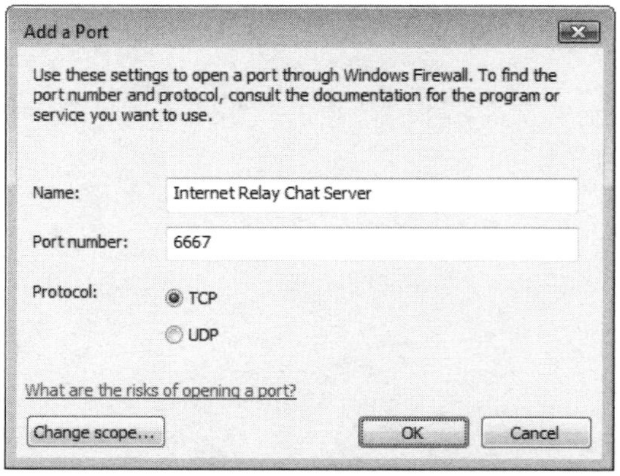

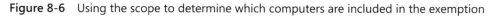

Figure 8-6 Using the scope to determine which computers are included in the exemption

---

Quick Check

1. In what type of scenarios would you select the Block All Incoming Connections check box in the General tab of the Windows Firewall Settings dialog box?

2. How can you ensure that only other computers on your network and not all computers on the Internet can view webpages on the web server that you were running off Windows Vista?

3. You are examining the firewall settings of a Windows Vista computer that you configured last week. When you configured the computer originally, you selected the Block All Incoming Connections check box. Now, when you look at the computer, the Block All Incoming Connections check box is not selected. No one else has reconfigured the computer. What might explain this?

Quick Check Answers

1. If your computer was located in a public place like a café with free wireless service or an airport lounge.

2. By configuring the scope settings of the exception that allowed access to the web server on your computer.

3. The network location has changed.

Windows Firewall with Advanced Security

Windows Firewall with Advanced Security allows you to be far more specific in the creation and implementation of firewall rules. For most users, the options that are available with Windows Firewall will be enough to keep their computers secure. The advantage of Windows Firewall with Advanced Security is that it allows greater nuance to be implemented in a computer's firewall configuration. The two products work in concert. Windows Firewall provides the baseline protection of a Windows Vista computer, and Windows Firewall with Advanced Security builds on top of that baseline protection.

The primary difference with Windows Firewall with Advanced Security is that you can use it to:

- Configure outbound and inbound exceptions. The basic version of Windows Firewall is limited to inbound exceptions only.
- Edit and apply firewall configuration for all network profiles. The basic version of Windows Firewall is limited to configuring the currently active network profile.
- Configure separate rules for IPSec traffic.

To open Windows Firewall with Advanced Security, perform the following steps:

1. Ensure that you are logged on with a user account that can use elevated privileges.
2. Click Start, and then click Control Panel.
3. Ensure that the Control Panel is in Classic View.
4. Open the Administrative Tools item.
5. Open Windows Firewall With Advanced Security.
6. Click Continue to close the User Account Control dialog box. This brings up the Windows Firewall With Advanced Security console, shown in Figure 8-7.

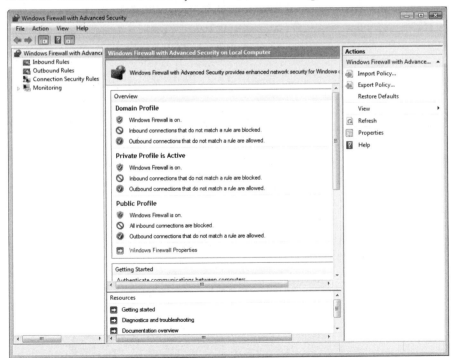

Figure 8-7   The Windows Firewall With Advanced Security console

You can also add the Windows Firewall with Advanced Security snap-in to a custom management console. Right-clicking the Windows Firewall With Advanced Security node at the top right of the console and selecting Properties allows you to bring up the dialog box that you can use to configure the basic settings for each profile by selecting the appropriate tab, as shown in Figure 8-8.

Figure 8-8   Using tabs in the Windows Firewall With Advanced Security On Local Computer Properties dialog box to configure basic firewall settings for each profile

For each profile, it is possible to turn the firewall on or off and configure the inbound and outbound connection settings to either block or allow traffic. There is a further setting for inbound connections, which is Block All Connections, which means that any configured inbound exceptions will be ignored. This is the default setting on the Public profile. It is important to note the difference between the default settings—for inbound traffic, it will block unless told otherwise and for outbound traffic, it will allow unless told otherwise. Most stand-alone products block by default in both directions, so if you are used to configuring other firewalls, it will be necessary to remind yourself that Windows Firewall with Advanced Security works differently.

Clicking the Customize button in the Settings area of each profile brings up the Customize Settings For The Selected Profile dialog box, as shown in Figure 8-9. From this dialog box, it is possible to configure whether a notification is displayed when a program is blocked from receiving an inbound connection, to configure how the computer responds to multicast or broadcast network traffic, and to deal with rules when you have configured some for Windows Vista and others are applied through Group Policy. It is unlikely that you will need to worry about the broadcast, multicast, or rule merging technologies on the 70-620 exam.

Figure 8-9 The Customize Settings For The Private Profile dialog box

---

NOTE **Advanced security and Group Policy**

If several Windows Vista computers are in a domain environment, it is possible to configure each computer to have the same settings using Group Policy. This vastly simplifies the management of firewalls in large environments. The 70-620 exam does not cover Group Policy topics.

The IPSec Settings tab allows you to configure how a Windows Vista computer establishes IPSec connections to other computers. IPSec is a technology that is used to encrypt network traffic in order to protect it from interception. Clicking Customize in the IPSec Settings tab brings up the Customize IPSec Settings dialog box, shown in Figure 8-10. This dialog box allows you to configure Key Exchange, Data Protection, and Authentication Method settings. Clicking Learn More About IpSec Settings provides more information on the technology. At present, IPSec is more likely to be configured on a corporate network than it is on a home network. This is likely to change, and IPSec will become more ubiquitous.

Figure 8-10   Using the Customize IPSec Settings dialog box to customize IPSec settings for different network profiles

Configuring Inbound and Outbound Rules

Inbound rules block or allow traffic coming to the Windows Vista computer through a network interface. Outbound rules block or allow traffic sent from the Windows Vista computer to external network locations. The configuration processes for inbound and outbound rules are very similar. The first step is to open the Windows Firewall With Advanced Security dialog box, right-click the type of rule that you want to configure, and select New Rule. Doing this brings up the New Inbound (or Outbound) Rule Wizard, the first page of which concerns Rule Types. On this page you can select between a program, port, predefined, or custom rule. The first two options are similar to the rules that can be generated using the basic firewall. A predefined rule allows you to build a rule around an aspect of the Windows Experience, from connecting to a network projector through to file and printer sharing. A custom rule allows you to configure a rule based on criteria not covered by any of the other options. The page that appears next depends on the type of rule that you choose.

If you choose to create a program rule and click Next, you are presented with the program page. This allows you to select a particular program and path for which the rule will apply. It is also possible to choose all programs on this page. If you choose to create a port rule, the next page asks you to specify whether the rule will apply to the TCP or UDP protocol and will ask for specific port numbers. It is also possible to choose all ports on a computer. If you choose a predefined rule, you will be able to modify aspects of how a particular part of Windows Vista, such as BITS Peercaching, is protected. The 70-620 exam's coverage of Windows Firewall with

Advanced Security is likely to focus on program-based and port-based rules rather than on predefined rules.

The next step after either specifying a program or a protocol and port is to specify what the firewall should do when traffic meeting that criteria is encountered. On this page, shown in Figure 8-11, you can select Allow The Connection, Allow The Connection If It Is Secure, or Block The Connection. You would use the blocking option if you wanted to keep someone who was using the computer from using a particular program or protocol. A good example of this is blocking the use of a file sharing program. After you have decided on an action, you need to specify the network profiles the rule will apply to and decide on a meaningful name and description for the rule. Names and descriptions are important because in 12 months time, when you are examining the firewall configuration of a Windows Vista computer that you set up, you will want to quickly ascertain what you were trying to accomplish with a particular rule. If you use something like "Ian's Rule," you will have to edit the properties of the rule to figure out what the rule actually does.

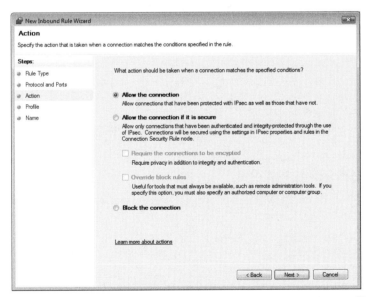

Figure 8-11 Specifying the action that should be taken when traffic meets specified conditions

Connection Security Rules

Connection security rules are special rules that deal with IPSec traffic. As mentioned earlier, IPSec is a technology that protects network traffic by encrypting it and using digital signatures to verify integrity and source information. The 70-620 exam does not examine this topic in detail, but it is helpful for candidates to have a basic familiarity with connection security rule functionality. Four types of connection security rule can be created, along with the ability to create custom rules. The four types of connection security rules are:

- **Isolation Rule**   This rule isolates Windows Vista computers based on authentication credentials such as a common domain. It is used to isolate groups of computers from others on the network.

- **Authentication Exemption Rule**   This rule prevents a Windows Vista computer from authenticating connections from computers specified in the rule. This is usually used in conjunction with an isolation rule to allow exceptions to that rule. For example, you want to restrict a computer from communicating with any computers except those in the same domain, but you also want it to communicate with two Mac OSX client computers.

- **Server-To-Server Rule**   This rule is used to protect connections between servers. An example might be between a web server application and a database hosting credit card information.

- **Tunnel Rule**   This rule is used to create encrypted tunnels across the Internet. Organizations often use this encryption technique to establish links between branch offices rather than to install dedicated data lines.

MORE INFO   Even more advanced firewall configuration

Although you will encounter only questions that relate to configuring Windows Firewall or Firewall with Advanced Security on the 70-620 exam, it is also possible to configure Windows Firewall from the command line using the netsh command in the advfirewall context. For more information, run a command prompt as an administrator and enter the command **netsh advfirewall /?**.

Importing and Exporting Policies

Rather than manually configuring Windows Firewall with Advanced Security each time you work on a new Windows Vista computer, it is possible to import and export firewall policy, significantly reducing your workload. Imagine that you work for a computer superstore and want to configure 30 different settings in Windows Firewall with Advanced Security for each Windows Vista computer that your store sells. By configuring the Windows Firewall with Advanced Security settings once and exporting that policy to a universal serial bus (USB) device, you can simply import it on every computer that you have to set up, drastically reducing configuration time. Another advantage of this function is that it allows you to save a firewall policy prior to making changes. If you make a mistake, you can simply import the policy configuration that you cleverly exported prior to making firewall configuration changes. To import or export policy, select Windows Firewall With Advanced Security in the console tree, and then click the Import Policy or Export Policy items located in the Actions area on the right-hand side of the Windows Firewall With Advanced Security console. If something goes wrong with firewall configuration, you can also click Restore Defaults to return Windows Firewall With Advanced Security to the state it was in when Windows Vista was first installed.

NOTE Advanced firewalls

Although it can do many things, the firewall that comes with Windows Vista is primitive compared with enterprise-level firewalls like ISA Server 2006 Enterprise edition. Not only can an enterprise-level firewall filter based on port, protocol, source, and destination, it can also inspect traffic and filter based on its content. For example, it is possible to block webpage downloads or e-mails at the firewall that contain specific words or file types. In terms of what fully featured enterprise-level firewalls can accomplish, Windows Vista's firewall is only the tip of the iceberg.

Practice: Windows Firewall Configuration

In these practices, you will perform several exercises that will familiarize you with the configuration of both the Windows Firewall and Windows Firewall with Advanced Security. To complete all these practices, you need to be logged on to Windows Vista with an account that can use elevated privileges.

▶ **Practice 1: Configuring an Exception By Using Windows Firewall**

In this practice, you will configure an exception in the standard Windows Firewall to allow incoming TCP traffic on port 6667 on the currently active profile. Normally, you would do this if you were running an Internet Relay Chat server off your Windows Vista computer.

1. Open the Windows Firewall item in the Control Panel.
2. Click Change Settings.
3. Click Continue to close the User Account Control dialog box.
4. In the General tab, ensure that the Block All Incoming Connections check box is cleared.
5. In the Exceptions tab, click Add Port.
6. In the Add A Port dialog box, type **IRC Server** in the Name text box and **6667** in the Port Number text box. Click OK to close this dialog box.
7. Click OK to close the Windows Firewall Settings dialog box.

▶ **Practice 2: Configuring an Inbound Rule By Using Windows Firewall with Advanced Security**

In this practice, you will create a rule that allows hosts on the subnet 10.10.10.0/24 to connect to a web server on your Windows Vista computer.

1. Open Windows Firewall with Advanced Security by opening the Administrative Tools item in Control Panel.
2. Click Continue to close the User Account Control dialog box.
3. In the Windows Firewall With Advanced Security console, click Inbound Rules.
4. In the Actions pane, click New Rule.
5. On the Rule Type page, select Custom, and click Next.

6. On the Program page, select All Programs, and click Next.

7. On the Protocol And Ports page, in the Protocol Type drop-down list, select TCP. In the Local Port drop-down list, select Specific Ports. In the Local Port text box, type **80**. Click Next.

8. On the Scope page, leave the default settings, and click Next.

9. On the Action page, select Allow The Connection, and click Next.

10. On the Profile page, click Next to accept the default settings.

11. On the Name page, type **Web Server Rule** in the Name text box, and click Finish.

12. Right-click Web Server Rule in the list of Inbound Rules, and select Properties.

13. Click the Scope tab. In the Remote IP Address area, select the These IP Addresses option, and click Add.

14. In the This IP Address Or Subnet text box, shown in Figure 8-12, type **10.10.10.0/24**.

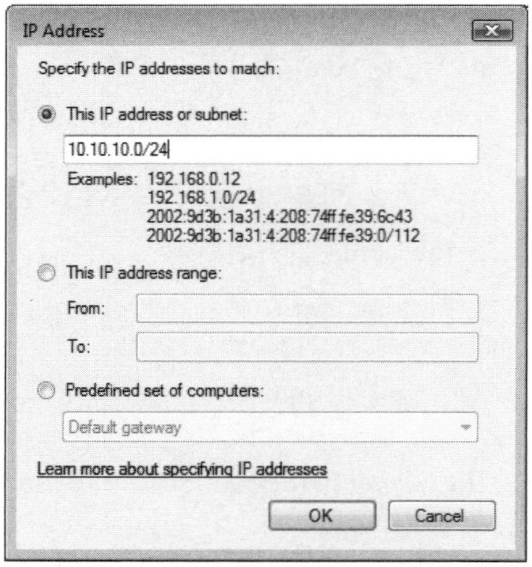

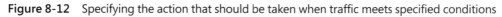

Figure 8-12   Specifying the action that should be taken when traffic meets specified conditions

15. Click OK twice to close the IP Address dialog box and the Web Server Rule Properties dialog box.

▶ **Practice 3: Exporting and Importing a Windows Firewall with Advanced Security Policy**

In this practice, you will export the current configuration, make alterations to the configuration, and then restore the configuration. Because you have made changes to the firewall rules in Practices 1, 2, and 3, you would not want to reset to the defaults because that would mean losing the changes already made. Reimporting the exported firewall configuration brings you back to the start of Practice 4 without having to perform the prior practices again. To complete the practice, perform the following steps:

1. Open the Windows Firewall With Advanced Security dialog box from the Administrative Tools item in Control Panel.
2. Select Windows Firewall With Advanced Security in the console tree.
3. Click Export Policy in the Actions Pane.
4. Save the policy as CH08Practice.wfw.
5. Examine the Overview pane in the center of the Windows Firewall With Advanced Security console. The Windows Firewall should be on in all three profiles.
6. Right-click Windows Firewall With Advanced Security in the console tree, and select Properties.
7. In the Domain Profile and Public Profile tabs, change the Firewall State to Off, and then click OK.
8. Examine the Overview pane in the center of the Windows Firewall With Advanced Security console. Verify that the Windows Firewall is turned off in the Domain and Public Profiles.
9. In the Actions pane, click Import Policy. Click Yes in the dialog box that asks if you want to import a policy now.
10. In the dialog box, select the policy CH08Practice.wfw, and click Open.
11. After the policy has been imported, verify that the Windows Firewall has been returned to its active state in the Domain and Public profiles.

Lesson Summary

- Windows Firewall can be applied on any or all interfaces.
- Windows Firewall allows all outbound traffic by default. Inbound traffic is also blocked by default unless an exception has been configured.
- It is possible to view and edit the configuration of Windows Firewall only for the current profile.
- Windows Firewall with Advanced Security works in concert with Windows Firewall.
- It is possible to configure both inbound and outbound rules in Windows Firewall with Advanced Security.
- Using Windows Firewall with Advanced Security, it is possible to edit rules and configurations that apply to all profiles.
- Windows Firewall with Advanced Security allows the creation of more nuanced rules.

Lesson Review

You can use the following questions to test your knowledge of the information in Lesson 1, "Configuring Security Settings in Windows Firewall." The questions are also available on the companion CD if you prefer to review them in electronic form.

NOTE   **Answers**

Answers to these questions and explanations of why each answer choice is correct or incorrect are located in the "Answers" section at the end of the book.

---

1. Which of the following is a limitation of Windows Firewall? (Choose all that apply.)

   A. It can be applied only to every network interface at the same time.

   B. It can be edited only on one network interface.

   C. It can be applied only to a single network interface.

   D. It can edit only the current network profile.

2. You want to block people using a computer running Windows Vista at the library from uploading files using File Transfer Protocol (FTP). What sort of rule would you configure? (Choose all that apply.)

   A. IPSec rule

   B. Inbound rule

   C. Outbound rule

   D. Connection security rule

3. You want to run a server for a popular multiplayer computer game off your Windows Vista computer. What type of rule would you configure to allow users from across the Internet to connect? (Choose all that apply.)

   A. Inbound deny rule

   B. Inbound allow rule

   C. Outbound deny rule

   D. Outbound allow rule

4. Which of the following should you do before making changes to the configuration of Windows Firewall with Advanced Security?

   A. Restore defaults

   B. Change profile

   C. Import policy

   D. Export policy

Lesson 2: Configuring Remote Support

Remote Assistance and Remote Desktop are two technologies that allow a user on a remote computer, whether on the same LAN or on the other side of the world, to see the screen of another computer. You use Remote Assistance primarily to support users who are currently working with their computers. You use Remote Desktop to connect to computers that are currently not being used. Both technologies have their uses when providing support to Windows Vista client computers. Understanding which of these technologies to implement in a particular situation is an important skill and is evaluated on the 70-620 exam.

After this lesson, you will be able to:
- Configure Remote Assistance.
- Configure and troubleshoot Remote Desktop.
    - ❑ Configure display settings.
    - ❑ Configure local resources.
    - ❑ Configure RDP performance.

Estimated lesson time: 40 minutes

Remote Assistance

Remote Assistance is a technology that allows support personnel to view the Windows Vista session of the person they are assisting. The person providing the assistance is often called the *helper*. The person who sends the invitation requesting assistance is often called the *host*. Remote Assistance greatly eases the desktop support process because it reduces the need for nontechnical users to accurately describe technical processes to support personnel. A helper connected through Remote Assistance might be able to see something in a few seconds that, without using this technology, would be uncovered only after minutes of questioning.

You can use Remote Assistance only with the permission of the person who requires the assistance. If you are a helper, you should reassure people that a Remote Assistance invitation can be used only for a limited time and that after the Remote Assistance application is closed, the host computer will automatically deny access. Sending a Remote Assistance invitation to a helper does not mean that the helper will always be able to connect to that computer in the future. You should also reiterate that even though a helper will have been sent an invitation, the host still has to approve access to that helper manually. Some people might worry that, after they grant a helper access to their computers, they will not be able to keep the helper from gaining access to confidential information stored on the computer. Part of your job supporting the Windows Vista client OS is to inform people that they can instantly terminate a Remote Assistance session if they want to and to explain how they can do this.

NOTE Remote Assistance in domain environments

It is possible to configure Group Policy in a domain environment so that a specific set of preap-proved user accounts, configured as Helper accounts, can be used to offer Remote Assistance to computers that are members of the domain. In this situation people using host computers are presented with a dialog box asking them if they want the helper to connect to the host computer and to view their desktops. If the person on the host computer does not acknowledge the offer for help, the dialog box will disappear, and the offer will need to be made again.

Again, the important thing to remember is that permission is required in this circumstance. A helper cannot seize control of a computer using Remote Assistance unless the operator of that computer gives permission. Because the 70-620 exam deals only with Windows Vista in nonenter-prise environments, you will not need to be familiar with the details of offering Remote Assistance help. It is only necessary to be familiar with generating and sending Remote Assistance invitations.

You cannot use Remote Assistance in situations where it is not possible to make a remote connection to the host computer. Remote Assistance does not require a connection to the Internet as long as both host and helper computers can connect to each other in another manner. It is possible to use Remote Assistance if the host computer has a modem and is configured to accept incoming connections. It is also possible to use Remote Assistance over ad hoc wireless networks. However, in this situation, helper and host are generally physically close enough that it is easier for the helper to be physically in front of the host's computer.

Improvements in Remote Assistance and Remote Desktop

Remote Assistance and Remote Desktop will be familiar to readers who have supported the Windows XP operating system. Windows Vista brings significant improvements in both these technologies, including the following:

- Remote Assistance and Remote Desktop achieve the same usability while reducing bandwidth requirements.
- Remote Assistance and Remote Desktop can now work through NAT firewalls.
- If the host computer must be rebooted as a part of the troubleshooting process, the Remote Assistance session is automatically reestablished. Previous versions of Remote Assistance required you to manually reestablish the connection. In some cases, it was necessary to transmit another invitation.

It is important for readers who have used the Windows XP version of Remote Assistance to know that the Windows Vista version does not support voice sessions. This means that you will have to use either a separate voice application or a telephone if you want communication between the helper and the host user.

Activating and Securing Remote Assistance

Windows Vista's default settings enable the sending of Remote Assistance invitations. Assuming that two Windows Vista computers can communicate with each other, the only way that one of them will not be able to request Remote Assistance is if a user with elevated privileges has explicitly disabled this functionality in the past. Of course, creating a Remote Assistance invitation is only the first step; it needs to be transmitted to and opened by the helper. We will cover these issues later in the lesson.

As mentioned, only a user who has elevated privileges can configure the setting that allows Remote Assistance invitations to be sent from a computer. Remote Assistance settings can also be configured using Group Policy if the Windows Vista computer is in a domain environment, but that topic is beyond the scope of the 70-620 exam. To enable a computer to receive Remote Assistance connections, perform the following steps:

1. Click Start, right-click Computer, and click Properties.
2. In the Tasks pane, click Remote Settings.
3. Click Continue to close the User Account Control dialog box.
4. In the Remote tab of the System Properties dialog box, ensure that the Allow Remote Assistance Connections To This Computer check box is selected, as shown in Figure 8-13.

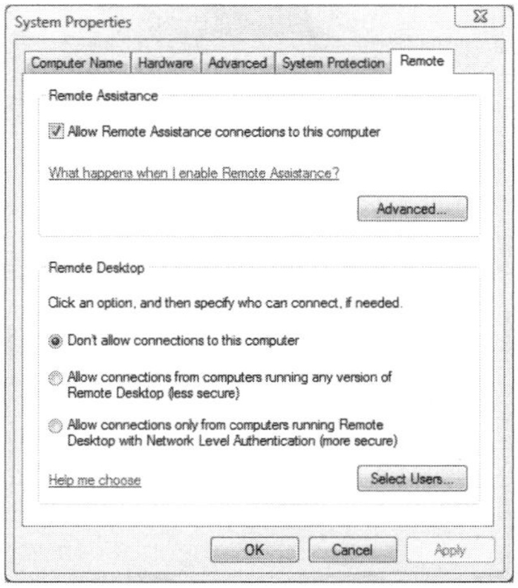

Figure 8-13   Allowing a computer to send Remote Assistance invitations

Only a user with elevated privileges is able to configure the security settings involved in Remote Assistance. Three security options apply to Remote Assistance invitations issued from computers running Windows Vista. These settings control:

- Whether the person connecting from the remote location can actually control the host computer.
- The length of time that an invitation can remain open.
- Whether invitations can be used only by computers running Windows Vista or later.

Each invitation issued by the computer has properties that are determined by the Remote Assistance settings. For example, this means that all invitations will be valid for the same amount of time. Remote Assistance settings cannot be configured individually each time an assistance invitation is issued.

The first security setting is used to determine whether the computer can be controlled remotely. This gives the person operating the host computer the highest degree of control over the Remote Assistance session. From a security perspective, it is important to remember that a helper can view everything on the desktop that the person hosting the remote session can. If the helper has control, the helper can access anything that the host user could normally access. For example, say that the Windows Vista computer used by the CEO of an organization is configured to allow the computer to be controlled remotely. The CEO is having some problems with her computer and sends a Remote Assistance invitation to a member of the help desk support staff. The helper connects to the computer to fix the problem plaguing the CEO. Rather than talking the CEO through the resolution, the CEO says that she needs to attend a meeting and leaves the helper connected to the host computer. In this situation, it is possible for the helper to view any document or information the CEO could because the helper is effectively logged on as the CEO. So although it can greatly simplify the assistance process to allow helpers to have full remote control over the host computer, in the case of certain sensitive computers you should allow the helper only to view the host computer's screen and to not be able to request control. In such a situation, the helper will have to direct the operator of the host computer to perform each action.

One problem that you might encounter with Remote Assistance relates to the elevation of privileges. When a user whose account is unable to elevate privileges tries to perform a task that requires elevated privileges, the user will be prompted for an administrator password. The same applies to allowing a helper to elevate privileges. The host will be asked for the password for an account that can elevate privileges in order to allow the helper to perform the same task. The helper cannot interact directly with the computer until this access is granted, hence the helper cannot enter the elevated account credentials by himself or herself. The only way that a helper can elevate privileges is if the user who has requested assistance has an account that can elevate privileges or if the host user knows the authentication credentials of an account that can elevate privileges. Most of the support scenarios covered in the 70-620 exam deal with users who are able to elevate privileges on their computers, so this particular issue is unlikely to arise. If you do have to remotely perform a task on a computer where the host user cannot elevate privileges but you know the credentials of an account that can, you should get the user to log off and then use Remote Desktop to complete the task securely. Remote Desktop is covered later in this lesson.

If the Take Control option is enabled, the host user still has safeguards that can be used to prevent abuse. The helper must request control from the host, and the person using the host computer must manually approve the helper taking control, using the dialog box shown in Figure 8-14. It is only when explicit permission is given by the host for the helper to take control that the helper will be able to interact with the host's desktop.

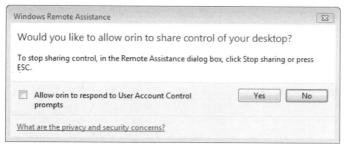

Figure 8-14   The host computer's user must manually approve a request to take control

When granting permission to control the desktop, the host can decide whether or not he or she wants to allow the helper to click through User Account Control requests. This is important only if the host's user has an account that can use elevated privileges. It allows the host computer's user to make a determination as to whether he or she wants the helper to be able to perform a task that requires elevated privileges even though the host has given the helper control of the desktop.

To configure settings so that that helpers are never able to take control of Windows Vista during Remote Assistance sessions, perform the following steps:

1. Open the Control Panel in Classic view.
2. Double-click the System item.
3. Click Remote Settings.
4. Click Continue to close the User Account Control dialog box.
5. Click Advanced, and then select the Allow This Computer To Be Controlled Remotely check box, as shown in Figure 8-15.

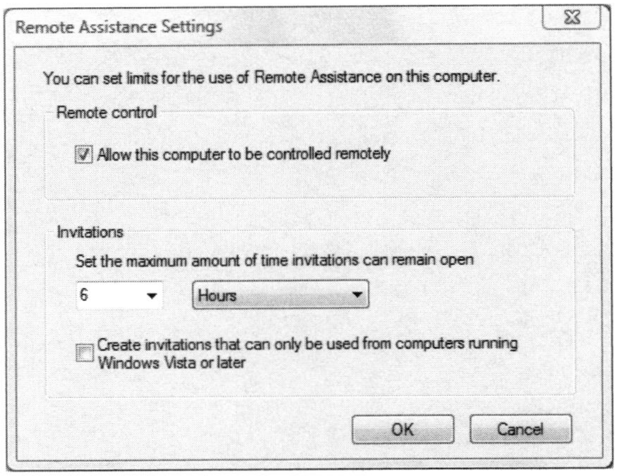

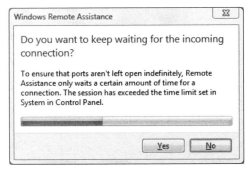

Figure 8-15 Allowing a computer to send Remote Assistance invitations

You can set invitation validity in minutes, hours, or even days. The minimum invitation validity period is one minute. The maximum invitation validity period is 30 days. In general, you should specify a period of time that is reasonable given the situation, but not excessive. Few people are going to keep the Remote Assistance application open for 30 days waiting for someone else to connect! Because Remote Assistance requires both the person at the host computer and the helper to be active at the same time, there is rarely a need to have an invitation period longer than 30 minutes. Although the terminology indicates otherwise, the validity period determines how long Windows Vista will wait before asking the host user whether or not he or she wants to wait for the incoming connection, as shown in Figure 8-16. The message has a countdown timer that will automatically close Remote Assistance if the host's user does not make a decision. If the host's user chooses to wait, Windows Vista waits until the invitation period expires again before presenting the same message one more time. This means that it is possible to use an invitation that is older than the validity period as long as the host user keeps clicking Yes when Windows Vista asks if the user wants to keep waiting.

Figure 8-16 After the invitation period expires, Windows Vista asks the host if he or she wants to keep waiting

If the host user decides to stop waiting or closes Remote Assistance manually at any time, the helper will be unable to connect. After Remote Assistance has been closed on the host's computer, a new invitation is required even if the previous invitation's validity period has not expired. If a helper attempts to connect with a valid invitation but Remote Assistance has been closed, the helper will receive the error message shown in Figure 8-17.

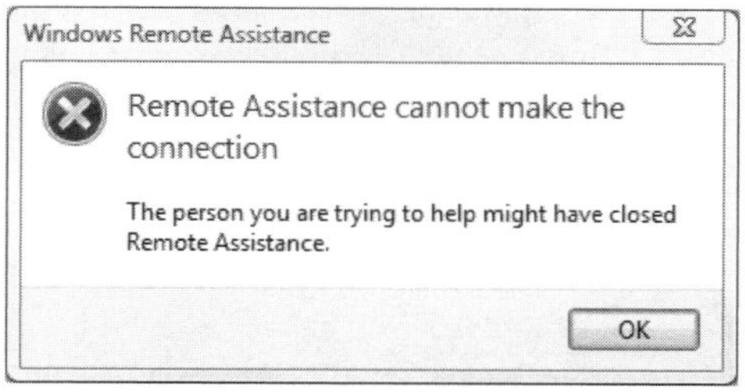

Figure 8-17   An error message explaining that Remote Assistance has been closed on the host's computer

---

NOTE   Dial-up support

Like previous versions of Windows, Windows Vista supports incoming dial-up connections. There might be a situation where a user of a Windows Vista computer who does not use the Internet requires Remote Assistance support. In such a situation, it is possible to use a modem to directly connect to the user's computer, retrieve the invitation from a shared folder, and use it to set up a Remote Assistance connection over the dial-up link. Because the 70-620 exam objectives do not mention dial-up at all, it is unlikely that such a scenario will arise on the exam.

The final security option is to restrict the helper using Windows Vista. Although it is possible for a helper using Windows XP, Windows Server 2003, or Windows 2000 to provide Remote Assistance, there are significant benefits in terms of security and performance when a helper is using a computer running Windows Vista.

NOTE   Vista only

When taking the exam, remember this setting if you see any question that asks about helpers using Windows XP who cannot connect to a Windows Vista computer using Remote Assistance.

Exploring a Remote Assistance Session

A Remote Assistance invitation is an Extensible Markup Language (XML) file that contains an encrypted string. Although it is possible to edit an invitation file with a text editor such as Microsoft Notepad, making any modifications to the file will make it unusable. Without going too far into the complex processes of encryption, the encrypted string in the text file is part of a key pair, the other key being stored on the host computer. Any change made to the key in the invitation file will be apparent because it will not be reflected in the paired key stored on the host computer.

Windows Vista makes the process of generating a Remote Assistance invitation far simpler than it was in earlier versions of Windows. This is a great boon to users because they rarely want to jump through hoops to send an invitation when all they really want is someone to help them fix their problem. The process can be started from Help and Support, available on the Start Menu, or by typing Remote Assistance in the search box on the Start Menu. To access Remote Assistance through Help and Support, users need to click the Windows Remote Assistance text that's located under the Ask Someone subheading, as shown in Figure 8-18.

Figure 8-18 Creating Remote Assistance invitations through Windows Help and Support

After a user activates Windows Remote Assistance, the user is asked whether he or she wants to invite someone the user trusts to help or to offer help to someone. Clicking the invite option brings up the dialog box that asks the user to select a method of invitation, as shown in Figure 8-19. The options are to send an invitation through e-mail or to save an invitation file. If previous invitations have been saved as files, it is possible to refresh them so that they can be retransmitted to the helper.

Clicking Use E-mail To Send An Invitation initiates the default e-mail program on the Windows Vista computer. If no e-mail program has yet been set up and configured, Windows Vista defaults to using Windows Mail and the host user will have to perform the e-mail account setup. The process of setting up Windows Mail is covered in more detail in Chapter 9, "Configuring Communications Applications." When you select e-mail as the way of transmitting the Remote Assistance invitation, the invitation is attached to a form e-mail, as shown in Figure 8-20. With everything already prepared, a user simply needs to add the helper's e-mail address.

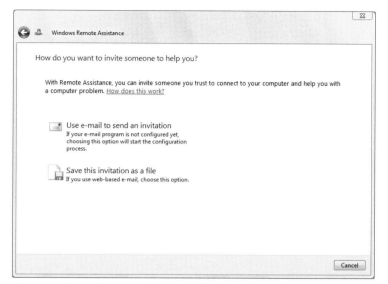

Figure 8-19   Selecting a method of invitation

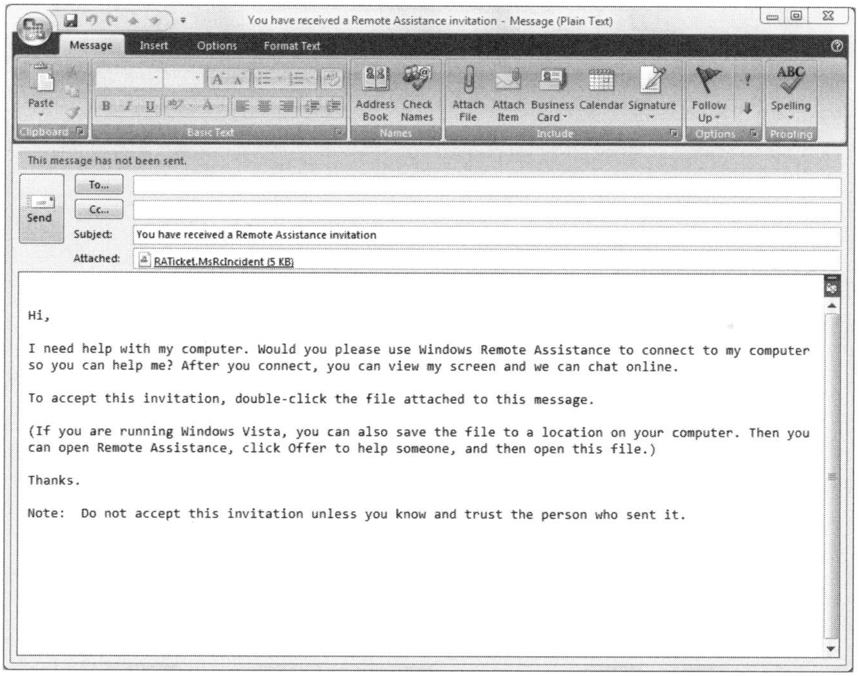

Figure 8-20   The default e-mail generated by Outlook 2007 when sending a Remote Assistance invitation

The other method is to save the invitation as a file and to come up with another method of getting it from the host to the helper. After an invitation is saved, it can be copied to a file server, uploaded to a support website, or sent as an attachment through webmail if the host does not use a traditional e-mail application with Windows Vista. In Windows XP it was possible to send an invitation directly through an instant messaging program. This is not the case with Windows Vista because Windows Vista does not ship with a default instant messaging application. If users want to use an instant messenger program to transmit an invitation to a helper, they must save the invitation as a file and then send it to the helper using the instant messaging program's file transfer function.

After a decision has been made on the method through which the invitation will be forwarded from the host to the helper, it is necessary to protect the invitation with a password, as shown in Figure 8-21. This password must be at least six characters long. Although the password should use mixed case letters, numbers, and symbols, Remote Assistance does not enforce this requirement.

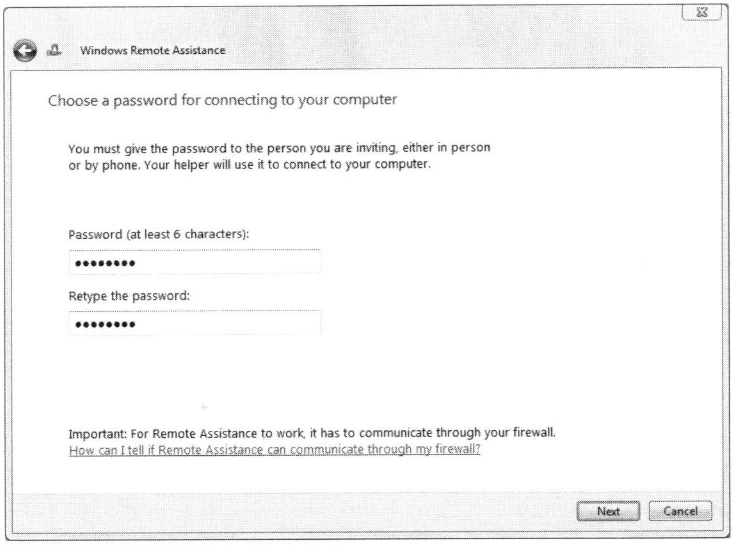

Figure 8-21   A password that has a minimum of six characters is required

You should teach users not to transmit this password with the invitation. The reason for this is straightforward. If a host accidentally transmits a password with the invitation and the invitation is intercepted, it is simpler for the person who made the interception to make a connection to the host's computer. The best way to transfer the password from the host to the helper is over the telephone. You should also remember to inform users that they need to keep the Remote Assistance panel open after they create the invitation. If they close the Remote Assistance panel, it will be necessary to generate a new invitation. The process of creating a Remote Assistance invitation is covered in detail in Practice 2 at the end of this lesson.

Using an Invitation to Make a Connection

After the invitation has been received, a helper can initiate a connection either by double-clicking the invitation file and entering the password set by the host or by starting Windows Remote Assistance, selecting the option to offer help, and loading the invitation file. At this point the helper must wait until the host accepts the incoming connection.

IMPORTANT   Remote Assistance by IP address

Although there is an option to enter the IP address of the host's computer, this functionality is only available in an Active Directory directory service environment that has been configured to support Remote Assistance technology. Using Remote Assistance in this manner is beyond the scope of the 70-620 exam.

After the helper opens the invitation and enters the password, the host will be prompted on whether he or she wants to accept the connection from the helper, as shown in Figure 8-22. The host is reminded that anything that he or she can see on the desktop can also be seen by the helper. This gives the host an opportunity to close any sensitive documents that might be open before the helper connects.

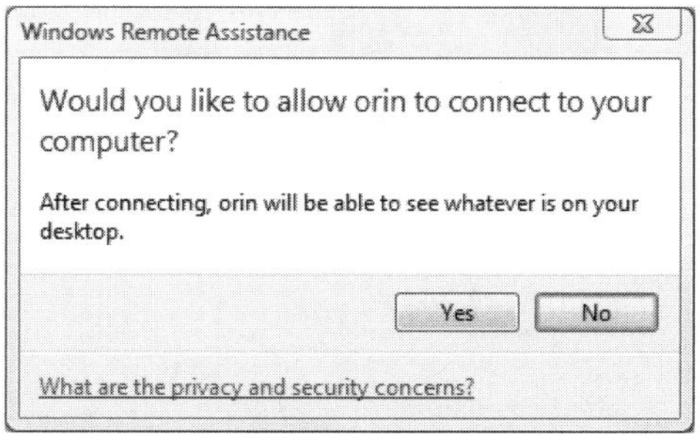

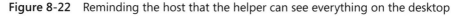

Figure 8-22   Reminding the host that the helper can see everything on the desktop

When the connection is accepted, the host will switch from using the Aero interface to using the Basic interface. The Aero interface will be restored when the Remote Assistance session is disconnected.

The Remote Assistance Session

After the Remote Assistance session has been established, it can be managed using the Remote Assistance panel. For the most part, the Remote Assistance panel is the same for the host and the helper with only one or two differences. The Remote Assistance panel icons do the following:

- **Disconnect**   This button allows either the host or the helper to terminate the Remote Assistance session.

- **Request Control**   This control allows the helper to request the ability to interact with the desktop. When granting this control, the host can decide whether the helper can view any user account control dialog boxes.

- **Stop Sharing**   This control keeps the helper from being able to interact with the desktop. It does not stop the helper from being able to view the desktop.

- **Pause**   This pauses the session. A host might need to check a sensitive document that he or she does not want the helper to see during the session. Pausing the session allows the host to do this without disconnecting the session.

- **Settings**   Several settings can be configured. Most settings can be configured only on the host computer.

  ❑ Use Esc key to stop sharing control.

  ❑ Save a log of this session. This is available to both the host or the helper.

    ● This log contains only Remote Assistance–associated activity. This means that it will log information about when the session was connected and whether a request for control was granted. The log file does not provide information on the tasks carried out during the session, such as which settings were changed or which applications were opened.

    ● Session logs include chat activity that occurs through the Remote Assistance chat application.

  ❑ Bandwidth Usage. This option is only available to the host. The bandwidth usage options are discussed further in Table 8-1.

- **Chat**   A basic text-based chat program through which the helper and host can send comments to each other.

- **Send File**   Allows files to be transmitted.

- **Help**   Brings up help and support.

The process of preparing a Remote Assistance invitation to connect to a remote computer is covered in detail in Practice 2 at the end of this lesson.

Table 8-1   Remote Assistance Bandwidth Usage Settings

Bandwidth Usage	Features
Low	Don't allow full window drag Turn off background Use 8-bit color
Medium	Don't allow full window drag Turn off background
Medium-High	Don't allow full window drag
High	No bandwidth optimization

Troubleshooting Remote Assistance

Remote Assistance cannot function if the computer requesting the Remote Assistance has no way of establishing connectivity between helper and host computers. If it is not possible to connect, check that both the host and the helper have network connectivity. Several procedures to check network connectivity were covered in Chapter 7, "Configuring Network Connectivity."

When a Windows Vista computer connects to another Windows Vista computer using Remote Assistance, it uses a range of ports. The range includes both the TCP and UDP protocols and ports between 49152 and 65535. When a Windows XP computer is used as a helper to a Windows Vista host, port 3389 TCP is used. If a connection cannot be made, but network connectivity exists, check whether appropriate exceptions have been configured in Windows Firewall or Windows Firewall with Advanced Security. Another firewall in between the two computers might be blocking connectivity.

Exam Tip   In the exam, if you are presented with a diagram of two Windows Vista computers attempting to communicate and there is a firewall in between them, carefully check the firewall settings.

> ### Quick Check
> 1. A user who is experiencing technical difficulties sends out an invitation to a helper at 1:30 P.M. The helper is busy assisting other users and is not able to open the invitation until 2:15 P.M. The invitations on the host computer are configured to remain open only for 25 minutes. Under what circumstances can the helper connect?
> 2. Which of the following, host or helper, is able to adjust the bandwidth configuration of the connection?
>
> ### Quick Check Answers
> 1. As long as the user who has sent the invitation manually keeps the invitation open, the helper will be able to connect even after the invitation period has expired.
> 2. Host. The helper cannot adjust the bandwidth configuration of the connection.

Remote Desktop

Remote Desktop appears superficially to be the same as Remote Assistance, although the two technologies are used for very different purposes. You use Remote Desktop for remotely logging on to a Windows Vista computer and using it in the same manner that you would if you were sitting in front of it. Remote Desktop does not require anyone to be logged on or to approve the session. The only people who can forcibly disconnect you from a remote desktop are the ones who would be able to log you off if you'd left your screen locked normally.

NOTE   Terminal Services

Windows Server 2003 and the subsequent version have a service that is superficially similar to Remote Desktop called Terminal Services. Unlike Remote Desktop, which allows only a single inbound connection, or two to a server operating system, Terminal Services allows multiple inbound connections. Each user is presented with his or her own separate desktop environment, and someone who is connected directly to the server using keyboard, monitor, and mouse might not even be aware that other users are connected to the same computer. Terminal Services connections must be licensed; Remote Desktop connections used for administering a server do not require extra licenses.

Configuring Remote Desktop

By default, Remote Desktop is disabled on computers running Windows Vista. Enabling Remote Desktop requires an account that can use elevated privileges, and this can be done through the System item in the Control Panel. When you enable Remote Desktop, you need to make a decision about the type of connections that are allowed. Three options are presented:

- **Don't Allow Connections To This Computer**   This disables Remote Desktop entirely, and no connections can be made.
- **Allow Connections From Computers Running Any Version Of Remote Desktop (Less Secure)**   Use this option if you want to connect to a Windows Vista computer from a computer with a Remote Desktop Protocol (RDP) client running Mac OS X, Linux, Windows Server 2003 R2, Windows Server 2003 SP1, Windows XP SP1, or Windows 2000. Using this option is less secure than using Network Level Authentication, although it might be necessary in situations where a worker with a home computer running Windows XP needs to connect to an office computer running Windows Vista.
- **Allow Connections From Computer Running Remote Desktop With Network Level Authentication (More Secure)**   Windows XP SP2, Windows Vista, and the next edition of the Windows Server operating system after Windows Server 2003. This is the most secure form of Remote Desktop authentication, and it allows the connection between host and remote user to be encrypted in the strongest possible way.

When connecting to another computer using Remote Desktop, a Windows Vista Remote Desktop client will always attempt to negotiate Network Level Authentication with a remote host before attempting a less secure authentication method. To the user, this happens transparently, and the client software that is included with Windows Vista cannot be configured to use differing levels of authentication.

To enable Remote Desktop on a computer running Windows Vista, follow these steps:

1. Click Start, right-click Computer, and select Properties.
2. In the Task pane of the System page, click Remote Settings.
3. Click Continue to close the User Account Control dialog box.
4. In the Remote Desktop area, shown in Figure 8-23, select either Allow Connections From Computers Running Any Version Of Remote Desktop or Allow Connections Only From Computers Running Remote Desktop With Network Level Authentication. If the currently selected power plan allows the computer to enter sleep or hibernation, a warning message is displayed.

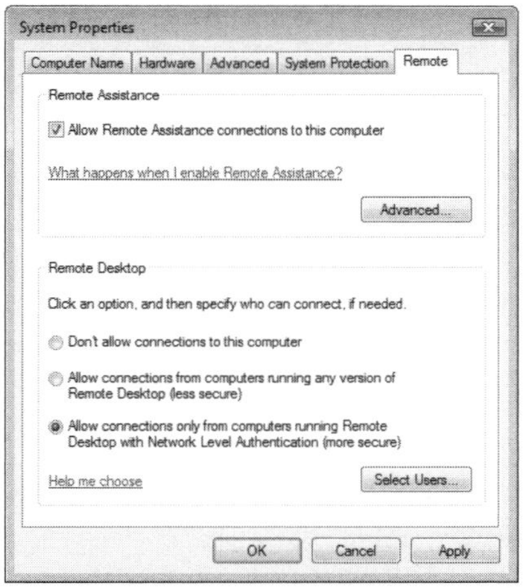

Figure 8-23 Selecting an authentication level that meets the user's needs

The Remote Desktop Users Group

Activating Remote Desktop on a computer does not mean that all users who have accounts on that Windows Vista computer will be able to make a Remote Desktop connection to it. By default, any member of the Administrators local group can make a Remote Desktop connection to a host computer. Other users need to be either added manually to the list of allowed users or added to the Remote Desktop Users local group if they are to have access to a computer running Remote Desktop. The most secure way is to use the Remote Desktop Users group.

To add a user account to the Remote Desktop Users group, perform the following steps while logged on with an account that is able to elevate privileges:

1. Click Start, right-click Computer, and select Manage.
2. Click Continue to close the User Account Control dialog box.

3. In the Computer Management Console, expand the Local Users And Groups node by clicking the triangle next to it.

4. Click the Groups folder, and then in the details pane of the console, double-click the Remote Desktop Users group. This opens the Remote Desktop Users Properties dialog box, shown in Figure 8-24.

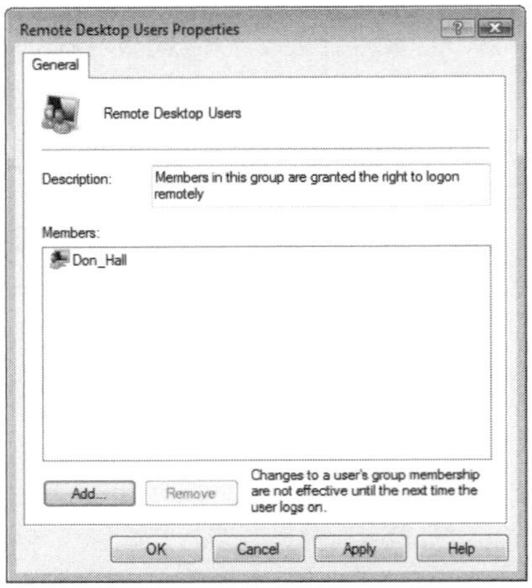

Figure 8-24   Adding users to the Remote Desktop Users group allows them access to Windows Vista through Remote Desktop

5. Click Add, and add the users to whom you want to grant Remote Desktop access by typing in their user account names.

6. When you are finished adding accounts, close the Select Users dialog box, and then click OK to close the Remote Desktop Users Properties dialog box.

Quick Check

1. Which technology allows you to connect remotely when no user is logged on?
2. You have a group of users who use the computer only to run office applications. You do not want to give these users the ability to elevate privileges. To which group should you add these users if you want them to access Windows Vista remotely?

Quick Check Answers

1. Remote Desktop does not require a logged-on user on the host computer. Remote Assistance has this requirement.
2. You should add these users to the Remote Desktop Users group.

Remote Desktop Connection Application

Unlike Remote Assistance, Remote Desktop allows the Aero interface to keep functioning. When using Remote Desktop over a LAN connection, it is even possible to view video without any loss of quality.

To open the Remote Desktop connection application, click Start, All Programs, Accessories, and Remote Desktop Connection. In the dialog box, you can enter the name or Internet Protocol (IP) address of the remote computer to which you want to connect. Clicking the Options button enables you to configure more options for a Remote Desktop session. The options on each tab are as follows:

- The General tab allows you to save or edit a set of credentials to use with Remote Desktop. It also can be used to save the current connection settings to a file or open another file that stores alternate connection settings. A user might save connection settings to a file that contains the user's computer's IP address. When the user gets home, the user can simply double-click the file to initiate a Remote Desktop connection.

- The Display tab allows you to configure a display size for the connection, from a specific resolution up to full screen. It is also possible to set the number of colors used by the connection. A check box allows the display of the connection bar when connected to a remote computer using the full screen mode. Configuring settings here, as well as on the Experience tab, can improve performance when limited bandwidth is available.

- On the Local Resources tab, it is possible to configure resources such as sound and printers.

    - By default, all sound on the host computer is transmitted to the remote computer. It is also possible to leave sound on the host computer or disable it. You should be careful about using the setting that leaves sound on the host computer because this will play at normal volume. Coworkers might be startled if the computer of an officemate who is telecommuting from home suddenly starts making unusual noises.

    - It is possible to configure keyboard combinations, such as 3D Flip, to work in full screen mode only (the default), on the host computer only, or on the computer making the Remote Desktop connection only.

    - The Local Devices And Resources box allows you to connect your local printer and clipboard to the Remote Desktop session. When it is connected to work through Remote Desktop, it allows you to print to your home printer from your work application. Clicking the More button brings up a new dialog box, shown in Figure 8-25, that allows you to connect volumes on your computer, smart cards, serial ports, and supported plug and play devices. Enable this setting if you want to copy files from your local hard disk drive to a host computer that you have connected to using Remote Desktop.

Figure 8-25   Using Remote Desktop to connect your local volumes

- The Programs tab allows you to configure an application to execute immediately after a connection is successfully established.

- The Experience tab, shown in Figure 8-26, allows you to configure how responsive Remote Desktop will be, given a particular bandwidth. It also allows you to configure automatic reconnection if a disruption occurs. It is possible to override the bandwidth setting and select individual components by placing a check in the box next to each one. The available speeds are:

  - Modem 28.8 Kbps.
  - Modem 56 Kbps.
  - Broadband (128 Kbps – 1.5 Mbps).
  - LAN (10 Mbps or higher).
  - Custom. Allows you to specify your own combination of features.

Figure 8-26   The Experience tab

- The Advanced tab contains the Server Authentication and Connect From Anywhere options.
  - Server Authentication verifies the identity of the computer that you are connecting to. This is done to protect you from connecting to a computer that might be impersonating the remote host as a way of stealing your authentication credentials. Only computers running Windows Vista or the next edition of the Windows Server operating system after Windows Server 2003 are able to verify their identities properly. The Authentication options are Connect Always, Warn If Authentication Fails, and Do Not Connect If Authentication Fails.
  - Connect From Anywhere configures Terminal Services Gateway settings. A Terminal Services gateway computer allows authorized users on the Internet to connect to remote computers on a protected network. It can be used as an alternative to connecting to a protected network through a VPN connection. The Terminal Services Gateway dialog box is available from the Advanced tab and is shown in Figure 8-27.

Figure 8-27   Terminal Services gateway servers provide an alternative to using a VPN to making a Remote Desktop connection to a computer on a protected network

Starting and Ending Sessions

This section examines several Remote Desktop usage scenarios. The examples will help you understand how Remote Desktop works.

- If a user account is logged on locally and the same user attempts to log on remotely, the remote user will automatically connect to the local session. This allows users to lock their Windows Vista computers at work while leaving their applications open. When they get home, they can launch a Remote Desktop session, and when they connect their applications will remain open.

- If a user account is logged on remotely and the same user account is used to log on locally, the local user will automatically connect to the remote session. This means that if a person has been up all night at home connected to a work computer through Remote Desktop and has left an application running, that application will still be running when the user connects locally when arriving at work the next day.

- If a Remote Desktop session disconnects, the session continues. For example, Kim Ackers is working with an application at work. At 6 P.M. she locks the screen and goes home. At 8 P.M. she makes a Remote Desktop connection to her computer and continues working with the same application. At 9 P.M. there is a power outage at Kim's home. After power is restored, she is able to connect to the session that is still running on her computer. Alternatively, she could reconnect to that session when she arrived at work the next day and logged on locally. The session will, of course, be lost if the power outage occurs at work, just like you would lose the session on a computer with a locked screen if power were shut off.

■ If a user attempts to connect remotely when a different user is logged on locally, the locally logged-on user will receive a prompt, shown in Figure 8-28, saying that the remote user wants to connect. If the user clicks OK, the local user will be logged off the computer. If the user clicks Cancel, the remote user is told that the request to connect was denied. If the local user does not respond to the prompt, the local user will be logged off after 30 seconds. Group membership has no influence over whether or not a person will be forcibly disconnected from an active session. If you are using the computer, you can reject any remote connection attempt by clicking Cancel.

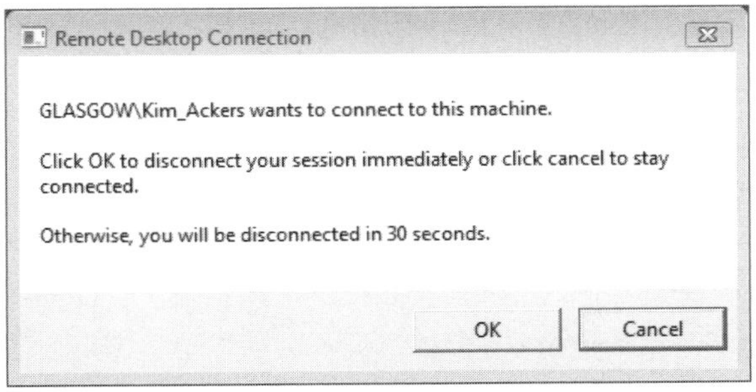

Figure 8-28 A user who is already logged on to a Windows Vista computer can refuse a local or remote logon request

■ If a user is logged on remotely and a user attempts to log on locally, the remote user will be informed that a local user wants to connect. As is the case when a remote user attempts to connect when a local user is logged on, the remote user in this case can deny or allow the local user's attempt to log on. User group membership is irrelevant, and no user can forcibly disconnect another user. This includes the local Administrator account, which is disabled by default.

Troubleshooting Remote Desktop

The troubleshooting rules for Remote Desktop are similar to those for Remote Assistance. When troubleshooting Remote Desktop, keep the following in mind:

■ If one user cannot connect through Remote Desktop and another can, it is because the first user is not a member of the Remote Desktop Users group.

■ If you can connect through Remote Desktop to one computer but not another, the first computer's firewall might not be configured to allow Remote Desktop connections.

■ If you cannot connect to any computers through Remote Desktop, a firewall rule in Windows Firewall with Advanced Security might be causing the problem.

■ If there is an extra firewall between the two computers that are trying to connect and you are certain that both computer's firewalls are correctly configured, this firewall might be blocking your connection.

Unlike Remote Assistance, a Remote Desktop user can always respond to User Account Control dialog boxes if the user has the appropriate permissions. If a Remote Desktop user cannot continue through a User Account Control dialog box, it is because the user would not be able to do so if he or she was logged on locally.

Practice: Providing Remote Support

In these practices, you will perform several exercises that will familiarize you with Windows Vista's Remote Assistance and Remote Desktop technologies.

▶ **Practice 1: Enabling Remote Assistance Security**

In this practice, you will configure Remote Assistance invitation settings. You will configure Remote Assistance invitations so that the helper cannot take control of the host computer, configure an invitation validity period of 30 minutes, and ensure that the host computer will accept only Remote Assistance connections made from computers running Windows Vista.

1. Click Start, right-click Computer, and select Properties.
2. Click Remote Settings.
3. Click Continue to close the User Account Control Dialog box.
4. Ensure that the Allow Remote Assistance Connections To This Computer check box is selected, and then click Advanced.
5. Clear the Allow This Computer To Be Controlled Remotely check box. This will allow helpers to view but not directly interact with the computer.
6. In the Invitations box, use the drop-down lists to set a maximum invitation length of 30 minutes.
7. Select the Create Invitations That Can Only Be Used From Computers Running Windows Vista Or Later check box. The Remote Assistance Settings dialog box should look like Figure 8-29.

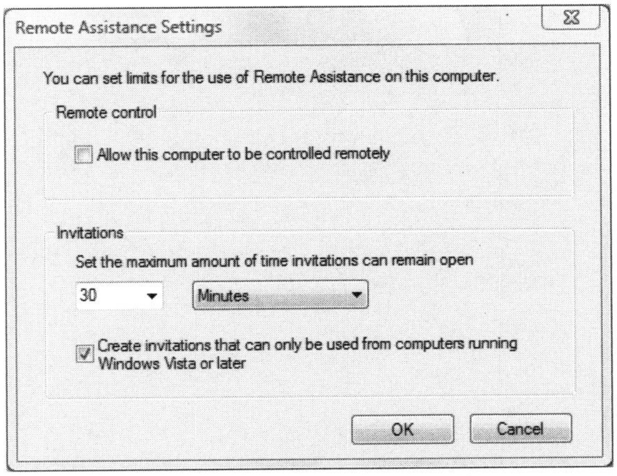

Figure 8-29 How the Remote Assistance Settings dialog box should look once you have finished this practice

8. Click OK to close the Remote Assistance Settings dialog box, and click OK to close the System Properties dialog box.

▶ **Practice 2: Preparing a Remote Assistance invitation**

In this practice, you will configure a Remote Assistance invitation and save it to your desktop. A Remote Assistance invitation that is saved to the desktop can be forwarded to the person who will be providing assistance as a helper using many means, including e-mail, instant messaging, and saving to a shared location.

1. Click Start, and then click Help And Support.

2. In Help And Support, click Windows Remote Assistance under the Ask Someone subheading.

3. In the Do You Want To Ask For Or Offer Help dialog box, shown in Figure 8-30, click Invite Someone You Trust To Help You.

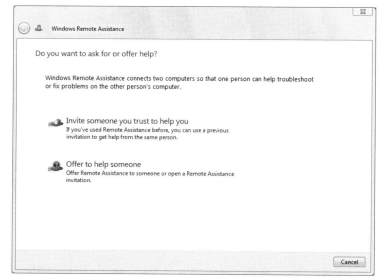

Figure 8-30   The Windows Remote Assistance page

4. On the How Do You Want To Invite Someone To Help You page, click Save This Invitation To A File.

5. By default, the invitation is saved to the desktop with the filename Invitation.msrcincident. You must also provide a password of at least six characters, as shown in Figure 8-21.

6. Click Finish to close the Windows Remote Assistance dialog box.

7. After you click Finish, the Waiting For Incoming Connection dialog box is displayed.

Lesson Summary

■ Remote Assistance is a technology that allows a helper to concurrently view the screen with the user of the host computer.

■ Remote Assistance requires a user to have an existing active session for a connection to be established.

■ Many safeguards are built into Remote Assistance to protect the host user. These include the requirement for a password, the need for desktop interaction to be granted separately after a connection is established, and quick disconnect.

■ The host, rather than the helper, is able to adjust the level of detail that is transmitted back to the helper.

■ Invitations can be sent directly through e-mail or saved as files that can be transmitted in other ways.

■ Remote Desktop allows a user to connect to an existing session or to create a new session on a remote computer.

- If another user is connected to a session on a computer when a Remote Desktop session is attempted, that user will be given the option to log off or dismiss the Remote Desktop connection attempt.

- If a user is logged on through Remote Desktop to a computer and a user attempts to log on locally, the remotely logged-on user will be given the option to log off or to dismiss the local logon attempt.

Lesson Review

You can use the following questions to test your knowledge of the information in Lesson 2, "Configuring Remote Support." The questions are also available on the companion CD if you prefer to review them in electronic form.

NOTE   Answers

Answers to these questions and explanations of why each answer choice is correct or incorrect are located in the "Answers" section at the end of the book.

1. You have configured a router that also functions as a firewall and wireless access point at your grandmother's home. You have a similar configuration at your own home. Yesterday, your grandmother sent you a Remote Assistance invitation using Microsoft Messenger. Which of the following conditions must be met so that you can connect using your grandmother's invitation? (Choose all that apply.)

   A. Grandmother must have kept her computer on and the Remote Assistance Panel open.

   B. Grandmother's computer and firewall must be configured to allow inbound Remote Assistance connections.

   C. Grandmother's computer must be configured to allow outbound Remote Assistance connections.

   D. Grandmother's computer must be running Windows Vista.

2. Orin's user account is a member of the local Administrators group. Ian's user account is a member of the Remote Desktop Users group. In which of the following situations will Orin always be able to make a successful Remote Desktop connection? (Choose all that apply.)

   A. Orin's user account is logged on to the host computer locally.

   B. Ian's user account is logged on to the host computer locally.

   C. No one is logged on to the host computer.

   D. Ian's user account is logged on to the host computer remotely.

3. Which of the following reasons might explain why a helper is unable to connect to a Remote Assistance session when both computers are located on the same LAN? (Choose all that apply.)

   A. A firewall is blocking the connection.

   B. The host is not configured to accept Remote Desktop sessions.

   C. The helper is not a member of the Remote Desktop Users group.

   D. The Remote Assistance panel has been closed on the host.

4. You want to allow several users of Windows Vista at home to connect to Windows Vista computers located on your company's internal network, which is located behind a firewall. Which of the following technologies could you implement to achieve this?

   A. Microsoft Exchange Server 2007

   B. Terminal Services Gateway

   C. Internet Information Services

   D. Microsoft SQL Server 2005

Chapter Review

To further practice and reinforce the skills you learned in this chapter, you can perform the following tasks:

- Review the chapter summary.
- Review the list of key terms introduced in this chapter.
- Complete the case scenarios. These scenarios set up real-world situations involving the topics of this chapter and ask you to create a solution.
- Complete the suggested practices.
- Take a practice test.

Chapter Summary

- Windows Vista Firewall has two aspects: the basic firewall and the firewall with advanced security.
- The basic firewall allows all outbound traffic and can be configured to have exceptions for inbound traffic. It can be configured only for the currently active network profile.
- The firewall with advanced security can be configured with inbound and outbound rules. It is also possible to configure rules for all network profiles, not just the active one.
- Remote Assistance allows a user to forward an invitation to a helper that enables that helper to concurrently view the user's screen. There are several safeguards in place to stop the helper from overriding the user and taking control of the user's computer.
- Remote Desktop allows a user to connect to an existing session that the user has created on a remote Windows Vista computer or to initiate a new session.
- A user logged on to a computer cannot be logged off if another user attempts to connect remotely. A remotely connected user cannot be logged off if another user attempts to connect locally.

Key Terms

Do you know what these key terms mean? You can check your answers by looking up the terms in the glossary at the end of the book.

- helper
- host
- inbound rule
- Internet Protocol Security (IPSec)
- outbound rule

Case Scenarios

In the following case scenarios, you will apply what you have learned about Windows Firewall, Remote Assistance, and Remote Desktop. You can find answers to these questions in the "Answers" section at the end of this book.

Case Scenario 1: University Firewalls

You are responsible for providing desktop support to three separate academics who have Windows Vista Tablet PCs that they use during their normal days.

1. Neil runs a personal website off his Tablet PC when he is presenting at a conference that users can connect to if they connect to his ad hoc network to download copies of his research. How would you configure Windows Firewall to handle this situation?

2. Several computers in the undergraduate laboratory have been used as file sharing servers distributing unlicensed copyright material. Describe the type of rule you would create if you knew the port, but not the program name, that was being used.

3. How might you deploy the Windows Firewall with Advanced Security profile to the 30 Windows Vista computers in the undergraduate lab that are not members of any domain?

Case Scenario 2: Antarctic Desktop Support

It is the middle of winter down at your organization's Antarctic research facility. The IT support person there has come down with a serious illness and has been confined to sick bay for the next two weeks. In her stead, you will be providing desktop support for the 50 scientists stationed at the facility. Your office in Tasmania is connected to the base by a high-speed Internet link. All computers have Remote Desktop and remote administration enabled.

1. A user needs help installing an application. You have the ability to elevate privileges on the computer, but the user does not. How should you approach this situation?

2. A user from the base needs to train you to use an application on their computer remotely. Which technology would you use?

3. Another staff member at the Tasmanian office needs to connect to a Windows Vista computer in Antarctica to check some scientific results but is unable to do so. You are able to connect to this computer. What steps might you take to resolve this problem?

Suggested Practices

To help you successfully master the exam objectives presented in this chapter, complete the following tasks.

Configure Security Settings in Windows Firewall

■ **Practice 1: Windows Firewall Exceptions**   Configure an exception for the program Calc.exe in the c:\windows\system32 directory.

Configure an exception for port 1138 for the UDP protocol for IP addresses between 10.10.10.1 and 10.10.10.255.

■ **Practice 2: Windows Firewall with Advanced Security**   Create an inbound predefined rule for Windows Media Player that blocks any connections.

Create an outbound rule that blocks the program Solitaire.exe from communicating with computers on the Internet.

Configure Remote Access

■ **Practice 1: Friendly Remote Access**   Organize for a friend or a study partner to connect to the Internet with a Windows Vista computer. Exchange remote access invitations and attempt to connect to each other's computers across the Internet.

■ **Practice 2: Remote Desktop**   Attempt to access your Windows Vista computer remotely using Remote Desktop. You might try to do this from work to your home computer or from a computer at the library to your home computer.

Take a Practice Test

The practice tests on this book's companion CD offer many options. For example, you can test yourself on just one exam objective, or you can test yourself on all the 70-620 certification exam content. You can set up the test so that it closely simulates the experience of taking a certification exam, or you can set it up in study mode so that you can look at the correct answers and explanations after you answer each question.

MORE INFO   **Practice tests**

For details about all the practice test options available, see the "How to Use the Practice Tests" section in this book's Introduction.

Chapter 9

Configuring Communications Applications Included with Windows Vista

Communication and collaboration are integral to productivity in the modern business environment. Windows Vista includes several new and important applications that can assist in easing the communication and collaboration process. Windows Mail functions in many respects like its predecessor Outlook Express, although users will quickly notice how resilient the application is in protecting the user against increasingly common Internet junk mail and phishing scams. Windows Contacts replaces the Address Book, but it also brings improvement in managing the information you keep about the people with whom you collaborate. In terms of new applications, Windows Calendar allows you to share your calendar with others and allows others to view yours, and Windows Meeting Space allows the sharing of desktops, applications, and files without requiring a server infrastructure. Understanding how these applications work by themselves and with each other is the key to gaining the productivity improvements available when you start using Windows Vista.

Exam objectives in this chapter:
- Configure Windows Mail.
- Configure Windows Meeting Space.
- Configure Windows Calendar.

Lessons in this chapter:

Before You Begin

You need to have completed the installation and upgrading practices in Chapter 1, "Installing Windows Vista Client," and Chapter 2, "Windows Vista Upgrades and Migrations." The result of this will be that you have installed Windows Vista Ultimate on a personal computer or within a virtual machine. This computer should also have a working connection to the Internet. You need a second Windows Vista computer to complete the third practice in Lesson 3.

No additional configuration is required for this chapter.

Real World

Orin Thomas

At a certain point it becomes impossible to deal with the amount of e-mail that you get unless you have configured some sort of rules and views. I've been using the same public e-mail address since 1995, which means that by now it is probably in the address book of everyone who has ever sent unsolicited commercial e-mail. I'm protected from this deluge by clever junk e-mail filters that spirit the junk e-mail away. Out of habit I check my junk e-mail folder once a month, but it has been quite some time since I've seen something that I wanted to read misdiagnosed as junk e-mail. Rules help me a great deal as well. I use rules to ensure that messages from my editors and co-author are safely placed in the same location and other rules to ensure that messages from other people are automatically categorized so that I have a fair idea what the message might be about prior to actually opening it. Rules take a lot of the hassle out of sorting e-mail. I know exactly where to find e-mails that are several years old without having to use search because rules that I created have placed those e-mails in the proper folder rather than letting them linger at the bottom of my inbox. With careful configuration, you will find that using Windows Mail makes your communication more efficient because when you open the application you will see everything nicely sorted, rather than a single pile as long as your arm waiting for you to start wading through it.

Lesson 1: Configuring Windows Mail

As an information technology (IT) professional, you are unlikely to need a lesson in how to send an e-mail. If you do not know how to send an e-mail, you really should not be taking this exam! What you will need to know to pass this exam is how to configure Windows Mail so that people can use it as an e-mail client and, if they are interested, as a tool to interact with Internet newsgroups. The common thread in Lesson 1 is the configuration of views and rules. Views and rules are a way of dealing with the flood of information provided by incoming messages.

- Views are a a configurable way of looking at messages.
- Rules are a way of processing those messages based on their properties.

The best way to use Windows Mail is to use views and rules in concert. You set a view so that you see only flagged messages, and you configure rules to ensure that interesting messages are flagged. When configured correctly, Windows Mail is a very powerful tool. Although even more powerful tools such as Outlook are available, after you understand what Windows Mail is capable of, you might choose to stay with Windows Vista's default messaging application rather than move to something that might have extra features that you will not necessarily need.

After this lesson, you will be able to:
- Configure Windows Mail.
- Set up Windows Mail inbox.
- Configure newsgroups.

Estimated lesson time: 40 minutes

Using Windows Mail as an E-mail Client

Windows Mail is primarily used as an e-mail client. It serves as a replacement for Outlook Express, the default mail client available with previous versions of Windows. The functionality of Windows Mail is relatively similar to that of Outlook Express. The main differences are improved ability to search through e-mail, integration with the new Contacts functionality of Windows Vista, and the junk e-mail filter.

Starting Windows Mail for the First Time

When you start Windows Mail for the first time, the setup wizard runs, helping you to configure your first e-mail account. The first question Windows Mail asks is which display name to use. People should answer this question formally because it is the name that Windows Mail attaches to every e-mail that they send. The second question that someone running Windows Mail for the first time is asked is what their Internet e-mail address is. This is the e-mail address for the messages that you will be using Windows Mail to read and respond to. Many people have multiple e-mail addresses—for example, an e-mail address assigned by their Internet service provider (ISP), a work-based e-mail account, and a webmail account, such as Windows Live. Before you set up Windows Mail, you need to decide which of these accounts will be used as the primary e-mail account. When you respond to an e-mail, even if you have multiple e-mail accounts, the default e-mail account is the address that all of your outbound messages will use. If you are unsure which e-mail account to designate, use the e-mail address assigned to you by your ISP.

Exam Tip   Because the 70-620 exam focuses on using Windows Vista in noncorporate environments, e-mail account information is likely to be provided by a person's ISP rather than by the organization's systems administrator. Almost all ISPs have a webpage that explains how customers can set up their own e-mail clients. When trying to determine e-mail settings, consult these pages. If there are no such pages, you will have to contact the ISP's help desk to get this information.

On the Set Up E-Mail Servers page, shown in Figure 9-1, you need to enter the incoming and outgoing e-mail server information. Before entering this information, you need to determine the answers to the following questions:

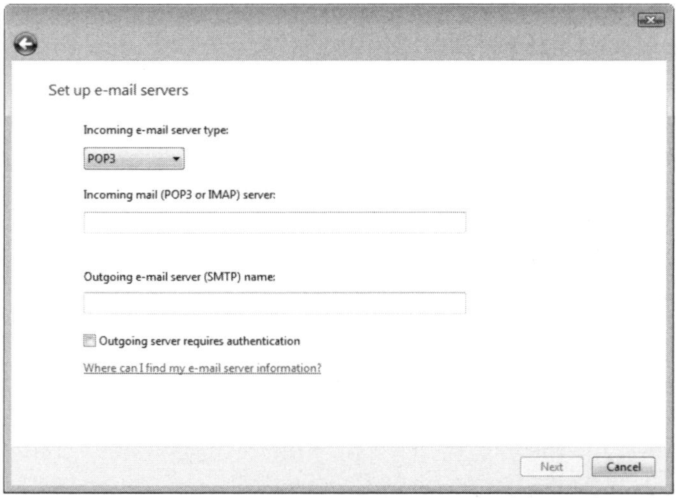

Figure 9-1   The Set Up E-Mail Servers page

- Does the e-mail server use the Post Office Protocol 3 (POP3) or Internet Message Access Protocol 4 (IMAP4) e-mail protocol? The difference between these two protocols is discussed later in this lesson.
- What is the fully qualified domain name (FQDN) of the incoming mail server? In some environments the name mail is enough, although this depends on the ISP's Domain Name System (DNS) server. If the computer is used on different networks, such as a Tablet PC being used at home and in airport lounges, the FQDN is necessary.

- What is the FQDN of the outgoing mail server? In some, but not all, cases this is the same as the incoming mail server's name.

- Does the outgoing mail server require authentication? Servers that process outgoing mail are increasingly requiring authentication as a way of ensuring that only authorized users send e-mail. This simple step can do much to reduce the incidence of unsolicited commercial e-mail.

Unlike previous versions of Outlook Express, Windows Mail does not support the Hypertext Transfer Protocol (HTTP) incoming e-mail server type. This incoming e-mail server type allowed users to use Outlook Express to read e-mail from services such as Hotmail, now known as Windows Live.

NOTE   Windows Live Desktop

You can use the Windows Live Desktop mail application, which you can download for free from Microsoft's website, to read and locally store e-mail sent to a Windows Live account.

After you have completed the Set Up E-Mail Servers page, you need to enter the mailbox name in the E-Mail Username text box and the mailbox password. It is not necessary to enter a password on this page. Clearing the Remember Password check box means that Windows Mail will prompt users for their mailbox passwords each time they open the application.

By default, Windows Mail is configured to download any e-mail stored in the configured mailbox when you complete the wizard, although you can turn this option off by selecting the Do Not Download My E-Mail At This Time check box. You should be careful with this if you are going to be reading messages from the same POP3 account on multiple computers. When most people read e-mail on multiple computers, they want the incoming messages to be available on those computers. If you have not configured an e-mail account to leave mail on the server, the first time it connects it downloads the messages and then deletes them from the server after that download completes. You might download an important message from your boss with instructions on what to do the next day when she is away but forget when you check your mail at work that you downloaded the message at home, and you do not have access to it because it has been removed from the mail server.

POP3, IMAP4, and SMTP

When you are configuring an incoming mail server, you need to know which incoming mail protocol the server uses. The two options are Post Office Protocol 3 (POP3) and Internet Message Access Protocol 4 (IMAP4). Sometimes an ISP offers both services and leaves it up to the customer to decide which one to implement. The differences between the two protocols are as follows:

- **POP3**   This protocol allows Windows Mail to retrieve e-mail stored on a POP3 server. Almost all ISPs use the POP3 protocol on their e-mail servers. If you are configuring e-mail for a home user, it is likely that you will use POP3 over IMAP4. POP3 clients such as Windows Mail usually connect to the POP3 server, retrieve all the e-mail stored in the configured account, and then delete the retrieved e-mail from the server. It is possible to leave downloaded e-mail on the POP3 server. POP3 periodically checks e-mail on the server and is a good solution for customers who use dial-up connections. POP3 uses Transmission Control Protocol (TCP) and User Datagram Protocol (UDP) protocols on port 110. If used in conjunction with Secure Sockets Layer (SSL), POP3 uses TCP and UDP protocols on port 995.

- **IMAP4** This protocol is more advanced than POP3 and is often used on corporate networks. IMAP4 differs from POP3 in that it allows a continuous connection to a mailbox on the incoming mail server. IMAP4 also allows you to connect multiple e-mail clients to the same mailbox simultaneously. IMAP4 clients can create mail folders on the incoming mail server and move messages between these mail folders.

Although there are multiple offerings for the incoming mail server, all outgoing mail servers use Simple Mail Transport Protocol (SMTP). SMTP uses TCP and UDP protocols on port 25. You can use SMTP only to send e-mail, you cannot use it to receive e-mail.

Windows Mail Settings

You can change Windows Mail settings using the Windows Mail Options dialog box. This dialog box is available through the Tools menu. These settings apply to all Windows Mail accounts. If you are unsure of which dialog box you use to configure a setting, consider whether the setting would apply to all e-mail accounts or to just a single e-mail account. Some of the settings that you can configure using the Options dialog box include:

- Whether a sound is played when new messages arrive. Many people disable this setting because it can distract them when they are concentrating on another task.
- Whether Windows Mail synchronizes at startup. If you open Windows Mail regularly when you are not connected to the Internet, you might want to disable the option and only synchronize manually using the Send And Receive button.
- How often Windows Mail checks for new messages. This depends on how much mail you receive and how quickly you need to be updated. You would not want to explain to your boss that the reason you have not responded to her request for information was because you had configured Windows Mail to check for new messages only every five hours!
- Whether a message is sent immediately or whether it will be sent the next time Windows Mail synchronizes. E-mail is sent immediately by default.
- Whether a signature is included on outgoing messages.
- Whether a spell check occurs prior to a message being sent. Enabling this can prevent embarrassing gaffes.

The list above is not exhaustive but includes almost all the important options. As a part of your studies, you should familiarize yourself with the Options dialog box so that you can see the full range of configuration settings that you can make in Windows Mail. The Options dialog box of Windows Mail is explored in more detail in Practice 1 at the end of this lesson.

Offline mode allows you to use Windows Mail without worrying about its attempting to synchronize. When you click Send on an e-mail, Windows Mail places the message in the outbox and does not forward it to the outgoing mail server until offline mode is disabled. You can enable and disable offline mode by choosing Work Offline on Windows Mail's File menu. If you click Send/Receive when Windows Mail is set to offline mode, you will be asked whether you would like to go online and perform synchronization.

Multiple Accounts and Advanced E-mail Account Settings

You can configure Windows Mail to receive e-mail from multiple e-mail accounts. To add an extra account, open the Internet Accounts dialog box from the Tools menu, click Add, and then click E-Mail Account. The setup process is the same as it is for the initial account configuration when you start Windows Mail.

Editing account properties allows you to configure advanced settings. It also allows you to rectify any mistakes that you might have made in the original configuration, such as the wrong outgoing server address or incoming server mail protocol. The Connection tab on a particular account's Properties dialog box allows you to specify what type of connection to make when synchronizing this particular account. This is very useful if an e-mail account can be accessed only over a virtual private network (VPN) connection, which is a special type of Internet connection that is often used to connect remotely to corporate networks. You use this setting only if an account requires a connection method different from the one specified in the Connections tab of Internet Explorer's Internet Options dialog box.

Windows Mail supports the use of signing certificates. Signing certificates are used to verify the identity of a sender. It is also possible if you have an appropriate certificate installed to encrypt messages to protect them. These types of certificates are usually implemented only in business environments, so although you should be aware of their functionality, they are unlikely to be covered in detail by the 70-620 exam.

The Advanced tab of an e-mail account's properties, shown in Figure 9-2, allows you to configure the e-mail account to use nonstandard ports, configure timeouts, leave messages on the server, and to break apart messages that are larger than a certain size into smaller parts. Configuring timeouts is useful when you are connected through a slow link when synchronizing mail. Leaving a copy of messages on the server is helpful when you check e-mail in multiple locations. For example, say that you have a POP3 account and you check your work e-mail account from home. In the Advanced tab of the e-mail account Properties dialog box on your Windows Vista computer, you can ensure that any message you read at home can be later accessed when you read your e-mail again at work by selecting the Leave A Copy Of Messages On Server check box. This is not a problem with IMAP accounts, which leave e-mail on the server unless you explicitly delete it.

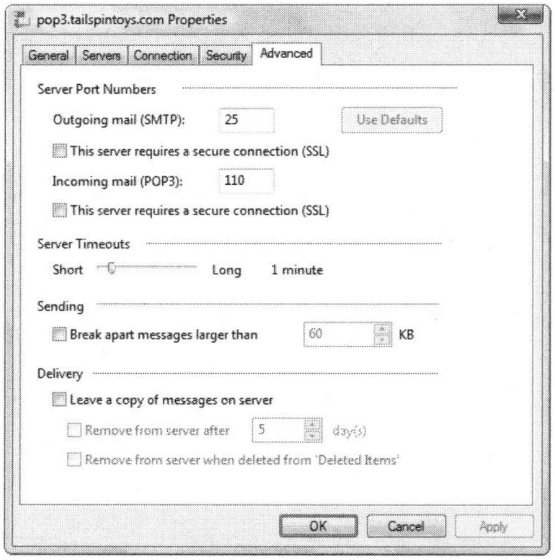

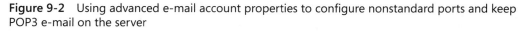

Figure 9-2   Using advanced e-mail account properties to configure nonstandard ports and keep POP3 e-mail on the server

IMAP accounts have a slightly different set of properties. The main difference in the advanced properties is that you can specify that Windows Mail will check for new messages in all folders on an IMAP server. You can also configure special folder properties for the Sent Items, Drafts, Deleted Items, and Junk E-Mail folders on the server.

Viewing the Windows Mail Inbox

When you use Windows Mail, you usually see all the messages that you have received, both read and unread. You can change this by altering the message views to one of the preconfigured options using the Current View option in the View menu. The preconfigured message views are as follows:

- **Show All Messages**   The default view shows all messages. Messages that have been read are displayed less prominently than unread messages.
- **Hide Read Messages**   This view is helpful if you want to quickly locate messages that you have not yet opened. After you have read a message, it will look as though it has been removed from the inbox. To make it reappear, you just need to switch the view to Show All Messages.
- **Hide Read Or Ignored Messages**   This is similar to hide read messages but allows you to use the power of message rules to designate less important messages and hide them from you. This can be a better option than having a message rule delete messages

because sometimes you might want to go back and look at a message you have ignored. You cannot do this if Windows Mail automatically deleted the message.

NOTE **Grouping messages**

Message grouping by conversation can be used with any of the above options. This is very useful when there are messages from several people that are all in response to one another.

It is possible to create custom views that you can then apply using the View menu. You can do this through creating a new view in the Define Views dialog box, and you can use this view to display or hide messages if the conditions are met. You can create views with a combination of the following conditions:

- Where the message is from one of a group of listed e-mail addresses.
- Where the Subject line contains one or more specific words.
- Where the sender has marked the message as a priority.
- Where the message has been received from a particular account. For example, if you read mail from two separate e-mail accounts using Windows Mail, you can limit the view to apply to only one of those accounts.
- Where the message was sent more than a specified number of days ago.
- Where the message is longer than a specified number of lines.
- Where the message has an attachment.
- Where the message has been read.
- Where the message body has been downloaded.
- Where the message is flagged.
- Where the message is watched or ignored.
- Where the message is secure.

You can use any or all of these conditions when creating a view in Windows Mail. The important thing to remember about views is that they are either used to show only messages that meet specific conditions or hide messages that meet specific conditions. You cannot use views directly to move messages between folders or to copy or delete messages from Windows Mail.

Message Rules and Folders

Message rules allow you to configure Windows Mail to process incoming mail prior to it reaching the inbox. Message rules differ from junk e-mail options in that you configure the rules yourself. Although it is possible to create message rules to flag an e-mail or display it in a different color, the most common usage is to have rules move e-mails into special folders on the basis of who sent the message or the information in the message's header.

Although it is possible to create a view that would display messages only from your best friend, you can also create a folder for all messages from your best friend and configure a message rule that automatically moves any future messages that you receive from your friend into that special folder. This saves you from having to constantly switch views; you can just look for certain types of e-mails in the folders that you have configured rules to copy them to.

Message rules have the same conditions as views except you cannot directly create a rule based on the account from which the message was retrieved. You can do this indirectly by using the extra conditions, which allow you to configure a rule based on the address that appears in the message's To or CC line. Whereas views only allow you to show or hide messages on the basis of the configured conditions, message rules allow you to perform the following tasks:

- Move the message to a specific folder.
- Copy the message to a specific folder.
- Delete the message.
- Forward the message to an e-mail address or set of e-mail addresses.
- Highlight the message using a chosen color.
- Flag the message.
- Automatically mark the message as read even though you will not have opened it.
- Mark the message as watched or ignored.
- Send an automatic reply.
- Not download the message from the mail server.
- Delete the message from the mail server.
- Stop processing more rules. This action is useful when there are multiple rules.

Although it is possible to combine actions on messages that meet the specified conditions, you need to be careful when doing this. For example, if you set the Move To The Specified Folder and the Delete actions, the message is moved and deleted from that folder. This is functionally the same as just deleting the message.

The order in which rules are applied is important and can be configured in the Rules dialog box. Unless you include the Stop Processing More Rules action in a rule, all rules that apply to a message will be invoked. For example, rule one might copy all messages from Kim into a folder named Kim. Rule two might delete all messages with the subject "Make Money Fast." If Kim sends you an e-mail with the subject "Make Money Fast," both rules will be applied. Adding the Stop Processing More Rules action to the first rule will mean that Kim's message will not be deleted because the second rule will not be applied.

Clicking Apply Now in the Message Rules dialog box allows you to apply new rules to a chosen folder and its subfolders. This can be very useful if you are asked to help sort the e-mail of someone with tens of thousands of messages in that person's inbox. You can create new rules and apply them directly to the messages in the inbox rather than sort them into folders manually.

Junk E-mail Options

Anyone who has an e-mail account knows the problem that junk e-mail causes. This problem is likely to get worse for you if you start posting to newsgroups because people who send unsolicited commercial e-mail often harvest newsgroups for e-mail addresses. Windows Mail allows you to enable a special set of junk e-mail filters to reduce the amount that appears in your inbox. Unlike message rules that you configure yourself, junk e-mail options have a set of algorithms configured by Microsoft that look for patterns in junk e-mail. Messages that display the characteristics that the algorithms are designed to detect are moved into the junk e-mail folder in the same way that a message rule you designed for e-mail from your best friend goes into a folder with your friend's name on it.

Depending on how you configure Junk E-Mail Options, shown in Figure 9-3, junk e-mail can either be moved to a junk e-mail folder or automatically deleted. The reason that you might want to use a junk e-mail folder is that for all its sophistication, the junk e-mail filter does generate false positives. A false positive with regard to junk e-mail is when a message is identified as junk e-mail when it is in fact a message that is not junk e-mail. From time to time, a message from someone you want to hear from is considered junk e-mail, which is why you should occasionally glance over your junk e-mail folder looking for false positives.

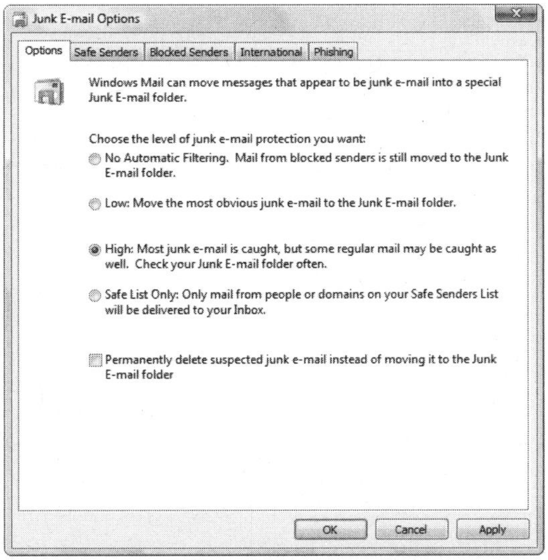

Figure 9-3   Configuring junk e-mail options

If you want to ensure that the messages of a particular correspondent of yours are never subjected to Windows Mail's junk filter, you should add that person to the Safe Senders list. All messages that come from an e-mail address on the Safe Senders list bypass any junk filters. It is also possible to add domain names to the Safe Senders list. You might do this if you want to ensure that Windows Mail never places e-mails from work in the junk e-mail folder. Similarly, you can also add e-mail addresses and domain names to the Blocked Senders list. Blocked senders and domains are automatically dumped in the junk-e-mail folder no matter what the content of the messages is.

On the International tab of the Junk E-Mail Options dialog box, the Blocked Top-Level Domain List offers comparable functionality, allowing you to block on the basis of top-level domain. This can only be done on the basis of country and not other top-level domains, such as .net, .com, .edu, and .org. The Blocked Encoding List allows you to block on the basis of a message's character encoding. Encoding allows non-ASCII characters, such as those in the Russian or Thai alphabet, to be displayed properly. Blocking on the basis of encoding stops messages written using nonfamiliar character sets from coming to your inbox. If you are in a country that uses a character set different from ASCII, it is possible to block all ASCII messages as well.

Phishing is the process by which an e-mail is sent asking a user to reenter his or her user name and password for a website that the user might regularly access. These messages often, but not always, appear to come from banks or other online financial institutions. The message is designed to appear legitimate, and when the recipient visits the site, it appears similar to the real site that the message claims to represent. In reality, the website is an elaborate trap designed to harvest user names and passwords. A person enters the user name and password that he or she uses to authenticate with the online financial institution, and those credentials are recorded and used later by the scammers to gain access to the real online financial institution and to clean out the recipient's account. Users of Windows Mail are protected by default from most of these attacks, but it is possible to disable this protection by making changes in the Junk E-Mail Options dialog box.

Searching E-mail

The quickest way to search e-mail is to type a query in the search box in the top right corner of the Windows Mail window. This performs a full-text search of all messages in the current folder. If you want to perform a more detailed search, it is necessary to use the Find Message dialog box, shown in Figure 9-4, which is accessible from the Edit menu. It is possible to search all mail folders for messages on the basis of sender, recipient, subject, message, date received, message text, whether the message had attachments, and whether the message was flagged.

Figure 9-4   The Find Message dialog box

Importing and Exporting Messages

At times, it is necessary to import messages from another computer. If you have not performed a full migration using Windows Easy Transfer, you might need to use Windows Mail's Import and Export functions. Windows Mail can import messages from the following applications:

- Microsoft Exchange 5.5, 2000, 2003, and 2007
- Microsoft Outlook personal folder (PST) files
- Microsoft Outlook Express 6
- Windows Mail

Except for the case of Exchange, it is necessary to perform an export using the previous e-mail application before attempting an import using Windows Mail. For example, if you have a Windows 2000 computer running Outlook 2003, you would need to export the mail in PST format and transfer it to a Windows Vista computer before attempting to import it into Windows Mail. To import mail, select Import from the File menu, select Messages, and then select the message format from which you want to import. Windows Mail can also import contacts, mail account settings, and news account settings.

Windows Mail itself can export messages only to a Microsoft Exchange Server through Messaging Application Programming Interface (MAPI) or to Windows Mail. For example, say that Tony has 3000 e-mails in 30 folders on his Windows Vista laptop computer. He wants to have a copy of these e-mails on his Windows Vista desktop computer. In this situation, you would perform an export from the laptop computer and then an import on the desktop computer. Microsoft Exchange Server is an enterprise product and is unlikely to be tested on the 70-620 exam.

Quick Check

1. Thomas calls you to complain that messages seem to be disappearing from his inbox after he reads them, even though he has not attempted to delete them. You check the deleted items folder and see no messages. What might you do to solve this problem?
2. Which e-mail protocol supports moving messages between folders on the incoming server?

Quick Check Answers

1. Thomas probably has his inbox configured to display only unread messages. Each time he reads a message, it is marked as read and is no longer displayed.
2. IMAP4.

Using Newsgroups with Windows Mail

Usenet is a set of distributed news servers that host newsgroups. Newsgroups are collections of threaded text messages. In general, anyone can post any message they like to a newsgroup, although some moderated groups exist. As web forums have become more prevalent, topical discussion on the Internet has moved away from Usenet. One advantage of Usenet is that anyone who still uses it tends to have been active on the Internet for some time. This means that if you ask a question in a newsgroup, you might find that you get a more knowledgeable answer than you might get asking the same question on a web forum. Because of its distributed nature, there are generally a lot more people reading an individual newsgroup than reading an individual web forum, although this will not always be the case.

Adding News Servers

Reading Usenet newsgroups for the first time is often likened to drinking from a fire hydrant. Usenet contains a staggering amount of information, and without judicious use of rules and views, it can be very hard to find the needles you are looking for in the haystack. Windows Mail is automatically configured to use Microsoft Communities, which carry Microsoft-related newsgroups. This server hosts Microsoft-specific newsgroups that are replicated around the world, which is great if you want to access only news about Microsoft products. If you want to access messages about role playing games or your favorite TV show, you will need to add Network News Transfer Protocol (NNTP) servers to Windows Mail.

Almost every ISP has a news server, and this should be your first port of call when looking for newsgroups that cover your peculiar interests. It is also possible to subscribe to news servers on a commercial basis. Commercial news servers tend to retain articles a lot longer than ISP news servers. Because Usenet has so much data, your ISP might retain new messages only for a couple of days before deleting them to make way for newer traffic. Commercial news servers always require subscribers to log on to access content, although some ISPs require this as well as a way of limiting access to people who are already paying for their service. To add another news server to Windows Mail, you need to know the FQDN of the news server and whether it requires authentication. Windows Mail also allows you to configure a separate reply to an e-mail address for each news server account. This option allows you to receive all of your work-related newsgroup traffic at one address for the Microsoft newsgroups and all of your recreational newsgroup-related traffic at another e-mail address.

To add a new news server to Windows Mail, perform the following steps:

1. Open Windows Mail. On the Tools menu, select Accounts.
2. In the Internet Accounts dialog box, click Add.
3. On the Select Account Type page, click Newsgroup Account, and click Next.
4. In the Display Name text box, enter the name that you want added to your messages. Unless you have a good reason to do otherwise, you should use the same name with which you configured Windows Mail. Click Next.
5. On the Internet News E-Mail Address page, enter the e-mail address of the account with which you configured Windows Mail. This allows you to receive any messages from other newsgroup readers in the same application that you use to read news. Click Next.
6. On the Internet News Server Name page, shown in Figure 9-5, enter the name of the NNTP server that you will connect to. If the news server requires you to log on, select the My News Server Requires Me To Log On check box. Click Next.

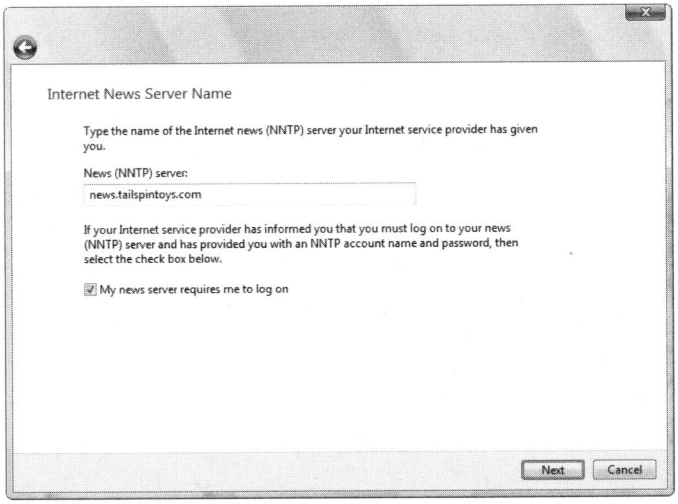

Figure 9-5   Adding a news server

7. If you have selected the My News Server Requires Me To Log On option, enter the authentication credentials and click Next. Otherwise click Finish. The new news server account is displayed in the Internet Accounts dialog box.

Subscribing and Unsubscribing to Newsgroups

There are tens of thousands of newsgroups on Usenet. Rather than provide a list of all newsgroups that a news server carries, which would be very long, you are given the option of searching through the list of available newsgroups and subscribing to those that interest you. Newsgroups that you subscribe to are placed under the NNTP server that carries them, as shown in Figure 9-6.

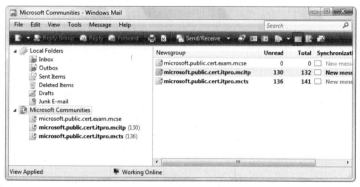

Figure 9-6   Three subscribed newsgroups under the Microsoft Communities news server

When you add a new news server, Windows Mail asks if you want to download a list of newsgroups that the server carries. Depending on the news server that you have subscribed to and the speed of your connection to the Internet, this might take some time. If you connect to your ISP's news server, do not be surprised if the number of newsgroups it downloads is well in excess of 50,000!

Finding the newsgroup that you need is simplified by the search box in the Newsgroup Subscriptions dialog box, shown in Figure 9-7. (You access this dialog box by selecting Newsgroups on the Tools menu.) It is possible to search for part of a newsgroup name. It is also possible to search newsgroup descriptions for keywords. After the search query results have been returned, you can select newsgroups that interest you and click Subscribe. It is not possible to preview a group unless you have subscribed to it and accessed its articles. If you find that the newsgroup does not meet your needs, you will then have to return to the Newsgroup Subscriptions dialog box to unsubscribe from that group. Clicking the Subscribed tab lists only those groups that you are subscribed to, which greatly simplifies unsubscribing.

Clicking the Reset List button in the Newsgroup Subscriptions dialog box instructs Windows Mail to retrieve the entire list of newsgroups from the server. Clicking the New tab shows only those newsgroups that have been added to the list since you last subscribed or unsubscribed to newsgroups. New newsgroups are added every day, although any relevant new groups will be returned when you perform a search. Each time you connect to a news server and it has new newsgroups, you are asked if you want to view them. If you want to turn this option off, you can do it in the General tab of the Windows Mail Optionsdialog box.

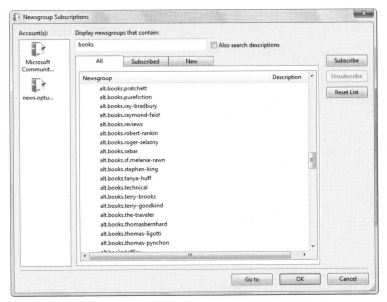

Figure 9-7 The Newsgroup Subscriptions dialog box

Downloading Articles

Some newsgroups receive hundreds of new messages each day. Rather than download the content of all new newsgroup messages, Windows Mail downloads a limited number of message headers when you open a newsgroup that you are subscribed to. When you open the newsgroup message, Windows Mail retrieves the content of the message from the news server. It is possible, using filters, to have Windows Mail automatically download messages that meet criteria that you have selected when you open a newsgroup.

> ### Real World
>
> *Orin Thomas*
>
> Newsgroups can be odd places. Some newsgroups have existed as communities for decades. I maintained a frequently asked questions (FAQ) for a newsgroup that I joined in 1992 for more than a decade, and a newsgroup that I was responsible for creating in 1995 is still going strong with many of the same people 12 years later! Many newsgroups have long-standing traditions. The virtual communities that some newsgroups host can be intimidating to newcomers. My advice, before posting to a newsgroup, is to get a feel for it by reading the messages it contains. You will quickly see if questions are answered or ignored. In the newsgroups where questions are answered, look for any FAQs that might be posted. FAQs deal with the most common questions that people who are new to the newsgroup might have. Most established newsgroups have informative FAQs because they got tired of new posters asking the same questions every day for many years!

Online and Offline Modes   Use online mode when you have a persistent connection to the NNTP server. In online mode, opening a message means that the body of that message is automatically retrieved from the NNTP server and displayed on your screen. Offline mode is used when you do not have a persistent connection to the NNTP server. For example, Tony connects to the Internet using a modem. Rather than using the line all of the time when reading newsgroups, he connects, downloads the headers, and then disconnects, switching to offline mode. He then looks through the headers, marks messages of interest for download, and then reconnects. He switches back to online mode, and Windows Mail downloads the messages of interest. He then disconnects and again switches to offline mode. He can read and respond to messages at his leisure. When he connects again and switches to online mode, his messages are posted to the news server. You can switch between online and offline modes by selecting or deselecting the Work Offline option in the File menu.

When you right-click a newsgroup under its newsgroup server, you can configure its synchronization settings. Synchronization settings determine what content is retrieved from the news server when you perform synchronization. The synchronization settings are:

- **All Messages**   Although it suggests all messages, this setting configures Windows Mail to download approximately 300 messages and their content. The reason for this limitation is that some news servers might store hundreds of megabytes of messages for a group. If you download all of them, you might be in for an unexpectedly long wait. It is possible to adjust this number on the Read tab of the Options dialog box. This dialog box is accessible through the Tools menu.

- **New Messages Only**   This downloads the content of messages that have been posted since the last synchronization with the news server.

- **Headers Only** This downloads all headers stored currently on the news server, which are checked against any headers that you have already downloaded so as to avoid duplication.

Right-clicking and selecting Catch Up marks all of the articles in the group as read. Doing this when you have finished reading the newsgroup allows you to concentrate only on new content the next time you open the newsgroup. It is also possible in the Read tab of the Windows Mail Options dialog box to have all messages marked as read when you exit a newsgroup.

Reading Newsgroups Newsgroups have been around for almost 30 years, which means that many terms are used to describe the same concepts. The terms used by Windows Mail to describe the most basic concepts of newsgroups are messages and conversations. When you read newsgroups, you see the terms posts and articles used to describe messages. A message is a single post made to a newsgroup. A conversation is a group of messages that are either direct or indirect responses to an original post. When reading newsgroups, you see the term thread used interchangeably with the term conversation.

When reading newsgroups, you will come across some messages or conversations that you want to follow or make note of. You can do this by using Windows Mail to *flag* the message or *watch* the conversation. You flag a message or watch a conversation by selecting a message and then choosing the appropriate option from the Message menu. The difference is as follows:

- Flags work on a per message basis. Flags are generally applied using filters. A filter is an automated routine that scans newsgroup content to bring to your attention messages that meet criteria you have specified.

- Watching works on a per conversation basis. Watching is generally used to keep track of an ongoing conversation. Conversations can last days, weeks, and even months. Watching allows you to quickly locate a conversation that you have been following.

Some newsgroup conversations can have thousands of replies. Because you are unlikely to have time to read all of the conversations, you can use rules to flag articles within a conversation that might be of particular interest. Using views, discussed later in this lesson, you can limit the display to only those items that are being watched and or flagged.

It is also possible to ignore a conversation. You might decide that you are simply not interested in a topic being discussed. If the conversation has been going on for some weeks and you read newsgroups every day, you might prefer that conversation not be displayed at all. You accomplish this by marking the conversation as ignored. You can ignore a conversation by selecting the conversation and then clicking Ignore Conversation on the Message menu. A blocking symbol appears next to the conversation and is dimmed. It is possible to use views, covered later in this lesson, to make ignored conversations invisible.

Occasionally, a message is posted in a basic code called ROT13. ROT13 is what is known as a substitution cipher, where one letter is substituted for a letter that is 13 letters along in the alphabet. For example, A becomes N, B becomes O, C becomes P, and so on. To decode a message posted in ROT13, select Unscramble (ROT13) from the Message menu.

Because news servers have limits to the size of messages that they accept, it is often necessary for people who post large files to newsgroups to split them up into multiple attachments. If you want to access the attachments from a group of newsgroup posts, it is necessary to combine and decode them. After you have done this, you can save the attachment locally. To combine and decode attachments from newsgroup posts, select all of the posts that contain part of the attachment by holding down the Ctrl key, clicking on each one. After you select all parts, from the Message menu, click Combine And Decode. This displays the Order For Decoding dialog box. Use the information provided in each message header to correctly order the messages, and then click OK.

IMPORTANT   A warning about viruses

Attachments posted to newsgroups are renowned for carrying viruses. Newsgroup posters are relatively anonymous, so you rarely have any way of verifying the identity of the person who uploaded the attachment. Before opening an attachment that you've downloaded from a newsgroup, be sure to subject it to vigorous testing for viruses. Some posters digitally sign their attachments and their posts. In these cases, you can verify the identity of the poster, although this does not guarantee that the attachment is safe for your computer.

Views and Newsgroups   By using the different options located in the View menu under current view, you can limit the number of posts that are displayed on screen. Used in conjunction with newsgroup rules, they can make the time you spend reading newsgroups more enjoyable. The default newsgroup views are:

- Show All Messages
- Hide Read Messages
- Show Downloaded Messages
- Hide Read Or Ignored Messages
- Hide Answered Messages
- Show Only Useful Conversations

Defining a view or customizing a view is similar to configuring a rule. The difference between them is that a rule is always applied after you create it, and a view is enforced only when you select it. You can think of a view as a temporary way to speed up your reading of newsgroups and a rule as a permanent way. Views also apply to all newsgroups, whereas rules apply only to the newsgroups that they are configured for. To define a view that displays only messages that have been flagged and that can be applied to all newsgroups you read using Windows Mail, perform the following steps:

1. In Windows Mail, click a newsgroup.
2. Hold down the Ctrl key, and click two messages in the newsgroup.
3. On the Message menu, click Flag Message.
4. Click Yes to add the Flagged Message column.

5. Click the View menu, click Current View, and then click Define Views.

6. In the Define Views dialog box, shown in Figure 9-8, click New.

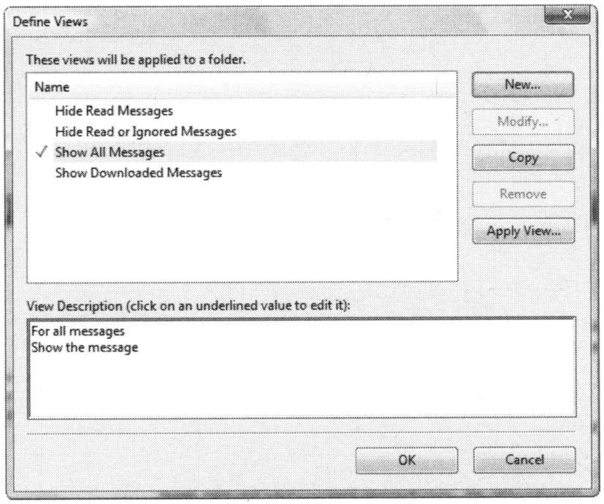

Figure 9-8   The Define Views dialog box

7. In the New View dialog box, scroll through the list of view conditions, and then select the Where The Message Is Flagged check box.

8. In the View Description box, click the words Show/Hide, which are in blue and underlined. In the Show/Hide Messages dialog box, verify that Show Messages is selected. Click OK.

9. In the Name Of The View text box, type **Show Only Flagged,** and click OK.

10. In the Define Views dialog box, verify that the Show Only Flagged view is selected, and click Apply View.

11. In the Apply View dialog box, verify that The Currently Selected Folder is selected, and click OK.

12. Click OK to close the Define Views dialog box.

13. Only the two messages that you flagged earlier are displayed. This view is retained for this newsgroup even if you restart Windows Mail unless you select another view.

Newsgroup Rules   In the same way that it is possible to create rules to sort incoming e-mail on the basis of its content, it is possible to create rules to sort newsgroup posts on the basis of their content. You configure these rules in an almost identical way to the way that you configure message rules for e-mail. The possible conditions are:

- Message is in a specified newsgroup.
- From line contains people. Right-clicking a message and selecting Create Rule From Message on the message menu automatically populates this rule with the message sender's e-mail address.
- Subject line contains specific words.

- Message is from the specific account.
- Message was sent more than X days ago.
- Where the number of lines in the message is more than X lines.
- All messages.

One or all of these conditions can be set, although it is redundant to set other conditions if you select the All Messages check box. After you set the conditions, it is possible to configure them specifically in the Rule Description box, as shown in Figure 9-9. This is done by clicking on each blue underlined item and using a dialog box to set the options.

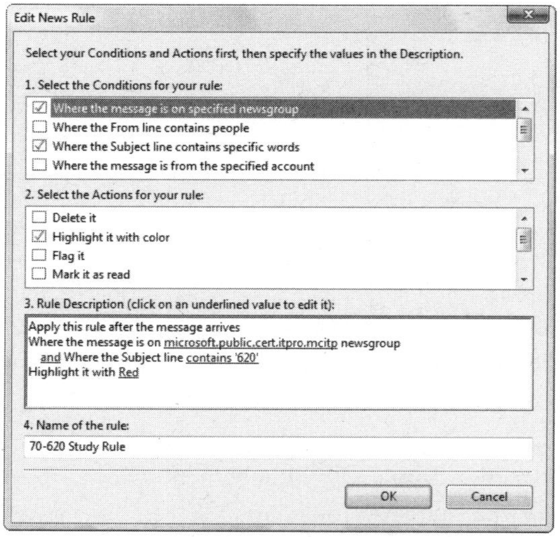

Figure 9-9   A newsgroup rule that highlights messages with specific words in the subject line

Seven possible actions can be taken when the conditions of a rule are met. You can configure the rule to:

- Delete the message.
- Highlight the message in a chosen color.
- Flag the message.
- Mark the message as read.
- Mark the message as watched or ignored.
- Mark the message for download.
- Stop processing rules.

You can use rules in conjunction with views or not at all. When used in conjunction with views, you see only the content you are interested in. If you have only a limited time to read each newsgroup, this can make your experience more fulfilling. Filtering is covered in more detail in Practice 4.

Rating Posts   Not all news servers support the rating of posts. To rate posts, you must be signed into the community with a Microsoft Passport account. To sign in, right-click a post that you want to rate, click Rate, and then click Please Sign In To Microsoft Communities. Enter your Microsoft Passport e-mail address and password in the dialog box shown in Figure 9-10, and then click Sign In. After you have signed in with your Microsoft Passport account, you can right-click any post on a supported news server and assign a rating. You can assign a post a rating of Useful or Not Useful. It is possible to define rules and views that will highlight, flag, or display only posts marked Useful. You can enable or disable the message rating feature in the General tab of the Windows Mail Options dialog box.

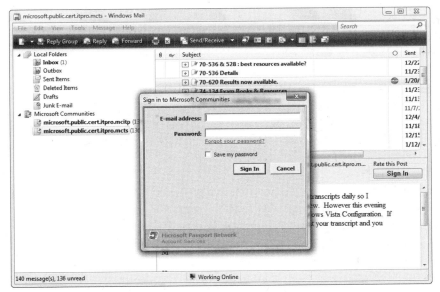

Figure 9-10 Signing in with a Microsoft Passport account

Posting and Replying   Posting a message to a newsgroup is as straightforward as sending an e-mail. Open the newsgroup that you want to post to and click the New Message icon. This brings up the New Message dialog box, shown in Figure 9-11. If you have multiple news servers configured, the message defaults to the news server to which the group you are reading belongs. You should post to this news server because there is no guarantee that other news servers that you have configured carry the newsgroup that you want to post to. In the *Newsgroups* field, verify that the group that you want to post to is selected. It is possible to post a single message to multiple newsgroups by separating them with a semicolon, although this is usually discouraged because it can lead to unnecessary duplication of answers. It is also possible to use the *Cc:* field to send a copy of the message through e-mail. The Format menu allows you to choose between Rich Text (HTML) and Plain Text. Plain Text is traditionally used on Usenet because there is a significant number of people who always use text-based newsreaders that do not display HTML messages.

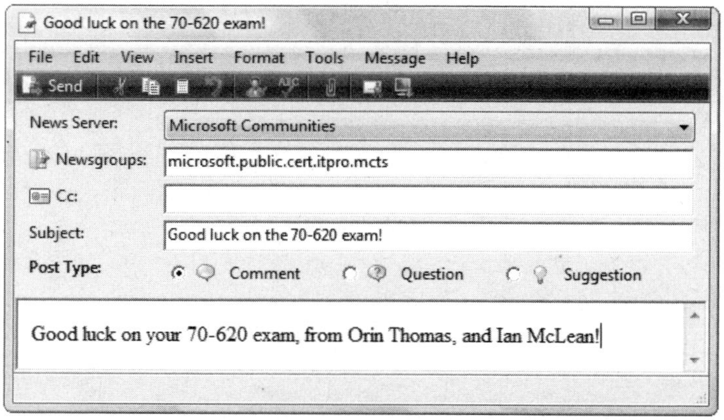

Figure 9-11   Posting a new message to the Microsoft.public.cert.itpro.mcts newsgroup

---

IMPORTANT   **Selecting a post type**

When posting to a Microsoft Communities newsgroup, you also have the option of selecting a post type. Post types can be Comments, Questions, or Suggestions. Although newsgroups in Microsoft Communities are replicated to other news servers across the Internet, not all of these news servers support these options.

Two options are available when responding to a post. You can click Reply To Group or Reply. Reply To Group sends your post back to the newsgroup as a follow-up to the post you are responding to. Reply allows you to reply directly through e-mail to the post originator. In general, you should reply to the group if you believe that your response will be of interest to other people besides the author of the post and reply through e-mail if you do not believe your response will be of interest, or you want to keep your response private. One thing to consider when responding privately is that many posters to newsgroups obfuscate their e-mail address. They do this because newsgroups are harvested by senders of unsolicited commercial e-mail, and if you post to a newsgroup with your real e-mail address, you can expect your inbox to be full of "offers that you can't refuse."

In some situations, you might want to retract a post that you have made to a newsgroup. It is possible to do this through the process of canceling messages. Canceling messages cannot be used to erase the memories of anyone who has read your post in between your sending it and canceling it, but it can reduce the number of people who do see the post. What canceling does not do is stop people who have seen the post from replying and quoting your original post's entire text in their response. Some news servers are also configured not to honor post-cancellation requests. An old Usenet rule is to never click Post unless you are absolutely sure that you want to send it. To cancel a post, select it, and click Cancel Message from the Message menu. You can cancel only one of your own messages.

Troubleshooting Windows Mail

Problems with Windows Mail are often caused by issues external to the application. For example, if you are unable to download messages, it might be because the computer has no network connectivity. Attempt to isolate the problem to Windows Mail. Also attempt to ascertain what might have changed to have caused the problem. When troubleshooting problems with Windows Mail, consider the following points:

- Ensure that you know whether the mail server supports POP3 or IMAP. If you are able to receive messages but not send them, check that you have configured the correct SMTP server address.
- If you are unsure whether Windows Mail is functioning correctly, send a test e-mail to yourself from within Windows Mail.
- Windows Mail displays an informative error message if the incoming or outgoing mail servers are not available. Sometimes a messaging problem is not caused by Windows Mail but by a problem on the mail server.
- If you have configured Windows Mail to leave messages on the server, keep an eye on your mailbox quota. If your mailbox becomes full, messages sent to you begin to bounce back to the people who sent them.
- When creating a view, ensure that you choose the correct view or hide option.
- If someone has sent you an e-mail and you cannot find it, check the junk folder and place the sender on your Safe Senders list.
- If a rule is not functioning as it should, verify that the message is not being intercepted by another rule with a higher priority.

Practice: Customizing Windows Mail

In these practices, you will perform several exercises that will familiarize you with features of Windows Mail. In the first practice, you will explore the options of Windows Mail. The second practice involves configuring junk e-mail settings. The third practice covers setting up a secondary news server account, and the final practice covers developing a newsgroup rule that can be used to filter content.

▶ **Practice 1: Exploring and Configuring Windows Mail Options**

In this practice, you will examine the Windows Mail options. Rather than exhaustively discussing each tab of the dialog box in the main text, this more practical example will take you through the options with the intent to accomplish the following result:

- Configure Windows Mail to check for new messages every five minutes.
- Configure Windows Mail to automatically expand grouped messages.
- Configure Windows Mail to automatically request a read receipt for all sent messages.
- Ensure that people replied to are not automatically added to the contact list.

- Configure Plain Text as the mail sending format.
- Create and add a signature to all outgoing messages except replies and forwards.

To complete this practice, perform the following steps:

1. Open Windows Mail.
2. Click the Tools menu, and then select Options.
3. In the General tab, change the Check For New Messages Every value to 5 minutes. This setting is suitable for people who receive a lot of e-mail during the day and want to know about it promptly.
4. In the Read tab, select the Automatically Expand Grouped Messages check box. This allows you to see all responses in a conversation rather than have them hidden.
5. In the Receipts tab, select the Request A Read Receipt For All Sent Messages check box. A read receipt is a request to the recipient of your message to acknowledge that they have received and read it.
6. In the Send tab, clear the Automatically Put People I Reply To In My Contacts List check box. Also change the Mail Sending Format option from HTML to Plain Text.
7. In the Signatures tab, click New.
8. In the Edit Signature text box, type **This is an e-mail signature**.
9. Select the Add Signatures To All Outgoing Messages check box, as shown in Figure 9-12.

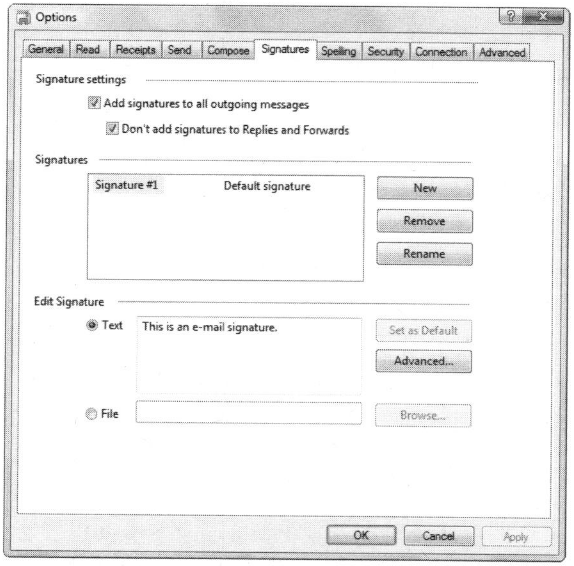

Figure 9-12   Adding signatures to all outgoing messages

▶ **Practice 2: Configuring Windows Mail Junk E-mail Options**

In this practice, you will configure the Windows Mail Junk E-Mail options so that most junk e-mail is caught and placed in the junk e-mail folder, that phishing e-mail is moved to the junk e-mail folder, and that any e-mail in Cyrillic, Greek, or Vietnamese is automatically blocked. These encodings were selected randomly, and the selection is not intended to imply anything about the frequency of junk e-mail sent using these character encodings.

1. Open Windows Mail. Click the Tools menu, and then click Junk E-Mail Options.

2. IIn the Options tab, change the junk e-mail protection level from Low to High. This improves junk e-mail protection but also leads to more false positives.

3. In the Phishing tab, ensure that both the Protect My Inbox From Messages With Potential Phishing Links and Move Phishing E-Mail To The Junk E-Mail Folder check boxes are selected.

4. In the International tab, click Blocked Encoding List. Scroll through the list of available encodings, and select the Cyrillic, Greek, and Vietnamese options. Click OK twice to close the dialog box.

▶ **Practice 3: Connecting to a News Server and Subscribing to Newsgroups**

In this practice, you will configure Windows Mail to connect to Microsoft's news server. This practice requires your Windows Vista computer to be connected to the Internet. To complete this practice, perform the following steps:

1. Open Windows Mail, click Microsoft Communities.

2. In the Subscribe To Newsgroups dialog box, shown in Figure 9-13, click Show Available Newsgroups And Turn On Communities.

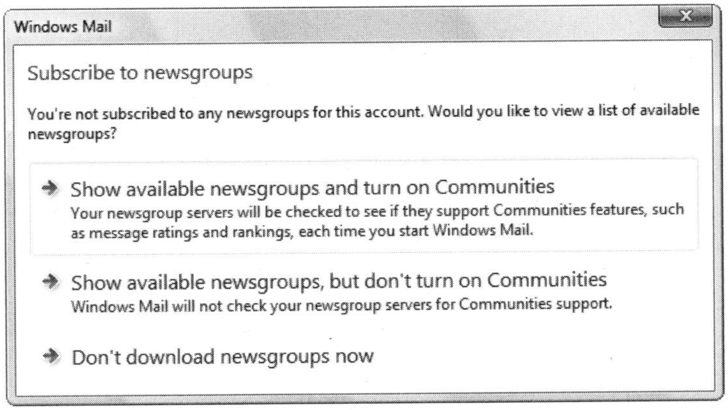

Figure 9-13 Turning on the Communities feature, which allows the rating and ranking of newsgroup posts

3. In the Newsgroup Subscriptions dialog box, enter the term **itpro**. Subscribe to the following newsgroups by selecting them and clicking Subscribe:
    - ❑ microsoft.public.cert.itpro.mcitp
    - ❑ microsoft.public.cert.itpro.mcts

4. Click OK to close the Newsgroup Subscriptions dialog box.

▶ **Practice 4: Viewing Newsgroups and Filtering Posts**

In this practice, you will open a Microsoft newsgroup that is relevant to the 70-620 exam. You will then create a News Rule that flags any posts that include the exam code 70-620 in their subject line that are posted to the microsoft.public.cert.itpro.mcts newsgroup. This will assist you in quickly locating any posts that are relevant to your study toward this exam in this newsgroup. To complete this practice, perform the following tasks:

1. Open the newsgroup microsoft.public.cert.itpro.mcts by double-clicking it under Microsoft Communities in Windows Mail.

2. Click the Tools menu, select Message Rules, and then select News. This opens the New News Rule dialog box, as shown in Figure 9-14.

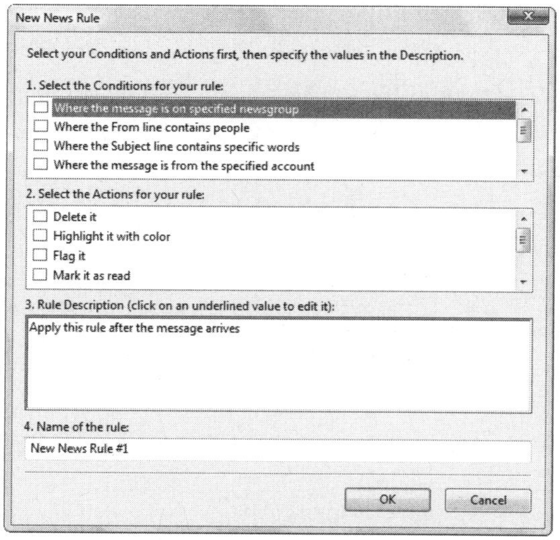

Figure 9-14   Using news rules to automatically highlight posts of interest to you

3. In the Select The Conditions For Your Rule box, select the check boxes for the following items:
    - ❑ Where The Message Is On Specified Newsgroup
    - ❑ Where The Subject Line Contains Specific Words

4. In the Select The Actions For Your Rule box, select the Highlight It With Color check box.

5. In the Rule Description box, click the Specified link. This brings up the Select Newsgroup dialog box. Expand Microsoft Communities, click microsoft.public .cert.itpro.mcts, and click OK.

6. In the Rule Description box, click the Contains Specific Words link. This brings up the Type Specific Words dialog box. Enter **70-620**, and click Add. Click OK to close the dialog box.

7. In the Rule Description box, click the Color link. Select the color Red, and click OK.

8. In the Name Of The Rule box, enter **70-620 Study Rule**, and click OK.

9. In the Message Rules dialog box, ensure that the 70-620 Study Rule check box is selected, and click Apply Now.

10. In the Apply News Rules Now dialog box, click Select All, and then click Apply Now.

11. Click OK when you are informed that your rule has been applied to the newsgroup.

12. Click Close and then OK to close the Message Rules dialog box.

13. Reexamine the newsgroup. You will notice now that all posts with 70-620 in their subject lines are now colored red.

Lesson Summary

■ Before running Windows Mail for the first time, you should know some details about the e-mail account that you are setting up. These details include whether the incoming mail server uses the POP3 or IMAP4 protocol, what the FQDNs of the incoming and outgoing mail servers are, and whether the outgoing mail server requires authentication.

■ When not in offline mode, Windows Mail checks for new messages every 30 minutes.

■ You can configure Windows Mail to check multiple e-mail accounts for new messages.

■ You use views to determine the properties of messages in a folder that are displayed or hidden. The default views allow for viewing all mail, viewing only unread mail, and viewing only unread mail and mail that is not configured to be ignored. It is possible to create custom views to hide or display only mail that meets certain user-configured conditions.

■ Rules process incoming messages and perform actions on them. They are triggered by user-configured conditions. Configuring rule priority determines the order in which rules apply to incoming messages. You most often use rules to sort mail into preconfigured folders based on subject or sender information.

■ Windows Mail has several levels of junk e-mail protection. You should take care when implementing the stricter levels of protection because it leads to a higher false-positive rate. You can protect your regular correspondents from the junk e-mail filter by adding them to the Safe Senders list.

■ It is possible to block incoming messages on the basis of country of origin or the character set used.

- News servers use the NNTP protocol. Some news servers require a client to authenticate before access is granted. Newsgroups are collections of messages that are replicated around the world to other news servers. Not every news server in the world carries every newsgroup that exists.

- The Microsoft Communities news server allows you to rate posts. You are able to rate posts only if you have authenticated with a valid Microsoft Passport account.

- Subscribing to newsgroups helps you find your favorite groups quickly.

- Using a combination of views and newsgroup rules, it is possible to reduce the number of threads and messages displayed in a high traffic newsgroup to a manageable level.

Lesson Review

You can use the following questions to test your knowledge of the information in Lesson 1, "Configuring Windows Mail." The questions are also available on the companion CD if you prefer to review them in electronic form.

NOTE Answers

Answers to these questions and explanations of why each answer choice is correct or incorrect are located in the "Answers" section at the end of the book.

---

1. One of your friends has had his e-mail address sold to a group of spammers working out of Vietnam. All of the e-mail sent by these spammers is in Vietnamese. Your friend cannot read Vietnamese and has to spend time each day manually removing e-mails that use this character encoding from his inbox. What steps can you take to ensure that all e-mail that is in Vietnamese is automatically blocked?

    A. Add the Vietnamese top-level domain to the blocked Top-Level domain list.

    B. Set the junk e-mail protection level to Safe List Only.

    C. Set the junk e-mail protection level to High.

    D. Block the Vietnamese character encoding.

2. How can you ensure that all e-mail from your lawyer is highlighted in pink?

    A. Create a view based on your lawyer's e-mail address.

    B. Create a rule based on your lawyer's e-mail address.

    C. Add your lawyer to the Safe Senders list.

    D. Add your lawyer to the Blocked Senders list.

3. Approximately half the time you receive an e-mail from Kim Ackers in your organization's sales department, Windows Mail automatically moves it to the junk e-mail folder. Which of the following steps could you take to ensure that none of Kim's e-mails are moved to your junk e-mail folder? (Choose all that apply.)

   A. Add Kim Ackers to your list of contacts.

   B. Add Kim Ackers to your Safe Senders list.

   C. Add Kim Ackers to your Blocked Senders list.

   D. Create a view based on Kim Ackers's e-mail address.

4. Tony uses Windows Mail to access e-mail from three separate e-mail accounts. Tony wants to be able to differentiate e-mail in his inbox on the basis of the account that the messages were received through. What method could you use to accomplish this?

   A. Create a view for each e-mail account.

   B. Create a rule for each separate e-mail account that copies messages from that account into a separate folder.

   C. Create a rule for the first e-mail account that highlights all messages in pink.

   D. Create a rule for the first e-mail account that flags all messages.

5. Messages from a particular poster in your favorite role-playing game newsgroup put your teeth on edge. You never want to see any of his messages again but still want to be able to view on the basis of flagged or watched conversations. Which of the following strategies should you use?

   A. Create a rule that deletes this poster's messages.

   B. Create a rule that marks this poster's messages as read.

   C. Create a view that deletes this poster's messages.

   D. Create a view that marks this poster's messages as read.

Lesson 2: Configuring Windows Contacts and Windows Calendar

Windows Calendar is a new application that allows you use a calendar to keep appointments, tasks, and reminders and to then share your calendar with others. It is also possible to use Windows Calendar to view your colleagues' appointments, tasks, and reminders by subscribing to their shared calendars. Windows Contacts is a replacement for the Windows Address Book application. Contacts can be accessed by any program that needs address information, whether it is a street address, an e-mail address, or a telephone number.

After this lesson, you will be able to:
- Configure and manage Windows Contacts.
- Configure Windows Calendar.
- Troubleshoot shared calendar issues.

Estimated lesson time: 20 minutes

Windows Contacts

Windows Contacts allow you to store information about people with whom you regularly communicate. Windows Contacts are particularly useful when you are synching information with your Windows Mobile device. All of the contact information is replicated to the device, meaning that a person's phone number that you got from an e-mail is automatically copied to your Windows cell phone.

Earlier versions of Windows stored contact information in an address book. The address book used a single file to store all contact information. This differs significantly from Windows Vista's contacts, which store each contact in a separate file in a special directory. Each Windows Vista user has his or her own contacts directory, so a contact added for Kim will not also exist for Tony when he logs on to the same computer. One significant advantage of Windows Contacts is that you can open the application and then send an e-mail or, if a modem is connected to the phone line, use your computer to dial the contact's phone number—although you need to lift the handset of your telephone to actually talk!

When creating a new e-mail in Windows Mail, if you click the envelope icon next to To: or Cc:, the Select Recipients dialog box will be populated with the contents of Windows Contacts, as shown in Figure 9-15.

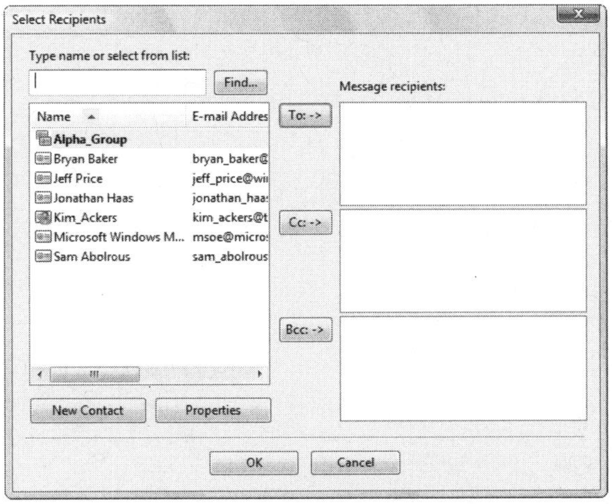

Figure 9-15   The Select Recipients dialog box in Windows Mail

---

NOTE **Windows Mobile**

Any contacts that are created on your Windows Mobile device are added to the list of contacts on your Windows Vista computer when you perform a synchronization. Windows Mobile devices are covered in greater detail in Chapter 13, "Configuring Mobile Devices."

Creating New Contacts Using E-mails Stored in Windows Mail   As discussed in Lesson 1, "Configuring Windows Mail," the default option in Windows Mail is for the details of everyone to whom you send a reply to be to automatically added to Windows Contacts. Although this can be useful in certain situations, if you receive a lot of one-off e-mail from people, such as responses to customer queries, this would cause Windows Contacts to become full of entries that you would never use. An alternative is to right-click an e-mail sent from someone whose contact details you want to retain and select the Add Sender To Contacts option.

Creating a New Contact Manually   To create a contact manually, all you need to do is click the New Contact button and enter one piece of name information. The Windows Contacts application needs only one piece of name information for you to be able to create a contact record. Creating a contact with just a phone number or an e-mail address does not work unless you also enter a first name, middle name, last name, or nickname. You might be on the phone with someone and not have time to enter everything relevant except a first name or a nickname. When you do this, a contact is created with that minimal information, and you will be able to come back later and add to it as necessary. This is one of the most important things about using Windows Contacts. You add information to Windows Contacts as it becomes necessary. A salesperson is going to enter very detailed information because the more the salesperson knows about the client, the better the chance of making a sale. Most users of Windows

Contacts will use a name and an e-mail address. If they synchronize with a mobile device, they are likely to include other information, such as a phone number.

The first tab that appears when you open a new contact is the Name And E-Mail tab, shown in Figure 9-16. In this tab, it is possible to enter name and title information, as well as e-mail address details. If you enter multiple e-mail addresses, you can select a preferred e-mail address by selecting one and clicking Set Preferred. It is also possible to associate a picture with a contact on this tab. If you have a picture of the person, you can associate it with the contact. This feature is especially useful for people who are good with faces but not so good at remembering names! If you have a Windows Mobile phone, you might take a picture of someone you meet at a conference using the phone's camera and add it to that person's contact information using the phone's Contacts utility. When you synchronize with Windows Vista, this picture appears as part of that person's contact information.

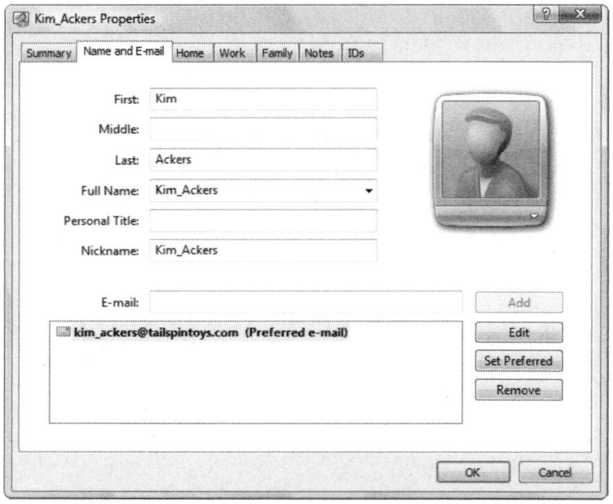

Figure 9-16   To create a contact, you must supply at least one piece of name information

The other tabs in a contact's properties allow for the input of the following information:

- **Home**   Street address, city, state/province, postal code, country/region, phone, fax, cell, and website address.
- **Work**   Street address, city, state/province, postal code, country/region, company, job title, department, office, phone, fax, pager, and website address.
- **Family**   Gender, birthday, anniversary, spouse/partner, and children.
- **Notes**   An area to enter miscellaneous notes about a contact.
- **IDs**   This tab allows you to associate digital certificates with particular e-mail accounts. This can be helpful in verifying that an e-mail was actually sent by a person from a specific e-mail address and is not a fake. To become a trusted contact for Windows Meeting Space, the contact must have a certificate associated with it.

To modify a contact, simply open the relevant item in Windows Contacts and make the changes you want to make. When you click OK, the updates made to the Contact item are saved.

Importing and Exporting Contacts

The Import and Export buttons are available on the Windows Contacts toolbar. Windows Contacts supports four formats for importing address data, as shown in Figure 9-17. CSV files are comma-delimited files that can be opened in a text editor or Microsoft Excel. If you are attempting to import contacts from Outlook Express, you would choose the Windows Address Book File format. In corporate environments, Lightweight Directory Access Protocol (LDAP) servers are often used to store contact information. The LDAP Data Interchange Format (LDIF) import format is used to support LDAP. vCards are slightly different from the other formats in that they usually contain only the contact information of a single person. vCard files are similar to digital business cards, and some people have them automatically attached to their outgoing e-mail.

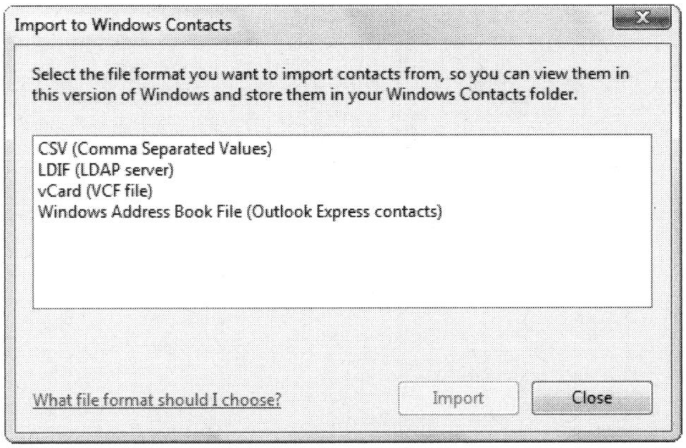

Figure 9-17   You can import data into Windows Contacts from four formats

You can export data from Windows Contacts using only two formats, CSV and vCards. When you perform an export, all your contacts are exported. You should export using the CSV format when you want the person with whom you are sharing your contacts to have access to all of your contacts. You should export using the vCard format when you want to be more selective about which contacts you want to share. Exporting using vCard format will provide you with a folder full of vCards, one for each contact. You then copy the ones you want to share and give them to the person you want to share them with. It is not possible to export a group contact to CSV or vCard format.

Using Contact Groups

Contact groups are collections of contacts that you can use to send a single e-mail to multiple people. For example, a contact group contains 15 e-mail addresses. If you send an e-mail to this contact group, Windows Mail sends it to those 15 e-mail addresses. The advantage of this to the user is that the user does not have to manually enter all of those e-mail addresses. When an e-mail is sent to a contact group, all of the e-mail addresses in that group will be visible to those who receive the message. If you do not want all of the e-mail addresses in the contact group to be visible to people who are members of the contact group, use the Bcc option when sending mail. To send an e-mail directly to all members of a contact group using your default mailing program from Windows Contacts, right-click the contact group, click Action, and then click Send E-Mail.

To create a new contact group, click the New Contact Group button in Windows Contacts. This opens the Contact Group Properties dialog box, shown in Figure 9-18. Clicking Add To Contact Group allows you to select an existing contact and add that contact to the group. Clicking Create New Contact allows you to create a new contact in the same way outlined above and then add that contact automatically to the Contact Group. You can also add people's e-mail addresses to a contact group without actually adding them as individual contacts. To do this, enter the person's e-mail address in the E-Mail text box, and click Create For Group Only. The Contact Group Details tab allows you to enter address, website, and notes information about the contact group.

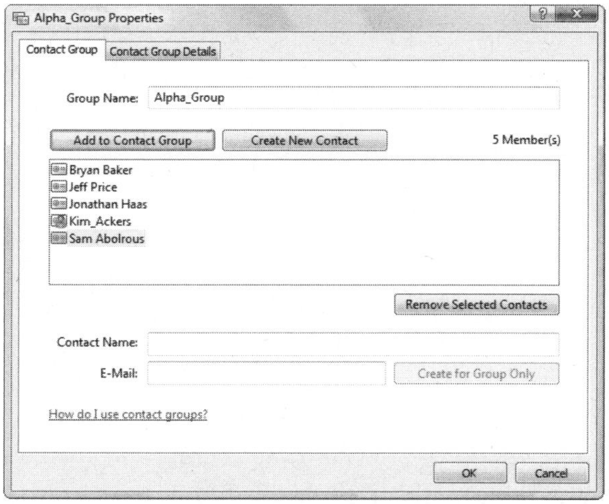

Figure 9-18   Using a contact group to send e-mails to many people using one alias

Quick Check

1. What is the minimum amount of information that you need to add to create a contact?
2. How can you add a person's e-mail address to a contact group without adding that person as a contact?

Quick Check Answers

1. You need to enter at least one piece of name information to create a contact.
2. Use the Create For Group Only button in the Contact Group Properties dialog box.

Windows Calendar

Windows Calendar is another collaboration tool new to Windows Vista. As with other calendaring software, it allows you to make appointments and reminders and to configure tasks. It works as a collaboration tool because for the first time an application that is included with the operating system allows you to publish and subscribe to shared calendars without any centralized infrastructure like a Microsoft Exchange server. To create a new appointment, click the New Appointment button in the tool bar. This adds a Details pane, shown in Figure 9-19, to the right side of the Windows Calendar screen. When you have finished providing appointment information, clicking elsewhere on the calendar closes the Details pane.

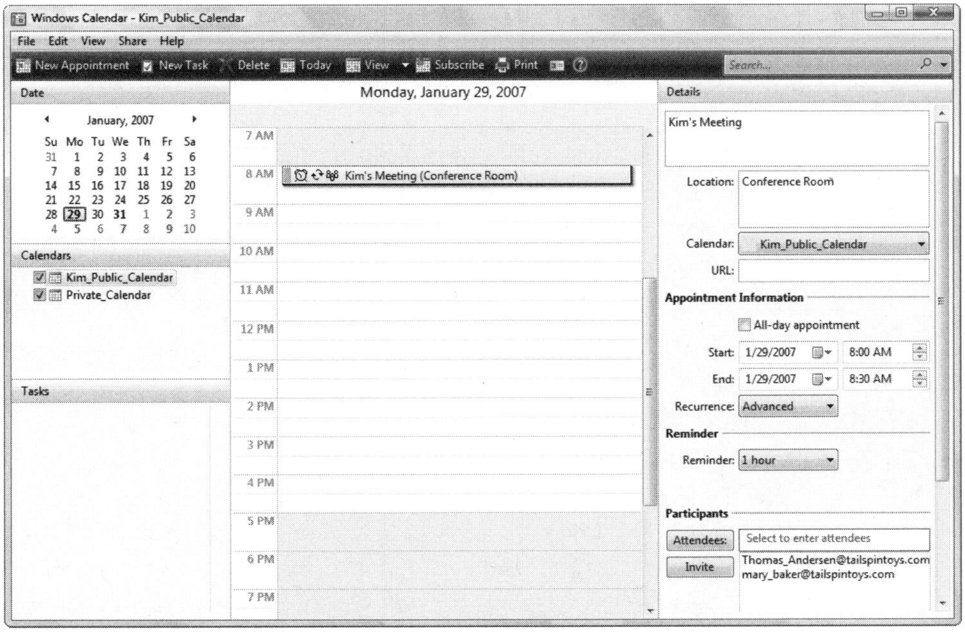

Figure 9-19   The Windows Calendar screen, displaying the details of an appointment

The important items to note when creating a new appointment are shown above in the exhibit. These items include:

- **Appointment Title**   In the figure it is Kim's Meeting. This is the title that will be used in other attendee's calendars if you invite them.
- **Location**   This tells people where the meeting is.
- **Calendar**   If you have multiple calendars, this drop-down menu allows you to select between them. If you examine the Calendars section on the left side of the figure, you will see that there is a public and a private calendar. Multiple calendars will be discussed later in the lesson in the section on publishing calendars.
- **URL**   Some meetings have an agenda. Placing the Uniform Resource Locator (URL) of the agenda in the meeting can ensure that participants know the meeting plan.
- **Appointment information**   Allows you to configure the date and time of the appointment. If other attendees of the meeting are in different time zones, an automatic adjustment is made for them when they import the meeting invitation into their own calendars.
- **Recurrence**   Allows you to specify how often, if at all, the meeting will recur. The default options are None, Every Day, Weekly, Monthly, Yearly, and Advanced. Selecting the Advanced option allows you to specify repetition on specific days of the week, the number of times to repeat the meeting, or an end date for the repeating of meeting. You would use this option if you wanted to have a meeting every Monday, Wednesday, and Friday between 8:00 A.M. and 8:30 A.M. for the next 10 weeks.
- **Reminder**   Has Windows Calendar displayed a dialog box on your screen reminding you of the appointment.
- **Participants**   Allows you to enter either contacts or e-mail addresses. Clicking the Invite button automatically generates an e-mail addressed to meeting participants with a calendar file that they can open. When they open the attachment, a compatible calendaring program appears displaying the details of the appointment and asking them whether they want to attend. You can also right-click an existing appointment and select Send, manually adding the addresses that you want to send it to using Windows Mail.
- **Notes area**   Not shown in the figure, this section allows you to add miscellaneous information t the appointment.

Sharing Calendars with Others

Publishing calendars allows others to view the information in your calendar. You can restrict the information that is viewed to appointments only or publish appointments and a combination of tasks, reminders, and notes. To allow people to see some, but not all, of your information, you might consider using multiple calendars. This allows you to publish the public calendar for subscribers to view while being able to add sensitive information to the private calendar. Multiple calendars are displayed together on the screen. It is possible to differentiate appointments on the basis of calendars because each calendar's items are displayed in their own color. For example, the items in Kim's public calendar might be displayed in blue, and the items in Kim's private calendar might be displayed in green. Subscribers to published calendars are not able to make changes to those calendars.

When you publish a calendar, you need to choose between publication on a website or on a file share. Although it is possible to create a website on a computer running Windows Vista, Internet Information Services (IIS) is not covered by the 70-620 exam. Using a shared folder with appropriately configured permissions is likely to be the way that this exam deals with publishing a shared calendar. Creating a shared folder was covered in Chapter 7, "Configuring Network Connectivity."

Published calendars cannot be password protected directly. Anyone who is able to access the shared calendar file is able to subscribe to its contents without having to authenticate. This has important privacy implications for calendars published to websites. Windows Calendar does not allow you to enter authentication credentials when accessing a shared calendar, so any calendar published to a website cannot require website authentication.

To publish a calendar, right-click the calendar in the Calendars list on the left side, and select Publish. This brings up the Publish Calendar dialog box shown in Figure 9-20. The calendar shown in the figure is published to a file share, and all changes that are made to the calendar will be published. The calendar will include any notes, reminders, and tasks that have been associated with it. Although persons subscribing to the calendar might find the notes interesting, they might find the reminders for tasks that do not apply to them annoying. Managers might find viewing subordinate's task lists informative. When you publish a calendar, you have the option of announcing it. An announcement is an e-mail sent out to selected people that informs them of the location on the network of the calendar file. Published calendars have a green arrow on their icon to remind you that they are public. To stop publishing a shared calendar, right-click it in the Calendars list, and select Stop Publishing. If a calendar is not configured to automatically update, you can right-click it and select Sync to update it.

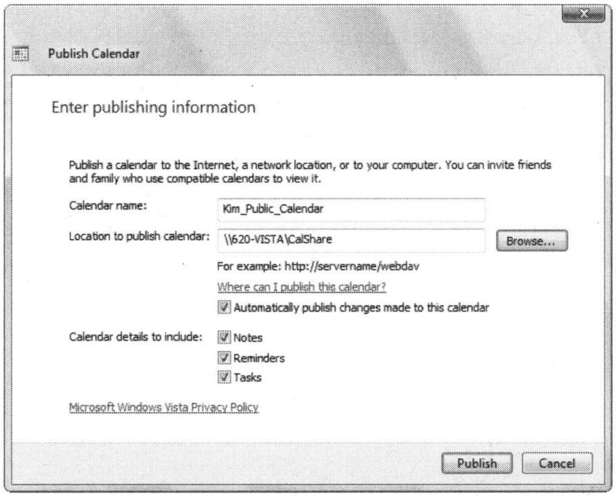

Figure 9-20 Publishing a calendar allows others to view it

Subscribing to Shared Calendars

To subscribe to a calendar, right-click in the Calendars area, and select Subscribe. To subscribe, you must know the calendar's location and name. Calendars can be located on network shares, which are discussed in Chapter 7, "Configuring Network Connectivity," or on websites. There is no capacity to browse, and you must have permissions to access the location that hosts the calendar file. After you have successfully entered the calendar location, you will need to configure the calendar subscription settings, as shown in Figure 9-21. Configuring the Update Interval determines how often the subscribed calendar is checked for updates. The available values are no update, 15 minutes, hourly, daily, and weekly. If reminders and tasks are published with the calendar, subscribers can determine whether they want to receive this information by selecting the appropriate options.

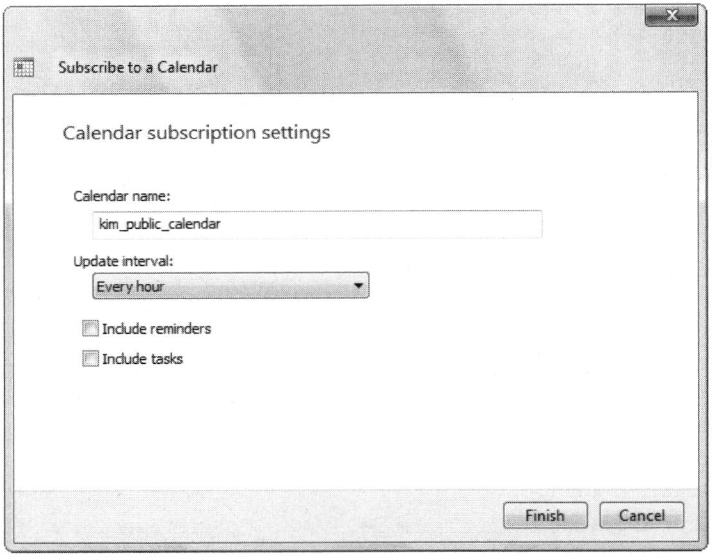

Figure 9-21   Using calendar subscriptions to view other people's appointments

Importing and Exporting Calendar Files

Importing and exporting calendar files differs from publishing or subscribing to a calendar in that the imported or exported file is static and cannot be updated. This method of calendar distribution can work well if publishing calendars is a problem because people are part of different organizations or behind firewalls that make calendar subscriptions problematic. For example, a university with students and staff spread across several campuses might make the academic calendar available for download to students and staff. When set, academic calendars remain static for the year, which makes subscriptions to them inappropriate.

It is not possible to selectively export or import calendar content. The entire calendar is written to a calendar file with the .ics extension. To export a calendar, select Export from the File menu, and then choose a location to save the file. When importing a calendar, you have a choice as to whether to merge the calendar data with an existing calendar or to create a new calendar with the imported data. The second option makes it easier to delete the imported data if you should decide that you do not want it. To delete a calendar, right-click it in the Calendars list, and select Delete. Only the data from that particular calendar are deleted, and all other calendar data are retained.

Real World

Orin Thomas

One area where calendar files are very useful to me is in scheduling conference calls. Working from Australia, almost everyone I have a conference call with is located in another time zone, often on the other side of the international date line. I very much appreciate when someone sends a calendar file along with an attachment because opening it instantly tells me what time it will be in Australia when that person wants to have the meeting as well as what time it will be where that person lives. Occasionally, someone on the East Coast of the United States will schedule a meeting for their early afternoon, not realizing that it will be around 5 A.M. where I live in Australia!

Troubleshooting Shared Calendars

The two things to look out for when troubleshooting shared calendars are access and updates. If security settings, such as file and share permissions or Windows Firewall configuration, are blocking access to a shared calendar, then subscribers are not going to be able to access it. A user who is publishing a calendar needs to have the necessary permissions to alter the calendar file. If the user has read only permissions to the shared calendar file, it will be impossible to process updates. If people appear not to be receiving updates to the calendar and there are no security or access issues to the shared calendar file, you should consider the following:

- Ensure that the person sharing the calendar has configured it so that changes are automatically published when they're made. If changes are not published, people do not receive updates.

- Ensure that the person sharing the calendar has not stopped publishing it. A person who has stopped publishing a calendar can still use it, and the originally shared file will still be available because these are not deleted when a user stops publishing a calendar.

- Ensure that the person subscribing to the calendar has set his or her update interval appropriately. Someone who has set the update interval to Every Week is not going to be able to see recent changes until the update occurs.

Practice: Windows Contacts and Windows Calendar

In these practices, you will perform several exercises that will familiarize you with using Windows Contacts and Windows Calendar.

▶ **Practice 1: Create Contacts and a Contact Group**

In this practice, you will create several contacts. Once these contacts have been created, you will add them to a contact group. Once the contact group is created, you will then add a group only contact.

1. Open Windows Contacts by clicking Start, All Programs, and then Windows Contacts.
2. Add the following contacts to Windows Contacts by clicking the New Contact button:
   - ❑ Thomas Andersen. thomas_andersen@tailspintoys.com
   - ❑ Jeff Price. jeff_price@wingtiptoys.com
   - ❑ Jonathan Haas. jonathan_haas@contoso.com
3. Click the New Contact Group button. Name the new contact group Beta_Team.
4. Click Add To Contact Group, and add the three contacts that you created in step 2.
5. In the Contact Name box, type **sam_abolrous@tailspintoys.com**, and then click Create For Group Only.

▶ **Practice 2: Export Contacts as vCards**

In this practice, you will export contacts as vCards. It is not possible to export individual contacts, but if you want to share some, but not all, of your contacts with another person, using the vCard export format allows you to be selective.

1. Open Windows Contacts.
2. Click Export.
3. Click vCards, and then click Export.
4. Click Desktop, and then click Make New Folder. Name the folder **vCard_Export**. Press Enter, and then click OK.
5. Click OK to close the message box stating that the export succeeded. Click Close to close the Export Windows Contacts dialog box.
6. Open the vCard_Export folder on the desktop to verify that the contacts that you created in Practice 1 have been exported.

▶ **Practice 3: Create and Publish a Calendar**

In this practice, you will create a new calendar, add some appointments, create a shared folder, and publish the calendar to the shared folder. To complete this practice, you need access to credentials that allow elevated privileges.

1. Click Start, click Computer, and then double-click the volume that Windows Vista is installed on.

2. Create a new folder called SharedCal.

3. Right-click the SharedCal folder, and click Properties. Click the Sharing tab.

4. Click Share. Click Share a second time.

5. Click Continue to close the User Account Control dialog box.

6. Make a note of the name of the shared folder. It will be similar to \\620-VISTA\SharedCal.

7. Click Done. Click Close to close the SharedCal Properties dialog box.

8. Click Start, All Programs, and then Windows Calendar.

9. Right-click in the Calendars area, and then click New Calendar. Enter the name **My_Public_Calendar**.

10. Click Today. Add three appointments at any time for your dentist, doctor, and lawyer. Ensure that they are for My_Public_Calendar and not the default calendar, which will have the user name with which you logged on to Windows Vista.

11. Right-click My_Public_Calendar, and then click Publish.

12. In the Location To Publish Calendar text box, enter the location you determined in step 6.

13. Select the Automatically Publish Changes Made To This Calendar check box, and then click Publish. Click Finish.

14. Verify that the Details pane of the Calendar shows that it is shared.

Lesson Summary

- Windows Contacts replaces the address books that were included in earlier versions of Windows. You can use Windows Contacts to launch Windows Mail or, if the Windows Vista computer has a modem, to dial a contact's phone number.

- To create a contact manually, you need only to provide a name. You can create a contact directly from Windows Mail by right-clicking on a message and selecting the Add Sender To Contacts option. Windows Mail adds a contact automatically for all correspondents you reply to.

- Contacts can be imported from vCard, CSV, LDAP, and from Outlook Express address books. Contacts can be exported using CSV and vCard. A CSV file exports all contacts to the same file. vCard exports all contacts to a folder, and each contact is exported as a separate file.

- Contact groups are collections of contacts that function as e-mail address aliases. It is possible to add e-mail addresses to contact groups without adding the addresses as contacts. You cannot export contact groups.

- A trusted contact is a contact that has a trusted digital certificate installed.

- Multiple calendars can be used and have their events, tasks, reminders, and notes displayed in a single instance of Windows Calendar.

■ You can publish calendars to shared folders or to websites. When a calendar is published, the publisher determines whether the calendar will be automatically updated when alterations are made. The publisher can also determine whether tasks, reminders, and notes are also shared. It is not possible to password protect a published calendar.

■ It is possible to subscribe to a shared calendar that is published on an accessible shared folder or website. When configuring a subscription, you specify how often the subscription will check for updates and whether the subscription will include downloading notes, reminders, and tasks.

■ An imported calendar is different from a subscription because it does not update. When you import a calendar, you can merge it with an existing calendar or create a new calendar.

Lesson Review

You can use the following questions to test your knowledge of the information in Lesson 2, "Configuring Windows Contacts and Windows Calendar." The questions are also available on the companion CD if you prefer to review them in electronic form.

NOTE Answers

Answers to these questions and explanations of why each answer choice is correct or incorrect are located in the "Answers" section at the end of the book.

---

1. Kim's Windows Contacts is full of several hundred entries, but she has never manually added a contact. What steps can you take to ensure that only explicitly added people are added to Windows Contacts? (Choose all that apply.)

    A. Edit Windows Mail's options.

    B. Manually delete the contacts.

    C. Create a rule to delete the contacts.

    D. Create a view that displays only flagged contacts.

2. Kim Ackers would like the contact information of two of your friends. You are going to e-mail this information to her. There are 200 separate entries in your Windows Vista computer's Contacts folder, some of which you do not want to share with Kim. Which format would you use to provide her with this information? (Choose all that apply.)

    A. vCard

    B. CSV

    C. Windows Address Book File

    D. LDIF

3. On Monday, Kim published her calendar to a network share. Tony and Thomas are subscribed to this calendar. On Tuesday, Kim added two appointments for Friday. Today is Wednesday. Tony is unable to locate these two appointments, but Thomas can. How can this situation be resolved?

    A. Configure Kim's calendar to automatically publish changes.

    B. Configure Tony's calendar to automatically publish changes.

    C. Reconfigure Kim's subscription settings.

    D. Reconfigure Tony's subscription settings.

4. On Monday, Kim published her calendar to a network share. Thomas and Tony are subscribed to this calendar. On Tuesday, Kim added two appointments for Friday. Both Thomas and Tony are unable to locate these two appointments. What steps need to be taken so that both Thomas and Tony are able to view Kim's updates?

    A. Configure Kim's calendar to automatically publish changes.

    B. Configure Tony's calendar to automatically publish changes.

    C. Reconfigure Kim's subscription settings.

    D. Configure Thomas's calendar to automatically publish changes.

5. What steps can Kim take to ensure that Tony and Thomas are able to subscribe to her published calendar but that Rob is unable to subscribe?

    A. Configure Rob as an untrusted contact.

    B. Share the calendar password only with Tony and Thomas.

    C. Configure Tony and Thomas as trusted contacts.

    D. Configure file and folder permissions in the location where the calendar is published.

Lesson 3: Configuring Windows Meeting Space

Windows Vista makes it easier for people to collaborate with one another by introducing Windows Meeting Space. Meeting Space allows for documents, applications, and desktops to be shared between a group of people without the need for a server in the middle. If everyone in the group has a wireless card, it is even possible to have Windows Meeting Space create an ad hoc network specifically for the meeting.

After this lesson, you will be able to:
- Configure Windows Meeting Space.
- Configure People Near Me.
- Create and manage meetings.
- Share files using Windows Meeting Space.

Estimated lesson time: 40 minutes

Windows Meeting Space Capabilities

Windows Meeting Space is a technology that allows desktop applications to be presented to groups of people running Windows Vista. It is important to note that Windows Meeting Space is not a complete meeting application. There is no way of broadcasting audio using Meeting Space, nor is there any way for all participants to chat with one another at the same time through text, although private messaging is allowed. This means that the bulk of the meeting's information exchange, which is almost always verbal, takes place over a conference call or across a meeting room table. What Meeting Space does is ensure that all meeting participants see the same thing on their computer screens at the same time. Consider the following situation. A group of eight engineers is gathered in a conference room, and each engineer has brought a laptop running Windows Vista. Most of the communication in the meeting is going to occur verbally. Windows Meeting Space will improve the meeting experience by allowing the engineers to share documentation quickly and by allowing each participant to make modifications to a shared schematic and display them to other participants as the meeting progresses.

When in a Windows Meeting Space meeting, users are able to:

- Share documents.
- Share desktops.
- Share applications, including applications with open documents.

Windows Meeting Space uses peer-to-peer technology rather than a centralized server. Although peer-to-peer programs have a bad reputation because they have historically been used for copyright infringement, they also form the backbone of productivity applications such as Windows Meeting Space and Microsoft Groove 2007. Using peer-to-peer rather than a client/server-based architecture means that you can create Meeting Space meetings in the absence of traditional network infrastructure.

As it is possible to create a meeting in an unsecured environment like the local café, Meeting Space ensures that data is secure. This is done through SSL encryption of network traffic. Even if someone in the coffee shop is capturing network traffic, that person will be unable to decipher the contents of that traffic because it is encrypted. Each meeting is also protected by a password, limiting the people who participate to the people who have explicitly been invited.

Configuring People Near Me

Before you can invite people to meetings, you and your meeting participants need to be connected to People Near Me. People Near Me is a Windows Vista technology that allows users on the same subnet to announce their availability. This announcement is made using the Web Services Discovery protocol. When making the announcement, People Near Me broadcasts the following identification information to the network:

- User configured nickname
- Computer's name
- Computer's IPv6 address
- Port number

When you first run People Near Me, you are prompted to allow elevation of privileges so that Windows Firewall can be configured to allow traffic to the Windows Peer-to-Peer Collaboration Foundation program. A user who is unable to access credentials that allow elevated privileges cannot use People Near Me until the firewall is appropriately configured to allow this traffic.

You activate People Near Me from the Control Panel in the Classic View. In the Settings Tab, shown in Figure 9-22, users can enter their People Near Me names. This defaults to the user's logon name, but it can be anything that the user chooses. In a meeting, a person's picture is always displayed even if the person has cleared the Make My Picture Available check box. The picture displayed is the same as the Windows Vista logon picture. Clicking Change Picture allows you to select a different picture. Changing this picture also changes the Windows Vista logon icon. The default setting allows invitations from Anyone and gives the user an audio prompt as well as a visual one when an invitation is received. It is possible to set up People Near Me so that invitations can be received only by Trusted Contacts. Trusted Contacts are entries within Contacts that have a digital certificate associated with them. Alternatively, it is possible to configure People Near Me so that all invitations sent to the user are blocked. If either of these settings is enabled, the user is not notified that an invitation has been automatically rejected. Blocking invitations does not block a user from joining Meeting Space meetings. It is still possible to view available meetings or to use an invitation file to connect to a meeting. The final option allows People Near Me to automatically start when the user logs on to Windows. This setting is configured on a per user basis, so just because one user on a Windows Vista computer has People Near Me configured to automatically start when he or she logs on does not mean that all users on the same Windows Vista computer have it similarly configured.

Figure 9-22   Using People Near Me settings to configure invitation settings and a screen name for Windows Meeting Space meetings

The Sign In tab, shown in Figure 9-23, allows you to sign in and out of People Near Me. The dialog box explains exactly what information becomes visible to people on the local network should you log on, which serves as an important reminder to users who sign on to People Near Me in public locations, such as airport lounges and coffee shops, that provide free wireless access to the Internet. Although people usually do not worry too much about who knows their name when they are in an environment like the office or home, people are less comfortable about broadcasting identity information when in a public place.

Figure 9-23   The sign-in settings for People Near Me, which remind users of the privacy implications of logon

Using Meeting Space

Because it requires exemptions to be configured in Windows Firewall, Meeting Space should first be run by a user who has access to elevated privileges. After Meeting Space has been successfully run for the first time, any user will be able to use the application.

When you run Meeting Space, you are given three options:

- Start A New Meeting.
- Join A Meeting Near Me. A list of available meetings is displayed beside this option, as shown in Figure 9-24. Clicking Update List shows any new meetings.
- Open An Invitation File.

Found: 2
⟲ Update list   Sort by: Name ▼

Start a new meeting

    Thomas Andersen 11:54 PM
    Started by Thomas Andersen
    1/26/2007 11:57 PM

Join a meeting near me

    Tony_Allen 11:57 PM
    Started by Tony_Allen
    1/27/2007 12:11 AM

Open an invitation file...

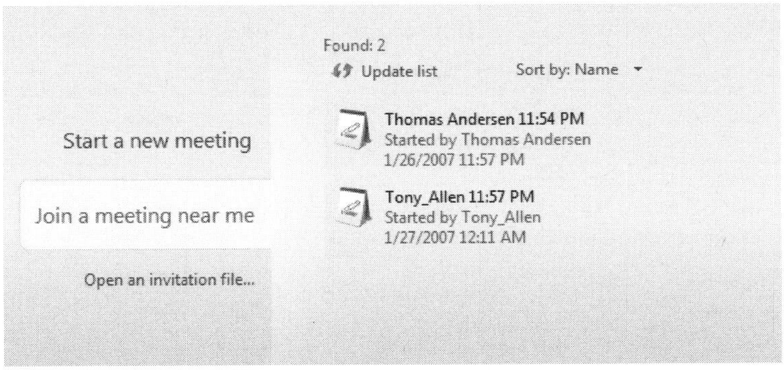

Figure 9-24   A list of available meetings is displayed when you start Windows Meeting Space

When you click Start A New Meeting, you are required to enter a meeting name and a password. The default meeting name is the People With Me name and the current time. You can change the meeting name to anything, but if you are setting up an Ad Hoc Wireless Meeting, as discussed later in this lesson, the name must contain fewer than 15 characters. The meeting password has the same security requirements as a user's logon password. On a stand-alone Windows Vista computer, this means a length of eight characters with mixed case, numbers, and symbols.

Meeting passwords need to be sent to participants prior to a meeting. Options include using the phone, Short Message Service (SMS), e-mail, or Instant Messenger, if participants have the appropriate software installed. Remember that you cannot use People Near Me as an instant messaging client to send this information even though the taskbar icon is similar to that of Windows Live Messenger.

Sending Invitations

After you have created the meeting, you can either wait for people to arrive or send them an invitation. Invitations are not required to join a meeting; only the meeting password is a necessity. There are three methods of sending invitations:

- Using People Near Me
- Sending an e-mail using the default e-mail application
- Generating an invitation file

Unless all of the participants are logged on to People Near Me, it is likely that you will need to e-mail them an invitation or forward them an invitation file through another means. The e-mail process creates an invitation file and invokes the default mail application in a process very similar to e-mailing a Remote Assistance invitation. Invitations cannot be personalized, so any user who has access to the invitation file and the meeting password can join the meeting.

To invite people who are currently logged onto People Near Me, perform the following steps:

1. In Windows Meeting Space, click Invite People.
2. In the Invite People dialog box, shown in Figure 9-25, select the check box for each person you want to invite to the meeting.

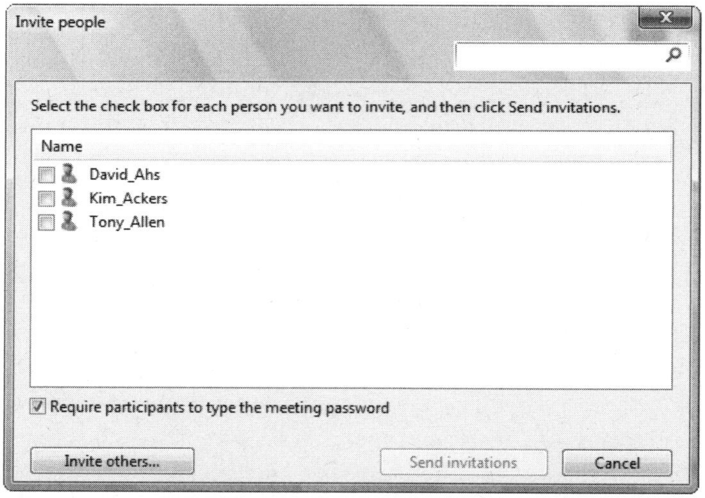

Figure 9-25 Inviting people signed into People Near Me to a Windows Meeting Space meeting

3. Click Send Invitations.

If you want to send invitations through e-mail or as invitation files, in step 3, click Invite Others, and then either click Send An Invitation In E-Mail or Create An Invitation File. The first option launches your default e-mail client; the second option asks you where you want to save the invitation file. Once invitations have been sent, the invited participants are dimmed in the Participants listing. A red X next to an invitee's name, shown in Figure 9-26, indicates that the user has declined the invitation.

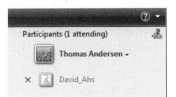

Figure 9-26   A red X is displayed if a participant rejects a meeting invitation

Conveners should be aware that any user who is connected to a meeting can send invitations to other people. For example, Kim Ackers convenes a meeting, inviting David Ahs and Thomas Andersen. After David has joined the meeting, he is able to invite Thomas Andersen, who Kim Ackers did not originally invite. Because Windows Meeting Space does not have any moderation tools, Kim will not be able to block Thomas from attending, nor will she be able to force him to leave the meeting.

When a meeting's convener disconnects from a meeting and there is still one participant attending, the meeting will continue. Meetings finish only after the final participant leaves. A convener who has disconnected from his or her own meeting can reconnect, assuming the meeting has continued, but is required to enter the meeting password to do so.

Quick Check

1. Thomas is visible in the list of available people when you attempt to send an invitation, but he is not notified that an invitation has been sent to him. What might explain this?
2. What happens to your logon picture if you change the picture associated with People Near Me?

Quick Check Answers

1. You either are not on Thomas's Trusted Users list, or Thomas has blocked all invitations. Because you can see him in the list of available people, no network or protocol problems are involved.
2. It also changes your Windows Vista logon picture.

Share an Application or Document

It is possible to share an individual application, a document, or the entire desktop with other users in the meeting. Although all users in a meeting can view an application, document, or desktop, only one person can interact with the shared object at a time. Applications are shared through streaming technology, meaning that the application executes only on the computer of the person sharing it. Similarly, if a document is shared, as opposed to being configured as a handout, the application that runs the document is opened with the document in focus and projected to other Meeting Space users. This means that someone can share a Microsoft Visio document so that other participants can see it even if only one person participating in the meeting has Microsoft Visio installed on his or her Windows Vista computer.

Only one meeting user can share an application at a time. Shared applications are displayed with a modified title bar, as shown in Figure 9-27, to remind the person sharing the application that everyone in the meeting can see it.

Figure 9-27   Shared applications use a green dot and display the words Currently Sharing on the title bar

It is possible to delegate control of a shared application to another meeting participant if you are the person who is currently in control of the application. It is also possible for another meeting participant to request control over a shared application. The controlling participant is notified when another user makes a request for control.

When control has been granted to another meeting participant, that participant is able to interact with that application as though it was on his or her desktop. To follow the earlier Microsoft Visio example, that means that the controlling user can modify the Visio diagram even if that user does not have Visio installed on his or her own Windows Vista computer.

The control is not complete, however. The person who is sharing the application is always able to interact with the application even when another person has control. For example, Kim shares Microsoft Notepad and then grants control to Thomas. Thomas starts typing. Kim is able to type in the Notepad window at the same time or close the application. Having two people provide input at the same time leads to a jumble of letters because although two people are typing there is only a single cursor! The person who is currently in control can pause the session. This might be necessary if some work needs to be completed, such as a quick fix in a presentation for an important client, that you do not want other participants seeing.

The person who is sharing the application can also take back control of the application from another user. To take back control of an application from another user to whom you have granted control, click the Control menu, and select Take Control, as shown in Figure 9-28. Alternatively, press the Windows key and the Esc key at the same time. For example, Kim has shared a Visio document to Thomas. Thomas is called away from his desk. While Thomas is away, Ian decides that he wants to make a contribution. Kim is able to take control of the application by using the Take Control menu option and then delegating control to Ian.

Figure 9-28 Taking back control of an application from another user

Handouts

Handouts are files that are replicated to each participant in the meeting. Any meeting user can open and edit the handout if the user has an application capable of performing that function. Once a participant makes a change to a handout and saves it, that change is replicated to all of the other participants in the meeting. If two or more participants are making changes to the document, the one who saves the document first will have his or her change replicated to all other users, and any other changes will be lost. The document replicated to meeting participants is a copy of the original document, not the original document itself. If participants want to save the modifications that have been made, they can save the document elsewhere on their computers. No matter what changes are made to the document within Meeting Space, the original document that was added as a handout remains unaltered.

In general, it is better to use sharing for documents that participants are going to change during the meeting and to use handouts for documents that are less likely to be changed during the meeting but that all participants should have access to. For example, if you were working on designing a new network for a customer, you would send out the job specification as a handout but share the Visio document containing the network design. This would allow participants to see changes in the document as they were discussed and also access the job specification, which is unlikely to change. Unless saved elsewhere, handouts are automatically deleted from participants' computers when the meeting ends. The original document itself is not deleted. To save a handout during a meeting, right-click the handout in the Handouts area, and click Save As.

To add a handout to a Windows Meeting Space meeting, perform the following steps:

1. Click the Add A Handout icon in the Handouts area. Or if handouts are currently distributed in the meeting, click the green plus icon in this area.
2. Click OK to close the message that reminds you that the handouts will be replicated to another participant's computer.
3. In the dialog box, select the handout you want to distribute, and click Open.

Any meeting participant is able to delete handouts. Deleting a handout removes the handout from the Meeting Space environment for all participants but does not delete the original file itself. The deleted handout is also placed in the Recycle Bin of the participant who deleted it. To delete a handout, right-click it in the Handouts area of the Windows Meeting Space screen and click Delete.

User Status and Passing Notes

Meeting participants are able to alter their status to inform other users how much attention they are paying to the meeting. By clicking on their own name, they are able to set their status to Busy, Be Right Back, or Away, as shown in Figure 9-29. Status is descriptive only. It is still possible to send notes and share applications to participants who have set a different status.

Figure 9-29   Using status to see how much attention other people are paying to the meeting

Right-clicking another user allows you to send that user a note. Windows Meeting Space does not allow you to send messages to all users at once, but you can send a private note to another user, as shown in Figure 9-30. This reinforces the idea that Meeting Space needs another medium, such as a conference call, for most of the information in the meeting to be transferred.

Figure 9-30   Sending private notes during a meeting

Ad Hoc Wireless Meetings

If a computer has a wireless adapter but is not currently connected to a wireless network, it is possible to set up an Ad Hoc Wireless Meeting using Windows Meeting Space. Other meeting participants who also have computers with wireless network adapters are able to join directly to this meeting without having to go through the process of configuring their computer's wireless network settings.

Although you could accomplish the same thing by setting up an ad hoc network through the Network And Sharing Center as covered in Lesson 2, "Troubleshooting Connectivity Issues," of Chapter 7, "Configuring Network Connectivity," this method is less complicated and does not require the convener or participants to understand anything about setting up a network. Rather than having to join a wireless network, meeting participants can open Meeting Space and join the ad hoc meeting using Meetings Near Me. The meeting password also functions as the ad hoc wireless network password.

The only times that setting up an ad hoc meeting will not work is if the wireless adapter is already connected to another network or if IPv6 has been disabled on the wireless interface. To start an Ad Hoc Private Meeting, perform the following steps:

1. Start Windows Meeting Space.
2. Click Start A New Meeting.
3. Select a meeting name and password.
4. Click Options. Select the Create A Private Ad Hoc Wireless Network check box, and select your country or region from the drop-down list.
5. When other users with wireless adapters in range of the convener's computer open Meeting Space, they see the meeting listed, as shown in Figure 9-31. They are able to join normally but need to provide the meeting password.

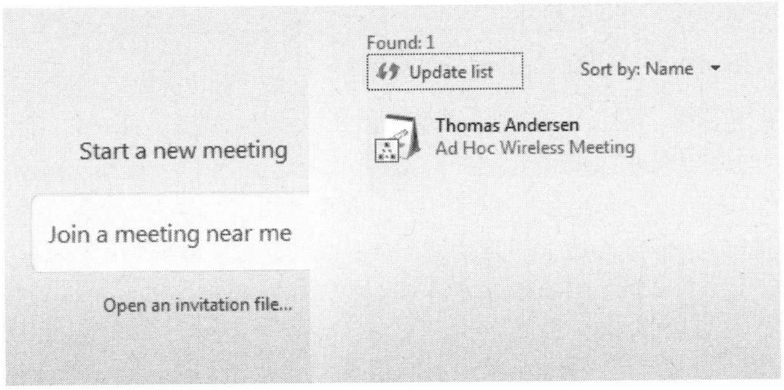

Figure 9-31 Detecting an Ad Hoc Wireless Meeting

It is possible to detect Ad Hoc Wireless Meetings only if the computer's wireless adapter is not currently connected to another wireless network. If the computer is connected to a wireless network and the user wants to connect to Ad Hoc Wireless Networking, the user will need to manually disconnect from his or her current network. After the user does this, available Ad Hoc Wireless Meetings are listed in Join A Meeting Near Me.

Troubleshooting Meeting Space

You can divide Windows Meeting Space troubleshooting into two categories—participants cannot connect to meetings to which they have been invited and poor Windows Meeting Space performance. To simplify things, we assume that everyone who has tried to connect to a meeting has actually typed in the correct password!

The two likeliest reasons a participant is unable to join a meeting are IPv6 address configuration and firewall configuration. If a client cannot connect, you should check that IPv6 has been enabled on all network interfaces. If IPv6 is enabled, also remember that users on separate IPv4 subnets can join the same meeting only if one of the following conditions is met:

- The routers between the subnets support IPv6.
- An Intra-site Automatic Tunnel Addressing Protocol Deployment (ISATAP) server is deployed on the network. Windows Server 2003 and later can be configured as ISATAP servers. An ISATAP server functions in a similar manner to an IPv6 DHCP server, leasing global IPv6 addresses as opposed to automatically configured link-local IPv6 addresses.
- Clients are using Teredo, an IPv4/v6 transition technology that ships with Windows Vista. Teredo allows IPv6 connectivity across the IPv4 Internet even when the two endpoint computers are located behind Network Address Translation (NAT) devices.

If IPv6 has been enabled, the computers are on the same local area network (LAN), or the above conditions have been met, you will need to check the firewall configuration. Remember that firewall configurations vary depending on the type of network that the computer is connected to. Check for the following exceptions:

- Windows Peer-To-Peer Collaboration Foundation
- Windows Meeting Space
- Connect To A Network Projector

If meeting performance is degraded, remember that meetings are limited to approximately 10 participants. This limit is not hard-coded into the technology, and it is possible to have more than 10 participants, but the performance of Windows Meeting Space might be unpleasant for all involved. There is also an adage in business that the number of people attending a meeting is inversely proportional to the amount that will be accomplished, so keeping this limit in mind might not be such a bad thing. If there are problems sharing applications, check which type of application people are trying to share. Video, audio, and DirectX applications cannot be shared using Windows Meeting Space.

Practice: Configuring People Near Me and Windows Meeting Space

In these practices, you will perform several exercises that will familiarize you with People Near Me and Windows Meeting Space. Practice 3 requires two or more Windows Vista computers because it involves participating in a meeting.

▶ **Practice 1: Setting Up People Near Me**

IIn this practice, you will set up People Near Me. Before any user on a Windows Vista computer can use People Near Me, it needs to be set up by a user with elevated privileges because setup involves creating Windows Firewall exceptions. After you perform this task, all other users of the Windows Vista computer are able to sign in to People Near Me. It is necessary to be signed into People Near Me if you want to join a Windows Meeting Space meeting.

1. Log on to Windows Vista with the Kim_Ackers account. This account was configured in Chapter 4, "Configuring and Troubleshooting Internet Access," Lesson 1, "Configuring and Troubleshooting Parental Controls and Content Advisor."

2. Click Start, and then click Control Panel. Ensure that the Control Panel is set to Classic View.

3. Click People Near Me.

4. In the Settings tab, change the name to **Kim Ackers**, and select the Make My Picture Available and Sign Me In Automatically When Windows Starts options.

5. In the Sign In tab, select the Sign In To People Near Me option, and then click OK.

6. Review the privacy information warning, and then click OK.

7. Click OK to close the User Account Control dialog box.

Quick Check

■ Why was it necessary to elevate privileges when configuring People Near Me in this practice exercise?

Quick Check Answer

■ Firewall exceptions are required to enable People Near Me. Firewall exceptions can only be configured using elevated privileges.

▶ **Practice 2: Starting a New Meeting Space Meeting**

In this practice, you will set up Windows Meeting Space and start a new meeting.

1. Log on to Windows Vista with the Kim_Ackers user account.

2. Click Start, click All Programs, and then click Windows Meeting Space.

3. In the Ready To Set Up Windows Meeting Space dialog box, click Yes, Continue Setting Up Windows Meeting Space. As shown in Figure 9-32, this dialog box is presented, because to run Windows Meeting Space, it is necessary to enable file replication and to correctly configure Windows Firewall.

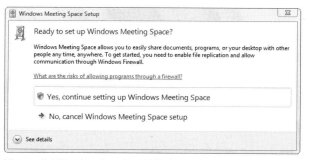

Figure 9-32   Configuring Windows Meeting Space by enabling file replication and allowing communication through the firewall

4. Click Continue to close the User Account Control dialog box.

5. On the Windows Meeting Space start page, click Start A New Meeting.

6. In the Meeting Name box, enter **70-640 Meeting**. In the Password box, enter the password **P@ssw0rd**.

▶ **Practice 3: Invite Users, Share an Application, and Send a Note**

Practice 3 requires two computers on the same LAN, each with users connected to People Near Me and each computer configured to allow Windows Meeting Space exceptions in Windows Firewall. This practice continues on directly from the completion of Practice 2.

1. In the active 70-640 meeting, click Invite People. This brings up the Invite People dialog box.

2. Select the check box for the user logged on to the second Windows Vista computer that you are using for this practice exercise.

3. Click Send Invitations.

4. On the second computer, click View, and then Accept to accept the invitation, as shown in Figure 9-33.

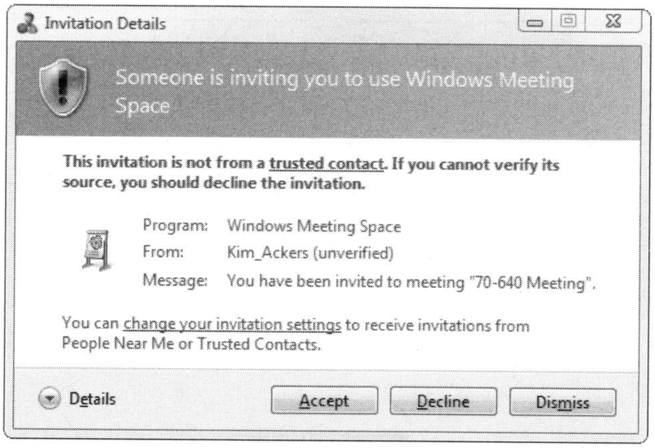

Figure 9-33   An alert informing you that you have been invited to a meeting by a person who is not on your trusted contacts list

5. On the second computer, enter the password **P@ssw0rd** to join the meeting.

6. On the first computer, verify that the invited user has joined the meeting.

7. On the first computer, open the Calculator application by clicking Start, All Programs, Accessories, and then Calculator.

8. On the first computer, click Share A Program Or Your Desktop.

9. Click OK at the prompt that asks if you want other people to see your desktop.

10. In the Start A Shared Session dialog box, shown in Figure 9-34, select Calculator, and then click Share.

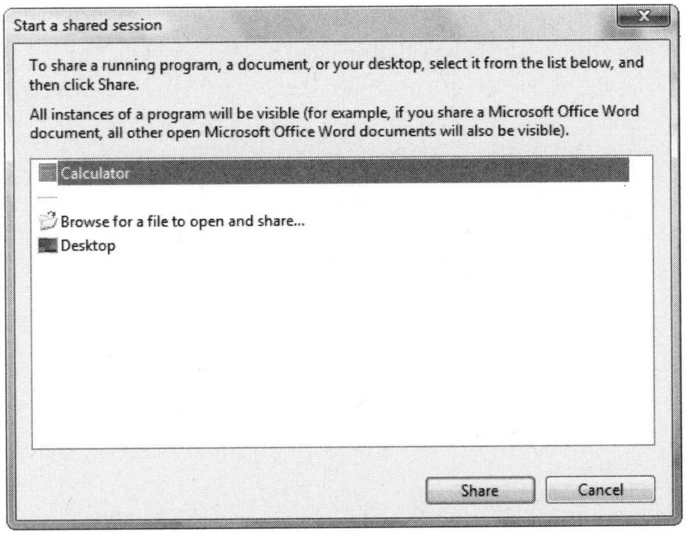

Figure 9-34   Sharing a running application by selecting it and clicking Share

11. Ensure that the Calculator application is on top of the Windows Meeting Space share area, and then check the display on the second computer. You should be able to see the Calculator application displayed there.

12. On the second computer, right-click the other meeting participant, and select Send A Note.

13. Type a message, and then click Send. Verify that this note appears in the Windows Meeting Space Window on the first computer.

14. Close Windows Meeting Space on both computers.

Lesson Summary

- Windows Meeting Space allows meeting participants to project applications to other users' desktops. It also allows the distribution of files through peer-to-peer replication.
- Windows Meeting Space relies upon People Near Me. Before joining a Meeting Space meeting, it is necessary to configure People Near Me settings.
- The initial configuration of People Near Me and Windows Meeting Space requires a user account that has access to elevated privileges. These privileges are necessary to configure Windows Firewall exemptions required to support People Near Me and Meeting Space.
- Windows Meeting Space relies upon IPv6. Users on separate LANs cannot by default join the same meeting unless they have global IPv6 addresses. It is possible to institute special technologies to overcome this limitation, but these are unlikely to be covered on the exam.
- Invitations can be sent to users logged on to People Near Me. It is also possible to send invitation files through e-mail or using other methods of file transfer. Any participant connected to a meeting can forward an invitation to another user.
- Windows Meeting Space has no moderation tools. It is impossible to kick a disruptive user out of a meeting or to block users from joining a meeting if they have a meeting password.
- Only one application can be shared at a time. It is possible to allow another user to have control of an application, but you can rescind that control at any time. Control can either be delegated to a participant, or the participant can request control, and that control can be granted.

Lesson Review

You can use the following questions to test your knowledge of the information in Lesson 3, "Configuring Windows Meeting Space." The questions are also available on the companion CD if you prefer to review them in electronic form.

NOTE   Answers

Answers to these questions and explanations of why each answer choice is correct or incorrect are located in the "Answers" section at the end of the book.

---

1. Scott has learned the password to Kim's Windows Meeting Space meeting, and he has also located the invitation file that Kim left on a network share for Tony to use to connect. Kim learns of this before any other meeting participants arrive. Which of the following strategies should she pursue to ensure that Scott cannot attend the meeting?

    A. Block Scott from joining.

    B. Rescind Tony's invitation and issue him a new one.

    C. Restart the meeting.

    D. Remove Scott from the list of trusted contacts.

2. Tony initially shared a computer-aided design (CAD) application to a Windows Meeting Space meeting initiated by Kim. During the meeting, Ian is granted control of the application to make modifications to the design but is then called away from his desk without relinquishing control. Kim wants to complete Ian's modifications to the design. How can Kim gain control of the application with a minimum of effort? (Choose two. Each forms a part of the answer.)

    A. Forcibly disconnect Ian from the meeting.

    B. Ask Tony to press the Windows Key and the Esc key.

    C. Ask Tony to close the application.

    D. Take control of the application.

    E. Ask Tony to give her control of the application.

3. Kim, Thomas, Tony, and Ian are in a Windows Meeting Space meeting. Kim adds a Microsoft Excel spreadsheet file as a handout. Each meeting participant opens the document and makes changes. Ian saves his changes first, Kim saves second, Tony third, and Thomas last. Whose changes will be replicated to all participants?

    A. Kim's

    B. Thomas's

    C. Tony's

    D. Ian's

4. Kim, Tony, Ian, and Orin are in an outback café and are all trying to join an Ad Hoc Wireless Meeting hosted by Tony. Each has a notebook computer with a functional wireless card. The café has no wireless access point, and no other users in the café have wireless devices. Kim, Ian, and Orin are able to join the Ad Hoc Wireless Networking, but Tony is unable to. Which of the following steps are likely to resolve the problem? (Choose all that apply.)

   A. Enable IPv6 on the wireless interface on Tony's computer.

   B. Disable IPv4 on the wireless interface on Tony's computer.

   C. Disable IPv6 on the wireless interface on Tony's computer.

   D. Enable IPv4 on the wireless interface on Tony's computer.

5. Kim wants to invite Tony to a meeting, but Tony has configured People Near Me to block invitations. Kim has used her mobile phone to SMS Tony the meeting password. How can she invite Tony to a meeting? (Choose all that apply.)

   A. Get Tony to add her to his Trusted Contacts.

   B. E-mail the invitation to Tony.

   C. Save the invitation to a network location that Tony can access.

   D. Add Tony to her list of Trusted Contacts.

Chapter Review

To further practice and reinforce the skills you learned in this chapter, you can perform the following tasks:

- Review the chapter summary.
- Review the list of key terms introduced in this chapter.
- Complete the case scenarios. These scenarios set up real-world situations involving the topics of this chapter and ask you to create a solution.
- Complete the suggested practices.
- Take a practice test.

Chapter Summary

- Before setting up an e-mail account, you need to know the FQDN of the incoming and outgoing mail servers and what protocol they use.
- Mail views are used to display and hide mail dependent on message properties. Mail rules can be used to sort mail based on content or modify the properties of messages.
- The junk e-mail folder should be checked periodically to locate legitimate messages that have been incorrectly identified.
- Windows Contacts stores address, telephone, and e-mail information about people you communicate with.
- Windows Calendars can be shared with other people, or you can subscribe to another person's published calendar.
- People Near Me allows you to see who else on the LAN is available. A person needs to be logged on to People Near Me to connect to a Windows Meeting Space meeting.
- Windows Meeting Space allows users to share documents, applications, and computer desktops with one another without having to connect to a centralized server.

Key Terms

Do you know what these key terms mean? You can check your answers by looking up the terms in the glossary at the end of the book.

- contact
- convener
- conversation
- false positive
- Internet Message Access Protocol 4 (IMAP4)

- Post Office Protocol 3 (POP3)
- Simple Mail Transport Protocol (SMTP)
- trusted contact
- Usenet

Case Scenarios

In the following case scenarios, you will apply what you have learned about configuring applications included with Windows Vista. You can find answers to these questions in the "Answers" section at the end of this book.

Case Scenario 1: University Calendars

You are responsible for providing desktop support and advice to the Department of Philosophy at the local university.

1. The university has finished finalizing the academic calendar for the next five years. The university has placed an exported calendar file on its website. What steps should staff and students take to add this information to their own calendars?

2. Kim manages five people in the office of the philosophy department at the university. She wants to be able to keep up to date on how they are completing their assigned tasks. How might she do this if all the people who work for her use Windows Vista?

3. Kim needs to make and update the head of the department's appointments. The head of the department views her calendar on her Windows Vista computer. The head of the department never creates or edits appointments. What method could Kim use to accomplish her goal?

Case Scenario 2: Presenting a Business Proposal Using Windows Meeting Space

The development team from Tailspin Toys is in Canberra this week to present a product proposal to the management of Wingtip Toys. Each member of the development team has an 802.11g-capable Tablet PC running Windows Vista Ultimate. The product design is stored as a file for a CAD application on the team leader's computer. No other team members have this CAD application installed.

1. When the development team arrives at their hotel in Canberra, they find that it does not have any wireless access points. They want to collaborate with each other using Windows Meeting Space. What options do they have?

2. During a brainstorming session, two members of the team think of some modifications that can be made to the product design. The team leader does not want the two team members to access his laptop directly because he has sensitive Human Resources information on his desktop. How can he grant the members access to the design when he is the only one with the CAD program installed?

3. The team's documentation developer finishes the product documentation half an hour before the Windows Meeting Space presentation to the Wingtip Toys management team begins. How can she best distribute this documentation to all participants?

Suggested Practices

To help you successfully master the exam objectives presented in this chapter, complete the following tasks.

Configure Windows Mail

- **Practice 1: Set Up Windows Mail to Handle Mail from a Friend**   Create a mail rule that copies all e-mail from a friend of yours into a folder that has your friend's name. Add your friend to the Safe Senders list.

- **Practice 2: Add Your ISP's News Server**   Add your ISP's news server to Windows Mail. Subscribe to a newsgroup that interests you.

Configure Windows Meeting Space

These practices require two computers running Windows Vista.

- **Practice 1: People Near Me**   Configure People Near Me to sign in automatically when Windows Vista starts.

- **Practice 2: Host a Meeting**   Host a Windows Meeting Space meeting. Invite the person logged on to People Near Me on that computer to the meeting. Share the Windows Calculator application.

Configure Windows Calendar

- **Practice 1: Create and Publish a Calendar**   With one Windows Vista user, create a public calendar, and then publish it to a shared folder on that computer.

- **Practice 2: Subscribe to a Calendar**   Log on to the same computer as used in Practice 1, and subscribe to the calendar that you just published.

Take a Practice Test

The practice tests on this book's companion CD offer many options. For example, you can test yourself on just one exam objective, or you can test yourself on all the 70-620 certification exam content. You can set up the test so that it closely simulates the experience of taking a certification exam, or you can set it up in study mode so that you can look at the correct answers and explanations after you answer each question.

MORE INFO   Practice tests

For details about all the practice test options available, see the "How to Use the Practice Tests" section in this book's Introduction.

Chapter 10

Configuring Faxes, Media Applications, and the Windows Sidebar

Windows Media Center is included in the Home Premium and Ultimate editions of Windows Vista. With the appropriate hardware, Media Center can allow a personal computer to replace your DVD player, video recorder, and audio CD players. All of your videos, DVDs, movies, TV, recorded television, photos, and music can be played through a single device that connects to your high definition television. Although it cannot be used to record television, Windows Media Player is available in all editions of Windows Vista and can be used to consolidate your music collection, adding it to a single library that all other compatible devices on the local area network can access.

Just as Windows Media Center eliminates the need for DVD players and videocassette recorders, Windows Fax and Scan removes the need for the fax machine. Fax and Scan is available with the Business, Enterprise, and Ultimate editions of Windows Vista. Fax and Scan allows documents to be faxed directly from Windows applications or scanned using an optical scanning device from hard copy to the computer and sent as a traditional fax. Synchronized with a mobile phone that supports modem functionality, the mobile worker can receive and send faxes anywhere that cell phone reception is available.

Exam objectives in this chapter:
- Configure and troubleshoot media applications.
- Configure Windows Fax and Scan.
- Configure Windows Sidebar.

Lessons in this chapter:

Before You Begin

To complete the lessons in this chapter, you must have done the following:

Completed the installation and upgrading practices in Chapter 1, "Installing Windows Vista Client," and Chapter 2, "Windows Vista Upgrades and Migrations." As a result, you will have installed Windows Vista Ultimate on a personal computer or within a virtual machine. This computer should also have a working connection to the Internet. It is not possible to complete all of the practices in this chapter unless you have Windows Vista Home Premium or Ultimate because practices involve Windows Media Center. Practices 1 and 2 in Lesson 1 require access to a TV tuner card or universal serial bus (USB) device.

No additional configuration is required for this chapter.

Real World

Orin Thomas

My father has a box in his cupboard containing all of the silent Super-8 film he took of my siblings and me as kids. Although it doesn't come out much and requires that he set up a special projector when he wants to play it, that box in the cupboard represents one type of important media archive to my family. Because of the hassle in setup, we get to see those old home movies only on special occasions, which suits me because my own son doesn't need to see his dad at the same age pretending to be Superman and jumping into a toddler pool.

Windows Media Center and the Media Center Extender allow me to take a different and more convenient approach. Since the birth of my son, all of the pictures and video that I have taken are digital. In the past, the primary drawback to this was that every time I wanted to show someone the video I'd taken, I'd either have to get that person to watch a computer screen or muck around with a set of cords to get the video camera to output directly to the television. The inclusion of Windows Media Center with Windows Vista Ultimate and my purchase of an Xbox 360 has completely changed how I display my family's memories. My digital media files are stored in my study on the Windows Vista computer that I am writing this book on. The Xbox 360 is configured as a Media Center Extender and is located in the family room, connected to the television. I can retrieve thousands of photographs and hours of footage all by remote control. Unlike my father, who must spend time setting up the projector and locating the delicate 30-year-old film, I can retrieve and replay my family's memories on the living room television in a matter of seconds.

Lesson 1: Configuring and Troubleshooting Media Applications

Windows Media Center is available in the Home Premium and Ultimate editions of Windows Vista. With the appropriate hardware, Media Center allows you to record and play back television programs, burn those television programs to DVD, or display recorded television programs in different parts of your home by streaming them through devices like the Xbox 360. Unlike Media Center, Windows Media Player is available in all versions of Windows Vista and does not require specialized hardware. Media Player allows the playback of all kinds of digital audio and video. Media Player is integrated with URGE, an online music store that allows you to purchase and legally download music from the Internet. You can also use Media Player to manage and sync audio with digital audio devices like Microsoft's Zune or Pocket PC edition mobile phones.

After this lesson, you will be able to:
- Configure Windows Media Center.
  - ❏ Install and configure extenders.
  - ❏ Install and configure digital cable devices.
  - ❏ Troubleshoot recording issues.
- Configure Windows Media Player.
  - ❏ Configure and troubleshoot Digital Rights Management (DRM).

Estimated lesson time: 50 minutes

Configuring Windows Media Center

Prior to setting up Windows Media Center, you should install the TV tuner device that you will use and connect it to the appropriate digital cable device. TV tuner devices either come as cards that you can install in the slots on your computer's motherboard or as USB devices that you can insert in any USB 2 slot. After you install the device, the process of connecting it to a signal is similar to that of connecting an antenna to the back of a television set or a VCR. At this point it is not necessary to make any configuration changes to the TV tuner other than to verify that Device Manager reports no problems.

The first time that you run Windows Media Center, you are presented with the setup wizard. The first few pages of the wizard deal with the Windows Media Center Privacy policy and the Customer Experience Improvement Program. After these steps are completed, you can determine whether Media Center periodically connects to the Internet to retrieve album and DVD cover art, TV Program Guide listings, and music and movie information. When you complete these steps, you can get on with the process of configuring Windows Media Center to display broadcast television.

Configuring TV Settings and Digital Cable Devices

After you have installed your TV tuner device, you need to set up Windows Media Center to receive all of the services that are available. You can do this by starting Windows Media Center and navigating to the Settings item under Tasks. You then need to open the TV item to get to the TV Settings menu, shown in Figure 10-1. This menu allows you to configure the TV Signal, the TV or Monitor, Audio, and Closed Caption settings. It is possible to set up a TV signal only if a TV tuner card is connected.

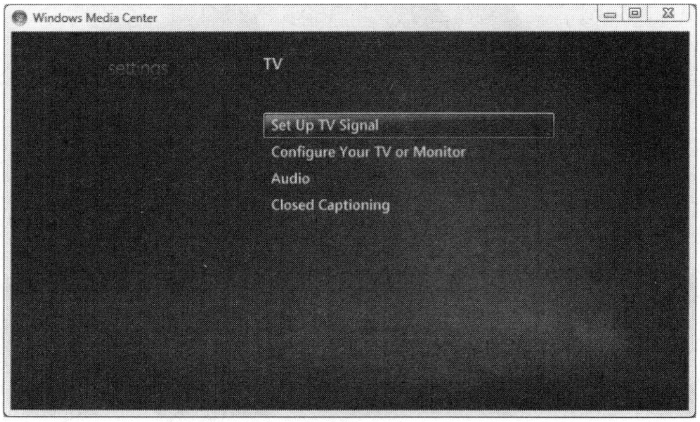

Figure 10-1 The TV Settings menu

If you do not have a TV tuner card, it is still possible to access some television programming through Media Center off the Internet. However, what is available legally over the Internet is a fraction of what is transmitted over free-to-air digital or pay TV digital channels. Free-to-air HDTV is generally the simplest to set up. Playing special cable services might require additional software or hardware, and you should check with your cable provider before you attempt this.

When you are configuring Media Center for TV reception, it scans for the following types of digital signal:

- **Antenna** In many countries, HDTV signals are broadcast over the airwaves. With an antenna plugged into your high definition TV card, you are able to view HDTV through Windows Media Center.

- **Direct cable connection** Rather than receiving your signal through an antenna, you receive it through a coaxial cable. This coaxial cable can plug directly into your PC's TV tuner.

- **Set top box** This option is selected if a box from your pay TV provider is present between the wall and the cable that goes into your PC's tuner hardware.

■ **Satellite** This option is similar to a direct cable connection except that the source of the signal is a satellite rather than an earthbound cable.

Windows Media Center should be able to configure these devices automatically. If it does not, you should verify that all connections are secure and that items such as the set top box are turned on. The process of configuring Windows Media Center to receive digital signals is covered in Practice 1 at the end of this lesson.

Setting Up Media Center and Configuring a Windows Media Center Extender

Although it is possible to connect your computer directly to a television if you have the appropriate cables, it is easier to use a device known as a Media Center Extender to act as an intermediary between your computer and your TV set. The most common form of Media Center Extender is the Xbox 360, although other products are available. Each product has the ability to connect to your local area network (LAN), either wirelessly or through an unshielded twisted pair (UTP) cable. The product retrieves content from the computer running Windows Media Center and displays it directly on the TV it is connected to. Media Center Extenders allow you to keep your computer out of the living room while enjoying all the benefits that Media Center has to offer.

Installing a Media Center Extender is easy. When you connect your Media Center Extender to the same subnet at the Windows Vista computer that has Media Center installed, a dialog box is displayed, as shown in Figure 10-2, informing you that a Media Center Extender has been found. This dialog box displays some information about the Media Center Extender. You have the option of dismissing this dialog box and selecting an option so that it is not displayed again. If you select the option not to be shown the notification again, you can start setting up the Media Center Extender through the Media Center menu.

Figure 10-2 A Media Center Extender is found on the LAN

Clicking Yes launches Windows Media Center. The Optional Setup page, shown in Figure 10-3, allows you to set up the Extender. It is also possible at this stage to set up the Pictures, Music, and Video libraries. You need to configure these libraries if you want to display more than TV and DVDs through your Media Center Extender. It is possible to come back and perform this configuration later. Windows Media Center is an application that requires a significant amount of configuration, but after you complete, its configuration does not require much in the way of maintenance.

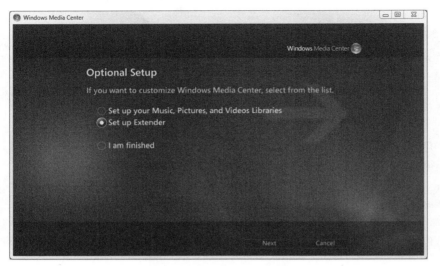

Figure 10-3   Configuring an extender with the Optional Setup menu

---

NOTE   Extender setup

The Media Center Extender setup is covered in the text, rather than in the practice exercises at the end of the lesson because we think most readers are unlikely to have both the required version of Windows Vista and access to an Xbox 360!

After you select the option to set up the Extender, you are presented with the Extender Setup page, shown in Figure 10-4. At this point, it is necessary to configure the extender itself. On the Xbox 360 this involves navigating in the console to the Media section and then using your controller to select the Media Center item. The Xbox 360 then provides information on how to complete the setup. A check is performed on the network and then an eight-digit setup key is displayed on the device that the Xbox 360 is connected to. You need to make a note of this number and then enter it on the Windows Vista computer in the Extender Setup page.

If the Media Center Extender device was not automatically detected, it might be necessary to reconfigure Windows Firewall settings. You also need to determine whether or not you want to have the computer running Windows Media Center use Away Mode. Away Mode is a high availability power setting that allows the Media Center Extender to connect at any time, even when the computer appears shut down. The benefit of this mode is that it allows you to wake the computer whenever you want to use the Media Center Extender to view digital content. The drawback of this mode is its increased power consumption because a certain level of functionality is required to wake the computer when it is contacted over the network. The final configuration step determines whether it is possible to view the folders that contain your media.

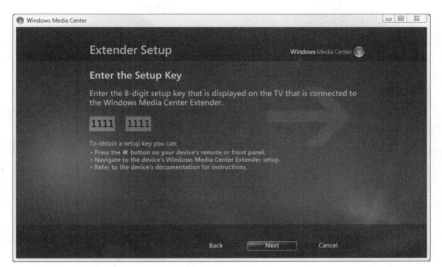

Figure 10-4   Obtaining the 8-digit setup key

Configuring Media Center Display

It can be necessary to calibrate Media Center's output for video on a computer screen or television. Similar in some ways to configuring a monitor's color properties in the Display Settings dialog box so that there is a direct match between the displayed color and the color output by the printer, the video output configuration ensures that the video output from Media Center is as accurate and true to life as possible. New digital video formats aim for the best possible fidelity, so it should not be surprising that you might need to alter some default settings to gain the best possible output.

The Video Setup Wizard queries you on which monitor you want to display content if there are multiple monitors connected and the type of monitor that video content will be displayed. When specifying the type of monitor, you provide information about the connection between your computer and the display, the monitor's aspect ratio, and the display resolution. When using LCD monitors, remember to configure them to use the native resolution even if higher resolutions are possible because native resolution provides the best display experience.

NOTE   Configuring captioning

Many programs are now broadcast with captioning, also known as subtitles, that allows people who are hearing impaired or who do not want to listen to audio to follow what is going on during the program. Windows Media Center can be configured to provide automatic captioning should the mute function be enabled. This captioning can be applied to both DVD, live TV, and recorded TV playback.

Troubleshooting Recording Issues

You can configure Windows Media Center to record TV broadcasts in the same way that you would record TV broadcasts with your VCR. It is possible to record on the basis of a program's title in the guide or by specifying a channel and a time. Although programming Windows Media Center to record your favorite program is simpler than programming a VCR, you can still run into problems when attempting to have your computer automatically record a program that you want to watch. These problems include:

- **Scheduled recording issues** The problem could lie with an inaccurate schedule, or there might be some time issues with the computer running Windows Vista. Ensuring that schedules are frequently updated is the best way to ensure that you record the program that you are interested in. If you want to record each episode of a program, select the Record By Series option. If you find that the schedule does not match the actual time the program you are interested in is broadcast, you should use the advanced recording function. The advanced recording function allows you to set up a recording to last between five minutes to three hours after a program is scheduled to finish. For example, your schedule indicates that the soccer game ends at 10:30 P.M., but you have found that it sometimes runs until 11:45 P.M. Using the advanced recording function allows you to record on the basis of schedule and extension.

- **Recording quality** To reduce the amount of disk space consumed by recordings, you can use the advanced recording function to reduce the quality of the recording.

- **Keep settings** Keep settings, shown in Figure 10-5, determine how long a recorded program is kept before it is automatically deleted. The possible settings are:
  - ❑ **Until Space Needed** Programs are not deleted until the amount of space allocated for recording programs is reached. Programs are then deleted on the basis of age.
  - ❑ **Until I Watch** Once a program is watched, it can be automatically deleted when the amount of space allocated for recording programs is reached.
  - ❑ **Until I Delete** All programs are kept until manually deleted.
  - ❑ **For One Week** All recorded programs are deleted after a week has elapsed.

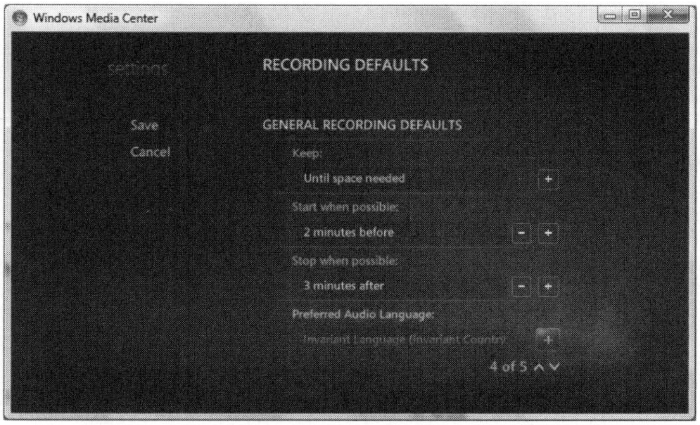

Figure 10-5 Keep settings

■ **Recorder storage** The recorder storage options, shown in Figure 10-6, allow you to configure the disk volume that you are recording to, the maximum amount of disk space to allocate to recording TV programs, and the Live TV Pause Buffer. It is important when configuring this option that you do not overallocate space to recorded TV data. For example, if you have 200 GB of free space on a 300-GB drive, you should not allocate more than 200 GB for the recording of TV. If you misconfigure these settings, the volume could become full, and that might cause other problems!

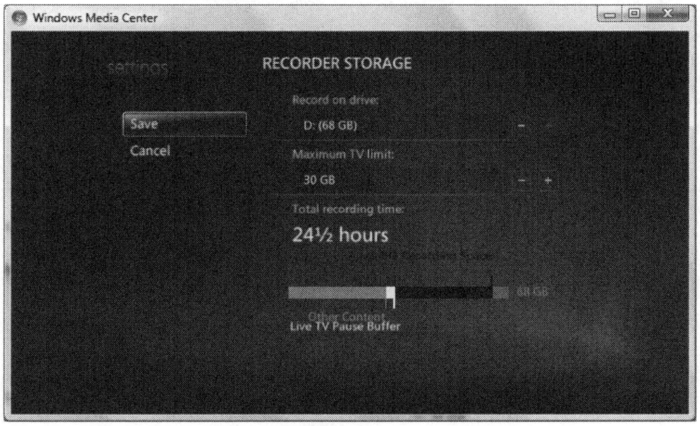

Figure 10-6 Recorder storage options

■ **Parental controls** Similar to the way it is possible to restrict children who use Windows Vista from using games or viewing web pages that are beyond a particular classification, it is possible to use Windows Media Center to block children from viewing live TV, recorded programs, or DVDs that are age-inappropriate. Unlike Windows Vista, which does this on a user account basis, Media Center requires an access code before restricted content can be viewed. Another difference compared to Windows Vista is that the limits cannot be applied on a per user basis. For example, if you have a 6-year-old and a 12-year-old, you have to decide on an appropriate level for both children.

■ **Configuring region** Windows Media Center uses region selection to determine cable connection settings and where it will locate program data. Windows Media Player configures its regional settings on the basis of the regional settings of the Windows Vista computer that it was configured on. It is possible to make alterations to these settings, as shown in Figure 10-7. For example, someone might work in a job overseas. That person might have a mobile PC with a USB digital cable device. If he or she left Media Center with the original regional settings and attempted to connect a digital signal to the digital cable device in the overseas location, that person might find that the disparity between each region's settings is enough to ensure that Windows Media Center is unable to access those signals.

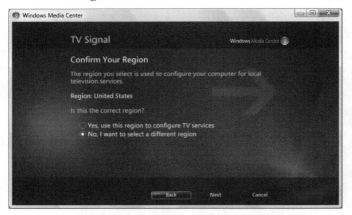

Figure 10-7 Selecting a different region

■ **Automatic vs. manual signal configuration** Windows Media Center provides the option of automatic or manual tuning for digital channels, as shown in Figure 10-8. This option is useful if the regional options do not include service information. In general, it is far simpler to allow Media Center to perform an automatic tuning than to perform a manual tuning. Only in rare instances, such as low digital signal quality, is it necessary to perform a manual configuration to get reception on a particular channel.

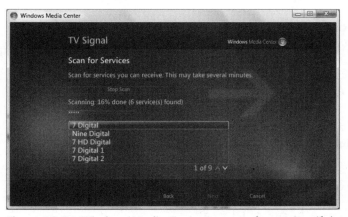

Figure 10-8   Windows Media Center can scan for services if data about your region is not found

- **Library issues**   Windows Media Center looks only in configured directories for content. It is possible to add new directories and have Windows Media Center regularly check them for content. If media files that you know are on your computer are not available through Media Center, use Add Folder To Watch. This brings up the dialog box, shown in Figure 10-9, which allows you to browse to the folder on the local or remote computer that you want Windows Media Center to monitor.

Figure 10-9   Informing Media Player where your media are located

Quick Check

1. What is the difference between Media Center and a Media Center Extender?
2. Which editions of Windows Vista are capable of running Media Center?

Quick Check Answers

1. A Media Center can record and play TV, DVDs, and audio. A Media Center Extender can display everything that can be shown on Media Center but does not store it locally.
2. Windows Vista Home Premium and Windows Vista Ultimate.

Configuring Windows Media Player

Windows Media Player is available with all editions of Windows Vista and does not require special hardware beyond the ability to output audio and video. There are many superficial similarities between Windows Media Player and Windows Media Center. Both can play back video and audio data, including CDs, DVDs, and home movies. The primary differences between the two products are as follows:

- Windows Media Center is available only in the Home Premium and Ultimate editions of Windows Vista. Windows Media Player is available in all editions of Windows Vista.
- Windows Media Center can record and play back broadcast television. Windows Media Player can play back only television broadcasts.
- Windows Media Center can be used to share media to other computers and mobile devices on the network. Windows Media Center can be used only to display media through a Windows Media Center Extender device.
- Windows Media Player can be used to rip audio from a CD to a variety of formats. Windows Media Center is incapable of ripping audio, although it can play audio ripped by Windows Media Player.

Ripping and Digital Rights Management

Ripping is the process of extracting multimedia data from a CD or DVD and converting it into a media file that can be played on a computer. Windows Media Player offers ripping as a prominent menu item, although it is possible to rip only audio CDs using Media Player. It is not possible to rip audio DVDs or video data from DVDs. The primary reason that you would want to use Windows Media Player's ripping functionality is to consolidate your audio CD collection in a single place. Rather than having to hunt around for a CD when you want to hear a particular song, you can locate it in your centralized media library.

You can rip audio data to the following formats:

- **Windows Media Audio**   Each CD ripped using this format consumes 56 MB of disk space.
- **Windows Media Audio Pro**   Each CD ripped using this format consumes 28 MB of disk space. It has a lower bit rate than Windows Media Audio and is useful for storing audio on mobile devices.
- **Windows Media Audio (Variable Bit Rate)**   A smart format, complex audio uses a higher bit rate, and simple audio uses a lower bit rate. It uses between 18 and 33 MB per CD.
- **Windows Media Audio (Lossless)**   The highest quality recording format. It uses between 206 and 411 MB per CD.
- **MP3**   Supported by almost all portable media devices, it uses approximately 57 MB per CD.
- **WAV (Lossless)**   An older format that has been in use since early versions of Windows. It uses 600 MB per CD.

You should remember that the higher the bit rate, the higher the quality of the audio and the more disk space that is consumed. Depending on the quality of your playback equipment, you might not notice a difference between some of the formats, even though they use a radically different amount of disk space. All of the Windows Media Audio formats support copy protection technology. The MP3 and WAV formats do not support copy protection technology.

When you rip to any of the Windows Media formats, you have the option of copy protecting the music. Copy protection, also known as Digital Rights Management (DRM), is a method of ensuring that people cannot make illegal duplicates of digital media that they have purchased. DRM ensures that someone cannot purchase the latest hot artist's track for one dollar and then sell it 500 times to other people for 50 cents. DRM is a method of controlling how media is used after it is purchased.

When you rip an audio CD into any Windows Media Audio format, the audio can be protected with copy protection. One reason you might choose to copy protect music is if you are a musician who wants some form of digital distribution of your music, but you do not want it to be given to just anybody. When a music file with copy protection is played, Media Player attempts to contact the rights server. When Windows Media Player encounters a copy protected file it attempts to obtain the rights to play that file. It is possible to configure such a rights server using Microsoft products, but this is beyond the scope of the 70-620 exam.

Unless you have a license for particular media, Windows Media Player will not be able to play it. DRM protects a file by encrypting it, and a license can be thought of as the decryption key. The keys are stored separately from the files within Media Player, and the files themselves cannot be played without access to a key. This does not apply to all digital media files, just those that the authors have decided to copy protect. Although this might all sound very Orwellian, the DRM features of Windows Vista allow artists and publishers to choose whether or not they want to apply copy protection restrictions on their works. The option is available but might not necessarily be used.

IMPORTANT   Rights backup

Windows Media Player does not allow you to back up your media usage rights. If media usage rights are lost, it is necessary to recover them through the service from which you purchased the digital media.

You can ensure that usage rights are immediately downloaded when you play or sync a file with a mobile device by setting configuration options in the Privacy tab of Windows Media Player Options dialog box, as shown in Figure 10-10. (You access this dialog box by clicking More Options at the bottom of any menu.) If you do not select the Download Usage Rights Automatically When I Play Or Sync A File check box, you will be prompted by Windows. If you do not acquire the rights, you will be unable to play the media file. If you have a permanent connection to the Internet, you should configure rights to be acquired automatically. This is the default setting for Windows Media Player.

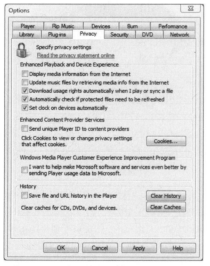

Figure 10-10   The Privacy tab

Adding Metadata

The Advanced Tag Editor, shown in Figure 10-11, allows you to configure metadata about files in your library. You can access this editor by right-clicking a file in your library and then clicking Advanced Tag Editor. Metadata is useful in constructing playlists. It is likely that you will collect thousands of separate music files, and finding the right one to play can be difficult. With correctly configured metadata, you can configure the computer to play your tracks based on your mood, comments you have made about the track, the genre, key, or any number of factors. It is not necessary to do this, but it does help if you need to organize a very large music collection. You might not remember all the songs that you associate with an old flame, but by using Windows Media Player, you can configure the computer to do it for you.

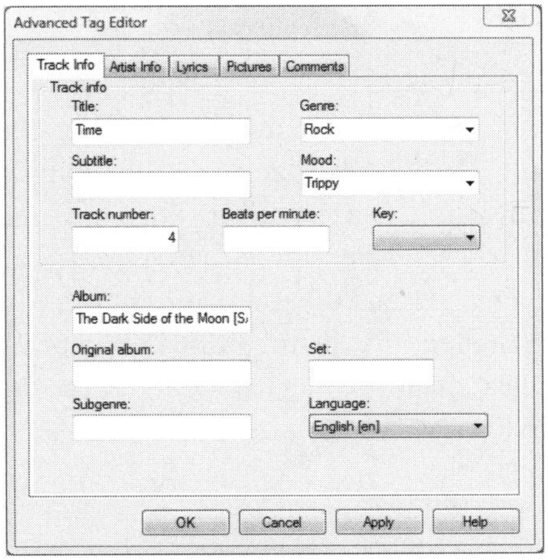

Figure 10-11 Using the Advanced Tag Editor to configure metadata

Media Sharing

Media Sharing allows you to share items in your library with other computers or devices on your network. Rather than duplicate your music library on every computer in the house, you can use media sharing to allow your Pocket PC phone to function as a portable media player accessing your entire library while you work out on the treadmill without having to copy files across to the phone before starting your workout. To configure media sharing, perform the following steps:

1. Click any tab menu, and then click More Options.
2. Navigate to the Library tab, and click Configure Sharing.
3. Select the Share My Media check box, as shown in Figure 10-12.

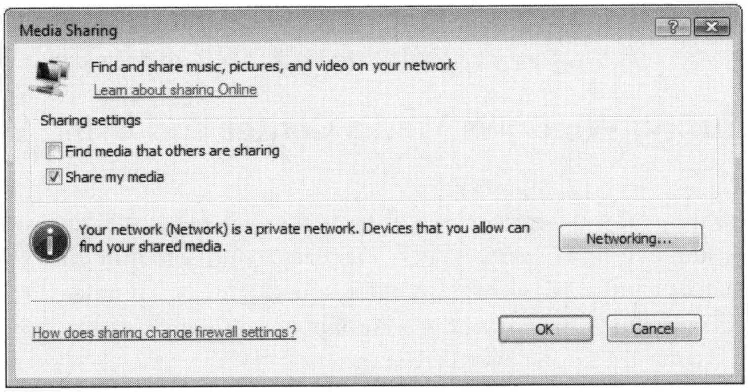

Figure 10-12 Sharing media to other devices on the network

4. When a compatible device connects to the network, you are alerted and you can decide whether you want to share your media with that device. You can also open the Media Sharing dialog box to allow or deny sharing to particular computers on the network.

Codecs

A codec is a method of encoding data. Each media format requires a separate codec. If you open a new media file, it might be necessary for Windows Media Player to obtain the codec to play that file from the Internet before you can listen to or watch it. The Download Codecs Automatically check box is selected by default in the Player tab of the Options dialog box, as shown in Figure 10-13. Clearing this check box means that the user is prompted when a codec is required. Unless the appropriate codec is installed, the file might not play correctly. In the case of digital video, this might mean that you can hear the playback but not see the playback or that the video might appear to be corrupted.

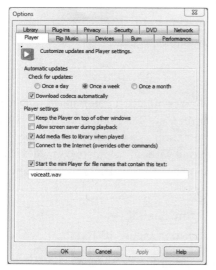

Figure 10-13   Automatically configuring Windows Media Player to download codecs

Practice: Configuring Windows Media Center and Using Windows Media Player

In these practices, you will perform several exercises that will familiarize you with Windows Media Center and Windows Media Player. Practices 1 and 2 require that you use either the Home Premium or Ultimate editions of Windows Vista. You can complete Practice 3 using any edition of Windows Vista, as long as the computer has an optical media drive.

▶ **Practice 1: Configuring TV Settings**

In this practice, you will configure TV settings. This practice requires either the Home Premium or Ultimate edition of Windows Vista and an already installed TV tuner card. The computer also requires an active Internet connection. To complete the practice, perform the following steps:

1. Open Windows Media Center, and navigate to Tasks using the arrow keys.
2. In Tasks, navigate sideways using the arrow keys to Settings.
3. Navigate to TV, and then, on the menu shown in Figure 10-14, navigate to Set Up TV Signal.

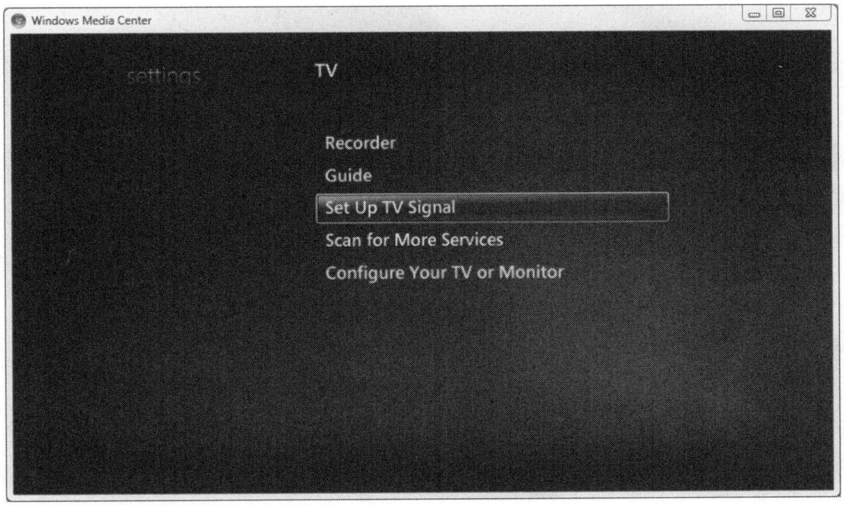

Figure 10-14   The TV menu allows you to set up the TV signal

4. On the Set Up Your TV Signal page, click Next.
5. On the Confirm Your Region page, verify that your region is selected, and click Next. If your region is not selected, click No, I Want To Select A Different Region. Scroll through the list of countries until you find yours. Select it, and click Next.
6. Windows Media Center now downloads settings from the Internet. When it is finished, you see the You Are Done! page. On this page, click Set Up Guide Listings, and then click Next.
7. Click Next on the Set Up Your TV Program Guide.
8. On the Guide Privacy page, select Yes. Click Next.
9. On the Guide Terms of Service page, select I Agree. Click Next.
10. On the Enter Your Postal Code page, enter your postal code, and click Next.

11. Windows now downloads your guide listings. If a guide listing is not available, click Next. Otherwise, select your TV signal provider, and click Next.

12. The TV Program Guide is now downloaded from the Internet. Depending on your connection speed, this might take between 5 and 20 minutes. When the download is complete, click Next.

13. On the Scan For Services page, click Start Scan. This process might take from 5 to 10 minutes. If your TV tuner device is not properly connected, no services are found. Click Next, and then click Finish.

▶ **Practice 2: Configuring Recording Options**

In this practice, you will configure recording options. This practice can be completed only on a computer running Windows Vista Home Premium or Ultimate. The computer must also have a functioning TV tuner card installed. To complete this practice, perform the following steps:

1. Using Windows Explorer, make a note of how much free space is available on Volume C.

2. Open Windows Media Center, and navigate to Tasks.

3. In Tasks, navigate to Settings.

4. In Settings, navigate to TV.

5. Select Recorder, and then select Recorder Storage.

6. Set the Maximum TV limit to 50 percent of the amount of free space available on Volume C. Select Save.

7. Navigate to Recording Defaults.

8. Change the Keep setting to Until I Delete, and change the Stop When Possible setting to 4 Minutes After.

9. Select Save, and close Windows Media Center.

▶ **Practice 3: Ripping and Copy Protecting Digital Audio**

Practice 3 can be performed on a computer running any edition of Windows Vista that has a CD-ROM or DVD-ROM drive installed. To perform Practice 3, you also need access to a standard non-copy protected audio CD. This type of CD is required to simplify the ripping process. To complete this practice, perform the following steps:

1. Insert an audio CD into the optical media drive.

2. If you have auto-play enabled, cancel the dialog box. In this practice, you do not want to play the CD; you are going to extract audio data from it.

3. Open Windows Media Player, and click Rip.

4. Hold down the Alt key, and from the Tools menu, select Options.

5. Click the Rip Music tab to bring up the ripping options, as shown in Figure 10-15.

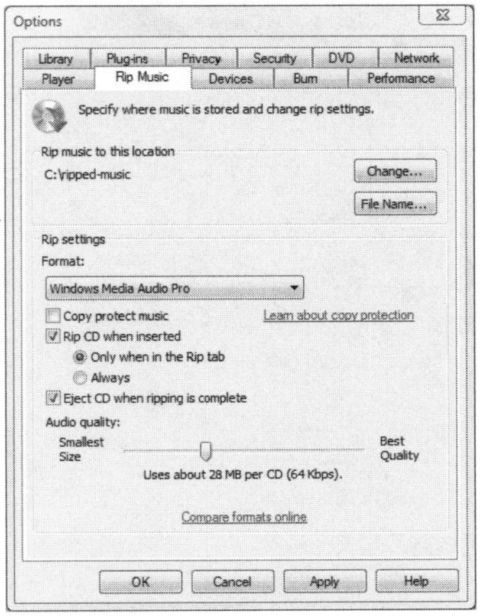

Figure 10-15 Configuring ripping options

6. Click Change to alter the Rip Music To This Location option. Set the new location as c:\ripped-music. You have to browse and create a new folder to complete this step.

7. In the Format drop-down list, select Windows Media Audio Pro.

8. Select the Copy Protect Music check box.

9. Select the Eject CD When Ripping Is Complete check box, and click OK.

10. In Windows Media Player, click the Start Rip button. If Windows Media Player cannot download media information for your CD, you can manually enter information. If you are presented with this dialog box, click OK, and then click Start Rip again.

11. Depending on the speed of your computer and the number and length of tracks on the album, the rip will take between 5 and 10 minutes.

12. When the rip has completed and the CD-ROM has been ejected, click Library on the Windows Media Player bar.

13. Click Recently Added, and verify that the audio tracks that you extracted are now in your library, as shown in Figure 10-16.

Figure 10-16   Newly ripped tracks in the music library

Lesson Summary

- The Windows Media Center feature is available only in Windows Vista Home Premium and Ultimate.
- With a TV Tuner Card, Windows Media Center can record, pause, and play back HDTV. Windows Media Center can also play back music, DVDs, and audio CDs and display digital photographs.
- A Windows Media Extender is a device that can be connected to a television and used to display content from a computer running Windows Media Center.
- Windows Media Player is available with all editions of Windows Vista.
- Windows Media Player can play back video files, audio files, DVDs, and audio CDs.
- Windows Media Player can rip data from audio CDs and import it into a media library, which can then be shared with compatible devices on the local network.

Lesson Review

You can use the following questions to test your knowledge of the information in Lesson 1, "Configuring and Troubleshooting Media Applications." The questions are also available on the companion CD if you prefer to review them in electronic form.

NOTE   Answers

Answers to these questions and explanations of why each answer choice is correct or incorrect are located in the "Answers" section at the end of the book.

1. Your friend has an Xbox 360 configured as a Media Center Extender for a desktop computer running Windows Vista Ultimate. The Xbox 360 is located on the ground floor of the house, and the Windows Vista computer is located on the house's third floor. Your friend wants to be able to view television shows recorded digitally on the Windows Vista computer automatically when he activates the Xbox 360. At present, he has to climb two flights of stairs to turn on the computer before he can return to the living room to view content through the extender. Which of the following configuration changes would you make to ensure that he does not need to manually activate the Windows Vista computer in this situation?

    A. Disable Away Mode.

    B. Enable Away Mode.

    C. Disable the screen saver.

    D. Configure the High Performance Power Plan.

2. Your friend is unable to browse the media folders on his PC from his Media Center Extender device located in his living room. Which of the following configuration changes should you make?

    A. Share the folders on the network.

    B. Alter the user account used by the Media Center Extender to access the media folders.

    C. Configure Extender Media Settings on the computer running Media Center to enable viewing of media folders.

    D. Configure Extender Media Settings on the Media Center Extender to enable viewing of media folders.

3. Although you have configured a limit that is currently less than the amount of free space available on the volume on which recordings are stored, you are concerned that you will not be able to record new programs because you have run out of hard disk drive space. You want Media Center to automatically delete programs that you have watched should you run out of disk space. Which Keep setting should you set in Media Center recording defaults?

    A. Until Space Needed

    B. For 1 Week

    C. Until I Watch

    D. Until I Delete

4. Kim wants to view several programs that she recorded using a TV tuner on the Windows Vista computer in her basement on the large plasma screen TV located in her living room. Kim has an Xbox 360 that is connected both to her home network and to the large TV in the living room. How can Kim view her recorded programs?

    A. Connect the Xbox 360 to the Windows Vista computer using an S-Video cable.

    B. Configure the Windows Vista computer to broadcast an HDTV signal through the TV Tuner.

    C. Configure the Xbox 360 as a Windows Media Center Extender.

    D. Configure the Windows Vista computer as a Windows Media Center Extender.

5. Ian wants to rip a DVD and add it to his media library. How can he accomplish this?

    A. He can rip the DVD using Windows Media Player or Windows Media Center.

    B. He can rip the DVD using Windows Media Player.

    C. He can rip the DVD using Windows Media Center.

    D. It is not possible to rip a DVD using Windows Media Player or Windows Media Center.

Lesson 2: Configuring Windows Fax and Scan

Windows Fax and Scan allows you to utilize a scanner and modem to create the functionality of a normal fax. Unlike previous versions of Windows, where Faxing and Scanning were separate applications, integrating both into one place simplifies the process of using your computer as a fax machine. Properly configured, Windows Fax and Scan allows people to stop using fax machines entirely, just as a properly configured computer with Windows Media Center can allow people to stop using DVD players and videocassette recorders.

After this lesson, you will be able to:
- Configure Windows Vista to send and receive faxes.

Estimated lesson time: 20 minutes

Setting Up Fax and Scan

To use the full functionality of Fax and Scan, a Windows Vista computer requires a modem and a scanner. It is possible to use Fax and Scan without either of these items if you do not need to transmit a hard copy document and a network fax server is available. Any modem that is compatible with Windows Vista can function as a fax modem. These fax modems can also be shared so that other computers on the network can send faxes using Fax and Scan.

Fax Accounts

The first step in setting up Fax and Scan is configuring a new fax account. You are asked to configure a fax account when you try to send your first fax. Or you can set one up by opening the Fax Accounts dialog box from the Tools menu. Each fax account allows you to configure a separate fax device. In general, this is done so that people who work with their Windows Vista mobile PCs are able to use a fax server when they are in the office and their fax modem when they are working remotely.

Multiple Fax Modems

If you have multiple fax modems installed on your computer, you can switch devices by opening up the Fax Settings dialog box and clicking the Select Fax Device button. This opens the Select Device dialog box, shown in Figure 10-17, which provides a drop-down list that lets you determine which device is used to send and receive faxes. This can be useful for people who usually use a land line to send and receive faxes but who find that they urgently need to send or receive a fax when they can connect only by using a compatible mobile phone.

Figure 10-17   The Select Device dialog box

Sending Faxes

There are three basic ways to send a fax using Windows Fax and Scan. After you have configured a fax account, a new printer with the name of the fax account becomes available in the Printers item in Control Panel. When using a normal Windows application like Microsoft Word, you can send a fax by printing a document to this printer, as shown in Figure 10-18. When you click OK, the New Fax dialog box is displayed. You enter the appropriate fax number or select an entry from Contacts that has the fax number configured, and you can send your fax. The second alternative is to click New Fax in Windows Fax and Scan, fill out the recipient's details, and then attach the document that you want to fax. The final option is to send a cover page fax. When you use this option, you do not attach a document but just edit the default cover page and add the message that you want to transmit.

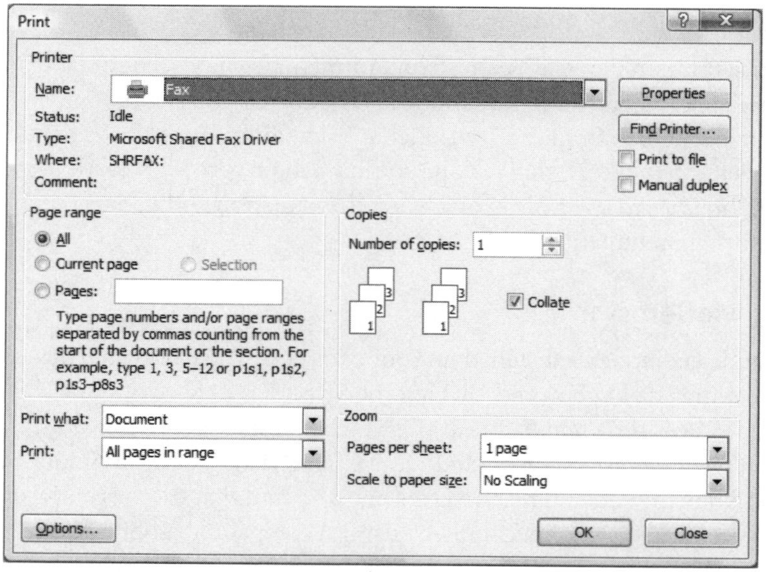

Figure 10-18   Printing to a fax

Configuring Scanners

Sometimes it is necessary to send a document using Fax and Scan that has not been entirely generated using an application running on your computer. For example, you might need to send a contract containing multiple signatures to a remote fax machine. You can do this only by using a scanner. When scanning faxes, remember that the resolution of faxes is significantly lower than that of normally printed documents. The low resolution of faxes allows them to be transmitted quickly across telephone lines using modems. If faxes had the same resolution as normal printer output, they would take much longer to transmit. For this reason, it is not necessary to scan documents that you want at the highest possible resolution, nor is it necessary to scan in color because faxes transmit in black and white.

Quick Check

1. What is the maximum number of fax accounts that you can configure if you have three fax modem devices connected to your computer?
2. How can you send a document that contains hand-written signatures using Fax and Scan?

Quick Check Answers

1. It is possible to configure only one fax account for local fax devices, even if multiple fax devices are connected to your computer.
2. You must first scan the document, and then you can fax it.

Receiving Faxes

There are two basic options for receiving faxes using Windows Fax and Scan. The first is to use the Manually Answer option. When this option is configured and an incoming call is detected, the computer's user is notified. The user can then choose to receive the fax. The second option is to have the computer automatically answer the call after a specified number of rings. Unless you share a voice line with a fax line, the second option is likely to be more useful. With the Manually Answer option, you must be present at your computer when the fax transmission occurs. This can be an issue if you are sent faxes when you are away from your computer. You configure these options by selecting Fax Settings from the Tools menu of Windows Fax and Scan.

Clicking the More Options button in the General tab of the Fax Settings dialog box brings up the More Options dialog box. From here, it is possible to configure the TSID and CSID settings and to specify what Fax and Scan should do when a fax is received. The identification settings are as follows:

- **TSID** Transmitting Subscriber Identification. This is the information about you that is sent to the fax machine that is receiving a fax you have sent.
- **CSID** Called Subscriber Identification. This is the identification information that is sent back to the person who is sending you a fax.

The other configurable options allow you to have each received a fax automatically printed to a printer that is already set up on your computer. It is also possible to save a separate copy of the incoming fax to another location. You might configure all incoming faxes to be saved to a server on the network if other people in the organization might need to see them.

Fax Options

The Fax Options dialog box, available by clicking Options in the Tools menu of Windows Fax and Scan, allows you to configure the sound that is played when a fax is received, whether the original message is included when a fax is replied to, and the font used with faxes for items such as the banner and the receipts setting. The Receipts settings, shown in Figure 10-19, allow you to have an e-mail sent to a configured address each time a fax is successfully transmitted. It is also possible to include a copy of the sent fax as an attachment, which can be useful for those organizations that need to meet legal requirements for data retention. If the Use One Receipt For Delivery To Multiple Recipients option is not selected, an e-mail receipt is sent for each separate destination number that the fax is transmitted to.

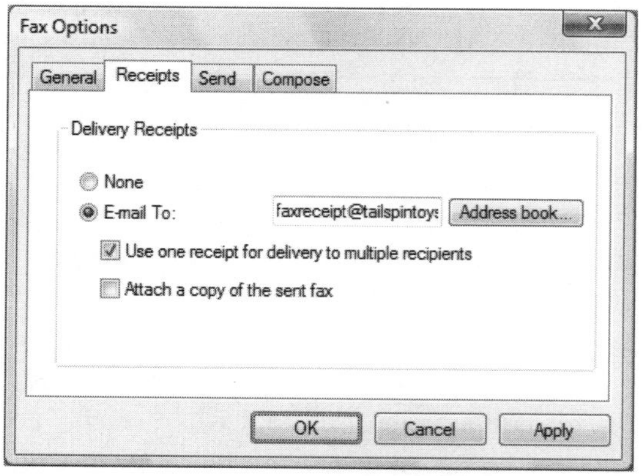

Figure 10-19   Using a receipt to confirm that a fax has been successfully transmitted

Advanced Fax Settings

If you have ever stood waiting at a heavily used office fax machine for the fax to redial after encountering a busy signal, you will appreciate Windows Fax and Scan's automatic redial option. Redialing allows Windows Fax and Scan to automatically reattempt transmission if the destination fax number is busy. Although traditional fax machines have this option, it can be tricky to configure, especially if there is a line of impatient workmates behind you who also want to use the fax!

To configure the number of redial attempts and the duration between attempts, open the Advanced tab of the Fax Settings dialog box from the Tools menu. This dialog box, shown in Figure 10-20, also allows you to configure transmission during periods when telephone charges are lower. This can be very helpful if the majority of the faxes that you send are to people in other states or other countries. The Advanced tab is also where you can configure whether the banner is included in all sent faxes. The banner is header text that is placed on each transmitted page and includes your TSID, the page number, and the recipient's fax number.

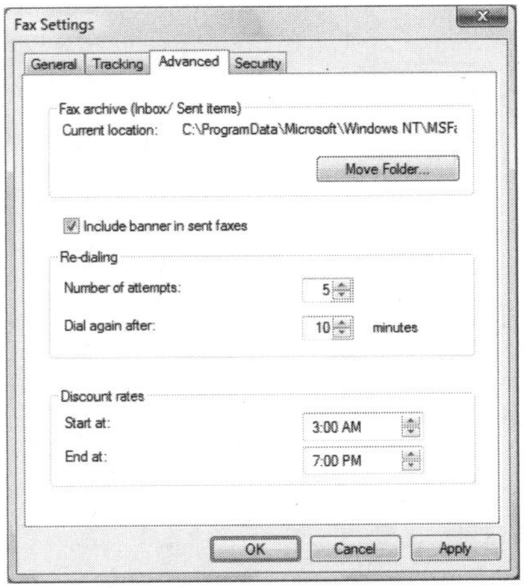

Figure 10-20   The Advanced tab of the Fax Settings dialog box

Practice: Setting up Windows Fax and Scan

In these practices, you will perform several configuration exercises using Windows Fax and Scan. The first configuration exercise is to set up a fax account, which is necessary prior to using Fax and Scan. The second configuration exercise involves configuring Fax and Scan to answer incoming calls after a preset number of rings and setting the fax's TSID and CSID settings.

▶ **Practice 1: Configuring a Fax Account**

In this practice, you will configure a fax account to be used with Windows Fax and Scan. It is necessary to create a fax account prior to sending or receiving faxes with Windows Fax and Scan. This practice requires your computer to have a modem. This practice can be completed on a computer with Windows Vista Business, Enterprise, or Ultimate. To complete the practice, perform the following steps:

1. Open Windows Fax and Scan.

2. On the Tools menu, click Fax Accounts. This brings up the Fax Accounts dialog box shown in Figure 10-21.

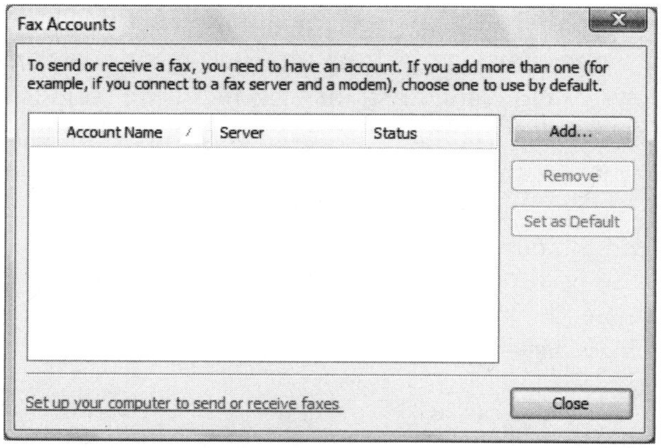

Figure 10-21   Configure a fax account for each fax device you use

3. Click Add.

4. On the Choose A Fax Modem Or Server page, click Connect To A Fax Modem.

5. On the Choose A Modem Name page, verify that the name Fax Modem is listed in the text box, and then click Next.

6. On the Choose How To Receive Faxes page, shown in Figure 10-22, click Notify Me.

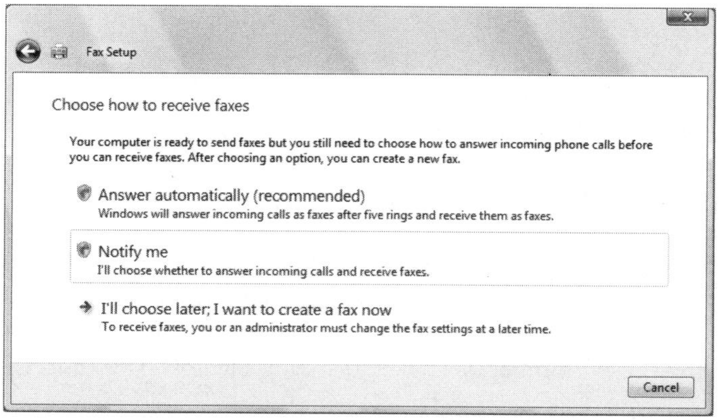

Figure 10-22   Select how to receive faxes

7. Click Continue in the User Account Control dialog box.

8. Click Close to close the Fax Accounts dialog box.

▶ **Practice 2: Configure Automatic Answering and Identification**

In this practice, you will configure the fax account that was configured in Practice 1 to automatically answer calls after 10 rings. To perform this practice, you need to have access to a fax modem attached to a Windows Vista computer and have completed Practice 1. To complete this practice, perform the following steps:

1. Open Windows Fax and Scan.
2. From the Tools menu, click Fax Settings.
3. Click Continue in the User Account Control dialog box.
4. In the Fax Settings dialog box, shown in Figure 10-23, select the Automatically Answer After option, and set the number of rings to 10.

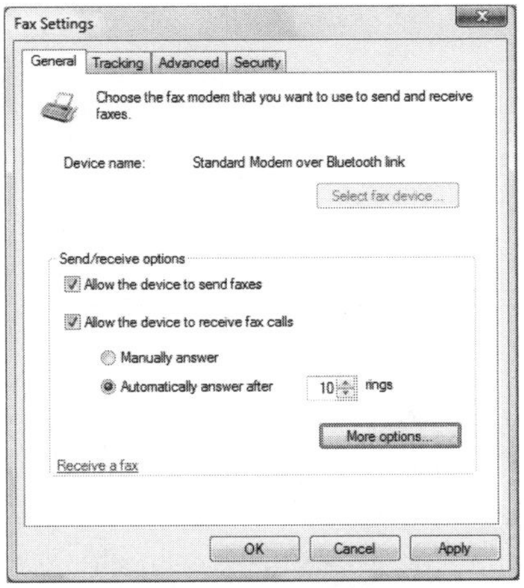

Figure 10-23   The Fax Settings dialog box

5. Click the More Options button to open the More Options dialog box.
6. In the TSID and CSID text boxes, enter **Tailspin Toys**.
7. Select the Print A Copy To box, and use the drop-down list to select Microsoft XPS Document Writer, as shown in Figure 10-24.

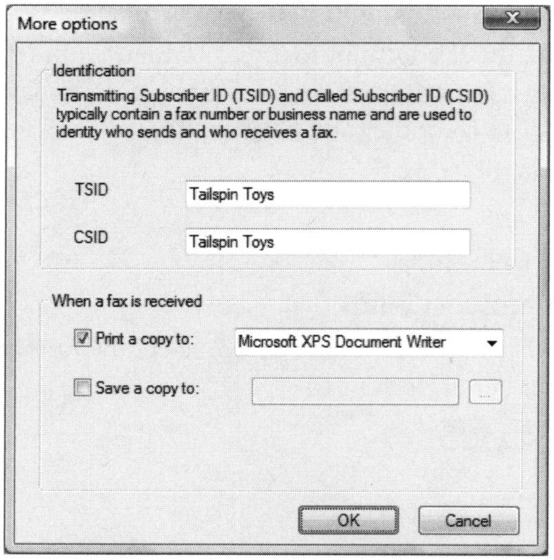

Figure 10-24   Configuring TSID and CSID settings

8. Click OK to close this dialog box.

Lesson Summary

- A fax account can be configured for all local fax modem devices or for network fax devices. The fax account determines the fax modem's answer settings.

- A fax device can be configured to send faxes or receive faxes, or both. A fax device can be configured to automatically answer an incoming call after a specific number of rings or to wait for the call to be manually received.

- You can configure a fax device to redial several times if the destination fax is busy. You can also configure a fax device to transmit faxes only when discount telephone rates are in effect.

- You can configure Fax and Scan to automatically output every received fax to a printer that Windows Vista is already configured to use. You can also configure Fax and Scan to e-mail a receipt and a copy of every successfully transmitted fax to a specified e-mail account.

- The CSID setting provides information to a transmitting fax about the receiver. The TSID setting provides information to a receiving fax about the sender. TSID information can be added to the header of all outgoing faxes using the Banner option.

Lesson Review

You can use the following questions to test your knowledge of the information in Lesson 2, "Configuring Windows Fax and Scan." The questions are also available on the companion CD if you prefer to review them in electronic form.

NOTE **Answers**

Answers to these questions and explanations of why each answer choice is correct or incorrect are located in the "Answers" section at the end of the book.

---

1. You are expecting a fax to arrive and have noted that your fax machine is out of ink. As a quick replacement, you hook up your Windows Vista Ultimate laptop to the phone line using the fax modem port. When the phone rings, you open Windows Fax and Scan for the first time but the fax is not received. What should you do to resolve the problem? (Choose two; each forms a part of the answer.)

    A. Configure the send/receive options to allow the device to send faxes.

    B. Configure modem properties.

    C. Configure a fax account.

    D. Configure the send/receive options to allow the device to receive faxes.

2. Your Windows Vista laptop has a built-in fax modem. Your mobile telephone has the ability to function as a Bluetooth modem, and you have already paired it with Windows Vista. When you are at home, you are able to send and receive faxes using the built-in modem. You are traveling to a conference and want to be able to send and receive faxes using your mobile telephone's Bluetooth modem functionality. What steps should you take to achieve this?

    A. Create a new fax account.

    B. Edit fax account properties.

    C. Use the Select Device option in Fax Settings.

    D. Delete the existing fax account.

3. Under which of the following conditions should you use more than one fax account?

    A. Your computer has a fax modem, and your office has a fax server.

    B. Your computer has more than one fax modem.

    C. You want to configure separate fax settings for each user.

    D. You want to share your fax modem with users on the network.

4. You want to ensure that a hard copy exists for each incoming fax received by your computer. What should you do?

   A. Configure Fax Settings.

   B. Configure Options.

   C. Configure fax account.

   D. Configure modem.

5. You want a record of each transmitted fax to be kept on a computer other than the one you use to send faxes with. Which of the following strategies should you pursue?

   A. Configure a receipt to be e-mailed after each fax transmission.

   B. Configure a receipt to be e-mailed after each fax is received.

   C. Include the banner in sent faxes.

   D. Configure the redialing options.

Lesson 3: Configuring Windows Sidebar

Windows Sidebar is a feature in all editions of Windows Vista that allows the display of useful information through gadgets. A gadget is a small application that displays information, such as the time, weather data, Really Simple Syndication (RSS) feed summaries, or Windows Vista performance information. You can configure the Sidebar to float above other windows on the Windows Vista desktop so that this information is always available, and you can configure gadgets with variable transparency so that it is possible to see the important information below them.

> **After this lesson, you will be able to:**
> - Configure Windows Sidebar properties.
> - Download, install, and configure gadgets.
>
> **Estimated lesson time: 20 minutes**

Configuring Sidebar Settings

You can configure Windows Sidebar from the Control Panel or by right-clicking the Sidebar and selecting Properties. This displays the Windows Sidebar Properties dialog box shown in Figure 10-25. This dialog box allows you to configure:

- Whether Windows Sidebar starts automatically when Windows Vista starts.
- Whether the Sidebar is displayed on top of all other windows. This does not make the Sidebar float above existing windows. Instead it reserves a certain amount of screen space for the Sidebar that maximized windows will not intrude upon. When it is configured this way, a minimized window can be dragged under the Sidebar.
- Which side of the screen Windows Sidebar is displayed on.
- Which monitor Windows Sidebar will be displayed on if more than one monitor is connected to Windows Vista.
- A list of running gadgets that you can view.

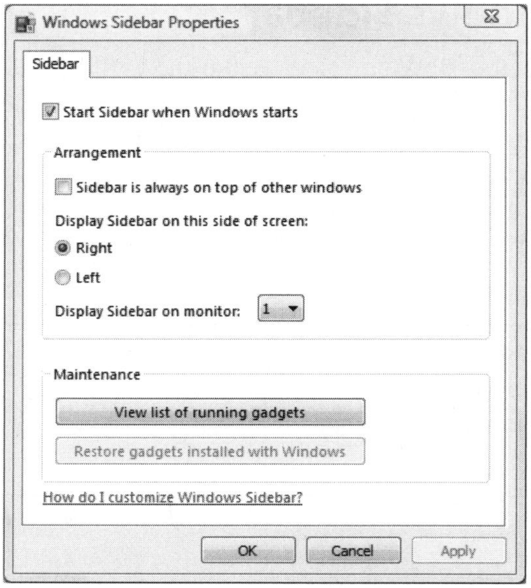

Figure 10-25   Windows Sidebar Properties

If youclick View List Of Running Gadgets, you see a list of all currently active gadgets that are on the Sidebar, as well as gadgets that have been detached and placed on the desktop. Selecting a gadget and then clicking Remove in this menu closes the gadget but does not uninstall the gadget from your computer. It is possible to uninstall gadgets only from the Gadget Gallery. If you close Windows Sidebar, you can open it again by clicking the Windows Sidebar item in the All Programs folder of the Start menu.

MORE INFO   Gadget hotkeys

To bring Windows Sidebar gadgets to the front, press the Windows key and the spacebar at the same time. To cycle through gadgets, press the Windows key and the G key at the same time.

Adding Gadgets to Windows Sidebar

Windows Vista ships with a set of default gadgets that you can add to Windows Sidebar. To add gadgets, click the plus sign on the top of the Sidebar. This opens the Gadget Gallery shown in Figure 10-26. You can drag a gadget from the gallery directly to the Windows Sidebar. Alternatively, double-clicking the gadget in the gallery automatically adds it to the Sidebar under other gadgets.

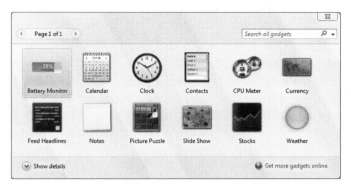

Figure 10-26 The gallery of gadgets included with Windows Vista

The gadgets included with Windows Vista represent only a fraction of those that are available. Clicking Get More Gadgets Online launches your web browser, allowing you to download gadgets from the online Gadget Gallery at *http://vista.gallery.microsoft.com/vista /SideBar.aspx?mkt=en-us*. Gadgets in the gallery are sorted by categories. It is important to note that most of these gadgets were created by the public, and although they are posted on Microsoft's website, Microsoft does not guarantee that they will work. You should always be careful when downloading any content from the Internet. Be especially careful of downloading free gadgets from websites other than Microsoft's. Once the gadget is downloaded and installed, it appears in the Gadget Gallery and can be added to Windows Sidebar.

It is possible to add more than one instance of a gadget. For example, you can configure Weather gadgets for Melbourne, Australia and Glasgow, Scotland. This can be especially useful if you need to work with people in other time zones. You simply add a Clock gadget for each separate time zone to the Sidebar. You can rearrange gadgets on the Sidebar by clicking the beveled area under the spanner icon and dragging the gadget into the appropriate position.

Quick Check

1. The Windows Sidebar appears on top of all windows. How can you change this?
2. What happens when you select a gadget from the list in the View Gadgets dialog box and click Remove?

Quick Check Answers

1. You can change whether the Windows Sidebar appears above all other windows by editing the Windows Sidebar Properties.
2. The gadget is removed from display. It is not uninstalled from the computer.

Configuring Gadgets

Each Windows Sidebar gadget has a set of properties that is unique to its function. For example, you can configure the Clock gadget with eight different appearances, with a particular name and a separate time zone, as shown in Figure 10-27. Alternatively, you might choose to use multiple instances of the Currency gadget to view the value of your native currency compared to that of countries where you travel. Or you might even configure multiple Weather gadgets so that you can see at a glance what the weather is like in distant cities where you have friends or family.

Figure 10-27   Using multiple clocks to display multiple time zones

Configuring Gadget Opacity

It is possible to configure a separate opacity for each Windows Sidebar gadget. Gadget opacity can be configured at 20%, 40%, 60%, 80%, and 100%. Varying gadget opacity is shown in Figure 10-28. Hovering the mouse over a Windows Sidebar gadget temporarily returns a gadget to full opacity. Gadget opacity is most useful if the Windows Sidebar is configured to always display on top of other windows. Configuring a low opacity allows you to view items below the gadgets, and you can bring a gadget you are interested in viewing to prominence by hovering the mouse over it.

Figure 10-28   Variable gadget opacity

Placing Gadgets on the Desktop

Placing Windows Sidebar Gadgets on the desktop allows you to keep gadgets without having Windows Sidebar running. Gadgets cannot directly be installed on the desktop but must be added to Windows Sidebar first and then dragged to an appropriate desktop position. An advantage of having gadgets on the desktop is that they can be displayed in their full size rather than their abbreviated site. For example, when displayed on the Sidebar, the Weather gadget shows only the current temperature, the location, and a picture of the weather. When detached to the desktop, the Weather gadget is larger and displays not only the current temperature but also the predicted temperature range and the three-day forecast, as shown in Figure 10-29.

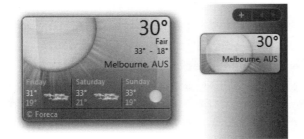

Figure 10-29   Detaching a Windows Sidebar gadget to the desktop to allow more information to be displayed

You can move detached Windows Sidebar gadgets by hovering the mouse over them until the side panel appears and then dragging them to a new position. If desired, it is possible to move detached Windows Sidebar gadgets back to the Sidebar. It is also possible to modify the properties of a detached gadget by right-clicking it. From this context menu, it is possible to alter the detached gadget's opacity. Detached gadgets are visible only when the area of the desktop on which they are located is visible, unless you have configured them to be always on top. Right-clicking the Windows Sidebar and clicking Bring Gadgets To Front also displays detached gadgets. If you close a detached Windows Sidebar Gadget, you can return the gadget to the desktop only by adding it again to the Windows Sidebar and then dragging it back onto the desktop.

Troubleshooting Gadgets

If a gadget displays the message "Service Unavailable," it is because the gadget is unable to contact the service it requires to display information. For example, the Weather gadget needs to be able to contact servers on the Internet. If your computer does not have Internet connectivity or the servers on the Internet are unavailable, the Weather gadget cannot display forecast information. Once connectivity is restored or the server that provides the information is returned to operational status, the gadget automatically begins to display the appropriate information.

If you uninstall a gadget from the Gadget Gallery, it is possible to restore it by opening Windows Sidebar Properties and clicking Restore Gadgets Installed With Windows. If the gadget that was uninstalled was downloaded from the Internet, it will be necessary to download it again.

Practice: Windows Sidebar and Gadgets

In these practices, you will perform several exercises that will familiarize you with the Windows Sidebar and the gadgets it can display. You can do this practice on a computer with any edition of Windows Vista installed, and it requires no other configuration.

▶ **Practice 1: Configure Windows Sidebar and Clock Gadgets**

In this practice, you will configure the Windows Sidebar to start when Windows Starts, ensure that the sidebar is displayed on top of other windows, add four separate clocks to the Windows Sidebar, and configure these clocks to use different time zone and display settings. To complete this practice, perform the following steps:

1. From the Start Menu, open Control Panel.
2. Ensure that Control Panel is set to Classic View, and open the Windows Sidebar Properties item.
3. Ensure that the Start Sidebar When Windows Starts check box is selected.
4. Select the Sidebar Is Always On Top Of Other Windows check box, and click OK.

5. Right-click the Sidebar, and select Add Gadgets.

6. Drag the Clock gadget to the Sidebar so that four clocks are present.

7. Right-click the second clock from the top of the Sidebar, and select Options. Enter the Clock name as Melbourne, click the arrows until clock 5 of 8 is displayed, and use the Time Zone drop-down list to select (GMT + 10:00) Canberra, Melbourne, Sydney. Click OK.

8. Right-click the third clock from the top of the Sidebar, and select Options. Enter the clock name as Glasgow, click the arrows until clock 8 of 8 is displayed, and use the Time Zone drop-down menu to select (GMT Greenwich Mean Time: Dublin, Edinburgh, Lisbon, London). Click OK.

9. Right-click the third clock from the top of the Sidebar, and select Options. Enter the Clock name as Tonga, click the arrows until clock 7 of 8 is displayed, and use the Time Zone drop-down menu to select (GMT+13:00) Nuku'alofa. Click OK.

▶ **Practice 2: Desktop Gadgets and Transparency Settings**

In this practice, you move gadgets to the desktop and adjust their transparency settings. The gadgets that you move were configured in Practice 1. To complete this practice, perform the following steps:

1. Drag the Clock gadget that displays the time in Melbourne and the Clock gadget that displays the time in Glasgow from the Windows Sidebar to the desktop.

2. Right-click the Clock gadget that displays the time in Melbourne and, using the Opacity menu, select a value of 60%.

3. Right-click the Clock gadget that displays the time in Glasgow and, using the Opacity menu, select a value of 40%.

4. Hover the mouse over each gadget. Notice how each gadget reverts to full opacity when the mouse is above it and reverts to the configured opacity when the mouse is moved away.

Lesson Summary

- The Windows Sidebar is used to host gadgets. The Windows Sidebar can be configured to appear above all other windows on the desktop.
- Gadgets are mini-applications that are used to display information. They are usually positioned on the Windows Sidebar but can also be positioned on the desktop.
- Opacity is configured on a per-gadget basis.
- The Gadget Gallery is a collection of all currently installed gadgets.
- Gadgets originally installed with Windows and deleted from the Gadget Gallery can be restored by using the Restore Gadgets button in Windows Sidebar Properties.

- Gadgets downloaded from the Internet and then deleted from the Gadget Gallery must be reacquired from the Internet.

- Gadgets removed from the Windows Sidebar or Desktop are not deleted. The only way to delete a gadget is to remove it from the Gadget Gallery.

Lesson Review

You can use the following questions to test your knowledge of the information in Lesson 3, "Configure Windows Sidebar." The questions are also available on the companion CD if you prefer to review them in electronic form.

NOTE Answers

Answers to these questions and explanations of why each answer choice is correct or incorrect are located in the "Answers" section at the end of the book.

1. What steps can you take to ensure that gadgets that have been added to the Windows Sidebar are always visible?
   A. Configure gadget opacity.
   B. Configure Sidebar opacity.
   C. Configure gadget properties.
   D. Configure Sidebar properties.

2. Kim has removed the default Clock and Calendar gadgets from the Windows Sidebar. What steps must she take to replace them?
   A. Download and install the gadgets from the Internet. Drag them to the Windows Sidebar.
   B. Drag the gadgets from the Gadget Gallery to the Windows Sidebar.
   C. Open the Windows Sidebar Properties, and click Restore Gadgets Installed With Windows. Drag the gadgets from the Gadget Gallery to the Windows Sidebar.
   D. Use Programs and Features to reinstall Sidebar gadgets. Drag the gadgets from the Gadget Gallery to the Windows Sidebar.

3. You have accidentally deleted two gadgets from the Gadget Gallery that you downloaded from the Internet. How can you restore these gadgets?
   A. Download the gadgets again from the Internet.
   B. Open the gadgets from the Windows Sidebar.
   C. Use the Restore Gadgets button in Windows Sidebar Properties.
   D. Refresh the Gadget Gallery.

4. You are finding it difficult to view several of the gadgets on the Windows Sidebar. When you move the mouse over the gadgets, they appear normally, but when you move the mouse elsewhere, they appear faded. How can you resolve this problem?

    A. Configure each gadget's opacity settings.

    B. Configure the Windows Sidebar opacity settings.

    C. Configure the Windows Theme opacity settings.

    D. Configure the Gadget Gallery opacity settings.

5. While viewing a list of running gadgets through Windows Sidebar Properties, you accidentally click Remove when a gadget you have downloaded from the Internet is selected. How can you restore this gadget to the Windows Sidebar?

    A. Drag the gadget from the Gadget Gallery to the Windows Sidebar.

    B. Use the Restore Gadgets option, and then drag the gadget from the Gadget Gallery to the Windows Sidebar.

    C. Download the gadget from the Internet, and then drag the gadget from the Gadget Gallery to the Windows Sidebar.

    D. Drag the gadget from the Recycle Bin to the Windows Sidebar.

Chapter Review

To further practice and reinforce the skills you learned in this chapter, you can perform the following tasks:

- Review the chapter summary.
- Review the list of key terms introduced in this chapter.
- Complete the case scenarios. These scenarios set up real-world situations involving the topics of this chapter and ask you to create a solution.
- Complete the suggested practices.
- Take a practice test.

Chapter Summary

- Windows Media Center is available in the Home Premium and Ultimate editions of Windows Vista. You can use the application to watch or record live television broadcasts in standard or high definition. Media Center can also play DVDs, audio CDs, and other digital media. Media Center can be used to watch television only if a TV tuner card is present and connected to a digital source, such as an antenna, satellite, direct cable, or set top box.
- It is possible to put ratings-based restrictions on DVD playback and to burn recorded TV to DVD using Media Center. A Windows Media Center Extender is a device that connects to Windows Media Center through a network and can display Media Center Content.
- Windows Media Player can be used to rip audio CDs to copy-protected digital audio format. It is sometimes necessary to obtain rights to play digital content. Content in the Media Player library can be shared with other Media Player compatible devices.
- Windows Fax and Scan allows you to send and receive faxes using your Windows Vista Business, Enterprise, or Ultimate edition computer. A fax account can be configured for all local fax devices or a network fax server. A fax device can be configured to automatically or manually receive incoming faxes and to print them out to a configured printer.

Key Terms

Do you know what these key terms mean? You can check your answers by looking up the terms in the glossary at the end of the book.

- Away Mode
- Called Subscriber Identification (CSID)

- Digital Rights Management (DRM)
- Media Center Extender
- rip
- Transmitting Subscriber Identification (TSID)

Case Scenarios

In the following case scenarios, you will apply what you have learned about configuring applications included with Windows Vista. You can find answers to these questions in the "Answers" section at the end of this book.

Case Scenario 1: Family Media Center Extender

Your family has two children aged five and nine. You have installed a computer running Windows Vista Home Premium in your living room and connected it to your large widescreen TV. TV tuning, DVDs, and TV recording are all displayed through Windows Media Center.

1. The five-year-old child has a favorite cartoon that you have configured Windows Media Center to regularly record. Unfortunately, the cartoon sometimes starts a few minutes earlier than the scheduled time. How can you ensure that the cartoon is recorded in its entirety each week?

2. You have added a removable hard disk drive to store digital media for Media Center. How can you ensure that the media stored here is available to Media Center users?

3. How can you ensure that the nine-year-old child is unable to play violent DVDs?

Case Scenario 2: Home Office Fax Solution

You use your Windows Vista Ultimate computer in your home office. You frequently send and receive faxes using Windows Fax and Scan. You want to make several configuration changes.

1. How can you ensure that the computer automatically answers fax calls after 10 rings?

2. You want to ensure that the TSID is printed on every page sent from Windows Fax and Scan. How can you ensure that this is done?

3. You want to ensure that a record is kept of each fax that is transmitted using Windows Fax and Scan. How can you achieve this?

Suggested Practices

To help you successfully master the exam objectives presented in this chapter, complete the following tasks.

Configure and Troubleshoot Media Applications

■ **Practice 1: Parental Restrictions**   Configure a code that must be entered by Media Center users to bypass parental restrictions.

Configure a restriction on the playback of DVDs that disallows all unrated content and all content not suitable for people under 18.

■ **Practice 2: DVD Options**   Configure closed captioning options for DVD playback so that captions are displayed when Media Center is muted.

Configure DVD remote control options.

■ **Practice 3: Ripping Options**   Use Windows Media Player to rip music at different qualities. Compare the difference by playing back tracks ripped at different qualities using your computer.

Attempt to play a track that you have ripped with copy protection on another computer.

Configure Windows Fax and Scan

■ **Practice 1: Change Fax Archive Location**   Change the fax archive location to c:\FaxArchive.

■ **Practice 2: Configure E-Mail Receipts**   Configure a delivery receipt to be e-mailed to faxreceipt@wingtiptoys.com for each fax sent.

Configure Windows Sidebar

■ **Practice 1: Download and Install More Gadgets**   Download a gadget from each of the following categories, and place it on the Windows Sidebar:

❑ Fun And Games

❑ Lifestyle

❑ Techy, Geeky, Cool

❑ Tools And Utilities

■ **Practice 2: Configure Opacity**   Drag three of the gadgets you downloaded in Practice 1 to the desktop, and set their opacity to 60%.

Add a second copy of each of the gadgets that you moved to the desktop to the Windows Sidebar.

Use the Windows+G keys to cycle through available gadgets.

Take a Practice Test

The practice tests on this book's companion CD offer many options. For example, you can test yourself on just one exam objective, or you can test yourself on all the 70-620 certification exam content. You can set up the test so that it closely simulates the experience of taking a certification exam, or you can set it up in study mode so that you can look at the correct answers and explanations after you answer each question.

MORE INFO **Practice tests**

For details about all the practice test options available, see the "How to Use the Practice Tests" section in this book's Introduction.

Chapter 11
Maintaining and Optimizing Windows Vista

Windows Vista offers a considerable number of features designed to enhance user experience, of which the Aero user interface is probably the most obvious example. Many other enhancements, particularly to security, work in the background invisible to the user. Microsoft has announced that Windows Vista contains more than 500 new features and enhancements.

It would be surprising if this number of enhancements came with no cost to overall performance. A user with a new Windows Vista-capable computer that has a reasonable specification is unlikely to notice any problems. If, however, you are supporting users who have upgraded from Microsoft Windows XP to Windows Vista, such users might report poorer performance—particularly if their computers are at the lower end of the hardware specification. A computer with 512 megabytes (MB) of random access memory (RAM) can run Windows XP quite happily, provided that the user does not run any high-end graphics applications. Such a computer will not be comfortable running Windows Vista.

Users do not expect a drop in performance when their machines have been upgraded—in fact, they expect the new operating system (OS) to make things smoother and faster. Managers are unlikely to be responsive to requests for hardware upgrades when they have just spent money on an OS upgrade. Home users are even less likely to be pleased about needing to buy more memory or a new graphics card. Fortunately, Windows Vista provides tools for tuning and optimizing performance and diagnosing reliability problems. This chapter discusses these tools.

Exam objectives in this chapter:
- Troubleshoot performance issues.
- Troubleshoot reliability issues by using built-in diagnostic tools.

Lessons in this chapter:

Before You Begin

To complete the lessons in this chapter, you must have done the following:

- Installed Windows Vista Ultimate on a personal computer, as described in Chapter 1, "Installing Windows Vista Client," and Chapter 2, "Windows Vista Upgrades and Migrations."

- Created an administrator account and standard accounts and enabled the Run command on the Start menu, as described in Practices 1, 2, and 3 of Lesson 1, "Configuring and Troubleshooting Parental Controls and Content Advisor," in Chapter 4, "Configuring and Troubleshooting Internet Access."

- Internet access is required for some of the practices.

- You need a USB 2.0 flash memory pen drive that supports ReadyBoost (almost all modern devices do) and a second flash drive that does not support ReadyBoost (less than 256 MB free) to carry out the practice session in Lesson 1.

Real World

Ian McLean

The first computer with which I came in contact in 1958 (I was 11 years old) had one kilobit of core store memory. You could see the individual magnetized cores. I counted them one day and there were 1024 of them. Having learned about the binary numbering system only a week before, I was rather pleased with this number. The computer filled a room and had lots of flashing lights, whirring tape drives, chattering line printers, and noisy Hollerith card readers. It impressed senior managers and visiting dignitaries.

The first computer of my own that I considered a professional machine had 32 MB of memory and a 250-MB hard disk. It was a Pentium 1 machine—P90 to be precise. I upgraded to 64 MB of RAM and added a second 1-GB disk. Colleagues thought I was crazy (they still do). Who could possibly need a whole gigabyte of hard disk space?

This was not an inconsiderable machine. I used it at a high level to run advanced courses in a well-known computer-aided vector graphics drawing package for professionals who used this software every day. The computer ran Microsoft Windows 95 and Microsoft Office 4.0 and did not break down once in 10 years. It was short on flashing lights, although the unbelievably fast 56 Kbps modem did make a most satisfactory noise when connecting to the Internet.

I now carry four times the total amount of storage that was on that computer on a universal serial bus (USB) flash memory pen in my inside pocket. This device makes no sound and is distinctly under-provisioned when it comes to flashing lights. I hardly ever show it to visiting dignitaries. In this chapter, I'm about to describe a laptop with 512 MB of RAM as a low-specification computer.

The point is that no matter how wildly you try to overestimate future technology advances, you will probably underestimate. But you can't sit on your hands and refuse to update until the next new gizmo comes on the market. That way lies stagnation and commercial disaster. At the same time, I often wonder whether a modern PC, technically wonderful though it is, will ever be quite as useful as my old P90. And if I want to impress senior management, I'm sure I can find a first generation computer with lots of flashing lights and whirring tape drives somewhere.

Lesson 1: Troubleshooting Performance Issues

Technology typically provides the answer to performance problems. Windows Vista-specific hardware, such as DirectX 10–compliant video cards and solid state or hybrid hard disks, will in the future (possibly by the time you read this book) provide significant improvements in Windows Vista performance. In the meantime, the tools provided by the Performance Information and Tools feature help you diagnose the areas where performance is less than optimal and to tune for best performance.

Where RAM is a bottleneck—and it frequently is—the new ReadyBoost feature makes use of considerable advances in USB and flash memory technology to provide a quick, easy, and inexpensive method to increase performance that is virtually foolproof and does not require technical knowledge or administrator privileges. This chapter looks at the tools Windows Vista provides for diagnosing bottlenecks and tuning performance and at how you, and the users you support, can use ReadyBoost to solve problems caused by insufficient RAM and excessive paging.

NOTE   Do not disable Aero

If a computer's hardware and OS is capable of supporting Aero—that is, the OS is not Windows Vista Starter or Windows Vista Home Basic—and the computer has a compatible graphics processor, you will get better performance with Aero enabled. Aero performs onscreen rendering and processing in the graphics processing unit (GPU), which frees your system's microprocessor for other tasks. This applies even if your graphics card uses shared RAM. The shared memory will still be allocated to the graphics adapter regardless of whether you are using Aero or not. The Aero rendering process is also inherently more reliable than a software renderer.

> **After this lesson, you will be able to:**
> - Use the features provided by the Performance Information and Tools feature to diagnose problems and tune performance.
> - Use the ReadyBoost feature to improve system performance.
> - Address problems that cause slow startup or shutdown or that cause programs to hang.
> - Explain the advantages of hybrid and solid state hard disk drives and prepare a technical case for using such devices.
>
> **Estimated lesson time: 50 minutes**

Implementing ReadyBoost

ReadyBoost uses spare space on USB-based storage devices—flash memory, for example—to improve computer performance. It does this by caching information to the USB device, which is typically faster than writing to a swap file on the hard disk drive. Information cached to the device is encrypted, so it cannot be read on other systems. The memory must be fast flash, and the computer needs a USB 2.0 port.

Swap File

A swap file is hard disk space used to extend RAM, and it allows your computer's OS to operate as if the computer has more RAM than it actually does. The least recently used files in RAM can be swapped out, or paged, to your hard disk until they are needed later and new files can be paged into RAM.

An advantage of a swap file is that it can be organized as a single contiguous space so that fewer input/output (I/O) operations are required to read or write a complete file. The disadvantage is that it takes time for a standard hard disk to access virtual memory. If a computer's memory is not sufficient for a memory-intensive operation, this can lead to excessive paging to hard disk and a consequent drop in performance.

Windows Vista (and other Windows OSs) provides a swap file, known as virtual memory, with default initial and maximum sizes. An administrator can reconfigure virtual memory size. The swap file is also known as the page file or paging file.

Configuring a Flash Memory Device for ReadyBoost

The user inserts a suitable flash memory device (typically, but not necessarily, a USB device) into a Windows Vista computer. The Autoplay dialog box appears, giving the user the option either to use the device to store files or to speed up the system. On choosing the second option, the user then needs to specify, in the ReadyBoost tab of the device's Properties dialog box, that Windows Vista should use the device for this purpose and how much flash memory it should allocate. By default, Windows Vista allocates 95 percent of free space on a flash memory device for ReadyBoost. Microsoft recommends configuring ReadyBoost with one to three times the amount of RAM that is installed in the system. So if a computer has 512 MB of RAM, the user should dedicate between 512 MB and 1.5 gigabytes (GB) of space for ReadyBoost. ReadyBoost recommends the ideal amount, based on the capacity of the device and the system's RAM. You enable ReadyBoost in the practice session later in this lesson.

NOTE Using the device's Properties dialog box

If the flash memory device is already connected or Autoplay is disabled, you can enable Ready-Boost by opening the device's Properties dialog box and selecting the ReadyBoost tab. If you want to disable ReadyBoost on a flash memory device, you can access the same tab and select Do Not Use This Device.

A user does not require elevated privileges to implement ReadyBoost. The operation can be completed in three mouse clicks if the default memory allocation is accepted. There is no requirement to open the computer's case and plug-in memory, and no technical knowledge is required. You can use ReadyBoost to improve performance on computers that already have the maximum amount of RAM that their motherboards allow installed. Flash memory not used for ReadyBoost can be used to store files. You can safely remove the USB device from the computer, if necessary, with no degradation of the computer's original performance, although the benefit of ReadyBoost would, of course, be lost.

Some Facts About ReadyBoost

The following information was extracted from answers given by Matt Ayers, the program manager in the Microsoft Windows Client Performance group, to questions about Ready-Boost. This appeared in a blog (online diary) written by Tom Archer, the program manager for the Windows Software Development Kit (SDK) Tools and Build Environment. The current URL is *http://blogs.msdn.com/tomarcher/archive/2006/06/02/615199.aspx*, but it is uncertain how long this will be available.

- ReadyBoost needs fast, consistent flash random performance memory—2.5 MB/sec throughput for 4 KB random reads and 1.75 MB/sec throughput for 512 KB random writes. Some devices have fast sequential performance but slow random performance. Other devices have 128 KB fast flash memory, but the rest is slow.

- You can use up to 4 GB of flash memory for ReadyBoost. This limitation is caused by FAT32 file system limits. The smallest flash memory cache you can use is 235 MB—which means you can use some, but not all, 256 MB devices, although larger capacities are recommended.

- ReadyBoost does not put the paging file on to flash memory. In fact, you cannot allocate ReadyBoost flash memory as virtual memory. ReadyBoost Memory is cache. The paging file is still stored on disk. If the data is not found in the Ready-Boost cache, Windows Vista reads it from the hard disk drive. ReadyBoost reduces paging because it increases the amount of RAM the system can use for caching, but ReadyBoost cache memory is not virtual memory.

- If a user pulls the ReadyBoost USB flash memory device out of the computer, Windows Vista does not crash but instead finds the information it needs on the hard disk. All pages on the USB device are backed by a page on disk. ReadyBoost is not a page-file store but rather a cache to speed up access to frequently used data.

- Everything that is written to a ReadyBoost device is encrypted by using the AES-128 algorithm. ReadyBoost is not a security risk.

- You can use only one ReadyBoost device per machine. This might change in future editions of Windows Vista. You can use some memory cards on internal buses for ReadyBoost, but you cannot currently use external card readers. USB hard disk drives (HDDs) are not (currently) fast enough for ReadyBoost, and there is in any case no benefit to using a USB HDD for ReadyBoost. MP3 players do not support ReadyBoost.

- Microsoft is currently working with manufacturers to create a program that will allow them to identify ReadyBoost-capable devices on their packaging. However, it is likely that most flash memory devices coming on the market will support ReadyBoost.

ReadyBoost Considerations

The main caveat is that flash memory used for ReadyBoost cannot be used for storing files. It is possible that an unsophisticated user might implement ReadyBoost by accident and be unable to store files on the flash drive. However, the default selection in the Properties dialog box is not to use the device for ReadyBoost, so the likelihood of a user's enabling ReadyBoost by accident is greatly reduced. Even if it does happen, enabling ReadyBoost does not delete any files on the device; nor is the USB device damaged by accidentally enabling ReadyBoost. You might need to assist the user to move his or her files to another storage device and reformat the flash memory, although given the current low price of such devices this might not be worth the effort.

In any case, if a flash memory device used for ReadyBoost does fail, nothing much is broken. The computer still works, although a bit more slowly. The user needs only to plug in another inexpensive device and configure it for ReadyBoost with three mouse clicks. However, with this in mind, it is probably a good idea to discourage your users from saving valuable files on the same device they use for ReadyBoost. It is also a good idea to persuade users to back up any valuable files, but, as any administrator knows, this is not an easy thing to do.

NOTE   Not all flash memory devices support ReadyBoost

Not all flash memory devices are fast enough to support ReadyBoost, and if you use a USB device, the computer must have a USB 2.0 port. You might need to explain to users you support that even some relatively new flash memory devices do not support sufficiently fast random performance for ReadyBoost or are a combination of fast and slow flash memory.

Quick Check

- You want to implement ReadyBoost on a computer running Windows Vista. The computer has 750 MB of RAM installed. Following Microsoft's recommendations, how much flash memory should you dedicate for this purpose?

Quick Check Answer

- Microsoft recommends dedicating between one and three times the capacity of the installed RAM—in this case, from 750 MB through 2.25 GB of RAM. You can dedicate more or less flash memory if you want to. The minimum amount of free space you need in flash memory is 235 MB. The maximum you can use is 4 GB.

A flash memory device that uses ReadyBoost to improve performance on a computer can improve performance only on that computer. You cannot plug it into another computer and expect it to automatically boost that machine's performance.

MORE INFO   USB flash memory

It is difficult to find authoritative documentation about USB flash memory without encountering large quantities of manufacturers' hype. You can find information by searching the Internet and accessing sites such as *http://www.intel.com/design/flash/articles/what.htm* and *http://www.pcdoctor-guide.com/wordpress/?page_id=408*. For more information about USB, access *http://support .microsoft.com/?kbid=822603* and *http://www.microsoft.com/whdc/system/bus/usb/default.mspx*.

Improving Performance with ReadyBoost

ReadyBoost works best on computers with limited memory. You will obtain a more significant improvement adding ReadyBoost flash memory to a computer with 512 MB of memory than to a high-specification workstation with 4 GB of RAM. A computer that has a limited amount of RAM needs to page information more often into and out of its swap file on hard disk. Ready-Boost flash memory provides a cache that reduces the need for paging and is therefore particularly effective on computers where RAM resource is a bottleneck.

As previously stated, Microsoft recommends configuring ReadyBoost with one to three times the amount of RAM you have installed in your system. So if you have 512 MB of RAM, you should try to dedicate between 512 MB and 1.5 GB of space for ReadyBoost on a flash memory device.

Chapter 3, "Troubleshooting Post-Installation System Settings," described the Windows Experience Index available from the Performance Information and Tools feature. If you are not familiar with this feature, you can access it by opening Control Panel, clicking System And Maintenance, and then clicking Performance Information And Tools. Figure 11-1 shows a Windows Experience Index analysis for a low-specification laptop with 512 MB of memory. Unsurprisingly, a low score is returned. However, you need to analyze the results with care. The lowest index score is for gaming graphics, which is not relevant because the PC is not used for gaming or 3D graphics.

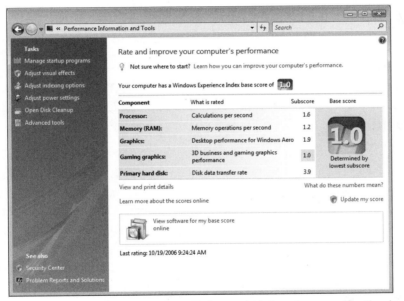

Figure 11-1   Windows Experience Index analysis for a low-specification laptop computer

A more significant figure is the 1.2 score for Memory (RAM). You can carry out problem analysis on a PC by clicking Advanced Tools in the Performance Information And Tools dialog box and then clicking Generate A System Health Report. Click Continue in the User Account Control dialog box. Figure 11-2 shows a system health report for the same low-specification laptop indicating that inadequate RAM is a major problem. In the practice session later in this chapter you use the ReadyBoost feature to improve the performance of a computer whose performance is limited by low RAM.

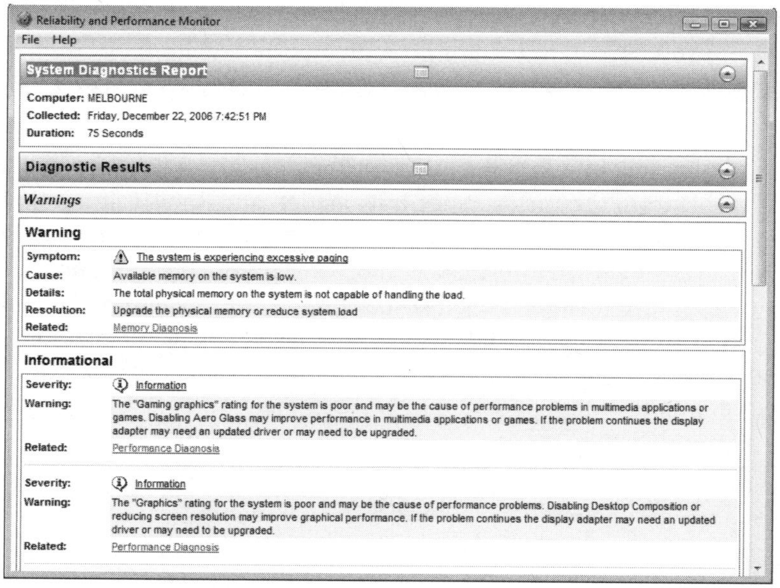

Figure 11-2   System Diagnostics Report for a low-specification laptop computer

Real World

Ian McLean

The first time I rebooted my laptop after configuring a USB flash memory device for ReadyBoost, I experienced a few moments of panic. The machine seemed to be completely dead. Fortunately, I noticed the light-emitting diode (LED) on my USB pen drive flashing and worked out what was happening. Instead of the noise of my hard disk drive thrashing about looking for files, the computer was silently finding the same files in flash memory. The screen soon lit up and all was well.

This demonstrated that ReadyBoost was working and also made me realize just how noisy the boot-up cycle on my computer previously had been. However, it is something you should warn your more nervous users about and be aware of yourself. Be prepared for support calls that start "it's completely dead" and continue "oh, it's working now." If ReadyBoost is implemented, you might also get calls from users reporting delays following logon. Although ReadyBoost improves overall performance, it can cause post-logon delays while Windows Vista copies information to ReadyBoost flash memory.

Transfer Rate Considerations

Flash memory is not as fast as RAM. It has a reasonable read speed but a slower write speed. The transfer rate for even fast flash is comparable with that of a good mechanical disk drive. The USB 2.0 standard offers a data transfer rate up to 480 Mbps. In practice, a USB flash memory device seldom achieves that speed and peaks at about 300 Mbps. An internal fiber channel hard disk drive can achieve a data transfer rate in excess of 200 Mbps, external FireWire hard disk drives claim data transfer speeds of up to 400 Mbps, and 7200 rpm Serial Advanced Technology Attachment (SATA) drives can hit data transfer speeds of almost 500 Mbps. Manufacturers appear to be constantly announcing new technologies and faster drives.

Where flash memory wins out is in access time. A disk head on a mechanical actuator takes time to find the correct position on the disk platter before data reading and writing can occur. Access to data on flash memory is, in comparison, instantaneous.

Microsoft has designed ReadyBoost very carefully. If flash memory were used for all operations that would otherwise require paging to hard disk, then the slower write performance of flash would reduce the effectiveness of the technique. Also, flash memory has a limited life in terms of read and write cycles, particularly write cycles. A system program can write to memory thousands of times per second and could dramatically reduce the life of a flash memory device. Rather than being used for general paging, ReadyBoost flash memory holds files that change seldom but are read many times. This results in significant performance gains with very little reduction in device life. In Microsoft's judgment a flash memory device used for ReadyBoost should last for approximately 10 years—although this has yet to be tested.

Page-File vs. Solid State Hard Disk Drive

Rather than implementing ReadyBoost, you can use the flash memory device to hold the page file. Lesson 2, "Troubleshooting Reliability Issues by Using Built-In Diagnostic Tools," describes how to configure virtual memory. In addition to moving virtual memory to a second hard disk, you can also allocate flash memory for this purpose, provided this flash memory has not already been allocated to ReadyBoost. Currently there is very little advantage to doing this, and there are several disadvantages. Flash memory used in this fashion does not boost performance as much as ReadyBoost and might not boost performance at all if the computer is paging large contiguous files. Using flash memory to hold the paging file can significantly reduce the life of the flash memory device and (unlike ReadyBoost) you can, and probably will, lose data if the device is removed while the computer is working.

However, hybrid and solid state storage devices with built-in RAM (as opposed to plug-in USB flash memory) could change this situation. We shall therefore look briefly at these technologies.

Hybrid Hard Disk Drives

Like many features that look like the answer we have all been waiting for when they are first introduced, ReadyBoost might be overtaken by other technologies. Hybrid hard disk drives (H-HDDs)—for example, the Samsung H-HDD or the Gigabyte i-RAM Storage Device—offer a combination of mechanical hard disk and RAM. In some cases, the solid state memory is synchronous dynamic RAM (SDRAM) and requires battery backup when the computer is switched off, while others—for example, the Samsung devices—use flash memory so that information is not lost in the case of battery failure.

Windows Vista's ReadyDrive feature takes advantage of H-HDD technology by using the built-in RAM to intercept data and then dispatching data to the hard disk for long-term storage. ReadyDrive improves battery life in laptops by reducing mechanical hard disk usage and enables faster recovery from the Sleep stage.

MORE INFO   ReadyDrive

For more information about ReadyDrive (and a very nice Microsoft PowerPoint presentation), access *http://download.microsoft.com/download/5/b/9/5b97017b-e28a-4bae-ba48-174cf47d23cd /STO008_WH06.ppt*.

However, H-HDDs are likely to be fitted as standard only on high-range workstations (until the price falls, as it almost certainly will). Most H-HDDs require Windows Vista as the client OS. On lower-specification client computers, and on older machines that have been upgraded from XP to Windows Vista, ReadyBoost provides a quick, easy, and inexpensive method of boosting performance.

MORE INFO   Hard disk speeds and H-HDDs

For more information about data transfer rates, access *http://www.pcwatch.com/QB/hard_disk /hard_disk.htm* and *http://www.pcmag.com/article2/0,1759,1046951,00.asp*. For more information about H-HDDs, access *http://www.samsung.com/Products/HardDiskDrive/whitepapers /WhitePaper_12.htm*.

Solid State Hard Disk

Although H-HDDs represent a significant advance in technology, they are generally seen as an interim solution. The explosion in compact MP3 players has led to a demand for inexpensive, reliable, high-capacity solid-state storage devices. Currently, 4 GB flash memory devices are common, and up to 64 GB are available. However, although larger capacity and faster flash memory devices might be the technology that provides solid state drives (SDDs), nobody can guarantee what the future will bring. Some other technology—for example, Phase-change Random Access Memory (PRAM)—might (and probably will) implement SSDs in the near future—possibly even by the time you are reading this book.

One thing is certain—expensive and unreliable mechanical devices will be phased out in future computers. Soon the only moving part will be the fan, and possibly future devices will be so efficient and generate so little heat that not even the fan will be needed.

MORE INFO   Solid state disks and PRAM

For more information about SSDs, access *http://www.tfot.info/content/view/100/*. For more information about PRAM, access *http://www.samsung.com/PressCenter/PressRelease /PressRelease.asp?seq=20060911_0000286481*.

Using Performance Information and Tools to Troubleshoot Performance Issues

The left pane of the Performance Information And Tools dialog box lists facilities that can help you tune the performance of those computers for which you are responsible. Elevated privileges are required to use some of the features. Standard users can use other features provided they are tuning only their own user experience. Adjusting settings for other users on the same computer requires elevated privileges.

However, unless your users are fairly sophisticated, you will probably be asked for your advice and support even for those tasks that do not require elevated privileges. Sometimes the implications of settings are not obvious, and many users are reluctant to change settings without first consulting their administrator or technical support person. The following features are available from the Performance Information And Tools dialog box:

- Manage Startup Programs
- Adjust Visual Effects
- Adjust Indexing Options
- Adjust Power Settings
- Open Disk Cleanup
- Advanced Tools

Benchmarking

Usually if you do something to improve the performance of a computer, it is sufficient for the user to tell you that it is working a lot better now. However, sometimes you are asked to prove and quantify performance improvements. Formal benchmarking is beyond the scope of this chapter, but it does discuss tools for measuring performance. You have already seen the Windows Experience Index and System Diagnostics Report outputs (Figures 11-1 and 11-2). If you have upgraded hardware, you can obtain an indication of the improvements you have made by obtaining a new Windows Experience Index and examining the subscores. This is not always as informative as you might like—for example, implementing ReadyBoost might not significantly increase the RAM subscore because of the way this is measured. If a system health report reported a problem and a new report following a hardware upgrade does not, you can be reasonably sure that the upgrade solved the problem.

To obtain figures for performance improvement, you need to use the tools described in Lesson 2, "Troubleshooting Reliability Issues by Using Built-In Diagnostic Tools." If you have identified an area of poor performance by examining resource usage in (for example) Task Manager or Reliability and Performance Monitor and then tuned performance settings, you can use the same tools under the same conditions to observe and quantify the improvement. Lesson 2 discusses this for each of these tools.

Managing Startup Programs

Some programs start automatically when you start Windows Vista. If too many of these programs open at the same time or if a program that opens automatically hangs or takes longer than it should to open—possibly because of corruption—this can slow down your computer's startup dramatically. You could encounter this problem if, for example, you or users you support purchase computers with the OS preinstalled. Many computer manufacturers install their own programs, which can impose significant performance burdens for questionable user benefit.

Selecting Manage Startup Programs opens Software Explorer in Windows Defender. Lesson 1, "Configuring Windows Defender," of Chapter 6, "Configuring Internet Explorer Security," discussed Windows Defender and Software Explorer in depth. If you suspect that a program is slowing a computer's startup, you can disable that program to check whether your suspicions are correct. If you discover that the program is the culprit, you might need to reinstall it. This facility also allows you to check whether any programs that you do not recognize or trust run at startup. Figure 11-3 shows the Software Explorer window. You do not need elevated privileges to run this task unless you want to manage startup programs for all users.

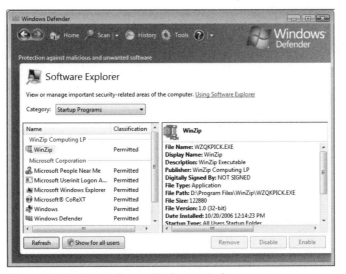

Figure 11-3   The Software Explorer window

MORE INFO   Managing startup programs

For more information, search for "Stop a program from running automatically when Windows starts" in Windows Help and Support.

Adjusting Visual Effects

You can optimize performance and change how menus and windows appear by clicking Adjust Visual Effects. This task requires elevated privileges. In the Visual Effects tab of the Performance Options dialog box, you can allow Windows to choose what is best for your computer (recommended), adjust for best appearance, and adjust for best performance, or you can select Custom and configure the visual effects individually.

NOTE   The Performance Options dialog box

The Performance Options dialog box is shown in Figure 11-11 as part of this lesson's practice session, which is more useful than having it here. However, some explanation is required to avoid confusion. Although you access the dialog box by clicking Adjust Visual Effects in Performance Information and Tools, you use only one tab in the dialog box for this purpose. The Data Execution Prevention tab lets you configure a security setting rather than tune performance, and the Advanced tab lets you configure processor scheduling and virtual memory. It can be confusing when you access these functions by clicking Adjust Visual Effects (at least it confused me).

In the Data Execution Prevention tab, you can ensure that data execution prevention (DEP) is enabled either for essential Windows programs and services or for all programs and services except those you specify. DEP is a security feature that can help prevent damage to a computer from viruses and other types of malware that attack Windows by attempting to execute code from system memory locations reserved for Windows and other authorized programs. DEP helps to protect the computer by monitoring programs to make sure that they use system memory safely. If DEP notices a program using memory incorrectly, it closes the program and notifies the user. You will need to provide administrative support for users who receive such messages and possibly disinfect their computers and ensure that antivirus and other security-related software is operating correctly.

MORE INFO   Data execution prevention

For more information about DEP, click How Does It Work in the Data Execution Prevention tab of the Performance Options dialog box. Note that, as the message on this tab informs you, some processors do not support hardware-based DEP.

Possibly the most significant tab in the Performance Options dialog box as far as performance tuning and troubleshooting is concerned is the Advanced tab. In this tab (which you can also access by clicking System And Maintenance in Control Panel, clicking System, clicking Advanced System Settings, and then clicking Settings), you can specify whether processor scheduling gives priority to programs or background services. In a client computer it is usually better to prioritize programs. You can click Change in the Virtual Memory section and adjust the virtual memory settings for the computer, as shown in Figure 11-4. If your computer has more than one hard disk drive, you can usually improve performance by putting the paging file on the disk that does not hold the system files (files used by the OS). If you have allocated all of USB flash memory to ReadyBoost, you cannot use it for paging. It is, in any case, not a good idea to page to flash memory, because it reduces the life of the device.

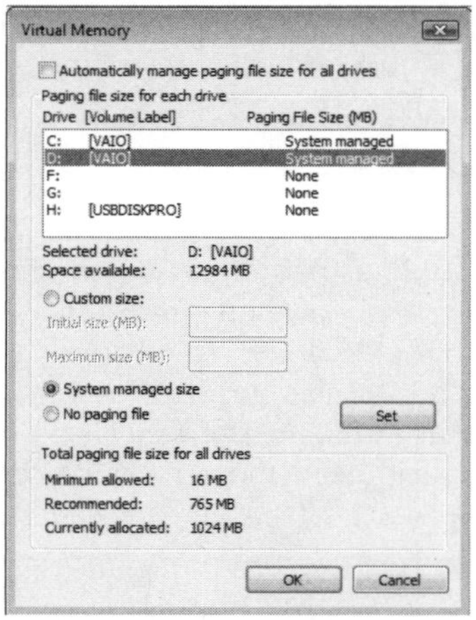

Figure 11-4   Virtual Memory settings

Adjusting Indexing Options

Indexing options can speed up the search function on a computer. You can narrow your search to focus on those files and folders in common use. You can obtain more information by clicking How Does Indexing Affect Searches in the Indexing Options dialog box. Configuring settings by clicking Advanced requires elevated privileges. In the Advanced Options dialog box, you can adjust indexing settings, restore defaults, specify where the index is stored, and specify the file types to be indexed. You can get more information by clicking Advanced Indexing Help in the Index Settings tab.

Adjusting Power Settings

The Adjust Power Settings facility lets you change power-related settings. You can increase performance at the cost of battery life and vice versa. You would normally adjust power settings only on laptop computers. You can choose a power plan and customize it by changing the settings that are listed in the left-hand pane of the Power Options dialog box. Elevated privileges are not required to choose a power plan but are needed for some settings, such as specifying whether a password is required on wakeup. For more information, click Tell Me More About Power Plans in the Power Options dialog box. Chapter 14, "Working with TabletPC," discusses power settings in detail.

NOTE   Power and Indexing Options

You can also access the Power and Indexing Options tools directly from the System And Maintenance dialog box that you open from Control Panel.

Performing a Disk Cleanup

When you click Open Disk Cleanup, you are prompted to select the disk drive you want to clean up and you then need to specify whether you want to clean up only your own files or files owned by all users of the computer. The latter option requires elevated privileges. You then select the drive you want to clean up and click OK. The Disk Cleanup tool deletes unnecessary or temporary files on your hard disk, so you can increase the amount of storage space available. It presents you with a list of files that can be deleted and identifies the types of file that it considers unnecessary by selecting the check box beside the file type. The tool gives you the option of viewing files and selecting or clearing files for deletion. Cleaning up files and defragmenting your disks regularly can significantly improve hard disk performance.

MORE INFO   Defragmentation

For more information about hard disk defragmentation, search for "What is disk defragmentation" in Windows Help and Support.

Using Advanced Tools

As a frontline support technician you will access advanced tools whenever the users you support report performance problems or ask you if you can make their computers go faster. If you provide remote help desk support, you will advise users who might have administrator accounts on their own computers how to use the advanced tools. System administrators and information technology (IT) professionals often use advanced system tools to solve problems.

By accessing the Advanced Tools dialog box, you can also view notifications about performance-related issues and what to do about them. If, for example, Windows Vista detects a driver that is reducing performance, it generates a notification. You can click the notification to learn which driver is causing the problem and to view help files that tell you how to update the driver. If Windows Vista detects a number of issues, those at the beginning of the list are affecting the system more than those later in the list.

Lesson 2 of this chapter, "Troubleshooting Reliability Issues by Using Built-in Diagnostic Tools," discusses the advanced tools. The Visual Effects tool described earlier in this lesson also appears in the advanced tool list, and an advanced tool was used to generate the System Diagnostics Report, shown in Figure 11-2. Figure 11-5 shows the tools that are available when you click Advanced Tools in Performance Information and Tools.

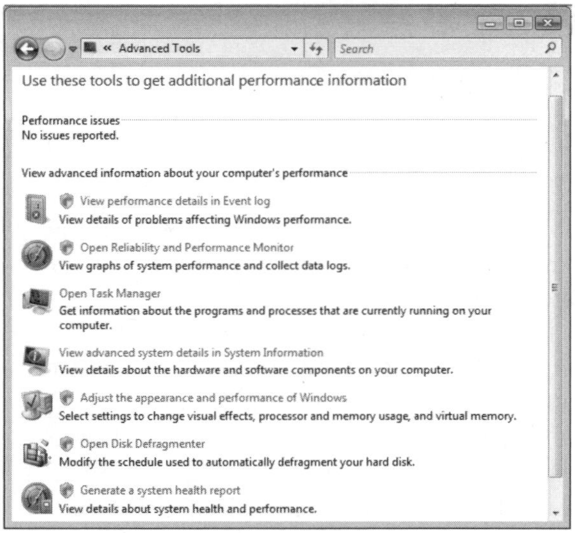

Figure 11-5 Advanced system tools

Resolving Startup, Shutdown, and Hanging Issues

The previous section described how you can use the Software Explorer tool in Windows Defender to identify programs that cause startup delays. Often, if a program or a driver causes startup delays, it can also cause shutdown delays. In this case, the issue might be listed in the Advanced Tools dialog box, and you can address it.

Sometimes a program or driver can be out of date or incompatible with Windows Vista. Configuring Windows Update so that the computers for which you are responsible regularly access the Microsoft Update site reduces this problem but does not eliminate it. Possibly a user you support has an item of hardware—for example, a digital camera—that does not have a corresponding Windows Vista-compatible driver. If the user has administrator privileges, he or she might have installed an unsigned driver located on the Internet, and this could be causing problems. Microsoft Update cannot help in this situation, and you need to explain to the user that he or she cannot use the hardware with a Windows Vista computer.

If a program—for example, Windows Defender—is performing a scan on a computer or if a disk is being defragmented, then the computer needs more time to shut down gracefully, without losing information, than would otherwise be the case. If a user has switched a computer off or pulled out the power cable rather than powering down in the correct fashion, the computer will take longer than normal to start up again. Both these situations are normal behavior, and there is nothing wrong with the computer.

Using the Problem Reports and Solutions Tool

Sometimes a program or driver simply hangs or operates unacceptably slowly during startup, shutdown, or normal operation. Millions of things need to go right for software to run normally, and only one thing need go wrong for it to crash. However, if slow startup or shutdown is a recurring problem or if the computer hangs frequently, there is probably a reason.

When a crash occurs, the user is given the option either to send an error report to Microsoft automatically or to be prompted to send such a report. Often, a solution to the problem is uploaded to the computer, and action can be taken. The Problem Reports And Solutions tool, available from System and Maintenance in Control Panel, displays problem solutions that are available and gives information on reported problems that do not have an immediately downloadable solution.

Sometimes a solution is not available when the user reports a problem but becomes available later. The Problem Reports and Solutions tool stores a problem history and provides the option to check for new solutions. This facility retransmits the information in the Problem History store to Microsoft to discover any new solutions. The report is available only if the user clicks the option to check for solutions when a problem occurs or if the user changes the settings to have Windows Vista automatically check for solutions. You can also view the problem history by using this tool. Figure 11-6 displays a problem history report.

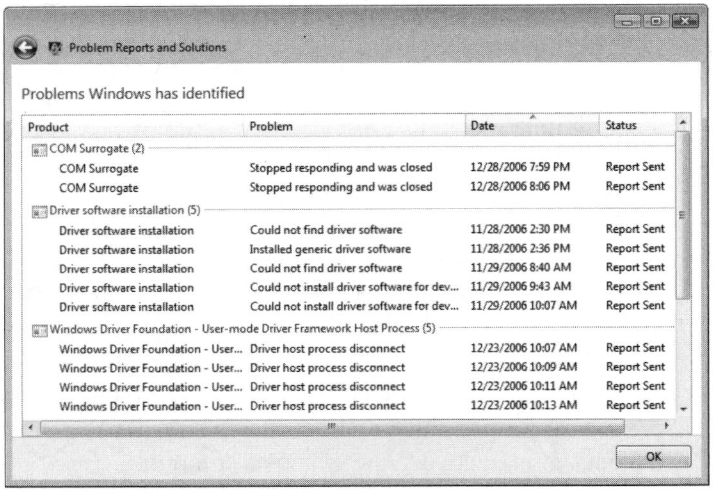

Figure 11-6   Problem history report

Dealing with Unresponsive Programs

A program that is not responding interacts more slowly than usual with Windows Vista (if it interacts at all). Typically, this occurs because a problem has occurred in the program. If the problem is temporary and the user chooses to wait, Windows Vista can often find the problem and fix it automatically so the program starts responding again. Otherwise, the user can choose to close or restart the program by using Task Manager.

If a user closes a program that stops responding, Windows Vista closes all files or documents that the user opened by using the program. Some programs might try to save information, but that depends on the program. You need to explain this to users you support and encourage them to save their work frequently.

If the program that stops responding is the computer's browser—typically Internet Explorer—this could be for one of several reasons. If this is the first time Internet Explorer stopped responding, the problem is probably temporary. Advise the user to restart the browser and all will be well.

If, on the other hand, Internet Explorer hangs regularly, the computer could be infected with spyware or a virus, the user could have installed an inappropriate add-on, or a file that Internet Explorer is trying to access could be corrupt. Chapter 6, "Configuring Internet Explorer Security," discussed Internet Explorer security in some detail, and you need to ensure that virus and malware protection is installed on any computer you support and regularly check for suspicious add-ons. Also, ensure that Windows Update settings include recommended as well as important updates. The Problem Reports and Solutions tool described earlier in this section lets you report problems with Internet Explorer (and other software) to Microsoft and check for solutions. Microsoft will notify you if there are steps you can take to solve problems and will use the information you send to generate new solutions.

Internet Explorer sometimes stops responding because it is trying to access a corrupted file stored in a temporary storage location. Temporary Internet files, cookies, and history files can all cause problems. If you suspect this is the problem, try deleting temporary Internet files first, then history files, and finally cookies. You need to warn your users that if cookies are deleted, they will lose personalization on websites that they visit regularly and might be required to reenter names and passwords for website access.

Practice: Implementing ReadyBoost and Adjusting Performance Options

In this practice session, you implement the ReadyBoost feature on a computer running Windows Vista. In an optional second practice, you attempt to implement ReadyBoost on a flash memory device that is not suitable for this purpose and observe the results. Both of these practices ask you to log on by using the standard account (parent_standard) that you created in Chapter 4, "Configuring and Troubleshooting Internet Access." If you have not created this account, or if you do not want to switch users before completing the third practice in the session, you can instead log on by using the Kim_Ackers account you created when installing Windows Vista. However, you should remember that implementing ReadyBoost does not require elevated privileges.

In the third practice, you adjust performance options—visual effects, for example—for maximum performance. This practice requires elevated privileges and asks you to log on by using the Kim_Ackers account that you created when you installed Windows Vista. If you want to, you can remain logged on with a standard account and provide credentials for the Kim_Ackers account when prompted.

You can complete the practices on any Windows Vista computer, but you will see the greatest effect if you use a computer at the lower end of the hardware specification range. The figures were captured on a laptop computer with 512 MB of RAM, and a 1 GB USB flash memory device was configured for ReadyBoost.

▶ **Practice 1: Implementing ReadyBoost**

In this practice, you implement ReadyBoost. You will need a USB flash memory device with a capacity between one and three times the capacity of your computer's RAM. You can use a flash memory device that already has files saved on it, or you can use part of the flash memory for file storage and the remainder for ReadyBoost. The practice as written uses the full capacity of a flash memory device.

1. Log on by using a standard account—for example, the parent_standard account that you created in Chapter 4, "Configuring and Troubleshooting Internet Access."

2. Insert the USB flash drive that you want to use to enhance system performance. You should see an Autoplay dialog box similar to that shown in Figure 11-7.

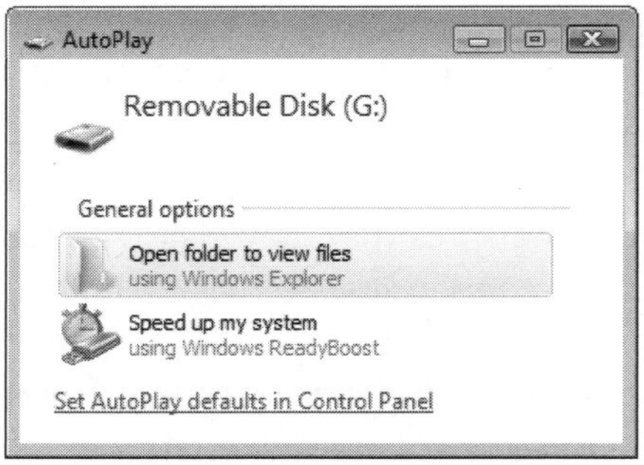

Figure 11-7   The Autoplay dialog box

3. Click Speed Up My System Using Windows ReadyBoost.

4. The ReadyBoost tab of the Properties dialog box for the USB flash drive opens, as shown in Figure 11-8. Select Use This Device.

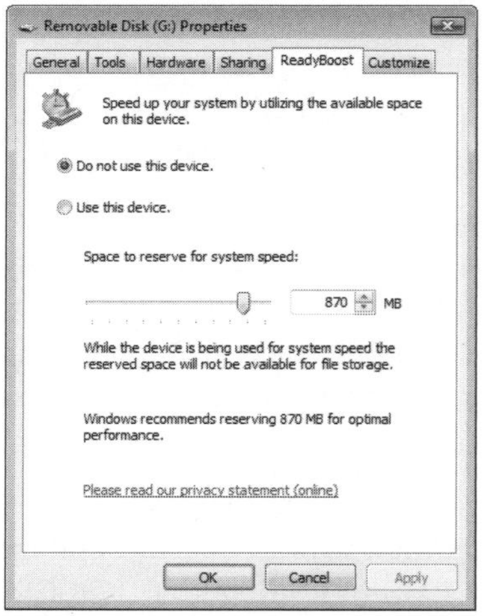

Figure 11-8   The ReadyBoost tab of the Properties dialog box for the USB flash drive

5. If you do not need to use any of the memory in the flash drive for file storage, you can increase the Space To Reserve For System Speed to the maximum capacity of the drive. Otherwise, accept the recommended setting. Click OK.

6. Use Windows Explorer to examine the contents of the USB flash drive. As shown in Figure 11-9, in this practice, all available flash memory is used for ReadyBoost cache.

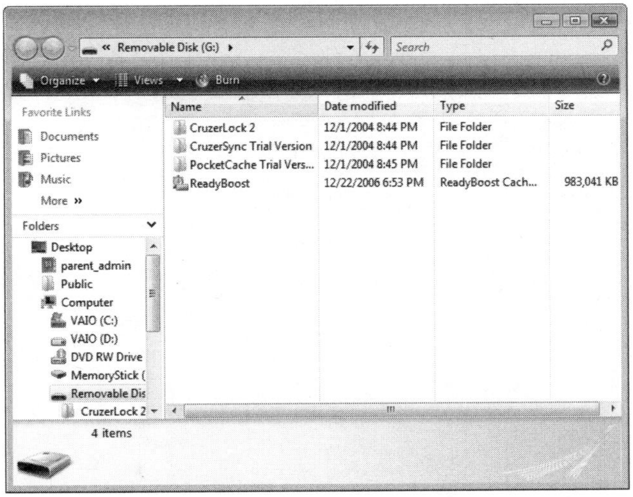

Figure 11-9   Flash memory used for ReadyBoost cache

► **Practice 2 (Optional): Attempting to Implement ReadyBoost on an Unsuitable USB Flash Memory Device**

In this practice, you attempt to implement ReadyBoost on a flash memory device that is unsuitable for the purpose. You could use a flash memory device with a capacity of less than 256 MB (the minimum is 235 MB, but devices come in standard sizes); you could use a larger capacity device that already holds files, so its spare capacity is less than 235 MB; or you could use a device that is not fast random access flash or a hybrid device with (say) 128 MB of fast random access flash and the rest slow flash.

Exam Tip   Implementing ReadyBoost is a straightforward process, and only a very limited number of examination questions can be asked about it. However, ReadyBoost implementation could fail in a variety of ways, and you could be asked to identify suitable and unsuitable flash memory devices.

---

1. If necessary, log on by using a standard account—for example, the parent_standard account that you created in Chapter 4, "Configuring and Troubleshooting Internet Access."

2. If you completed Practice 1, disable ReadyBoost on the device you configured by accessing the ReadyBoost tab on the device's Properties box (refer to Figure 11-8 in the previous practice), selecting Do Not Use This Device, and clicking OK. Alternatively, if you are short of USB slots, you can simply unplug the device.

3. Insert the USB flash drive that is unsuitable for ReadyBoost. Click Speed Up My System Using Windows ReadyBoost in the Autoplay dialog box.

4. Depending on the device you inserted, you should see one of the two messages shown in Figure 11-10.

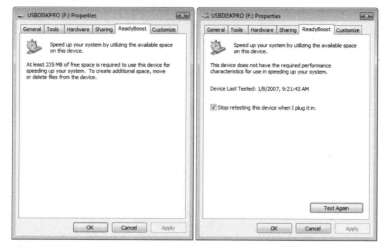

Figure 11-10 ReadyBoost implementation failure dialog boxes

NOTE Stop Retesting This Device When I Plug It In

Figure 11-10 shows that when the performance of a device is inadequate, the Stop Retesting This Device When I Plug It In check box is selected by default. This prevents the Speed Up My System Using Windows ReadyBoost option appearing in the Autoplay dialog box whenever the device is plugged in. The same check box is not available when the device has inadequate capacity because Windows Vista assumes you might want to delete some files and attempt to configure ReadyBoost again.

---

5. If you want ReadyBoost enabled on your computer, reenable it on the flash memory device you used in Practice 1 by accessing the Properties dialog box for that device, selecting Use This Device in the ReadyBoost tab, and clicking OK.

▶ **Practice 3: Configuring Visual Effects and Virtual Memory for Maximum Performance**

In this practice, you configure the visual effects on a computer to maximize performance. You would do this on a computer with a modest hardware specification that needs the best performance boost it can get and on which attractive effects, such as shadows under the mouse pointer and under menus, are not required.

The practice also asks you to move virtual memory from the C partition to the D partition. If the computer you use does not have two hard disk drives or a hard disk drive with two partitions, you cannot perform this part of the practice as written. In this case, reconfigure the other virtual memory settings as described. If the computer has only one hard disk drive but two partitions, you can perform the practice as written, but you should be aware that you will not boost computer performance as you would if the partitions were on separate disks.

1. If necessary, log on by using the account that you created when you installed Windows Vista.

2. From Settings on the Start Menu, select Control Panel.

3. In Control Panel, Click System And Maintenance, and then Performance Information And Tools.

4. On the left pane, click Adjust Visual Effects. Supply administrator credentials or click Continue as prompted to close the UAC dialog box.

5. In the Visual Effects tab of the Performance Options dialog box, select Adjust For Best Performance. This disables all visual effects. If you prefer, you can select Custom and select or clear the check box for each visual effect in turn to meet user requirements.

6. Click Apply. Applying the new visual effects settings can take some time, especially if you have several windows open. When the settings have been applied, the Apply button is dimmed, as shown in Figure 11-11. You should also notice that the appearance of the Start button has changed.

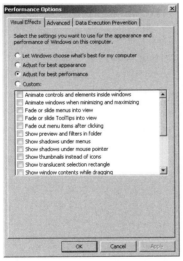

Figure 11-11   Visual effects settings have been applied

7. In the Data Execution Prevention tab of the Performance Options dialog box, ensure that Turn On DEP For Essential Windows Programs And Services Only is selected. Click How Does It Work to find out more about this setting. Close Windows Help And Support when you are finished reviewing this topic.

8. In the Advanced tab of the Performance Options dialog box, ensure that Adjust For Best Performance Of Programs is selected, as shown in Figure 11-12.

Figure 11-12 Allocating processor resources for best performance of programs

9. Click Change in the Virtual Memory section of the Advanced tab. In the Virtual Memory tab, clear the Automatically Manage Paging File Size For All Drives check box, as shown in Figure 11-13.

Figure 11-13 Disabling automatic virtual memory allocation

10. If the computer has a D partition, select it. Select System Managed Size, and then click Set. Figure 11-14 shows the result of this modification.

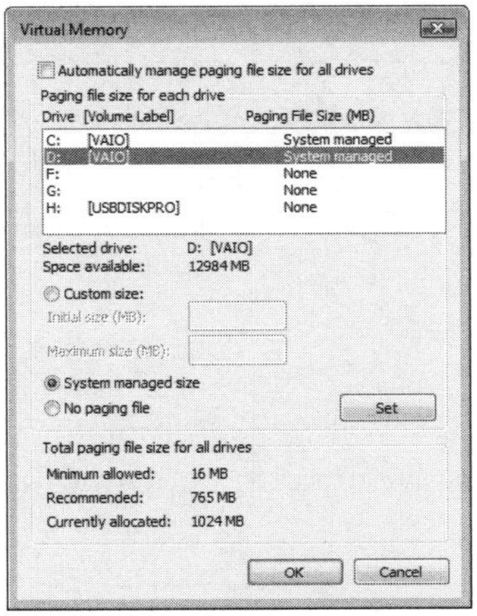

Figure 11-14   Allocating virtual memory to the D drive

11.   If you do not have a D drive, you should instead select the Automatically Manage Paging File Size For All Drives check box.

CAUTION   Let the system manage virtual memory

It is tempting to select No Paging File for the C drive so that all paging is done to the D drive. However, if you do this, problems can occur with error reporting. You could select Custom for the C drive and allocate 200 MB of virtual memory on that drive to prevent such problems, but in general, it is better to let the OS sort this out automatically. By the same token, you could select Custom for both drives and allocate virtual memory manually to each. Long experience with several OSs has taught me that the system can usually allocate virtual memory better than I can.

---

12.   When you are happy with the virtual memory settings, click OK. You might be prompted to overwrite a d:\page file.sys file. If so, click OK.

13.   Restart the computer.

Lesson Summary

■   You can use ReadyBoost to improve hardware performance, especially in computers where the RAM resource is a bottleneck.

■   You can use the Manage Startup Programs option in Performance Information and Tools to disable a program that is causing delays from running at startup. This option opens Software Explorer in Windows Defender.

- You can improve performance by configuring visual effects settings and virtual memory settings in the Performance Options dialog box. You access this dialog box by selecting Adjust Visual Effects in Performance Information and Tools.

- You can improve search performance by modifying indexing settings in the Indexing Options dialog box. You access this dialog box by selecting Adjust Indexing Options in Performance Information and Tools.

Lesson Review

You can use the following questions to test your knowledge of the information in Lesson 1, "Troubleshooting Performance Issues." The questions are also available on the companion CD if you prefer to review them in electronic form.

NOTE   Answers

Answers to these questions and explanations of why each answer choice is correct or incorrect are located in the "Answers" section at the end of the book.

---

1. Ian McLean is writing Chapter 11 of a book about Windows Vista. He is changing settings in the Performance Options dialog box and capturing screen dumps. Ian finds that screen dumps of dialog boxes no longer have a black line all the way around them. What setting has he changed to cause this?

    A. He has changed virtual memory settings.

    B. He has adjusted the allocation of processor resources to achieve best performance of background services.

    C. He has adjusted visual effects for best performance.

    D. He has adjusted visual effects for best appearance.

2. You receive a help desk request from a colleague whose computer has recently been upgraded from Windows XP to Windows Vista. He is running a graphics application and reports poor performance. He also reports that his hard disk indicator LED is lit almost continuously. He does not have an administrator account on the computer. He needs to finish the project he is working on by the close of business that day. What do you advise?

    A. The user needs to install a faster, higher capacity hard disk.

    B. The user can insert a USB flash memory device and configure it for ReadyBoost.

    C. The user needs to install more RAM.

    D. The user should change the virtual memory settings.

3. You want to implement ReadyBoost on a laptop computer with 750 MB of RAM. You have four new USB flash memory devices of different capacities. You intend to use the full capacity of the device you choose. According to Microsoft guidelines, which of the following devices can you use for this purpose? (Choose all that apply.)

    A. 256 MB flash memory

    B. 512 MB flash memory

    C. 1 GB flash memory

    D. 2 GB flash memory

4. You want to reconfigure virtual memory settings on a computer. You already have the Performance Information And Tools dialog box open on the desktop. You want to use the quickest method of accessing the Virtual Memory dialog box. What do you click next?

    A. Adjust Visual Effects

    B. Adjust Indexing Options

    C. Adjust Power Settings

    D. Advanced Tools

5. Two weeks ago, Windows Vista encountered a problem that caused a data analysis program to hang. Although you automatically send information about such events to Microsoft, you received no solution to this problem. Tomorrow you intend to use this program again. How can you quickly check whether a solution has been found in the meantime?

    A. On the Start menu, select Windows Update. In the Windows Update dialog box, click View Update History.

    B. In Control Panel, select System And Maintenance. In the System And Maintenance dialog box, under Problem Reports And Solutions, click Check For New Solutions.

    C. On the Start menu, select Windows Update. In the Windows Update dialog box, click Restore Hidden Updates.

    D. In Control Panel, select System And Maintenance. In the System And Maintenance dialog box, under Problem Reports And Solutions, click View Problem History.

Lesson 2: Troubleshooting Reliability Issues by Using Built-in Diagnostic Tools

Lesson 1, "Troubleshooting Performance Issues," discussed various methods you can use to improve performance on a computer that is not working as quickly as its user believes it should. At worst, the computer might occasionally hang or take longer than expected to start up or shut down. In summary, Lesson 1 is about performance tuning.

Sometimes, however, the problems associated with a computer go beyond the scope of tuning. If a hardware component is inadequate for the task that the computer needs to perform, you should identify that component and either upgrade or replace it. If a driver or OS component needs to be updated, you might need to download an executable file from the Microsoft Update site and also find out why that file was not downloaded automatically. If a problem occurs regularly but is not reported to Microsoft, you might not be informed about a downloadable Microsoft solution. You need to both implement the solution and find out why the problem was not reported.

The Windows Experience Index tool (sometimes known as the System Performance Rating tool) was discussed in Chapter 3, "Troubleshooting Post-Installation System Settings," and mentioned again in Lesson 1 of this chapter, "Troubleshooting Performance Issues." This lesson also discusses the tool. Chapter 3 and Lesson 1 also introduced the Problem Reports and Solutions tool, and this lesson looks at this tool in more depth.

Selecting Advanced Tools in the Performance Information And Tools dialog box lets you access a number of tools that help you diagnose and address performance issues. You can view performance details in the event log, view graphs of system performance and collect data logs in the Reliability and Performance Monitor, get information about currently running programs and processes in Task Manager, view details about hardware and software components in System Monitor, adjust the appearance and performance of the computer by accessing the Performance Options dialog box, schedule disk defragmentation, and generate a system health report. Lesson 1, "Troubleshooting Performance Issues," discussed the Performance Options dialog box, and Figure 11-2 showed a system health report. This lesson discusses the other diagnostic tools.

NOTE **Disk defragmentation**

If you subscribe to Microsoft Windows One-Care, one of the features of this package is that it defragments the computer's hard disks regularly.

> **After this lesson, you will be able to:**
> - Use the Windows Experience Index tool to determine which hardware components are generating performance bottlenecks on your computer and to get an indication of overall computer performance.
> - Use the Problem Reports and Solutions tool to control when Windows Vista reports faults to Microsoft and to access any new solutions to faults that were previously reported.
> - Use event logs to obtain information about significant events on a computer.
> - Use the Reliability and Performance Monitor, Task Manager, and the system monitor to obtain information to help you diagnose performance and reliability problems.
>
> **Estimated lesson time: 45 minutes**

Using the Windows Experience Index Tool

Chapter 3, "Troubleshooting Post-Installation System Settings," discussed the Windows Experience Index tool. However, this tool is included in the objectives specified for this chapter and is therefore also mentioned here. You can access the tool either by opening the Performance Information And Tools dialog box or by opening the System And Maintenance dialog box from Control Panel and clicking Check Your Computer's Windows Experience Index Base Score under System. In either case, clicking Update My Score recalculates the Windows Experience Index score.

You can use the Windows Experience Index score to determine whether a computer running Windows Vista has sufficient resources to run a particular application. An application has a recommended Windows Experience Index rating. If your computer meets that score, the application should perform adequately. If your computer has a Windows Experience Index rating below that score, the application might still run but might not do so in an acceptable way.

In practice, you need to analyze the index base score carefully. It is not an average score but is instead the score returned by the least adequate component. If, for example, the application has no requirement for three-dimensional (3D) graphics but the gaming graphics component returns a low score, then the application might run satisfactorily even though the index score is below what it specifies. If the index base score is above what an application specifies, that application will perform adequately. If the index base score is below the value specified, the application might still run adequately depending upon which component returned the low subscore.

Table 11-1 lists the components that are tested when calculating the Windows Experience Index base score. This table is also in Chapter 3 but is repeated here for convenience.

Table 11-1   Components Used to Determine System Performance

Component	Measurement
Processor	Calculations per second
Physical Memory (RAM)	Memory operations per second
Graphics	Windows Aero Desktop performance
Gaming graphics	3D graphics performance
Primary hard disk	Disk data transfer rate

A computer that is rated between 1 and 2 can usually perform basic tasks adequately but should not be used for games or multimedia. A computer rated at 3 can run Aero and play DVDs but might have problems displaying high-definition television (HDTV). A computer rated 4 or above will run software and multimedia applications well. Currently, an index score of 5 is seen only on a state-of-the-art high-performance workstation, but this situation will change as more powerful client computers designed to run Windows Vista come on the market.

The Windows Experience Index base score is generated automatically during the installation of Windows Vista. You can reevaluate the score at any time, but you would typically do so if you add a new graphics adapter, processor, motherboard, RAM, or hard disk drive. As described earlier in this lesson, you generate a new Windows Experience Index score by clicking Update My Score in the Performance Information And Tools dialog box. You need to supply administrator credentials and to be connected to the Internet to perform this operation.

If you are attempting to identify the component in your computer that could be causing performance or reliability problems, it is a good idea to look at both the Windows Experience Index score and a system health report, as we did in Lesson 1, "Troubleshooting Performance Issues." You can obtain a system health report by selecting Advanced Tools in the Performance Information And Tools dialog box and clicking Generate A System Health Report. This operation requires elevated privileges and Internet access. It can also take quite a long time to complete.

Quick Check

1. What system components are evaluated when calculating a Windows Experience Index score?

2. Which system component is rated by calculations per second when calculating a Windows Experience Index score?

Quick Check Answers

1. Processor, physical memory (RAM), graphics, gaming graphics, and primary hard disk

2. Processor

Using Event Viewer

You can access Event Viewer from the Advanced Tools dialog box (refer to Figure 11-5 earlier in this chapter) or from the Administrative Tools menu. You can supply administrator credentials if you have logged on by using a standard account, but some event logs might not then be accessible. It is easier to use this tool if you log on as an administrator.

Event Viewer displays event logs, which are files that record significant events on a computer—for example, when a user logs on or when a program encounters an error. You will find the details in event logs helpful when troubleshooting problems with the Windows Vista OS, drivers, and application programs. The events recorded fall into the following categories:

- Critical
- Error
- Warning
- Information

The security log contains two more event categories that are used for auditing purposes: Audit Success and Audit Failure.

Figure 11-15 shows details of a critical event. This is a failure in a USB driver that could (and did) cause information in a file to be lost.

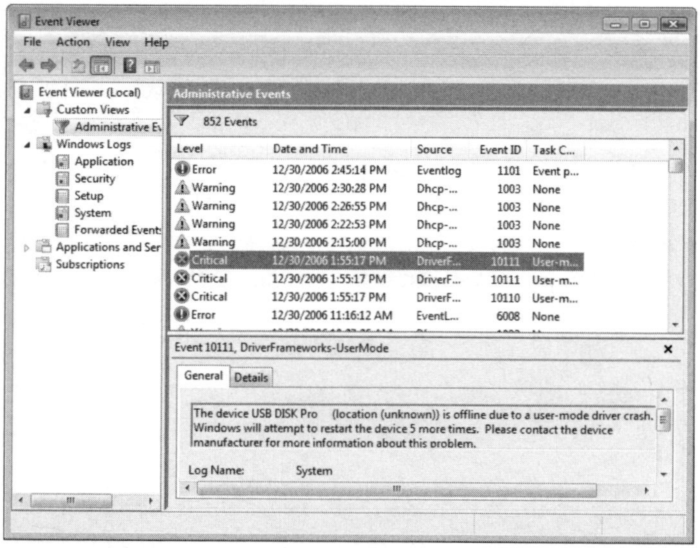

Figure 11-15   A critical event

Event Viewer tracks information in different logs. Windows logs include the following:

- **Application**   Stores program events. Events are classified as error, warning, or information, depending on the severity of the event. An error is a significant problem, such as loss of data. A warning is an event that is not necessarily significant but might indicate a possible future problem. An information event describes the successful operation of a program, driver, or service. The critical error classification is not used in the Application log.

- **Security**   Stores security-related audit events that can be successful or failed. For example, the Security log records an audit success if a user trying to log on to the computer was successful.

- **Setup**   Stores setup events. Computers that are configured as domain controllers in an Active Directory directory service domain have log files displayed here.

Exam Tip   The 70-620 examination objectives do not specify Active Directory domains, and you are unlikely to encounter any questions about the Setup log.

- **System**   Stores system events that are logged by Windows Vista and Windows Vista system services. System events are classified as critical, error, warning, or information.

- **Forwarded Events**   Stores events that are forwarded by other computers.

Custom Views

You can create custom views by clicking Create Custom View in the Event Viewer Action menu, specifying the source logs or events and filtering by level, time logged, event identity (ID), task category, keywords, user, or computer. You are unlikely to specify all of these criteria, but this facility enables you to refine your search to where you think a problem might be occurring rather than searching through a very large number of events. Figure 11-16 shows a custom view specification.

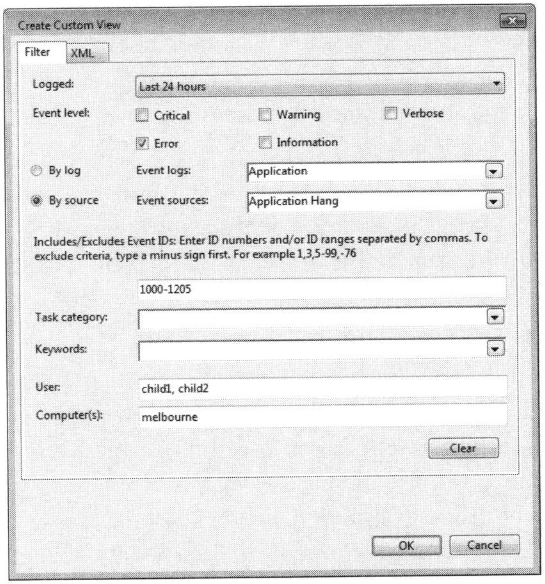

Figure 11-16   Specifying a custom view

Windows Vista provides the Administrative Events custom view by default. This view contains critical, error, and warning events from all administrative logs.

Applications and Services Logs

Event Viewer provides a number of Applications and Services logs. These include logs for programs that run on the computer and detailed logs that store information about specific Windows services. For example, these logs can include the following:

- Distributed file system (DFS) replication log
- Encrypted file system (EFS) debug log
- Function discovery provider host service tracing log
- Hardware events log
- Internet Explorer log

- Key management service log
- Media center log
- A large number of Microsoft Windows logs
- Microsoft Windows services performance diagnostic provider diagnostic log

Attaching Tasks to Events

Sometimes you want to be notified by e-mail if a particular event occurs, or you might want a specified program to start—for example, one that activates a pager. Typically, you might want an event in the Security log—such as a failed logon or a successful logon by a user who should not be able to log on to a particular computer—to trigger this action. To implement this functionality, you attach a task to the event so that you receive a notification.

To do this, open Event Viewer, and navigate to the log that contains the event you want to be notified about. Typically, this would be the Security log in Windows logs, but you can implement this in other Windows logs or in Applications and Services logs if you want to. You can select the event and click Action, click the event and go to the Actions pane, or right-click the event, and then select Attach Task To This Event.

This opens the Create Basic Task Wizard. You name and describe the task and then click Next. The When A Specific Event Is Logged page summarizes the event, and you can make sure that you have chosen the correct event before clicking Next. The Action page gives you the option of starting a program, sending an e-mail, or specifying a message. When you make your choice and click Next, you configure the task. For example, if you want to send an e-mail, you would specify source address, destination address, subject, task, attachment (if required), and the name of the Simple Mail Transfer Protocol (SMTP) server. You click Next, and then click Finish.

Using Network Diagnostics with Event Viewer

When you run Windows Network Diagnostics, any problem found, along with solutions, is displayed in the Network Diagnostics dialog box. If, however, more detailed information about the problem and potential solutions is available, Windows Vista saves this in one or more event logs. As a network administrator or technical support technician, you will use the information in the event logs to analyze connectivity problems or help interpret the conclusions.

Chapter 7, "Configuring Network Connectivity," described how you run Network Diagnostics from the Network And Sharing Center, which you access by clicking Network And Internet in Control Panel. You can also start the tool from the message that Internet Explorer returns if you fail to connect to a webpage. You can filter for network diagnostics and Transmission Control Protocol/Internet Protocol (TCP/IP) events by specifying Network-diagnostics and Tcpip event sources and capturing events from these sources in a custom view. You do this in the practice session later in this lesson.

If Network Diagnostics identifies a problem with a wireless network, it saves information in the event logs as either helper class events or informational events. Helper class events provide a summary of the diagnostics results and repeat information displayed in the Network Diagnostics dialog box. They can also provide additional information for troubleshooting, such as details about the connection that was diagnosed, diagnostics results, and the capabilities of the wireless network and the adapter being diagnosed.

Informational events can include information about the connection that was diagnosed, the wireless network settings on the computer and the network, visible networks and routers or access points in range at the time of diagnosis, the computer's preferred wireless network list, connection history, and connection statistics—for example, packet statistics and roaming history. They also summarize connection attempts, list their status, and tell you what phases of the connection (such as preassociation, association, and security setup) succeeded, failed, or did not start.

There can be one or more helper class events per diagnostics session, but only one informational event per session.

Using the Problem Reports and Solutions Tool

If a program stops working or responding, Windows Vista, by default, automatically reports the problem to Microsoft and checks for a solution. You can verify or change this default by opening the Problem Reports and Solutions tool. You access this tool by clicking System And Maintenance in Control Panel and then clicking Problem Reports And Solutions. The Problem Reports and Solutions tool is shown in Figure 11-17.

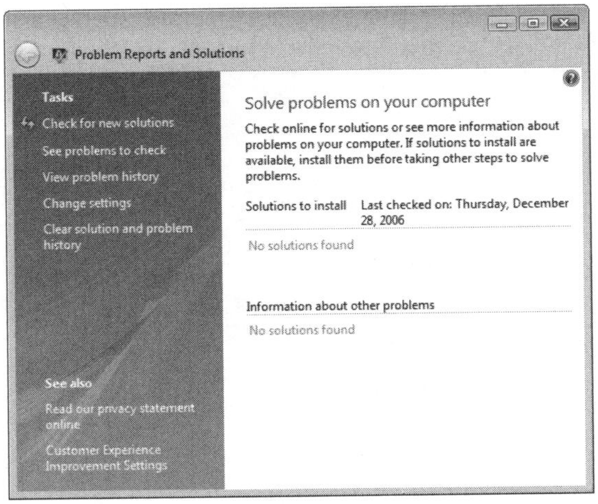

Figure 11-17   The Problem Reports and Solutions tool

To check current settings, click Change Settings in the tool's left pane. Unless you have a good reason for changing it (for example, no Internet connectivity), the default setting Check For Solutions Automatically (Recommended) should be enabled, as shown in Figure 11-18.

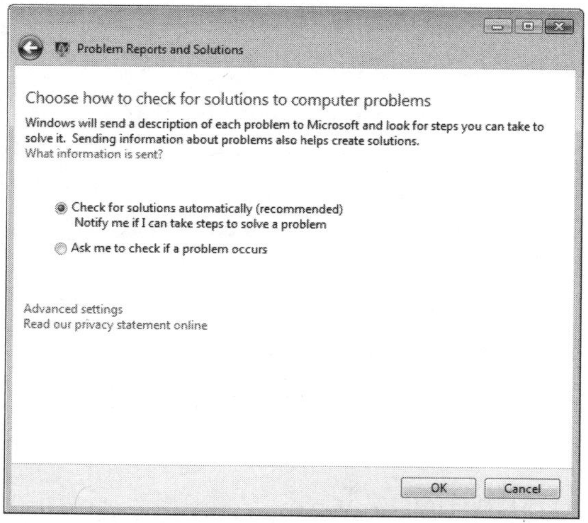

Figure 11-18   The Problem Reports and Solutions tool settings

Clicking Advanced Settings in the dialog box, shown in Figure 11-18, lets you specify whether all users on a computer can alter the settings for the Problem Reports and Solutions tool or if they can specify whether they want to send reports to Microsoft or not, as shown in Figure 11-19. Changing advanced settings on the tool requires elevated privileges.

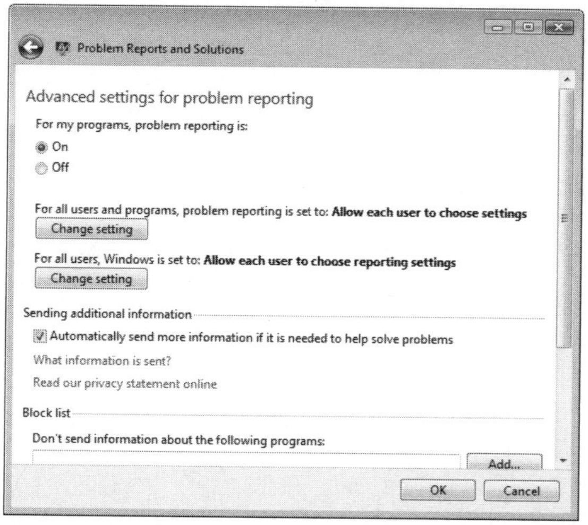

Figure 11-19   The Problem Reports and Solutions tool advanced settings

If a problem occurs, Windows Vista automatically sends information to Microsoft, except when the problem is such that sending information could reveal details about the user or the computer, in which case Windows Vista asks the user for permission to send problem details. If there are steps the user can take to prevent or solve the problem or if Microsoft needs more information to find or create a solution, the user is notified. This happens whether the user has logged on by using a standard or an administrator account, and you need to advise users you support what is happening and what the implications are.

Windows Vista uses the information in the report that is sent to Microsoft and any information Microsoft uploads about the problem to match the problem description to a solution. Windows Vista notifies the user when steps can be taken to solve the problem or to find more information. If a solution is not yet available, the information that a user sends in a problem report can help Microsoft find or create a new solution.

Sometimes the suggested solution requires elevated privileges. In this case, you need to assist the users you support to implement the solution.

If the Problem Reports and Solutions tool is not configured to report problems to Microsoft automatically, the user is prompted to check for a solution whenever a problem occurs. The tool records the details of any problems that occur in a Problem History file. Figure 11-6 showed such a file. If problems are not sent automatically to Microsoft and the user chooses not to send details when a problem occurs, then the user can click See Problems To Check in the Problem Reports and Solutions tool. The tool then uses the Problem History file to populate the Check For Solutions To These Problems dialog box, as shown in Figure 11-20. The user can select the check boxes for all or some of the problems listed and click Check For Solutions. Alternatively, you can send details of all the problems in the Problem History file by clicking Check For New Solutions in the left-hand pane of the Problem Reports and Solutions tool.

If no solution was available for a particular problem when it occurred, a user can determine whether Microsoft has developed a solution by clicking Check For Solutions in the Check For Solutions To These Problems dialog box or by clicking Check For New Solutions in the left pane of the Problem Reports and Solutions tool, as previously described.

The Problem Reports and Solutions tool also lets users clear the solution and problem history. You need to impress on users you support that they should do this only if they are confident that all current problems have been solved. Clicking Clear Solution And Problem History generates a warning, but this operation does not, by default, require elevated privileges.

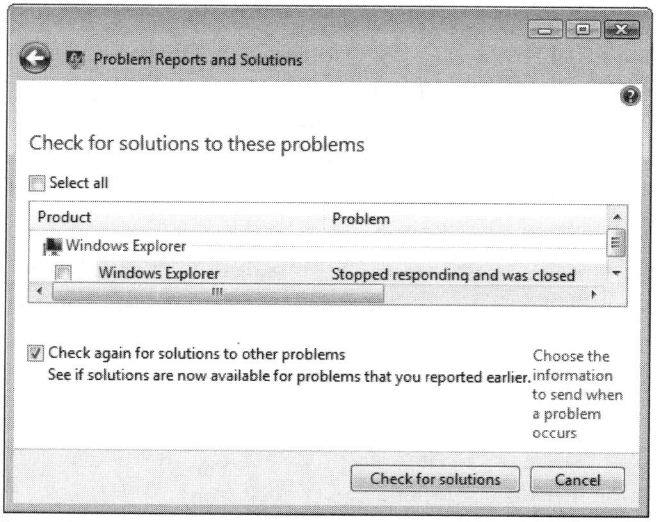

Figure 11-20   The Check For Solutions To These Problems dialog box

Using Advanced Diagnostic and Analysis Tools

The Reliability and Performance Monitor, Task Manager, and System Information tools are available from the Advanced Tools dialog box that you access from Performance Information and Tools. You can also open the Reliability and Performance Monitor from the Administrative Tools menu or as a Microsoft Management Console (MMC) snap-in. You can open Task Manager by right-clicking the taskbar at the foot of the screen and selecting Task Manager or by pressing Ctrl+Alt+Del. Usually, you can open Task Manager even when the computer appears to have crashed completely and use it to close the application that is causing the crash.

Reliability and Performance Monitor

You use the Reliability and Performance Monitor to analyze system performance. This tool lets you monitor application and hardware performance in real time, customize the data you want to collect in logs, define thresholds for alerts, generate reports, and view past performance data.

NOTE   Windows XP equivalents

Reliability and Performance Monitor combines the functionality of several Microsoft Windows XP stand-alone tools, including Performance Logs and Alerts (PLA), Server Performance Advisor (SPA), and System Monitor.

Reliability and Performance Monitor provides three monitoring tools: Resource View, Performance Monitor, and Reliability Monitor. This tool performs data collection and logging by using data collector sets.

MORE INFO   Data collector sets

For more information about data collector sets, access http://technet2.microsoft.com /WindowsVista/en/library/53582ab0-24a0-411c-9c7a-7b24667416991033.mspx?mfr=true, http:// technet2.microsoft.com/WindowsVista/en/library/55ae9400-d7a9-4bf0-838a-ec981be903641033 .mspx?mfr=true, and http://technet2.microsoft.com/WindowsVista/en/library/b37b4bd8-2e2d- 4a0c-a850-09899d6cb9dd1033.mspx?mfr=true.

As an administrator, you can use all the features of Reliability and Performance Monitor. Standard users can view log files in Performance Monitor and change the display properties while viewing historical data. They can also use Reliability Monitor.

NOTE   Other user groups

If you want to give other users more privileges when using Reliability and Performance Monitor, you can add their accounts to the Performance Monitor Users group or to the Performance Log Users group. However, this is typically done in an Active Directory domain that has a lot of users and several levels of administration and is beyond the scope of this chapter.

Resource View   The Resource Overview window is the Windows Reliability and Performance Monitor home page, as shown in Figure 11-21. This view lets you monitor the usage and performance of CPU, disk, network, and memory resources in real time. You can get information about which processes are using which resources by clicking the down-arrow beside each resource.

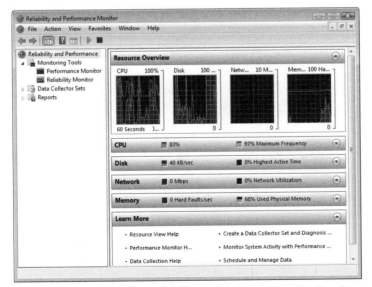

Figure 11-21   Windows Reliability and Performance Monitor Resource Overview

Performance Monitor   Performance Monitor, shown in Figure 11-22, provides a visual display of built-in Windows performance counters—for example, the Memory:Pages/sec and Processor:%Processor time counters—either in real time or as performance data collector sets that let you create baselines and review historical data. You can add performance counters to Performance Monitor by dragging and dropping or by creating custom data collector sets. Performance Monitor provides multiple views—you can view data in a report format or in real time as a line graph or histogram. You can create custom views in Performance Monitor that can be exported as data collector sets for use with performance and logging features.

MORE INFO   **Performance counters**

There are a lot of performance counters, and many have multiple instances (for example, if a computer has two processors, two instances of Processor:%Processor time exist). It is impractical to list every counter or to state acceptable and unacceptable values for each—for example, a value in excess of 80 percent for a significant period returned by Processor:%Processor time indicates CPU problems, and a value greater than 20 for Memory:Pages/sec could indicate RAM problems. However, if you want more information about performance and reliability monitoring and performance counters, access *http://technet2.microsoft.com/WindowsVista/en/library/ab3b2cfc-b177-43ec-8a4d-0bfac62d88961033.mspx?mfr=true*.

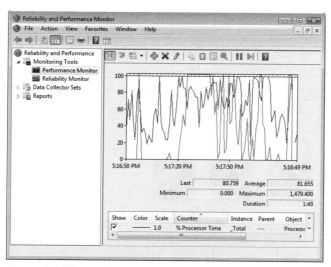

Figure 11-22   Performance Monitor

NOTE **Benchmarking with Performance Monitor**

One of the most important functions of performance monitoring is to obtain benchmarks for system performance. You can use the Performance Monitor tool to collect data from counters that measure resource usage during a quiet period, at the peak of a day's activity, and at a period of average usage. You can then repeat the process later (particularly if the computer is experiencing performance problems) and see what has changed. If you are tuning performance or upgrading hardware, it is a good idea to capture benchmark data before and after you make the changes to determine what improvement, if any, has been made. You need to take care that you capture both sets of performance data under (as much as possible) the same load conditions.

Reliability Monitor Reliability Monitor, shown in Figure 11-23, provides an overview of system stability and trend analysis. It lets you view detailed information about individual events that could affect the system's overall stability, such as software installations, OS updates, and hardware failures. It starts collecting data as soon as Windows Vista is installed.

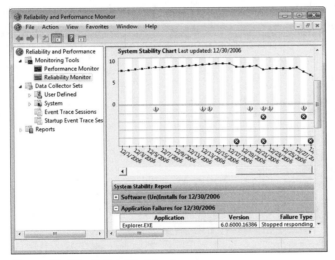

Figure 11-23   Reliability Monitor

MORE INFO **Windows Reliability and Performance Monitor**

For more information about this powerful and versatile tool, access *http://technet2.microsoft.com /WindowsVista/en/library/53582ab0-24a0-411c-9c7a-7b24667416991033.mspx?mfr=true.*

Task Manager

If a program stops responding, Windows Vista tries to find the problem and fix it automatically. Alternatively, if the system seems to have crashed completely and Windows Vista has not resolved the problem, the user can end the program by opening Task Manager and accessing the Applications tab.

NOTE Encourage users to wait

Using Task Manager to end a program might be faster than waiting, but any unsaved changes will be lost. Encourage the users you support to wait a few minutes and let Windows Vista try to fix the problem first, rather than immediately pressing Ctrl+Alt+Del.

The Performance tab in Task Manager provides details about how a computer is using system resources—for example, RAM and CPU. As shown in Figure 11-24, the Performance tab has four graphs. The first two show the percentage of CPU resource that the system is using, both at the moment and for the past few minutes. A high percentage usage over a significant period indicates that programs or processes require a lot of CPU resources. This can affect computer performance. If the percentage appears frozen at or near 100 percent, a program might not be responding. If the CPU Usage History graph is split, the computer either has multiple CPUs, a single dual-core CPU, or both.

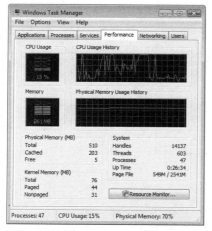

Figure 11-24 Task Manager Performance tab

NOTE Processor usage

If processor usage is consistently high—say 80 percent or higher for a significant period—you should consider installing a second processor or replacing the current processor even if the Windows Experience Index subscore does not identify the processor as a resource bottleneck. However, before you do so it is worth capturing processor usage data by using Performance Monitor rather than relying on snapshots obtained by using Task Manager.

The next two graphs display how much RAM is being used, both at the moment and for the past few minutes. The percentage of memory being used is listed at the bottom of the Task Manager window. If memory use appears to be consistently high or slows your computer's performance noticeably, try reducing the number of programs that are open at one time (or encourage users you support to close any applications they are not currently using). If the problem persists, you might need to install more RAM or implement ReadyBoost.

NOTE Benchmarking with Task Manager

Task Manager is not the primary tool for benchmarking. The Performance Monitor tool in Reliability and Performance Monitor can capture and display historical data, but Task Manager can display information only over the last few minutes. Nevertheless, if you are testing the effect of reconfiguring a setting or upgrading hardware, it can be useful to look at resource usage in Task Manager before and after the change.

Three tables below the graphs list various details about memory and resource usage. In the Physical Memory (MB) table, Total is the amount of RAM installed on your computer, Cached refers to the amount of physical memory used recently for system resources, and Free is the amount of memory that is currently unused and available.

In the Kernel Memory (MB) table, Total is the amount of memory being used by the core part of Windows, called the kernel; Paged refers to the amount of virtual memory the kernel is using; Nonpaged is the amount of RAM memory used by the kernel.

The System table has five fields: Handles, Threads, Processes, Up Time, and Page File. A detailed description of these parameters is beyond the scope of this chapter, but if you want more information, search for "See details about your computer's performance using Task Manager" in Windows Help and Support.

If you need more information about how memory and CPU resources are being used, click the Resource Monitor button. This displays the Windows Reliability and Performance Monitor Resource View that was described earlier in this lesson. You require elevated privileges to access Resource Monitor.

You can determine how much memory an individual process uses by selecting the Task Manager Processes tab. As shown in Figure 11-25, the Memory (Private Working Set) column is selected by default. A private working set indicates the amount of memory a process is using that other processes cannot share. This information can be useful in identifying a "leaky" application—an application that, if left open, uses more and more memory resource and does not release memory resource that it is no longer using.

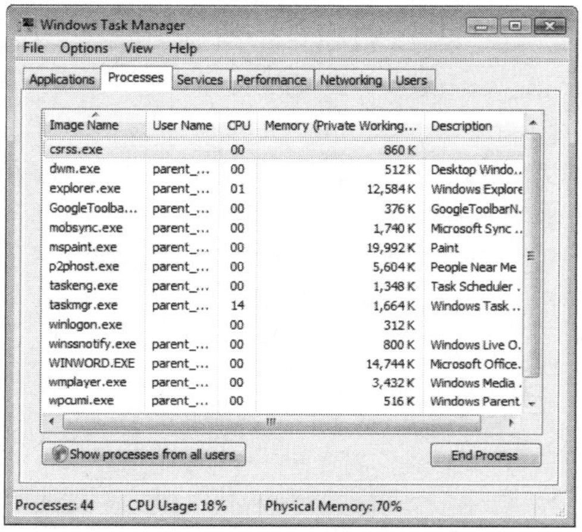

Figure 11-25   Task Manager Processes tab

You can click View, click Select Columns, and then select a memory value to view other memory usage details on the Processes tab, for example:

- **Memory - Working Set**   Amount of memory in the private working set plus the amount of memory the process is using that can be shared by other processes
- **Memory - Peak Working Set**   Maximum amount of working set memory used by the process
- **Memory - Working Set Delta**   Amount of change in working set memory used by the process
- **Memory - Commit Size**   Amount of virtual memory that is reserved for use by a process
- **Memory - Paged Pool**   Amount of committed virtual memory for a process that can be written to another storage medium, such as the hard disk
- **Memory - Nonpaged Pool**   Amount of committed virtual memory for a process that cannot be written to another storage medium

You can use the Task Manager Processes tab to end a process, to end a process tree (stops the process and all processes on which it depends), and to set process priority.

The Task Manager Services tab shows which services are running and which are stopped. You can stop or start a service or go to a process that depends on that service. If you want more details about or more control over the services available on a computer, you can click Services to access the Services administrative tool. You require elevated privileges to use the Services tool.

The Task Manager Networking tab lets you view network usage. The Users tab tells you what users are connected to the computer and lets you disconnect a user.

System Information

System Information shows details about hardware configuration, computer components, and software, including drivers. (You open System Information by clicking Start, All Programs, Accessories, System Tools, and then System Information.) As shown in Figure 11-26, System Information lists categories in the left pane and details about each category in the right pane. The categories include the following:

- **System Summary**   Shows general information about the computer and its OS, such as the computer name and manufacturer, the type of basic input/output system (BIOS), and the amount of memory that is installed
- **Hardware Resources**   Displays details about a computer's hardware
- **Components**   Displays information about disk drives, sound devices, modems, and other components
- **Software Environment**   Shows information about drivers and network connections and displays other program-related information

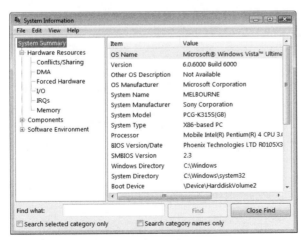

Figure 11-26   System Information

If you want to find specific details in System Information, type the information you are looking for in the Find What text box at the bottom of its window. For example, if you want to determine a computer's Internet Protocol (IP) address, type **ip address** in the Find What box, and then click Find.

Quick Check

■ You want to change the priority of a process on a computer. How do you do this?

Quick Check Answer

■ Open Task Manager. In the Processes tab, right-click the process. Click Select Priority. You can choose Realtime, High, Above Normal, Normal, Below Normal, or Low.

Practice: Creating a Custom View and Capturing Network Diagnostic Event Logs

In this practice session, you create a custom view in Event Viewer to record Network Diagnostic and TCP/IP events. You then generate some events to populate the view. These are administrator tasks, and you should log on by using an administrator account as the practices stipulate.

As written, you carry out Practice 2 on a wireless-enabled PC connected to a wireless network. If you do not have a wireless-enabled PC, you can still carry out the practice. However, your view will not record events that are specific to diagnosing a wireless connection.

▶ **Practice 1: Creating a Custom View**

In this practice, you create a custom view in Event Viewer to capture network diagnostic and TCP/IP events.

1. If necessary, log on by using the account that you created when you installed Windows Vista (Kim_Ackers).

2. Open Control Panel, click System And Maintenance, click Performance Information and Tools, click Advanced Tools, and click View Performance Details In Event Log.

3. As prompted, supply administrator credentials or click Continue to close the UAC dialog box.

4. In Event Viewer, right-click Custom Views, and select Create Custom View, as shown in Figure 11-27.

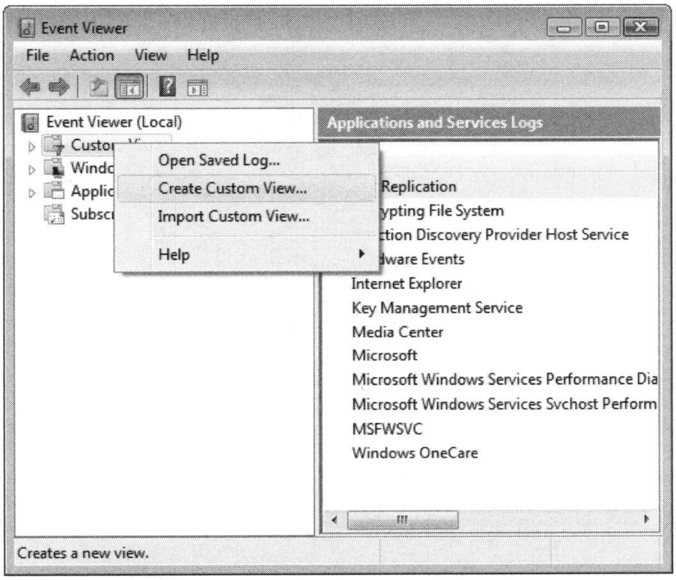

Figure 11-27   Creating a custom view

5. In the Filter tab of the Create Custom View dialog box, select the Critical, Error, Warning, and Information event level check boxes.

6. Select By Source. In the Event Sources drop-down list, select the Diagnostics-Networking, TCP/IP, and Tcpip check boxes. The Custom View dialog box should look similar to Figure 11-28.

NOTE   Configuring your custom view filter

In this practice, it is (arguably) sufficient to configure your filter to include only events with the Diagnostics-Networking event source or even to include only events with Event ID 6100. However, Diagnostics-Networking sourced events with Event IDs 1000, 2400, and 4000 can give useful information, as can Tcpip sourced events with Event ID 4201. By the same token, it is arguably unnecessary to include Critical events, which are unlikely to have these event sources. Although too much information is a bad thing, it is also unwise to specify your filtering criteria too narrowly because you might miss valuable information.

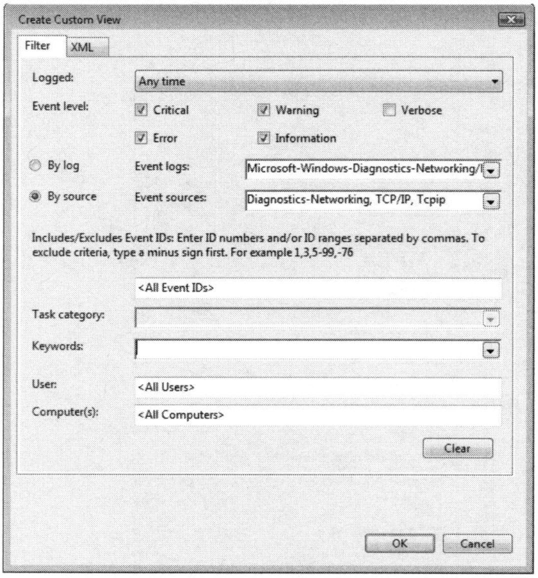

Figure 11-28   The Custom View dialog box

7. Click OK. In the Save Filter To Custom View dialog box, enter a name and description for the custom view, as shown in Figure 11-29.

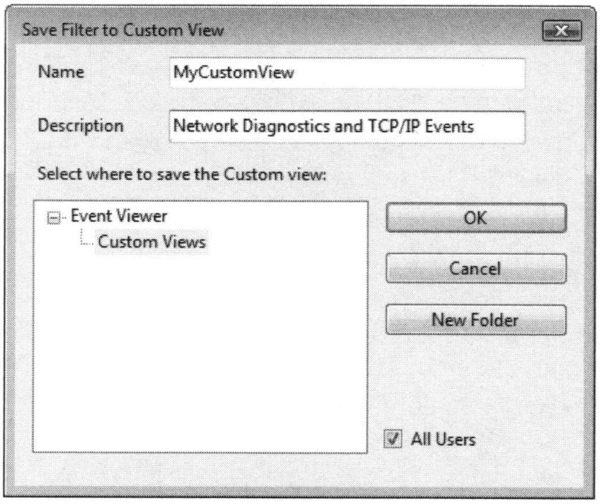

Figure 11-29   Naming the custom view

8. Click OK.

9. In Event Viewer, select the custom view you have created (unless it is already selected). As shown in Figure 11-30, the view might already show events from the last time you ran Network Diagnostics.

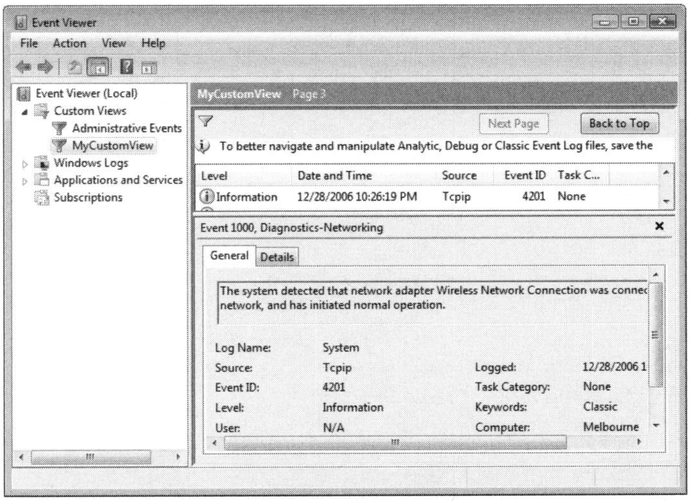

Figure 11-30   Selecting the custom view

▶ **Practice 2: Diagnosing a Network Problem and Viewing Related Events**

In this practice, you use Network Diagnostics to diagnose and repair a network problem and then examine the events that this process has generated in Event Viewer.

1. If necessary, log on by using the account that you created when you installed Windows Vista (Kim_Ackers).

2. Open Control Panel, click Network And Internet, click Network And Sharing Center, and click Manage Network Connections.

3. Right-click the network connection (preferably wireless) that you use to connect to the Internet, and click Disable, as shown in Figure 11-31.

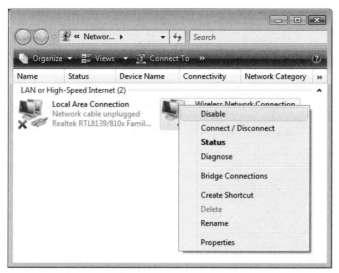

Figure 11-31   Disabling a network connection

4.   As prompted, supply administrator credentials or click Continue to close the UAC dialog box.

5.   The Network And Sharing Center should show you are no longer connected to the Internet. Click Diagnose And Repair.

6.   Windows Network Diagnostics diagnoses the fault, as shown in Figure 11-32. Enable the network adapter you previously disabled.

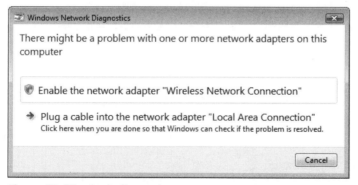

Figure 11-32   Fault diagnosis

7.   As prompted, supply administrator credentials or click Continue to close the UAC dialog box.

8.   In the Network And Sharing Center, check that network connectivity has been restored.

9. If necessary, open Event Viewer as described in Practice 1, and select the custom view you created earlier.

10. Select an event that has been added to the custom view. You can identify such events by date and time. Double-click the event to read its properties, as shown in Figure 11-33. Repeat the process for other events.

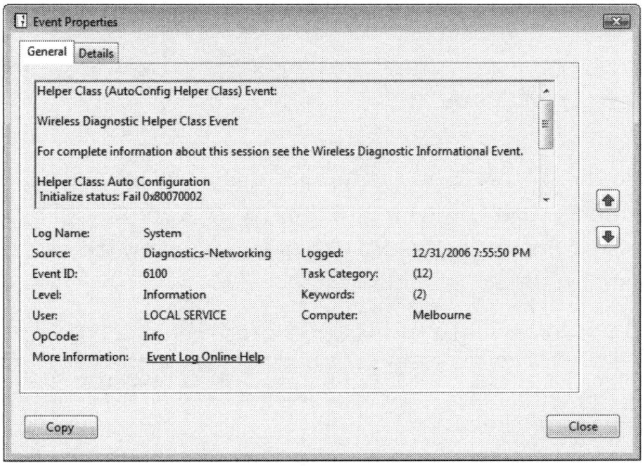

Figure 11-33   Properties of a Network Diagnostics event

Lesson Summary

■ You can use the Windows Experience Index tool to calculate a base index score whenever you change a computer's hardware configuration. The base index score indicates how well a computer will run various programs.

■ The Problem Reports and Solutions tool lets you configure whether problem reports are sent automatically to Microsoft. The tool generates a problem history, lets you review problems, and lets you resubmit problems to find out whether a solution has been found since a problem was previously submitted.

■ Event Viewer collects events on the computer in various event logs. Events can have critical, error, warning, or information levels. The System log contains system auditing events classed as audit success and audit failure.

■ The Reliability and Performance Monitor lets you monitor counters that measure resource usage on a computer and provides both real-time and historical data. It can generate an alert if a counter goes above or below a predefined value. The Reliability Monitor gives a graphical record of system stability.

■ Task Manager gives a snapshot of resource usage and lets you control services and processes. System Information gives you advanced information about system details.

Lesson Review

You can use the following questions to test your knowledge of the information in Lesson 2, "Troubleshooting Reliability Issues by Using Built-In Diagnostic Tools." The questions are also available on the companion CD if you prefer to review them in electronic form.

NOTE   Answers

Answers to these questions and explanations of why each answer choice is correct or incorrect are located in the "Answers" section at the end of the book.

1. You have upgraded the hardware on a computer that a mathematician in your company uses for highly complex calculations that require a large amount of processor resource. You use the Windows Experience Index tool to generate a new base score. The subscores for each component are shown in Table 11-2.

   Table 11-2   Windows Experience Index Subscores

Component	Subscore
Processor	4.1
Physical Memory (RAM)	3.3
Graphics	3.6
Gaming Graphics	2.3
Primary Hard Disk	4.4

   Based on these figures, what is the Windows Experience Index base score?

   A. 2.3

   B. 3.5

   C. 4.1

   D. 4.4

2. You have an administrator account on a computer in your organization's workgroup. You want to set a default so that every other user who has an account on the computer automatically checks for solutions when a problem occurs. You do not want to give users the option of changing this default behavior. How do you do this?

   A. Open Problem Reports And Solutions. Click Change Settings. Select Check For Solutions Automatically.

   B. Open Problem Reports And Solutions. Click See Problems To Check. Select the problems you want to check. Click Check For Solutions.

   C. Open Problem Reports And Solutions. Click Change Settings. Select Advanced Settings. Under Allow Each User To Choose Settings, click Change Setting. Select For All Users Turn Windows Problem Reporting On.

     D. Open Problem Reports And Solutions. Click Change Settings. Select Advanced Settings. Under Allow Each User To Choose Reporting Settings, click Change Setting. Select Automatically Check For Solutions (Recommended).

3. Which Event Viewer Windows log records Audit Success and Audit Failure events?

     A. Application

     B. Security

     C. Setup

     D. System

4. You are troubleshooting reliability problems on a computer running Windows Vista. You want to obtain data about critical driver crashes, errors caused by application failures, and warnings and information events that were generated when applications accessed the registry. You are interested only in events that occurred in the last 24 hours. How best can you obtain this information?

     A. Access the System log because only this log stores critical events.

     B. Access the Applications log. Drivers are applications, so all the required information is in this log.

     C. Create a new Applications and Services log.

     D. Create a custom view.

5. You want to record information such as the number of paging operations carried out per second and the percentage of available processor time used when a computer is carrying out several resource-intensive tasks simultaneously. For the purposes of comparison, you want the same information for a time when the computer is only lightly used. In addition to recording historical data, you want to see what is happening in real time when the computer's performance appears to drop. How do you access the best tool for this purpose?

     A. In Control Panel, select System And Maintenance. Click Problem Reports And Solutions. Select View Problem History.

     B. In Control Panel, select System And Maintenance. Click Performance Information And Tools. Click Advanced Tools. Select Open Task Manager.

     C. In Control Panel, select System And Maintenance. Click Performance Information And Tools. Click Advanced Tools. Select View Performance Details In Event Log.

     D. In Control Panel, select System And Maintenance. Click Performance Information And Tools. Click Advanced Tools. Select Open Reliability And Performance Monitor.

Chapter Review

To further practice and reinforce the skills you learned in this chapter, you can perform the following tasks:

- Review the chapter summary.
- Review the list of key terms introduced in this chapter.
- Complete the case scenarios. These scenarios set up real-world situations involving the topics of this chapter and ask you to create a solution.
- Complete the suggested practices.
- Take a practice test.

Chapter Summary

- Features such as ReadyBoost can improve hardware performance. Future developments in solid state hard disk technology could eventually make such techniques unnecessary.
- Performance Information and Tools provide options that you can use to adjust computer performance. These include Manage Startup Programs, Adjust Visual Effects, and Adjust Indexing Options.
- The Windows Experience Index base score gives a measure of a computer's hardware performance and how well it can run specified programs.
- The Problem Reports and Solutions tool lets you control problem reporting and obtain solutions from Microsoft.
- Event Viewer, Reliability and Performance Monitor, Task Manager, and System Information provide powerful tools for diagnosing problems that affect system performance, reliability, and stability.

Key Terms

Do you know what these key terms mean? You can check your answers by looking up the terms in the glossary at the end of the book.

- bottleneck
- DirectX 10–compliant
- FireWire
- flash memory
- hybrid hard disk
- paging

- solid state hard disk
- swap file
- transfer rate
- universal serial bus (USB)
- virtual memory

Case Scenarios

In the following case scenarios, you will apply what you have learned about maintaining and optimizing Windows Vista. You can find answers to these questions in the "Answers" section at the end of this book.

Case Scenario 1: Troubleshooting Performance Issues

You provide frontline technical support for Trey Research, a small organization that uses a workgroup structure and does not have an Active Directory domain. Trey Research has recently upgraded its computer OSs from Windows XP to Windows Vista. Currently only a very small budget is available for hardware upgrades. You have improved hardware performance by implementing ReadyBoost on all the machines. Answer the following questions:

1. A colleague reports that she cannot back up any files to a USB flash memory device on her machine. She has accessed the device properties and cannot see any files stored on it, although all the memory space on the device is shown as being used. She asks you if there is a hardware fault. What do you tell her?

2. A supervisor reports that his computer is taking a very long time to start whenever he reboots it. You check that Windows Defender is running on his computer and that no malware has been reported. What should you advise him to do next?

3. A researcher wants to use a new analysis program that uses 3D graphics. The program has a required index rating of 1.0 and a recommended rating of 2.7. The current Windows Experience Index base score on his computer is 2.0, which is also the subscore for 3D business and gaming graphics performance. What do you advise?

Case Scenario 2: Troubleshooting Reliability Issues

You work for a company that supplies computer equipment to small businesses. One such business reports that computers are hanging and that its network is generally unreliable. Further questions tell you that most of the problems occur on two machines that are used for high-resolution multimedia applications. The machines both have adequate hardware specifications. You visit the customer to investigate the problems as part of an extended warranty agreement. Answer the following questions:

1. You inspect the settings on the Problem Reports and Solutions tool on one of the computers that are experiencing problems and find that it is not configured to report problems automatically. You want to obtain details about problems that have occurred and select problems to report to Microsoft and find out if solutions are available. What option should you use in the Problem Reports and Solutions tool?

2. You suspect that hardware problems in the RAM in one of the computers could be causing unreliability. However, the customer does not want you to take the computer offline and remove the case to replace the RAM hardware until you are sure this is the problem. You want to record memory usage over a 24-hour period. How do you do this?

3. You suspect that critical system errors linked with device drivers could be causing one of the computers to crash. How would you obtain information about such events?

4. You want to see a graphical display of system stability since a computer was installed and find out on which days applications failures, hardware failures, Windows failures, and miscellaneous failures occurred. What tool should you use for this purpose?

Suggested Practices

To help you successfully master the exam objectives presented in this chapter, complete the following tasks.

Troubleshoot Performance Issues

■ **Practice 1: Implement ReadyBoost**   If you have access to a number of computers that are used for different purposes, implement ReadyBoost, and observe the effect on performance on each computer. Find out whether computers that perform a lot of graphics or run multimedia applications benefit from ReadyBoost or whether the improvement is more noticeable on computers that do a lot of number-crunching.

■ **Practice 2: Configure Performance Options**   Open Performance Information and Tools, and select Adjust Visual Effects. In the Visual Effects tab, select Custom, and determine the effect on both performance and appearance of changing individual display options. In the Advanced tab, experiment with virtual memory settings. Perform the last practice on a test computer, not on a production machine.

■ **Practice 3: Adjust Indexing Options**   Open Performance Information and Tools, and select Adjust Indexing Options. Click Advanced, and experiment with the options available.

Become Familiar with the Built-in Tools for Troubleshooting Reliability Issues

- **Practice 1: Use Event Viewer** Event Viewer is a powerful tool that can provide you with a great deal of information about what is happening on a computer. Look at the contents of the Windows logs. Become familiar with some of the more common events and what they indicate. If you know the Event IDs of events that are of interest, you will find this helps you create custom views quickly and easily. Experiment with custom views.

- **Practice 2: Use Task Manager** Although Task Manager mainly provides snapshots of performance and closes crashed applications, this tool has other features, particularly linked to processes and services, which you will find very useful when you become familiar with them.

- **Practice 3: Use Performance Monitor** The Performance Monitor tool in Reliability and Performance Monitor is both complex and powerful. A very large chapter, if not an entire book, would be required to describe this tool in depth. However, you will learn more by using it than by reading about it. Learn how to generate performance data collector sets in addition to looking at performance in real time. Find out about reports. Learn how to use alerts. In the Add Counters dialog box, select Show Description, and find out what the various counters measure.

Take a Practice Test

The practice tests on this book's companion CD offer many options. For example, you can test yourself on just one exam objective, or you can test yourself on all the 70-620 certification exam content. You can set up the test so that it closely simulates the experience of taking a certification exam, or you can set it up in study mode so that you can look at the correct answers and explanations after you answer each question.

MORE INFO   **Practice tests**

For details about all the practice test options available, see the "How to Use the Practice Tests" section in this book's Introduction.

Chapter 12

Configuring Updates and Protecting Data

Possibly the two most important things that users require from a computer are that the operating system (OS) remains up to date and as secure as possible from attacks from the Internet and that personal files are not lost. Microsoft Windows Update can ensure that Windows Vista and important applications (for example, Microsoft Office) remain up to date. Because many updates are a response to known security threats from the Internet, the update process also helps keep the computer secure.

Windows Vista lets you configure automatic backups and restores files from backup. If a user loses a file or folder, it can be restored, and only recent changes are lost. Windows Vista also implements restore points whenever any updates are implemented (or other changes occur). You can restore a computer system to the last restore point without losing user data. If a user has amended a file since the last restore point, Windows Vista creates a shadow copy of the file when a new restore point is created. This enables users to remove changes to a file and revert to a version they saved earlier if they want to. You can also back up an image of the whole computer and restore this in the event of major problems—a hard disk failure, for example.

This chapter discusses Windows Update and the Windows Vista Backup and Restore service.

Exam objectives in this chapter:
- Configure Windows Update.
- Configure Data Protection.

Lessons in this chapter:

Before You Begin

To complete the lessons in this chapter, you must have done the following:

■ Installed Windows Vista Ultimate edition on a personal computer, as described in Chapter 1, "Installing Windows Vista Client," and Chapter 2, "Windows Vista Upgrades and Migrations."

■ Created an administrator account and standard accounts and enabled the Run command on the Start menu, as described in Practices 1, 2, and 3 of Chapter 4, "Configuring and Troubleshooting Internet Access," Lesson 1, "Configuring and Troubleshooting Parental Controls and Content Advisor."

No additional configuration is required for this chapter. Internet access is required to complete the practices.

Real World

Ian McLean

I expect it has happened to most of us.

You get to work and go straight to your computer or you decide to look at your home computer and check your e-mail before breakfast. The computer tells you it has installed updates and needs to restart.

The sensible thing to do is restart the computer and go get some coffee. You don't (at least I don't). Instead you restart the computer and watch it do its thing. Watching a computer powering up is marginally less exciting than watching grass grow and makes watching paint dry seem like an enthralling spectator sport. Compared to a rebooting computer, a kettle boils with the velocity of greased lightning.

If Windows Vista is your first OS, you are very lucky. I'm not saying it never needs a restart. Some exclusive or stand-alone updates require you to reboot the computer, but thankfully these are few and far between. Windows XP seemed to need a restart every morning (it was probably about once per week, but it *seemed* like every morning). Windows 98 wasn't happy unless you rebooted on a very regular basis.

Windows Vista has many neat, technically advanced features that make it well worth the inconvenience and expense of an upgrade. However, the one that will most likely endear it to its users is that they hardly ever need to restart it first thing in the morning.

Lesson 1: Configuring Windows Update

To protect your computer and computers you support from threats from the Internet and to ensure that the OS, and applications that ship with the OS, such as Microsoft Internet Explorer and Microsoft Windows Defender (and, optionally, other important applications such as Office), remain up to date, you need to ensure that Windows Vista obtains the appropriate updates from the Microsoft Update site at *http://update.microsoft.com/microsoftupdate /v6/vistadefault.aspx?ln=en-us*.

Typically, users do not need to access this site directly. You can configure the Windows Update settings to control what updates Windows Vista downloads, the time that it downloads them, and whether or not updates install automatically when they download.

Microsoft's Update Release Schedule

Although the users you support do not need to access the Microsoft Update website directly, as an administrator, you need to be more proactive. At the very least, you should check for updates that Microsoft releases on the second Tuesday of each month.

Microsoft introduced this release schedule in order to reduce the costs related to the deployment of updates. Security updates are dispatched all at once on an anticipated date for which system administrators can prepare. Microsoft chose a Tuesday because it is not too close to the beginning of the week and yet far enough from the end of the week to allow any problems that might arise to be resolved before the weekend.

You can mark the second Tuesday of the month in advance as the day during which most updates are published and plan accordingly. Many software vendors follow Microsoft's lead and issue vulnerability updates on the same day.

Not every update is published on the second Tuesday of each month—for example, Windows Defender definitions are updated more often, and Microsoft issues updates its classes as highly critical whenever these are required. However, this regular release schedule gives you, as an administrator, the opportunity to find out what updates Microsoft is publishing and what impact these will have on your users. For more information, access *http://www.microsoft.com/athome/security/update/bulletins /default.mspx*. You can register to receive security bulletins and advisory notices by following the links at *http://www.microsoft.com/technet/security/bulletinsandadvisories /default.mspx*.

Changing Windows Update settings requires elevated privileges. If you are supporting colleagues in a small office environment and they do not have administrator accounts, you need to make any changes required. If you are advising home users who have administrator accounts—for example, through a help desk—you might need to explain the Windows Update settings. The default settings are sensible, and hopefully you will not need to reconfigure them too often.

NOTE   Updates apply to the computer, not to the user

If a computer has several users, any user can download and install updates (although *optional updates* require that a user supplies administrator credentials). Typically, recommended and important updates download and install automatically at a time when no user is likely to be logged on. Updates apply to the computer and the computer's OS. They are not applied on a per-user basis.

Windows Server Update Services

In larger organizations it is sometimes impractical to have all the computers on a network accessing the Microsoft Update site to obtain updates. In this situation, Windows Server Update Services (WSUS) is installed on one or more WSUS servers. This server accesses the Internet and downloads the updates, which it then distributes to the other computers on its network. WSUS reduces Internet bandwidth requirements and enables an administrator to control updates from a central point, test updates, and specify the updates that are downloaded and installed on client computers.

However, although it is possible to add a WSUS server to workgroup, WSUS is typically implemented in Active Directory directory service domain environments. It is unlikely that WSUS will be tested in any depth in the 70-620 examination. If you want to find out more about WSUS, access: *http://technet2.microsoft.com/windowsserver/en /technologies/featured/wsus/default.mspx, http://www.microsoft.com/windowsserversystem /updateservices/default.mspx* and *http://www.microsoft.com/windowsserversystem /updateservices /downloads/WSUS.mspx.*

After this lesson, you will be able to:
- Configure Windows Update settings.
- Install updates and troubleshoot update problems.
- Hide updates and restore hidden updates.
- View update history.
- Uninstall updates.

Estimated lesson time: 40 minutes

Configuring Windows Update Settings

You configure Windows Update settings by selecting Windows Update from the All Programs Menu. In the Windows Update dialog box, you click Change Settings. The Change Settings dialog box is shown in Figure 12-1.

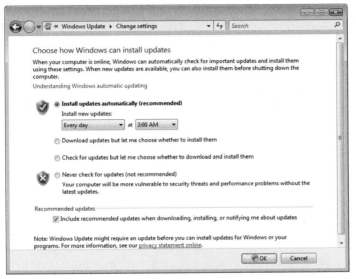

Figure 12-1   The Change Settings dialog box

You can set Windows to automatically install important and recommended updates or to install important updates only. Important updates offer significant benefits, such as improved security and reliability. Recommended updates address noncritical problems and help enhance the computing experience. Optional updates (for example, device driver updates) are not downloaded or installed automatically.

NOTE   **Critical updates**

Microsoft sometimes refers to important updates as critical updates and uses this classification for its security bulletins. However, Windows Update for Windows Vista uses the term important updates.

If you automatically download and install updates, you can choose a time to do so. By default, updates are downloaded from the Microsoft Update site at 3:00 A.M. This is typically a time of low activity, when the computer is likely to be doing very little else. You would change this setting if, for example, a computer is not switched on or connected to the Internet overnight (for example, where there is a dial-up connection) or in businesses that operate overnight and for which 3:00 A.M. is a busy time.

Instead of downloading and installing updates automatically, you can configure Windows Update to notify the user when updates are available for a computer. The user can then download and install the updates. Although elevated privileges are required to change Windows Update settings, standard users can download and install important and recommended updates when notified.

You can also configure Windows Update to automatically download updates and then notify the user so he or she can install them. Finally, you can choose never to download updates, although this is not recommended. If you choose to select the last option, you need to ensure that you or the users you support manually check for updates regularly.

Updates and Service Packs

Users might sometimes ask you what the difference is between updates and service packs. Some users believe that downloading updates is pointless because they will all be included in the next service pack.

Microsoft issues updates to fix known vulnerabilities and reliability and performance problems and in response to possible threats from the Internet. Updates can include security updates, hotfixes, drivers for new devices, and sometimes executables that implement new or improved OS features. If users do not download and install updates, their systems become vulnerable to attack. You need to convince them that they should not wait months (sometimes years) for the next service pack.

A service pack is a collection of updates, fixes, or enhancements (or all three) to an OS (or a software program) delivered in the form of a single installable package. In addition to bug fixes, a service pack can contain entirely new features. Microsoft typically releases a service pack when the number of individual updates to a given program reaches a certain arbitrary limit. Service packs are downloadable and can also be ordered on CD-ROM or DVD-ROM. New versions of the OS typically have the latest service pack included.

For more information about the Microsoft support lifecycle, which includes Microsoft's updating and service pack policies, access *http://support.microsoft.com/lifecycle/*.

Quick Check

- What Windows Update settings are available in the Change Settings dialog box?

Quick Check Answer

- Install Updates Automatically
- Download Updates But Let Me Choose Whether To Install Them
- Check For Updates But Let Me Choose Whether To Download And Install Them
- Never Check For Updates

You can also specify the day and time at which updates are automatically downloaded and installed and whether Windows Update should include recommended updates when automatically downloading and installing updates or when informing the user when updates are available to download or install.

Installing Updates

When you open Windows Update, the Windows Update dialog box, shown in Figure 12-2, tells you if updates are available for download and installation. In the scenario illustrated in Figure 12-2, the Microsoft Update site has published two important updates that Windows Update has detected at 9:32 A.M. If you take no action, these updates will be downloaded and installed at 3:00 A.M. on the following day.

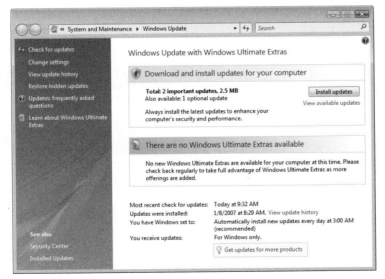

Figure 12-2   The Windows Update dialog box

If you want to find out more about these updates, you can click Check For Updates in the left pane of the Windows Update dialog box to access the View Available Updates dialog box, shown in Figure 12-3. If you want detailed information, you can right-click an update and select View Details.

NOTE   **Windows Vista editions**

The figures and descriptions in this book are based on Windows Vista Ultimate, as is the 70-620 examination. In other editions, such as Windows Vista Enterprise, some dialog boxes look slightly different. For example, the Windows Update dialog box in Windows Vista Enterprise uses View Available Updates instead of Check For Updates and does not have the Learn About Windows Ultimate Extras link.

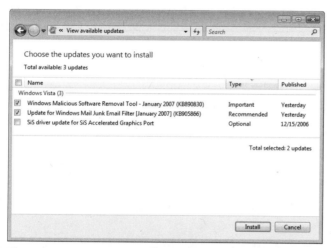

Figure 12-3   The View Available Updates dialog box with updates selected for installation

In this scenario, you might decide to install the important and recommended updates but not to install the optional update because the computer does not have a Silicon Integrated Services (SiS) Accelerated Graphics port. In this case, you select the check boxes beside the updates you want to install, as shown in Figure 12-3 (above).

NOTE   **Important and recommended updates**

The Windows Update dialog box categorizes all nonoptional updates as "important." Provided the setting to include recommended updates is enabled, this classification covers both important and recommended updates. However, the Check For Updates dialog box differentiates between important and recommended updates.

You can install the selected updates by clicking Install in the View Available Updates dialog box or Install Updates in the Windows Update dialog box. (The Install Updates command is only available if there are important or recommended updates ready to be installed.) Windows Vista downloads the updates, as shown in Figure 12-4, and then installs them. Although a standard user can download and install important and recommended updates, elevated privileges are required to stop a download or installation.

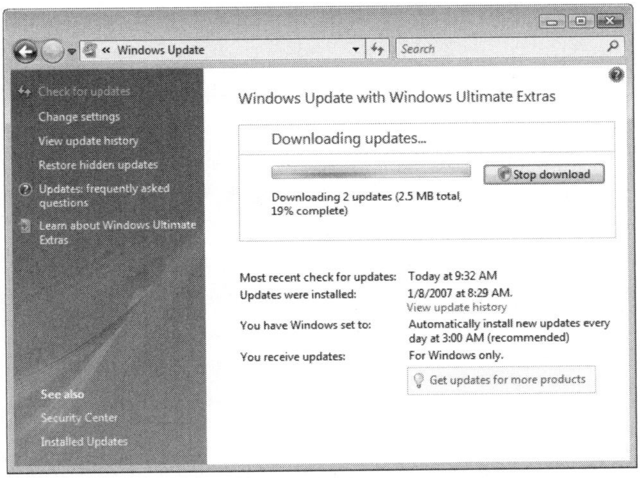

Figure 12-4   Downloading updates

NOTE   **Installing optional updates**

Because optional updates include, for example, device driver updates that might not be appropriate for the computer, elevated privileges are required to download and install optional updates.

Troubleshooting Update Problems

Typically, Windows Update operates at night, without user intervention. Windows Vista, unlike Windows XP, seldom needs a restart when updates are installed, so the user is not aware that updates have occurred. However, updating can occasionally go wrong. The most common reasons include the following:

■ **The user needs to provide credentials**   This can happen when a computer uses a proxy server to connect to the Internet and obtain updates. In this case, Windows Update returns Error 8024401B and the user needs to click Check For Updates and provide logon credentials. The user account does not require elevated privileges.

■ **Firewall settings are blocking downloads**   Windows Vista Firewall does not block update downloads. However, some small business networks are protected by third-party firewalls. Update downloads use the Background Intelligent Transfer Service (BITS). This enables interrupted downloads to resume at the point of interruption and throttles the bandwidth used by the download to reduce disruption to normal network operations even when a user chooses to download updates in the middle of the working day. If a firewall blocks the bitspeer port (User Datagram Protocol [UDP] and Transmission Control Protocol [TCP] port 2178), problems can occur. This is more commonly seen in large networks, and a solution is to use WSUS rather than allow individual downloads.

MORE INFO   The Background Intelligent Transfer Service

The 70-620 examination is unlikely to test your knowledge of BITS in any depth. Nevertheless, if you want to find out more, access *http://www.microsoft.com/technet/community/en-us/management/bits_faq.mspx*.

■ **The user did not accept the Microsoft software license terms**   Some updates require that a user agrees to Microsoft software license terms. If the user fails to accept the license terms, the update will not install. You can check whether this has happened by opening Windows Update and reviewing error messages. You can then click Try Again and, when prompted, agree to the license terms. The update should then install.

■ **Insufficient free disk space**   If a computer does not have sufficient disk space to either download or install the update, updating will fail. In this case, you need to delete or transfer files to create space. Typically, you can free disk space by deleting temporary Internet files, emptying the Recycle Bin, or performing a disk cleanup. However, if hard disk space has become insufficient to download or install updates, you will almost certainly encounter other disk-related problems and should consider a hard disk upgrade.

■ **The user cancelled the installation process or the computer disconnected from the Internet**   Sometimes an update can take a considerable time, and a user might cancel it through inexperience or impatience (this is probably why Microsoft designed Windows Update to require elevated privileges in order to stop a download or installation). Sometimes an Internet connection is required to install an update, and it is always required to download the update files. Disconnection from the Internet can happen for a wide variety of reasons. If the disconnection is transient, download will resume when the connection is reestablished, but if the interruption lasts for too long, the download times out. If the installation process was cancelled, the update can be installed again. If a download failed, the update will be downloaded the next time a scheduled download occurs, or it can be downloaded manually.

■ **A user installs an update and a device stops working**   Installing an optional update such as a new device driver requires elevated privileges. You can therefore control such updates when you are supporting standard users. However, a home user who has an administrator account might install an unsuitable device driver that conflicts with computer hardware. In this case, you need to advise the user how to roll back to the previous device driver or access a manufacturer's site to download and install a device driver.

NOTE Troubleshooting device drivers

For more information about installing and troubleshooting device drivers, see Lesson 3, "Installing, Updating, and Troubleshooting Windows Vista Device Drivers," of Chapter 1, "Installing Windows Vista"; Lesson 1, "Troubleshooting Post-Installation Configuration Issues," of Chapter 3, "Troubleshooting Post-Installation System Settings"; and Lesson 2, "Troubleshooting Connectivity Issues," of Chapter 7, "Configuring Network Connectivity."

■ **The update cannot complete because a restart is required**   Some updates apply to files or services that Windows is using and cannot be installed while Windows is running. In this case, you should advise the user to save his or her work, close any open programs, and then restart the computer to complete the update process.

NOTE Stand-alone or exclusive updates

Some updates cannot be installed at the same time as other updates, usually because they require a computer restart before they can take effect. For example, an update for the Windows Update service might be required before the service can check for other updates, or an update might be a new version or a service pack for software that is currently running. To make sure that a computer is ready to install these updates, you (or users you support) must first install all important updates on the computer. It is highly advisable, but not essential, to also install recommended updates. After you have installed these updates, Windows Update will prompt you to install the stand-alone or exclusive update.

■ **The computer was turned off at the time at which the update was scheduled**   If the computer is on during the next scheduled installation, the update will be installed at that time. However, if an organization you support turns off all its computers at night, you should consider rescheduling updates. If home users do the same, you might need to advise them how to change Windows Update settings. If new updates are ready to be installed and a user shuts down a computer, Windows Update will prompt the user to install the updates before shutdown.

■ **The computer was in a power-saving state (sleep or hibernate) when the update was scheduled**   If a computer (typically a laptop) is in one of the power-saving states during a scheduled update and the computer is plugged in to a power source, Windows Vista wakes the computer for long enough to install new updates. If, however, the computer is running on battery power, the new updates will not install. Windows Update instead tries to install them at the next scheduled installation time. If this behavior presents a problem, you should consider rescheduling the updates.

If you cannot identify the problem in the list supplied in this section, you can learn more about what happened and what to do next by reviewing error messages displayed in the Windows Update dialog box. If you want to see examples of Windows Update errors and error message numbers, search for "Windows Update error" in Windows Help and Support.

If you encounter an error that you cannot identify and resolve, you can post details on the Discussions in Windows Update website at *http://www.microsoft.com/communities/newsgroups /en-us/default.aspx?dg=microsoft.public.windowsupdate&lang=en&cr=US*. If somebody has already come across the problem and reads your post, that person will probably help you. You might even see a solution to your problem already posted on the discussion forum.

MORE INFO   Windows Update problems

You can get more information about Windows Update and Windows Update problems on the Microsoft Windows Update Help and Support site at *http://support.microsoft.com/ph/6527/*. You can get detailed information about Windows Update problems at *http://support.microsoft.com/kb /906602*. If you want to report a problem to Microsoft online, access *http://support.microsoft.com /gp/wusupport*.

> ## Quick Check
> 1. What type of update requires elevated privileges to download and install?
> 2. What updates cannot be installed at the same time as other updates?
>
> ### Quick Check Answers
> 1. Optional
> 2. Stand-alone or exclusive updates

Hiding Updates and Restoring Hidden Updates

If you decide not to install an update, you probably do not want it to appear on the update list in the Check For Updates dialog box. If you have configured Windows Update to notify you (or other users) when updates are available for download or installation, you do not want an update that you previously decided not to install to trigger a notification. You can prevent both these occurrences by hiding the update.

Hiding updates and restoring hidden updates both require elevated privileges, so you will need to carry out these tasks for users with standard accounts. You might need to advise home users with administrator accounts why they should hide updates and how they can do so.

You can hide an update by right-clicking it in the View Available Updates dialog box and selecting Hide Update, as shown in Figure 12-5. If you need more details before you decide to do so, you can click View Details first.

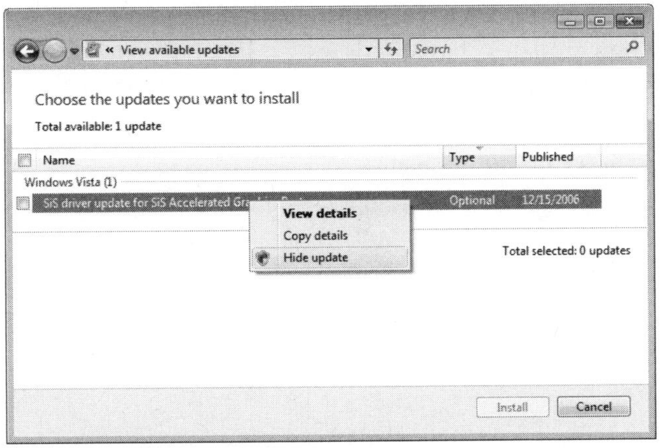

Figure 12-5   Hiding an update

Elevated privileges are required to hide updates, so you need to either supply credentials or click Continue as prompted to close the User Access Control (UAC) dialog box. If you then press F5 to refresh the Check For Updates dialog box, the hidden update should no longer be listed.

If you decide that you should not have hidden an update after all, you can first restore it and then (if you want to) install it. To do this, you open Windows Update and click Restore Hidden Updates. In the Restore Hidden Updates dialog box, you select the update or updates that you want to restore, as shown in Figure 12-6, and click Restore.

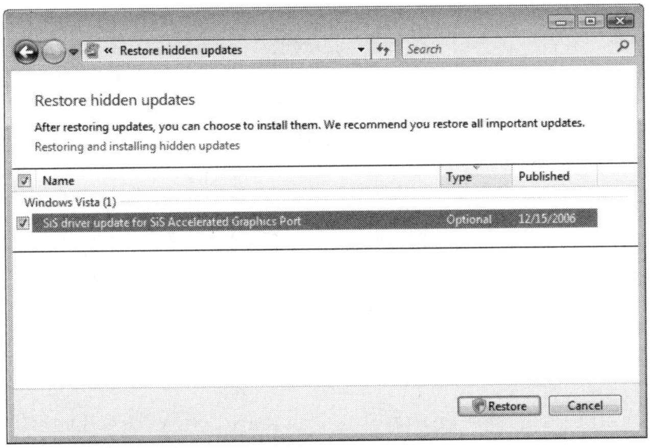

Figure 12-6   Restoring an update

As with hiding updates, the restore operation requires elevated privileges, so you need to clear the UAC dialog box. After you have restored hidden updates, Windows Update scans the Microsoft Update site to discover whether any new updates have been published. You can then check for updates. The restored updates are now listed in the View Available Updates dialog box together with any new updates that Windows Update has detected, and you can decide whether to install the updates.

NOTE   **Sometimes hidden updates do not appear**

Updates that you have previously hidden might not appear on the list. This happens when a subsequent update addressed the same problem. If an optional update contained a device driver file, for example, and a subsequent update contained a new version of the same file, only the second update would be available.

Viewing Update History

To find out which Windows updates are installed on your computer, you open Windows Update and click View Update History in the left pane of the Windows Update dialog box. The View Update History dialog box, shown in Figure 12-7, shows the installed updates, when they were installed, the update type, and whether the installation was successful.

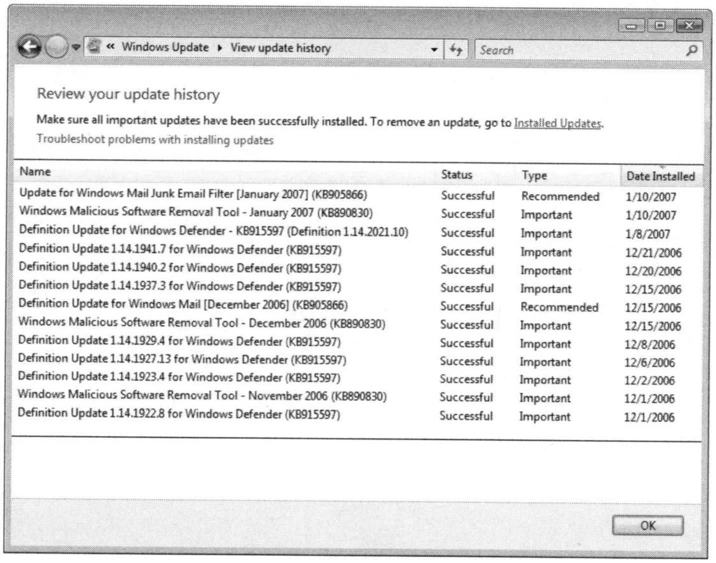

Windows Update ▸ View update history   Search

Review your update history

Make sure all important updates have been successfully installed. To remove an update, go to Installed Updates.
Troubleshoot problems with installing updates

Name	Status	Type	Date Installed
Update for Windows Mail Junk Email Filter [January 2007] (KB905866)	Successful	Recommended	1/10/2007
Windows Malicious Software Removal Tool - January 2007 (KB890830)	Successful	Important	1/10/2007
Definition Update for Windows Defender - KB915597 (Definition 1.14.2021.10)	Successful	Important	1/8/2007
Definition Update 1.14.1941.7 for Windows Defender (KB915597)	Successful	Important	12/21/2006
Definition Update 1.14.1940.2 for Windows Defender (KB915597)	Successful	Important	12/20/2006
Definition Update 1.14.1937.3 for Windows Defender (KB915597)	Successful	Important	12/15/2006
Definition Update for Windows Mail [December 2006] (KB905866)	Successful	Recommended	12/15/2006
Windows Malicious Software Removal Tool - December 2006 (KB890830)	Successful	Important	12/15/2006
Definition Update 1.14.1929.4 for Windows Defender (KB915597)	Successful	Important	12/8/2006
Definition Update 1.14.1927.13 for Windows Defender (KB915597)	Successful	Important	12/6/2006
Definition Update 1.14.1923.4 for Windows Defender (KB915597)	Successful	Important	12/2/2006
Windows Malicious Software Removal Tool - November 2006 (KB890830)	Successful	Important	12/1/2006
Definition Update 1.14.1922.8 for Windows Defender (KB915597)	Successful	Important	12/1/2006

OK

Figure 12-7   The View Update History dialog box

If you want more detail about an update, you can right-click it and click View Details. The View Details information box, shown in Figure 12-8, includes a hyperlink that enables you to obtain more information if required. You do not need to supply administrator credentials to view update history or obtain update details, but it is an activity that an administrator rather than a standard user is more likely to carry out.

NOTE The View Details information box

The information box shown in Figure 12-8 is the View Details information box. The Windows Update legend at the top of the information box is generic, although it looks as if it is the information box title.

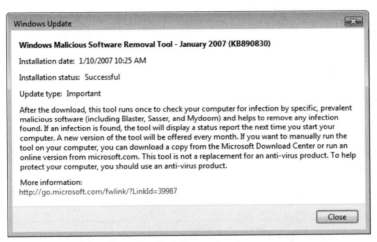

Figure 12-8 The View Details information box

Sometimes updates can cause unforeseen problems. In an enterprise environment (i.e. in large organizations), WSUS is used to distribute updates, and updates are rigorously tested before distribution. Typically, in the Small Office/Home Office (SOHO) environment, every important and recommended update is automatically installed. You might, therefore, need to uninstall an update that is causing problems. If you want to uninstall an update, you can click Installed Updates in the View Update History dialog box or the Windows Update dialog box. This opens the Uninstall An Update dialog box, shown in Figure 12-9. You can also access this dialog box by clicking Programs in Control Panel, selecting Programs And Features, and selecting View Installed Updates.

Not all of the updates in the View Update History dialog box appear in the Uninstall An Update dialog box. Windows Defender definitions, for example, cannot be uninstalled. To uninstall an update, select the update, and click Uninstall. This operation requires elevated privileges.

NOTE Features accessible from the Uninstall An Update dialog box

By clicking the links in the left pane of this dialog box you can select a program to uninstall, access the Windows Marketplace website, view purchased programs in digital locker, and enable or disable Windows features such as Games or the Index Service. None of these facilities have anything to do with updates (although Windows Ultimate Extras is one of the features you can disable). They are items included in Programs and Features, as is Uninstall Updates.

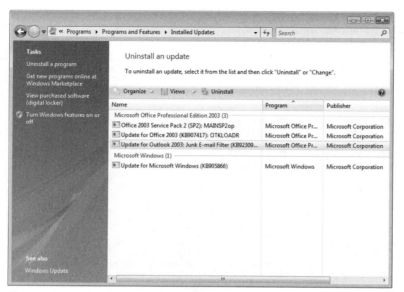

Figure 12-9   The Uninstall an Update dialog box

Windows Ultimate Extras

If a computer is running Windows Vista Ultimate edition, the Windows Update dialog box contains a link to Windows Ultimate extras. If a Windows Ultimate extra is available, the user can download and install it. Windows Ultimate extras are programs, services, and premium content (for example, publications) for Windows Vista Ultimate edition. You can obtain more information by clicking Learn About Windows Ultimate Extras in the Windows Update dialog box. This accesses the Windows Ultimate Extras information box.

You can download Windows Ultimate extras (if available) from the Windows Ultimate Extras information box by selecting Download Programs, Services, And Unique Content From Windows Ultimate Extras. You can also access the Windows Vista Ultimate website from this dialog box or directly at *http://www.microsoft.com/windowsvista/getready /editions/ultimate.mspx*.

Practice: Configuring Windows Update

In this practice session, you configure Windows Update to obtain updates for more products. You configure the settings so that Windows Update scans for important and recommended updates, but the user is prompted to download and install them.

Configuring Windows Update settings requires elevated privileges, and the practices, as written, ask you to log on by using the administrator account (Kim_Ackers) that you created when you installed Windows Vista. If you prefer, you can use the parent_admin account that you created in Chapter 4, "Configuring and Troubleshooting Internet Access." If you want to, you can use a standard account—for example, the parent_standard account that you created in Chapter 4—and supply administrator account credentials in the UAC dialog box when prompted.

IMPORTANT   Practice 1 is a one-off procedure

Configuring Windows Update to obtain updates for more products is a one-off procedure that ensures Windows Update uses the Microsoft Update site, which provides updates for additional Microsoft products rather than the Windows Update site, which provides only OS updates. If you performed a clean install of Windows Vista, as described in Chapters 1 and 2, you need to carry out this procedure. If, however, you instead performed an OS upgrade or if someone else has previously carried out the procedure, there is no need for you to configure Windows Update to obtain updates for more products. In this case, you will not see the Get Updates For More Products link in the Windows Update dialog box, as described in step 3 of the Practice. In this situation, you can connect manually to the Microsoft Update site at *http://update.microsoft.com/microsoftupdate/v6 /vistadefault.aspx?ln=en-us* and read the Microsoft Update Privacy Statement and Terms of Use.

▶ **Practice 1: Configuring Windows Update to Obtain Updates for More Products**

By default, Windows Update obtains updates for Windows only. To configure it to obtain updates for more products, follow these steps:

1. If necessary, log on by using the Kim_Ackers account that you created when you installed Windows Vista.

2. On the All Programs menu, select Windows Update.

3. In the Windows Update dialog box, click Get Updates For More Products, as shown in Figure 12-10. If this link is not available, then you do not need to configure Windows Update to obtain updates for more products—refer to the Important note that precedes this practice.

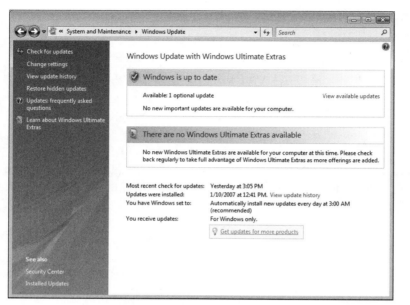

Figure 12-10   Getting updates for more products

4. On the Windows Vista Microsoft Update website, click Microsoft Update Privacy Statement. This accesses the Microsoft Online Privacy Notice Highlights website. A number of links exist on this website, and you can find out as much as you want to about the Microsoft Update Privacy statement.

NOTE   Windows Update and privacy

The Microsoft Update Privacy Statement contains a lot of information. What it boils down to is that Windows Update contains software tools that detect information about a computer, such as the make and model and the version of Windows and other Microsoft software that the computer is running. Microsoft uses that information to install only the updates the computer needs. Microsoft does not gather personal information about users or information that would uniquely identify a computer.

---

5. Click the Back button on your browser until you return to the Windows Vista Microsoft Update website. Click Terms Of Use. As with the privacy statement, this accesses a lot of information. Read what you need to. When you are happy with the terms of use, return to the Windows Vista Microsoft Update website.

6. On the Windows Vista Microsoft Update website, select I Accept The Terms Of Use, as shown in Figure 12-11.

Figure 12-11   Accepting the terms of use

7. Click Install. As prompted, click Continue to close the UAC dialog box. The website informs you that Microsoft Update is successfully installed, as shown in Figure 12-12. Close the website.

Figure 12-12   Microsoft Update is successfully installed

8. Windows Update now automatically checks for new updates. Access the Windows Update dialog box, which should still be open.

9. As shown in Figure 12-13, Windows Update will probably find several new updates. View and install these updates (if available) as described earlier in this lesson.

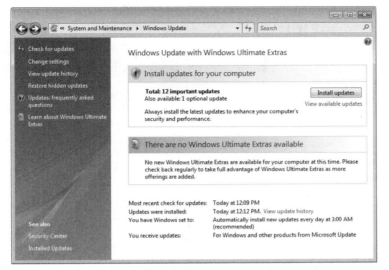

Figure 12-13   Windows Update detects new updates

▶ **Practice 2: Configuring Windows Update Settings**

In this practice, you configure Windows Update settings so that Windows Update informs you when important and recommended updates are available for download. You then decide whether to download and install them. The configuration does not take very long, but you might need to wait for some time, possibly a few days, before you see the notification displayed in the final figure in this procedure (Figure 12-15). If you want to reduce the time you need to wait, carry out the procedure on the second Monday in a month—the day before Microsoft usually releases updates. To configure Windows Update settings, follow these steps:

1. If necessary, log on by using the Kim_Ackers account that you created when you installed Windows Vista.
2. On the All Programs menu, select Windows Update.
3. In the Windows Update dialog box, click Change Settings.

4. In the Change Settings dialog box, ensure that the Include Recommended Updates When Downloading, Installing, Or Notifying Me About Updates check box is selected.

5. Select Check For Updates But Let Me Choose Whether To Download And Install Them. The new settings in the Change Settings dialog box are shown in Figure 12-14.

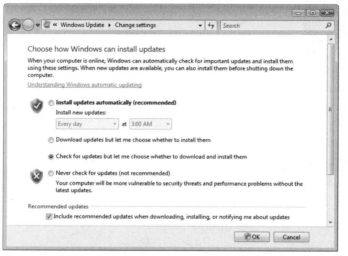

Figure 12-14   New Windows Update settings

6. Click OK. As prompted, click Continue to close the UAC dialog box.

7. When the Microsoft Update site next publishes new updates, you (or any other user using the computer) will see the new update icon appear on the screen and will be informed that new updates are available, as shown in Figure 12-15.

Figure 12-15   New updates are available

8. Clicking the New Updates Are Available message opens Windows Update. You can then click Check For Updates and select the updates you want to download and install as described previously in this lesson.

Lesson Summary

- You can configure Windows Update to automatically download and install updates, to automatically download updates and prompt you to install them, or to prompt you to download and install updates. Optional updates are not installed automatically.
- By default, both important and recommended updates install automatically or generate user prompts. You can change this setting so that only important updates do that.
- If you choose not to install an update, you can hide it so that Windows Vista does not keep reminding you about it. You can restore and install hidden updates.
- You can view a history of the updates that Windows Update has installed and, if required, uninstall an update.

Lesson Review

You can use the following questions to test your knowledge of the information in Lesson 1, "Configuring Windows Update." The questions are also available on the companion CD if you prefer to review them in electronic form.

NOTE Answers

Answers to these questions and explanations of why each answer choice is correct or incorrect are located in the "Answers" section at the end of the book.

---

1. What type of update can you configure either to be installed or not to be installed automatically if the Install Updates Automatically setting is enabled in Windows Update?
   - A. Important
   - B. Recommended
   - C. Optional
   - D. Stand-alone
2. The installation of which types of update never requires elevated privileges? (Choose all that apply.)
   - A. Important
   - B. Recommended
   - C. Optional
   - D. Stand-alone

3. A user you support is aware that her computer is updated automatically every evening at 7:00 P.M. However, she has been on vacation for two weeks, and her computer has been turned off. She is concerned that she might have missed some important updates. You are at a meeting off-site, and firewall restrictions prevent you from using Remote Assistance or Remote Desktop to access the user's computer. The user is not confident that she can manually download updates. What do you tell her?

   A. She has missed any updates that occurred during the last two weeks. You need to access the Microsoft Update site directly from her computer and download these updates. You cannot do this until the following morning.

   B. No method exists for downloading the missed updates. However, you can manually update her virus and spyware definitions when you return to the office on the following morning.

   C. You can manually download and install all the updates she has missed when you return to the office on the following morning.

   D. She should not power down her computer overnight. All the important updates she has missed will be installed automatically that evening.

4. Windows Update is configured for users you support, so they are prompted to download and install updates. A user has decided not to install a recommended update. He does not want to be notified about this update in the future. The user has a standard account. How do you prevent this from happening?

   A. Log on to the user's computer and hide the update.

   B. Log on to the user's computer. Access Windows Update settings, and clear the Include Recommended Updates When Downloading, Installing, Or Notifying Me About Updates check box.

   C. Ask the user to hide the update.

   D. Ask the user to access Windows Update settings, and clear the Include Recommended Updates When Downloading, Installing, Or Notifying Me About Updates check box.

Lesson 2: Configuring Data Protection

You do not want to lose your files. As an administrator, you encourage users you support to create regular backups. If you lose a significant amount of your own data for any reason whatsoever, your credibility is zero. We all make mistakes. You need to ensure that your mistakes do not seriously affect the information you store.

You need to advise your users about backup. Accept that all inexperienced users, most senior managers, most home users, and all family members will have a serious mental block about backing up data, and any file they lose is entirely your fault. You need to ensure that you and your users back up important files regularly. You can manually back up your files any time or set up automatic backups. Whenever possible, implement the automatic option.

NOTE Automatic backups

You cannot implement automatic backups in Windows Vista Starter and Windows Vista Home Basic editions.

After this lesson, you will be able to:
- Use Windows backup and restore settings to schedule automatic backups.
- Carry out full and updated files only backups manually.
- Create restore points and use System Restore.
- Restore damaged or deleted files by using backup and shadow copies.
- Use Complete PC Backup to create an image.

Estimated lesson time: 45 minutes

Real World

Ian McLean

Once upon a time, a user whom I refuse to name because she's married to me was working on a rather large document. She decided to copy the information in its entirety into another document, so she pressed Ctrl+A. She meant to then press Ctrl+C, but missed the Ctrl key, so the entire document now contained only the letter c. She didn't realize what had happened (a simple Edit/Undo would have retrieved the situation) and decided she had better call on me for advice. However, she remembered that I was always advising her to save her work.

So first she saved and closed the file.

Yesterday an author who shall remain anonymous, although he should not be too difficult to identify, was writing Chapter 12 of a book about Windows Vista. Usually he saves his work to hard disk and then saves it again to a universal serial bus (USB) flash memory pen. If either the disk or the flash memory were to develop a fault, the work would still be safe. However, he was in a hurry. He saved his work regularly to hard disk (this is by now a reflex) but not to flash memory. At the end of the day, hurrying to keep an appointment, he closed the file, realized the updated file wasn't on the pen drive, and copied it (he thought) from the hard disk to the pen drive.

He copied from the pen drive to the hard disk.

Everybody makes mistakes, no matter how experienced they are. Hardware is a lot more reliable than it used to be, but disks still fail. We all need to back up our work. Regular daily backups ensure that you will, at worst, lose a day's work. Backups need to be scheduled to occur automatically, otherwise you will forget (I know I will). Shadow copies provide additional protection, particularly if you decide that you want to revert to a file that you created a few days ago. Fortunately, in both cases described, a shadow copy of the user file had been created earlier that day, so only a couple of hours work was lost—annoying, but not a disaster.

Using Windows Backup and Restore

You can use the Back Up Files and Restore Files wizards to configure automatic backup settings, perform manual backups, determine what files have been backed up, and perform restores.

Configuring Automatic Backup Settings

To configure automatic file backup on a computer, you click System And Maintenance in Control Panel and click Backup And Restore Center. In the Backup And Restore Center, shown in Figure 12-16, you click Back Up Files beside Create Backup Copies Of Your Files And Folders.

Any user can create a copy of a file or folder at any time by simply copying it to another location. However, taking a backup is not the same as making a file copy, as we shall see when we have discussed backup more fully in this lesson. Using or configuring the Back Up Files wizard requires elevated privileges, and you need to do this for nonadministrator users you support. You might also need to guide home users with administrator accounts through the procedure.

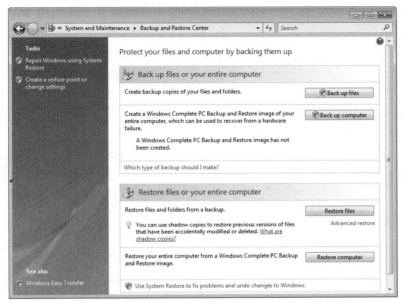

Figure 12-16   The Backup And Restore Center

When you close the UAC dialog box by clicking Continue or by supplying administrator credentials as prompted, the Back Up Files wizard starts. You specify where you want to store the backup, what you want to back up, and when you want backup to occur. As shown in Figure 12-17, the first thing you need to specify is the location of the backup files.

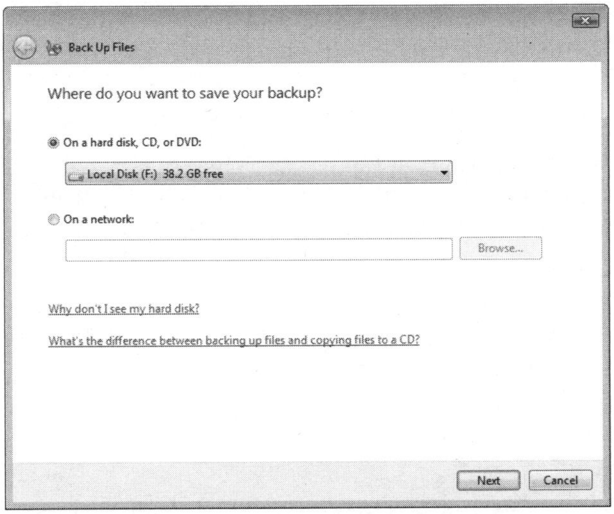

Figure 12-17   Choosing the backup destination

Choosing Backup Media You can back up files onto the following:

- Another fixed hard disk on the computer
- Removable media such as a USB or FireWire hard disk
- CD-R, CD-RW, or DVD rewritable disks (previous OSs did not allow backup to optical media)
- Another computer on the network
- A stand-alone network drive

Arguably, for SOHO networks the best choice might be a USB or FireWire hard disk. If a user's computer fails, you can easily unplug the removable hard disk and plug it into another computer to allow the user to continue working. This is not so easy if you use a second internal hard disk.

You need to be reasonably sure that a backup device will be there when the backup is scheduled. A USB or FireWire hard disk is typically left plugged in to a computer. There might not be a suitable disk in a CD-RW or DVD-RW drive.

Exam Tip Windows Help and Support is careful to specify CD-R, CD-RW, and DVD rewritable disks as backup media, rather than read-only CD-ROM and DVD-ROM disks. Be wary of any answer in the 70-620 examination that specifies a CD-ROM or DVD-ROM disk as a backup medium.

If a backup does not fit on one CD-R, CD-RW, or DVD rewritable disk, you need to be present during the backup to feed additional disks into the drive. This rather negates the advantage of automatic backups scheduled at midnight. The amount of space that a backup requires depends on the size of the files that are backed up. Windows Vista keeps track of the files that have been added or modified since the last backup, so the automatic backup process backs up only these files that have been changed. This saves time and disk space.

If you use a hard disk (removable or fixed), it should be formatted by using the new technology file system (NTFS). You can back up to a hard disk that is formatted by using the file allocation table (FAT) filing system—that is, FAT16 or FAT32—but Microsoft recommends NTFS.

NOTE Files stored in a FAT filing system

It is possible (if inadvisable) to specify a hard disk formatted by using FAT as a backup destination. However, you *cannot* back up files that are stored on FAT media. For this reason, you typically cannot back up files stored on a USB flash memory device because flash memory is by default formatted by using FAT.

A major advantage of NTFS is you can use the Encrypting File System (EFS) to protect the backed-up data (although you cannot back up files that are already encrypted). EFS is discussed in more detail later in this lesson.

> ## FAT and NTFS
>
> You can format hard disks used with Windows OSs in NTFS, FAT32, and FAT (also known as FAT16). NTFS is the preferred file system for Windows Vista (and Windows XP). NTFS is more reliable, having the capability to recover from some disk-related errors, such as bad sectors, automatically. It is sometimes described as self-healing.
>
> NTFS (introduced with Microsoft Windows NT) provides better security because you can use file-level permissions and encryption to restrict access to specific files to approved users. It also supports larger hard disks and larger files. You cannot create a FAT32 partition greater than 32 GB, and you cannot store a file larger than 4 GB on a FAT32 partition.
>
> FAT and FAT32 were used with Windows 95, Windows 98, and Windows Millennium Edition OSs. Except in the case of a client that needs to dual boot between Windows Vista and one of these legacy systems, there is no good reason for having a hard disk formatted in FAT32 or FAT. You can use the convert command-line utility to convert from FAT or FAT32 to NTFS without loss of data.
>
> Floppy disks (now largely obsolete) needed to be formatted in FAT because they had insufficient capacity to support NTFS. Flash memory devices typically use FAT.

Using another computer or a stand-alone network drive has advantages as far as single-seat centralized administration is concerned, but this technique is more likely to be used on large Active Directory networks.

CD-R, CD-RW, and DVD rewritable disks are more commonly used for archiving. You might schedule backups every night but back up the backups once a week onto disk media and archive them in a fireproof safe, preferably off-site. Files backed up on optical disk media can be encrypted.

A user can copy files manually to a second partition on the same hard disk or even to another folder on that disk. This is better than nothing. If a user accidentally deletes a file, the copy will still be there. However, if the hard disk fails or is wiped in a virus attack, both the user files and the file copies will be lost. Microsoft does not recommend backing up onto the same disk that holds a user's files, and the Back Up Files wizard does not permit you to specify the source disk as a backup destination.

A user can also copy a file or folder on the computer to a USB pen drive or even a flash memory card (the device you use to store pictures in a digital camera). However, you cannot specify these devices in the File Back Up wizard. The wizard also does not permit you to back up files to tape drive.

Choosing the Files to Back Up   When you have specified a destination for the backup files and clicked Next, the wizard prompts you for the disks you want to include in the backup (if your computer has more than one hard disk drive) and then for the type of file to back up, as shown in Figure 12-18. The wizard will automatically detect all the files of the specified types that are stored on the computer. You can move your mouse pointer over any file type to obtain more details. For example, Figure 12-18 shows that document files include spreadsheets and presentations.

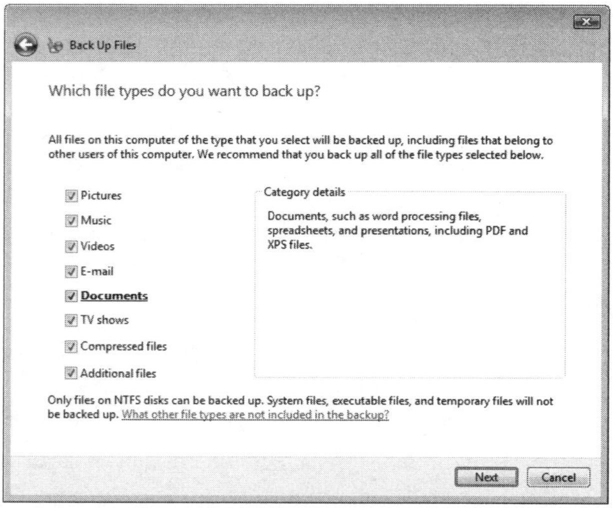

Figure 12-18   Choosing the file types to back up

The Back Up Files wizard backs up most common file types. If several users log on to the computer, all of these users' files are backed up, although a user can access only his or her own personal files to restore. The following files are *not* included:

- Files that have been encrypted by using EFS.
- System files (the files that Windows Vista needs in order to run).
- Program files.
- Files stored on media that are formatted using the FAT file system. You cannot, for example, specify files on a USB flash memory device.
- Web-based e-mail that is not stored on the computer's hard disk.
- Files in the Recycle Bin.
- Temporary files.
- User profile settings.

NOTE Encrypted files

If a user has chosen to encrypt files by using EFS, only that user can copy these files, and you cannot use the File Back Up wizard to implement or schedule a backup. In this case, you need to encourage the user to regularly copy the files and paste them to NTFS-formatted backup media. As an administrator, you can obtain a recovery certificate and decrypt files that another user has encrypted, but you would normally do this only in exceptional circumstances—for example, if a user has left an organization and you need access to that user's files. For more information, search for "Create a recovery certificate for encrypted files" in Windows Help and Support.

> ## Real World
>
> *Ian McLean*
>
> When it comes to protecting files, the nightmare user is the one who carries files around in a USB flash memory pen drive so that they can be worked on anytime, anywhere there is a computer to plug the pen drive into. The very, very worst of these users are known as authors. USB flash memory is formatted as FAT and is more likely to lose data than an NTFS hard disk. Also, a device carried around in a pocket or briefcase is doubly vulnerable.
>
> Once, one such author was on vacation. He decided to do some writing under a sun parasol with a long, cool drink in his hand. It was a soft drink—honest. He borrowed a laptop from some trusting soul in the next-door apartment, plugged in his trusty pen drive, and wrote for a couple of hours about SQL Server 2005. It's nice work if you can get it.
>
> Our hero saved his file, unplugged the pen drive, and put it in the pocket of his swimming shorts. He then returned the laptop to its owner and decided that another long, cool drink was in order. He finished his drink, relaxed in the sun for a while, and then jumped in the pool to cool off.
>
> You cannot schedule automatic backups of a USB flash memory device. It is even more difficult to protect the files on a device that lives in its owner's pocket. You need to persuade the owner in question to download from portable memory to hard disk. Many administrator tasks involve dealing with people problems rather than technical problems. Hopefully, most of your users won't be as dumb as that author.

Scheduling Backups   When you select the check boxes for the types of files you want to back up and click Next, the wizard asks you to schedule your backups, as shown in Figure 12-19. If you have not previously used the wizard to back up files, a backup will be performed immediately, as well as at the next scheduled backup time.

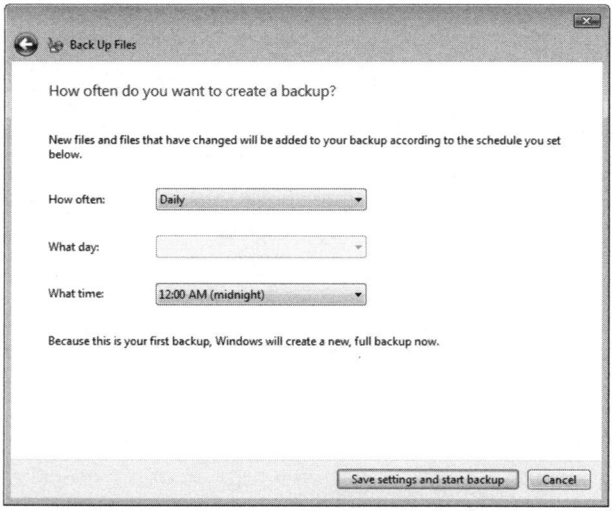

Figure 12-19   Scheduling automatic backups

You should schedule automatic backups for a time of low activity. Users can continue to work at the computer during a backup. If any file is changed while it is being backed up, the changes to the file will not be backed up until the next scheduled backup. However, the performance of the computer degrades significantly during a backup.

You should also avoid scheduling backups to occur at the same time as automatic Windows Update download and update installation or downloads of Windows Defender or virus definitions. Typically, backups are scheduled for around 7:00 P.M. If, however, a computer is heavily used in the evening (many home computers are), you might decide to schedule backups at midnight.

When you have specified when backups should occur, click Save Settings And Start Backup. This saves the automatic backup settings and (if no backup has been made previously) starts the backup. The wizard scans for files to back up and then backs up these files to the location you have specified.

NOTE   **Backups and Windows Vista editions**

You cannot implement automatic backups in Windows Vista Starter and Windows Vista Home Basic editions. However, Windows will periodically remind users to back up their files.

Accessing and Encrypting Backup Files

Because a backup contains the files created by all of a computer's users, you need to elevate permissions at every stage of the process if you want to access them by using Windows

Explorer. In this situation, you will find it is much more convenient if you log on by using an administrator account.

Backups are saved in the format: <backup location>\<computer name>\Backup Set <year-month-day> <time>. For example, if your computer name is GLASGOW, your backup location is F, and you backed up on January 15, 2007, at 11:08:30 (24-hour clock), the backup would be located in F:\GLASGOW\Backup Set 2007-01-15 110830, as shown in Figure 12-20. Backup files are zipped, and you need to use decompression software such as WinZip if you want to view them. Files are automatically unzipped during the restore process.

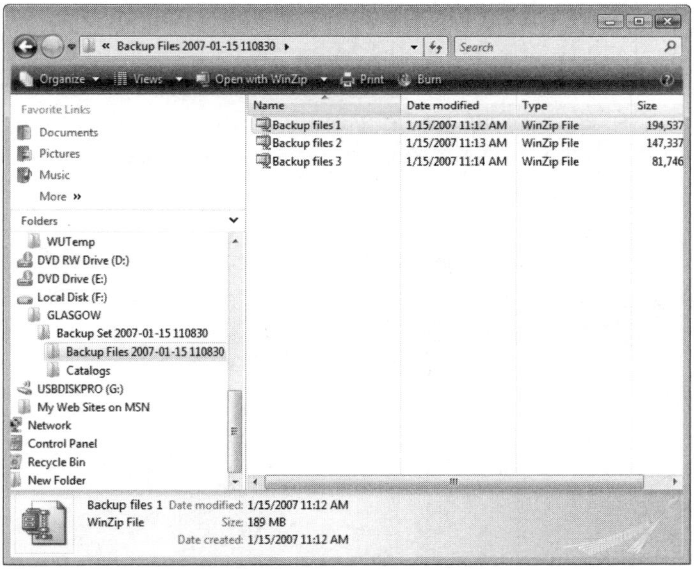

Figure 12-20   Viewing backup files

When you make a full backup, a backup folder is created and labeled with the date for that day. As you add updates, that date stays the same. However, the backup is not out of date. A new backup folder will not be created and labeled with a new date and time until the next time you make a full backup. Scheduled backups that occur automatically perform updates—that is, they back up only files that have changed. You can use the Backup and Control Center to perform an unscheduled manual full backup.

Encrypting Backed-Up Files   For extra security, you can use EFS to encrypt backup files with your personal encryption certificate. This could be inconvenient if several users log on to the computer because you would need to decrypt the files before another user could carry out a restore. Also, files that have been backed up are unencrypted in their original locations (otherwise they could not have been backed up), and it is debatable whether encrypting them in their backup location is worthwhile. This is something you need to decide on a case-by-case basis.

NOTE **EFS and Windows Vista editions**

EFS is not included in Windows Vista Starter, Windows Vista Home Basic, and Windows Vista Home Premium editions.

However, one situation in which it is a good idea to encrypt files is after you have copied them to CD-R, CD-RW, or DVD rewritable removable disks for archiving off-site. Personal files stored off-site should be encrypted. As an administrator, you will almost certainly be involved if files need to be restored from archived copies, so you can decrypt the files as required in this situation.

To encrypt all backed-up files, you right-click the parent folder, select Properties, and click Advanced in the General tab of the folder's Properties dialog box. In the Advanced Attributes dialog box, you select the Encrypt Contents To Secure Data check box, as shown in Figure 12-21, click OK, click OK again to close the Properties dialog box, and apply changes to the folder, subfolders, and files.

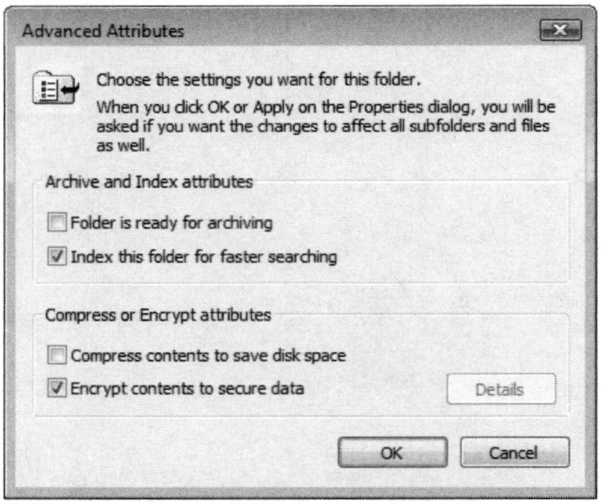

Figure 12-21 Encrypting backup files

Viewing Backup Files   You can view a list of files that have been backed up by opening the Back Up and Restore Center, clicking Restore Files, selecting files from either the latest backup or an older backup, and then clicking Add Files. As shown in Figure 12-22, you can then browse through the folder structure and see the files that are available for restore. However, if you open the Users folder, you will see only your own folder and the Public folder. Also, you cannot access folder or file properties. For example, you could not use this procedure to encrypt files or folders.

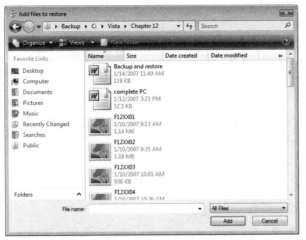

Figure 12-22 Using the Restore Files feature to view backed-up files

Changing Backup Settings

The first time you open the Backup and Control Center and click Back Up Files, the Back Up Files wizard guides you through the process of configuring automatic backup settings. However, when these settings have been configured, clicking Back Up Files implements a manual full backup.

If you want to change automatic backup settings, you need to open the Backup and Restore Center and click Change Settings under the Back Up Files button. This opens the Backup Status And Configuration dialog box, shown in Figure 12-23.

Figure 12-23 The Backup Status And Configuration dialog box

From this dialog box, you can disable automatic backup, start a manual backup, or click Change Backup Settings. If you choose the last option and clear the UAC dialog box as prompted, the Back Up Files wizard opens and you can reconfigure backup settings as described previously in this lesson.

Copying Files Manually

A user can at any time copy files and paste them to a folder on the preferred storage device. This is a good idea if you, or a user you support, have made significant changes to a file or have created some new and important files. However, if you want to carry out a manual backup of all the files selected for backup on the computer rather than wait for a scheduled backup, you should use the Back Up Files wizard. This requires elevated privileges, and you will need to carry out the procedure if a user you support requests it.

If you back up your work by copying and pasting rather than by using the Back Up Files wizard, you need to manually select each file and folder that you want to back up. If you want to back up only files that have changed since the last backup, you need to remember or check which files were amended recently. This can be time-consuming and tedious.

Backing up every file might be less tedious, but it is a lot more time-consuming. If, on the other hand, you use the Back Up Files wizard, Windows Vista keeps track of which files and folders are new or modified. You can then choose to either back up all of the specified files on your computer or just the files that have changed since the last time you made a backup. If you open the Backup and Restore Center and click Back Up Files, this creates a full backup. If you click Change Settings and then click Back Up Now, Windows Vista scans for new or updated files and backs them up. In both cases, elevated privileges are required, and you need to clear the UAC dialog box as prompted before backup starts.

You can choose to use the Back Up Files wizard to regularly back up changed files. However, you need to remember to do so. The one time you forget will be the time an important file is lost or corrupted. By all means back up manually when something significant has changed, but also configure the wizard to schedule automatic backups—for yourself and the users you support.

Backups vs. Copies

Most users, and some books and technical magazines, use the terms backups and copies interchangeably. The main purpose of both is to protect user data. However, they have significant differences:

- When a file is backed up, the archive attribute of the file is set. The file will not be backed up again during a scheduled backup. If the file is modified, the archive attribute is reset, and the file will be backed up. A manual full backup backs up all files whether they have been modified or not.
- A backup backs up all users' files. A user can copy only his or her own files.
- You cannot save registry settings or other system settings by using file copying. The use of restore points and System Restore is discussed later in this lesson.
- You cannot use file copying to create a complete image of a computer. Complete PC Backup is discussed later in this chapter.
- Backups are zipped and take up less disk space than copies. Compression and decompression happen automatically and are invisible to the user.
- You cannot use the Restore Files wizard to restore files you have copied.
- Copies are not marked as previous versions. You cannot restore them using the Restore Previous Versions feature discussed later in this lesson.
- You can copy files from any medium to any medium. You cannot back up files on FAT media. You can back up files only to hard disk (internal, external, or network drive), optical media, or another computer.
- You can copy files that you have encrypted. You cannot back up encrypted files.

Restoring Files

Any user can restore his or her files, and this operation does not require elevated privileges. Earlier in this lesson we saw how to use the Restore Files wizard to view backed-up files. To restore a file or a folder, you (or users you support) open the Backup and Restore Center and click Restore Files. You can choose to restore from the latest backup or from a previous backup. Usually, a restore from the latest backup is required, and this is the default. If you want to restore an entire folder (and all the subfolders and files it contains), select Add Folders. If you want to restore a particular file, select Add Files.

If you are not sure where a file or folder is located, you can select Search. Figure 12-24 shows the result of a search for a file called Backup and restore.doc.

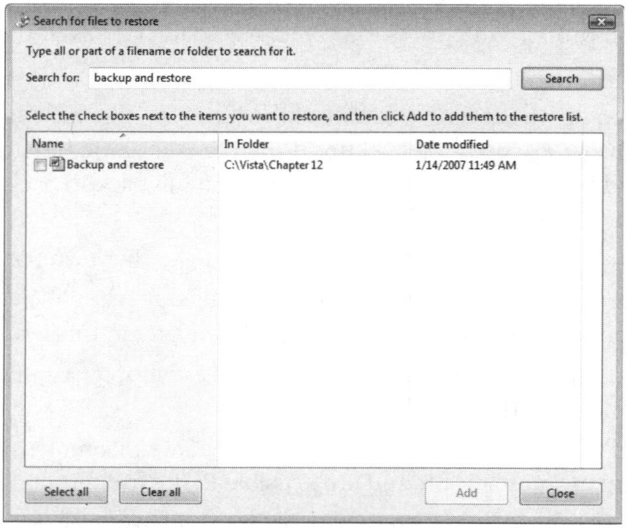

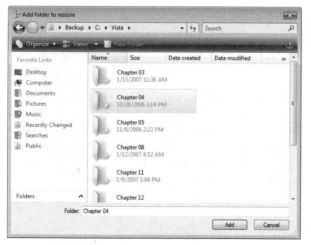

Figure 12-24   Searching for a file to restore

If you have found a file or folder you want to restore by using the Search facility, you can select the check box next to it and click Add. If you find the file or folder by using Add Folders or Add Files, you can select the folder you want to restore by clicking it, as shown in Figure 12-25, and then click Add.

Figure 12-25   Selecting a folder to restore

When you have selected all the files and folders you want to restore, you click Next in the Restore Files wizard. By default, you restore the files and folders to their original locations, overwriting the information that has been corrupted and that you need to restore. However, you have the option of restoring to another location. Restoring to a different location is sometimes called a dummy restore, and you can use it to test that the backed-up files and folders are not corrupt and that the restore process is working satisfactorily.

When you specify the location and click Start Restore, the backed-up files will be restored to the location you select. If this is the original location, the Copy File dialog box will likely indicate conflicts with the files already stored there. You can decide whether to replace each file in turn, or you can select Do This For All Conflicts and specify whether to copy and replace, not to replace, or to replace but keep both files.

Advanced Restore

If you have specified another computer as your backup medium or if you want to restore from a backup older than the most recent one, you click Advanced Restore in the Restore section of the Backup and Restore Center. This opens the Backup Status And Configuration dialog box but, as Figure 12-26 shows, this dialog box looks different from the one previously shown in Figure 12-23 because the restore options now display. If you click Restore Files, you can choose to restore from the most recent backup or from a previous backup. If you click Advanced Restore, you can restore from a backup made on another computer or restore files for all users of a computer.

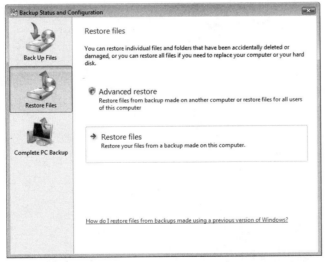

Figure 12-26   The Restore Options in the Backup Status And Configuration dialog box

---

NOTE Users do not need to unzip backed-up files

Although backups are stored as zipped files, this is invisible to the user when carrying out a restore. The restore process automatically unzips the files when a restore takes place.

Using System Restore

You can use System Restore to restore a computer's system files to an earlier point in time. It lets you undo system changes to a computer without affecting the computer users' personal files. System Restore is useful if a recently installed program or device driver is causing problems that uninstalling the program or rolling back the driver does not fix. System Restore restores the computer's system to an earlier date when everything worked correctly, but any user file that has been created since that earlier date is not affected.

System Restore uses the System Protection feature to regularly create and save restore points on a computer. A restore point is created automatically before any significant change is made to system settings. Restore points are also created on a daily basis by default, typically round about midday. They contain information about registry settings and other system information. You can also create restore points manually.

To restore a system to a previous restore point, open System And Maintenance from Control Panel, click System, click System Protection, clear the UAC dialog box as prompted, and click System Restore in the System Protection tab of the System Properties dialog box. The System Restore wizard opens, as shown in Figure 12-27.

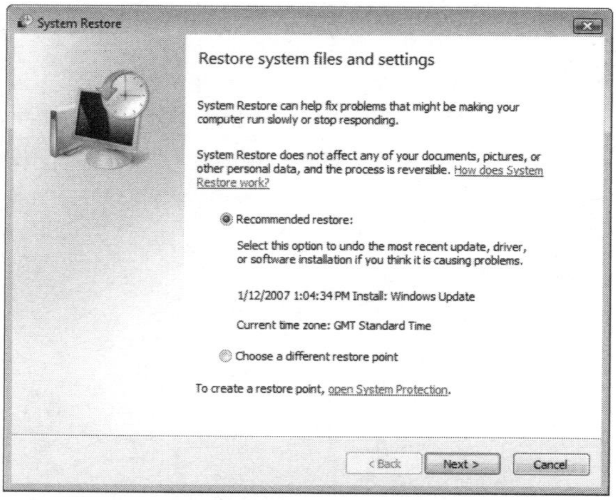

Figure 12-27 The System Restore wizard

Typically, you want to restore to the last restore point. In this case, you click Next and then click Finish to confirm the restore point and close the wizard. A computer restart is needed to complete the system restore process

System restore points are created automatically on a daily basis and also just before updates, applications, and device drivers are installed. If, however, you intend to make changes that might affect the system, it is a good idea to first create a system restore point manually. To do this, you access the System Protection tab of the System Properties dialog box as before, select the hard disk or disks on which you want to create system restore points (you should always select the disk where system files are located—typically the C drive; you might also choose to specify other disks where important files are stored), click Apply, and then click Create. Figure 12-28 shows the System Properties dialog box with a hard disk selected and the Create button enabled.

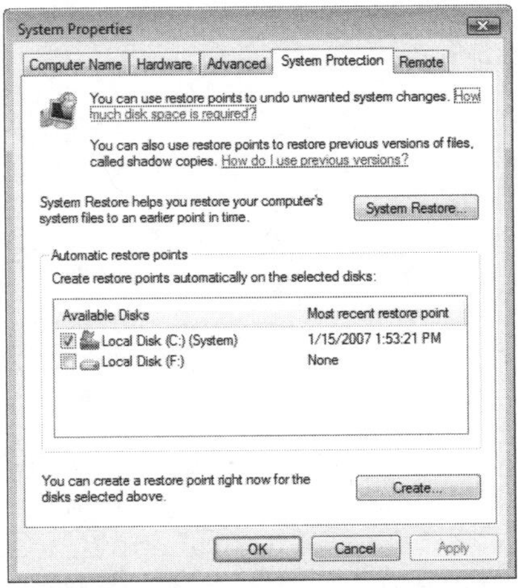

Figure 12-28   The System Properties dialog box configured to create a restore point

You click Create in the System Properties dialog box, give the restore point a name, and then click Create in the System Protection dialog box to create the restore point.

Restore points are saved until the hard disk space that System Restore reserves is filled up. System Restore reserves 300 MB of hard disk space initially and might use up to 15 percent of hard disk capacity. When the reserved hard disk space has been used up, System Restore will delete the oldest restore points to make room for new ones.

Shadow copies are automatically saved as part of a restore point in System Properties. If System Protection is turned on, Windows automatically creates shadow copies of files that have been modified since the last restore point was made.

NOTE   Scheduling shadow copies

In enterprise systems where user files are held on file servers rather than on client computers, you can schedule when shadow copies are created. On a computer running Windows Vista in a SOHO, shadow copies of user files that have changed since the last restore point are created with the next restore point. Typically, this happens around about the middle of the day—so if you create backups every night, you should always have a previous version of a frequently modified file that is only a few hours old. For more information about scheduling shadow copies on servers, access *http://technet2.microsoft.com/WindowsServer/en/library/4a10eb9b-611e-4a3f-a20b-9b2f8722cc171033 .mspx?mfr=true.*

If you turn off System Protection on a disk, all restore points are deleted from that disk. When you turn System Protection back on, new restore points are created. System Protection is enabled by default. To turn off System Protection for a hard disk, access the System Protection tab of the System Properties dialog box as before and clear the check box next to the disk. In the System Protection dialog box, click Turn System Restore Off.

NOTE   System Restore limitations

System Restore is not intended for backing up personal files, so it cannot help you recover a personal file that has been deleted or damaged (although a shadow copy of that file might have been saved when a restore point was created). System Restore does not work on hard disks with a capacity of less than 1 GB.

Using Complete PC Backup

Windows Complete PC Backup creates a backup image, which contains copies of your programs, system settings, and files. The backup image is then stored in a separate location from the original programs, settings, and files. You can use this backup image to restore the contents of a computer if a hard disk or computer ever stops working.

A Complete PC backup enables you to restore your OS and any other files to the state that existed when the complete PC backup was made. You should create a Windows Complete PC Backup image when you install Windows Vista. If the computer has more than one partition, the backup will typically include all files and programs on all partitions. Microsoft recommends creating a new Windows Complete PC Backup image every six months. You can save the backup image to a disk on which Windows Vista is not installed. You should also keep a backup on an external disk or on a set of CD-R, CD-RW, or DVD rewritable disks.

Creating a Windows Complete PC Backup Image

If you want to create a Windows Complete PC Backup image, your hard disk must be formatted to use the NTFS filing system. If you want to save the backup to an external hard disk, that disk must also be formatted with NTFS. The hard disk that you save the backup to must be a basic disk, not a dynamic disk.

MORE INFO   Basic and dynamic disks

For more information, search for "What are basic and dynamic disks?" in Windows Help and Support.

To create a complete PC backup, click System And Maintenance in Control Panel, select Backup And Restore Center, and then click Back Up Computer. Close the UAC dialog box as prompted and the Windows Complete PC Backup wizard starts. You can back up a complete PC image to a hard disk that can be internal or external but cannot be the hard disk that contains your system files (or any other hard disk that you include in the image). The Windows Complete PC Backup wizard warns you if there is insufficient space on a hard disk to create a Complete PC image. You can save a Complete PC image on CD-R, CD-RW, DVD rewritable, or hard disks. If you use CD-R or CD-RW disks, you might need a lot of them. Even if you use DVD rewritable disks, you are unlikely to get the entire backup onto a single disk. You create a Complete PC Backup image in the practice session later in this lesson.

NOTE   Using a removable hard disk drive

If you plug a removable (USB or FireWire) hard disk drive (HDD) into a computer and if you have not used the drive before with that computer, Windows Vista will install the device driver for the HDD. As part of this process, it will create a restore point and make shadow copies of files that have been altered since the last restore point. If you start a Complete PC Backup onto that HDD as soon as it becomes active and while Windows Vista is still creating shadow copies, the backup might fail. This is not a huge problem—repeat the backup and it will succeed. However, in this situation, it is better to wait a few minutes between plugging in the HDD and starting the backup.

Restoring a Computer from a Complete PC Image

When you use a Windows Complete PC Backup image to restore your computer, it is a complete restoration. You cannot choose individual items to restore, and all of your current programs, system settings, and files are replaced. A Windows Complete PC Backup image is a complete image that you can use to restore the contents of a computer if a hard disk or entire computer stops working.

If the computer you are restoring came with a Windows Vista installation disk, insert the installation disk, and restart the computer. The computer should boot from the installation disk.

NOTE   Computer not configured to start from an installation disk

If the computer is not configured to start from an installation disk, refer to Chapter 1, "Installing Windows Vista Client."

On the Start menu, click the arrow next to the Lock button, and click Restart. Choose the language settings, click Next, and then click Repair Your Computer. You then need to select the OS you want to repair and click Next. On the System Recovery Options menu, shown in Figure 12-29, click Windows Complete PC Restore. This procedure was previously described in Lesson 3, "Troubleshooting Installations and Upgrades," of Chapter 2, "Windows Vista Upgrades and Migrations."

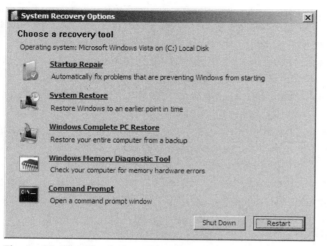

Figure 12-29   The System Recovery Options menu

Some vendors do not supply a Windows installation disk but instead install the System Recovery tools on a separate partition. In this case, restart the computer. On the Start menu, click the arrow next to the Lock button, and click Restart. If the computer has only one OS installed, press the F8 key repeatedly as the computer restarts and before the Windows logo appears.

If the computer has more than one operating system installed, you need to use the arrow keys to highlight the operating system you want to repair and then press F8. On the Advanced Boot Options menu, use the arrow keys to highlight Repair Your Computer, and then press Enter.

You then select a keyboard layout and click Next. You select a user name, type the password, and click OK. On the System Recovery Options menu, shown previously in Figure 12-29, you click Windows Complete PC Restore.

Whether you access the System Recovery tools from the installation disk or from a separate partition, the procedure after you have clicked Windows Complete PC Restore is the same and is straightforward. If Complete PC Restore detects the image on an internal or external hard disk drive, it involves clicking Next and Finish. If you choose to back up the image to optical media, you are prompted to insert the disks in the order in which they were created. If you have used third-party imaging software, such as Norton Ghost or Acronis True Image, the process will seem familiar.

Complete PC Restore restores the disk image exactly as it was when it was backed up. The backup consists of a large virtual hard disk (VHD) file and a number of small Extensible Markup Language (XML) documents. If you have included more than one hard disk in the image, all included hard disks will be restored. The OS installation disk is used only to load the System Recovery tools. It does not install the OS. You would use Complete PC Restore if, for example, a virus attack has corrupted or erased the disk partition that contains your OS and wiped out all your restore points.

MORE INFO   **VHD files**

For more information about VHD files, access *http://www.microsoft.com/technet/prodtechnol/virtualserver /2005/proddocs/vs_tr_a_virtualhd.mspx?mfr=true.*

If your entire hard disk suffers a hardware failure and you replace it, you will need to use an OS installation disk to load the System Recovery tools. If the computer came without an installation disk but was supplied with a recovery partition, you need to contact the manufacturer or retailer. You can specify only hard disk (internal or external) or optical media when creating a Complete PC Backup, so these are your only restore options.

If you carry out a Complete PC Restore, you will need to revalidate your OS. Otherwise, there would be nothing to prevent dishonest persons from creating a Complete PC Backup on optical media from a computer with a validated OS and applying the image to other computers.

NOTE   **Windows Vista editions**

Windows Complete PC Backup and Restore is not included with Windows Vista Home Basic or Windows Vista Home Premium editions.

Restoring Damaged or Deleted Files by Using Previous Versions

Previous versions are either backup copies (copies of files and folders that you back up by using the Back Up Files wizard) or shadow copies (copies of files and folders that Windows Vista automatically saves when it creates a restore point). You can use previous versions of files to restore damaged files or files that you, or users you support, accidentally modify or delete. You can open previous versions, save them to a different location, or restore a previous version of a damaged file to its original location.

Shadow Copies

Shadow copies are automatically saved as part of a restore point. If System Protection is enabled, Windows Vista automatically creates shadow copies of files that have been modified since the last restore point was created. Typically, new restore points are created once a day.

NOTE   Multiple partitions

If a hard disk is partitioned or if you have more than one hard disk on a computer, you need to turn on System Protection on the other partitions or hard disks. If, however, a hard disk is used solely to back up files, you probably will not gain much from creating restore points on that disk.

You can access previous versions of a file or folder by right-clicking the file or folder in Windows Explorer and clicking Restore Previous Versions. As shown in Figure 12-30, you then see a list of available previous versions of the file or folder. The list includes both backed-up files and shadow copies if both types are available.

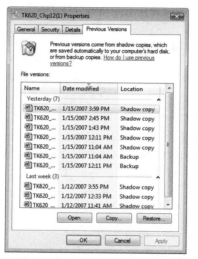

Figure 12-30   Previous versions

If you want to restore a previous version of a file or folder, right-click the file or folder, and click Restore Previous Versions. Click the item you want to restore, and then click Restore. You need to be careful to select the previous version that you want to restore because the file or folder will replace the current version on the computer, and you cannot undo the replacement. If the Restore Previous Versions option is unavailable, you cannot restore a previous version of the file or folder. You might, however, be able to open the previous version or save it to a different location.

On a computer that is running Windows Vista Business, Windows Vista Enterprise, or Windows Vista Ultimate, you can use shadow copies to recover previous versions of files directly from your hard disk rather than from a backup. If, however, you need to restore a backup copy, as opposed to a shadow copy, you carry out the same procedure, but you click the backup version of the file in the Previous Versions tab. When you click Restore, Windows Vista opens the Restore Files wizard.

If you cannot find shadow copies of some files, System Protection might not be turned on for that hard disk or the files might be offline files. Offline files, discussed in more detail in Chapter 13, "Configuring Mobile Devices," are copies of files that are stored on shared network folders. Shadow copies are not available for offline files. Shadow copies are unavailable for files and folders that are required for Windows Vista to work. For example, there is no shadow copy of the system folder (the folder that Windows Vista is installed in) and files in that folder.

You can restore a file or folder that was deleted or renamed from a shadow copy, but you need to know the location that the file or folder was saved to You do this in the practice session in this lesson.

Summary of Backup and Restore Types and When to Use Them

Windows Vista offers you several backup and restore methods, all designed for specific purposes. These have been described in this lesson but are summarized here for convenience:

- Use the Back Up Files wizard to back up personal files such as pictures, music, and documents.
- Create restore points to store system settings and create shadow copies.
- Use Windows Complete PC Backup to create an image of your entire computer when it is new and subsequently every six months.
- Use the Restore Files wizard to restore personal files such as pictures, music, and documents.
- Use previous copies if you want to restore personal files from either a shadow copy or a backup (whatever is the most recent) or if you want to go back to a previous version of a file before it was amended.
- Use System Restore if a change to the OS, a new program, or a new device driver is causing problems and you want to restore system or registry settings. System Restore does not alter personal files.
- Use Windows Complete PC Restore if a virus or hardware fault has corrupted your OS and deleted your restore points. Windows Complete PC Restore will restore personal files to the way they were when the Complete PC Backup was made, so you will probably need to use the Restore Files wizard after a Complete PC Restore to restore more recent versions of personal files.
- Make copies of files stored on USB flash memory devices and of your encrypted files. Always copy your encrypted files onto NTFS-formatted hard disk or optical storage so they remain encrypted.

Practice: Recovering Files and Creating a Complete PC Backup

In this practice session, you recover the previous version of a file you have renamed. You can use the same procedure to recover the previous version of a file you have deleted. You also create a Complete PC Backup. To carry out the second procedure, as written, you need a DVD-RW drive (internal or external) connected to your computer. However, if you prefer, you can create the backup on an external hard disk or on a second internal hard disk.

▶ **Practice 1: Recovering a Deleted or Renamed File**

In this practice, you select a file that has a number of previous versions and rename it. You then discover that you need to recover an older version of the file. You recover the previous version with its original filename.

You do not need to elevate privileges to complete this practice, and the procedure, as written, asks you to log on by using a standard account. However, if you want to, you can complete the practice logged on with an administrator account, such as the Kim_Ackers account that you created when you installed Windows Vista.

The procedure asks you to find a file (for example, a Microsoft Word document or Microsoft Excel spreadsheet) that has a number of previous versions. Hopefully, several such files exist on the computer. If not, you will need to create a file, perform a backup, edit the file, perform another backup, and create a restore point. The procedures for performing manual backups and manually creating a restore point were described earlier in this lesson. The figures in the practice show a file called Backup and restore.doc being used for this purpose. To recover a previous copy of a renamed file, follow these steps:

1. If necessary, log on by using a standard account—for example, the parent_standard account you created in Chapter 4, "Configuring and Troubleshooting Internet Access."
2. Open Windows Explorer by double-clicking My Computer on the Start menu.
3. Navigate to a folder in which you store personal files.
4. Open the folder, and right-click a file that you amend regularly. Select Restore Previous Versions.
5. Check that previous copies of the file exist, as shown in Figure 12-31.

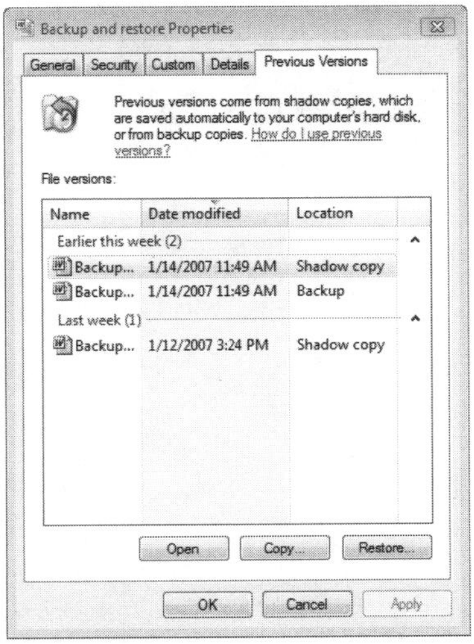

Figure 12-31   Previous versions of the Backup and restore file

6. Close the file Properties dialog box.

7. Right-click the file, and rename it.

8. Right-click the renamed file. As shown in Figure 12-32, the Restore Previous Versions option is no longer available.

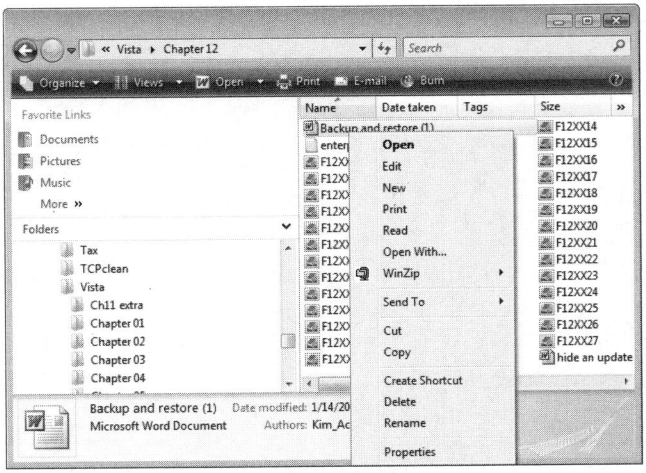

Figure 12-32   No previous versions of the renamed file are available

9. To restore a previous version of the file, right-click the folder in which it is saved in the left Windows Explorer pane, as shown in Figure 12-33, and click Restore Previous Versions.

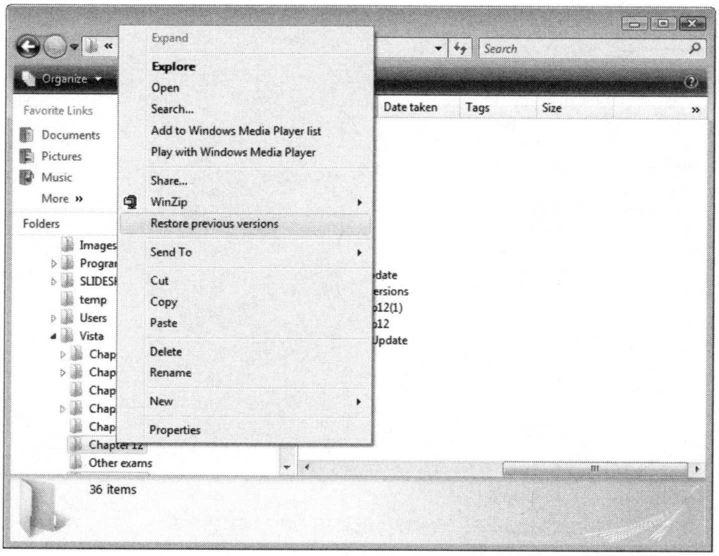

Figure 12-33   Restoring previous versions of a folder

10. Select a previous version of the folder that is likely to contain the file you want to restore, as shown in Figure 12-34, and then click Open.

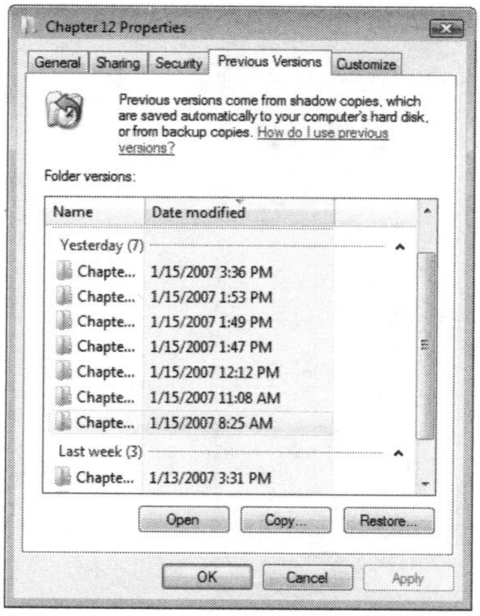

Figure 12-34   Selecting the previous version of a folder that contains the file you want to restore

11. As shown in Figure 12-35, the previous version of the file you want to restore should be in the previous version of the folder. Right-click the file, and copy it.

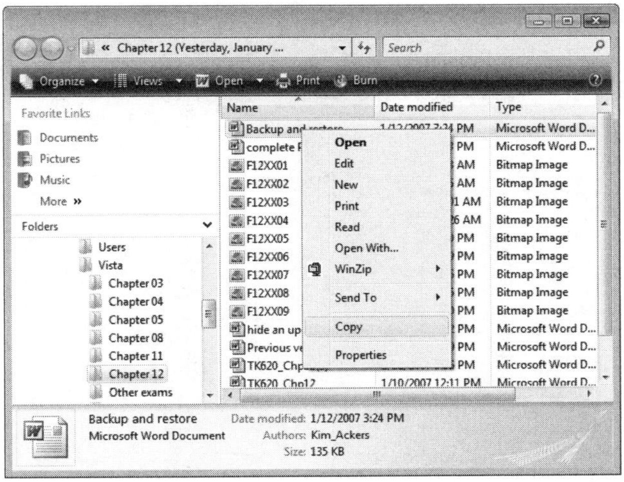

Figure 12-35   Copying the previous version of the file you renamed

12. Close the previous version of the folder. Paste the file to wherever you want to store it. It is a good idea to open it and make sure it is the version that you want.

NOTE   Recovering deleted files

You can also use the procedure outlined in Practice 1 to recover a previous version of a file you deleted and that is no longer in the Recycle Bin.

▶ **Practice 2: Creating a Complete PC Image**

In this practice, you create a Complete PC Backup image on DVD rewritable disks. If you prefer, you can create the image on an external hard disk drive. Complete PC Backup also lets you use an internal hard disk dive, provided that this drive is not included in the disks to be backed up.

Complete PC Backup requires elevated privileges, and the practice asks you to log on by using an administrator account. If you prefer, you can log on by using a standard account and supply administrator credentials to clear the UAC dialog box as prompted. To create a Complete PC Backup image, complete the following steps:

1. If necessary, log on by using the account (Kim_Ackers) that you created when you installed Windows Vista.

2. In Control Panel, under System And Maintenance, click Back Up Your Computer.

3. In the Create A Windows Complete PC Backup And Restore Image Of Your Entire Computer section of the Backup And Restore Center, click Back Up Computer.

4. Click Continue as prompted to close the UAC dialog box. Windows Complete PC Backup searches for backup devices.

5. Select the DVD-RW drive, as shown in Figure 12-36. Click Next.

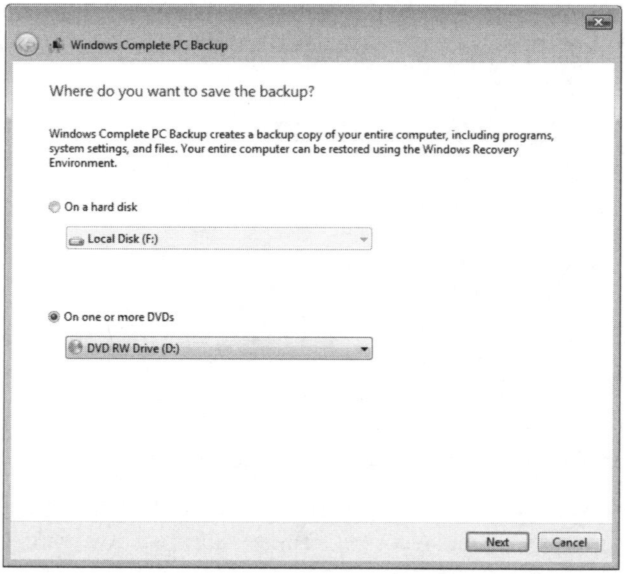

Figure 12-36   Selecting a destination for your Complete PC image

6. Select the disk or disks you want to back up. In the scenario shown in Figure 12-37, the F drive is used for file backups only and is not included in the backup. Click Next.

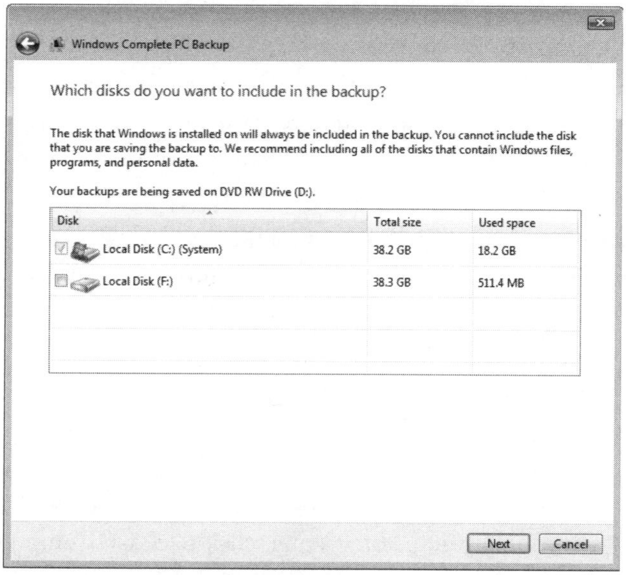

Figure 12-37   Selecting disks to include in the image

7. In the Confirm Your Backup Settings dialog box, note the number of blank DVD rewritable disks you need. Make sure you have these handy. Click Start Backup.

8. Windows creates the backup. Insert labeled blank DVD rewritable disks as instructed. Figure 12-38 shows the prompt to insert a new blank disk. If required, click Format to format the disks when prompted.

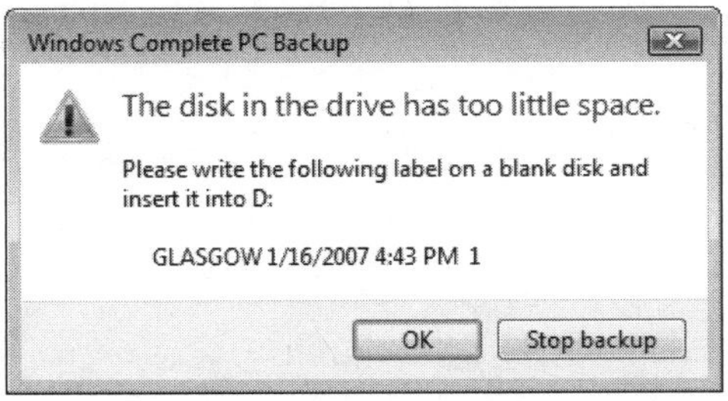

Figure 12-38   Prompt to insert a new blank disk

9. The backup finishes, as shown in Figure 12-39.

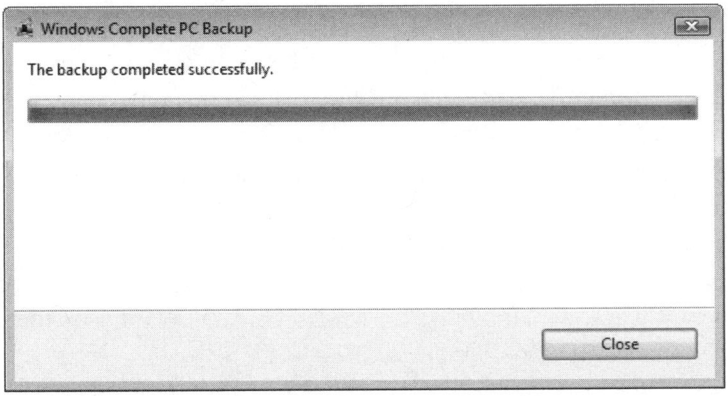

Figure 12-39   Complete PC Backup finishes successfully

Lesson Summary

- You can configure Windows File Back Up Wizard to regularly back up specified types of files. The first backup that is made is a full backup of all specified files. Subsequent scheduled backups back up only files that have been updated since the previous backup. You can also implement full or updated file backups manually.

- System Restore lets you restore the computer system to a previously created restore point. When a restore point is created, Windows Vista creates shadow copies of user files that have been amended since the previous restore point was created.

- You can restore files from backup or shadow copies.

- You can create a Complete PC Backup and use this to restore your computer to the point when the full backup was made.

Lesson Review

You can use the following questions to test your knowledge of the information in Lesson 2, "Configuring Data Protection." The questions are also available on the companion CD if you prefer to review them in electronic form.

NOTE Answers

Answers to these questions and explanations of why each answer choice is correct or incorrect are located in the "Answers" section at the end of the book.

---

1. You want to be notified if the Microsoft Update site publishes a new important update. You do not want to be notified about recommended updates. You want to decide when to download and install updates. What settings do you configure in the Windows Update Change Settings dialog box?
   A. Select Download Updates But Let Me Choose Whether To Install Them. Clear the Include Recommended Updates When Downloading, Installing, or Notifying Me About Updates check box.
   B. Select Download Updates But Let Me Choose Whether To Install Them. Select the Include Recommended Updates When Downloading, Installing, or Notifying Me About Updates check box.
   C. Select Check For Updates But Let Me Choose Whether To Download and Install Them. Clear the Include Recommended Updates When Downloading, Installing, or Notifying Me About Updates check box.
   D. Select Check For Updates But Let Me Choose Whether To Download and Install Them. Select the Include Recommended Updates When Downloading, Installing, or Notifying Me About Updates check box.

2. Kim Ackers has an administrator account on a computer running Windows Vista Ultimate edition. Don Hall has a standard account on the same computer. Both users have Word and Excel files saved in their My Documents folders. Don stores Microsoft Power-Point presentations in a subfolder of his My Documents folder named Presentations. He also stores digital photographs in his My Pictures folder. Don has created a folder called Secret in My Documents and has encrypted the folder and all its contents. He stores confidential files in that folder. When Don last logged on, he deleted some personal files but did not empty his Recycle Bin. Kim is logged on to the computer. She has plugged in a USB flash memory that holds personal files but has not yet copied any of these files onto the computer. She has never formatted the flash memory device. Kim

configures automatic backup settings, accepting the default setting for the file types to back up, and a full backup occurs. Which files are backed up? (Choose all that apply.)

    A. The Word and Excel files in Don's My Documents folder

    B. The Word and Excel files in Kim's My Documents folder

    C. The PowerPoint files in Don's Presentation folder

    D. The digital photographs in Don's My Pictures folder

    E. The files in Don's Secret folder

    F. The files in Don's Recycle Bin

    G. The files on Kim's USB flash memory device

3. A user telephones you at 4:00 P.M. She has just accidentally deleted a file she was working on earlier that afternoon. You have configured her computer to carry out backups every evening. How should you advise the user to retrieve her file?

    A. Use the Restore Files wizard.

    B. Use the Restore Previous Versions feature.

    C. Open her Recycle Bin, right-click the file, and click Restore.

    D. Perform a System Restore.

4. A home user telephones your support help desk. A virus attack has deleted his hard disk. He carried out a Complete PC Backup on his computer three months ago and automatically backs up his personal files every night. He uses an external FireWire hard disk drive to hold his backups. All his personal files are in his My Documents folder. What do you advise? (Choose two answers; each answer forms part of the solution.)

    A. Carry out a Complete PC Restore.

    B. Carry out a System Restore.

    C. Use Restore Previous Versions to restore his My Documents folder from a shadow copy.

    D. Use the Restore Files wizard to restore his My Documents folder.

Chapter Review

To further practice and reinforce the skills you learned in this chapter, you can perform the following tasks:

- Review the chapter summary.
- Review the list of key terms introduced in this chapter.
- Complete the case scenarios. These scenarios set up real-world situations involving the topics of this chapter and ask you to create a solution.
- Complete the suggested practices.
- Take a practice test.

Chapter Summary

- Windows Update lets you specify whether and when updates install automatically. You can hide updates if you do not want to be prompted to install them.
- You can view update history and uninstall updates if required.
- The Windows Back Up Files wizard can select files to back up and create automatic scheduled backups. You can also use the wizard to create manual backups.
- The System Protection feature creates restore points automatically. You can also create them manually. You can use System Restore to restore the computer system to a previous restore point. Windows Vista creates shadow copies of amended files when a restore point is created.
- The Complete PC Backup feature implements a full computer backup.

Key Terms

Do you know what these key terms mean? You can check your answers by looking up the terms in the glossary at the end of the book.

- dummy restore
- full backup
- hidden updates
- image
- important updates
- optional updates
- recommended updates
- restore point
- shadow copy

- stand-alone or exclusive updates
- updated files only backup

Case Scenarios

In the following case scenarios, you will apply what you've learned about configuring Windows Update and configuring data protection. You can find answers to these questions in the "Answers" section at the end of this book.

Case Scenario 1: Configuring Windows Update

You provide technical support for Lucerne Publishing, a small publishing company that has only one office. Lucerne's network does not use Active Directory and is configured as a workgroup. All computers on the network run Windows Vista Ultimate. You have an administrator account on all Lucerne's computers. All other employees have standard accounts except for the boss, Don Hall, who has an administrator account on his own computer but not on any others. Unfortunately, Don is not as knowledgeable about computers as he thinks he is. Answer the following questions:

1. Don is not convinced that automatic scheduled updates are a good idea. He wants Lucerne employees to download and install updates during quiet periods. However, he does not believe the other employees have sufficient permissions to do this, and he asks you to create administrator accounts for them on their own computers. What advice do you give him?

2. You manage to convince Don that automatic updates should be scheduled on all Lucerne's machines. He then reports that although you have configured automatic updates, some updates on his computer have not been installed. When he opens the View Available Updates dialog box, he can see uninstalled device driver updates. What do you tell him?

3. Don installs an optional update and can no longer configure optimum resolution and color depth settings for his monitor. What do you advise him to do?

Case Scenario 2: Configuring Data Protection

You work for a large computer retailer and provide help desk advice to home users. The retailer sells mostly computers that run Windows Vista. Answer the following questions:

1. A user has deleted all the data in a file and then saved the file to hard disk and closed the application. He has not scheduled automatic backups. He has been working with the file for over a week. What do you tell him?

2. A user has configured automatic backup to take place at midnight every night. A file that her son is working on for a school project has been corrupted. She is concerned that

because she did not specify her son's personal files he will not be able to restore the file from backup. What do you tell her?

3. A user recently installed third-party software that is causing problems on his computer. He also has problems uninstalling the software. He understands that he can use System Restore to restore the computer to its last restore point, but he is afraid he might lose some important files he has created recently. What do you tell him?

4. A user's computer has a single hard disk that contains two partitions. She has tried to create a Complete PC Backup on the partition that does not hold her OS, but the Complete PC Backup wizard does not give her that option. She wants to know how she can create such a backup. What do you advise her?

Suggested Practices

To help you successfully master the exam objectives presented in this chapter, complete the following tasks.

Configure Windows Update

- **Practice 1: Experiment with Update Settings**   Change the update settings available in the Change Settings dialog box, and determine the effect of each change. You might need to do this over time because you need to wait until Microsoft publishes updates on the Microsoft Update websites before you can see the effect of your changes. It is best to try this on the second Monday of the month because updates will probably be published on the following day.

- **Practice 2: Review Update History**   Review update history, and uninstall an update. If available, choose a recommended rather than an important update. Configure the Change Settings dialog box so that Windows Update informs you when updates are available to download and install. When Windows Update informs you that the update is available, download and reinstall it.

- **Practice 3: Hide and Restore an Update**   Hide an update listed in the View Available Updates dialog box. Restore the hidden update, and install it.

Configure Data Protection

- **Practice 1: Configure Automatic Backups**   If you have not already done so, configure automatic backups. If you have already done this, change the automatic backup settings.

- **Practice 2: Carry Out Manual Backups**   Create a full manual backup. Manually back up only those files that have been changed since the last backup. Use the Back Up Files Wizard for both tasks.

- **Practice 3: Manually Create a Restore Point** Manually create a restore point. Use System Restore to restore the computer system to that restore point.
- **Practice 4: Restore a Computer from Complete PC Backup** If you completed the practice that asked you to create a Complete PC Backup, use this backup to restore the computer. Back up any important files before you do this.

Take a Practice Test

The practice tests on this book's companion CD offer many options. For example, you can test yourself on just one exam objective, or you can test yourself on all the 70-620 certification exam content. You can set up the test so that it closely simulates the experience of taking a certification exam, or you can set it up in study mode so that you can look at the correct answers and explanations after you answer each question.

MORE INFO **Practice tests**

For details about all the practice test options available, see the "How to Use the Practice Tests" section in this book's Introduction.

Chapter 13
Configuring Mobile Devices

Mobility is one of the current buzzwords. People who travel expect their work and resources to travel with them. They expect to be able to access a wireless network wherever they are, without needing to remember where in the Control Panel hierarchy they can find the settings. They expect to be able to attend a meeting, set up an ad hoc network, and give a presentation by extending their screen on to a plasma display or by connecting to a network projector. They do not want to memorize the locations of the icons that control these features—they want a single, easily accessible tool that does everything.

When users are out of the office, they want access to the files they were working on back at base. When they return, they want the files on the office network server to automatically update with the changes they made while away. A home user wants to be able to connect her digital camera or camera phone with a computer and automatically upload any new photographs on to the computer. Another user wants to copy any new tunes that his computer downloads to a portable mp3 player. The same user wants to back up files on his personal digital assistant (PDA) on his computer, copy files from the computer to the PDA, and install software on the computer on to the PDA. Still another user wants to be able to access e-mail on her computer while sitting on the other side of the room without needing to walk over to the computer or even turn it on. She wants to check the status of her mobile PC while it is hibernating, and she does not want to pull it right out of her carrying case.

As administrators, we are all accustomed to unrealistic user expectations—except these are not unrealistic. They are here, now. Windows Vista does all this and more. This chapter tells you how.

NOTE **Mobile PCs vs. mobile devices**

This chapter discusses both mobile PCs and mobile devices extensively. Sometimes, there's confusion about the difference between them. This is understandable. A mobile PC is by definition mobile, and many mobile devices, such as PDAs, are undeniably computers. In the context of this chapter, and the 70-620 examination, a mobile PC is a wireless-enabled laptop PC running Windows Vista. A mobile device is a handheld device such as a PDA, mobile phone, or mp3 player.

Exam objectives in this chapter:
- Configure Mobile Display Settings.
- Configure Mobile Devices.

Before You Begin

To complete the lessons in this chapter, you must have done the following:

■ Installed Windows Vista Ultimate on a personal computer, as described in Chapter 1, "Installing Windows Vista Client" and Chapter 2, "Upgrading Windows Vista Migrations and Upgrades." For this chapter, you need Windows Vista running on a mobile PC. You also need a second computer on your network that is acting as a network server (it does not need to be running Windows Vista). Before you start Practice 2 in Lesson 2, you need to enable a folder for offline use on the network server and place two files in that folder, as described in the introduction to the Practice. You also need an additional monitor.

■ Created an administrator account and standard accounts and enabled the Run command on the Start menu, as described in Practices 1, 2, and 3 in Lesson 1, "Configuring and Troubleshooting Parental Controls and Content Advisor," of Chapter 4, "Configuring and Troubleshooting Internet Access."

No additional configuration is required for this chapter. Internet access is required to complete the practices.

If you want to try out all the technologies described in this chapter, you need access to a network projector, a mobile device (for example, a PDA or mobile phone) running Microsoft Windows Mobile 2003 or Windows Mobile 2003 Second Edition, and either an integrated or connectable SideShow-compatible device. However, you can study the chapter and complete all the practice sessions without this equipment.

Real World

Ian McLean

I've always been a bit of a dinosaur.

This has less to do with having a very large body and very small brain or smelling as if I became extinct millions of years ago and more to do with always being marginally behind the latest cutting-edge technology.

I remember turning up to do a demonstration and unpacking a large computer and even larger (and much heavier) monitor, a mouse, a keyboard, and a pile of cables tied in a Gordian knot. Having staggered up two flights of stairs with all of it, I entered the demonstration room where a fellow demonstrator showed me a new concept in computer hardware. In those days, it was called a portable computer. Now we would call it a laptop.

I recall carefully preparing transparencies from a PowerPoint file for use with an overhead projector, walking into a lecture room, and meeting my first data projector.

Now, of course, I am mobile. I can take my wireless laptop almost anywhere and connect to the Internet. I can set up or join an ad hoc network during a meeting and connect wirelessly to a projector to give a presentation. I have a handheld device about a hundred times more powerful than the old AT personal computer that I used to drag up stairs. I think I might finally have evolved.

Friends and colleagues sigh and shake their heads. One attends meetings and conferences all over the world and often gives presentations. He only ever leaves his desk to go to a net-conferencing room. Another hardly ever leaves her home but holds down a full-time job at a senior level and has an international reputation.

Of course, there are times when you need to be there. I've used every remote teaching gadget and technique available. I still believe students learn better when you're there to show them. I prefer to seal deals with a handshake. Most dinosaurs do.

Mobile computing has its place, and Windows Vista offers some neat and useful facilities. It's a completely up-to-date technology, and I'm not denigrating it in any way. However, don't be fooled into thinking it's the only technology, the only way of doing things. To coin a cliché—horses for courses.

Lesson 1: Configuring Mobile Display Settings

Windows Vista offers a number of facilities for configuring display settings on a mobile PC. Most of these facilities are designed for users who give presentations, talks, and lectures. Sometimes, as a technical support person, you will be called on to give a demonstration of Windows Vista features, possibly as an induction talk for new staff. If you provide system support for a school, college, or university, you could be called on to prepare presentation settings for teachers or academics.

This lesson discusses the Windows Mobility Center, which is a collection of panes that provide a single tool, or "one stop shop," for configuring mobile PC settings. It then goes on to look at specific presentation settings and how you would configure multiple monitors and network projectors.

> **After this lesson, you will be able to:**
> - Access and use the Mobility Center.
> - Turn presentation settings on and off.
> - Connect to an additional monitor.
> - Configure presentation settings for additional monitors.
> - Connect to a network projector and configure settings.
>
> **Estimated lesson time: 40 minutes**

Using the Windows Mobility Center

The Mobility Center is available only on mobile PCs. It lets you quickly access your mobile PC settings in one convenient location. You could, for example, check the status of your wireless network connection, adjust the speaker volume, and adjust the display brightness all from one location. You access the Mobility Center by clicking Mobile PC in Control Panel and selecting Windows Mobility Center. You can also press the Windows logo key and the X key simultaneously.

The Mobility Center, shown in Figure 13-1, is especially useful if you need to adjust settings so you can use your mobile PC at your desk, at off-site meetings, or sitting in an airport. It lets you, and users you support, adjust all the required settings from a single tool, rather than needing to remember how to access each one from Control Panel. The Mobility Center on your mobile PC might not have the same tiles that are shown in the figure.

Figure 13-1   The Windows Mobility Center

Depending on your system configuration, the following tiles might appear in the Mobility Center window:

- **Brightness**   Temporarily adjusts the brightness of your display. To adjust the display brightness settings for your power plan, click the icon on the tile to open Power Options in Control Panel.

- **Volume**   Adjusts the speaker volume of your mobile PC and lets you select the Mute check box.

- **Battery Status**   Shows how much charge remains on your battery and lets you select a power plan from the list.

- **Wireless Network**   Indicates the status of your wireless network connection and lets you select a network to connect to or turn your wireless adapter on or off.

- **Screen Rotation**   Lets you change the screen orientation from portrait to landscape or vice versa.

- **External Display**   Lets you connect an additional monitor to your mobile PC and customize display settings.

- **Sync Center**   Lets you view the status of an in-progress file synchronization, start a new synchronization, set up a synchronization partnership, and adjust your synchronization settings.

- **Presentation Settings**   Lets you adjust presentation settings, such as the speaker volume and the desktop background image.

If you need to access Control Panel to make additional adjustments, you can click the icon on a tile to open Control Panel for that setting. If a tile does not appear, it might be because the required hardware or drivers are missing.

NOTE   Additional tiles

Your mobile PC manufacturer might add tiles to the Mobility Center. For more information, check the manufacturer's documentation or access the manufacturer's website.

Configuring Presentation Settings

Presentation settings are a collection of options on a mobile PC that you can apply when you or a user you support needs to give a presentation. For example, you can change the volume level and block notifications and reminders. Enabling presentation settings also blocks instant messaging—the last thing a lecturer or salesperson wants is for private instant messages to pop up on the screen when giving a presentation.

When presentation settings are turned on, the mobile PC stays awake and system notifications and instant messages are turned off. You can also choose to turn off the screen saver, adjust the speaker volume, and change your desktop background image. The settings can be automatically saved and applied every time the computer is used to give a presentation, unless you, or the computer's user, manually turns them off. You can turn on presentation settings when connecting the mobile PC to a network projector or connecting it to an additional monitor.

You can enable presentation settings by clicking Turn On in the Presentation Settings tile of the Mobility Center. You can configure presentation settings at any time by clicking Presentation Settings in the Presentations Settings tile of the Mobility Center. Figure 13-2 shows the Presentation Settings dialog box. You typically configure display and audio settings when connecting to an additional monitor or a network projector. You configure presentation settings in the practice session later in this lesson.

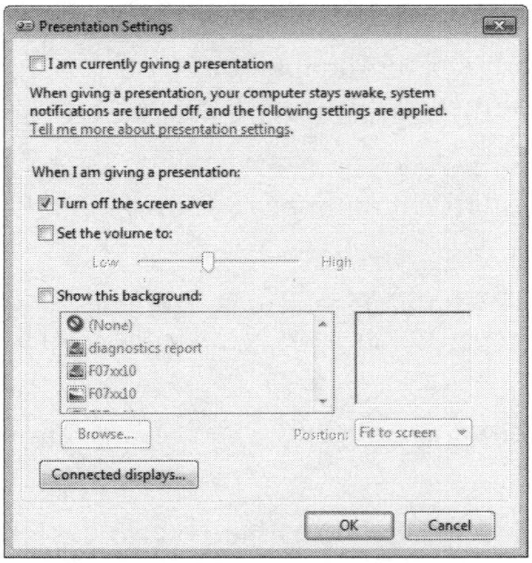

Figure 13-2 Presentation Settings dialog box

Presentation settings automatically turn off when you disconnect a mobile PC from a network projector or additional monitor or when you shut down or log off from the mobile PC. You can manually turn off presentation settings by opening the Mobility Center and clicking Turn Off in the Presentation Settings tile.

Configuring Multiple Monitors

If you, or a user you support, are using a mobile PC to give a presentation or demonstration to a small number of people—for example, in a conference room—it is usually sufficient to connect a large monitor such as a wall-mounted plasma display or TV-type monitor to the PC for this purpose. You can also treat a non-networked data projector as if it were an additional monitor.

Also, smaller and neater mobile PCs have a limited screen size—probably acceptable for working on a train but inconvenient when working in the office. In this case, you can connect a second, larger monitor for your own use.

You can connect an additional monitor to your mobile PC and configure presentation settings for that monitor. These presentation settings are disabled when you disconnect the monitor from the PC. If you have the appropriate hardware, you can connect multiple monitors to your mobile PC and configure presentation settings for each of them.

If you connect an additional monitor to your mobile PC, Windows Vista might (depending upon the monitor you connect) automatically detect the monitor and display your computer's desktop. You can then choose how you want your desktop to appear and customize the display settings, such as screen resolution and color depth.

If Windows Vista cannot identify the monitor, press the keyboard shortcut that opens the New Display Detected dialog box by using the keyboard shortcut that turns on an additional display. In most mobile PCs this is FN+F5, but if this does not work on your mobile PC, check the manufacturer's documentation or go to the manufacturer's website.

You can also use the Mobility Center to connect to the monitor by clicking Connect Display on the External Display tile. If Windows Vista detects the new monitor, the New Display Detected dialog box appears. The following display options are available:

- **Mirrored**   Mirrors, or duplicates, your desktop on each display that you connect. This is the default display option and is useful if you plan to use your mobile PC to give a presentation on a data projector or a fixed display.
- **Extended**   Extends your desktop across all of the displays to which you connect. You can use this if you want to increase your desktop area.
- **External Display Only**   Shows your desktop on each display to which you connect, but not on the mobile PC display. You can use this if you are employing a mobile PC to give a demonstration and want to conserve battery power. You can also use this option when you play a digital versatile disk (DVD) on a mobile PC that supports full-screen video playback on only one display.

If Windows Vista cannot identify the connected monitor but only the monitor type, it automatically applies the last display settings that you used for that type of monitor and asks whether you want to keep the settings. You can click OK to keep these settings; if you click

Cancel or do nothing or if no settings are available for the type of monitor selected, the Display Settings dialog box appears, as shown in Figure 13-3. You can then manually choose the display settings.

Figure 13-3 The Display Settings dialog box

Any time you want to change your display settings you can access the Display Settings dialog box, shown in Figure 13-3, by opening Control Panel, clicking Appearance And Personalization, clicking Personalization, and clicking Display Settings. You can also use this method to install external monitors that Windows Vista does not automatically detect or to install more than one external monitor. You manually configure an external monitor and extend your desktop onto it in the practice session later in this lesson.

Quick Check

■ You want to play an educational video from the DVD-ROM drive on your mobile PC on a wall-mounted plasma display. Your mobile PC supports full-screen video playback on only one display. What display option should you select in the New Display Detected dialog box?

Quick Check Answer

■ External Display Only

Using a Network Projector

A Windows Network Projector is a display device such as a conference room projector that uses Remote Desktop Protocol (RDP) over an Internet Protocol (IP) network (typically a wireless network) to display the desktop of a Windows Vista-based mobile PC. Using this technology, you can quickly connect your mobile PC to a conference room projector over the local wireless network.

MORE INFO   Remote Desktop Protocol (RDP)

For more information about RDP, access *http://msdn2.microsoft.com/en-us/library/aa383015.aspx*. Although this article does not mention Windows Vista, the information it gives is valid for the Windows Vista operating system (OS).

The following connection scenarios exist:

- **Infrastructure Network Connection** The network projector is part of an organization's infrastructure. If it is on the same subnet as the computer you want to connect to it, you can use the connection wizard or specify a Universal Naming Convention (UNC) path to the projector. A step-by-step procedure for doing this is given later in this lesson. If the network projector is a component in an Internetwork, you can identify it by using a URL.

- **Ad Hoc Connection** Ad hoc connections were described in Chapter 7, "Configuring Network Connectivity." If you are at a meeting (for example, in a hotel conference room) where you and other participants have formed an ad hoc network, a network projector can be included in that network, enabling you or any other participant to give a presentation.

- **Connection through a Network Projector Adapter** If you or the organization for which you work does not have a network projector, you can use an existing data projector for that purpose by connecting to it through a network projector adapter. Typically, the adapter connects to the network wirelessly but has a wired connection to the projector.

Figure 13-4 illustrates the various network projector connection scenarios.

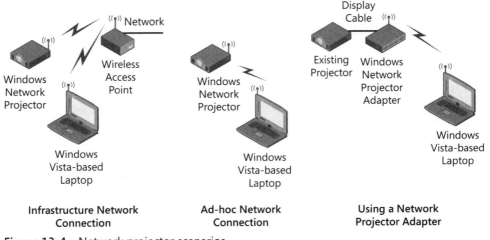

Figure 13-4 Network projector scenarios

MORE INFO Network projector design and specification

Microsoft issues specifications for the hardware and software design of network projectors. For example, a wireless connection is mandatory, while a wired connection is optional. A network projector consists of a data projector controlled by microprocessor and memory chips. The control section is in effect a built-in computer and is called the network projector server. If you want more information about the network projector specification, access *http://msdn2.microsoft.com /en-us/library/aa934274.aspx*. This URL goes into much more depth than is required for the 70-620 examination.

You can use a network projector to support the following business scenarios:

- Microsoft PowerPoint presentations with simple animations and still image display
- Displays to a single projector (one-to-one connection)
- Mirrored or extended display

A network projector uses RDP for display and can support wired or wireless network connections between the computer and the projector, although wireless is more common. It is important to distinguish between a connection through a wired network between a computer and a network projector, both of which are network components, and a direct connection through a port between a computer and a (non-network) data projector. In the latter case, Windows Vista treats the data projector as an additional monitor rather than as a network projector.

Connecting to a Network Projector

You can use the Connect To A Network Projector wizard to find a network projector by searching for one on the network or by entering a projector's network address (this can be a UNC path or a URL, or you can use the network projector's IPv4 address). If you search for a network projector, the wizard can find it only if the projector is connected to the local subnet (the network segment that your computer is connected to). However, when you enter a projector's network address, the wizard can find the projector regardless of where it is located on the network.

To open the Connect To A Network Projector wizard, click Accessories in the All Programs Menu, and then select Connect To A Network Projector. Depending on your firewall settings, you might then need to give permission to communicate with the network projector through the firewall and clear a UAC dialog box. The Connect To A Network Projector wizard is shown in Figure 13-5.

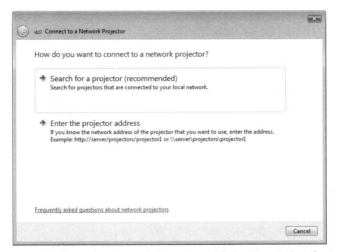

Figure 13-5   The Connect To A Network Projector wizard

To find a network projector on your local subnet automatically, click Search For A Projector (Recommended). The wizard searches, as shown in Figure 13-6.

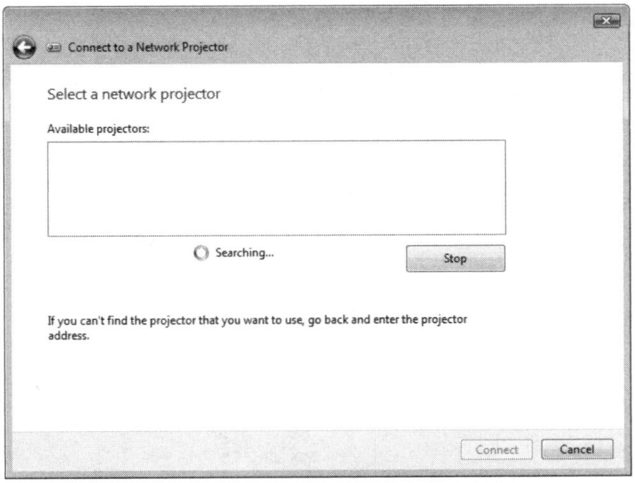

Figure 13-6   The wizard searches in the local subnet

You can then choose from a list of available network projectors. Projectors you used recently are at the top of the list. Projectors can be either security enabled (password-protected) or unsecured. An icon beside the projector on the list indicates whether a password is required, as shown in Figure 13-7.

Unsecured network projector

Security-enabled network projector

Figure 13-7   Security enabled and unsecured network projector icons

You connect to a projector by selecting it from the list and clicking Next. You then supply a password if necessary.

If you know the network address of the projector and want to enter this directly, or if the projector is not on the local subnet, in the Connect To A Network Projector wizard, you can click Enter The Projector Address. You then enter a network address for the projector and (if necessary) a password, as shown in Figure 13-8. If the projector is on the same subnet as your computer, you can enter a UNC address, such as *myserver**projectors**myprojector*. If the projector is elsewhere on a network, you need to enter a URL—for example, *http://myserver/projectors /myprojector*. You then click Connect to connect to the projector.

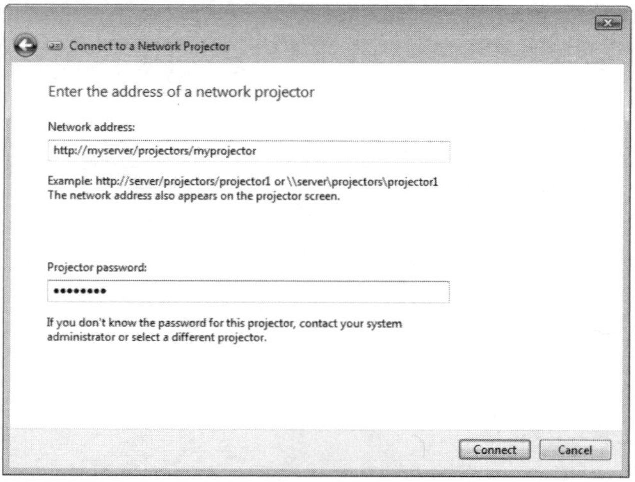

Figure 13-8   Entering the projector network address

Whether you choose to search for a projector or specify a network address, when you connect, the Network Presentation dialog box opens and then minimizes on the Windows taskbar. You can use this dialog box to pause or resume your presentation or to disconnect from the network projector. When you have chosen and connected to a network projector, you can open the Mobility Center and configure and enable presentation settings for that projector. You configure presentation settings in the practice session later in this lesson.

Troubleshooting Network Projector Problems

In general, if you can connect to a network projector, it should work. Problems with network projectors are mainly network connection problems, which were discussed in Chapter 7, "Configuring Network Connectivity." The following are common problems:

- **No projectors appear on the list when you search for projectors in the Connect To A Network Projector wizard**   First you need to make sure your computer is connected to a wireless or wired local area network (LAN). To do this, you click Network on the Start menu and then click Network And Sharing Center. If your computer is not connected to the LAN, Not Connected appears. To see which network connections on your computer are not working, click Manage Network Connections in the left pane of the Network And Sharing Center. A red "X" on the connection icon indicates that the connection is not working. If your computer is connected to a network but the Connect To A Network Projector wizard does not list any projectors, it is likely that the network does not include any shared network projectors.

- **You connect to a network projector, but then nothing happens**   In this case, turn off the projector, and then restart it. If this does not work, check whether someone else is already using the projector.

- **You entered the correct network address, but the Connect To A Network Projector wizard did not find the projector**   If you are certain that the network address of the network projector is correct, try turning off the projector and then restarting it. If the wizard still cannot find a projector, try refreshing the Domain Name System (DNS) cache. To do this, right-click Command Prompt on the Accessories menu, select Run As Administrator, and supply administrator credentials or click Continue as prompted to clear the User Access Control (UAC) dialog box. At the command prompt, enter **ipconfig / registerdns**. Restart the projector, and try to connect to it again.

MORE INFO   DNS

For more information about DNS, see Chapter 7, "Configuring Network Connectivity."

- **You click Resume in the Network Presentation dialog box, but your presentation does not restart**   Your computer's central processing unit (CPU) might be busy with another system task. Wait a few minutes, and try again. If the problem persists, examine CPU usage as described in Chapter 7, "Configuring Network Connectivity." Some presentations are processor-intensive, and you might need to close down other processes or upgrade your processor.

- **A video clip in a presentation plays for a few seconds, stops, and then restarts**   Network projectors are designed to transmit and display still images, such as photographs and Microsoft PowerPoint slides, not high-bandwidth transmissions such as video streams. The projector can transmit video, but the playback quality is sometimes poor. You might need to upgrade your equipment or use a data projector or plasma TV screen that is directly connected to your computer.

- **Firewall settings prevent connection**   If firewall settings block protocols or services that are required for connection, you might need to configure the firewall on your mobile PC. This tends to happen when third-party firewalls are enabled. You need to reconfigure your firewall settings. Alternatively, you can try disabling the third-party firewall and enabling Windows Firewall instead. If the DNS service is not working, the Search option will not find a projector, and entering a UNC path or a URL will not work either. In this case, if you know the IP address of the network projector, click Enter A Projector Address in the Connect To A Network Projector Wizard, and then type in the IP address.

Practice: Connecting to an External Monitor and Configuring Presentation Settings

In this practice session, you connect to an external monitor that is not detected automatically. You can use the same procedure to connect to a plasma screen monitor or a directly connected (non-network) data projector. You then enable and configure presentation settings.

▶ **Practice 1: Manually Connecting an External Monitor and Configuring Colors and Resolution Settings**

In this practice, you connect a second monitor and extend the Windows Vista desktop to this monitor. When Windows Vista detects the monitor automatically and applies the optimum settings for this monitor, the procedure is trivial. However, you might be called upon to install an older monitor or a lesser-known make of monitor that is not automatically detected. You might also need to install several external monitors. For these reasons, you should be familiar with the manual procedure.

Although this procedure does not require elevated privileges, an administrator is most likely to carry it out. For that reason, the procedure asks you to log on by using an administrator account.

1. Log on by using the account (Kim_Ackers) that you created when you installed Windows Vista.

2. Connect an external monitor, and turn it on.

3. In Control Panel, click Appearance And Personalization, click Personalization, and click Display Settings.

4. In the Display Settings dialog box, shown in Figure 13-9, select the second monitor (the box that contains the number 2), and select the Extend The Desktop Onto This Monitor check box.

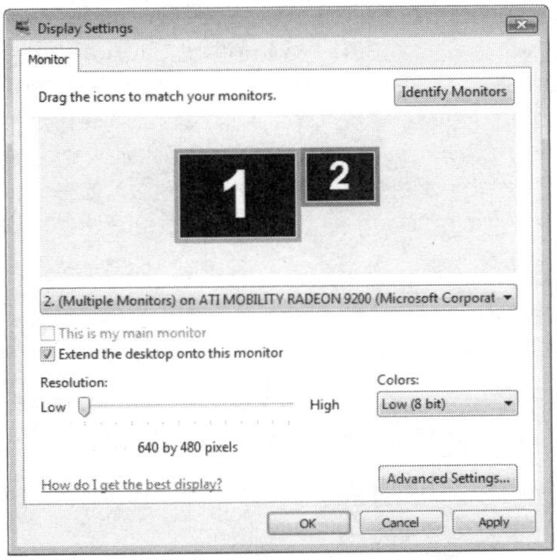

Figure 13-9   The Display Settings dialog box

5. Click Apply. Your second monitor should show a Windows Vista desktop, possibly at a very low resolution and color setting.

6. Click Yes to keep display settings.

7. Click Identify Monitors. You should see a large "1" on your mobile PC monitor and a large "2" on your external monitor.

8. In the Display Settings dialog box, ensure that your external monitor is still selected, and configure a suitable Colors setting, as shown in Figure 13-10.

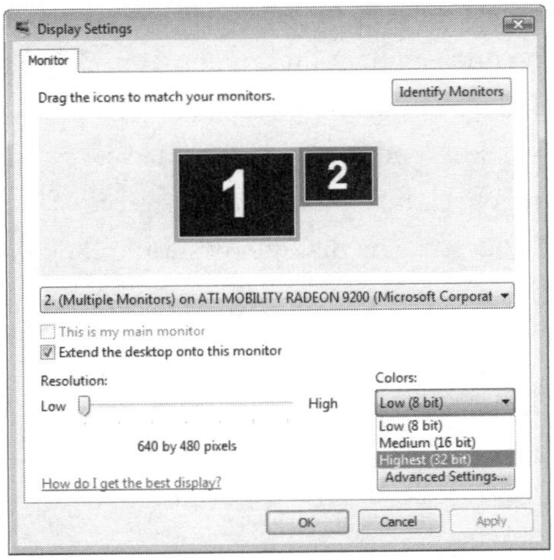

Figure 13-10   Configuring a Colors setting

9. Move the Resolution slider to select a suitable resolution. Click OK.

NOTE   Extended Display Identification Data (EDID)

Most modern monitors and projectors support Extended Display Identification Data (EDID). This is a standard video data format that contains basic information about a display's capabilities, including maximum screen size, screen resolution, refresh rate, color depth, and orientation. If a display is EDID-enabled, Windows Vista automatically identifies the display and applies the appropriate display settings, so manually setting the color and resolution settings is unnecessary. However, an EDID-enabled display will be detected automatically, and the procedure described in this practice for manual setup will be required only if you are setting up more than one additional monitor.

---

10. Click Yes to keep display settings.
11. Open the Windows Mobility Center.
12. In the Presentation Settings tile, in the Mobility Center, click Turn On.
13. Drag the Mobility Center window past the right edge of your mobile PC screen. It should appear on the left side of your external screen.

▶ **Practice 2: Configuring Presentation Settings**

It is not essential that you carry out this practice directly after completing Practice 1, but you will see the results of the procedure much more plainly if you do. For that reason, you are asked to log on with the same account as before, although elevated privileges are not required to complete this practice.

1. If necessary, log on by using the Kim_Ackers account that you created when you installed Windows Vista.
2. Open the Windows Mobility Center.
3. In the Presentations Settings tile, click the icon beside either Presenting or Not Presenting.
4. If necessary, select the I am Currently Giving A Presentation check box.
5. If necessary, select the Turn Off The Screensaver check box.
6. Select the Set The Volume To check box, and move the slider to set volume as appropriate.
7. Select the Show This Background check box. Select a background—for example, Img8.
8. Ensure that the Position is Fit To Screen. The dialog box should look like Figure 13-11.

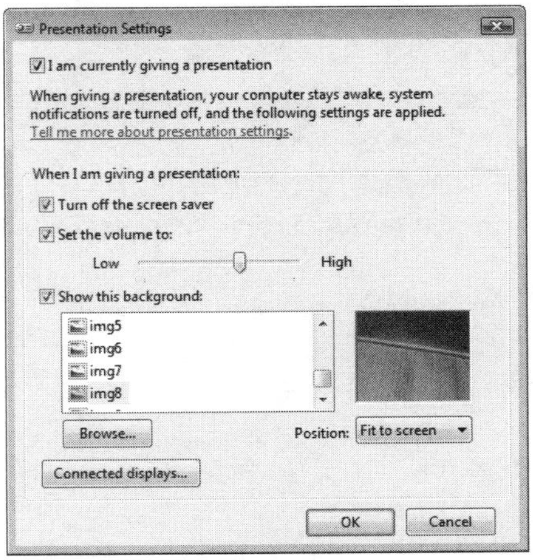

Figure 13-11   Presentation settings

9. Click OK. The background in your external monitor should now be the one selected in the Presentations Settings dialog box.

Lesson Summary

■ The Mobility Center provides a single tool for configuring mobile PC settings.

■ You can extend the display on a mobile PC to use an external monitor.

■ You can connect to a network projector to give presentations. Typically, this connection is wireless.

■ You can configure presentation settings that apply to an external monitor, a network projector, or both.

Lesson Review

You can use the following questions to test your knowledge of the information in Lesson 1, "Configuring Mobile Display Settings." The questions are also available on the companion CD if you prefer to review them in electronic form.

NOTE Answers

Answers to these questions and explanations of why each answer choice is correct or incorrect are located in the "Answers" section at the end of the book.

1. Which of the following functions can you perform directly from the Windows Mobility Center? (Choose all that apply.)

    A. Mute the speaker.

    B. Access offline files.

    C. Select a power plan.

    D. Turn presentation settings on or off.

    E. Access Sync Settings.

    F. Open your My Documents folder.

2. Which of the following functions can you perform from the Presentation Settings dialog box? (Choose all that apply.)

    A. Change the screen background.

    B. Connect to a network projector.

    C. Select a new screensaver.

    D. Turn off system notifications.

    E. Access a list of connected displays.

    F. Set the speaker volume.

3. You are extending the screen of your mobile PC on to a second monitor. You connect the monitor and access the Display Settings dialog box. You then click the icon for the second monitor to select it. You notice that the icon for the second monitor is much smaller than the icon for the first, and a colleague has advised you that you will get the best results if both icons are approximately the same size. What control will resize the monitor icon?

    A. Identify Monitors. When Windows Vista identifies the second monitor, it will adjust the size of the icon.

    B. This Is My Main Monitor. To extend a Mobile PC display on to an external monitor, you need to make this the main monitor.

    C. Resolution. Increasing resolution increases the size of the icon.

    D. Colors. Increasing color depth increases the size of the icon.

4. You are connecting to a network projector so you can give a presentation at an off-site meeting. You start the Connect To A Network Projector wizard and choose to search for a network projector. The projector to which you want to connect appears on the list but has a padlocked icon beside it. What does this indicate?

   A. You can connect to the projector, but you will need to specify a password.

   B. The projector is unsecured. You can connect to it, but this is at your own risk and is not recommended.

   C. The projector is turned off. You cannot connect to it.

   D. The projector is on a different subnet. You need to specify a URL in order to connect to it.

5. You identify a projector by using the Search function in the Connect To A Network Projector wizard but cannot connect to the projector. You try turning the projector off and back on again and wait a short while, but then you still cannot connect. What should you check next?

   A. Whether the projector is on the same subnet as your computer

   B. Whether someone else is connected to the projector

   C. Whether the projector is showing streamed video

   D. Whether the projector is security-protected

Lesson 2: Configuring Mobile Devices

A mobile PC is, by definition, mobile, but it is not normally regarded as a mobile (handheld) device. Users will travel on business with their mobile PCs and expect their work in progress to travel with them. But a mobile PC, no matter how small and neat it is, probably does not fit in a pocket or purse. PDAs, digital cameras, mobile camera phones, and even mp3 players and digital sound recorders are computers in all but name. These devices are truly mobile—users take them everywhere.

This lesson discusses both the synchronization between a mobile PC and a network server and a PC (mobile or static) and mobile handheld devices. It also discusses SideShow devices—computers within computers.

After this lesson, you will be able to:

- Use the Microsoft Sync Center to synchronize network files.
- Set up synch partnerships between mobile devices and computers.
- Use the Windows Mobile Device Center (WMDC) to set up Windows Mobile partnerships and manage compliant handheld devices.
- Configure and troubleshoot Windows SideShow devices.

Estimated lesson time: 55 minutes

Real World

Ian McLean

I'm told education isn't as good as it used to be—but then it never was.

The nature of my rather strange mode of employment means that I travel at odd times. Sometimes, as a result, I share a train with a crowd of young people going to or coming from school. Usually, most of them spend the journey working with mobile devices—some use mobile phones or music players, but most access PDAs. These kids are a serious bunch.

All around me I can see configuring and text-messaging. Spreadsheets surround me. Styluses and young fingers blur as data is entered at speeds I could never match. When they get to school, the students will be using computers during a high percentage of their lessons. After school they will use a home PC or a complex games console. Technology is second nature to them.

In 1970 I attended a postgraduate computer programming course. I didn't even get to see the computer, never mind being able to get my grubby fingers on it.

Today's technically aware kids *are* educated. They continue their education on public transport and just about anywhere else. Mobile devices are an integral part of their lives and seldom out of their hands. These devices are much more powerful than the computer I didn't get to see in 1970.

Technology has changed education. The schoolchildren might not know that the plural of stylus is styli and *not* styluses, as I typed earlier. You see, styli is *not* in their spellcheckers. Nevertheless, they are unlikely to be freaked out by new devices coming on the market. As an old traditionalist, I have only one complaint. Today's kids are literate in text-message abbreviation rather than English. Truly, text-messaging has a lot 2 &sr 4.

Using the Sync Center to Synchronize Network Files

If you, or users you support, store files in several locations—for example, on a mobile PC, on a static computer (file server) in your company network, and on mobile devices such as portable music players, PDAs, or mobile phones—keeping track of these files and ensuring that they remain synchronized can be a major problem. If your users take their mobile PCs on business trips or use them at home, they want to be sure that the files they are working on are the most recent versions. When they return to base, they want any updates they have made to be implemented in the files on the static office computer. Home users might want to synchronize music files so that downloads they store on their Windows Vista computers are also available on their portable music players.

Copying files manually can be tedious and is an irksome task when a user is in a hurry to get home. It is error prone, and a user can all too easily copy an old version of a file over the most recent version rather than vice versa, losing several hours of work. In Windows Vista, the easiest, most efficient, and safest way is to sync files automatically by using Sync Center.

Sync is short for synchronization. In Windows Vista, sync is the process of storing two or more matching versions of the same file in different locations. If you add, change, or delete a file in one location, Windows Vista adds, changes, or deletes the same file in the other locations whenever you choose to sync. Sync Center allows you to sync information between your computer and mobile devices that you plug in to your computer or to which you connect wirelessly. It also permits you to sync information with files stored in folders on another computer (on larger networks, a network file server). These files are called offline files because you can access them even when your computer or the server is not connected to the network. You can sync files with programs that support Sync Center.

You can access the Sync Center through the Mobility Center. You can also open it from Accessories in the All Programs menu. The Sync Center is shown in Figure 13-12.

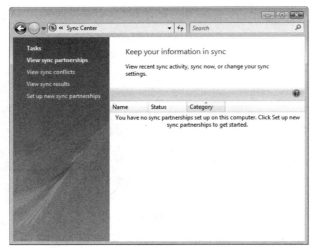

Figure 13-12   The Sync Center

NOTE   **Windows Vista editions and network folders**

The ability to sync with network folders is not included in Windows Vista Starter, Windows Vista Home Basic, and Windows Vista Home Premium.

Each time you sync files between two or more locations, the Sync Center compares the files in each location to see if they have changed. If the file details differ (one file was amended more recently than the other), the Sync Center determines which version of each file to keep and copies that version to the other location, overwriting the existing files at that location.

If the file details are identical, the Sync Center does nothing. If the Sync Center finds a new file in one location (such as on a computer but not on a mobile device set up to sync with the computer), it copies the file to the other location. If you delete a file in one location, Sync Center deletes the file in the other location.

Sync Partnerships

To sync between your computer and a mobile device, or to sync your mobile PC with a static PC that acts as a network server on a company network, you need to form a sync partnership. Clicking Set Up New Sync Partnerships in Sync Center lists the available partnership devices, as shown in Figure 13-13.

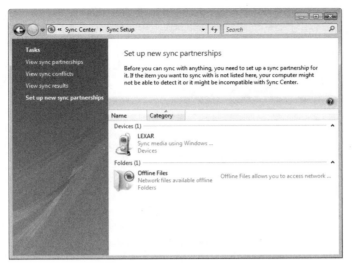

Figure 13-13 Available sync partnership devices

You can set up a partnership by selecting a device on the list and clicking Set Up. Alternatively, you can right-click a device and either access the device's sync properties or click Set Up. During the setup process, you select the files and folders that you want to sync. Clicking View Sync Partnerships in Sync Center lists the available partnerships. In Figure 13-14, we set up a partnership between the mobile device and the computer. You set up a partnership to sync offline files in the practice session later in this lesson.

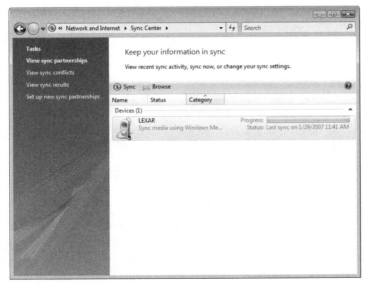

Figure 13-14 A sync partnership

You can select the device and click Browse to view the files that the sync process has placed on the device and to sync additional files. Figure 13-15 shows the files that sync has placed on the device.

Figure 13-15   Files on mobile device

Sync partnerships can be one-way or two-way. In one-way sync partnerships, files are copied from the primary location to the secondary location, but no files are copied back to the primary location. In two-way sync partnerships, Sync Center copies files in both directions to keep the two locations in sync. Most sync partnerships are automatically set up to perform either one-way or two-way sync (depending upon the device chosen). Some sync partnerships let you select one-way or two-way.

You could set up a one-way sync partnership with, for example, a portable music player where new music files you download to your computer are copied to the mobile device, but music files are never copied from the mobile device to the computer. Typically, you would use two-way sync partnerships when you sync offline files with another computer. Offline files are discussed in detail later in this lesson.

You can sync most types of files, including documents, music, and photographs. If your mobile phone supports Sync Center, you can sync information such as schedules and contacts. You can find out if your device is compatible with Sync Center by plugging it into your computer and (if necessary) installing any software that came with the device. If your device is able to sync using Sync Center, it appears in the list when you click Set Up New Sync Partnerships in Sync Center. If this does not happen, visit the device manufacturer's website where you might be able to download additional software that implements Sync Center support. The device manufacturer must support Sync Center for sync to work.

Sync Conflicts

In most sync partnerships the Sync Center automatically keeps the most recent version of a file and overwrites the older versions. Sometimes, however, the Sync Center prompts you to choose which version of a file to keep. This usually occurs when a file has changed in both locations since the last sync. When this happens, Sync Center notifies you of a sync conflict, which you must resolve before it can sync the items in conflict.

For example, if you have changed a document on your computer since the last sync and made a different change to the same document in a network folder set up to sync with your computer, a sync conflict will occur. Sync Center will ask how you want to resolve the conflict, allowing you to choose which version you want to leave unchanged and which version you want to update.

If you have a sync conflict, the Sync Center icon in the notification area on your taskbar changes to display a black exclamation mark on a yellow triangle superimposed on the normal icon. You can point to this icon to see if there are any conflicts. (Depending on how you have your taskbar configured, this icon might not be visible.) If there are conflicts, Windows will display a summary of them. You can right-click the Sync Center icon at any time and click View Conflicts to open Sync Center and check for sync conflicts.

You can also open Sync Center from the Accessories menu or the Mobility Center (on a mobile PC) and click View Sync Conflicts. If conflicts are listed, you can select one or more of them and click Resolve. You create, detect, and resolve a sync conflict in the practice session later in this lesson.

NOTE Sync conflicts, errors, and warnings

A sync conflict occurs when differences cannot be reconciled between file versions stored in different locations. This stops sync from completing until you reconcile the differences. A sync error is a problem—such as a mobile device not plugged in or an unavailable network server—that prevents sync from being completed. Sync errors are not caused by problems reconciling two versions of a file. A sync warning is typically less severe than a sync error and usually does not prevent the sync from completing. For example, Sync Center might warn you when it detects low battery power on your cell phone. If the cell phone died completely, this would create a sync error.

Offline Files

You, or users you support, can use offline files to access files stored in shared network folders even when the network copies are unavailable. You can do this by using Sync Center to sync with network files that you have made available offline. This automatically creates a copy of the network files (offline files) on your computer. Sync Center will automatically sync your offline files and open them when the network versions are unavailable.

NOTE   **Offline files are on the mobile PC**

Files on the network server are made available for offline use. However, offline files are the files that Sync Center copies to the mobile PC. It is important to remember that using files offline is a two-stage process. You need to make files on the network server available offline, and then you need to sync so these files are copied to the mobile PC.

Offline files enable you and users you support to edit files when out of the office and to continue to work on files in the office if the network becomes unavailable. Usually, permissions are set on the network sever so that only the owner of the files marked for offline use can access them. However, in collaborative projects it might be possible for more than one person to access a file. In this case, it is possible for one user to change a file on a mobile PC and another to change the file on the server. In this case, conflicts can occur, and the Sync Center can be used to resolve them.

If Windows Vista encounters a problem when trying to sync offline files between your computer and a network folder (for example, the network server is unavailable) a sync error occurs. Sync warnings are unusual when you sync offline files and are more typically associated with devices such as mobile phones and music players.

Network Servers

A network server (or file server) is any computer on a network that holds the personal files for one or more users and makes these files available as network shares. In the enterprise environment, a network server typically runs a server OS, such as Windows Server 2003. However, in a limited small office/home office (SOHO) network, the network server can be a computer running a client OS, such as Windows Vista or Windows XP. Any computer that shares files and folders on a network is a network server.

Figure 13-16 shows a folder being configured for offline use on a computer running Windows Vista Ultimate that is used as a network server. You can access this dialog box by clicking Advanced Sharing in the Sharing tab of the folder's Properties dialog box, clearing the UAC dialog box as prompted, and clicking Caching.

MORE INFO   **File and printer sharing**

If you are using an OS other than Windows Vista, or if Windows Vista is set not to display the Sharing tab, search for "File and printer sharing" in the computer's help files for more information on how to configure files for offline use.

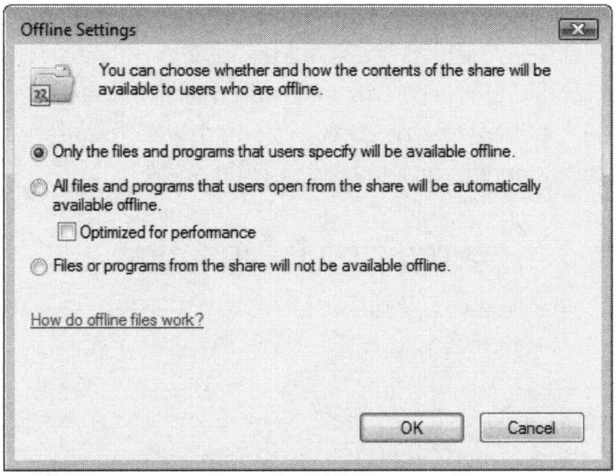

Figure 13-16   Configuring a folder for offline use

Using the Windows Mobile Device Center

The Windows Mobile Device Center (WMDC) replaces Microsoft ActiveSync in Windows Vista and provides device management features for Windows Mobile-powered devices, including setting up a desktop partnership and synchronization with the desktop. WMDC includes the following features:

- An enhanced user interface that helps you to quickly access critical tasks and configure your device
- A partnership wizard and improved partnership management
- Device browsing that lets you quickly browse files and folders and open documents on your device directly from your computer
- Synchronization of e-mail, calendars, contacts, tasks, favorites, and files
- Synchronization and shuffling of Microsoft Windows Media Player music files
- Picture management that detects new photos on a Windows Mobile device, tags them, and imports them to Windows Vista Photo Gallery

WMDC runs on Windows Vista Ultimate, Enterprise, Business, Home Premium, and Home Basic editions. It is compatible with Microsoft Outlook 2000, Outlook XP, Outlook 2003, and Outlook 2007 messaging and collaboration clients (Microsoft recommends Outlook 2007).

WMDC does not (currently) ship with Windows Vista, and you need to download it. Microsoft recommends connecting your mobile device to your Windows Vista PC by using a universal serial bus (USB) cable so it installs through plug and play and then using Windows Update to scan for updates. Windows Update detects your mobile device and downloads and installs the WMDC driver as an update.

Unfortunately, life is seldom that easy. The device drivers for some mobile devices are not in the Windows Vista plug and play library, and you need to install the necessary software from the CD-ROM that came with the device. Windows Update might not recognize the connected device, in which case you need to navigate to the Windows Mobile Device Center webpage at *http://www.microsoft.com/windowsmobile/devicecenter.mspx* and click the link as instructed to download and install the 32-bit or 64-bit WMDC driver. When the driver installation has completed, Windows Update automatically checks for the latest updates to install.

Establishing a Partnership and Synchronizing Information

When you connect a mobile device and install WMDC or when you connect a new mobile device to a computer that has WMDC installed, you need to decide whether to set up a Windows Mobile partnership in WMDC. If you want to synchronize information between your device and the computer, a desktop partnership is required. When you set up this partnership, your selected synchronization settings are saved. WMDC will recognize your device when you reconnect and use your synchronization settings.

A computer can set up Windows Mobile partnerships with many Windows Mobile-powered devices, but a device can have synchronization relationships with at most two computers. So if you use a number of computers, you need to decide carefully what computers you need to synchronize with.

To establish a partnership and set up synchronization (assuming the device is connected to the computer and WMDC has opened), click Set Up Your Device on the first WMDC screen, as shown in Figure 13-17.

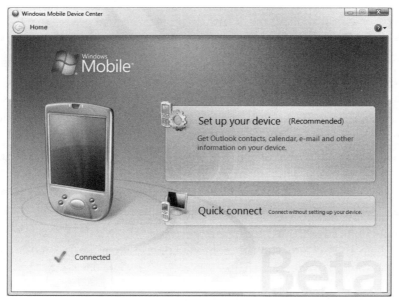

Figure 13-17   Choosing to set up a partnership

The Set Up Windows Mobile Partnership wizard opens and asks you to select the content type that you want to synchronize, as shown in Figure 13-18. When you make your selections and click Next, the wizard prompts you to give your device a name. You then click Set Up to create the Windows Mobile partnership.

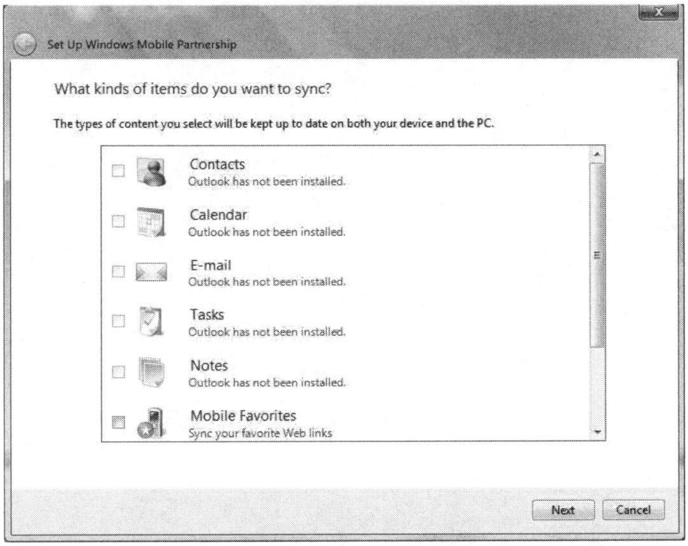

Figure 13-18   The Set Up Windows Mobile Partnership wizard asks what you want to synchronize

After you have configured a partnership, you can change your synchronization selections at any time from WMDC. When you connect the device to the computer, WMDC opens with the page shown in Figure 13-19, and you click Mobile Device Settings.

The mobile device settings you can configure are shown in Figure 13-20. You can click Change Content Sync Settings, select the check box for the information type that you want to synchronize, click Sync Settings (if available) for each content type whose settings you want to change, and then select the options you require.

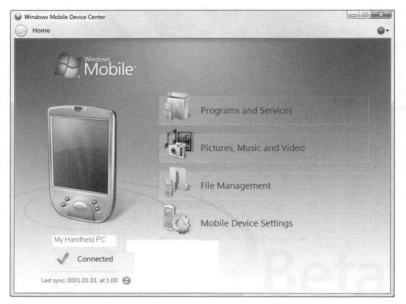

Figure 13-19   WMDC window when a device is connected

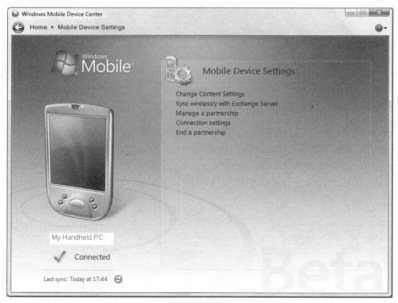

Figure 13-20   Mobile device settings

You can end a Windows Mobile partnership at any time. You would do this if you no longer use the device or if you want to set up a partnership between the device and another computer. You need to ensure that the device is not connected to your computer and then open WMDC and click Mobile Device Settings. On the screen shown in Figure 13-20, click End A Partnership, select the device whose partnership you want to end, and then click End Partnership. You should see the screen shown in Figure 13-21.

Figure 13-21   Ending a partnership

Connecting Without Setting Up a Partnership

If you do not intend to connect your device to the computer on a regular basis or to synchronize with the computer, you can connect the device without setting up a partnership. You are then able to browse and open files on the device, import pictures from the device, and perform other tasks that do not require a partnership with the computer. In this case, plug your device into the computer, and click Quick Connect when WMDC opens with the screen shown previously in Figure 13-17.

Opening WMDC

When you have installed the WMDC driver, WMDC opens automatically whenever you connect a mobile device to the computer. If you want to open WMDC without plugging in a mobile device—for example, if you want to end a partnership—you can access it from the All Programs menu or click Network And Internet in Control Panel and then select Windows Mobile Device Center.

Typically, you install WMDC with your device connected to the computer through a USB cable. After WMDC has been installed and a partnership has been established (if required), you can remove the device for normal use, and you need to reconnect it only when you want to synchronize it with your PC. Devices can connect by using a USB or FireWire connection, a USB cradle, a wireless network, or a Bluetooth connector. Connecting your device to the computer opens WMDC.

Using Bluetooth

Using a Bluetooth connection to create a direct connection between your device and computer can be an advantage when switching between multiple devices because you do not need to change any cables or adapters. Before you begin, ensure that both your computer and your device are Bluetooth enabled and that you have logged on to the computer using an administrator account.

If your computer does not have built-in Bluetooth and you want to use Bluetooth connections, ensure that a USB Bluetooth adapter is attached. To Bluetooth-enable the computer, click Hardware And Sound in Control Panel, and click Bluetooth Devices. Click the Options tab, select the Allow Bluetooth Devices To Find This Computer check box, and click OK. To use Bluetooth, you must ensure both that it is enabled on your computer and that the mobile device is discoverable.

To connect by using Bluetooth, click Menu in ActiveSync on the mobile device (or tap Menu if your device is touch screen–enabled), and then click or tap Connect Via Bluetooth. When asked if you would like to set up a partnership, click or tap Yes. On some devices, you might need to click or tap Add New Device. When the name of the computer appears in the list, select it, and click Next. Enter a passcode when prompted, and then click Next.

On the computer, you will be prompted that a Bluetooth device is attempting to connect with the computer. Click To Allow This Connection, Click This Message. In the Add Bluetooth Device Wizard, enter the same passcode that you entered on your device, and then click Next. Finally, ensure that the check box for the ActiveSync service appears and is selected on the mobile device, complete the Bluetooth Wizard on the computer, and complete the Add Bluetooth Device Wizard on the mobile device.

Changing Connection Settings

When yourr device is connected to WMDC, it can use the network connection on your computer to connect to your SOHO network or to the Internet. If you want to change this setting, you need to open the Connection Settings dialog box. First, you connect your device to the computer, and WMDC starts automatically. If you have set up a partnership, the screen shown previously in Figure 13-19 appears. Otherwise, you click Quick Connect (refer to the screen shown in Figure 13-17) to access this screen. You then click Mobile Device Settings and select Connection Settings (refer to the screen shown in Figure 13-20). In the This Computer Is Connected To list, you can select Automatic to use the most common settings or select the specific device connection that you want to use the network connection on the computer to "pass through" WMDC.

NOTE　**Saving a personal identification number**

If you use a personal identification number (PIN) to lock your device, you will need to enter that PIN when you connect the device and WMDC opens. If you want to, you can save the PIN on your computer so that you do not have to enter the PIN the next time you connect your device with your computer. In a SOHO, this is normally permitted. However, if you have a device that contains a security setting from a corporate deployment of Microsoft Exchange Server, your company might require you to enter the PIN each time you connect your device with your computer.

Working with Device Files

If you want to store data files on your mobile device or to find specific files by browsing, connect the device to your computer. When WMDC starts, access the screen shown previously in Figure 13-19 (if you have set up a partnership, this screen opens automatically), and click File Management. This opens the Mobile Device folder for your device, and you can browse the files on your device as you would files on the computer. Note that when you double-click a folder in the Mobile Device folder, it might take a few seconds for the folder to open because it is being read from the device.

You can also copy information from the computer to the device and vice versa. Copying a file creates separate versions of the file on your device and computer. Because the files are not synchronized, any changes made to the file will not affect the copied file. To copy files, you open the Mobile Device folder as described in the previous paragraph. You can then right-click any file on your device, copy it, and paste it into a folder on your computer. Alternatively, you can right-click any file on your computer, copy it, and paste it into a folder on your device. WMDC also supports drag-and-drop operations. When you browse device contents, you can open, copy, delete, or rename any file on the device or access file properties.

If your mobile device is running Windows Mobile 2003 or Windows Mobile 2003 Second Edition, you can back up files on the mobile device onto your computer. To back up information automatically, you connect the device to the computer, WMDC opens, and, if synchronization occurs, you wait for it to finish. You then click Mobile Device Settings and select Backup And Restore. Click the Backup tab, and select Automatically Back Up Each Time The Device Connects. If you want to back up to a different backup file than the one you used previously, click Change and select the file to use.

Automatic backup is available only on devices that have a Windows Mobile partnership with the computer. If you want to back up information that is on a device that does not have a partnership configured (is set up as a guest), you need to manually back up the information. To do this, connect the device to your computer and WMDC starts automatically. As before, you click

Mobile Device Settings, select Backup And Restore, and click the Backup tab. To back up all information, you select Full Backup; to back up only new and changed information, you select Incremental Backup. You then click Back Up Now.

If you have created files on your device since the last backup and do not want them deleted during the restore process, you need to move those files from your device to your computer before restoring information. To restore information to your device, connect your device to the computer and WMDC starts (if your device is already connected, disconnect it, and connect it again). Click Quick Connect, and exit from any running programs on your device that do not automatically close. Click Mobile Device Settings, select Backup And Restore, click the Backup tab, click Restore Now, and select the name of the partnership you want to restore. Do not use your device until the restore process is complete.

Synchronizing Music, Video, and Pictures

If you want to transfer music files and other digital media files to your mobile device, WMDC can connect to Windows Media Player to synchronize these files. All media synchronization settings are set in Windows Media Player. To connect to Windows Media Player, first connect your device to the computer. WMDC starts automatically, and you click Pictures, Music, And Video, as shown in Figure 13-22. This opens the Windows Media Player. You can then click Add Media To Your Device From Windows Media Player and select the files to synchronize.

Figure 13-22   Selecting pictures, music, and video

Importing Pictures and Videos from Your Device

If your Windows Mobile–powered device has a camera, you can import still pictures and video clips from the device to your computer. Connect your device to the computer, and WMDC starts automatically. If synchronization starts at this point, first allow it to finish, and then click Pictures, Music, And Video. You can then click Import Pictures/Video From Your Device, and pictures and video are imported automatically.

Working with Sync Center

As described earlier in this lesson, Sync Center provides an overview of all of the partnerships that have been created with the computer. This includes partnerships between Windows Mobile–powered devices and the computer. Sync Center provides information about the partnership, including synchronization status and error information, and you can use it to perform simple tasks such as starting and stopping synchronization, browsing the files on your device, and opening WMDC.

You can access WMDC from Sync Center, provided you have already created a partnership with the device. To do this, click the Sync Center notification area icon (green circle with arrows), and double-click the Windows Mobile Powered Device icon in Windows Sync Center.

Adding and Removing Programs on a Mobile Device

If you install a program on your computer, you can also install it on your mobile device, provided the device is compatible with the software. Be careful, however, that this does not breach the licensing conditions for using the program.

You can install a program on your device that is already installed on your computer by opening WMDC (or connecting the device so WMDC starts automatically), clicking Programs And Services, clicking More, and clicking Add/Remove Programs. You then select the program from the list that appears, as shown in Figure 13-23, and click OK. Note that the names of the programs have been changed in this figure for copyright reasons. Some simple programs are implemented by a single .exe file, and you can use File Management in WMDC to copy this from the computer and paste it into the Program Files folder on the device. However, this will not work for most software packages.

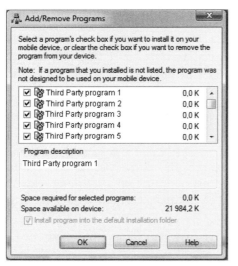

Figure 13-23   Add/Remove Programs

You can remove a program only from your device or from both your device and your computer. If you remove a program from your device but not from your computer, you can add it back to your device later, as described in the previous paragraph.

If the check box for the program is dimmed, you must use Remove and remove the program from both your device and your computer. If the program is not listed, but you know its file name, you can delete it from your device. For more information about deleting files from your device, see the documentation that came with your device. You remove a program by opening WMDC (or connecting the device so WMDC starts automatically), waiting until synchronization stops (if necessary), clicking Programs And Services, and selecting Add/Remove Programs. To remove a program from both your device and your computer, select it, and click Remove. To remove a program from the device only, clear its check box. If the check box is dimmed, you cannot remove the program from the device without removing it from the computer.

Configuring and Troubleshooting Windows SideShow Devices

Windows SideShow implements a secondary display that you can use with devices such as mobile phones, PDAs, or TVs, or by Windows software packages known as SideShow gadgets. Two types of Windows SideShow-compatible devices exist: those that are integrated into a computer—for example, small color displays embedded in a laptop lid—and wireless or plug-in devices that you connect to a computer, such as mobile phones, keyboard displays, and remote control devices.

NOTE **SideShow gadgets**

This lesson describes SideShow gadgets. There are other types of gadgets—for example, Sidebar gadgets. It is important to distinguish these from SideShow gadgets that run on SideShow devices.

SideShow-compatible devices provide a way to interact with a mobile PC when it is off or when the user does not have access to keyboard, mouse, and monitor. For example, you can look at an auxiliary display (aux display) on a mobile PC, find out how many new e-mails you have received, and read them immediately without turning the mobile PC on, waking it from hibernation, or even pulling it right out of its bag.

The aux display is a small computer that is always on even if the mobile PC is turned off. It can periodically power up the mobile PC to perform tasks such as e-mail synchronization and then shut it down again. SideShow-compatible devices can also act autonomously. For example, a device might alert you about a meeting without needing to interact with the mobile PC because it downloaded meeting information the last time the mobile PC was active. Figure 13-24 shows a mobile PC with a built-in SideShow-compatible device.

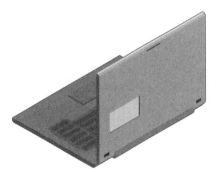

Figure 13-24 Mobile PC with a built-in SideShow-compatible aux display

NOTE **Status information on aux displays**

Aux displays can be built into portable computers on places other than the lid. They can, for example, replace light-emitting diode (LED) displays to indicate status information, such as whether the mobile PC is running on battery or is plugged into a power source.

SideShow-enabled devices can be used to remotely control applications on the main PC. For example, you could use such a device to control Windows Media Player and play songs without having to open a mobile PC lid or to check your e-mail from the other side of the room. Figure 13-25 shows an emulator for such a device. The figure (obviously) does not show a real device but is instead an emulation provided as part of the Windows SideShow software development kit (SDK).

Figure 13-25   SideShow device used to remotely access e-mail (emulation)

NOTE   SideShow and static PCs

SideShow devices are not confined to mobile PCs, although the technology plays an important role in mobility. SideShow devices could, for example, enable a system administrator to check the status of a server, or a set of rack-mounted servers, without ever having to connect a monitor and a keyboard. The SideShow device could (if so designed) enable the administrator to perform simple tasks, such as resetting a service or rebooting a computer.

Using SideShow Gadgets

A SideShow gadget is an add-in program that runs on a SideShow-compatible device and updates the device with information from the computer. SideShow gadgets can include familiar programs such as Windows Mail, Windows Media Player, and Windows Picture viewer, or third-party packages such as mapping gadgets that let you obtain travel directions without booting up your PC.

You can view SideShow gadgets that are installed on your device or download additional SideShow gadgets for your device in SideShow by clicking Hardware And Sound in Control Panel and selecting Windows SideShow. The Windows SideShow dialog box is shown in Figure 13-26. As yet, no devices are added to SideShow.

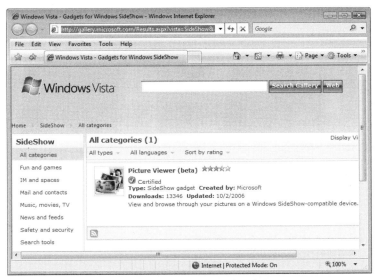

Figure 13-26 The Windows SideShow dialog box

You can view SideShow gadgets that are available for download and installation by clicking Get More Gadgets Online. This accesses the website shown in Figure 13-27.

Figure 13-27 SideShow gadget download website

Installing and Uninstalling Devices and SideShow Gadgets

There is no limit to the number of devices that you can install to use with SideShow. To determine whether a device is SideShow-compatible, look for the Windows SideShow logo on the device or refer to the manufacturer's documentation. To install a SideShow-compatible device, you follow the manufacturer's instructions. This typically involves connecting the device, inserting an optical disk, and running a wizard.

When the device is installed, it appears in the Windows SideShow dialog box, shown previously in Figure 13-26. Under the device, the dialog box provides a check box for each installed SideShow gadget, and you specify the SideShow gadgets you want to use on the device.

Exam Tip Because different installation procedures might apply to devices from different manufacturers, the 70-620 examination is unlikely to ask questions about how to install a device.

When you download a SideShow gadget and run the installation (msi) file, an installation wizard asks you to agree to license terms and then installs the SideShow gadget. You then typically enable the SideShow gadget for one or more devices in the Windows SideShow dialog box. However, if you install a third-party device, the device manufacturer might have installed and enabled some SideShow gadgets on the device, and these SideShow gadgets might not appear in the dialog box. Check the documentation that came with the device or access the manufacturer's website.

Although there is no limit to the number of SideShow gadgets that you enable for a device, the device has a fixed amount of space to store information, and this space is shared by all of the SideShow gadgets. If you need to increase the amount of space for a SideShow gadget on a device, turn off other SideShow gadgets that you do not need.

You can uninstall a device from the Windows SideShow dialog box. However, SideShow gadgets are programs. If you want to uninstall a SideShow gadget, you need to click Programs And Features in Control Panel, select Uninstall Or Change A Program, and then uninstall the Side-Show gadget as you would any other application. SideShow gadgets such as Windows Media that are built into the OS cannot be uninstalled.

MORE INFO Using the SideShow simulator

If you do not have access to a SideShow device but want to learn more about the technology before tackling the examination, you can run the SideShow simulator. This is provided in the Windows SideShow SDK, which is part of the Microsoft Windows SDK for Windows Vista, downloadable at *http://www.microsoft.com/downloads/details.aspx?FamilyID=c2b1e300-f358-4523-b479-f53d234cdccf&DisplayLang=en*. Note the name and path of the Windows SDK install folder.

You can find instructions for installing and launching the simulator at *http://msdn2.microsoft.com/en-us/library/ms744169.aspx*.

Changing Device and SideShow Gadget Settings

Installed devices are listed in the left-hand tile of the Windows SideShow dialog box. Clicking a device lists the settings available. Clicking a SideShow gadget name accesses the settings for that SideShow gadget. You cannot configure a device unless it is connected to your PC. The following settings are available for devices:

- **Lock The Device** This setting lets you specify how long the device remains inactive before it is automatically locked. It also lets you specify a four-digit PIN for the device. If your device is protected by using a PIN, this helps protect your data if the device is lost or stolen.

- **Turn Off The Device Backlight Automatically** To save power, the backlight on some devices turns off before the screen turns off, so the screen appears to dim. If this bothers you (or a user you support), you can clear the Turn Off The Backlight Automatically check box and then click OK. Not all devices have this feature.

- **Show Notifications For Gadgets On This Device** Notifications are small pop-up windows that are displayed in the notification area of the device screen. If you want to disable notifications on a device, clear the Show Notifications For Gadgets On This Device check box under Gadgets, and then click OK. This check box does not appear if the device does not offer notifications.

- **Change The Order In Which SideShow Gadgets Appear** You can change the order of most (not all) SideShow gadgets for each device. Only SideShow gadgets that are turned on and that appear in the Windows SideShow dialog box can be reordered. If more than one device is installed, you need to select the name of the device for which you want to reorder SideShow gadgets. In the list, click a gadget name, and then use an arrow button to move the gadget up or down in the list. Click OK when you have finished. Not all Side-Show gadgets support reordering.

NOTE Device-specific SideShow gadgets

Some SideShow gadgets are specific to a particular SideShow-compatible device and are installed on the device by the manufacturer. If these device-specific gadgets do not appear in The Windows SideShow dialog box, you need to change the gadget settings directly on the device. Check the documentation that came with your device or go to the manufacturer's website.

Troubleshooting SideShow Devices

Typically, your SideShow device is either integral to the computer or connects through a cable, a wireless network, or a Bluetooth adapter and works more or less automatically. Sometimes, however, problems occur.

The Device Is Not Connected to the Computer   If the device has never connected, you might have installed the wrong driver or not installed a driver at all. Refer to the manufacturer's documentation for more information. The device might itself be faulty, or the cable or Bluetooth connector might be the source of the problem. If you are connecting across a network, you could encounter network problems. To troubleshoot network connection problems, refer to Chapter 7, "Configuring Network Connectivity." If you have installed a third-party firewall, check that it is not blocking the connection.

If the device has been connected but the connection is lost, the cable might have become unplugged. If the device connects to your computer by a Bluetooth adapter or wireless network, you might have lost your connection. In this case, restart your device to try to restore the connection.

The device might have been removed from Device Manager, or the device driver might be corrupt. You access Device Manager by clicking System And Maintenance in Control Panel, selecting System, clicking Device Manager, and clearing the UAC dialog box as prompted.

Updated Information Does Not Appear on the Device   Start with the simple checks—ensure that the device is turned on and check the connection to the device. If you have set Windows Vista to automatically wake your computer to update information on your device, make sure you are logged on. Unlike with Windows Update, updating information on a device requires a valid user logon.

Some Device Content Is Missing   Your device has a fixed amount of space to store information, and all your SideShow gadgets share this space. The more SideShow gadgets you add, the less space there is for each gadget. If you recently added a SideShow gadget, content associated with gadgets already enabled on the device can be lost. Disable any SideShow gadgets you do not currently need on the device.

The Device Failed   Reasons for device failure typically depend on specific device settings. You can often get the device working again by restarting it. Check the manufacturer's documentation, or go to the manufacturer's website for more details.

The Device Screen Dims   As stated earlier in this section, the backlight on some devices turns off before the screen turns off, so the screen appears to dim. Users sometimes identify this as a fault, although it is normal operation for the device. If you want to change this behavior, configure the Turn Off The Device Backlight Automatically setting.

MORE INFO SideShow

For more information about SideShow and SideShow-enabled devices, access *http:// msdn2.microsoft.com/en-us/library/e56672bc-c341-4c5d-b5bb-5aa3a68debbb.aspx* and *http://www.markusegger.com/Articles/Article.aspx?quickid=0512122.*

Practice: Recovering Files and Creating a Complete PC Backup

In this practice session, you synchronize offline files and schedule synchronization. You then create a sync conflict and resolve it. Standard users should be able to perform all these tasks, and the practices ask you to log on by using a standard account. You simulate disconnection from a network by disabling a network adapter (probably wireless because this chapter is about mobile PCs and devices), and this action requires elevated privileges, but in practice, users will be disconnecting from office networks by hibernating their laptops and taking them home.

You need a network connection to another PC that will act as your network server. This PC does not need to be running Windows Vista.

▶ **Practice 1: Synchronizing Offline Files and Scheduling Synchronization**

In this practice, offline files have been enabled in a folder called Offline Files on a network server called Office. You might choose to use a different server and give the folder a different name. Enabling offline files on a computer that is running Windows Vista is described earlier in this lesson. For any other OS, refer to the Help files. (Note that in Windows XP you need to disable fast user switching before you can enable offline files). You need to set permissions so that the account you use to log on has permission to access the folder on the network server that holds the offline files. In the Practice 2 text files, *mydoc1.txt* and *mydoc2.txt* have been created in the Offline Files folder. In the real world, you would copy other files (for example, Microsoft Word files) into it.

1. Log on by using a standard account—for example, the parent_standard account that you created in Chapter 4, "Configuring and Troubleshooting Internet Access."

2. On the Start Menu, click Network.

3. Browse to the shared folder that has been enabled for offline files on the network server. In Figure 13-28, this is \\Office\Offline files. It will probably be a different folder in your network.

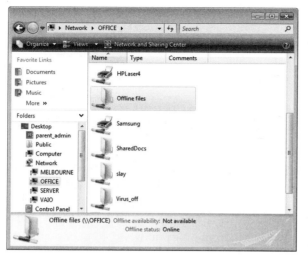

Figure 13-28   Browsing to the folder that contains the offline files

4. Right-click the folder that contains the offline files, and click Always Available Offline, as shown in Figure 13-29.

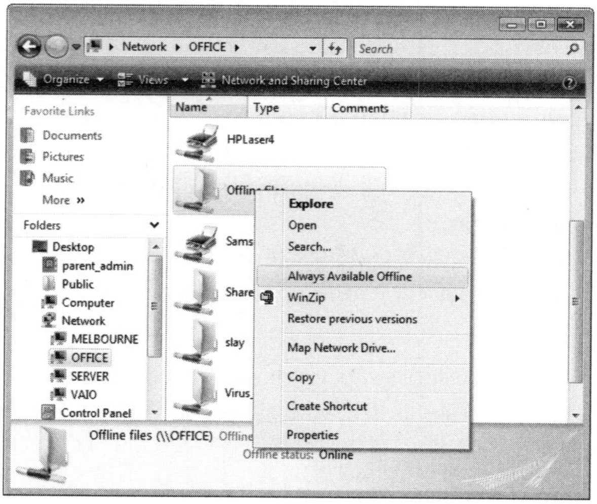

Figure 13-29   Marking a folder as available offline

5. The Sync icon appears beside the selected folder, as shown in Figure 13-30.

Figure 13-30   The Sync icon appears beside the selected folder

6. Open the Mobility Center, and click the Sync icon on the Sync Center tile.

NOTE Using a desktop computer

Typically, file synchronization is required when users intend taking their laptops off-site. However, you can sync files between a file server and a desktop computer if you want to. In this case, you would use the Sync Center because you cannot use the Mobility Center on a desktop PC.

---

7. If necessary, click View Sync Partnerships. Offline Files is set up as a sync partnership, as shown in Figure 13-31.

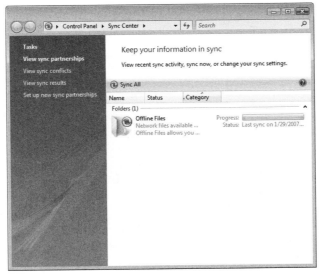

Figure 13-31   Synchronizing offline files

8. Click Sync All to sync immediately.

9. To schedule sync, select Offline Files, and click Schedule.

10. Select the item (or items) you want to schedule, as shown in Figure 13-32, and click Next. If you do not see any files listed, check that you clicked Sync All in Step 8.

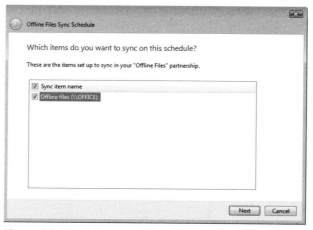

Figure 13-32 Selecting offline files to schedule

11. Click On An Event Or Action (if you prefer, you can select a scheduled time), and click Next.

12. Specify when you want sync to occur, as shown in Figure 13-33. Click Next.

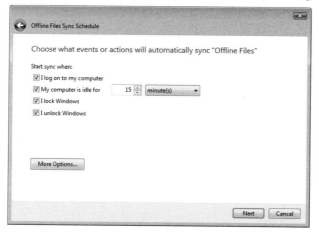

Figure 13-33 Specifying when sync occurs

13. Save the schedule.

▶ **Practice 2: Creating and Resolving a Sync Conflict**

In this practice, you edit the *mydoc1.txt* file on your mobile PC while it is disconnected from your network. You also change the file on the network server. When you reconnect the mobile PC to the network, a sync conflict occurs. You resolve this conflict.

You need to complete Practice 1 in this lesson before starting this practice. Sync must have occurred, and the *mydoc1.txt* file must be saved on your mobile PC (typically in your My Documents folder) as well as on the network server.

In this practice, you log on to your mobile PC with the same account as before. However, you need to provide administrator credentials (for example, for the Kim_Ackers account that you created when you installed Windows Vista) in order to enable and disable the network connection.

1. Log on by using the same account that you used in Practice 1.
2. Simulate removing the mobile PC from the network by opening the Network and Sharing Center, clicking Manage Network Connections, and disabling the network adapter. If you have forgotten how to do this, refer to Chapter 7, "Configuring Network Connectivity." Supply administrator credentials to close the UAC dialog box as prompted.
3. Search for the *mydoc1.txt* file on the mobile PC. Open it, amend it, and save it.
4. Log on to the network server (because the network adapter is disabled, you cannot do this through Remote Desktop, and you need to log on at the actual PC that you are using as a file server). Open the *mydoc1.txt* file in the Offline Files folder in that server. Amend it, and save it.
5. On the mobile PC, enable the network adapter. As before, supply administrator credentials to close the UAC dialog box as prompted.
6. The Sync icon on the toolbar should indicate that sync conflicts have occurred. Click this icon. As shown in Figure 13-34, one conflict has occurred.

Figure 13-34 One conflict has occurred

7. Click "1 Conflicts." This lists the conflicts (in this case, only one), as shown in Figure 13-35. Select the conflict, and click Resolve.

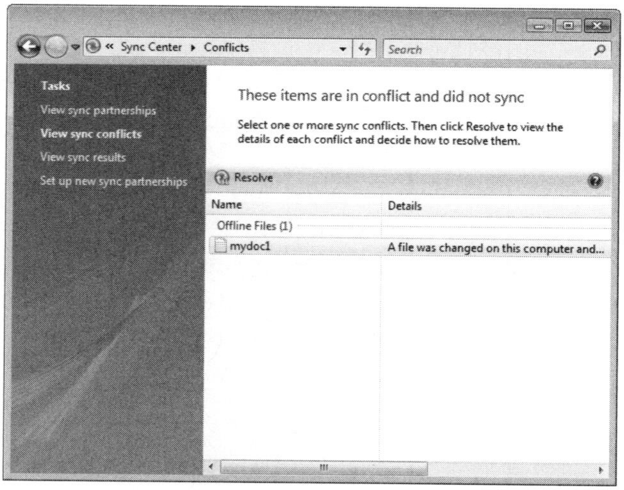

Figure 13-35 Listing the conflicts

8. As shown in Figure 13-36, you are given the choice of keeping the version on the mobile PC, keeping the version on the network server, or keeping both versions but renaming the version on the mobile PC. Select to keep the version on the network server.

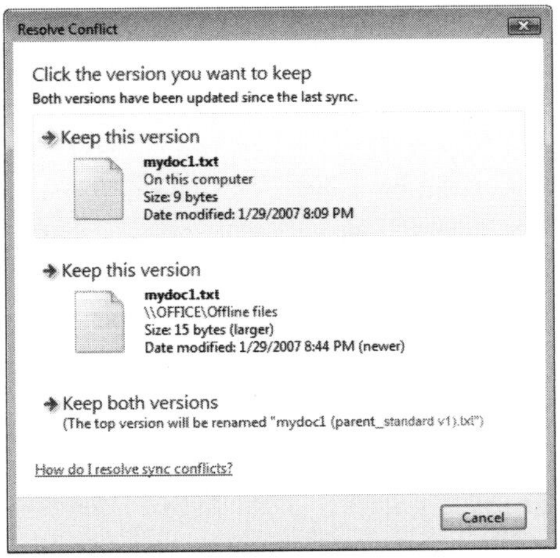

Figure 13-36   Conflict resolution choices

9. Check that the contents of the file on the mobile PC are now the same as the contents of the file on the network server.

Lesson Summary

- You can use the Sync Center to synchronize files on your mobile PC with files on a handheld device such as an audio player or digital camera. You can also synchronize offline files on a network server with your mobile PC.
- WMDC lets you set up Windows Mobile partnerships with compatible handheld devices. You can synchronize files, perform backup and restore, install and remove programs, and arrange picture, video, and music files. You can also connect a compatible device without forming a partnership.
- SideShow devices are computers within computers that let you access information on your computer even when it is turned off. SideShow devices can be connected devices or built-in devices.

Lesson Review

You can use the following questions to test your knowledge of the information in Lesson 2, "Configuring Mobile Devices." The questions are also available on the companion CD if you prefer to review them in electronic form.

NOTE Answers

Answers to these questions and explanations of why each answer choice is correct or incorrect are located in the "Answers" section at the end of the book.

1. A worker has decided to synchronize her personal laptop with the desktop computer that she uses in the office. She configures her My Documents folder on the desktop computer to be available for offline use. She brings her laptop into the office and tries to set up a sync partnership with the Offline Files folder on her desktop computer but is unable to. Her desktop computer is running Windows Vista Ultimate and has 2 GB of RAM and a 400-GB hard disk. Her laptop is running Windows Vista Home Premium and has 1 GB of RAM and a 100-GB hard disk. Both hard disks have more than 75 percent free disk space. Her company uses a workgroup configuration and not an Active Directory directory service domain. What is the problem?

    A. There is insufficient RAM in the laptop computer.

    B. There is insufficient hard disk space in the laptop computer.

    C. The office computer needs to be a member of an Active Directory domain before files can be configured for offline use.

    D. Her laptop is running the wrong version of Windows Vista.

2. You see a colleague checking her e-mail on a handheld device and ask her if she has purchased a new mobile phone. She tells you that the device is not a mobile phone, and she is accessing e-mail on her computer. Her mobile PC is on the other side of the room. The lid is closed, and the computer appears to be turned off. What type of device is your colleague likely to be using?

    A. A PDA that has formed a Windows Mobile partnership with the mobile PC through WMDC

    B. A SideShow-enabled device

    C. A PDA that has been configured to sync with the mobile PC through the Sync Center

    D. A PDA running Outlook 2007 that connects to the mobile PC by using a Bluetooth connection

3. A user reports that he has downloaded several new SideShow gadgets and enabled them on his SideShow-enabled multifunction handheld device, but now some of the information that was stored for previously installed devices is missing. What do you advise him to do?

    A. Disable any SideShow gadgets he does not currently need.

    B. Use Windows Update to download updated SideShow gadgets.

    C. Change the order in which SideShow gadgets appear.

    D. Disable notifications for SideShow gadgets on the device.

4. You decide to remove software from a handheld device that is connected to your computer and has been configured with a Windows Mobile partnership through WMDC. You do not want to remove the software permanently from the computer. You access Add/Remove Programs on the device, but the check box beside the software is blanked out. How do you remove the software?

   A. You cannot remove this software.

   B. Hold down the Ctrl key, and click the check box. This will clear the check box and remove the program.

   C. Click Remove. Reinstall the software on the computer.

   D. End the partnership. This automatically removes any software from the handheld device that was installed by running the software installation file on the PC.

5. You connect a Windows Mobile-enabled PDA to your computer and WMDC opens. You do not create a partnership. You decide to configure automatic backup to back up files on the PDA to the computer. You have not previously backed up any files on the PDA. You click Mobile Device Settings, click Backup And Restore, and select the Backup tab, but the Automatically Back Up Each Time The Device Connects option is not available. How do you back up the files on the PDA with the least effort?

   A. Disconnect the device. Connect the device again, and form a partnership. Follow the same procedure as before. This time the Automatically Back Up Each Time The Device Connects option will be available.

   B. Manually select each file on the PDA that you want to back up, and copy it to a folder in the computer.

   C. Perform an Advanced Restore on the computer, and identify the PDA as the device from which files should be restored.

   D. Select Full Backup, and then click Back Up Now.

Chapter Review

To further practice and reinforce the skills you learned in this chapter, you can perform the following tasks:

- Review the chapter summary.
- Review the list of key terms introduced in this chapter.
- Complete the case scenarios. These scenarios set up real-world situations involving the topics of this chapter and ask you to create a solution.
- Complete the suggested practices.
- Take a practice test.

Chapter Summary

- The Mobility Center provides a single tool for configuring mobile PC settings, including presentation settings and connection to an external monitor.
- You can use the Connect To A Network Projector Wizard in the Accessories menu to connect to a network projector on either a local or a remote subnet.
- Sync Center lets you synchronize files with a mobile device or with a network server that stores files marked for offline use.
- You can use WMDC to configure compatible handheld devices and synchronize them with your computer. SideShow devices let you access information on your computer even when it is turned off.

Key Terms

Do you know what these key terms mean? You can check your answers by looking up the terms in the glossary at the end of the book.

- mobile PC
- mp3 player
- network projector
- personal digital assistant (PDA)
- plasma display
- presentation settings
- screen orientation
- synchronize

Case Scenarios

In the following case scenarios, you will apply what you've learned about configuring mobile display settings and configuring mobile devices. You can find answers to these questions in the "Answers" section at the end of this book.

Case Scenario 1: Configuring Mobile Display Settings

You are a frontline technician providing technical support to teaching staff at a small college. The classrooms at the college are not part of the college's Active Directory domain but instead contain computers connected wirelessly in workgroups. A network projector is installed in each classroom. Typically, staff members prepare lecture material on their mobile PCs and then take the PCs to the classrooms, where they join the relevant workgroup and connect to the network projector. Answer the following questions:

1. A lecturer is having difficulty preparing detailed lecture material on the small screen of his laptop. He is happy enough presenting lectures when the laptop is connected to a network projector. He does not want to prepare his material on a desktop machine and transfer it to his laptop. How can you help him?

2. A staff member lectures at several locations in the college and needs to access the wireless network at each one. She needs to access her presentation settings and adjust them. She needs an easy method of disabling and enabling presentation settings. She does not want to search for all these features through the Control Panel hierarchy. What do you tell her?

3. An inexperienced lecturer is worried that his laptop might go into sleep mode during a lecture or might display system notifications that would detract from his lessons. How do you reassure him?

Case Scenario 2: Configuring Mobile Devices

You work for a large computer retailer that also sells handheld mobile devices. Sometimes customers purchase a mobile PC running Windows Vista and one or more mobile devices as a package, and you need to provide support. Answer the following questions:

1. A customer places a helpline call. She reports that a small display on the outside of her laptop remains lit even when she powers the computer down and shuts the lid. She is concerned that this might drain her battery. What do you tell her?

2. A customer connects his PDA to his Windows Vista computer, and the drivers for the device install through plug and play. He has heard that the WMDC should then open and let him form a partnership and synchronize his PDA and his computer. This does not happen. What do you advise?

3. A commercial customer wants to configure offline files on a network server, so he can synchronize a laptop computer in a sync partnership, download the files to the laptop, and work on them at home. He has recently purchased a laptop computer running Windows Vista Business for that purpose. A work colleague has told him he needs Windows Vista Ultimate to synchronize with offline files. What do you tell him?

Suggested Practices

To help you successfully master the exam objectives presented in this chapter, complete the following tasks.

Configure Mobile Display Settings

Do all the practices in this section for which you can access suitable hardware.

- **Practice 1: Connect to an External Monitor**   The practice session asks you to connect an external monitor manually and extend your mobile PC screen on to it. Experiment with both a modern flat-screen monitor and an older monitor, possibly a cathode-ray tube (CRT) monitor, and find out whether the monitors require different procedures or different presentation settings.
- **Practice 2: Connect to a Plasma Screen Monitor**   If you have access to a plasma screen monitor, extend your mobile PC screen to this monitor.
- **Practice 3: Connect to a Network Projector**   If you have access to a network projector, connect your mobile PC to it, and configure presentation settings. Connect from both the same subnet as the network projector and from another subnet.

Configure Mobile Devices

Do all the practices in this section for which you can access suitable hardware.

- **Practice 1: Use Sync Center**   Use Sync Center to synchronize with your digital camera so all new pictures are downloaded to the computer when you connect the camera.
- **Practice 2: Use WMDC to Synchronize with Your PDA**   Use WMDC to form a Windows Mobile partnership with your PDA. Install programs on your computer on to your PDA. Back up and restore your PDA files.
- **Practice 3: Run the SideShow Simulation**   If you have not already done so, run the Side-Show simulation. If you have access to a SideShow device, apply what you have learned in the simulation to the device. Note the differences between a simulation and working with a real device.

Take a Practice Test

The practice tests on this book's companion CD offer many options. For example, you can test yourself on just one exam objective, or you can test yourself on all the 70-620 certification exam content. You can set up the test so that it closely simulates the experience of taking a certification exam, or you can set it up in study mode so that you can look at the correct answers and explanations after you answer each question.

MORE INFO **Practice tests**

For details about all the practice test options available, see the "How to Use the Practice Tests" section in this book's Introduction.

Chapter 14
Working with a Tablet PC

With Windows Vista, the Tablet PC experience has reached a new level. Tablet PC functionality is built into most editions of Windows Vista, and it is not necessar to install a separate edition of the operating system, as it was with Microsoft Windows XP, to take advantage of these remarkable devices. Tablet PCs are mobile PCs into which you use a pen device to enter data. Although entering text with a pen rather than a keyboard might seem quaint, the ability to write and draw makes the Tablet PC an excellent note-taking and brainstorming device. When used on battery power, the Tablet PC becomes like the ultimate clipboard, used by a variety of people, from doctors in hospital wards to students in lecture theatres.

The downside of that portability is the limited capacity of the battery. Anyone who has used a battery-powered laptop knows the stress of being in the middle of writing an important document with notifications popping up informing you that the computer is almost out of power and that you need to shut it down right now or risk losing everything. Power settings allow mobile computers to make the most out of a limited battery supply. You can configure a mobile computer to display all bells and whistles when connected to an external power supply and then have it shift into a mode where it conserves every last bit of energy to extend your working time when external power is not available.

Exam objectives in this chapter:
■ Configure Tablet PC software.
■ Configure Power Options.

Lessons in this chapter:

Before You Begin

■ Unlike in other chapters, performing the practices in the first lesson of this chapter requires that you have access to a Tablet PC that has Windows Home Premium, Business, Enterprise, or Ultimate installed.

■ Performing the practices in Lesson 2 require only that you have access to a computer running Windows Vista.

Real World

Orin Thomas

One of the reasons I learned to type is that my teachers found my handwriting incomprehensible. The fact that my Windows Vista Tablet PC has quickly come to terms with my messy scrawl is to me one of the most amazing things about Windows Vista. Although I type very fast, I enjoy using the Tablet PC for taking notes when I'm attempting to nut out a problem. The interface allows you to be nonlinear in a way that typing text directly into Microsoft Word does not. The Tablet PC is a wonderful replacement for the traditional notepad and, even though I've only had one for a couple of months, it is hard for me to imagine my life without it.

Lesson 1: Configuring Tablet PC Software

To get the most out of a Tablet PC, you have to know how to use the pen and train the computer to understand your handwriting. If you are lucky or have very neat handwriting, Windows Vista's handwriting recognition routines will recognize everything you input every time you do it. If you have relatively normal handwriting, Windows Vista will make a few mistakes at first but will soon learn your style, and recognition mistakes will become rare. If your handwriting is so bad that people wince whenever they try to read your notes, you might have to run the routine that allows you to enter a significant sample of your handwritten text before the computer understands the information you are attempting to enter. The handwriting recognition routines in Windows Vista are remarkable in that with enough data they can be trained to interpret even the roughest scrawl.

After this lesson, you will be able to:

■ Configure Tablet PC applications.
  ❑ Configure the Handwriting Recognition Personalization tool.
  ❑ Configure pen flicks.
  ❑ Configure pen input devices.
  ❑ Configure Input Panel settings.

Estimated lesson time: 30 minutes

Tablet PC

Tablet PC functionality is available only if you have a Tablet PC device and the appropriate editions of Windows Vista. The Business, Enterprise, Home Premium, and Ultimate editions of Windows Vista have Tablet PC functionality included, but this functionality is active only if the appropriate Tablet PC hardware exists. Tablet PC hardware includes a special screen that can process input from a pen, sometimes known as a stylus. Pressing the pen quickly against the screen is called a tap. Prolonged contact, such as when using the pen for handwriting, is called applying ink. Tablet PCs come in two general categories:

■ **Slate** This type of Tablet PC looks like a notebook monitor with a thick back. Slates do not have dedicated keyboards. Although slates support landscape display orientation, the default orientation that most computers use, with the width of the screen being longer than the screen's height, slates are most often used in portrait mode. Portrait mode is when the screen's height is longer than its width.

■ **Convertible** A convertible Tablet PC looks like a normal laptop computer. The screen can be rotated and folded down across the keyboard so that it resembles a slate. Driver software switches the display from landscape when in laptop mode to portrait when in slate mode.

If you want to manually change the screen orientation, you can use the Windows Mobility Center's Screen Orientation function. For example, you might have a slate Tablet PC but want to display a DVD movie. Movies tend to be presented in aspect ratios where the width is longer than the height. If your slate Tablet PC does not have a screen reorientation button, you can use screen orientation to rotate the screen appropriately. It is also possible to adjust the screen orientation through Tablet PC Settings in the Control Panel, as shown in Figure 14-1.

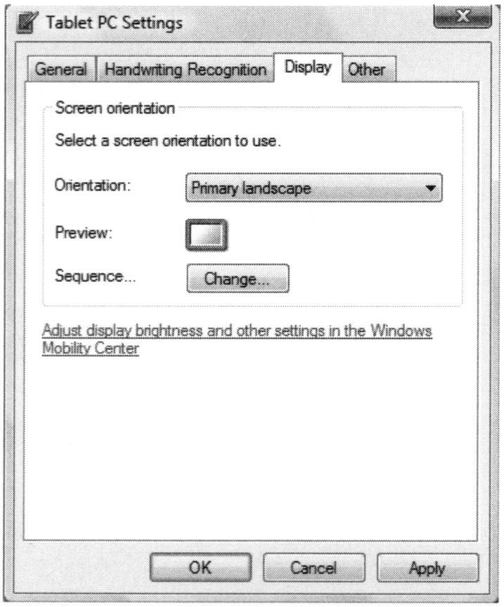

Figure 14-1 Using Tablet PC Settings to alter orientation settings

The four screen orientations are:

- **Primary Landscape** This is the default for most laptops, with the base of the display near the hinge that connects the screen to the keyboard area. This mode is useful for slate mode Tablet PCs when displaying movies.
- **Primary Portrait** The default for slate mode Tablet PCs, with the aspect ratio favoring height over width. Convertible Tablet PCs shift between the Primary Landscape and Primary Portrait modes when they are converted.
- **Secondary Landscape** An orientation that is not often used and is rotated 180 degrees from the Primary Landscape orientation.
- **Secondary Portrait** Another orientation that is not often used and is rotated 180 degrees from the Primary Portrait orientation.

Exam Tip Because secondary orientation options are less commonly used, they are likely to turn up on the 70-620 exam only as distracters.

The Tablet PC Settings item in the Control Panel is available on all editions of Windows Vista that can be used with a Tablet PC, even if the Tablet PC hardware is not present. Opening Tablet PC Settings in Control Panel and navigating to the General tab, as shown in Figure 14-2, allows you to configure whether the menus appear to the left or right of your hand. If the place where you tap on the screen does not match the underlying display, this tab allows you to initiate the calibration routine. The routine itself involves tapping on several crosshairs located in different places across the screen.

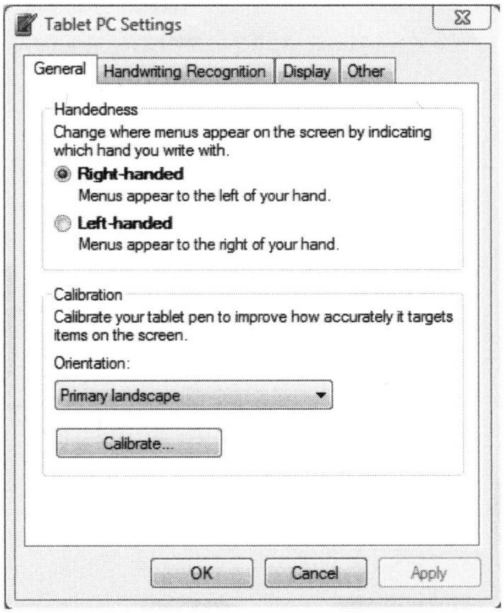

Figure 14-2 Using Tablet PC Settings to configure whether menus are right-handed or left-handed and to recalibrate your pen

Configuring Handwriting Recognition

Handwriting recognition is one of the core components of the Windows Vista Tablet PC experience. The default settings allow Windows Vista to learn your handwriting style over time, making note of corrections and adjusting appropriately. If Windows Vista is making a specific recognition error or you are impatient and want the computer to learn your handwriting style more quickly, you can use the Personalize Handwriting Recognition routines that are built into Windows Vista. The handwriting recognizer collects different data for different languages, depending on which language is currently selected in the Regional And Language Options section of the Control Panel. For example, if you use handwriting in English and Russian to input data into your Windows Vista Tablet PC computer, the recognizer will use a different data set depending on which input language is selected. Of course, if you start writing in Russian when your computer is configured to use English, no amount of correction is going to get the recognizer to identify your handwriting!

Targeting Specific Recognition Errors

The handwriting recognition routines included with Windows Vista can do only so much when people write different characters in very similar fashions. Consider the characters O, 0, o, and D. Even when looking at typed text it can be difficult to tell the difference between O and 0, so it is not a surprise that a computer might have difficulties in sorting one from the other. The Target Specific Recognition Errors routine allows you to either select a specific character or word or set of characters with similar shapes, such as the O and 0 characters. When you choose a specific character or word, you are asked to enter it using the on-screen keyboard. Once you have done this, you must provide four written examples of the character or word before you can update the recognizer.

The characters with similar shapes routine works in a similar fashion. You select one of six sets of similar characters and then provide Windows Vista with examples of your handwriting for those characters, as shown in Figure 14-3. If you are unhappy with the way you have written the characters, you can choose not to update the recognizer and start again from the beginning.

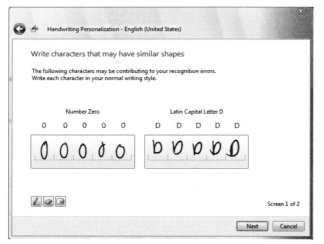

Figure 14-3 Writing out similar characters several times when targeting specific recognition errors

Teaching the Recognizer Your Handwriting Style

Teaching the recognizer your handwriting style is useful if you are impatient and want to reduce recognition errors immediately or if your Windows Vista Tablet PC computer finds it difficult to recognize your handwriting style. This process involves entering a series of 50 sentences, as shown in Figure 14-4, or providing examples of each available character to the computer. It is possible to save your progress if you do not have time to write all 50 sentences in a single session. Writing 50 sentences by hand can be tedious, although it will greatly improve Windows Vista's chances of identifying your handwriting.

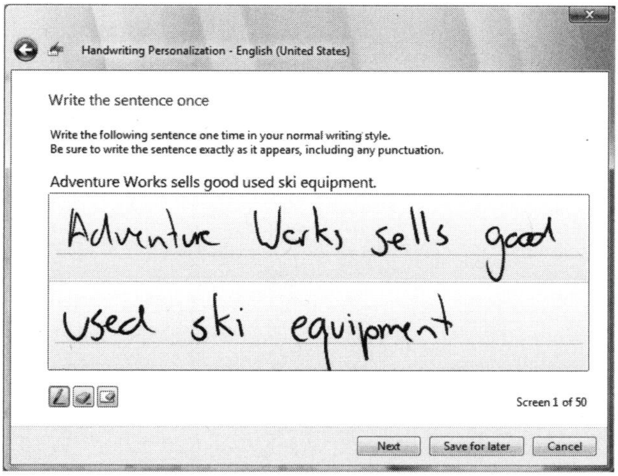

Figure 14-4   How Windows Vista learns to decipher handwriting

Managing Handwriting Recognition Data

When someone has used handwriting input on a Windows Vista Tablet PC for some time, the handwriting recognition routines will learn that person's style to the point where inaccurate interpretations are rare. Handwriting recognition data is stored as a part of a user's profile. This means that if someone logs on to the Windows Vista Tablet PC with another user account, that person will have to teach the recognizer about his or her handwriting over from the beginning, even if the computer has already learned to recognize the handwriting.

If a person needs to shift from one Windows Vista Tablet PC to another or use a new user account, it is possible to transfer the handwriting recognition data. You can do this by using the Windows Easy Transfer Wizard. When using the Windows Easy Transfer Wizard, make sure that the Handwriting Recognition check box is selected when performing the Select User Accounts, Files, And Settings To Transfer step, as shown in Figure 14-5. By performing careful selection at this step, you can transfer only handwriting selection data should this become necessary.

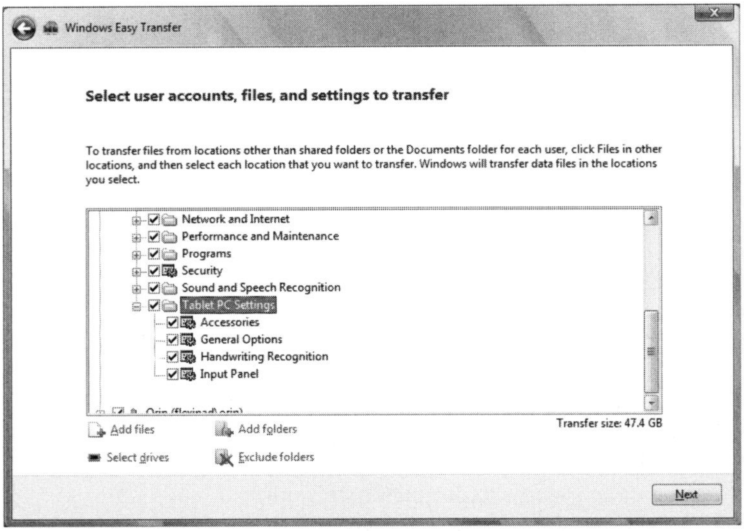

Figure 14-5 Using Windows Easy Transfer to move handwriting recognition data between computers

When a person is replaced at an organization, it is common practice to assign the replacement the old person's user account. This grants the new person access to all of the files and data needed without having to go through the complex practice of creating a new user account and configuring exactly the same security settings. If this is done after the handwriting recognition routine has learned the original person's particular style, it can cause recognition errors when the new person attempts to use that feature. It is possible to delete existing handwriting recognition data by turning off automatic learning in Tablet PC Settings in the Control Panel, as shown in Figure 14-6. After the data is cleared, you can turn automatic recognition back on, and the Windows Vista Tablet PC begins to learn the new person's handwriting style.

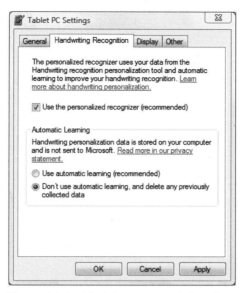

Figure 14-6 Disabling automatic learning removes existing handwriting recognition data

Configuring Pens and Input Devices

Tablet PC pens interact with the screen through magnetic resonance and not through pressure, which eliminates the chance that touching the screen or applying accidental pressure with an object that is not the pen will lead to input. The Pen And Input Devices item in Control Panel allows you to customize how a pen or stylus used with a Tablet PC interacts with the operating system. The basic options allow you to configure pen taps to mimic mouse clicks. As Figure 14-7 shows, you can configure specific pen actions to mouse actions. The settings enable you to configure double-tap speed in a way similar to how you would configure double-click speed using the Mouse item of the Control Panel. Some pens that come with Tablet PC computers have a button along the shaft and another at the end. Pressing down on the button on the shaft alters the small magnetic field around the end of the pen; depressing the one at the end by pushing it against the screen allows the pen to act as an eraser. The pen button can be configured so that tapping with the pen while holding down this button performs the same action as a mouse's right-click. If the stylus is appropriately configured, you can use it to erase ink writing input from the pen in a way similar to how you would use an eraser to remove pencil marks from paper.

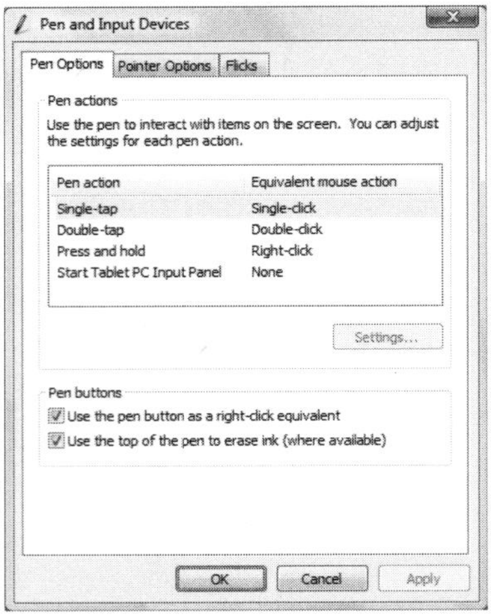

Figure 14-7   The Pen And Input Devices item in Control Panel allows you to customize pen settings

The other tabs within this Control Panel item allow you to configure the visual feedback from each type of tap. A single tap displays small ripples, and a double tap displays slightly larger ripples. Holding the pen to the screen displays a gray ring, and pressing the pen button and tapping, which is equivalent to the right-click of a mouse, displays a glowing blue ring. You can also configure the pen to show a different pointer to the mouse, differentiating both input devices, although only one cursor can be present on the screen at any time. The pointer differentiation essentially lets you see which device currently has control of pointing-based input. It is not uncommon for people to pair a Bluetooth mouse with a Tablet PC until they are used to navigating around the screen using only the pen.

NOTE   **Tapping instead of clicking**

Given the Tablet PC-specific nature of this lesson, the term "tap" rather than "click" is used to describe click-like input from the stylus device. A tap is a short, sharp connection of the stylus with the Tablet PC screen. Windows Vista's Tablet PC functionality is able to distinguish between a tap and the more prolonged stylus-to-screen contact that is used in activities like handwriting, drawing, or dragging.

You can perform a pen flick by quickly dragging the pen in a straight line across the screen for approximately an inch (2.5 cm). Windows Vista performs a different action depending on the direction of the flick. The default configuration of pen flicks allows you to use them in a way similar to that of the scroll wheel on a mouse. The default flicks are scroll up, scroll down, forward, and back; and they are assigned to the up, down, right, and left flicks, respectively. These default flicks are primarily used for navigating the Internet using a web browser. More advanced users can go beyond the default four directions and configure Windows Vista to understand up to eight. You do this by selecting the Navigational Flicks And Editing Flicks option in the Flicks tab of Pen And Input Devices. If this option is selected, it is also possible to launch the Customize Flicks dialog box, shown in Figure 14-8. The Customize Flicks dialog box allows advanced Tablet PC users to assign custom actions to eight directions rather than the default four. You can select actions through a drop-down list. If a desired action is not there, you can create a custom action and assign it to a flick, such as creating a screenshot by flicking in a particular direction with the pen.

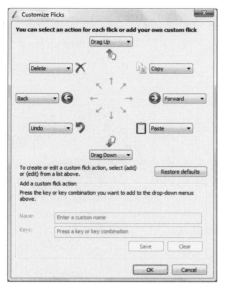

Figure 14-8   The Customize Flicks dialog box

NOTE   Graphics tablets

A graphics tablet is an input device that uses a stylus and a tablet device that is possible to draw on but that is not the screen of a Tablet PC. Graphics tablets are often used by artists who find using a pen with a graphics tablet more accurate than using a mouse. Tablet PC functionality requires input through a compatible screen and is not activated by the addition of a graphics tablet to a computer with a standard monitor.

Quick Check

1. You want to create a shortcut to save a document when you move your stylus in a particular manner. Which technology should you implement?
2. Your Windows Vista Tablet PC always recognizes your handwritten O as 0. Other recognition problems are rare. How should you resolve this issue?

> **Quick Check Answers**
> 1. Customized pen flicks.
> 2. Use the Target Specific Recognition Errors function of Handwriting Personalization.

Tablet PC Input Panel

The Tablet PC Input Panel is the primary method through which Tablet PC users input data. The three ways that you can input information into the Tablet PC Input Panel are:

- On-screen keyboard
- Character pad
- Writing pad

The on-screen keyboard, shown in Figure 14-9, can be used with a pen or a mouse to input text. Text input using this method is generally slower than other methods, but it allows for precision. During normal use, each key is highlighted when it is tapped to provide feedback to the user. The exception to this is when data is entered in password dialog boxes. This visual feedback is not provided, ensuring that anyone watching is not given visual clues to a user's password. It is possible to provide visual feedback by lowering the password security slider on the Advanced tab of the Input Panel Options dialog box.

Figure 14-9   The on-screen keyboard

The character pad uses a letter-by-letter handwriting recognition routine. If a letter is not recognized correctly, you can use a drop-down list under each letter to correct it, as shown in Figure 14-10. Entering handwriting this way is slower than using the writing pad because you must work character by character. Because it allows corrections character by character during input, this method is useful if you have to enter a significant number of symbol-based characters that might not easily be recognized when entered through the writing pad. You can adjust the thickness of the ink on the character pad through the Input Panel Options dialog box.

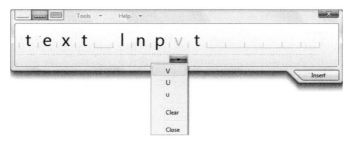

Figure 14-10   The character pad

The writing pad, shown in Figure 14-11, allows you to handwrite full words and have Windows Vista recognize them. The handwriting recognition algorithm uses probabilistic reasoning to determine what each word is based on the characters it contains. This allows Windows Vista to provide a best guess if the recognition routine does not fully recognize all the characters that make up a word. Clicking on a recognized word allows you to select near match alternatives or to provide corrections on a per-character basis. As you continue to write, the writing pad automatically enlarges. Tapping Insert clears the pad, entering the existing text into whatever document you are working on.

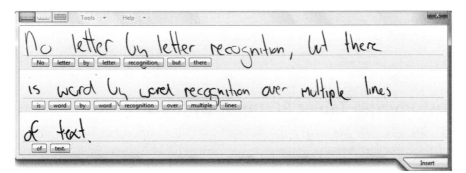

Figure 14-11   Using the writing pad to achieve recognition at the word level

You can dock the Tablet PC Input Panel at the top or bottom of the screen or as a floating panel that flies out from the side of your screen when you hold your stylus or pointing device above it and tap or click on it. To change this option, tap on the Tools menu, and select from:

- Float
- Dock At Top Of Screen
- Dock At Bottom Of Screen

Other options that can be applied to the Tablet PC Input Panel are to have the panel fly out by pointing the pen at its location rather than having to tap on it, as shown in Figure 14-12. You can configure the Input Panel tab to hide on the left or right side of the screen. You can also configure both the character and writing pads to perform a text insert by holding the pen over the Insert button rather than having to tap on it. Finally, you can configure strike-out gestures. Strike-out gestures allow you to delete text from the writing pad by striking it out with the pen. Through configuration options you can allow a range of common gestures used with popular PDAs, use only the strike-out gesture used with Windows XP Tablet PC edition, or to disable strike-out gestures entirely. These options are useful for advanced users who are confident using the pen and are not recommended for users with little experience. You can configure all these settings through the Input Panel Options dialog box.

Figure 14-12   Using the Input Panel Options dialog box to configure Input Panel behavior

Practice: Customizing Tablet PC Input Options

After someone becomes familiar with using a Tablet PC computer, that person is likely to want to customize the way it reacts to the stylus to better suit his or her habits.

Completing this practice requires that you have access to a Tablet PC computer with Windows Vista Business, Enterprise, Home Premium, or Ultimate edition installed.

▶ **Practice 1: Customizing Pen Flicks**

In this practice, you will configure pen flicks. Pen flicks are used as navigation shortcuts, usually to scroll up or down a page or forward and back between pages in a web browser. You can assign other keystroke combinations to flips, where Windows Aero displays the window switching animation, and even create your own key combinations. This practice requires an attached keyboard if you have a Tablet PC slate or for you to have the computer in laptop mode if you have a convertible model. To complete the practice, perform the following steps:

1. Open the Control Panel, and switch to Classic View.
2. Open the Pen And Input Devices item, and navigate to the Flicks tab, as shown in Figure 14-13.

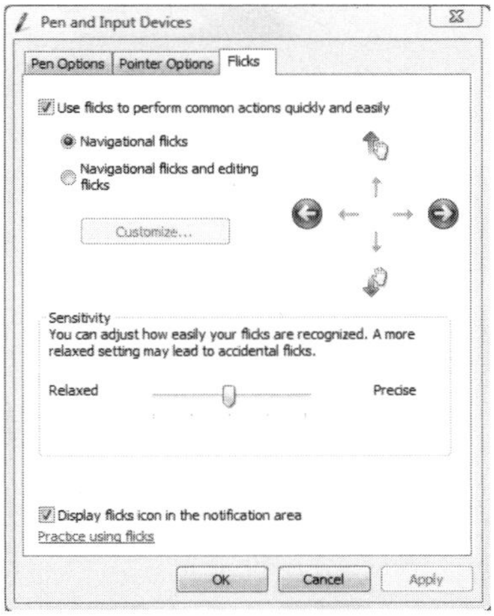

Figure 14-13   Configuring pen flicks

3. Select the Navigational Flicks And Editing Flicks option, and then tap Customize.
4. Use the drop-down list to change the right arrow flick, by default assigned to Forward, to Save.
5. Use the drop-down list to change the left arrow flick, by default assigned to Back, to Add.
6. In the Name text box, enter **Flip**.
7. Tap in the Keys text box, and then, on the attached keyboard, hold down the Alt key, and press the Tab key. If you have a convertible Tablet PC, you can do this step in laptop mode.
8. Click Save. When you have finished this practice, the Customize Flicks dialog box should look as it does in Figure 14-14. Test your combination by using left flick to perform a flip on your Tablet PC computer.

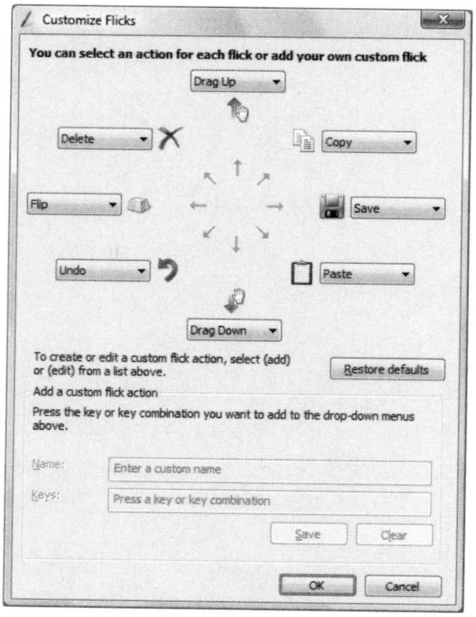

Figure 14-14   Configuring pen flicks

▶ **Practice 2: Configuring Input Pad Options**

In this practice, you will customize input pad options. The Input Panel defaults are excellent for users new to the Tablet PC platform, but experienced users are likely to want to try advanced options to optimize their text input experience. To complete this practice, perform the following steps:

1. Tap the input pad to bring it to the center of the screen if it is not already fully visible.

2. Tap on the Tools menu, and then tap on Options. This brings up the Options dialog box, shown in Figure 14-15.

Figure 14-15   The Settings tab of the Input Panel Options dialog box

3.   In the Settings tab, select Pointing To The Insert Button Inserts Text. This allows inserting of text without having to tap the insert button, which can improve text input speed for experienced users.

4.   Tap on the Opening tab, and select the Point To The Input Panel icon or the tab to open Input Panel. This allows the Input Panel to fly out automatically rather than having the user tap on it.

5.   Tap on the Gestures tab, shown in Figure 14-16, and change the scratch-out gesture to Only The Z-Shaped Scratch-Out Gesture That Was Available In Microsoft Windows XP Tablet PC Edition.

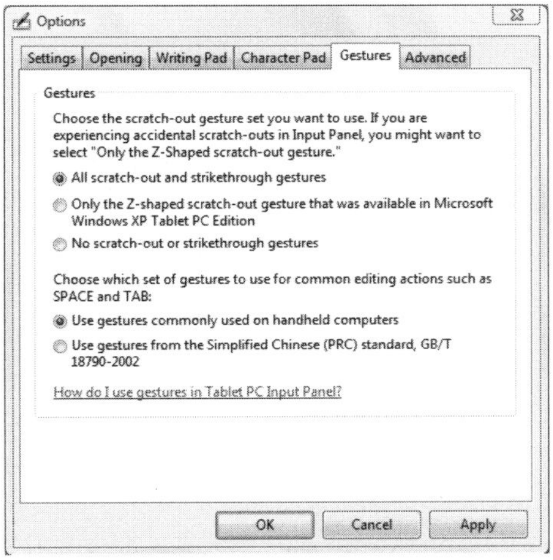

Figure 14-16   Configuring input pad gestures

6.   Tap the Advanced tab, and change the password security to High. This ensures that only the on-screen keyboard, and not the character pad or writing pad, can be used for password entry.

▶ **Practice 3: Targeting Specific Recognition Errors**

In this practice, you will run through the target specific recognition errors routine. This routine is used to improve character recognition if Windows Vista consistently incorrectly identifies specific letters or words. To complete the practice, perform the following steps:

1.   Open the Input Panel, tap on the Tools menu, and then tap on Personalize Handwriting Recognition.

2.   Tap on Target Specific Recognition Errors.

3.   On the Target Specific Recognition errors page, tap on Characters With Similar Shapes.

4.   On the Choose A Character Set You Want To Target page, shown in Figure 14-17, tap on 0 D o O.

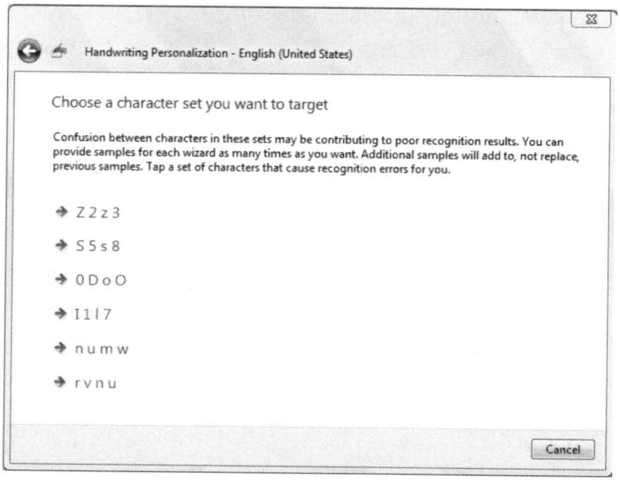

Figure 14-17 Improving character recognition

5. On the Write Characters That May Have Similar Shapes page, write the characters required, and then tap Next.

6. Repeat your actions from step 5, and then click Save.

7. Click Update and exit.

Lesson Summary

- Tablet PC functionality is available in the Business, Enterprise, Home Premium, and Ultimate editions of Windows Vista. Tablet PC functionality can be used only if a computer has Tablet PC hardware.

- There are two general versions of the Tablet PC computer, the slate and the convertible. A slate has no attached keyboard. A convertible can change from a standard laptop computer to the slate form by rotating the display 180 degrees and then folding it back across the keyboard.

- The most often used display orientations are Primary Portrait for slate mode and Primary Landscape for laptop mode.

- Text input on a Tablet PC is most often performed through the Input Panel. There are three input options for the Input Panel—an on-screen keyboard; the character pad, which recognizes written text one character at a time; and the writing pad, which recognizes text one word at a time.

- Gestures and pen flicks can be used as shortcuts to perform functions like deleting text, scrolling down and up through webpages, or saving documents. Pen flicks can be configured through the Pen And Input Devices item in the Control Panel.

- Windows Vista can be configured to automatically learn from your handwriting so that recognition is improved. Using the handwriting personalization routine, you can teach Windows Vista about your handwriting through extensive examples or target specific recognition errors.

Lesson Review

You can use the following questions to test your knowledge of the information in Lesson 1, "Configuring Tablet PC Software." The questions are also available on the companion CD if you prefer to review them in electronic form.

NOTE Answers

Answers to these questions and explanations of why each answer choice is correct or incorrect are located in the "Answers" section at the end of the book.

---

1. You are having trouble using the stylus to select or open items on your Tablet PC. Each time you tap an item, the single tap visual feedback appears half an inch away from where the stylus touched the screen. How can you resolve this issue?

   A. Calibrate Tablet Pen in Pen And Input Devices

   B. Enable Automatic Learning in Tablet PC Settings

   C. Use Handwriting Personalization

   D. Configure Orientation Calibration in Tablet PC Settings

2. There is a problem with hardware that initiates the display orientation change on your Tablet PC when you convert it from laptop mode to slate mode. When you convert, the display usually automatically rotates by 90 degrees. Now, when you perform a conversion, the screen remains in its laptop rather than its slate mode setting. You want to manually change your screen so it is displayed in its usual slate mode orientation. Which orientation should you set it to using Windows Mobility Center?

   A. Primary Landscape

   B. Primary Portrait

   C. Secondary Landscape

   D. Secondary Portrait

3. Orin enjoys using the character pad to input text into his Tablet PC during meetings. Orin has an unusual writing style, and his Tablet PC almost always incorrectly recognizes several letters that he scribbles on the screen. How can Orin ensure that these letters are correctly recognized in the future?

   A. Enable Use Automatic Learning in Tablet PC Settings.

   B. Disable Use Automatic Learning in Tablet PC Settings.

    C. Use Target Specific Recognition Errors in Handwriting Personalization.

    D. Use Teach The Recognizer Your Handwriting Style in Handwriting Personalization.

4. Ian often finds that text entered through the Input Panel is inadvertently scratched out. He wants text scratched out only when he makes a deliberate gesture. Which of the following actions should he take?

    A. Use Teach The Recognizer Your Handwriting Style in Handwriting Personalization.

    B. Configure the computer to use all scratch-out and strikethrough gestures in Input Panel options.

    C. Configure the computer to use only the Z-shaped scratch-out gesture in Input Panel options.

    D. Configure the computer to use no scratch-out or strikethrough gestures in Input Panel options.

5. You have noticed that several users are entering passwords on their Windows Vista Tablet PC computers using the character pad or writing pad from the Input Panel. This could allow someone to read their passwords while they are entering them. How can you ensure that passwords can be entered only from the on-screen keyboard?

    A. Configure Password Security in the Input Pad Options dialog box.

    B. Configure Password Security through the User Accounts item.

    C. Disable Writing Pad on the Input Panel.

    D. Disable Character Pad on the Input Panel.

Lesson 2: Configuring Power Options

Power options allow you to customize the way your computer uses energy. This is rarely an issue for desktop computer users, but if you are using a laptop computer without power in a meeting or in a library, an extra 15 minutes of battery power can be very important. Or if you frequently come and go from your computer, you are unlikely to want to use a power plan that requires you to regularly wake the computer from sleep. Power plans can have a significant impact on how a computer is used and often it needs to be customized to meet a person's needs.

After this lesson, you will be able to:
- Configure power options.
- Configure power profile settings.

Estimated lesson time: 30 minutes

Power Option Basics

Windows Vista is able to conserve power by reducing the flow of electricity to hardware that is currently not being used. A power plan is a collection of device power settings. The applied power plan determines when the computer's display is shut off and when the Windows Vista computer itself enters a powered-down state. Windows Vista has three powered-down states. These states are:

- **Shut Down** This mode is the most familiar to people. In this state, the computer is without power and when power is returned through pressing the power button, the computer performs a cold boot. A cold boot occurs when a computer is started up from a powered-off state.

- **Sleeping** Windows Vista computers in sleep mode still require a small amount of power. This trickle of energy is used to keep available all data that was in active memory when the computer was being used. This allows the computer to quickly become reoperational when awakened from sleep. This active memory data is also written to a file on the hard disk drive. If the computer is not awakened after 15 minutes, Windows Vista cuts power and data in RAM is discarded. When the computer is awakened, data is retrieved from the hard disk drive in a way similar to returning from hibernation. After 15 minutes the sleep process is the same as hibernation. You can awaken a computer that is sleeping by pressing a key on the keyboard. You can awaken a computer that is in hibernation only by using the power buttons.

- **Hibernating** Hibernation is similar to sleep in that the data in active memory is written to the hard disk drive, but after this is completed, the computer is completely powered off. Hibernation allows for a quicker resumption than a cold boot. Although resumptions from hibernation and a cold boot both start up from a powered-off state, recovery from hibernation involves dumping an active computer state into memory. Cold booting involves loading the operating system from scratch and is a much longer process. You can awaken a computer that is in hibernation only by pressing one of the power buttons.

Power Plans

Windows Vista ships with three plans—Power Saver, Balanced, and High Performance. You set the active power plan in the Power Options dialog box, shown in Figure 14-18. This dialog box displays the default power plans as well as any custom power plan that has been created on the computer. In general, the Power Saver power plan turns off devices quickly when the computer is not in use to conserve battery power, and the High Performance plan turns off devices less quickly because you would select this plan when conservation of battery power is not a priority. The process is actually a little more complicated because advanced power options allow you to restrict how much power the wireless adapters use and to configure a maximum level of processor usage. Advanced power options are covered later in this lesson.

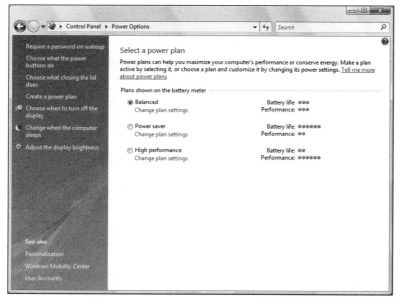

Figure 14-18   Using the Power Options dialog box to assign a power plan

Which power plan options are available depends on the hardware installed on the computer. For example, the plan settings shown in Figure 14-19 allow for the adjustment of screen brightness. Screen brightness is available as a power plan option only on some computers, and you might not be able to configure this option on your computer. You can configure power settings only for compatible hardware. How a power plan works depends on whether the computer is running off a battery or is plugged in to an external power supply. Settings for battery operation are always less power-intensive than the equivalent plugged-in setting. As you will note from the figure, there is a significant difference in the period of inactivity that causes the computer to go to sleep from when the computer is running on battery compared to when the computer being plugged into an external power supply.

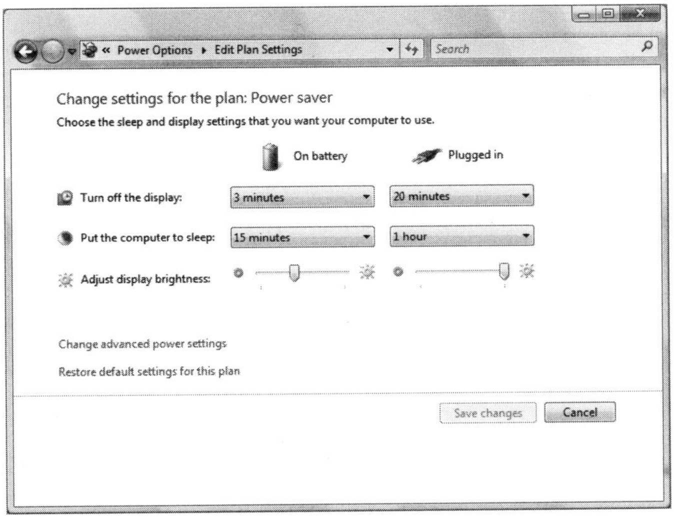

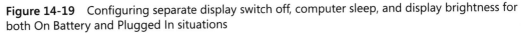

Figure 14-19   Configuring separate display switch off, computer sleep, and display brightness for both On Battery and Plugged In situations

Advanced Settings

Each power plan has a set of basic and advanced settings. The basic settings, seen earlier, determine when significant items, such as the display and computer, will be turned off. You can use the advanced power settings, shown in Figure 14-20, to apply a greater level of detail to a computer's power usage pattern. As with basic power plans, you can configure settings for both On Battery and Plugged In states. For example, you can have the computer require a password when it is awakened from sleep on the battery but not to require a password when awakened from sleep when plugged in.

Figure 14-20   Configuring advanced power options

Advanced settings allow you to configure the following for both the battery and plugged-in states:

■ Whether a password is required on wakeup.

■ How long to wait before turning off the hard disk.

■ The power and performance settings for wireless adapters. Limiting an adapter's range can reduce the amount of power it uses.

■ How much inactivity there is prior to sending the computer into sleep mode.

■ How much inactivity there is prior to sending the computer into hibernation.

■ How long to wait before suspending supported universal serial bus (USB) devices.

■ What action to take when pressing the power button. Power button configuration will be covered later in the lesson.

■ What action to take when shutting the lid. This setting will also be covered later in the lesson.

■ PCI express card power management. This setting determines whether built-in PCI express card power savings are implemented.

■ Processor power management. This allows you to throttle your processor as a way of reducing power output. The Power Saver plan limits the processor to 50 percent of its normal capacity.

- Search and Index performance settings. The more searching and indexing that is done, the more power is used. Limiting these processes can increase the amount of time a computer can run off a battery.
- Display power settings. This functions in a manner similar to the basic power settings.
- Multimedia settings. This setting relates to the sharing of media through Media Center or Windows Media Player.
- Battery warning thresholds. These settings determine when you are notified that the battery is running low and at what level the computer automatically enters hibernation.

You can modify all of the settings that can be configured when editing a power plan at a basic level when you are editing a power plan at the advanced level. The advanced editor brings all of the power-related settings together in one dialog box. In enterprise environments, you can apply power settings through Group Policy. Although enterprise environments are not tested on the 70-620 exam, you can imagine how an organization with thousands of Windows Vista computers might lower its electricity bill by optimizing the applied power plan.

Quick Check

1. How long does a computer put to sleep continue to use power?
2. Why is it possible to configure display brightness through the power settings of some computers and not others?

Quick Check Answers

1. A computer that is put to sleep uses power for 15 minutes before shutting down completely.
2. The options that can be configured through power settings depend on the hardware installed. Not all hardware supports being controlled through power settings.

Custom Plans

Sometimes the default settings will not suit your needs. For example, say that you are running your laptop using a car charger device while camping. Windows Vista would recognize a car charger in the same way it would recognize a computer plugged into an electrical outlet and the Plugged In state would be set. In this situation, you would want to make the power drain from the car battery as little as possible for fear of running the battery down. When you need to make changes to power plans to suit your situation, you can either edit an existing plan or create one of your own. The benefit of creating your own plan is that the existing plan is still available. It is far simpler to switch between plans than it is to edit the settings of plans each time circumstances change.

To create a custom plan, click Create A Power Plan in the Power Settings dialog box. This starts the Create A Power Plan wizard. The first page of the wizard, displayed in Figure 14-21, asks which existing power plan to use as the basis of the new custom plan. After you have selected an existing power plan and then clicked Next, the next page allows you to configure the power plan settings, such as when to turn off the display and when to put the computer to sleep. As with editing normal plans, it is also possible to configure advanced settings for custom power plans. When you finish creating your custom power plan, it is set as the default. You can still use the Power Settings dialog box to switch between the default power plans and your new custom plan.

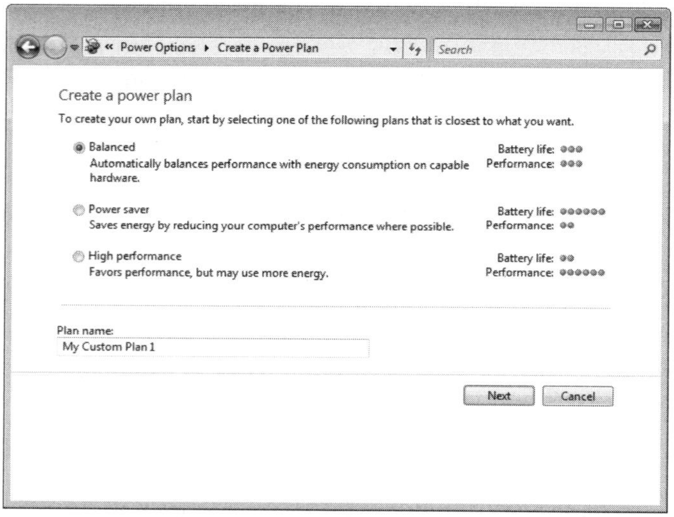

Figure 14-21 When you create a custom plan, you base it on an existing plan

Although you can delete custom power plans after you create them, you can do this only if the custom power plan is not currently in use. To delete a custom power plan, switch to another power plan, click Change Plan Settings, and then click Delete This Plan. You cannot delete the default plans that ship with WindowsVista.

Configuring Button Behavior and Security

Clicking Require A Password On Wakeup, Choose What The Power Buttons Do, and Choose What Closing The Lid Does in the Power Options dialog box brings up the Define Power Buttons And Turn On Password Protection dialog box, shown in Figure 14-22. The settings configured in this dialog box are applied generally and are not tied to any one power plan. From this dialog box, you can configure what the power button and sleep button do when pressed. The options you can assign to each button are Do Nothing, Sleep, Hibernate, and Shut Down.

If your computer is a laptop, you can also configure one of these actions to be initiated if the lid is shut.

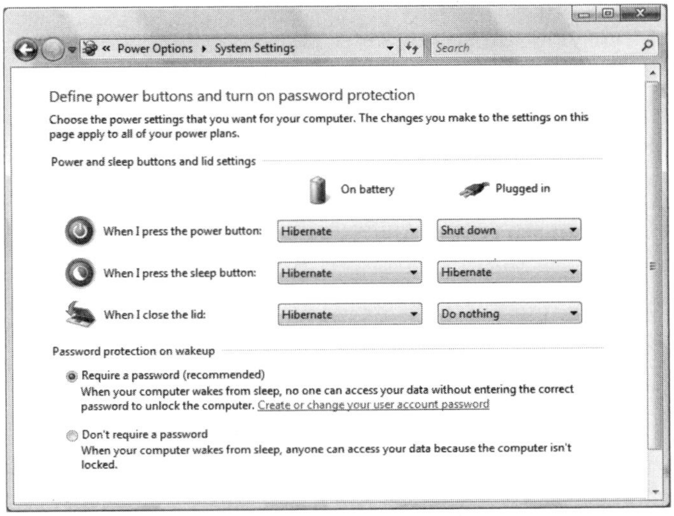

Figure 14-22   Configuring a computer's power buttons

You can also use the Define Power Buttons And Turn On Password Protection dialog box to force the user to enter a password when the computer wakes from sleep mode. A Windows Vista computer always requires a password when starting up for the first time or returning from hibernation, but sometimes you want to require a password to be entered after waking from sleep mode and sometimes, as when working in a secure environment, it is less of a priority—when you are working with a Tablet PC computer in a meeting, for example. Allowing the computer to move in and out of sleep mode decreases battery usage, but you do not want to have to enter your password repeatedly when you want to add some notes after a period of inactivity.

NOTE   **Advanced power buttons**

As discussed earlier in the lesson, it is also possible to configure button behavior and password security on a per plan basis using a power plan's advanced options. The advanced settings for a power plan override the more general settings configured through this dialog box.

Practice: Customizing Windows Vista Power Options

In this practice, you will perform several operations that will familiarize you with the Windows Vista power options. These include setting and then modifying one of the default power plans, editing advanced power saving options, and then creating a custom power plan. To best perform this practice, you should have access to Windows Vista installed on a laptop computer.

Practice 1 involves configuring an action for when the lid is closed, and you cannot configure this option on a desktop or virtual computer. You can still perform the rest of this practice if you do not have access to a laptop computer.

▶ **Practice 1: Setting and Modifying the Power Saver Plan**

In this practice, you will configure a computer to use the Power Saver power plan and then modify that plan to ensure that the display is only turned off after five minutes rather than three and that shutting the lid does nothing except send the computer into hibernation. To complete the practice, perform the following steps:

1. Log on to Windows Vista with a user account that is a member of the local administrators group.
2. From the Start menu, open the Control Panel in Classic View.
3. Open the Power Options item.
4. Set the Preferred Plan to Power Saver.
5. Click Change Plan Settings.
6. Change the Turn Off The Display drop-down value under the On Battery Category to 5 minutes. Click Save Changes.
7. In the Power Options dialog box, click Choose What Closing The Lid Does.
8. Change the When I Close The Lid under the On Battery category to Do Nothing. Click Save Changes.

▶ **Practice 2: Configuring Advanced Power Plan Settings**

In this practice, you will configure the Advanced settings of the Balanced Power Options Plan. Advanced settings give a finer level of control than the basic plan settings. In this plan, you will configure the wireless adapter power settings, search and indexing settings, and battery actions. To complete the practice, perform the following steps:

1. Log on to Windows Vista with a user account that is a member of the local administrators group.
2. From the Start menu, open the Control Panel in Classic View.
3. Open the Power Options item.
4. Set the Preferred Plan to Balanced.
5. Under Balanced, click Change Plan Settings.
6. In the Change Settings For The Plan: Balanced dialog box, click the Change Advanced Power Settings text.
7. In the Power Options dialog box, scroll down, and expand the Wireless Adapter Settings. Change the On Battery setting from Maximum Performance to Medium Power Saving.
8. Scroll further down to Search And Indexing. Expand this node, and change the On Battery setting from Balanced to Power Saver.

9. Navigate down to the bottom of the Power Options Advanced Settings dialog box, and expand the Battery node. Expand the Low Battery Level, and raise the On Battery figure from 10% to 15%.

10. Click OK to close the dialog box, and then click Save Changes.

▶ **Practice 3: Creating a Custom Power Plan**

In this practice, you will create your own power plan. To complete the practice, perform the following steps:

1. Log on to Windows Vista with a user account that is a member of the local administrators group.

2. From the Start menu, open the Control Panel in Classic View.

3. Open the Power Options item.

4. Click Create A Power Plan. On the Create A Power Plan page, select Power Saver, and enter the plan name as Power Saver II. Click Next.

5. In the Change Settings For The Plan: Power Saver II, configure the settings to never turn off the display or put the computer to sleep if the computer is plugged in, as shown in Figure 14-23. Click Create to create the plan.

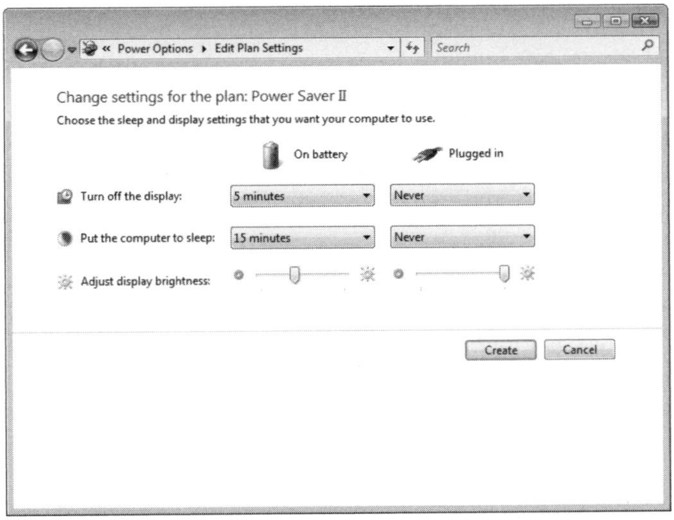

Figure 14-23   Changing settings for a custom power plan

6. Verify that the Power Saver II plan is now being used.

7. To restore your computer to its default power saver configuration, select the Balanced plan. Click Change Plan Settings, and then click Restore Default Settings For This Plan.

Lesson Summary

- Power plans control how hardware features work and are primarily used with mobile computers to vary the drain on battery charge.

- Power plans can also control when a computer shuts down or hibernates due to inactivity. Power plans can also be used to customize the behavior of power and hibernation buttons.

- The default power plans are Balanced, Power Saver, and High Performance.

- Away mode is a specific configuration that allows a media center extender to wake a media center computer.

- Custom power plans allow specialized power settings to be stored.

- Editing the advanced power settings allows power plans to be configured with greater detail. Users need to be able to elevate their privileges in order to edit the advanced power settings.

Lesson Review

You can use the following questions to test your knowledge of the information in Lesson 2, "Configure Power Options." The questions are also available on the companion CD if you prefer to review them in electronic form.

NOTE   Answers

Answers to these questions and explanations of why each answer choice is correct or incorrect are located in the "Answers" section at the end of the book.

---

1. A Windows Vista laptop computer has six power plans: the default three plans and three custom plans. The custom plans are named Custom 1, Custom 2, and Custom 3. The laptop is currently using plan Custom 2. Your user account is a member of the local administrators group. Which of these plans can you delete? (Choose all that apply.)

    A. Custom 1

    B. Custom 2

    C. Custom 3

    D. Balanced

    E. Power Saver

    F. High Performance

2. Your Windows Vista laptop computer is configured to use the Power Saver power plan, which means that it enters power saving mode if not used after a short time. You regularly leave your desk and do not want someone who might encounter your computer in power saving mode to be able to access your data. Which of the following should you do?

    A. Configure a screen saver password.

    B. Enable User Account Control.

    C. Disable User Account Control.

    D. Require a password to wake from sleep.

    E. Change to the High Performance power plan.

3. An executive at your company complains that her laptop shuts down unexpectedly when she is in meetings. The power configuration is shown in Figure 14-24. Which of the following changes should you make to resolve this problem?

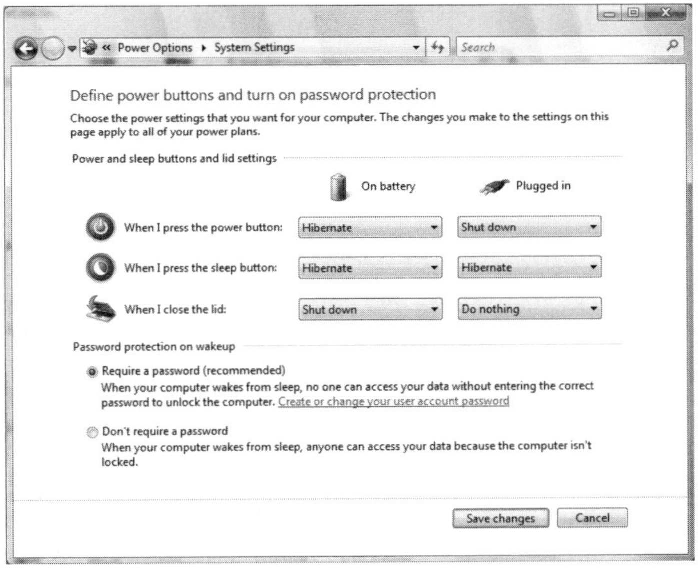

Figure 14-24   Power configuration

    A. Change the When I Close The Lid setting for when the laptop computer is on batteries.

    B. Change the When I Close The Lid setting for when the laptop computer is plugged in.

    C. Change the When I Press The Power Button setting for when the laptop computer is plugged in.

    D. Change the When I Press The Power Button setting for when the laptop computer is on batteries.

4. You are currently using the High Performance power plan. You want the computer to ask for a password when it wakes from sleep when plugged in but not when using the battery. How can you do this with a minimum of effort?

    A. Create a custom power plan.

    B. Edit the Advanced Power Settings of the High Performance plan.

      C. Change to the Balanced power plan.

      D. Change to the Power Saver power plan.

5. You want to have a particular set of power settings that are not available in the current power plans. You do not want your settings lost if the Restore Plan Defaults button is used. You want individualized display brightness and computer sleep settings. Which of the following should you do?

      A. Change advanced power settings.

      B. Create a power plan.

      C. Adjust the display brightness.

      D. Change when the computer sleeps.

Chapter Review

To further practice and reinforce the skills you learned in this chapter, you can perform the following tasks:

- Review the chapter summary.
- Review the list of key terms introduced in this chapter.
- Complete the case scenarios. These scenarios set up real-world situations involving the topics of this chapter and ask you to create a solution.
- Complete the suggested practices.
- Take a practice test.

Chapter Summary

- There are three options for entering text through the Input Panel—the on-screen keyboard, the character pad, and the writing pad. The on-screen keyboard gives the best precision but the slowest speed, the writing pad gives the fastest experience, and the character pad strikes a balance between the two.
- By default, the handwriting recognition system improves recognition based on corrections made. It is also possible to improve recognition by running the personalize handwriting recognition routines. You can either provide a significant sample of handwriting for Windows Vista to analyze or target specific recognition errors.
- Power plans are collections of hardware and system settings that determine how a computer uses power. The default plans, from lowest power usage to highest, are Power Saver, Balanced, and High Performance. It is possible to create a custom plan and to configure more detailed power plan settings.

Key Terms

Do you know what these key terms mean? You can check your answers by looking up the terms in the glossary at the end of the book.

- cold boot
- hibernation
- pen flick
- power plan
- slate
- sleep
- tap

Case Scenarios

In the following case scenarios, you will apply what you have learned about configuring applications included with Windows Vista. You can find answers to these questions in the "Answers" section at the end of this book.

Case Scenario 1: Tablet PCs at Tailspin Toys

All the executives at Tailspin Toys have Tablet PC computers running Windows Vista Ultimate. They use the Tablet PC computers for meetings and conferences. All the Tablet PC computers are convertible, which gives the executives the greatest amount of flexibility. Because the executives are now experienced users, you have been asked to provide some tips on how they might use their Tablet PCs more efficiently.

1. Several of the executives are left-handed. How can you optimize their experience?
2. Several executives want to speed up the editing of their documents while in slate mode. Specifically, they want to be able to quickly copy and paste data. What steps can you take to help them?
3. The company's CEO has just been given a brand new Windows Vista Tablet PC. She is concerned that she will have to teach the computer how to read her handwriting again. How can you ensure that the new computer will recognize her handwriting as well as the old one does?

Case Scenario 2: Individualized Power Plans

Five people in the research and development division of Wingtip Toys use Windows Vista laptop computers. Each of them has different requirements with regard to performance and battery life. Kim almost always has her laptop plugged into an AC outlet, Ian spends a fair amount of time in meetings with his computer, and Orin likes to go to the park as often as he can and work there.

1. Ian uses his laptop to read the morning news and then drives to work at Wingtip Toys. He takes 45 minutes to commute and wants to quickly restart using the laptop when he arrives at work with a minimal impact on the battery charge. Which of the following power down modes should he use?
2. Which of the default power plans would best suit Kim given what you know about her computer usage habits?
3. Orin has some special requirements. Given his usage habits, which of the default power plans would you use as the basis for creating a custom power plan for his computer?

Suggested Practices

To help you successfully master the exam objectives presented in this chapter, complete the following tasks.

Configure Tablet PC Software

- **Practice 1: Modify Security Settings**   Vary the security options on the on-screen keyboard, and determine which level provides keyboard feedback when entering a password.
- **Practice 2: Calibrate the Pen**   Perform pen calibration.
- **Practice 3: Perform Handwriting Recognition**   Teach Windows Vista to understand your handwriting better by running the Teach The Recognizer Your Handwriting Style routine in Handwriting Personalization.

Configure Power Options

- **Practice 1: Basic Power Plans**   Set your computer to each of the available default plans.
- **Practice 2: Shut the Lid**   Configure the computer to enter hibernation when the lid is shut.
- **Practice 3: Create a Custom Plan**   Create a custom plan, and then edit the advanced power settings. Configure a computer running using your custom plans.

Take a Practice Test

The practice tests on this book's companion CD offer many options. For example, you can test yourself on just one exam objective, or you can test yourself on all the 70-620 certification exam content. You can set up the test so that it closely simulates the experience of taking a certification exam, or you can set it up in study mode so that you can look at the correct answers and explanations after you answer each question.

MORE INFO   Practice tests

For details about all the practice test options available, see the "How to Use the Practice Tests" section in this book's Introduction.

Answers

Chapter 1: Lesson Review Answers

Lesson 1

1. **Correct Answers: B and C**
   A. **Incorrect:** The Windows Vista Upgrade Advisor does not support Windows 2000 Professional.
   B. **Correct:** The Windows Vista Upgrade Advisor runs on all 32-bit versions of Windows XP and Vista.
   C. **Correct:** The Windows Vista Upgrade Advisor runs on all 32-bit versions of Windows XP and Vista.
   D. **Incorrect:** The Windows Vista Upgrade Advisor does not run on Windows Me.

2. **Correct Answer: D**
   A. **Incorrect:** A 10-megabit network card does not fall below Windows Vista's minimum recommended requirements. The requirements for Windows Vista do not specify a minimum speed for a network adapter.
   B. **Incorrect:** A 100-megabit network card does not fall below Windows Vista's minimum recommended requirements. The requirements for Windows Vista do not specify a minimum speed for a network adapter.
   C. **Incorrect:** A 900 MHz Pentium III Processor exceeds Windows Vista's minimum recommended requirements. An 800 MHz processor or better is the minimum required to run Windows Vista.
   D. **Correct:** Windows Vista has a minimum recommended RAM requirement of 512 MB.

3. **Correct Answers: B and D**
   A. **Incorrect:** Windows Vista has a minimum requirement of an 800 MHz processor. A 3.0 GHz Pentium IV exceeds this.
   B. **Correct:** Windows Vista has a minimum requirement of an 800 MHz processor. This processor falls below that speed.
   C. **Incorrect:** Windows Vista has a minimum requirement of an 800 MHz processor. This processor exceeds that speed.
   D. **Correct:** Windows Vista has a minimum requirement of an 800 MHz processor. This processor falls below that speed.

Lesson 2

1.   **Correct Answer: B**

   A.   **Incorrect:** Using recommended settings causes Windows Vista to attempt to download updates from the Windows Update website.

   B.   **Correct:** Clicking Ask Me Later allows you to configure Windows Vista to use a local update server rather than having the computer automatically contact the Microsoft Update servers on the Internet.

   C.   **Incorrect:** Configuring the computer's location does not influence whether updates are downloaded from Windows Update or WSUS.

   D.   **Incorrect:** Configuring the computer's location does not influence whether updates are downloaded from Windows Update or WSUS.

2.   **Correct Answer: C**

   A.   **Incorrect:** To perform an install, you need to boot off the DVD-ROM drive, not the RAID array.

   B.   **Incorrect:** If you have reached this portion of the install, the computer is already configured to boot off the DVD-ROM drive.

   C.   **Correct:** If no disk drive is present when you reach the portion of the install where you need to select a disk and partition to install Windows Vista on, you need to load a disk driver.

   D.   **Incorrect:** Rolling back driver software is possible only once Windows Vista has been installed, and multiple drivers have been installed.

3.   **Correct Answer: A**

   A.   **Correct:** Purchasing a second hard disk drive is the only option that allows you to dual boot Windows XP and Windows Vista.

   B.   **Incorrect:** Disk partitioning software does not work in this instance because only 3 GB are free, which is not enough to install Windows Vista.

   C.   **Incorrect:** Upgrading does not allow dual booting to occur.

   D.   **Incorrect:** Deleting the partition with Windows Vista does not allow you to configure dual booting.

Lesson 3

1.   **Correct Answers: A and B**

   A.   **Correct:** Windows Update can be used to detect updated drivers as they become available.

   B.   **Correct:** It is possible to detect and update drivers from Device Manager by right-clicking a specific device and selecting Update Driver.

    C. **Incorrect:** It is not possible to detect updated drivers using Network and Sharing Center.

    D. **Incorrect:** It is not possible to detect updated drivers using Add Hardware. Add Hardware is used only to detect non–Plug and Play Hardware. Non–Plug and Play hardware is hardware that is not automatically detected by Windows Vista.

2. **Correct Answer: C**

    A. **Incorrect:** In this case, there is no need to uninstall the driver because you can roll back to a previous version that worked.

    B. **Incorrect:** If the driver has just been released on the vendor's website, it is unlikely that the Windows Update site has a newer version.

    C. **Correct:** Because previous versions of the driver worked, the best course of action is to roll back the driver.

    D. **Incorrect:** Rolling back using System Restore might undo other changes that you have implemented since the last restore point was taken. System Restore is covered in more detail in Chapter 2, "Windows Vista Upgrades and Migrations."

3. **Correct Answer: A**

    A. **Correct:** The default behavior for Windows Vista is to automatically check Windows Update for new drivers when you attach a new hardware device. You can ensure that Windows Vista will ask you prior to making this connection by adjusting the Windows Update Driver Settings.

    B. **Incorrect:** User Account Control relates to administrative privileges. It is covered in more detail in Chapter 4, "Configuring and Troubleshooting Internet Access."

    C. **Incorrect:** You cannot configure the Windows Update Driver Settings using Device Manager. You must configure these settings using System Properties.

    D. **Incorrect:** You cannot configure the Windows Update Driver Settings using Startup and Recovery.

Chapter 1: Case Scenario Answers

Case Scenario 1: Recommending Windows Vista Editions

1. Windows Vista Home Basic. If home users do not require multimedia functionality, Aero, or Tablet PC functionality, Windows Vista Home Basic will meet their needs well.

2. Windows Vista Home Premium. If home users need Tablet PC functionality but do not need to connect to an Active Directory domain, the Home Premium SKU is most appropriate.

3. Windows Vista Ultimate is the only version of Windows Vista that provides Media Center functionality with the ability to join with Active Directory domain environments.

Case Scenario 2: Diagnosing and Troubleshooting Device Driver Problems

1. Try to update the driver, either through Windows Update or by checking the vendor's website.
2. Roll back the driver to a previous version.
3. Clear the Automatically Restart check box in the Startup And Recovery dialog box. This leaves the STOP error on the screen until the computer is manually rebooted.

Chapter 2: Lesson Review Answers

Lesson 1

1. **Correct Answer: D**
   A. **Incorrect:** Windows Easy Transfer can transfer only files from a computer running Windows 2000 Professional to Windows Vista. Only the User State Migration Tool is able to migrate user settings and data from a computer running Windows 2000 Professional to Windows Vista.
   B. **Incorrect:** The File Settings and Transfer Wizard is a utility that works with Windows XP. You cannot use it to migrate user settings and data from a computer running Windows 2000 Professional to Windows Vista.
   C. **Incorrect:** You use Windows Anytime Upgrade to upgrade one edition of Windows Vista to another. You cannot use it to migrate user settings and data from a computer running Windows 2000 Professional to Windows Vista.
   D. **Correct:** Only the User State Migration Tool is able to migrate both user settings and data from a computer running Windows 2000 Professional to Windows Vista.

2. **Correct Answer: A**
   A. **Correct:** Only the User State Migration Tool can take user data and settings from a computer running Windows Vista and transfer them to a computer running Windows XP.
   B. **Incorrect:** You can use Windows Easy Transfer to transfer data only to computers running Windows Vista. You cannot use it to transfer data to computers running Windows XP.
   C. **Incorrect:** You use Windows Anytime Upgrade to upgrade between editions of Windows Vista. It is not used to transfer data between computers running different operating systems.
   D. **Incorrect:** The File Settings and Transfer Wizard is the Windows XP equivalent of Windows Easy Transfer. The File Settings and Transfer Wizard does not run on Windows Vista and so cannot be used to migrate data to Windows XP.

3. **Correct Answers: A and C**

  A. **Correct:** Checking with the vendors is the best course of action because they will have a definite answer to the question "Does your application work with Windows Vista?"

  B. **Incorrect:** The User State Migration Tool is used to transfer files and settings from one computer to another. It cannot be used to determine whether an application will run under Windows Vista.

  C. **Correct:** The Windows Vista Upgrade Advisor can identify applications that are known to have problems running under Windows Vista.

  D. **Incorrect:** Windows Anytime Upgrade cannot be used to detect possible application compatibility issues.

4. **Correct Answer: B**

  A. **Incorrect:** If the computer has the Windows Vista Capable logo attached, it has enough RAM to run Windows Vista.

  B. **Correct:** Given the customer's use of digital videos, it is likely that the upgrade has failed because of a lack of free space on the volume. There needs to be at least 11 GB free to upgrade Windows XP to Windows Vista.

  C. **Incorrect:** A laptop that has the Windows Vista Capable logo attached will have a graphics adapter that has a WDDM driver.

  D. **Incorrect:** Although you cannot use Windows Anytime Upgrade without activating your copy of Windows Vista, it is possible to upgrade Windows XP to Windows Vista without activating the software.

Lesson 2

1. **Correct Answers: A and D**

  A. **Correct:** Windows Vista Home Basic can be upgraded only to Home Premium and Ultimate editions.

  B. **Incorrect:** Windows Vista Home Basic cannot be upgraded to the Business edition. Windows Vista Home Basic can be upgraded only to Home Premium and Ultimate editions.

  C. **Incorrect:** Windows Vista Home Basic cannot be upgraded to the Enterprise edition. Windows Vista Home Basic can be upgraded only to Home Premium and Ultimate editions.

  D. **Correct:** Windows Vista Home Basic can be upgraded to the Ultimate edition.

2. **Correct Answer: B**

  A. **Incorrect:** The new edition of Windows Vista that you want to upgrade to is purchased during the Windows Anytime Upgrade process, not prior to it.

    B. **Correct:** It is possible to run Windows Anytime Upgrade only if your current edition of Windows Vista has been activated.

    C. **Incorrect:** It is not necessary to run the Windows Vista Upgrade Advisor prior to running Windows Anytime Upgrade. Any program that works on one edition of Windows Vista will work on another edition of Windows Vista, as long as both editions are of the same processor architecture.

    D. **Incorrect:** It is not necessary to install MSXML version 6 or .NET Framework version 2.0 or higher to run Windows Anytime Upgrade.

3. **Correct Answer: B**

    A. **Incorrect:** Windows Vista Business cannot be upgraded to Windows Vista Home Premium. Only Windows Vista Ultimate has Tablet PC and Media Center functionality.

    B. **Correct:** Only Windows Vista Ultimate has Tablet PC and Media Center functionality.

    C. **Incorrect:** Only Windows Vista Ultimate, not Enterprise, has Tablet PC and Media Center functionality.

    D. **Incorrect:** Windows Vista Business cannot be upgraded to Windows Vista Home Basic.

Lesson 3

1. **Correct Answer: A**

    A. **Correct:** System restore points are automatically created whenever a new application or device driver software is installed. This means that you can return the computer to the state it was in prior to installing the application by using the restore point taken at that point in time.

    B. **Incorrect:** A startup repair will not work in this circumstance because the startup files are not missing or corrupted.

    C. **Incorrect:** Running the command prompt will not solve this problem. It is not possible to return a computer to the point at which it was prior to the installation of an application using the command prompt. Although it is possible to delete application files, things such as registry settings are impossible to manually modify from the command prompt.

    D. **Incorrect:** Although a Windows Complete PC Restore might work, nothing was mentioned in the question about a full backup of the entire computer being taken. A full backup is required prior to performing this action, whereas a restore point is automatically created prior to the installation of any application or device driver software.

2. **Correct Answer: A**

   A. **Correct:** Startup Repair should be your first port of call with any startup problem encountered by a computer running Windows Vista.

   B. **Incorrect:** You should try Startup Repair first. System Restore is generally used to roll back configurations rather than to repair them.

   C. **Incorrect:** You should try Startup Repair first. Windows Complete PC Restore is used when a computer's operating system has been lost, and you want to rebuild it.

   D. **Incorrect:** You should try Startup Repair first because a memory problem would not manifest itself in this way. If the memory problem were serious, the computer would not be able to get past the POST test. If there were a minor error in the RAM, it would likely not become apparent until after the computer had booted.

3. **Correct Answer: D**

   A. **Incorrect:** The problem is not with compatibility mode but with the program's way of using administrative rights conflicting with Windows Vista's User Account Control.

   B. **Incorrect:** No problems were reported with the application's display, so this answer is incorrect.

   C. **Incorrect:** No problems were reported with the application's display, so this answer is incorrect.

   D. **Correct:** Older programs, especially those written for Windows 95, 98, and Me, sometimes expect that every user who runs them is an administrator. This can cause problems with the User Account Control system in Windows Vista. One solution is to configure the application to run as an administrator. You still need to be an administrator to execute it, but this technique bypasses some of the problems older programs have with User Account Control.

Chapter 2: Case Scenario Answers

Case Scenario 1: Upgrading and Migrating

1. Migration. Windows 2000 cannot be upgraded to Windows Vista. SKU choice: Windows Vista Home Premium. Computer is capable of running Aero. DVD playback hints that Media Center functionality. Home Basic does not provide Aero or Media Center.

2. Upgrade. Windows Vista Business would best suit this customer. The customer does not need Enterprise features such as BitLocker and Virtual PC. Business edition supports direct upgrade from Windows XP Tablet PC. The computer has enough free space to allow upgrade.

3. Upgrade. Windows Vista Home Basic. The couple does not appear to need Aero, nor do they need features such as Media Center or BitLocker.

Case Scenario 2: Troubleshooting

1. You should use the Windows Memory Diagnostic to check that the computer's physical memory has no errors. Physical memory errors often manifest as unusual freezes that require a reboot to undo.
2. You should use Startup Repair. Startup Repair fixes the most common problems that stop a Windows Vista computer from booting properly.
3. You can use the command prompt option to copy the corrupted files from the Windows Vista installation media.

Chapter 3: Lesson Review Answers

Lesson 1

1. **Correct Answer: C**
   A. **Incorrect:** If the problem was refresh rate, the complaint would be about flickering rather than a blurry or blocky display.
   B. **Incorrect:** If the problem was the number of colors, the complaint would be color-related rather than a blurry or blocky display.
   C. **Correct:** Laptop computers use LCD screens, which should always be set to their native resolution. If an LCD screen is set to a resolution other than its native one, the display appears blurry and blocky.
   D. **Incorrect:** Monitors are not incompatible with operating systems. Windows Vista displays on any monitor that supports the Video Graphics Adapter (VGA) standard.

2. **Correct Answers: C and D**
   A. **Incorrect:** The Device Manager is helpful only if a device is incorrectly configured. It does not help you determine which device or software is causing system instability.
   B. **Incorrect:** The Add New Hardware Wizard is used to add legacy hardware to a computer running Windows Vista. It cannot help you diagnose which component is causing system instability.
   C. **Correct:** The Problem Reports And Solutions log might give you an idea of what device failed, although the Reliability Monitor graph might help you more quickly zero in on when the problems began to arise.

      D. **Correct:** The Reliability Monitor graph is helpful because it will show a sharp dip when the offending component or software was installed.

3. **Correct Answer: C**

      A. **Incorrect:** Adjusting the number of colors displayed will not stop a monitor from flickering. The amount a monitor flickers is determined by its refresh rate.

      B. **Incorrect:** Although some people get headaches from squinting at monitors that are configured to use too high a resolution, monitor flickering is caused by the refresh rate setting.

      C. **Correct:** Adjusting the monitor's refresh rate will reduce the amount of screen flicker. Some people can get headaches from using monitors that are set to use lower refresh rates.

      D. **Incorrect:** The color management settings ensure that the image on the screen matches the image output to other devices, such as printers. Altering the color management settings will not change how much a monitor flickers.

4. **Correct Answer: B**

      A. **Incorrect:** Changing the number of colors from 32-bit to 16-bit will not mean that the colors displayed on the screen will match those output by the printer. The only way to ensure a match is by using the Color Management utility.

      B. **Correct:** The Color Management utility is designed to ensure that all devices connected to a Windows Vista computer, such as printers and monitors, output the same set of colors. Because the number of colors a printer outputs is usually less than what is possible for a monitor to output, using Color Management means reducing the number of colors displayed on the screen. The benefit is that what is output on the screen will match what is output on the printer.

      C. **Incorrect:** Changing the refresh rate on the monitor reduces or increases the amount of flicker that is perceptible to the eye. It will not ensure that the color displayed on the screen matches the color output on the printer.

      D. **Incorrect:** Changing the resolution changes the amount of information displayed on the screen. It will not ensure that the color displayed on the screen matches the color output on the printer.

5. **Correct Answer: D**

      A. **Incorrect:** Unless the device is in Device Manager, it is not possible to install the drivers manually.

      B. **Incorrect:** Unless the device is already in Device Manager, it is not possible to manually configure the hardware resources the device uses.

      C. **Incorrect:** Scan For Hardware Changes will detect plug and play devices. This hardware component is a non-plug and play, also known as legacy, device.

D. **Correct:** Because this component is non-plug and play, it needs to be installed by using the Add Legacy Hardware command in the Device Manager.

6. **Correct Answer: D**

A. **Incorrect:** Because the device is critical, you should try altering the resource settings before disabling the device.

B. **Incorrect:** Because the device is critical, you should try altering the resource settings before uninstalling the driver. Uninstalling the driver is a good option to pursue when you have an alternative driver, but you are unable to update the one that is currently being used.

C. **Incorrect:** Because the device is critical, you should try altering the resource settings before uninstalling the device.

D. **Correct:** You should try to alter the resources that the device uses to see if that resolves the conflict.

Lesson 2

1. **Correct Answer: D**

A. **Incorrect:** Because Aero has functioned in the past on this computer, a WDDM graphics driver is already installed.

B. **Incorrect:** When a user changes a theme, it applies only to that user's account. The only way that your account's theme can be forcibly changed is if another user has disabled Aero by changing the number of colors displayed. It is possible for another user to do this without administrative permissions.

C. **Incorrect:** Changing the monitor refresh rate will not force Aero to stop working.

D. **Correct:** The only way that your account's theme can be forcibly changed is if another user has disabled Aero by changing the number of colors displayed. It is possible for another user to do this without administrative permissions. Returning the number of colors displayed back to 32-bit will restore Aero.

2. **Correct Answer: A**

A. **Correct:** The device with the lowest score determines the Windows Experience Index base score. In this example, it is the processor. Replacing the processor would increase the index score.

B. **Incorrect:** The device with the lowest score determines the Windows Experience Index base score. Replacing the RAM would not increase the score.

C. **Incorrect:** The device with the lowest score determines the Windows Experience Index base score. Replacing the graphics adapter would not increase the score.

D. **Incorrect:** The device with the lowest score determines the Windows Experience Index base score. Replacing the hard disk drive would not increase the score.

3. **Correct Answers: A, B, and D**

   A. **Correct:** The computer name is not collected during a WGA check.

   B. **Correct:** Your name is not collected during a WGA check.

   C. **Incorrect:** BIOS revision date information is sent to Microsoft during a WGA check.

   D. **Incorrect:** As standard procedure, your Internet Protocol (IP) address is temporarily logged when your computer connects to an MGA website or server. These logs are routinely deleted.

4. **Correct Answers: B and C**

   A. **Incorrect:** To run Windows Aero, a graphics adapter must have a minimum of 64 MB of total graphics memory. This adapter has only 32 MB.

   B. **Correct:** To run Windows Aero, a graphics adapter must have a minimum of 64 MB of total graphics memory. This adapter has 128 MB.

   C. **Correct:** To run Windows Aero, a graphics adapter must have a minimum of 64 MB of total graphics memory. This adapter has 256 MB.

   D. **Incorrect:** To run Windows Aero, a graphics adapter must have a minimum of 64 MB of total graphics memory. This adapter has only 48 MB.

5. **Correct Answer: C**

   A. **Incorrect:** See explanation for correct answer.

   B. **Incorrect:** See explanation for correct answer.

   C. **Correct:** Windows Vista must be activated within 30 days of installation.

   D. **Incorrect:** See explanation for correct answer.

Chapter 3: Case Scenario Answers

Case Scenario 1: Post-Installation Troubleshooting

1. Use the Add New Hardware Wizard to detect the legacy device.
2. Edit the device's resources in Device Manager.
3. Disable COM 1.

Case Scenario 2: Troubleshooting Aero and Display Settings

1. By setting the color settings to 16-bit.
2. That the monitor will be able to display only lower resolutions.
3. Yes, resolution settings are global across profiles.

Chapter 4: Lesson Review Answers

Lesson 1

1. **Correct Answer: C**

   A. **Incorrect:** You are either logged on with an administrator account or have supplied administrator credentials; otherwise, you could not have accessed this dialog box. You do not need to switch accounts.

   B. **Incorrect:** Using the New User dialog box creates a standard account by default.

   C. **Correct:** If you clear the User Must Change Password At Next Logon check box, this activates the User Cannot Change Password and the Password Never Expires check boxes, and you can then select them.

   D. **Incorrect:** M.Hanson is a valid user name. Changing this to Mark_Hanson has no effect on the check boxes.

2. **Correct Answer: D**

   A. **Incorrect:** This solves the problem for the particular bulletin board site, but you would need to add other bulletin board and educational sites to the list. This involves additional administrative effort.

   B. **Incorrect:** Content Advisor ratings apply to all users, including the administrator account that you created during installation.

   C. **Incorrect:** You know that this particular site contains no offensive content. This setting enables you to access bulletin board and discussion sites where strong language is permitted. In this instance, this is not the case.

   D. **Correct:** Some bulletin board and technical information sites have no ratings specified. Changing the configuration of Content Advisor as described enables access to such sites.

3. **Correct Answer: A**

   A. **Correct:** No direct method exists for blocking card games specifically. The EVERYONE classification is deemed suitable for a child of seven, but you need to block any card games that meet this classification. You do this in the Game Overrides dialog box.

   B. **Incorrect:** You block specified games in the Game Overrides dialog box, not the Game Restrictions dialog box.

   C. **Incorrect:** You specify a rating classification in the Game Restrictions dialog box, not the Game Overrides dialog box.

   D. **Incorrect:** The EVERYONE 10+ classification is suitable for children aged 10 years and older. It does not block card games.

4. **Correct Answer: B**

    A. **Incorrect:** This procedure blocks every program except the ones you want to block.

    B. **Correct:** This selects all programs in the list so that the child can run them. Clearing the check boxes for specific programs blocks them.

    C. **Incorrect:** This works, but it is much easier to clear three specific programs than to select every program except these three.

    D. **Incorrect:** The Browse button is used to add programs to the list and is typically used when you have installed new applications on the computer. Right-clicking an executable file does not enable you to block it.

5. **Correct Answers: A and E**

    A. **Correct:** This is the recommended procedure for accessing the User Controls dialog box.

    B. **Incorrect:** You use the supervisor password when reconfiguring Content Advisor or allowing Internet access to sites that Content Advisor blocks. It is not required to configure Parental Controls.

    C. **Incorrect:** Right-clicking an account in the Users container enables you to delete it, rename it, change group membership, reset the password, or change password properties. It does not permit you to set Parental Controls.

    D. **Incorrect:** This is an alternative procedure for accessing a user account in the Users container. It does not permit you to set Parental Controls.

    E. **Correct:** You can access the User Controls dialog box by using this procedure. The procedure requires more steps than are listed in answer A, but the question asks whether the procedure works, not whether it is the most efficient.

6. **Correct Answer: D**

    A. **Incorrect:** You might be able to achieve the appropriate level of safety by choosing Custom and blocking every category of unacceptable content. However, not all content in these areas can be automatically blocked. You should instead specify the High restriction level that permits access only to websites approved for children.

    B. **Incorrect:** A restriction level of None does not automatically block any content.

    C. **Incorrect:** A Medium restriction level blocks unratable content, mature content, pornography, drugs, hate speech, and weapons. However, not all content in these areas can be automatically blocked. This rating lets older children explore the web in relative safety but is not considered suitable for a six-year-old.

    D. **Correct:** A High restriction level permits access only to websites approved for children.

Lesson 2

1. **Correct Answer: B**

   A. **Incorrect:** You do not need a third-party aggregator. IE7+ provides built-in aggregator functions.

   B. **Correct:** IE7+ provides built-in aggregator functions that do what you require.

   C. **Incorrect:** A search aggregator returns an up-to-date set of search results. This is not what you require.

   D. **Incorrect:** IE7+ does not implement Clouds.

2. **Correct Answer: C**

   A. **Incorrect:** If you click the View Full Width button, you cannot access the controls for adjusting the margin. In any case, dragging provides a quick but inaccurate method of adjusting the margins. If you want to specify accurate margin sizes, you need to use the Page Setup dialog box.

   B. **Incorrect:** You cannot type margin sizes into the Print Preview dialog box. You need first to click the Page Setup button in Print Preview. Alternatively, you can access Page Setup directly from IE7+. Clicking the View Full Page button does not affect this.

   C. **Correct:** You can specify accurate margin sizes in the Page Setup dialog box.

   D. **Incorrect:** Dragging the margin symbols provides a quick method of adjusting margins. However, if you want to specify accurate margin sizes, you need to use the Page Setup dialog box.

3. **Correct Answer: A**

   A. **Correct:** This prints the footer as specified.

   B. **Incorrect:** This prints the footer right-justified rather than center-justified.

   C. **Incorrect:** This prints the total number of pages first and the actual page number at the end.

   D. **Incorrect:** This prints the total number of pages first and the actual page number at the end. Also, it prints the footer right-justified rather than center-justified.

4. **Correct Answer: D**

   A. **Incorrect:** Change Search Defaults lets you set the default search provider or delete a search provider. You cannot use it to add a search provider.

   B. **Incorrect:** This is an alternative method of accessing the Change Search Defaults dialog box. This dialog box lets you set the default search provider or delete a search provider. You cannot use it to add a search provider.

C. **Incorrect:** Add To Favorites adds the current webpage (in this case, Add Search Providers to Internet Explorer 7) to your favorites list. It does not let you add a search provider.

D. **Correct:** This procedure adds the search provider to your search providers list.

Chapter 4: Case Scenario Answers

Case Scenario 1: Advising Users on How to Configure Parental Controls

1. For the 6-year-old, the customer should block all games that have no rating and specify the EVERYONE rating. For the 11-year-old, he should block all games that have no rating and specify the EVERYONE 10+ rating. For the 15-year-old, he should specify the TEEN rating. He could probably allow his oldest child to play games that have no rating, but you should advise him to enable activity reporting and periodically check what his children are accessing. For all three children, he should block Blood and Gore, Fantasy Violence, Violence, and Intense Violence. He probably does not need to block Mild Violence, but this is a judgment call.

2. You should advise the customer to enable Content Advisor and block all sites that do not have a rating. Educational and bulletin board sites are often unrated. She can then use the supervisor password that she creates if she wants to allow her son to access an unrated site.

3. You need to remind the user that *Child* Can Only Use The Programs I Allow means just that. The child cannot use any programs that are not part of the operating system— including Microsoft Office programs such as Word—unless the parent specifically allows access to them. He should select the check box next to WINWORD.EXE and probably EXCEL.EXE, as well.

Case Scenario 2: Printing Webpages

1. She should access Print Preview. At the top of the Print Preview window, she should see a drop-down list (to the right of the Page View box). The list probably has As Laid Out On Screen selected. In this box, she should select All Frames Individually.

2. He should select Shrink To Fit rather than 100%. The Shrink To Fit setting adjusts the print size so that the webpage fits on the paper and adjusts the bottom margin so that single lines at the bottom of pages (orphans) are moved to the next page.

3. She should switch to single page view, select to view the full page, and then manually adjust her margins by dragging the margin symbols. When she is satisfied with the first page, she should then view all the other pages and make sure she is happy with them.

You should remind her that a margin change made on any page affects all pages, so if she makes any changes, she needs to check all the pages again.

4. Page &p of &P&b&w.

Chapter 5: Lesson Review Answers

Lesson 1

1. **Correct Answer: B**

   A. **Incorrect:** He cannot open an application until he closes the UAC dialog box by clicking either Cancel or Continue.

   B. **Correct:** By default, Secure Desktop is enabled. This means that the computer cannot perform any operation, including Print Screen, until you close the UAC dialog box.

   C. **Incorrect:** By default, UAC applies to all administrator accounts except the disabled built-in Administrator account.

   D. **Incorrect:** The account Ian created when he installed Windows Vista is an ordinary administrator account. It is not the built-in Administrator account.

2. **Correct Answer: A**

   A. **Correct:** This setting causes administrator accounts to run continuously with elevated privileges. Standard accounts cannot supply administrator permissions to run administrator tasks. This is legacy Windows XP mode, and UAC is disabled.

   B. **Incorrect:** This is the default setting. UAC is enabled.

   C. **Incorrect:** This setting permits an administrator to perform a task that requires elevated privileges to do it without being prompted. However, the administrator account runs as a standard user account except when performing an administrator task, and the user experience of the standard user is unaffected. UAC is not, therefore, disabled.

   D. **Incorrect:** This setting increases UAC security by requiring administrators to provide credentials every time they perform tasks that require elevated privileges.

3. **Correct Answer: D**

   A. **Incorrect:** This setting prevents unsigned application files from running. However, legacy files that attempt to write to protected parts of the registry or file system are not necessarily unsigned.

   B. **Incorrect:** This is the default setting. It allows unsigned files to run, although it gives a warning. It does not affect legacy files that attempt to write to protected parts of the registry or file system.

C. **Incorrect:** This is the default setting. It permits legacy files that attempt to write to protected parts of the registry or file system to run by cloning these locations to unprotected areas in the user's profile.

D. **Correct:** This setting prevents legacy files that attempt to write to protected parts of the registry or file system from running.

4. **Correct Answer: A**

A. **Correct:** The UAC options are at the end of the list of security policies.

B. **Incorrect:** Audit policy lets you determine who is doing what on the computer. It does not affect UAC.

C. **Incorrect:** User rights assignment controls who has permission to perform specified tasks on a computer. UAC does not directly affect user rights but rather under what circumstances these rights are used.

D. **Incorrect:** You can use software restriction policies to identify software and to control its ability to run on your local computer. UAC can control whether, for example, unsigned programs can run. However, software restriction policies have a more general application. You cannot configure UAC settings by accessing software restriction policies.

NOTE **Software restriction policies**

For more information about software restriction policies, access *http:// technet2.microsoft.com/WindowsServer/en/library/697cf804-36ae-4925-a56a- bc91b44dfcd91033.mspx?mfr=true.*

---

5. **Correct Answers: B, D, E, and F**

A. **Incorrect:** By default, UAC is not applied to the built-in Administrator account.

B. **Correct:** By default, applications that attempt to write to protected areas are permitted to write instead to virtual areas in the user profile.

C. **Incorrect:** By default, unsigned applications can run provided that the user provides appropriate credentials.

D. **Correct:** By default, UIAccess applications can run only if they are installed in secure locations.

E. **Correct:** This setting enables UAC. UAC is enabled by default.

F. **Correct:** By default, Windows Vista switches to Secure Desktop when prompting for elevation.

6. **Correct Answer: C**

A. **Incorrect:** You can run such programs by specifying that the program runs under the context of an administrator account in the Program Compatibility Wizard.

      B. **Incorrect:** This setting is enabled by default. It lets Windows Vista run legacy pro-grams that attempt to write to protected areas. It does not affect the account under which such programs run.

      C. **Correct:** Specifying this setting in the Program Compatibility Wizard allows a leg-acy program to run in the context of an administrator account.

      D. **Incorrect:** This setting prevents unsigned programs from running. It does not determine whether a program runs under the context of an administrator account.

Chapter 5: Case Scenario Answers

Case Scenario 1: Giving Advice On User Account Control

1. If an administrator is not warned when he or she initiates an administrator-level task, that administrator could accidentally install malware with full administrative privileges. UAC ensures that an administrator account runs as a standard user account except where an operation needs to run in the context of an account with elevated privileges. This conforms to the Principle of Least Privilege.

2. Don should set User Account Control: Behavior of the elevation prompt for administra-tors in Admin Approval mode to Elevate without prompting.

3. If Don changes this configuration, he can no longer log on as a standard user to carry out tasks such as editing Microsoft Word documents with the facility of performing admin-istrator tasks by supplying his administrator account credentials. However, if he wants to implement this change in user experience, he can set User Account Control: Behavior of the elevation prompt for standard users to Automatically deny elevation requests.

4. Don can disable UAC. This results in administrators being able to carry out administra-tor tasks without being prompted to continue while standard users cannot perform such tasks and are not prompted for administrator credentials. Don can do this by setting User Access Control: Run all administrators in Admin Approval mode to Disabled. How-ever, this reduces the overall security of Don's network.

Case Scenario 2: Running Legacy Programs

1. Kim should set User Access Control: Virtualize File And Registry Write Failures To Per-User Locations To Disabled.

2. Don should run the Program Compatibility Wizard and select the Run This Program As An Administrator check box.

3. You should not use the Program Compatibility Wizard to run legacy virus checking programs.

Chapter 6: Lesson Review Answers

Lesson 1

1. **Correct Answer: B**
   A. **Incorrect:** By default, Windows Defender real-time protection does not notify you about software that has not yet been classified for risks. You need to configure this setting under Real-Time Protection Options in the Options dialog box.
   B. **Correct:** You need to select this check box to configure real-time protection to notify you about software that has not yet been classified for risks.
   C. **Incorrect:** You do not need to perform a custom scan to obtain Windows Defender real-time protection. The check box you need to select is in the Options dialog box, not the Scan Options dialog box.
   D. **Incorrect:** You want to configure Windows Defender real-time protection to notify you about software that has not yet been classified for risks. Although it is possible to use Software Explorer to list all the executable files on a computer so you can manually list the unclassified ones, this is not what the question requires.

2. **Correct Answers: A, B, D, and F**
   A. **Correct:** The Startup Programs category contains programs that run automatically with or without the user's knowledge when Windows starts.
   B. **Correct:** The Currently Running Programs category contains programs that are currently running on the screen or in the background.
   C. **Incorrect:** Auto Start is an attribute of a program that Software Explorer lists. It indicates whether the program is registered to start automatically when Windows starts. Although this is similar to the Startup Programs category information, Auto Start is a program attribute, not a category.
   D. **Correct:** The Network-Connected Programs category contains programs or processes that can connect to the Internet or to a home or office network.
   E. **Incorrect:** When Software Explorer lists the attributes of a program, it indicates whether the program ships with the operating system. This is a program attribute, not a category.
   F. **Correct:** The Windows Sockets (Winsock) Service Providers category contains programs that perform low-level networking and communication services for Windows and programs that run on Windows.

3. **Correct Answer: A**
   A. **Correct:** You cannot select a default action for software items with a severe alert rating because Windows Defender automatically removes the item or alerts you to remove it.

    B. **Incorrect:** For high, medium, and low alert items, you can specify either Remove or Ignore, or you can leave the action at its default setting, which is Default Action (Definition-Based).

    C. **Incorrect:** This answer is incorrect for the reason given for answer B.

    D. **Incorrect:** This answer is incorrect for the reason given for answer B.

4. **Correct Answer: C**

    A. **Incorrect:** The Scan The Contents Of Archived Files And Folders For Potential Threats advanced setting locates spyware and other potentially unwanted software that can install itself in archives. It does not enable you to recover files that Windows Defender deletes.

    B. **Incorrect:** The Use Heuristics To Detect Potentially Harmful Or Unwanted Behavior By Software That Has Not Been Analyzed For Risks setting enables Windows Defender to detect and alert you about potentially harmful or unwanted software that is not yet listed in a definition file. It does not enable you to recover files that Windows Defender deletes.

    C. **Correct:** The Create A Restore Point Before Applying Actions To Detected Items setting enables you to restore system settings if you want to use software that you did not intend to remove.

    D. **Incorrect:** The Do Not Scan These Files Or Locations setting might prevent Windows Defender scanning for and deleting specified files or files in specified locations. It does not, however, enable you to recover files that Windows Defender does delete.

Lesson 2

1. **Correct Answer: C**

    A. **Incorrect:** The Internet zone contains all the sites that are not included in the other zones. Protected mode is necessary to protect users from malicious software that some Internet sites attempt to install.

    B. **Incorrect:** Malware is sometimes distributed internally by malicious insiders. Protected mode is enabled for the Local Intranet zone, and you should retain this setting, particularly on large intranets.

    C. **Correct:** Trusted Sites are sites that you know are reputable and carefully controlled and from which you frequently download files. Protected mode is disabled for the Trusted Sites security zone, although you can enable it if you want to.

    D. **Incorrect:** Restricted Sites are not trusted and the highest predefined level of security settings is applied. This includes enabling protected mode.

2. **Correct Answer: B**

    A. **Incorrect:** The Information bar does not appear if a pop-up is blocked when the pop-up blocker filter level is set to High.

    B. **Correct:** Pressing Ctrl+Alt when clicking a link overrides the High pop-up filter setting.

    C. **Incorrect:** Adding the site to the Allowed Sites list enables pop-ups to appear whenever the site is accessed. This is not what the user wants.

    D. **Incorrect:** A Medium pop-up blocker filter level blocks most, but not all, pop-ups. This is not what the user wants.

3. **Correct Answer: A**

    A. **Correct:** This setting does not display the red warning when a user tries to access a known phishing site. Instead, an icon appears at the foot of the browser window and the user can, optionally, obtain information about the status of the site.

    B. **Incorrect:** This setting displays the red warning when a user tries to access a known phishing site. The user can still choose to access the site.

    C. **Incorrect:** This setting disables the phishing filter, and no indication is given if the user tries to access a known or suspected phishing website. The user can still click Tools, select Phishing Filter, and click Check This Website.

    D. **Incorrect:** This is not a phishing filter setting but a feature that allows a user to check an individual website.

4. **Correct Answer: D**

    A. **Incorrect:** The site is almost certainly in the Internet zone at present. Sites cannot be added to the Internet zone in any case.

    B. **Incorrect:** This would result in the highest possible security settings being applied to every site in the Internet zone, which would severely limit the user's browsing options. A High security level disables all downloads.

    C. **Incorrect:** Adding the site to the Trusted Sites zone would reduce the level of security settings that are applied to that site. This is not what is required.

    D. **Correct:** The user can still visit the site and obtain information. He cannot, however, download anything from that site because the High security level applies to sites in the Restricted Sites zone. Note that not even fonts can be downloaded. This is an increase in security from Internet Explorer 6, which permitted no downloads from the Restricted Sites zone apart from fonts, which were at a security setting of Prompt.

Chapter 6: Case Scenario Answers

Case Scenario 1: Giving Advice on a Windows Defender Setting

1. By default, Windows Defender creates a restore point before applying actions to detected items. If the user restores his system to that restore point (or you do it for him), the deleted application should be reinstated. However, if Windows Defender has identified the application as a high alert item, the user should think carefully about the possible risks before he restores and uses it.

2. She should configure Windows Defender to quarantine high alert items. A quarantined application cannot run or do any damage, but she can inspect quarantined items and decide whether to delete or reinstate them.

3. By default, the user is a member of the SpyNet community. She can submit the item to SpyNet for analysis. She can also visit the SpyNet website to see if any other members of the SpyNet community have discovered the item and what action they took.

Case Scenario 2: Advising Customers About IE7+ Security Settings

1. The customer has almost certainly been targeted for an identity theft scam. The e-mail that purported to be from his bank was most probably from a scammer, especially if it was addressed to "Dear <bank> Customer." The link is almost certainly to a phishing site that simulates his bank's site. The phishing filter in IE7+ is doing its job. The customer should *not* access the site. If he is still concerned about his account, he should contact his bank directly.

2. The customer should access Internet Options and select the Security tab. She should then click Set All Zones To Default Level. She should then select each security zone in turn, select Custom, and click Reset. Finally, she should close and reopen her browser. IE7+ defaults provide good protection without seriously compromising the user experience. If the problem persists, the customer should also check the sites on her Trusted Sites and Local Intranet zones and ensure that only sites that she completely trusts are in these zones.

3. The customer should configure her pop-up filter to allow pop-ups specifically from her work OWA site.

4. Add-ons that run without requiring permission are generally either digitally signed by a trusted organization or are downloaded with the user's permission from a source that the user trusts—for example, the Microsoft Corporation. They are necessary for running some applications. If, however, the user sees any source that he does not recognize, he should inform you so you can investigate further.

Chapter 7: Lesson Review Answers

Lesson 1

1. **Correct Answer: C**

    A. **Incorrect:** The ping command is used to test connectivity. It does not display the IP configuration of a computer's interfaces.

    B. **Incorrect:** The tracert command is used to test connectivity to a device on a remote network and return information about the intermediate hops. It does not display the IP configuration of a computer's interfaces.

    C. **Correct:** The ipconfig command displays the IP configuration of a computer's interfaces.

    D. **Incorrect:** You can enter cmd in the Run box to access the Command Prompt console. It is not a command-line command, and it does not display the IP configuration of a computer's interfaces.

2. **Correct Answers: B, C, and D**

    A. **Incorrect:** This accesses the Local Area Network (LAN Settings) dialog box. You can select automatic configuration, specify an automatic configuration script, or specify a proxy server. The dialog box does not display connection properties.

    B. **Correct:** This procedure accesses the Local Area Connections Properties dialog box.

    C. **Correct:** This is an alternative method of accessing the Local Area Connections Properties dialog box.

    D. **Correct:** Although this procedure requires one more step than that described in Answer C, it accesses the Local Area Connections Properties dialog box.

3. **Correct Answers: A and D**

    A. **Correct:** The 801.11a specification can achieve a bandwidth of up to 54 Mbps.

    B. **Incorrect:** The 802.11b specification can achieve a bandwidth of up to 11 Mbps.

    C. **Incorrect:** 802.11d is a wireless network communications specification for use in countries where systems using other standards in the 802.11 family are not allowed to operate. The 802.11d specification is similar in most respects to 802.11b and supports bandwidths of up to 11 Mbps.

    D. **Correct:** The 801.11g specification can achieve a bandwidth of up to 54 Mbps under optimal conditions.

4. **Correct Answer: A**

    A. **Correct:** 802.11a uses the 5 GHz frequency. Although some mobile phones use this frequency, most domestic appliances use the 2.4 GHz 802.11a networks and are therefore the least affected by interference from other devices.

B. **Incorrect:** 802.11b uses the 2.4 GHz frequency. This frequency is prone to interference from microwave ovens, cordless phones, and other appliances.

C. **Incorrect:** 802.11d is similar in most respects to 802.11b. It uses the 2.4 GHz frequency.

D. **Incorrect:** 802.11b uses the 2.4 GHz frequency. As with 802.1 b and 802.11d, 802.11d networks are prone to interference.

5. **Correct Answer: D**

A. **Incorrect:** The user needs to use Public Folder Sharing to share files without administrator intervention.

B. **Incorrect:** If you disable Password Protected Sharing, all users on the network can access the shared files. Access is not limited to users that have accounts on the computer.

C. **Incorrect:** If you disable Network Discovery, the user cannot access files shared on the computer from another workstation.

D. **Correct:** Enabling Public Folder Sharing allows the user to share files without requiring administrator intervention. Enabling Password Protected Sharing ensures that only users who have accounts on the computer can access the files. Enabling Network Discovery enables the user to access her files from another workstation. The user will not use the file sharing method because this requires administrator intervention, so in this scenario, it does not matter whether this setting is enabled or disabled. However, it is good practice to disable any feature that is not used.

Lesson 2

1. **Correct Answers: B, C, E, and F**

A. **Incorrect:** The modem is working okay because you can access other websites.

B. **Correct:** The computer's DNS Resolver cache has stored the information that the website URL cannot resolve. Rebooting the computer clears the cache.

C. **Correct:** Negative caching has occurred only on the computer that failed to access the website. You should be able to access the site from another computer.

D. **Incorrect:** The ipconfig /flushdns command requires that you run the Command Prompt console as an administrator.

E. **Correct:** This procedure clears the DNS Resolver cache, and you should be able to access the website.

F. **Correct:** The computer's DNS Resolver cache has stored the information that the website URL cannot resolve. The cache is periodically cleared, so waiting for about half an hour and trying again is likely to work.

2. **Correct Answer: C**

    A. **Incorrect:** The user's computer works fine in the office. There is no need to reconfigure the office network.

    B. **Incorrect:** The order in which the user's computer accesses networks is not a problem. The problem occurs when her computer is within range of two wireless networks and switches between them.

    C. **Correct:** The likely cause of the reported behavior is that the lounge area of the hotel is within range of (and possibly equidistant between) two wireless networks and keeps switching between them. You can disable this feature or tell the user how to do so. You need to warn the user that if she moves to another part of the hotel, she might need to reconnect to a network.

    D. **Incorrect:** The user's laptop is working in the office and her hotel room. There is nothing wrong with her wireless adapter.

3. **Correct Answer: A**

    A. **Correct:** The MAC address is unique to an interface and does not change. MAC address control ensures that only computers whose wireless interfaces have one of the listed MAC addresses can access a wireless network. Be aware that if a new computer needs to access the network or if you replace the wireless adapter in a computer, you need to register the new MAC address in the WAP.

    B. **Incorrect:** Most networks are configured by using DHCP so IPv4 addresses can change. Even in networks where IPv4 addresses are statically configured, it is unlikely that the WAP supports IPv4 address control.

    C. **Incorrect:** WEP is an encryption method that ensures that third parties cannot read messages if they intercept them. It does not determine which computers can access a network.

    D. **Incorrect:** Like WEP, WPA is an encryption method and does not determine which computers can access a network.

4. **Correct Answers: C, E, and F**

    A. **Incorrect:** The Network Diagnostic tool is not a system tool and cannot be accessed from the System Tools menu.

    B. **Incorrect:** You run the Network Diagnostic tool when you have a problem. It is not a tool that you schedule to run on a regular basis, and it is not in the task scheduler library.

    C. **Correct:** You can run the Network Diagnostic tool from the Network And Sharing Center.

    D. **Incorrect:** You cannot access the Network Diagnostic tool from the Adapter Properties dialog box. This dialog box is used for configuration, not diagnosis.

    E. **Correct:** You can run the Network Diagnostic tool when you fail to connect to a webpage.

    F. **Correct:** You can run the Network Diagnostic tool for a specific connection by accessing the Network Connections dialog box.

5. **Correct Answers: A, C, and E**

    A. **Correct:** The Public profile is used when a computer connects to a network other than a private network and not as a member of an Active Directory domain. Public profile settings are typically more restrictive than Private profile settings.

    B. **Incorrect:** No specific firewall settings exist for wireless-enabled computers. Such computers are likely to have both Public and Private profiles configured.

    C. **Correct:** The Domain profile is used in computers that are members of an Active Directory domain.

    D. **Incorrect:** The Public profile is used when a computer is connected to an external network. There is no External profile.

    E. **Correct:** The Private profile is used when a computer is connected to a private network that is accessed through a router or gateway. Private profile settings are typically less restrictive than Public profile settings.

Chapter 7: Case Scenario Answers

Case Scenario 1: Advising Customers About Network Configuration

1. The customer needs to set up ICS on the computer that connects to his modem. He needs to ensure that the other computers on his network obtain their TCP/IP configuration automatically. When he has configured ICS on the first computer, he should reboot the other two.

2. The customer found the WAP setup easy because she accepted all the defaults and did not set up any security. She needs to change her SSID from its default value, configure encryption, and set up a passphrase. She should also change the access password on her WAP's web interface. She should consider restricting access by MAC address.

3. The customer needs to create a standard account for his deputy on his personal workstation and configure permissions on his shares so that his deputy has the Reader role.

Case Scenario 2: Troubleshooting a Network

1. In this scenario, it is likely that Trey Research's wireless network has MAC address control enabled while the client's wireless network does not. You need to obtain the MAC address of the customer's wireless adapter and register it in the WAP.

2. You can tell your boss that you can set up Public and Private profiles for the laptop computers. The Public profile can be enabled any time a laptop is used outside the office.

3. The computer is receiving its configuration through APIPA. All the other computers are okay, so DHCP is working on the WAP, and the network hub is probably okay. Either the NIC on the computer is faulty or (more likely) the Ethernet cable is not making a proper connection.

Chapter 8: Lesson Review Answers

Lesson 1

1. **Correct Answer: D**
   A. **Incorrect:** Windows Firewall can be applied to all, some, or none of a computer's network interfaces.
   B. **Incorrect:** Windows Firewall can be edited only on the current profile, not the current interface.
   C. **Incorrect:** Windows Firewall can be applied to all, some, or none of a computer's network interfaces.
   D. **Correct:** It is possible to modify the Windows Firewall configuration only for the currently active profile.

2. **Correct Answer: C**
   A. **Incorrect:** IPSec revolves around encrypted network communication and is not relevant in this situation.
   B. **Incorrect:** Uploading is outbound traffic rather than inbound traffic.
   C. **Correct:** Uploading is outbound traffic, hence an outbound rule would be appropriate.
   D. **Incorrect:** Connection security rules are used to isolate computers on networks by limiting which computers they can authenticate with.

3. **Correct Answer: B**
   A. **Incorrect:** An inbound deny rule would block inbound connections to the game server.
   B. **Correct:** Users who connect are making inbound connections, hence an inbound allow rule is appropriate.
   C. **Incorrect:** Users who connect are making inbound connections, hence an outbound rule is inappropriate.
   D. **Incorrect:** Users who connect are making inbound connections, hence an outbound rule is inappropriate.

4. **Correct Answer: D**

    A. **Incorrect:** Prior to making changes, you should export the current firewall policy. Restoring defaults will wipe out any existing changes.

    B. **Incorrect:** Prior to making changes, you should export the current firewall policy. It is not necessary to change profile prior to editing firewall configuration for Windows Firewall with Advanced Security.

    C. **Incorrect:** Prior to making changes, you should export the current firewall policy. Importing a policy might lead to unpredictable results.

    D. **Correct:** Prior to making changes, you should export the current firewall policy. If something goes wrong, you can import that policy to roll back to the original configuration.

Lesson 2

1. **Correct Answers: A and B**

    A. **Correct:** After she has sent you the invitation, your grandmother must keep the Remote Assistance Panel open for you to make a successful connection.

    B. **Correct:** To allow a successful connection, your grandmother's computer firewall and the router/firewall must be configured to allow inbound Remote Assistance connections.

    C. **Incorrect:** The connection will be inbound, so outbound rules will be irrelevant in this case.

    D. **Incorrect:** Your grandmother's computer could be running Windows XP and still send a Remote Assistance invitation. It is only if a Windows Vista computer has been configured to only allow other Windows Vista computers to connect to it that there might be a problem with Windows XP.

2. **Correct Answers: A and C**

    A. **Correct:** Orin will be able to take over his existing session.

    B. **Incorrect:** Ian has the option of denying Orin's connection if he is logged on locally.

    C. **Correct:** Orin can always log on if no one else is logged on at the same time.

    D. **Incorrect:** Ian has the option of denying Orin's local logon if Ian is already logged on remotely.

3. **Correct Answers: A and D**

    A. **Correct:** It is possible that a firewall might block a Remote Assistance connection, even on a LAN.

    B. **Incorrect:** Remote Assistance does not rely on Remote Desktop settings.

C. **Incorrect:** A helper does not log on, and it does not matter if the helper is a member of the Remote Desktop Users group.

D. **Correct:** Closing the Remote Assistance panel will stop any possible Remote Assistance connection.

4. **Correct Answer: B**

A. **Incorrect:** Exchange Server 2007 is used for e-mail and calendaring. It cannot be used to provide Remote Desktop access to computers behind a firewall.

B. **Correct:** A Terminal Services Gateway provides an alternative to using a VPN to access computers behind a firewall using Remote Desktop.

C. **Incorrect:** Internet Information Services is used for displaying webpages. It cannot be used to provide Remote Desktop access to computers behind a firewall.

D. **Incorrect:** Microsoft SQL Server 2005 is a database server. It cannot be used to provide Remote Desktop access to computers behind a firewall.

Chapter 8: Case Scenario Answers

Case Scenario 1: University Firewalls

1. You would configure an exception that allowed incoming web traffic on the local subnet.
2. You would create a port-based outbound rule to block the port.
3. You could export the profile from one computer and import it on the others.

Case Scenario 2: Antarctic Desktop Support

1. Installing an application requires the ability to elevate privileges. You will need to connect through Remote Desktop and elevate privileges.
2. Remote Assistance is an excellent technology for training because it allows two people in different locations to view the same screen.
3. If the user cannot connect, it is likely that that the user's user account is not a member of the Remote Desktop Users group. Add the user to this group to resolve the issue.

Chapter 9: Lesson Review Answers

Lesson 1

1. **Correct Answer: D**

A. **Incorrect:** Although this might reduce the problem, the question did not state that the messages were coming from Vietnam, only that they were encoded in the Vietnamese character set.

B. **Incorrect:** This option will not automatically deal with e-mail encoded in Vietnamese.

C. **Incorrect:** This option will not automatically deal with e-mail encoded in Vietnamese.

D. **Correct:** Configuring a block based on a message's character encoding will work in this particular instance.

2. **Correct Answer: B**

A. **Incorrect:** Views can only show or hide. They cannot highlight in pink.

B. **Correct:** You can configure rules to apply a highlight color based on the message sender's address.

C. **Incorrect:** Adding a sender to the Safe Senders list ensures that the sender's e-mail is never treated as junk mail. It cannot be used to highlight an e-mail.

D. **Incorrect:** Adding a sender to the Blocked Senders list ensures that you do not get e-mail from that person.

3. **Correct Answer: B**

A. **Incorrect:** Unless added to the Safe Senders list, someone in Contacts can still have their e-mail recognized as junk e-mail.

B. **Correct:** Addresses on the Safe Senders list are never recognized as junk e-mail.

C. **Incorrect:** Messages from addresses on the Blocked Senders list are automatically discarded.

D. **Incorrect:** Creating a view will not stop false positives from occurring with the junk e-mail filter.

4. **Correct Answer: A**

A. **Correct:** Creating a view for messages from each separate e-mail account will accomplish this task.

B. **Incorrect:** Although this would differentiate e-mail, the question specified differentiation within the inbox, not within separate folders. In all exams you must be careful to answer exactly what the question is asking.

C. **Incorrect:** This answer will differentiate only one e-mail account from the two others. It will not differentiate all three e-mail accounts.

D. **Incorrect:** This answer will differentiate only one e-mail account from the two others. It will not differentiate all three e-mail accounts.

5. **Correct Answer: A**

A. **Correct:** Creating a rule allows you to delete this poster's messages before you become aware of them. Deleting messages does not remove them from the news server. It just means that you will not be able to see them.

B. **Incorrect:** Marking the messages as read still allows you to see these messages, depending on the view being used.

    C. **Incorrect:** Views cannot be used to delete messages.

    D. **Incorrect:** Views cannot be used to mark messages as read.

Lesson 2

1. **Correct Answer: A**

    A. **Correct:** The default settings in Windows Mail automatically add the address of anyone whose messages are replied to as a contact. You have to disable this option to ensure that contacts must be added explicitly.

    B. **Incorrect:** Manually deleting the contacts clears out the contacts folder but does not stop the automatic adding of contacts.

    C. **Incorrect:** You cannot create a rule to delete the contacts, and it does not stop the automatic addition of contacts.

    D. **Incorrect:** You cannot create a view in contacts, and it does not stop the automatic addition of contacts.

2. **Correct Answer: A**

    A. **Correct:** Although this would result in a folder full of 200 vCard files, it allows you to share only specific contacts with Kim instead of sharing all of them.

    B. **Incorrect:** CSV exports all contacts in a single file, so Kim would get the ones she wants as well as the contacts that you do not want to share.

    C. **Incorrect:** Contacts supports only export to CSV and vCard. Contacts supports import from the Windows Address Book File format.

    D. **Incorrect:** Contacts supports only export to CSV and vCard. Contacts supports import from the LDIF format.

3. **Correct Answer: D**

    A. **Incorrect:** If Thomas can locate changes on Kim's published calendar, it means that Kim's published calendar is configured to automatically publish changes.

    B. **Incorrect:** Kim is not subscribed to Tony's calendar, so whether his changes are published is irrelevant.

    C. **Incorrect:** Kim is not subscribed to Tony's calendar, so her subscription settings are irrelevant.

    D. **Correct:** If Thomas can locate changes on Kim's published calendar, it means that Kim's published calendar is configured to automatically publish changes. It also follows that Tony's subscription is not configured to refresh.

4. **Correct Answer: A**

    A. **Correct:** If Thomas and Tony are subscribed but are unable to see updates, either both of their subscription settings are incorrect or Kim's publishing settings need to be revised. The first is not presented as an option in this list of answers, so the only solution is that Kim needs to fix her publishing settings.

    B. **Incorrect:** No mention is made in the question of subscriptions to Tony's calendar.

    C. **Incorrect:** Kim is publishing her calendar. No mention is made of problems to calendars to which Kim is subscribed.

    D. **Incorrect:** No mention is made in the question of subscriptions to Thomas's calendar.

5. **Correct Answer: D**

    A. **Incorrect:** The only way to lock down access to a calendar is to lock down access to the published calendar's location. Contact trust is irrelevant to shared calendars.

    B. **Incorrect:** Published calendars cannot be configured with passwords.

    C. **Incorrect:** Contact trust is irrelevant to shared calendars.

    D. **Correct:** The only way to lock down access to a calendar is to lock down access to the published calendar's location. The way to accomplish Kim's goal is to configure file and folder permissions so that Kim, Tony, and Thomas have access and Rob does not.

Lesson 3

1. **Correct Answer: C**

    A. **Incorrect:** It is not possible to block a user from joining a Windows Meeting Space meeting if he or she knows the meeting password and has an invitation file.

    B. **Incorrect:** It is not possible to rescind an invitation for a Windows Meeting Space meeting.

    C. **Correct:** After a meeting is started, the password cannot be changed. To change the password, start a new meeting.

    D. **Incorrect:** The Trusted Contacts list can be used to block incoming invitations but not to block users from joining meetings.

2. **Correct Answers: B and E**

    A. **Incorrect:** It is not possible to forcibly disconnect a user from a Windows Meeting Space meeting.

    B. **Correct:** Pressing the Windows key and Esc returns control to the person who is sharing the application.

    C. **Incorrect:** It is not possible to take control of an application but only to request control of an application.

    D. **Incorrect:** It is not possible to take control of an application but only to request control of an application.

    E. **Correct:** After Kim has requested control of the application, Tony can grant it to her.

3. **Correct Answer: D**

   A. **Incorrect:** The first changes made to the document will be replicated. When participants open the spreadsheet again, they will find that Ian's changes have been saved, and their changes have been discarded.

   B. **Incorrect:** The first changes made to the document will be replicated. When participants open the spreadsheet again, they will find that Ian's changes have been saved, and their changes have been discarded.

   C. **Incorrect:** The first changes made to the document will be replicated. When participants open the spreadsheet again, they will find that Ian's changes have been saved, and their changes have been discarded.

   D. **Correct:** The first changes made to the document will be replicated. When the participants open the spreadsheet again, they will find that Ian's changes have been saved, and their changes have been discarded.

4. **Correct Answer: A**

   A. **Correct:** To join any Windows Meeting Space meeting, IPv6 needs to be enabled. It does not matter if the meeting is ad hoc wireless or over a cabled LAN.

   B. **Incorrect:** Windows Meeting Space requires IPv6. Enabling or disabling IPv4 will not resolve the problem.

   C. **Incorrect:** To join any Windows Meeting Space meeting, IPv6 needs to be enabled.

   D. **Incorrect:** Windows Meeting Space requires IPv6. Enabling or disabling IPv4 will not resolve the problem.

5. **Correct Answers: B and C**

   A. **Incorrect:** If Tony is blocking all invitations, adding Kim to his list will not resolve the problem.

   B. **Correct:** If Tony opens an invitation sent to him through e-mail and uses the password sent through SMS, he will be able to join Kim's meeting.

   C. **Correct:** If Tony opens an invitation stored on a network share and uses the password sent through SMS, he will be able to join Kim's meeting.

   D. **Incorrect:** Adding Tony to Kim's list of trusted contacts will not resolve the problem.

Chapter 9: Case Scenario Answers

Case Scenario 1: University Calendars

1. Download the calendar file and import it. When no updates will be made to the calendar, importing is a better option than subscribing.

2. Kim should get the five people to publish their calendars and tasks. She should then subscribe to them to monitor their task list.

3. Kim should create a calendar for the head of the department and publish that calendar. She should then subscribe the head of the department's Windows Calendar application to the published calendar.

Case Scenario 2: Presenting a Business Proposal Using Windows Meeting Space

1. They can initiate an Ad Hoc Wireless Meeting.
2. The team leader can share the application using Windows Meeting Space to the two team members.
3. Add the documentation as a handout.

Chapter 10: Lesson Review Answers

Lesson 1

1. **Correct Answer: B**

    A. **Incorrect:** Disabling Away Mode allows the computer to be fully shut down. When a computer is fully shut down, it cannot be awakened by a paired Media Center Extender.

    B. **Correct:** Away Mode ensures that even when the computer is shut down, it will still be responsive to requests made by the Media Center Extender.

    C. **Incorrect:** Disabling the screen saver has no effect on whether the computer can be awakened by a Media Center Extender.

    D. **Incorrect:** The High Performance Power Plan does not make the Windows Vista computer responsive to requests made by the Media Center Extender because it is possible to completely shut down the computer when this plan is active.

2. **Correct Answer: C**

    A. **Incorrect:** Although Media Center can be configured to watch network folders, watched folders must be configured through Windows Media Center on the computer running Windows Vista.

    B. **Incorrect:** Although permissions can be an issue when configuring watched folders, it is necessary to configure the folders that can be viewed on the extender from within Media Center on the Windows Vista computer first. If these folders could not be seen through Media Center, you would start to look at issues such as permissions.

    C. **Correct:** It is necessary to configure the folders that can be viewed on the extender within the Media Center application on the Windows Vista computer.

    D. Incorrect: It is not possible to configure which media folders are visible on the Media Center Extender. This operation must be completed on the computer running Media Center.

3. **Correct Answer: C**

    A. Incorrect: The Until Space Needed setting might allow programs that you have not watched to be deleted.

    B. Incorrect: The For 1 Week setting might allow programs that you have not watched to be deleted.

    C. Correct: The Until I Watch setting deletes programs that you have watched in an effort to minimize the amount of disk space used by recordings.

    D. Incorrect: The Until I Delete setting might mean that you run out of recording space if you forget to delete watched programs.

4. **Correct Answer: C**

    A. Incorrect: Media Center Extenders such as the Xbox 360 are connected to Windows Media Center through the network, not through audio visual cables.

    B. Incorrect: Windows Vista computers with TV tuners cannot be configured to broadcast television signals. They can be used only to receive and record television signals.

    C. Correct: Configuring the Xbox 360, which is already connected to the plasma screen TV, as a Windows Media Center Extender allows content recorded and stored on the Windows Vista PC to be viewed through the Xbox 360.

    D. Incorrect: Windows Vista computers cannot be configured as Media Center Extenders. Only special devices such as the Xbox 360 can be configured as Media Center Extenders.

5. **Correct Answer: D**

    A. Incorrect: See explanation for correct answer.

    B. Incorrect: See explanation for correct answer.

    C. Incorrect: See explanation for correct answer.

    D. Correct: It is not possible to rip DVDs using any default application or feature included with Windows Vista. Only audio CDs can be ripped.

Lesson 2

1. **Correct Answers: C and D**

    A. Incorrect: Configuring the device to send faxes does not help in receiving them.

    B. Incorrect: It is not necessary to configure modem hardware properties to enable a computer to receive faxes.

    C. **Correct:** To receive faxes, it is necessary to configure a fax account and to configure the send/receive options to allow the modem attached to the fax account to receive faxes.

    D. **Correct:** To receive faxes, it is necessary to configure a fax account and to configure the send/receive options to allow the modem attached to the fax account to receive faxes.

2. **Correct Answer: C**

    A. **Incorrect:** Separate fax accounts allow you to select between a fax modem and a fax server; they cannot be used to configure multiple modems.

    B. **Incorrect:** It is not possible to edit fax account properties.

    C. **Correct:** The Select Device option in Fax Settings allows you to set which fax modem is used to send and receive faxes.

    D. **Incorrect:** Deleting the existing fax account does not allow you to switch between fax devices.

3. **Correct Answer: A**

    A. **Correct:** Fax accounts allow you to shift between using a built-in fax modem and a fax server on the network.

    B. **Incorrect:** If your computer has more than one fax modem, you can switch between them using fax settings. You cannot configure more than one fax account for local fax devices.

    C. **Incorrect:** Like printers, faxes use a single set of central settings.

    D. **Incorrect:** Fax modems can be shared like printers. Multiple fax accounts are not possible for local fax devices.

4. **Correct Answer: B**

    A. **Incorrect:** It is not possible to specify a printer to output incoming faxes using Fax Settings.

    B. **Correct:** The Options dialog box allows you to configure every incoming fax to be automatically printed out by a selected printer.

    C. **Incorrect:** Fax accounts cannot be modified once created.

    D. **Incorrect:** Configuring a redirect to a printer is specified in options rather than by configuring hardware options.

5. **Correct Answer: A**

    A. **Correct:** Configuring an e-mail to be sent after each fax transmission meets the goal of storing a record on another computer.

    B. **Incorrect:** It is not possible to send a receipt when a fax has been received.

    C. **Incorrect:** Including the banner in sent faxes provides information on the sent fax; it does not provide an independent receipt.

D. **Incorrect:** Configuring redialing options might ensure that a fax is received if the recipient is busy, but it does not provide a receipt.

Lesson 3

1. **Correct Answer: D**

   A. **Incorrect:** Gadget opacity does not determine whether a gadget is always visible above other windows. Only the Windows Sidebar itself can be configured to stay above other windows.

   B. **Incorrect:** It is not possible to configure Sidebar opacity. Only gadget opacity can be configured.

   C. **Incorrect:** Individual gadgets cannot be configured to stay above other windows. Only the Windows Sidebar itself can be configured to stay above other windows.

   D. **Correct:** The Windows Sidebar can be configured through its properties to always stay on top of other windows.

2. **Correct Answer: B**

   A. **Incorrect:** Only gadgets that were originally installed from the Internet need to be redownloaded if they are removed from the Gadget Gallery.

   B. **Correct:** Because the gadgets were removed from the Windows Sidebar and not the Gadget Gallery, they are still present in the Gadget Gallery. They can be dragged from here back to the Windows Sidebar.

   C. **Incorrect:** Only if default gadgets are deleted from the Gadget Gallery is it necessary to use the Restore Gadgets Installed With Windows option.

   D. **Incorrect:** If default gadgets are deleted from the Gadget Gallery, use the Restore Gadgets Installed With Windows option in Windows Sidebar Properties to restore them. Deleted gadgets cannot be restored using Programs and Features.

3. **Correct Answer: A**

   A. **Correct:** If you delete a gadget from the Gadget Gallery that you have downloaded from the Internet, you need to redownload the gadget from the Internet.

   B. **Incorrect:** Gadgets downloaded from the Internet and deleted from the Gadget Gallery must be redownloaded. They cannot be opened from the Windows Sidebar.

   C. **Incorrect:** The Restore option in Windows Sidebar Properties can be used only to restore the set of default gadgets, not gadgets downloaded from the Internet.

   D. **Incorrect:** If you delete a gadget from the Gadget Gallery that you have downloaded from the Internet, you need to redownload the gadget from the Internet.

4. **Correct Answer: A**

   A. **Correct:** Opacity is configured on an individual basis for each gadget.

      B. **Incorrect:** Gadget opacity cannot be configured through Windows Sidebar Properties. Opacity is configured on an individual basis for each gadget.

      C. **Incorrect:** Windows Theme opacity determines how opaque the window borders are when the Aero theme is enabled. Opacity is configured on an individual basis for each gadget.

      D. **Incorrect:** Opacity settings cannot be configured from the Gadget Gallery. Opacity is configured on an individual basis for each gadget.

  5. **Correct Answer: A**

      A. **Correct:** Using the Remove button in the View Gadgets dialog box only removes the gadget from the Sidebar or the desktop and does not delete the gadget from the gallery. The gadget can be returned to its position by dragging it back from the gallery.

      B. **Incorrect:** Using the Remove button in the View Gadgets dialog box only removes the gadget from the Sidebar or the desktop and does not delete the gadget from the gallery. There is no need to use the Restore Gadgets function.

      C. **Incorrect:** Using the Remove button in the View Gadgets dialog box only removes the gadget from the Sidebar or the desktop and does not delete the gadget from the gallery. There is no need to redownload the gadget from the Internet.

      D. **Incorrect:** Gadgets cannot be placed in nor removed from the Recycle Bin.

Chapter 10: Case Scenario Answers

Case Scenario 1: Family Media Center Extender

  1. Modify the recording settings so that the season recording starts several minutes before the time the cartoon is scheduled to start.

  2. Use the Add Folder To Watch function to ensure that Media Center checks the folder.

  3. Configure parental controls to limit the rating of DVDs that can be played.

Case Scenario 2: Home Office Fax Solution

  1. Configure fax settings so that incoming calls are automatically answered after 10 rings.

  2. Configure the banner to be included with each page.

  3. Configure Receipt options. Ensure that a copy of the sent fax is e-mailed as a part of the receipt.

Chapter 11: Lesson Review Answers

Lesson 1

1. **Correct Answer: C**
    A.   **Incorrect:** Virtual memory settings control how much hard disk space is used for paging. They do not affect the appearance of dialog boxes.
    B.   **Incorrect:** This setting is used in certain Microsoft BackOffice servers (for example, Microsoft Exchange Servers). It does not affect the appearance of dialog boxes.
    C.   **Correct:** Adjusting visual effects for best performance removes features such as drop shadows on menus or under the mouse symbol. It also affects the appearance of dialog boxes.
    D.   **Incorrect:** Adjusting visual effects for best appearance ensures that features such as menus and dialog boxes look good on the screen. This setting ensures there is a black line around dialog boxes.

2. **Correct Answer: B**
    A.   **Incorrect:** Continuous hard disk access is usually a sign of memory problems rather than hard disk problems. A faster hard disk, particularly an H-HHD or SSD device, would probably improve performance because paging would be faster. However, he is unlikely to be able to obtain, configure, and install a hard disk by the close of business, and he probably is not technically competent to do so.
    B.   **Correct:** ReadyBoost provides a quick, easy, and inexpensive solution when a computer is experiencing memory problems. The user can install a USB flash memory device merely by plugging it into the computer and can easily configure Ready-Boost without needing elevated privileges.
    C.   **Incorrect:** Before ReadyBoost was available, this was the standard solution to this problem, and you should consider adding more RAM as a long-term solution (provided the computer's motherboard permits this). However, the user probably cannot obtain and install RAM in the time specified and is unlikely in any case to have the necessary technical expertise. ReadyBoost provides a quick, easy, and inexpensive solution in this scenario.
    D.   **Incorrect:** The problem is excessive paging caused by inadequate RAM capacity. Adjusting the size of the virtual memory that stores the page file is unlikely to provide a solution. In any case, the user needs administrator privileges in order to configure virtual memory.

3. **Correct Answers: C and D**
    A.   **Incorrect:** Microsoft guidelines specify a flash memory capacity between one and three times the capacity of the computer's RAM. 256 MB is too small.

Answers

B. **Incorrect:** Microsoft guidelines specify a flash memory capacity between one and three times the capacity of the computer's RAM. 512 MB is too small.

C. **Correct:** Microsoft guidelines specify a flash memory capacity between one and three times the capacity of the computer's RAM. 1 GB falls within this range, although you are likely to see a more significant improvement in performance if you use a larger capacity flash memory device.

D. **Correct:** Microsoft guidelines specify a flash memory capacity between one and three times the capacity of the computer's RAM. 2 GB fall within this range.

4. **Correct Answer: A**

A. **Correct:** You click Adjust Visual Effects, close the UAC dialog box, and select the Advanced tab in the Performance Options dialog box. On this tab, you click Change in the Virtual Memory section.

B. **Incorrect:** Clicking Adjust Indexing Options takes you to the Indexing Options dialog box. You cannot access Virtual Memory settings from this dialog box.

C. **Incorrect:** Clicking Adjust Power Settings takes you to the Power Options dialog box. You cannot access Virtual Memory settings from this dialog box.

D. **Incorrect:** You can click Advanced Tools, and then select Adjust The Appearance And Performance Of Windows. You then close the UAC dialog box, and select the Advanced tab in the Performance Options dialog box. On this tab, you click Change in the Virtual Memory section. Although this procedure lets you access the Virtual Memory dialog box, it requires one more operation than the answer given in option A. The question asks for the quickest method.

5. **Correct Answer: B**

A. **Incorrect:** Update History tells you all the updates that a computer has downloaded. Although it is possible that a recent update could have solved the problem you encountered, it is very difficult to deduce this from the information given in Update History.

B. **Correct:** Check for new solutions resends details of all the problems recorded in Problem History to Microsoft. If solutions have been found since a problem was first reported, Microsoft informs you about that solution.

C. **Incorrect:** Hidden updates are updates you have asked Windows Vista not to notify you about or install automatically. To enhance the security and performance of your computer, you should restore all important and recommended updates. However, this will not tell you whether Microsoft has subsequently found a solution to the problem you encountered.

D. **Incorrect:** Problem History lists the problems you encountered and whether you reported them to Microsoft. However, it will not tell you whether Microsoft has subsequently found a solution to the problem you encountered.

Lesson 2

1. **Correct Answer: A**

    A. **Correct:** The lowest subscore determines the base score, even though this computer is not primarily used for 3D graphics and gaming.

    B. **Incorrect:** 3.5 is the average of the subscores. However, the lowest subscore determines the base score—not the average.

    C. **Incorrect:** 4.1 is a significant score because the computer is used for processor-intensive operations. However, the question asks for the base score, and the lowest subscore determines the base score.

    D. **Incorrect:** 4.4 is the highest subscore. The lowest subscore, not the highest subscore, determines the base score.

2. **Correct Answer: C**

    A. **Incorrect:** This is the default setting. It ensures that any problem you encounter (other than those that require personal information to be sent) is forwarded to Microsoft. It does not, however, enable this behavior for all computer users.

    B. **Incorrect:** This lets you scan for solutions for problems that ocurred but have not yet been resolved. It does not, however, set a default so that every other user who has an account on the computer automatically checks for solutions when a problem occurs.

    C. **Correct:** This turns on Windows Problem Reporting for all users.

    D. **Incorrect:** If you have allowed each user to change settings in Advanced Settings, this ensures that all users report problems by default. However, users can change this default, which is not what the question requires.

3. **Correct Answer: B**

    A. **Incorrect:** The Application log stores program events. Events are classified as error, warning, or information.

    B. **Correct:** The Security log stores security-related audit events that can be Audit Success or Audit Failure.

    C. **Incorrect:** Computers that are configured as domain controllers in an Active Directory domain have events displayed in the Setup log. The log does not store security-related audit events.

    D. **Incorrect:** The System log stores system events that are logged by Windows Vista and Windows Vista system services. System events are classified as critical, error, warning, or information.

4. **Correct Answer: D**

    A. **Incorrect:** The System log does not store warnings and information events that were generated when applications accessed the registry.

  B. **Incorrect:** Driver failures are not stored in the Applications log, although if a driver failure causes an application to fail, the application failure would be recorded. Application log events are classified as error, warning, or information, but not critical.

  C. **Incorrect:** Windows Vista creates Applications and Services logs depending upon the applications and services that are installed. The user cannot create such a log directly.

  D. **Correct:** You can create a custom view that contains events from several Windows logs. You can also configure the view to display events that occurred in the previous 24 hours.

 5. **Correct Answer: D**

  A. **Incorrect:** The Problem History window shows you the problems that have occurred in computer operation since the last time the history was cleared. It does not give you the information the question stipulates.

  B. **Incorrect:** Task Manager gives you a snapshot of current resource usage and resource usage over the past few minutes. You cannot use it to record activity and resource usage during quiet and busy times.

  C. **Incorrect:** Event Viewer logs record events that occur on the computer. The tool is not designed to record activity and resource usage during quiet and busy times.

  D. **Correct:** You can open the Reliability and Performance Monitor and then select Performance Monitor. This allows you to record information about resource usage and use this information as historical (or baseline) data. The tool also enables you to view resource usage in real time.

Chapter 11: Case Scenario Answers

Case Scenario 1: Troubleshooting Performance Issues

 1. The USB device in your colleague's computer is being used to implement ReadyBoost. If she wants to save files to flash memory, she needs to plug a second USB flash memory device into another slot.

 2. You should advise the supervisor to open Performance Information and Tools and click Manage Startup Programs. He can then disable any programs that he does not recognize or trust. If this does not improve performance, he can disable each program in turn and find out which one is causing the performance problem. Although none of these operations require elevated privileges, you will likely need to assist the user in this scenario.

 3. You should advise the researcher that the program will run but might not run efficiently. If the researcher needs to use the program regularly, the computer requires a hardware upgrade.

Case Scenario 2: Troubleshooting Reliability Issues

1. Click Check For New Solutions in the Problem Reports and Solutions tool.

2. Select Performance Monitor in the Reliability and Performance Monitor tool. Capture a performance data collector set over a 24-hour period that monitors memory-related counters—for example, Memory:Pages/sec.

3. You can find information about critical system events such as driver failures in the System Log in Event Viewer.

4. You should open the Reliability and Performance Monitor tool and select Reliability Monitor.

Chapter 12: Lesson Review Answers

Lesson 1

1. **Correct Answer: B**

   A. **Incorrect:** Important updates are always installed automatically if the Install Updates Automatically setting is enabled in Windows Update.

   B. **Correct:** By default, recommended updates are installed automatically if the Install Updates Automatically setting is enabled in Windows Update. However, you can change this setting by clearing the Include Recommended Updates When Downloading, Installing, Or Notifying Me About Updates check box in the Change Settings dialog box.

   C. **Incorrect:** Optional updates cannot be installed automatically.

   D. **Incorrect:** Stand-alone updates cannot be installed at the same time as other updates. They can be important, recommended, or optional. Because you don't know what type of update a stand-alone update might be, you cannot predict or configure whether it is installed automatically.

2. **Correct Answers: A and B**

   A. **Correct:** Important updates can be installed without requiring elevated privileges. They can also be installed automatically even if no user is logged on to the computer.

   B. **Correct:** Like important updates, recommended updates can be installed without requiring elevated privileges. They can also be installed automatically even if no user is logged on to the computer.

   C. **Incorrect:** Installing optional updates requires elevated privileges.

   D. **Incorrect:** Stand-alone updates can be important, recommended, or optional. If they are optional, installation requires elevated privileges.

3. **Correct Answer: D**

   A. **Incorrect:** You do not need to obtain the updates from the Microsoft Update website. Windows Update can detect published updates that have not been installed on the user's machine.

   B. **Incorrect:** Windows Update can download and install the missed updates.

   C. **Incorrect:** You can install updates manually the following morning if any uninstalled updates exist. However, this should not be necessary because Windows Update will install them that evening.

   D. **Correct:** Windows Update will identify any important (and, by default, any recommended) updates that have not been installed on the user's computer. In this scenario, these updates will download and install at 7:00 P.M. that evening.

4. **Correct Answer: A**

   A. **Correct:** When you hide the update, the user will no longer be notified about it.

   B. **Incorrect:** This prevents notifications for all recommended updates. The user wants you to stop Windows Update from notifying him about only one specific update.

   C. **Incorrect:** Hiding an update requires elevated privileges. It is usually a very bad idea to give administrator passwords to standard users, so you need to hide updates for your users rather than ask them to do it themselves.

   D. **Incorrect:** Configuring Windows Update settings requires elevated privileges. This answer is therefore incorrect for the reason given for Answer C. Also, changing this setting does not have the required result for the reason given in Answer B.

Lesson 2

1. **Correct Answer: C**

   A. **Incorrect:** These settings download important uploads and notify you so you can install them. You want to choose when to download them.

   B. **Incorrect:** These settings download important and recommended uploads and notify you so you can install them. You want to choose when to download important updates, and you do not want to be notified about recommended updates.

   C. **Correct:** These settings notify you that important updates are available for downloading and installing.

   D. **Incorrect:** These settings notify you that important or recommended updates, or both, are available for downloading and installing. You do not want to be notified about recommended updates.

2. **Correct Answer: A, B, C, and D**

    A. **Correct:** Don's personal document files (including Excel spreadsheets) on the hard disk are backed up by default. Don does not need to initiate the backup or to be logged on to the computer.

    B. **Correct:** Kim's personal document files on the hard disk are backed up by default.

    C. **Correct:** Document files include PowerPoint presentations for backup purposes.

    D. **Correct:** Image files, including digital photographs, are backed up by default.

    E. **Incorrect:** Encrypted files and folders are not backed up.

    F. **Incorrect:** Files in the Recycle Bin are not backed up.

    G. **Incorrect:** By default, a USB flash memory device is formatted with the FAT filing system. Files on such a device are not backed up.

3. **Correct Answer: C**

    A. **Incorrect:** The Restore Files wizard will restore the version of her file that existed on the previous evening. She will lose the changes she made today.

    B. **Incorrect:** Previous versions will include the backup version created on the previous evening and shadow copies. It is unlikely that the last shadow copy made contains exactly the same information as the file the user accidentally deleted. In any case, it is easier to restore a recently deleted file from the Recycle Bin.

    C. **Correct:** The user deleted the file recently. It will still be in her Recycle Bin. It will contain all the information that it contained when it was deleted.

    D. **Incorrect:** A System Restore will not restore a deleted user file. In any case, a System Restore requires elevated privileges, and the user probably will not have an administrator account.

4. **Correct Answers: A and D**

    A. **Correct:** A Complete PC Restore will restore the computer to how it was three months ago.

    B. **Incorrect:** All restore points were deleted when the hard disk was wiped, so a System Restore will not help. The user needs to reinstall any software he installed in the last three months, install (or allow Windows Update to install) three months of updates, and ensure his virus and spyware definitions are up to date, but these options were not given in the question.

    C. **Incorrect:** Shadow copies are made of files, not folders. In any case, all shadow copies were deleted when the hard disk was wiped.

    D. **Correct:** A Complete PC backup ensures that the user has a working computer. However, the contents of his My Documents folder will be three months out of date. He needs to restore this folder from backup.

Chapter 12: Case Scenario Answers

Case Scenario 1: Configuring Windows Update

1. Users do not need administrator accounts to download and install recommended and important updates, and giving administrator accounts to all users lets them reconfigure other important settings. You can also tell Don that updates can be downloaded and installed even when no user is logged on, so you can configure this to happen in the evening or during the night when it does not interfere with work.

2. Optional updates do not download and install automatically. As an administrator, Don can install optional updates, such as device driver updates, on his own computer.

3. Don has installed a device driver that is unsuitable for his graphics adapter. He needs to open Device Manager and roll back the driver. If this fails, he needs to carry out a System Restore. You will probably need to assist him.

Case Scenario 2: Configuring Data Protection

1. In this situation, shadow copies of the file probably exist. You should advise the user to recover his file by right-clicking it, selecting Restore Previous Versions, and selecting the most recent shadow copy.

2. Automatic scheduled backups back up specified types of files for all users with accounts on the computer. The user's son can use the Restore Files wizard to restore his file from backup.

3. System Restore can restore the computer system to a restore point created before the new software was installed without deleting or modifying the user files currently on the computer. However, it is still a good idea to back up important files before carrying out a System Restore (or any other major operation).

4. The user cannot place a Complete PC Backup on the same disk that holds her OS. She needs to create the backup on an external hard disk or on removable CD-R, CD-RW, or DVD rewritable disks.

Chapter 13: Lesson Review Answers

Lesson 1

1. **Correct Answers: A, C, D, and E**
   A. **Correct:** You can mute the speaker in the Volume tile of the Mobility Center.
   B. **Incorrect:** You can access Sync Settings and configure offline file synchronization. However, you cannot access offline files directly from the Mobility Center.

C. **Correct:** You can select a power plan in the drop-down box in the Battery Status tile of the Mobility Center.

D. **Correct:** You can click the Turn On/Turn Off button in the Presentation Settings tile of the Mobility Center.

E. **Correct:** You can access Sync Settings from the Sync Center tile of the Mobility Center.

F. **Incorrect:** You cannot access your personal files directly from the Mobility Center. You need to open Windows Explorer.

2. **Correct Answers: A, D, E, and F**

A. **Correct:** You can select the Use This Background check box and then either select a background from the list provided or browse for a background file.

B. **Incorrect:** You cannot connect to a network projector from this dialog box. You need to click Accessories in the All Programs Menu and then select Connect To A Network Projector.

C. **Incorrect:** You can turn off the screen saver, but you cannot select a new one.

D. **Correct:** When you select the I Am Currently Giving A Presentation check box, this automatically turns off system notifications.

E. **Correct:** You can click Connected Displays to access a list of connected displays.

F. **Correct:** You can select the Set Volume To check box and then use a slider control to adjust speaker volume.

3. **Correct Answer: C**

A. **Incorrect:** This control displays the number 1 on the main monitor and 2 on the additional monitor to help you identify which monitor is which. It does not affect the size of the monitor icon.

B. **Incorrect:** You do not need to make the external monitor your main monitor, although you can if you want to. This does not affect the size of the monitor icon.

C. **Correct:** The higher the resolution, the larger the screen monitor icon. If the second icon is significantly smaller than the first, you probably need to increase the resolution to get a satisfactory display.

D. **Incorrect:** You probably need to increase the color depth to get a satisfactory display, but this will not affect the size of the monitor icon.

4. **Correct Answer: A**

A. **Correct:** The padlock indicates a security-protected network projector. You can connect, but you will need to supply a password.

B. **Incorrect:** The padlock indicates a security-protected network projector, not an unsecured network projector. Securing a network projector ensures that unauthorized users cannot use it. There is no risk to the user in using an unsecured network projector.

    C. **Incorrect:** If the projector were turned off, it would not appear on the list.

    D. **Incorrect:** You need to specify a URL in order to connect to a network projector that is not on the subnet, but this is not relevant to this scenario because Search finds the projector.

5. **Correct Answer: B**

    A. **Incorrect:** You know the projector is on the same subnet as your computer because you could locate it by using the Search function.

    B. **Correct:** In this scenario, it is likely that somebody else was connected to the projector when you tried to connect and has reconnected as soon as the projector restarted.

    C. **Incorrect:** Network projectors are designed to transmit and display still images, not high-bandwidth transmissions such as video streams. The projector can transmit video, but the playback quality is sometimes poor. However, in this scenario, your concern is that you cannot connect to the projector, not that the playback is of poor quality.

    D. **Incorrect:** If the projector were security-protected, you could still connect, although you would need to supply a password.

Lesson 2

1. **Correct Answer: D**

    A. **Incorrect:** Both computers have enough RAM to run Windows Vista and to form synchronization partnerships.

    B. **Incorrect:** It is unlikely that the size of the user's My Documents folder is greater than 75 GB, and if it were, her desktop computer would not have more than 75 percent free disk space.

    C. **Incorrect:** Computers in both workgroups and Active Directory domains can sync offline files.

    D. **Correct:** Windows Vista Home Premium does not support offline file synchronization.

2. **Correct Answer: B**

    A. **Incorrect:** If WMDC is used to connect a handheld device, the computer must be powered on.

    B. **Correct:** A SideShow device can access a mobile PC even when the PC is turned off.

    C. **Incorrect:** Mobile devices can be synchronized through Sync Center, but the computer needs to be turned on.

    D. **Incorrect:** A handheld device that is not SideShow-compatible needs the computer to be powered on before the device can interact with it. Whether the device is connected through a cable, over a wireless network, or through Bluetooth is irrelevant.

3. **Correct Answer: A**

A. **Correct:** The device has a limited amount of memory space, and the new Side-Show gadgets are using space, resulting in information being lost. Disabling unneeded SideShow gadgets frees memory space.

B. **Incorrect:** It is unlikely that the newly downloaded SideShow gadgets require updates. Downloading SideShow gadget updates is unlikely to free memory space on the device.

C. **Incorrect:** The order of the SideShow gadgets does not affect the amount of memory they use.

D. **Incorrect:** Notifications are pop-up information boxes that appear on the device screen. Disabling notifications is unlikely to solve the problem.

4. **Correct Answer: C**

A. **Incorrect:** You can remove the software by clicking Remove.

B. **Incorrect:** Holding down the Ctrl key and clicking the check box has no effect.

C. **Correct:** Clicking Remove removes the software from both the PC and the hand-held device. You need to reinstall it on the PC.

D. **Incorrect:** Ending a partnership does not remove software installed on the hand-held device.

5. **Correct Answer: D**

A. **Incorrect:** Automatic backup is available only on devices that have a Windows Mobile partnership with the computer. If you want to configure automatic backup, the procedure described in this answer is the one to follow. However, the question does not ask you how to configure automatic backup. It asks you how you back up the files with the least effort in the situation described. In this scenario, this involves a manual backup.

B. **Incorrect:** Copying the files manually requires more effort than performing a manual backup.

C. **Incorrect:** You cannot use Restore (whether advanced or not) to copy files that have not been backed up.

D. **Correct:** This performs a manual backup and requires only two mouse clicks. You need to select Full Backup because you have not previously backed up the files on the PDA.

Chapter 13: Case Scenario Answers

Case Scenario 1: Configuring Mobile Display Settings

1. You can either replicate his laptop screen to a larger external monitor or extend the screen to a second monitor. The lecturer can probably use the same presentation settings for the external monitor that he does for the network projector. If not, it is easy to change them.

2. She needs only to access the Mobility Center by either clicking Mobile PC in Control Panel and selecting Windows Mobility Center or by pressing the Windows logo key and the X key simultaneously. The Mobility Center lets her access all the settings she requires from a single tool.

3. When he enables presentation settings or selects the I Am Currently Giving A Presentation check box in the Presentation Settings dialog box, it automatically prevents his laptop from going into sleep mode or displaying system notifications.

Case Scenario 2: Configuring Mobile Devices

1. This is a SideShow device that lets her check information such as e-mails without turning on the computer. It uses very little power and should not drain the battery on her laptop.

2. He needs to access Windows Update to download the WMDC driver. Alternatively, he can download it from the Windows Mobile Device Center webpage at *http:// www.microsoft.com/windowsmobile/devicecenter.mspx*.

3. Windows Vista Business will let him sync with network folders marked as offline. The ability to sync with network folders is not included in Windows Vista Starter, Windows Vista Home Basic, or Windows Vista Home Premium editions.

Chapter 14: Lesson Review Answers

Lesson 1

1. **Correct Answer: A**
   A. **Correct:** Calibrate Tablet Pen in Pen and Input Devices allows you to calibrate your pen taps with the specific place on the screen where you are tapping.
   B. **Incorrect:** Enable Automatic Learning in Tablet PC Settings allows Windows Vista to learn your handwriting style.
   C. **Incorrect:** Handwriting Personalization is used for handwriting recognition and not for pen calibration.

    D. **Incorrect:** Configure Orientation Calibration in Tablet PC Settings is used to set portrait or landscape mode.

2. **Correct Answer: B**

    A. **Incorrect:** Primary Landscape is the orientation used when a computer is in laptop mode. If the screen is meant to be reoriented when changed to slate mode, the orientation cannot be Primary Landscape.

    B. **Correct:** Primary Landscape is the orientation used when a computer is in laptop mode. If the screen reorients when used in slate mode, it will be displayed in Primary Portrait mode.

    C. **Incorrect:** The Secondary Landscape mode is an upside-down version of the normal laptop display mode.

    D. **Incorrect:** Although it is possible to use Secondary Portrait mode with a convertible Tablet PC in slate mode, the Primary Portrait mode is the default tablet display mode in convertible laptops.

3. **Correct Answer: C**

    A. **Incorrect:** Although enabling automatic learning will help and the option is enabled by default, you should use the Target Specific Recognition Errors function when trying to resolve specific rather than general recognition problems.

    B. **Incorrect:** Disabling automatic learning will stop Windows Vista from attempting to improve its handwriting recognition.

    C. **Correct:** The Target Specific Recognition Errors function is designed to prevent Windows Vista from consistently misidentifying certain words or letters. If only certain items are misidentified, this will resolve the problem more quickly than Windows Vista's standard learning routines.

    D. **Incorrect:** Although the Teach The Recognizer Your Handwriting Style function helps Windows Vista better identify your handwriting, the function that targets specific recognition errors does this much faster.

4. **Correct Answer: C**

    A. **Incorrect:** Having Windows Vista become better at handwriting recognition will not resolve the problem with accidental scratch-outs. You should limit the recognition of scratch-outs to a specific marking.

    B. **Incorrect:** The problem in the question is caused by the recognition of multiple scratch-out gestures. Limiting the number of recognized scratch-out gestures to one will likely resolve the problem because it will be difficult to inadvertently use the Z scratch-out marking.

    C. **Correct:** Configuring this option will limit Windows Vista to a single scratch-out gesture, the Z-shaped one used with Windows XP Tablet PC edition. This option is useful when you want to use scratch-out gestures when using the input pad but

find that the expanded gestures included with Windows Vista mean that you inadvertently scratch out text when you do not intend to.

    D. **Incorrect:** Configuring this option will mean that Ian is unable to use any strikethrough gestures.

5. **Correct Answer: A**

    A. **Correct:** On low levels of security, it is possible for some users to use the writing pad or character pads of the Input Panel to enter their passwords. The downside to this is that the full text of the password is displayed on the screen and is not hidden. Configuring the highest security level in the Input Panel Options means that users can enter their passwords only through the on-screen keyboard, which does not provide any information about which characters have been tapped during password entry.

    B. **Incorrect:** Several aspects of password security can be configured using Local Policies, but these policies cannot be configured through the User Account item in Control Panel.

    C. **Incorrect:** It is not possible to disable the writing pad in the Input Panel.

    D. **Incorrect:** It is not possible to disable the character pad in the Input Panel.

Lesson 2

1. **Correct Answers: A and C**

    A. **Correct:** Custom plans can be deleted as long as they are not in use.

    B. **Incorrect:** It is not possible to delete the active plan, even if the plan is a custom one.

    C. **Correct:** Custom plans can be deleted as long as they are not in use.

    D. **Incorrect:** Default plans cannot be deleted.

    E. **Incorrect:** Default plans cannot be deleted.

    F. **Incorrect:** Default plans cannot be deleted.

2. **Correct Answer: D**

    A. **Incorrect:** Configuring a screen saver password will not ensure that a password will be required to wake from sleep.

    B. **Incorrect:** Enabling User Account Control has no influence on whether a password is required when the computer wakes from sleep.

    C. **Incorrect:** Disabling User Account Control has no influence on whether a password is required when the computer wakes from sleep.

    D. **Correct:** Configuring the computer to require a password to wake from sleep will ensure that a password is always required to access data after the computer powers up from a sleep state.

    E. **Incorrect:** Changing to a different power plan will not ensure that a password will be required to wake from sleep. It will depend on the power plans settings, which might have been modified.

3. **Correct Answer: A**

    A. **Correct:** The laptop is likely to be running on batteries during meetings. The only setting that could inadvertently shut down the computer is closing the lid because this would be expected behavior for using the power button.

    B. **Incorrect:** The current setting will not shut down the computer if the lid is closed.

    C. **Incorrect:** Although pressing the power button will shut the computer down when it is plugged in, the executive said that the shutdowns were unexpected.

    D. **Incorrect:** Although pressing the power button will hibernate the computer down when plugged in, the executive said that the shutdowns were unexpected.

4. **Correct Answer: B**

    A. **Incorrect:** Although you can achieve the goal by creating a custom power plan, you still have to edit the advanced settings of the new plan. Simply creating a new custom power plan will not resolve the problem.

    B. **Correct:** Editing the Advanced Power Settings of the current plan allows you to modify whether a password is required when the computer is woken up, depending on whether the computer is using the battery or is plugged in.

    C. **Incorrect:** Although you can achieve the goal by switching to the Balanced power plan, you still have to edit the advanced settings of the new plan. Simply switching to a new plan will not accomplish the goal.

    D. **Incorrect:** Although you can achieve the goal by switching to the Power Saver plan, you still have to edit the advanced settings of the new plan. Simply switching to a new plan will not accomplish the goal.

5. **Correct Answer: B**

    A. **Incorrect:** Changing advanced power settings is a way of customizing a current plan. These changes will be lost if the Restore Plan Defaults button is used.

    B. **Correct:** Creating a custom plan ensures that you can configure the settings you want without worrying that they will be lost if the Restore Plan Defaults button is pressed.

    C. **Incorrect:** Adjusting the display brightness is a way of customizing a current plan. These changes will be lost if the Restore Plan Defaults button is used.

    D. **Incorrect:** Changing when the computer sleeps is a way of customizing a current plan. These changes will be lost if the Restore Plan Defaults button is used.

Chapter 14: Case Scenario Answers

Case Scenario 1: Tablet PCs at Tailspin Toys

1. Configure the menus to work for left-handed people rather than the default, which suits right-handed people.
2. Configure advanced pen flicks, which will enable them to copy and paste data using pen flicks rather than normal menu commands.
3. Use the Windows Easy Transfer Wizard to transfer handwriting data across to the new Tablet PC.

Case Scenario 2: Individualized Power Plans

1. Ian should use hibernation because he will not be accessing the computer within the next 15 minutes. Sleep uses power to keep the computer's state in active memory for 15 minutes. After that period has elapsed, sleep is functionally equivalent to hibernation.
2. Because Kim rarely takes her laptop computer far away from an AC outlet, the High Performance default power plan would best suit her usage needs.
3. Because Orin spends a lot of time away from AC outlets in the park, if you were building him a custom power plan, you would base it on the Power Saver default plan.

Glossary

access token   When a user is authenticated, the Local Security Authority (LSA) creates an access token for that user. An access token contains a security identifier (SID) for the user, all of the SIDs for the groups to which the user belongs, and the user's privileges.

account escalation   If a program requires to perform a task that requires elevated privileges (a full administrator access token), the user is required to elevate the privileges under which the task runs by supplying administrator credentials or (if an administrator) by giving permission to continue. This process is known as account escalation.

ActiveX   A set of technologies that share information among different applications. ActiveX controls are routines that use these technologies and that can be automatically downloaded and executed by a web browser.

add-on   An optional software module that supplements or enhances the original software it is adding on to. Add-ons are also known as plug-ins, extensions, and snap-ins.

Admin Approval mode   The user experience when both administrator and standard accounts run as standard accounts without elevated privileges until the user initiates a task that requires such privileges. At this point, the standard user is prompted to supply administrator credentials, and the administrator is prompted for permission to continue.

administrator application   An application that runs in the context of an account with elevated privileges.

Aero   The new Windows Vista GUI, which is more efficient and aesthetically pleasing than the Windows XP or Windows 2000 interfaces.

age rating   A rating system for games, films, and other entertainment based on the age of the potential audience. Age rating systems include the Entertainment Software Rating Board (ESRB), the Computer Entertainment Rating Organization (CERO), and the Pan European Game Information (PEGI) systems.

aggregator   Client software that uses a web feed to poll feed sites (for example, news feed sites) and retrieve syndicated web content.

Away Mode   A power setting applied to a Windows Vista computer running Media Center that allows a Media Center Extender to wake it to retrieve content.

binary digit (bit)   A digit in the binary numbering system. A bit can take the value 1 or 0.

BIOS   The set of essential software routines that tests hardware at startup, assists with starting the operating system, and supports the transfer of data among hardware devices. The BIOS is stored in read-only memory (ROM) so that it can be executed when the computer is started. Although critical to performance, the BIOS is usually invisible to computer users. Configuration settings are accessible during boot.

bottleneck   A resource (memory, disk, processor, or network) is considered to be a bottleneck if high usage of the available resource, in comparison to the other resources, is limiting system performance.

Called Subscriber Identification (CSID)   Provides information to a transmitting fax about the receiving station.

cold boot   The action that occurs when a computer is started from a powered-off state and must load the operating system from scratch. This is the standard way that a computer starts up.

compatibility mode   A way of running applications that emulates the environment of previous versions of Windows.

contact   A person with whom you communicate through mail, telephone, or e-mail.

Content Advisor   A web browser feature that enables you to prohibit or allow access to websites based on a voluntary content-rating system. You can decide whether to allow access to unrated sites and provide a supervisor password to allow access to sites that are blocked.

content rating   A system by which website content is rated for nudity, pornography, strong language, and violence. Content rating is voluntary, but Content Advisor can block access to unrated sites.

context   Applications run with the privileges (or access token) of an account. An application is said to run in the context of that account.

convener   A person who initiates a Windows Meeting Space meeting.

conversation   A group of messages that is either direct or indirect to an original message.

credentials   An account user name and password. Typically, a user selects an account and then enters the corresponding password to supply credentials.

default gateway   The Internet Protocol (IP) address to which a host on a subnet sends a packet (or IP datagram) when the packet's destination IP address is not on the local subnet. The default gateway address is usually an interface belonging to the border router of the local area network (LAN). In the case of a small office/home office (SOHO) network, the default gateway is the static IP address of the wireless access point (WAP) or the Internet connection sharing (ICS) computer.

destination operating system   The operating system that the user has when the upgrade or migration process is complete.

Digital Rights Management (DRM)   A copy protection mechanism applied to digital media such as music and video.

digitally signed   An executable program that has been through an approval and validation process and has been issued with a digital certificate is said to be digitally signed.

DirectX   Software within Windows Vista that is used to manage multimedia output.

DirectX 10–compliant   Describes a graphics processing unit (GPU) that meets the DirectX 10 specification for gaming and 3D graphics—in simple terms, a very high specification graphics card.

driver rollback   The act of switching back to a previously installed hardware device driver.

driver signing   The process by which a digital certificate is created that verifies the publisher identity and driver file integrity. It is possible to check the publisher identity and validate the certificate's authenticity by examining special code within the certificate. The certificate is used to validate the driver file's integrity so that the user can be sure the driver files have not been tampered with.

dual booting   When a computer is configured to dual boot, each operating system is installed on a separate volume.

dummy restore   A process that occurs when files and folders are restored to a location other than that in which the original files are stored. You can use dummy restores to check the restore process and to ensure that backup files are not corrupt.

false positive   An e-mail that you want to receive that Windows Mail identifies as junk mail.

FireWire   A high-speed serial interface that conforms to the IEEE 1394 specification.

flash memory   A form of nonvolatile computer memory that can be electrically erased and reprogrammed.

flicker   Perceptible distortion caused by the updating of information on a cathode ray tube (CRT) monitor.

full backup   A type of backup that backs up all files and folders whether or not they have been updated since the previous backup.

Hardware Pixel Shader   A capability built into a graphics adapter that improves visual performance.

helper   A person who remotely connects to a host using a Remote Assistance invitation.

heuristics   The application of experience-derived knowledge to a problem. In simple terms, a program can use heuristics to obtain the best possible answer when it does not have enough information to guarantee a correct one.

hibernation   A state that involves writing the data that is in active memory to disk and then powering off the computer. Restart is faster because it is not necessary to go through the boot process but just to return the data to active RAM.

hidden updates   Updates that are not installed but are not listed in an installation list and do not cause Windows Update to notify the user.

host   A computer that hosts a Remote Assistance or a Remote Desktop session.

hybrid hard disk   A storage device that uses both magnetized platters and solid state RAM to store large amounts of data.

image   A read-only copy of all the files and folders on the system disk (and other specified hard disks) on a computer. You can use a computer image to restore the computer to exactly what its configuration was when the image was created.

important updates   Updates that offer significant benefits, such as improved security and reliability.

inbound rule   A rule that applies to the network traffic that is generated on the network and is destined for the local host.

Internet connection sharing (ICS)   A system that allows one computer on a small office or home network to access the Internet

through an Internet service provider (ISP). Other computers on the network in turn access the Internet through that computer.

Internet device discovery and control (IGDDC)   A Windows feature that allows computers on a network to access the Internet through a gateway device—for example, a computer running Internet connection sharing (ICS).

Internet Message Access Protocol 4 (IMAP)   An e-mail protocol that supports server folders and persistent connections. It supports multiple mailboxes and can only be used to receive e-mail.

Internet Protocol (IP) address   A unique address on a computer network that devices use in order to identify and communicate with each other.

Internet Protocol (IP) datagram   The fundamental unit of information passed across any Internet Protocol (IP) network. An IP datagram contains source and destination addresses along with data and a number of fields that define such things as the length of the datagram, the header checksum, and flags that indicate whether the datagram can be (or has been) fragmented.

Internet Protocol Security (IPSec)   A technology that can encrypt the contents and verify the source of network traffic.

legacy hardware device   A device that is not automatically detected and installed on a Windows Vista computer. Often an older device.

legacy programs   Executable programs that have been designed to run under previous operating systems (OSs)—for example, Windows XP and Windows 98. Compatibility problems can exist when a user attempts to run a legacy program in Windows Vista.

local administrators group   A local group on a computer. Members of this group (administrators) are granted full administrator access tokens to the computer, and software that needs to run with elevated privileges can run in the context of an administrator account.

malware   Any form of malicious software. Spyware, viruses, worms, and Trojan horses are all examples of malware.

Media Center   A centralized application that allows a computer to play live and recorded standard and HDTV movies, music, and pictures. It differs from Media Player in that it can also be used to transmit this information over a network to a Media Center Extender, such as an Xbox 360 attached to a high-definition television.

Media Center Extender   A device that can retrieve and display content from Windows Media Center over a local area network.

migration   The process whereby a user's files, application, and operating system settings are moved from an original operating system to a destination operating system.

mobile PC   A personal computer that is designed to be used in multiple locations. Typically, a wireless-enabled laptop.

mp3 player   An audio device that plays MPEG-1 Audio Layer 3 (mp3) files. Mp3 is a popular digital audio encoding and compression algorithm that is designed to greatly reduce the amount of data required to represent audio yet still sound like a faithful reproduction of the original. MPEG stands for Moving Picture Experts Group.

multiprocessor support   The ability to use more than one processor.

network projector   A data projector that can connect through a network and has a network address.

octet   An eight-bit binary number.

optional updates   Updates (for example, device driver updates) that are not downloaded or installed automatically.

original operating system   The operating system the user has prior to the upgrade or migration process.

outbound rule   A rule that applies to network traffic that is generated by the local host and sent out onto the network.

paging   Writing information to hard disk when there is insufficient space in RAM to store the data. Hard disk space allocated for this purpose is called virtual memory.

Parental Controls   An IE7+ feature that allows a responsible adult to configure a child's access to web content, games, and executable programs; to limit logon hours; and to generate activity reports. Parental Controls are configured on a per-child basis.

pen flick   A gesture in which the pen is dragged in a straight line for an inch across the screen. Can be assigned to shortcuts such as scrolling up and down or cutting and pasting.

personal digital assistant (PDA)   A handheld computer. PDAs were originally designed as personal organizers but have since become much more versatile and powerful. PDAs are also known as pocket computers or palmtop computers.

phishing   An identity theft scam that attempts to fraudulently obtain (for example) details of a user's bank account, credit card number, social security number, or personal identity number for dishonest purposes.

plasma display   A flat panel display commonly used for large television displays. Plasma displays contain inert gases (neon and xenon) that are electrically turned into plasma, which then excites phosphors to emit light. Sometimes known as a plasma display panel (PDP).

plug and play   A type of device that can be automatically detected and installed on a Windows Vista computer.

pop-ups   Additional windows generated when you open a webpage. Pop-ups are typically generated by online advertisers, although some are intended to increase web traffic or capture e-mail addresses. Some websites—for example, sites that allow employees to access e-mail through OWA—use pop-ups as part of their normal operation.

Post Office Protocol 3 (POP3) An e-mail protocol often used by ISPs. It supports a single mailbox, does not support persistent connections, and can only be used to receive e-mail.

Power Management A device configuration option that allows a hardware device to be powered off to save energy.

power plan A collection of power settings. The High Performance power plan uses up battery charge faster, but it uses hardware features at full power. The Power Saver plan uses up battery charge more slowly, but at the cost of screen brightness.

preferred wireless network A wireless network to which a wireless client will attempt to connect and authenticate. Typically, the list of preferred networks contains networks to which the client has previously connected, listed in order of preference.

presentation settings Settings that are applied when a mobile PC is used to give a presentation but are typically disabled for normal use.

private network A network that uses Request for Comments (RFC) 1918 Internet Protocol (IP) address space. Computers can be allocated addresses from this address space when it is necessary for them to communicate with other computing devices on an internal network but not directly with the Internet.

privileges The rights and access permissions granted to a user account. User privileges are included in a user's access token.

protocol A convention or standard that controls or enables the connection, communication, and data transfer between two computing endpoints. A protocol contains rules governing the syntax, semantics, and synchronization of a communication. At its lowest level, a protocol defines the behavior of a hardware connection.

protocol stack A particular software implementation of a computer networking protocol suite or group of interrelated protocols—for example, Transmission Control Protocol/Internet Protocol (TCP/IP).

public address An Internet Protocol (IP) address that identifies a device on the Internet (or is allocated to a local area network [LAN]). Public addresses must be unique on the Internet.

recommended updates Updates that address noncritical problems and help enhance the computing experience.

refresh rate How many times, per second, a monitor is updated. Measured in Hertz.

resolution Measured in pixels, resolution is specified in horizontal and then vertical terms.

resources Parts of the computer's hardware that the device interacts with.

restore point A restore point contains information about registry settings and other system information. Windows Vista generates restore points automatically before implementing significant system changes. You can manually create restore points and restore a computer system to a selected restore point.

rip A slang term for extracting and creating a digital media file from a traditional source such as an audio CD-ROM. Used in the Windows Media Player interface.

rollback The act of reverting to the original state of the computer.

RSS feed (news feed) A facility provided by some webpages that sends updated content to subscribers. IE7+ polls RSS feeds on a regular basis and refreshes the feed contents automatically.

screen orientation The manner in which a screen is laid out. Orientation can be portrait (taller than it is long) or landscape (longer than it is tall).

search provider A search engine, such as Ask Jeeves or AOL Search, that you can add to your search provider list and use to implement Internet searches. You can specify a default search provider.

Secure Desktop Windows Vista can take a screenshot of the desktop and switch into Secure Desktop. When Secure Desktop is in force, the user cannot perform any operations on the computer until he or she has dealt with the dialog box that initiated Secure Desktop. Secure Desktop is initiated when any of the UAC dialog boxes appear and is also used by Windows Vista's welcome/logon window.

security zone Placing websites in a security zone enables you to apply a group of predefined security settings (known as a security level) to all the websites in the zone. The security settings for any site that you access through the Internet and that you have not placed in another security zone are determined by the security level you allocate to the Internet zone.

shadow copy A previous version of a file created at the same time as a restore point.

side-by-side A migration in which user data is moved from one computer to another.

Simple Mail Transport Protocol (SMTP) An e-mail transport protocol that transmits messages between mail servers. It can be used only to send and not to receive e-mail.

slate A Tablet PC without a keyboard. A convertible Tablet PC can use slate mode, and its keyboard is often folded away under the screen.

sleep The act of keeping the data in active memory and writing a copy of that data to disk. This enables a very fast resumption of the computer because the data still exists in active memory. Retaining data in active memory requires power. After 15 minutes, data in active memory is discarded, and resumption requires reading data from disk back into active memory, which is functionally similar to resumption from hibernation.

solid state hard disk A storage device that holds large amounts of data in a solid state RAM device and has no moving parts.

spyware A form of malware that attempts to record a user's browsing patterns for the purposes of marketing. Spyware can also generate pop-up advertisements, in which case it is known as adware.

stand-alone or exclusive updates Updates that cannot be installed at the same time as other updates, typically because they require a computer restart.

Stock Keeping Unit (SKU) A Windows Vista SKU is another way of saying an edition of Windows Vista.

subnet An identifiably separate part of an organization's network. Typically, a subnet might represent all the computers at one geographic location, in one building, or on the same local area network (LAN). An IPv4 address consists of the address of a subnet (subnet address) combined with the address of a device on the subnet (host address).

subnet mask A number that defines what bits in an Internet Protocol (IP) address represent the subnet address and what bits represent the host address.

swap file Hard disk space used to extend RAM.

synchronize In this context, to make the same. Files are synchronized when modifications made to the current version are applied to a previous version.

System Restore A tool that allows you to revert the operating system to an earlier state.

Tablet PC A computer that accepts pen-based input from the screen.

tap The pen equivalent of a mouse click.

transfer rate The rate, usually expressed in bits per second, at which data is read from, or written to, a storage device.

Transmitting Subscriber Identification (TSID) Provides information to the receiving fax about the transmitting fax.

trusted contact A contact who has a digital certificate associated with that contact's contact information.

universal serial bus (USB) A serial bus standard that applies to interface devices. Current USB standards are USB 1.1 and USB 2.0.

updated files only backup A backup of the files that were updated since the previous backup.

upgrade The process in which a new operating system is installed over the original operating system while retaining all user data, settings, and applications.

Usenet The collection of news servers around the Internet that replicates newsgroup posts to one another.

User Account Control (UAC) A feature in Windows Vista that helps prevent unauthorized changes to your computer by running administrator accounts as standard accounts and asking for permission or for administrator credentials before performing actions that could potentially affect a computer's operation or that change settings that affect other users.

User State Migration Tool A toolset for migrating user data and settings from one Windows operating system to another.

virtual memory Windows implementation of a swap file.

Windows Anytime Upgrade An application that allows users of one edition of Windows Vista to upgrade to another.

Windows Easy Transfer A user-friendly application that allows the migration of user data and settings to Windows Vista.

Windows Product Activation (WPA) The method by which Microsoft ensures that Windows Vista is installed only on a limited number of computers.

Windows Vista Display Driver Model (WDDM) Display drivers that are specifically designed to work with Windows Vista.

wipe-and-load A migration strategy in which user data is exported, the computer is wiped, a new operating system is installed, and the user data is imported.

wireless fidelity (Wi-Fi) A wireless networking 802.11 standard. A Wi-Fi interface card enables a computer to act as a wireless access point (WAP).

wireless router A device in a wireless local area network (WLAN) that determines the next network point to which a packet should be forwarded toward its destination. In a small office/home office (SOHO) network the wireless router connects to an Internet service provider (ISP) and hence to the Internet through a modem. Sometimes known as a wireless access point (WAP).

Index

Reliability Monitor, 107–109, 123, 566, 569
Remote Assistance
  compared to Windows XP version, 386
  configuring, 387–388, 390, 396, 406–407
  connections, opening, 387, 389–395, 407–408
  connections required, 386
  in domain environments, 386
  limitations, 385–386
  over dial-up connections, 391
  privileges, elevating, 388–389
  security options, 387–391
  sessions, managing, 395–396
  troubleshooting, 397
  uses, 365–366, 385
Remote Desktop
  access to, 399–400
  Aero interface and, 401
  compared to Terminal Services, 398
  compared to Windows XP version, 386
  configuring, 398–399, 401–404
  connection process, 398
  connections, opening/closing, 401, 404–405
  troubleshooting, 405–406
  Users group, 399–400, 405
  uses, 365–366, 385, 397
Remote Desktop Protocol (RDP), 654–656
removable hard drives, transferring migration data via, 58
renamed files, recovering, 631–637
repartitioning, 59, 63
resolution, monitor, 111–112, 118
Resource View tool, 566–567, 571
restarts
  updates requiring, 597
  Windows Vista compared to other OSs, 588
Restore Files wizard, 612, 633
restore points
  creating, 90–91, 626–628, 631
  deleting, 628
  reverting to, 91–93, 256, 626
  uses, 587, 633
restoring computer image, 88, 629–631, 633
restoring files. See also Back Up And Restore Center;
    Restore Files wizard; System Restore
  about, 633
  advanced options, 625
  to a different location, 625
  files, searching for, 624
  with previous versions, 631–637
  privileges needed, 623
  process, 623–626
restoring hidden updates, 598–600

Restricted Sites security zone, 276, 278
ripping data, 492–493, 498–500
ROT13 substitution cipher, 433
routers, configuring wireless, 326–330
RSS 2.0 specification, 179
RSS (really simple syndication) feeds, 177–179, 184–186
rules, e-mail, 416–417, 423–425, 439
Run command, adding to Start menu, 161
runas feature, 199

S

safe mode, 86
Safe Senders list, 426
Same Service Set Identifier (SSID), 322, 344–345
SATA (Serial Advanced Technology Attachment) drives, 537
saved cookies, 280
Scanstate.exe, 61
scratch-out gestures, 716, 719
screen orientation, 651, 705–706
screen saver, 121, 124, 662
SDDs (solid state drives), 539
search. See also Internet Explorer 7 (IE7), Search facility
  optimizing speed, 543
  power plan settings, 727
  for system information, 574
search aggregators, 179
secondary landscape screen orientation, 706
secondary portrait screen orientation, 706
Secure Desktop, 203, 213–214, 224
secure websites, 282, 284
security. See also DEP (data execution prevention); Local
    Security Policies; User Account Control; Windows
    Defender; Windows Firewall
  about, 237
  attacks on, 368. See also phishing; spyware
  browsers, 546
  importance, 199
  improving, 199, 202
  online, resources for, 282
  screen saver, 121
  user precautions, 238–239
security bulletins, 589
security logs, 559–560. See also Event Viewer
Serial Advanced Technology Attachment (SATA) drives, 537
servers
  mail, 419, 421
  migrating data from, 56
  status-checking SideShow applications, 684
  on workstations, 56

System Requirements

We recommend that you use an isolated network that is not part of your production network to do the practice exercises in this book. The computer that you use to perform practices requires Internet connectivity. It is possible to perform almost all of the practices in this training kit if you decide to use a virtual machine instead of standard computer hardware.

Hardware Requirements

Your computer or computers should meet (at a minimum) the following hardware specifications:

- Personal computer with a 1-GHz or faster processor.
- 512 MB of RAM (1.5 GB if you plan to use virtual machine software).
- 40 GB of available hard disk space (80 GB if you plan to use virtual machine software).
- DVD-ROM drive.
- DirectX-capable graphics card with a Windows Display Driver Model (WDDM) driver, Hardware Pixel Shader 2.0 support, and a minimum of 128 MB of graphics memory. Graphics cards with lower specifications might work, but it will not be possible to use Windows Aero.
- Keyboard and Microsoft mouse or compatible pointing device.
- To complete the practice in Lesson 1, "Upgrading and Migrating to Windows Vista," of Chapter 2, you should have access to a Windows XP computer with Service Pack 2 installed. The optional practice involves performing an upgrade of a Windows XP computer, but you should attempt this only under the circumstances outlined in the practice.
- The practices in Chapter 7, "Configuring Network Connectivity," require a wireless router or wireless fidelity interface card.
- The practice in Lesson 3, "Configuring Windows Meeting Space," of Chapter 9 requires a second computer with Windows Vista installed.
- Practices 1 and 2 in Lesson 1, "Configuring and Troubleshooting Media Applications," of Chapter 10 require access to a TV tuner card or universal serial bus (USB) device.
- The practice in Lesson 1, "Troubleshooting Performance Issues," of Chapter 11, requires a USB2 flash memory pen drive that supports ReadyBoost (almost all modern devices do) and a second flash drive that does not support ReadyBoost (less than 256 MB free).

- The practices in Chapter 13, "Configuring Mobile Devices," require Windows Vista running on a mobile PC. You also need a second computer on your network that is acting as a network server (it does not need to be running Windows Vista).
- The practices in Lesson 1, "Configuring TabletPC," of Chapter 14 require access to a Tablet PC that has Windows Home Premium, Business, Enterprise or Ultimate installed.

Software Requirements

The following software is required to complete the practice exercises:

- Windows Vista Ultimate edition.

What do you think of this book?

We want to hear from you!

Do you have a few minutes to participate in a brief online survey?

Microsoft is interested in hearing your feedback so we can continually improve our books and learning resources for you.

To participate in our survey, please visit:

www.microsoft.com/learning/booksurvey/

...and enter this book's ISBN-10 number (appears above barcode on back cover*). As a thank-you to survey participants in the United States and Canada, each month we'll randomly select five respondents to win one of five $100 gift certificates from a leading online merchant. At the conclusion of the survey, you can enter the drawing by providing your e-mail address, which will be used for prize notification only.

Thanks in advance for your input. Your opinion counts!

* Where to find the ISBN-10 on back cover

ISBN-13: 000-0-0000-0000-0
ISBN-10: 0-0000-00000-0

00000

0 000000 000000

Example only. Each book has unique ISBN.

www.microsoft.com/learning/booksurvey/

Save 15%

on your Microsoft® Certification exam fee

Present this discount voucher to any of 5,000 testing centers worldwide for 15% off one Microsoft Certification exam fee. Or, use the discount code on the voucher to register online or via phone with the Microsoft Certified Exam Provider of your choice.

Microsoft | Learning

Good for 15% off one exam fee in the Microsoft Certified Professional Program

Offer expires 12/31/2011

Your voucher discount code

Redeemable at Microsoft Certified Exam Providers worldwide.
For locations, visit: **www.microsoft.com/mcp/exams**

Promotion Terms and Conditions:

- Offer good for 15% off one exam fee in the Microsoft Certified Professional Program.
- Voucher code can be redeemed online or at Microsoft Certified Exam Providers worldwide.
- Exam purchased using this voucher code must be taken on or before December 31, 2011.
- Inform your Microsoft Certified Exam Provider that you want to use the voucher discount code at the time you register for the exam.

Voucher Terms and Conditions

- Expired vouchers will not be replaced.
- Each voucher code may only be used for one exam and must be presented at time of registration.
- This voucher may not be combined with other vouchers or discounts.
- This voucher is nontransferable and is void if altered or revised in any way.
- It may not be sold or redeemed for cash, credit, or refund.

X12-41824